Goodnight Sweetheart
A Guide to the Classic Sitcom

Goodnight Sweetheart

A Guide to the Classic Sitcom

Paul Burton

Foreword by Victor McGuire

Introduction by Laurence Marks and Maurice Gran

First published in 2024 by Fantom Publishing, an imprint of Fantom Films
www.fantompublishing.co.uk

Copyright © Paul Burton 2024

Paul Burton has asserted his moral right to be identified as the author of this work in accordance with the Copyright, Designs and Patents Act 1988.

All rights reserved.

A catalogue record for this book is available from the British Library.

Hardback edition ISBN: 978-1-78196-365-4

Typeset by Phil Reynolds Media Services, Leamington Spa
Printed and bound by CPI Group (UK) Ltd, Croydon, CR0 4YY
Cover design by Stuart Manning

All photographs in plate section © Fremantle Media/Shutterstock

*This book is dedicated to Nicholas Lyndhurst
and Laurence Marks and Maurice Gran*

Contents

Foreword *by Victor McGuire*		xi
Acknowledgements		xii
Introduction *by Laurence Marks and Maurice Gran*		xiv
1	A Passage of Time	1
2	The Singing Spy	63
3	Blitz and Pieces	113
4	A New Dimension	172
5	West End Living	218
6	Closed for the Duration	262
7	Many Happy Returns	328
List of Episodes		351
Sources		382

Gary Sparrow: My wives exist in different temporal aspects of a four-dimensional space-time continuum.

Ron Wheatcroft: Typical bigamist's excuse.

Foreword

THE GREAT AMERICAN COMEDIAN Bob Newhart performed a sketch called 'Introducing Tobacco to Civilisation'. The gag was a phone call between Sir Walter Raleigh and the head of the West Indies Company in London. Basically, he wants to ship leaves back to England from America. A tough pitch by any standard. I imagine the pitch for *Goodnight Sweetheart* was also an interesting meeting.

Executive:	Hold all my calls, Martha, I'm with Marks and Gran. So, what have you got for me boys? We want you to know we are very excited!
Maurice:	It's a sitcom and the hero is a time-travelling bigamist.
Executive:	The boys are leaving now, Martha. You can put through all calls.
Laurence:	Nicholas Lyndhurst is on board.
Executive:	Martha…

Sitcom is hard to get right. You need great writing, chemistry between the players, a fine production team, but most importantly – luck! *Goodnight Sweetheart* had all of these. It was also fun to make. The chemistry between Nicholas and firstly Dervla and Michelle, and then Elizabeth and Emma, was incredibly special and key to the success of the show. This was so important in getting people to believe they could root for a bigamist, which fans of the show certainly did. This was due in no small part to Nicholas's great skill as an actor. However, the heart of the show was, of course, the impeccable performances of Reg and Ron. A point that is often missed, which I find surprising, but there you go!

Goodnight Sweetheart was a joy from start to finish. I hope you enjoy this book.

Victor McGuire

Acknowledgements

WHEN THE OPPORTUNITY AROSE to write a book about *Goodnight Sweetheart* for Fantom Publishing, I was delighted. From the first time I watched an episode of the sitcom, I quickly became hooked, ley line and sinker. Therefore, it has been an absolute pleasure to write and research the story behind the making of the unique time-travelling series.

To say that I'm indebted to many people for their time and help while I was working on this publication is an understatement. Firstly, my huge thanks must go to Laurence Marks and Maurice Gran for granting me permission to write this book and for writing the introduction. I am also grateful for all their patience, support and cooperation.

In addition, I would like to thank Dexter O'Neill at Fantom Publishing and Dominic Burns and Jane Foster at FremantleMedia for also making this book possible.

My deepest gratitude goes to Nicholas Lyndhurst for allowing me to interview him at length about working on the series. I am also extremely beholden to Victor McGuire for not only writing the foreword but also providing me with his invaluable recollections for this book. I also cannot thank Elizabeth Carling, Emma Amos and Christopher Ettridge enough for all their memories and kind support.

I'm incredibly grateful to the following people for their reminisces of appearing in the long-running sitcom: Suzy Aitchison, Darren Bancroft, Martin Beaumont, David Benson, Richard Braine, Allie Byrne, Helena Calvert, Rowena Cooper, Kenneth Cope, Esme Coy, Jeannie Crowther, Peter Czajkowski, Yvonne D'Alpra, Nicholas Day, Sally Dexter, Sam Douglas, Norman Eshley, Regina Freedman, Michael Garner, Jon Glover, Tom Goodman-Hill, Paul Goodwin, Maria Gough, Paul Grunert, Jason Hall, Andrew Havill, Pippa Haywood, Polly Hemingway, Adam Henderson, Chris Humphreys, Angus Kennedy, Diana Kent, Gary Lammin, Bryan Lawrence, Phil Nice, Ellen O'Grady, Patrick Pearson, Anthony Pedley, Tim Preston, Matt Rippy, Ted Robbins, Rolf Saxon, Paul Shearer, Simon Sherlock, Lee Sheward, Jay Simon, Roger Sloman, Penelope Solomon, Colin Spaull, Steve Speirs, Belinda Stewart-Wilson, Nick Stringer, Danny Swanson, Richard Syms, Danielle Tarento, Harriet Thorpe, Susan Tracy, Michael Troughton, Robert Whitelock and Gordon Winter.

My sincere appreciation goes to the following production team members for their invaluable insight into working behind the scenes on the comedy: Paul

Alexander, Trevor Brown, Christopher Clayton, Mandy Demetriou, Martin Dennis, Dave Ferris, David Harsent, Simon Haveland, Claire Hinson, Denny Hodge, Micheál Jacob, Terry Kinane, Sam Lawrence, Gary Lawson and John Phelps, Julia Morpeth, Anthea Nelson, Robert Newton, Susie Parriss, Paul Peppiate, Nic Phillips, Jon Rolph, Anthony Sadler and Gaynor Sadler, Keith Strachan, Julie Sykes and Chris Wadsworth.

Furthermore, I would like to sincerely thank: Francis Abbott, Kim Barry, Leanne Batwell-Peters, Eamonn Bedford, Victoria Blackburn, Melvyn Bragg, Andrew Braidford, Gary Brannan, Malcolm Browning, Alice Burton, Sharry Clark, Amy Clarke, Shane Collins, Simon Copley, Lou Coulson, Roger Davidson, Chris Dean, Darren Deans, Jean Diamond, Sarah Espino, Donna French, Imogen Fuller, Michael Gattrell, Jonathan Hall, Humphrey Hendrix, Adrian Huckfield, David Jason, Holly Jenkins, Ben Kellett, Max Latimer, Michael Linnit, Maureen Magee, Emma Marchant, John Markham, Sarah Mitchell, Sarah Mowat, Izzy Parriss, Jasmine Parris, Meg Poole, Sarah Redmond, Anah Ruddin, Simon Sharkey, Jane Shepperd, Sue Taylor and Paul White for their invaluable help.

I would also like to credit Lynda Baron, John Bartlett, Harry 'Aitch' Fielder, Terrence Hardiman, Mia Jupp, Anna Karen and Harry Landis for their time and contributions during my research. Sadly, they passed away before this book was published.

Finally, an extra special thank you is due to the editor and typesetter Phil Reynolds for all his tireless efforts.

I hope you will enjoy this celebration of *Goodnight Sweetheart*.

Paul Burton

Introduction

PAUL BURTON CLEARLY LOVES the entertainment industry for he seems to have spent his whole life producing, directing, and writing about television, film, and the stage. His knowledge of our industry is encyclopaedic, so we knew he was the man to write the story of *Goodnight Sweetheart*, which of all our comedies has the most dedicated and enthusiastic fans. These 'Sweeties', as some term themselves, run *Goodnight Sweetheart* websites and forums, organise conventions and create fan fiction. We bet they know more about Gary Sparrow than we do. But they can't possibly know as much as Paul, whose book is full of revelations and reminders of what a complex world we managed to create. If either of us applied to *Mastermind*, with *Goodnight Sweetheart* as his specialist subject, he'd have to hope Paul wasn't setting the questions or he'd risk ending up with a big fat zero!

In his opening pages, Paul retells the *Goodnight Sweetheart* creation story, how a chance remark from Laurence sparked a reaction from Maurice that led to the birth of Gary. That was in late 1990. We spent more than a year mulling over how to turn an intriguing idea – that a modern man could somehow find himself in London during the Blitz – into a long-running series. The first question was, 'How does he do it?' As we weren't quantum physicists, we decided not to worry too much about that.

The second and more important question was why would Gary risk returning repeatedly to such a dangerous era? It couldn't just be that he hated his present-day life, though he certainly didn't love it. Neither did we want him to go back because he hated his present-day wife; it would be too easy and obvious to make Yvonne the bad girl, although undeniably she gave Gary a hard time. Was the appeal of 1940s barmaid Phoebe enough to make Gary risk his life? Not really, though the attraction was real and mutual. Then what was it Gary was getting in 1940 that he couldn't get in 1993?

The answer is 'respect'. In his own era Gary is a television repairman, a profession about to be made redundant by technological progress; televisions had simply stopped breaking down. But in the past he could impress the locals as a man of mystery, a spy, and a brilliant songwriter.

Many fans find Gary's musical piracy the most enjoyable element of his alternative life. Yet when we began to write the show, that was never part of the plan. Everything changed when we sat Gary at the piano in episode one and he started to pick out the opening chords of Elton John and Bernie Taupin's 'Your Song'. Phoebe asks if Gary learned it when he was in Hollywood. Gary hesitates, then says, 'Actually I wrote it.'

That was as much a surprise to us as it was to Phoebe, but as soon as those words left Gary's lips we knew we had stumbled upon a vein of pure gold. Writers sometimes say that when a script is going well you don't feel as if you're making it up; it's more like you're taking dictation. This was one of those moments. Gary Sparrow had taken over the show, and we knew that with his supposed musical prowess he would repeatedly get himself into and out of all kinds of comedic trouble.

Goodnight Sweetheart duly became our third big television hit of the Nineties. That was an extraordinary decade for us. We can only appreciate it in hindsight, because while it was happening there wasn't time to take it all in. In 1988, we had set up our own production company, ALOMO, to produce *Birds of a Feather* for the BBC. We then embarked upon a comedy-drama, *Love Hurts*. Today we have no explanation for how we managed that workload, especially as around the same time we were also writing another BBC sitcom *Get Back* and Rik Mayall's *The New Statesman* for ITV. It must have been the drugs – we were each drinking at least five large mugs of coffee per day!

The process of writing the first series of *Goodnight Sweetheart* was enormous fun. We found it liberating to return with Gary to the 1940s, and vicariously experience the togetherness and determination of the residents of the East End of London. Sometimes it felt as if the Forties were seeping into the present day. While we were plotting the first series, we arranged to meet one of the producers in a Hampstead pub. We'd never been there before, but when we entered it was as if we had been transported into the past. The pub was almost exactly as we had envisioned the Royal Oak: battered brown furniture, sticky tabletops, and ancient regulars playing cribbage and puffing away at pipes and roll-ups. It was only the lack of gummed brown paper criss-crossed on the windows that assured us an air raid wasn't in the offing.

A few weeks later we went to Laurence's local Cotswold railway station to catch the train to London for a *Goodnight Sweetheart* rehearsal. The indicator board said our train had been cancelled, and the next one wasn't for half an hour. We'd have had a consoling cup of tea if the buffet hadn't been closed. Then we saw a train in the distance. Perhaps our service hadn't been cut after all. Thirty seconds later a gleaming steam locomotive thundered through the station, pulling half a dozen pre-war cream and brown dining carriages. A tourist special (the Cotswolds Express) of course; but, for a moment, it felt like the Forties.

Fans of the show will know how wonderfully the actors, the actresses and the production team responded to the script. Nicholas Lyndhurst, of course, was perfect, and so were the rest of the cast. Robin Nash directed them with sensitivity and style, and the production designer, Roger Andrews, was superb. We had worked with Roger before, so we knew he was a true artist, but he excelled himself with his sets for *Goodnight Sweetheart*. The first time we saw the Royal Oak we felt transported.

We hope this book will transport you too, to those days when a television repairman could walk into a wartime pub, sit at the piano, and make millions love him, despite his rather dubious morals.

Laurence Marks and Maurice Gran

Goodnight Sweetheart
A Guide to the Classic Sitcom

1
A Passage of Time

Laurence Marks and Maurice Gran, best known collectively as Marks and Gran, and the original writers and creators of *Goodnight Sweetheart*, were both raised in the Finsbury Park area of north London. In 1960, they became members of the Jewish Lads' Brigade, Finsbury Park Company. However, they didn't properly become acquainted until 1965 when they discovered that, by coincidence, they were on the same holiday at Butlins in Saltdean, near Brighton; and the pair have been firm friends ever since.

In 1973, Laurence and Maurice discovered a scriptwriting club called Player Playwrights that was based at the British Drama League offices in Fitzroy Square in central London. The club congregated on Monday nights and there they both witnessed a host of plays of varying quality written by members. This led to both men separately submitting material to the club's sketch-writing competition and regularly winning competitions at the weekly meetings. As a result, the playwright and club secretary, Don West, suggested that they should team up and write together. This appealed, not least because their comedy-writing heroes included Galton and Simpson, Took and Feldman and Clement and La Frenais. Thus Marks and Gran were born.

Taking time off from their day jobs, the new writing duo penned a half-hour script about a suicidal inventor called *The World's Not Ready for You Yet, Sylvester*. Sending their script to James Gilbert, the then BBC head of comedy, at BBC Television Centre resulted in him inviting the pair for an informal meeting at the BBC's White City base on Friday 11 October 1974. Although this meeting offered little more than valuable advice, Television Centre would later prove incredibly important to their careers.

The subsequent sitcom scripts they wrote and sent to the BBC and various ITV companies of the time were not proving fruitful. For a while, it looked as though they would both have to stick with their day jobs. During this period, Laurence was working as a researcher on Thames Television's current affairs programme *This Week* and writing occasionally for the *Sunday Times* and Maurice as the manager of the Tottenham Job Centre. Then fate took a hand when Laurence happened to meet one of his comedy-writing heroes, Barry Took, on a train in April 1977. Barry, whose credits included co-writing the BBC radio comedy series *Round the Horne* with Marty Feldman, agreed to read some of Laurence and Maurice's sitcom scripts. Laurence was later surprised with a phone call from Took who said, 'I've read your scripts and I think it would be a great loss to British comedy if you two didn't persevere.'

Within months, Barry contacted Richard Willcox, the producer of *The Frankie Howerd Variety Show* on BBC Radio 2, and this resulted in him calling Laurence and Maurice. Richard commissioned them to write twenty minutes of comedy material for each of the six hour-long editions of the aforementioned radio series. Happy with their work, Frankie, always a supporter of new writers, then asked Laurence and Maurice to write a monologue for his unannounced appearance on that year's *Royal Command Performance*. This proved hugely successful and in a roundabout way led them to write for the long-running children's series, *Playaway*. Also in 1978, the opportunity arose for Laurence and Maurice to become part of the writing team for *The Marti Caine Show*. Although they liked and respected Marti, they felt that writing for variety performers was not for them.

It was Barry also who recommended Laurence and Maurice to Linda Seifert, who became their agent and arranged for them to meet Humphrey Barclay, the then head of comedy at LWT (London Weekend Television), in early 1979. That meeting led to the commissioning of a pilot of a sitcom called *Holding the Fort*, the recording of which in August 1979 was interrupted by the ITV strike. When that was resolved, Michael Grade commissioned a series of *Holding the Fort*, which saw Peter Davison play house-husband Russell Milburn, Patricia Hodge as his army wife Penny, and Matthew Kelly as Russell's friend, Fitz.

With this sitcom commissioned, the reality of the projected workload that the series would demand made them realise they could no longer continue to write while holding down full-time jobs. Despite there being no guarantee that success and financial security would continue to come their way, they nevertheless took the big step and left their day jobs. They then progressed to writing an eclectic mix of television series. Their other sitcoms included *Roll Over Beethoven*, featuring Liza Goddard as prim piano teacher Belinda Purcell and Nigel Planer as Nigel Cochrane, a reclusive rock star. Later, they created *The New Statesman*, a hugely popular vehicle for Rik Mayall that saw him take on the role of Tory MP Alan B'Stard.

One of their most successful sitcoms is undoubtedly *Birds of a Feather*, with the heavenly pairing of Pauline Quirke and Linda Robson as Cockney sisters Tracey Stubbs and Sharon Theodopolopodous, whose husbands were originally in prison, and added Lesley Joseph to the mix as their wealthy, snobbish, man-eating neighbour, Dorien Green. Not content to rest on their laurels, they also devised *Get Back*, with Ray Winstone as self-made man Martin Sweet, who finds himself going from riches to rags when the recession of the early 1990s hits. The cast also included Carol Harrison as Loretta Sweet, Larry Lamb as Albert Sweet and a young, pre-*Titanic* Kate Winslet as Eleanor Sweet.

Later, in 1998, they wrote *Unfinished Business*, starring Harriet Walter as Amy, Henry Goodman as Spike and Jaye Griffiths as Tania. The year 2002, meanwhile, saw them write *Believe Nothing*, a sitcom made for ITV, which starred Rik Mayall.

Meanwhile, their comedy dramas have included *Shine on Harvey Moon*, a post-war series that saw Kenneth Cranham, and later Nicky Henson, play demobbed RAF serviceman Harvey Moon; and *Love Hurts*, featuring Adam Faith as Frank Carver, Zoë Wanamaker as Tessa Piggott and Jane Lapotaire as Diane Warburg.

Never wanting to be pigeonholed as just comedy writers, their dramas have included *Mosley*, a four-part miniseries based on British fascist Sir Oswald Mosley's life in the period between the two world wars. Jonathan Cake played Sir Oswald 'Tom' Mosley and the cast also included Jemma Redgrave as Lady Cimmie Curzon and Hugh Bonneville as Bob Boothby.

In addition to writing and creating for television, Laurence and Maurice have also written productions for the theatre. Their credits include *Playing God*, about the controlling behaviour of a terminally ill and controlling rock star, a play commissioned by Alan Ayckbourn for the Stephen Joseph Theatre in Scarborough. They also wrote *The Blair-B'Stard Project*, a stage version of *The New Statesman* which toured the country and played at the Trafalgar Studios (later renamed the Trafalgar Theatre) in London's West End. A quartet of 1960s-set musicals called *Dreamboats and Petticoats*, *Save the Last Dance for Me*, *Dreamboats and Miniskirts* and *Dreamboats and Petticoats: Bringing on Back the Good Times* have also proved crowd-pleasers at various theatres. Meanwhile, fans of *Birds of a Feather* were able to take in a touring version of the long-running sitcom, which the writing partners co-wrote with Gary Lawson and John Phelps.

Summarising why he believes Laurence and Maurice have continued to be so successful in their long careers, the broadcaster Melvyn Bragg said, 'The accurate but short answer is that they have a great eye for a subject, have superb sense of structure and can write completely convincing dialogue. They're also distinctive.'

In late 1990, Laurence and Maurice were working on the first series of *Love Hurts*. They were planning a scene in which two of the main characters, Frank Carver and Rabbi Diane Warburg, were going to have lunch at Bloom's kosher restaurant in Whitechapel. Laurence happened to say, apropos of nothing at all,

'If you walk two or three streets behind where we are setting this scene, you'd find they haven't changed since the Blitz.' Maurice replied, 'Thank you. I think you've just created our next series.' Laurence had no idea at all what Maurice was talking about. He'd merely spoken about two or three streets that he knew well. Indeed, his first wife's family lived in one such street. What Maurice had imagined was somebody strolling down a street in the 1990s and emerging in the 1940s. He didn't know how or why; in fact, he was clear even then that the time-travel process should never be dwelt on as they didn't want to write a sci-fi series. '*Goodnight Sweetheart* almost came down a passage of time,' said Laurence. 'It was merely a passing comment that would inexplicably lead to the creation of one of the UK's most successful sitcoms.'

However, like all good ideas, it needed the time and room to grow. 'We discussed the idea over and over during 1991 and 1992,' said Laurence. 'We even brought it up and tried to explain it at a SelecTV executive weekend meeting in a very posh Hampshire hotel, but nobody seemed to understand the idea or see its comedy potential. Maurice and I felt just a little isolated. What we knew was, it was about a man who was, in the eyes of his wife, an abject failure, a man without ambition or hope, who then becomes a hero to the woman he meets in 1940. I think there was little more than that at the beginning.'

Once Laurence and Maurice had set upon the idea of a man that was going to cross backwards and forwards in time, they realised they had to create a character that would want to keep doing this and, in doing so, be willing to keep taking risks. They realised it had to be someone that wasn't satisfied with his life in the present. Eventually, they decided upon a double love story. In short, the main character would become a two-timing time traveller.

With the subject of adultery set to become a prominent theme of *Goodnight Sweetheart*, the right casting of the lead was always going to be vital. For the as-then-unnamed lead character, Laurence and Maurice had just one actor in mind: Nicholas Lyndhurst. They were convinced that Nicholas would be able to play the character, whose sex drive spans two time zones, while still making the sitcom appealing to a family audience.

An accomplished actor, Nicholas trained at the Corona Academy in London. His theatre credits include playing Bob and Brindsley Miller in a tour of Peter Shaffer's one-act plays *The Private Ear* and *Black Comedy*, and Bob in the Jimmie Chinn comedy *Straight and Narrow* at both Wyndham's Theatre and the Aldwych Theatre in London's West End, with Carmel McSharry. He has also played Norman in Ronald Harwood's funny and beautifully observed play *The Dresser*, opposite Julian Glover's Sir, on tour and at the Duke of York's Theatre, London, and Trinculo in Trevor Nunn's production of the William Shakespeare play *The Tempest* at the Theatre Royal Haymarket, London. The actor's more recent stage roles include the Starkeeper and Dr Seldon in the Rodgers and Hammerstein musical *Carousel*, appearing alongside Katherine Jenkins and Alfie Boe, and the Innkeeper and the Captain in the Dale Wasserman, Mitch Leigh and Joe Darion musical *Man of La Mancha*, with Kelsey Grammer, which were both staged at the Coliseum Theatre, London.

As a child actor, Nicholas played Peter in a television adaptation of *Heidi* and Davy Keith in *Anne of Avonlea*. He was then cast in the lead roles of Tom Canty and Prince Edward in the drama series *The Prince and the Pauper* and Tootles in the Anthony Newley and Leslie Bricusse musical version of J. M. Barrie's *Peter Pan*. After a short spell as a presenter on the Saturday-morning series *Our Show*, Nicholas played Karl Brandt in the children's drama *The Tomorrow People* and Raymond Fletcher in the *Porridge* spin-off *Going Straight*, opposite Ronnie Barker. This led to him being cast as Adam Parkinson in Carla Lane's sitcom *Butterflies*, Dobson in the drama *To Serve Them All My Days* and playing Rodney Trotter in the John Sullivan sitcom *Only Fools and Horses*, alongside David Jason. Viewers then saw the actor play Ashley Phillips in the flat-sharing sitcom *The Two of Us*, with Janet Dibley, and MI5 agent Peter 'Piglet' Chapman in the secret-agent sitcom, *The Piglet Files*. Nicholas also took on the roles of Uriah Heep in an adaptation of *David Copperfield*, Dr Graham Moss in the thriller *Thin Ice* and handyman Jimmy Venables in the sitcom *After You've Gone*, with Celia Imrie, Dani Harmer and Ryan Sampson. In 2010, he was given the chance to play Frederick 'Freddie the Frog' Robdal, Rodney Trotter's biological father, in the *Only Fools and Horses* comedy-drama prequel, *Rock and Chips*. Since then, his television credits have included playing Dan Griffin in the police procedural comedy drama *New Tricks* and Johnny in an episode of the children's sitcom, *So Awkward*. More recently, Nicholas joined the cast of the revival series of the sitcom *Frasier* to play the role of Alan Cornwall, Frasier's old college buddy turned university professor.

Nicholas has also played various film roles. They include Chalky in the adventure *Sky Bandits*, Buckle in the comedy drama *Lassie* and George Williams in the biographical drama, *A United Kingdom*.

In August 1992, Laurence and Maurice contacted Nicholas's agent and invited the actor to lunch to discuss the possibility of taking on the lead role in their proposed new sitcom. By this stage, they had agreed upon the show's theme and that it would be set in two time zones: 1993 and 1940. The task was now to explain their ideas as best they could to him.

Marks and Gran first met Nicholas for lunch at Orso's, Covent Garden, on Thursday 6 August 1992. The two writers arrived first and then Nicholas, wearing a cap designed to help prevent him from being recognised, duly joined them. With introductions out of the way, Laurence, Maurice and Nicholas now had three courses and two hours to get to know each other. They had some people in common, not least John Sullivan and Tony Dow, the writer and director respectively of *Only Fools and Horses*, and this helped to break the ice. The conversation moved on to *Goodnight Sweetheart*, which Nicholas was keen to know more about. Laurence and Maurice discussed the subject as fully as they possibly could because, of course, there was absolutely nothing written down, and Nicholas added his own contributions. 'I didn't know much about their idea for the series prior to meeting Lo and Mo at the restaurant,' said Nicholas. 'I thought the combination of comedy, drama and time travel was really intriguing and that's what sold it to me. Also, I was keen to get away from the "oh no, it's the neighbours" type of sitcom.'

They also discussed one of Nicholas's potential leading ladies. Laurence and Maurice had been talking about Linda Robson. However, Linda would not have been available if they were to write and record the first series during the summer of 1993. Nicholas, in any case, felt that she might not be a good idea; not because she isn't a sterling actress, but because of the baggage brought to the project by casting two stars from the two biggest comedy series on television. Laurence and Maurice felt that Nicholas had a point. Maurice was not unduly worried; he has always believed that casting is 'a fun element'.

By the end of the meeting, Nicholas had expressed his desire to star in the new series. Not surprisingly, Laurence and Maurice were delighted. By now, they were convinced he would bring all his best qualities to the series that they would need.

They all departed Orso's having had a good Italian lunch, with the plan to meet each other again when Maurice was back in London. Laurence suggested that Maurice went to see the West End play Nicholas was currently appearing in and that the three of them should meet in a restaurant after the performance. Nicholas liked this idea and Laurence formalised the arrangements. After the meeting, Laurence wrote in his diary:

> I do believe Maurice and I would like Nicholas to play whatever we call the character, and that we three between us shall be able to produce the most unusual comedy of the year.

On the evening of Tuesday 8 September 1992, Laurence and Maurice went to the Aldwych Theatre to see Nicholas star in the play *Straight and Narrow* by Jimmie Chinn. 'This was a comedy about a gay couple out and proud and getting laughs,' recalled Laurence. 'Afterwards, we returned to Orso's, where the three of us got to know one another so much better and realised it would be great fun to work together on this strange and magical idea Maurice and I had.'

With Nicholas on board, it was time for the writers to formally approach the BBC about the series. To put the subsequent meeting they had with then head of comedy, Martin Fisher, fully into context, we have to go back further in time.

In 1982, Laurence and Maurice first met Allan McKeown, one of the first independent television producers in the UK, when they worked together on the very first series of *Shine on Harvey Moon*. Allan started his working life as an apprentice ladies' hairdresser at Vidal Sassoon's salon in Bond Street, London. Before he turned twenty, he had his own salon and soon found his talents were in demand on television programmes such as the variety series *Sunday Night at the London Palladium* and films including the Lindsay Anderson satirical drama *If...* and the crime drama, *Get Carter*. He decided that film and TV production looked a lot more fun than hairdressing, and changed direction to join the James Garrett advertising agency, initially to make commercials. Before long, though, he became the agency's managing director.

In 1979, Allan formed ground-breaking WitzEnd Productions with multiple BAFTA-winning comedy writers Dick Clement and Ian La Frenais. WitzEnd's early projects included the Elton John documentary *To Russia with Elton* and the film version of the classic sitcom, *Porridge*. The company went on to make series including the comedy-dramas *Auf Wiedersehen, Pet* and *Lovejoy*. Meanwhile, Allan somehow found time to marry the British-American actress, comedienne, singer, writer, producer and director Tracey Ullman in 1983.

The year 1988 saw Allan mastermind WitzEnd's acquisition of SelecTV, a publicly listed company. The day he closed the deal Allan proposed to Laurence and Maurice that they form their own production company under the SelecTV banner. They named the company ALOMO (AL for Allan, LO for Laurence and MO for Maurice).

In 1991, after the runaway success of ALOMO's first show, *Birds of a Feather*, ALOMO signed an exclusive three-year deal with the BBC. At the time, it was the first output agreement between an independent production company and the public service broadcaster. In return for development funds, and a commitment to a six-part half-hour sitcom series a year, the BBC received first option on ALOMO's upcoming projects. It also meant that the BBC had exclusive call on Laurence and Maurice's services.

Despite the new BBC deal, Allan announced that this would not affect his plans to participate in the ITV franchise auction that was taking place that year.

Indeed, as a result of a successful franchise bid, he become a founder of Meridian Television, who took over the South and South East of England ITV franchise from TVS at the start of 1993.

Allan also produced for the theatre. He co-produced the first fully staged production of the Richard Thomas and Stewart Lee musical *Jerry Springer – The Opera* at the National Theatre, London, and the Cambridge Theatre, London, and *Lennon*, Don Scardino's musical about John Lennon, which featured many of the late performer's songs, at the Broadhurst Theater, New York.

The veteran producer later died of prostate cancer in Los Angeles on Christmas Eve 2013, aged sixty-seven. Maurice said, 'We still miss him, and remember him as a television visionary with ideas ahead of his time.'

Having digressed somewhat, we return to the meeting at which Laurence and Maurice pitched *Goodnight Sweetheart* to Martin Fisher at the BBC. 'We met Martin in his fourth-floor office at BBC Television Centre, an office we had come to know well,' said Laurence. Martin, having listened to us explain this bizarre idea, admitted he couldn't understand it. Maurice was feeling mischievous when he was asked for the strapline and said, "It's about a man who's in love with a woman of over eighty who may well be dead." Martin asked, "Will it be funny?" We told him we thought so, and he asked for six episodes.'

As with all of Laurence and Maurice's television series of the period, *Goodnight Sweetheart* was set to be made by ALOMO who, along with Witzend, were a subsidiary of SelecTV at the time.

The story of how *Goodnight Sweetheart* came to be given its title is an interesting one. One morning, the ALOMO managing director Michael Pilsworth called Laurence. 'He said he had just received the contracts for the new series from the BBC, which needed signing and returning,' recalled Laurence. 'But because this new show didn't have a title, we had to fill one in, just for the sake of the legal document. "Have you any ideas for a title?" he asked. I said, "Maurice and I hadn't given it any thought just yet," to which he said, "Well, I need one now." I swung my revolving chair around, in thought, and there on one of the bookshelves was a book. I just blurted out, "Call it *Goodnight Sweetheart* for now. We'll think of something later." Michael responded, "Okay. It's just so I can put something on the contract." Thus, *Goodnight Sweetheart* was born.'

Claire Hinson began working for SelecTV in 1990. 'I initially worked in production management on shows including *Birds of a Feather, Nightingales, The Old Boy Network* and *Get Back*,' she said. 'I was made managing director of ALOMO in May 1993 after Michael Pilsworth left as managing director of SelecTV, specifically to oversee development and production of the ALOMO slate, headed up by Laurence and Maurice.' Although Claire was inexplicably not given an onscreen credit in the first two series of *Goodnight Sweetheart*, she was involved in all the episodes of the original run.

'Prior to early 1996, I was based full time at Teddington Studios along with all the other production personnel working for ALOMO,' Claire explained. 'The legal team, accounts department, PR department etc. were all based in SelecTV's Derby Street office in London. For a while, all SelecTV permanent employees (not production freelancers) worked together in Fouberts Place, W1, later on, and I would just spend recording days at Teddington and visit the rehearsal rooms for read-throughs and technical runs.'

Claire's other television credits include the sitcoms *Unfinished Business*, *The House That Jack Built*, and *Believe Nothing*.

John Bartlett was chosen by Laurence and Maurice to produce the first series of *Goodnight Sweetheart*, and would continue to produce the time-travelling sitcom until the end of series five. 'I first worked with Marks and Gran as an associate producer on a sitcom they'd written called *Snakes and Ladders*, which starred John Gordon Sinclair and Adrian Edmondson,' said John. 'I then became the executive producer on *The New Statesman* for ALOMO in 1992. Lo and Mo invited me to lunch one day and asked me to work on *Goodnight Sweetheart*. However, I was under contract at Yorkshire Television and I thought this would prevent me from working on the series. In the end, ALOMO "rented me" from the company for the first series. However, I was later advised to go freelance.'

The early part of John's career saw him writing for performers including Dave Allen and Frankie Howerd. He was also a writer and script editor and, for a time, an associate producer on the Ted Rogers game show, *3-2-1*. He went on to produce programmes including the Carla Lane sitcom *Searching*, with Prunella Scales, and the comedy special *The Joe Pasquale Show*. Later, he worked for DLT Entertainment where his credits included two specials of the sitcom *As Time Goes By*, with Judi Dench and Geoffrey Palmer, and the long-running sitcom *My Family*, with Robert Lindsay and Zoë Wanamaker. Quite unexpectedly, John died on Tuesday 3 January 2023.

Engaging John as producer proved to be a smart move. 'We shouldn't underestimate John's contribution to *Goodnight Sweetheart*,' emphasised Laurence. 'He worked tirelessly, and way beyond the call of duty. His casting ideas were spot on, and his enthusiasm for the world of Gary Sparrow never diminished. *Goodnight Sweetheart* would have been a lesser show without him. Because when Maurice and I were not there during the casting or planning period, due to us writing other shows at the time, he was a tower of strength and he really took it on as his show as much as ours.'

To direct the first series of *Goodnight Sweetheart*, Laurence and Maurice decided they needed someone who could at least remember the Second World

War. The only director they could think of was Robin Nash. The writers arranged to meet Robin at BBC Television Centre. During the meeting, he admitted that he didn't begin to understand the idea for *Goodnight Sweetheart* that the writers had described to him. However, he said, 'I'm all for it, let's see what happens.'

'Robin was thrilled to be back in the directing saddle again,' said Claire Hinson. 'He and producer John Bartlett made a great team with their shared attention to detail and understanding and respect for the period setting.'

Robin began his career by working for twelve years as an actor and stage manager. For nine months he entertained the troops in India, even coming face to face with then future co-writer of *Dad's Army*, David Croft.

Famed for his bow ties, moustache and old-school manner, Robin joined the BBC in 1955 and became a highly regarded producer, director and executive producer. The programmes he worked on for the BBC included the gentle sitcom *Marriage Lines*, which starred Richard Briers and Prunella Scales, the police drama series *Dixon of Dock Green*, with Jack Warner playing PC George Dixon, and the sitcom *Meet the Wife*, featuring the ups and downs of a middle-aged couple played by Freddie Frinton and Thora Hird. Robin's credits also included the long-running music programme *Top of the Pops*, the popular game show *The Generation Game*, with first Bruce Forsyth and later Larry Grayson, and Roy Clarke's corner-shop sitcom, *Open All Hours*. Also benefiting from his involvement were the sitcom *No Place Like Home*, with William Gaunt and Patricia Garwood, the variety show *The Les Dawson Show* and the quintessential suburban sitcom *Terry and June*, which paired Terry Scott and June Whitfield.

Uniquely, Robin had tenures as both the head of variety and head of comedy at the BBC before becoming a freelance director. During his years as a freelancer, his credits included the sitcom *Searching* for Carlton Television and the sketch series *Harry Hill*, broadcast by Channel 4. Harry is quoted as saying, 'I couldn't have met a better person so early on in my career.' After a well-deserved period of retirement, Robin died on 18 June 2011, aged eighty-four.

'Robin was the ideal director for *Goodnight Sweetheart*,' said Laurence. 'He was vastly experienced, his direction was unflashy and precise, and his charm ensured the production was smooth and harmonious.'

To help with writing the series, Laurence and Maurice realised that they would need to do a considerable amount of research on the Second World War to ensure that the episodes were factually correct; for instance, with colloquialisms of the period, and the bombings. 'Maurice and I went along to the Blitz Museum, in Tooley Street, for the day to get a feel of life at that time,' said Laurence. 'In the eponymous shop on the way out after a long day, during which we spent time in an air-raid shelter that was supposedly experiencing a heavy

Luftwaffe raid, we purchased about four books, two of which told us of every bombing raid in the East End throughout the Second World War.

'Maurice reminds me that we bought the books for our research, then realised it would be a good idea if the main character had the same books, so he knew when it was relatively safe to go back. We lent these books to the production designers and not only do they exist, Maurice and I still own them.'

Although real day-to-day life and events of the Second World War would inspire and influence the storylines of *Goodnight Sweetheart*, Laurence and Maurice deliberately didn't want to explain the manner in which the lead character could go back and forth in time. They felt that aspect would be quite boring, and frankly they didn't know how he did it either! In the early part of the series, they didn't want any other characters that could do the same, either from the past to the present or vice versa. The writers realised they might have to explain it one day, but it wasn't something they wanted to address back in 1993.

The first series of *Goodnight Sweetheart* was written by Laurence and Maurice in Suite 7 of St Peter's House, Beaconsfield. This was a period building where one could rent an office by the week. They needed it for longer than that, however, because Laurence had just moved to the Cotswolds from London, but Maurice was still preparing to do the same. 'Having worked out the first episode storyline in just one whole day on Tuesday 11 May 1993, we began writing the episode on Wednesday 12 May 1993,' said Laurence. 'We finished the first draft on Tuesday 18 May 1993.'

In his diary, Laurence wrote:

> It is going to be overlong and we shall have to make many cuts, but when we reach the end, we shall see what happens. I also have to say that the piece is quite surreal in a real kind of way; not at all like *Snakes and Ladders* in which we were dealing with the future. Here we are dealing with the past and present.

While on Tuesday 18 May 1993, Laurence wrote in his diary:

> By four o'clock we complete the first draft of the very first episode and write 'The End' at the bottom of the page. I will not pass comment upon it, only to say it is a piece of original work and it has a certain flavour not common in television comedies. I think the script will need refining, but once we finish this first script, we comment that it is our intention to start working on the storyline of episode two and see if we can't make a start upon the next script tomorrow, if not Thursday at the latest. If, by wonderful chance, we manage to complete two scripts in this month of May, then Maurice and I will be on target to complete the six by September, which is what we are really aiming at.

Two days later, on Thursday 20 May 1993, Alan Yentob, the then controller of BBC One, asked Laurence and Maurice for an update on the first draft for the first episode of *Goodnight Sweetheart*. Laurence made a note of this encounter in his diary on the same date:

> Alan Yentob asks us all about *Goodnight Sweetheart* and we are pleased to be able to report that we have indeed completed it, albeit in first draft. It's the first and most important episode and we are pleased, at least we think we are, with what we have done, or rather the way it has evolved. First scripts are unusual for they seem to take on a life of their own and they start wandering in directions you sometimes have no idea of half an hour earlier. This script is a prime example of this. We knew only the storyline, we didn't know the tone, yet it is the tone of the piece that is, in my opinion, so interesting and will allow us to go forward and write the further episodes. I just hope Nicholas Lyndhurst and Robin Nash feel about the script as we do.

When it comes to naming characters, writers are inspired in various ways. In the case of *Goodnight Sweetheart*, it was people who came into Laurence and Maurice's orb while penning the first episode that helped inspired the names of the main characters. 'For Gary, either one of us believed he – whoever "he" was – should possess the name of a bird,' said Laurence. 'Perhaps there may have been a subconscious feeling that he was about to take flight having had his wings clipped by Yvonne. My diary tells me that we played about with Nightingale, but rejected that because of the ALOMO comedy, *Nightingales*. We discussed for some time the name Wren, dismissed it and settled on Sparrow. Where Gary came from there is no record. Clearly his had to be a short name to match nicely with Sparrow, a two-syllable name. But it has not been chronicled as to where Gary came from.'

'The lady who managed St Peter's House, and who we used to meet around the communal coffee machine, was a Mrs Deadman. We borrowed her name for no good reason other than it made us laugh. We met not only Mrs Deadman in the coffee room there, but a chap who introduced himself as Eric and a woman called Phoebe. Maurice and I consciously or otherwise must have taken this information back to our desk and thought we could use those names in our new series. I can tell you too that the name Ron was taken from an old friend of Maurice and mine called Ron Tabor. He would be pleased to know that. Where Yvonne came from remains a mystery. I certainly didn't chronicle its origins in my diary.'

On Friday 28 May 1993, Laurence and Maurice met Nicholas, along with John Bartlett and Robin Nash, for lunch at the Belvedere restaurant in Holland Park, London, to discuss the first episode. 'John and Robin simply adored the script,' revealed Laurence. 'Nicholas had yet to read it because his agent hadn't sent it to him. But he was on board, all the same.' John gave Nicholas his copy of the script and then everyone sat back and waited for his verdict. Thankfully, it was favourable.

'After reading the first script, I was hooked and keen to make a series,' enthused Nicholas. 'I like to look at things from an audience's point of view and I was convinced the series would be of interest to the viewers too. One of the other selling points was that the story and the characters had layers to them. I didn't say anything at the time, but I thought to myself, can the BBC do big budget any more? Fortunately, I discovered they could. Lo and Mo insisted on high production values, which helped, of course.'

With Nicholas confirming he was happy with the first script, Laurence and Maurice finally began writing the remaining episodes of the first series on 1 June 1993. These were completed by mid-August 1993.

With Nicholas Lyndhurst already cast as the time-travelling television repair man, Gary Sparrow, casting directors Susie Parriss and Paddy Stern were assigned the task of casting the other roles. 'For leading roles, we'd discuss with the writers, director and producer what calibre of performer they were hoping to get for the role,' explained Susie. 'We'd then refer back to the budget to see what we could afford, make lists of ideas, check availabilities and then discuss with the creative team who they liked, who they thought could bring certain skills to the pertinent roles. Most of the artists would audition, but in some cases, there would be direct offers. It was the same process with all the smaller roles but those were generally either just discussed with the director or we just invited who we wanted to audition to the casting sessions. Once decisions were made on who to cast, we then negotiated with the agent over the fees. When all was agreed, we issued the details on a casting advice note and passed it on to the production office who took over giving calls, sending scripts out etc. We would attend the read-throughs and most of the live studio recordings. I loved attending the recordings and rarely missed one.'

Susie's other credits as a casting director include the BBC historical drama *Poldark*, with Aidan Turner and Eleanor Tomlinson, the drama series *Noughts + Crosses*, an adaptation of Malorie Blackman's 2001 novel series with Masali Baduza and Jack Rowan, and the quirky crime drama *Agatha Raison*, with Ashley Jensen.

Paddy worked in the casting department at Yorkshire Television for many years before Susie and Paddy formed a business partnership. Her credits at the ITV franchise included the sitcom *Home to Roost*, that saw John Thaw and Reece Dinsdale play father and son respectively, and the comedy dramas *A Bit of a Do*, with David Jason and Gwen Taylor playing a down-to-earth married couple from Yorkshire, and *Stay Lucky*, which cast Dennis Waterman as a London wheeler-dealer and Jan Francis as a self-sufficient businesswoman.

Although Susie was to work on every episode of *Goodnight Sweetheart*, Paddy passed away in 1998. 'Paddy and I were a great team,' she said. 'We would go to drama school showcases, write our notes separately and then the next day we'd compare them and ninety-nine per cent of the time we would have written identical notes!'

Several actresses were auditioned for the character of Phoebe Bamford, who became Gary Sparrow's East End wartime girlfriend and later his wife, including the actress Emma Amos, who went on to play Yvonne Sparrow from series four onwards. This was at the time when Laurence and Maurice were considering making Phoebe a blonde. In the end, the coveted role went to Dervla Kirwan. 'I remember the director Robin Nash showing surprise when we brought in Dervla to play a Londoner as she was Irish!' recalled Susie. 'Dervla's accent was excellent and Paddy and I had always been of the same mind, that actors become actors not to play themselves but to be challenged in other roles/accents.' Laurence admired Dervla's ability to retain the East End accent: 'I only ever heard her drop it once,' he recalled. 'It wasn't during a recording, but at a read-through.'

Dervla (meaning 'daughter of a poet') was born in Churchtown, Dublin, Ireland. 'I started acting when I was fifteen,' she said. 'I came over to England to do a play called *A Handful of Stars* by Billy Roach and that's where I got my big break.' Her television breakthrough, meanwhile, came in 1992 when she played Bernadette Kennedy in Melvyn Bragg's BBC drama, *A Time to Dance*. This was incidentally the series that first brought the actress to the attention of Laurence and Maurice.

The actress has worked extensively in the theatre. Her credits include playing Rosa in the April De Angelis drama *Hush* at the Royal Court Theatre, London, Alice in the revival of Brian Friel's 1979 play *Aristocrats* at the National Theatre, London, and Valerie in the Conor McPherson drama *The Weir* at both the Donmar Warehouse and Wyndham's Theatre in London. Dervla has also played Peg in Ian Kelly's riotously funny play *Mr Foote's Other Leg* at the Hampstead Theatre, London, Mary Jane Hanrahan in Stephen Adly Guirgis's critically acclaimed dark comedy *Jesus Hopped the 'A' Train* at the Young Vic, London, and Lady Macbeth in the William Shakespeare tragedy *Macbeth* at the Chichester Festival Theatre.

On television, Dervla's many other roles include playing the landlady Assumpta Fitzgerald opposite Stephen Tompkinson as Father Peter Clifford in three series of the popular Sunday night drama *Ballykissangel*, Jaye Dackers and Angel Gabriel in the comedy *The Flint Street Nativity* and Emma Rose in two series of the drama series *Hearts and Bones*, alongside Damian Lewis and Sarah Parish. Her other parts have included villain Miss Mercy Hartigan in 'The Next Doctor', the 2008 Christmas special of *Doctor Who*, with David Tennant in the title role, Davina Bailey in the comedy drama *Material Girl* and Annabelle Degalais in the intense drama, *The Reunion*.

The award-winning actress has also appeared in several films. Amongst these titles, she has played Rosie Boyd in the drama *With or Without You*, opposite Christopher Eccleston, Maura in the romantic drama *Ondine*, with Colin Farrell and Stephen Rea, and Christine in the fantasy film *Luna*, appearing with Ben Daniels and Stephanie Leonidas.

Meanwhile, Michelle Holmes was cast in the role of Yvonne Sparrow, Gary Sparrow's wife in 1993. Laurence and Maurice first became aware of the actress when she played Sue in Andrea Dunbar's black comedy film *Rita, Sue and Bob Too* with George Costigan, Siobhan Finneran and Lesley Sharp. Born Corinne Michelle Cunliffe in Rochdale, Lancashire, Michelle changed her name in order to be able to join Equity. Despite being a shy child, Michelle attended Oldham Theatre Workshop, and this stood her in good stead for when she became a professional actress.

Her theatre roles have included Doreen in the Barry Heath play *Me Mam Sez* at Oldham Coliseum Theatre, Sue in playwright Dave Simpson's *The Beauty Game* at the Library Theatre, Manchester, and Carol in Jim Cartwright's seminal play *Road* at the Octagon Theatre, Bolton.

In the early part of her career, Michelle played young receptionist Susan Turner in the medical drama series, *The Practice*. The cast also included John Fraser and Brigit Forsyth. Subsequently, her television credits have included playing Rovers Return barmaid Tina Fowler in the soap opera *Coronation Street*, Maggie Coles in the drama series *Firm Friends* alongside Billie Whitelaw and Madhur Jaffrey, and Britt Woods, the feisty wife of Woolpack landlord Terry Woods, in the soap opera *Emmerdale*. She has also played Marie in the comedy drama *Common as Muck*, Theresa in Paul Abbott's black comedy *Shameless* and Mary, a café owner, in the heart-warming comedy drama *Cold Feet*.

The actress has also played Jane in the short drama film *Jean*, opposite Doreen Mantle, best known for playing Mrs Warboys in the David Renwick sitcom *One Foot in the Grave*.

Laurence and Maurice were keen to cast Victor McGuire for the role of eloquent artisan Ron Wheatcroft, Gary Sparrow's best friend, because they had seen him play a journalist called Tim Crawford in an episode of *Love Hurts*. 'I recall Lo and Mo, Robin, the director, John, the producer, and Nick were all in the room at my audition,' said Victor. 'I had played the role of Jack in the sitcom *Bread* before *Goodnight Sweetheart*, and Robin had directed some of the episodes, so he knew my work. We had a chat and Nick and I read a scene together. I think they were keen to see what we looked like together and if there was any rapport between us.' The audition went well, and Victor was duly offered the part.

Victor was born in Tuebrook, Liverpool. After leaving school, he started to attend Everyman Youth Theatre. It was there that the actor found he had a talent for acting. 'I loved the Everyman,' he said. 'It was quite a vibrant time to be there then, in the days of the McGanns, Cathy Tyson and Ian Hart.' He then successfully applied to attend Bristol Old Vic Theatre School and became a classically trained actor.

Victor's theatre credits include playing Tony Lumpkin in the Oliver Goldsmith comedy *She Stoops to Conquer* at the Belgrade Theatre, Coventry, Snug in the William Shakespeare comedy *A Midsummer Night's Dream* at the Everyman Theatre, Liverpool, and Jack Boswell in the stage version of the Carla Lane sitcom *Bread* at the Dominion Theatre, London, on tour and at the Pavilion Theatre, Bournemouth. His roles also include Amos Hart in the Kander and Ebb musical *Chicago* at the Cambridge Theatre, London, Inspector Lestrade in the Mark Catley play *Sherlock Holmes: The Best Kept Secret* at the West Yorkshire Playhouse (rebranded the Leeds Playhouse in 2018) and on tour, and Joe Bell in Richard Greenberg's stage adaption of the Truman Capote novel *Breakfast at Tiffany's* on tour and at the Theatre Royal Haymarket, London.

On television, Victor's other roles have included Mike in the Liverpool-based soap opera *Brookside*, Jack Boswell in the sitcom *Bread* and Barry Gage in the comedy drama *Sunburn*. He also appeared as Luis Banks in the sitcom *A Many Splintered Thing*, with Alan Davies and Kate Ashfield, Dave Green in the crime drama *Dalziel and Pascoe* and Ian in the supermarket sitcom, *Trollied*. The actor also played Phil Sirkin in the drama *Shakespeare and Hathaway: Private Investigators*, Mr Mulholland in Andy Hamilton and Guy Jenkin's sitcom *Kate and Koji*, with Brenda Blethyn, and Trevor in the crime drama, *The Responder*.

Victor's film parts include Gary in Guy Ritchie's crime comedy *Lock, Stock and Two Smoking Barrels*, Piangi in the Andrew Lloyd Webber musical *The Phantom of the Opera* and Gerald Hardy in the horror film *The Woman in Black*. He has also played Andy in the biographical drama *My Week with Marilyn*, with Michelle Williams as Marilyn Monroe, Deputy Chief Constable Nadin in the Mike Leigh historical drama *Peterloo* and Creakle in Armando Iannucci's comedy drama, *The Personal History of David Copperfield*.

Laurence and Maurice had seen Christopher Ettridge playing Colin Sterne, a dodgy accountant, in an episode of *Love Hurts* and had kept him in mind for the role of PC Deadman, also known as Reg Deadman.

A Passage of Time

Christopher was born in Isleworth, London. Having enjoyed drama at school, he went on to join a local amateur acting group in Teddington, where he was brought up. 'In my heart, I wanted to become an actor,' revealed Christopher. 'I remember clearing up one day after an amateur production, when our director, Eric Yardley, said I was good enough to go to drama school.' Christopher later attended the Drama Centre in London and then went on to work in repertory theatre. 'It was hard work, because we would be rehearsing all day for the next show and on stage in the evening for the current one.'

Christopher's many theatre appearances include playing Ernest in the Alan Ayckbourn comedy *Bedroom Farce* at the New Wolsey Theatre, Ipswich, Walter Cunningham and Judge Taylor in Christopher Serge's adaptation of Harper Lee's *To Kill a Mockingbird* at the Open Air Theatre, Regent's Park, London, and Peregrine Brand in Robin French's *Heather Gardner*, which is based on Ibsen's *Hedda Gabler*, at the Birmingham Rep. He has also played Juror 11 in the Reginald Rose courtroom drama *Twelve Angry Men* at the Garrick Theatre, London, the headmaster in a tour of Alan Bennett's award-winning drama *The History Boys* and Horace Mundy and Mr Wilson in Hattie Naylor's play *The Nightwatch*, adapted from Sarah Waters's novel, at the Royal Exchange Theatre, Manchester. Christopher's roles also include Colonel Pickering in George Bernard Shaw's *Pygmalion*, a humane comedy about love and the English class system, at the English Theatre of Frankfurt in Frankfurt, Germany.

Christopher began directing in 2000. His first production was a version of Goldoni's comedy *Mirandolina*. Retitled *Dinner at Mirandolina's*, the play was staged at Komedia, Brighton. This gave the audience the novel chance of eating a three-course Italian dinner while watching the play.

His television roles have included Scarus, one of Antony's commanders, in the William Shakespeare tragedy *Antony and Cleopatra*, which was directed by Sir Jonathan Miller, Dr Cattrell in the police drama *Juliet Bravo* and an interrogator in the action drama *The Professionals*. Christopher has also played a Jehovah's Witness in the comedy drama *Minder*, Eric Dunn in the medical drama *Casualty* and General Kurt von Schleicher in the miniseries *Hitler: The Rise of Evil*. He has also appeared as Mr King in the department-store drama *Mr Selfridge*, Harvey in the revived sitcom *Birds of a Feather* and Nicola's father in the comedy *Nutritiously Nicola*.

For the big screen, Christopher's credits have included playing Sid Thomas, a removal man, in the Jack Rosenthal comedy drama *The Chain*, the postman in the comedy *Kevin and Perry Go Large*, which starred Harry Enfield and Kathy Burke, and a station bystander in the romantic comedy *I Capture the Castle*.

Finally, for the main characters of the first series of *Goodnight Sweetheart*, David Ryall was cast as Phoebe's patriotic father and landlord of the Royal Oak,

Eric Elward. Born David John Ryall in Shoreham-by-Sea, Sussex, he attended RADA (Royal Academy of Dramatic Art) and went on to enjoy a long and successful acting career.

David's first professional theatre role was as Smiler in the Arnold Wesker drama *Chips with Everything* at the Phoenix Theatre, Leicester. His other roles included playing Sir William Honeywood in the Oliver Goldsmith comedy *The Good-Natured Man*, and Ambassador in Tom Stoppard's absurdist, existential tragicomedy *Rosencrantz and Guildenstern are Dead* for Laurence Oliver's company at the National Theatre at the Old Vic, London. David later played Fence and Lockit in the John Gay play *The Beggar's Opera*, with Imelda Staunton and Paul Jones, at the National Theatre, London, and Theatre Royal, Bath, Polonius in the William Shakespeare tragedy *Hamlet* at the Barbican Theatre, London, and Louis in Patrick Marber's sprightly update of Molière's comic morality play *Don Juan in Soho*, with Rhys Ifans and Laura Piper, at the Donmar Warehouse, London. His last theatre role saw him playing King Lear in William Shakespeare's play of the same name in a fringe production staged at the Cockpit Theatre, London.

His television credits included playing Sextus Parker in the 1974 adaptation of Anthony Trollope's *The Pallisers*, Bretherton in the drama series *Love for Lydia* and Selman in the sci-fi series *Blake's 7*. David also took on the roles of George Gunn in the sitcom *Two's Company*, alongside Donald Sinden and Elaine Stritch, Herr Glass in the classic drama *Reilly: Ace of Spies* and Mr Hall in Dennis Potter's singalong noir series, *The Singing Detective*. Later in his career, he became known for playing Frank, the grandfather and dementia sufferer, in the critically acclaimed sitcom *Outnumbered*. David's appearance as Tommy Mills in the period drama *Call the Midwife* would turn out to be his last television role.

The actor's film parts included playing the Man with Whores in David Lynch's *The Elephant Man*, Froude in the crime comedy *Wilt*, which starred Mel Smith and Griff Rhys Jones, and George in the fantasy drama *Truly, Madly, Deeply*. David was also cast as Elphias Doge in the J. K. Rowling fantasy *Harry Potter and the Deathly Hallows – Part One*, Tom Tit in the horror comedy *The League of Gentlemen's Apocalypse* and Harry in the Dustin Hoffman comedy drama, *Quartet*.

David died on Christmas Day in 2014, aged seventy-nine. One of the many tributes he received came from Mark Gatiss, who said he was 'a twinkling, brilliant, wonderful actor I was privileged to call a friend'.

As part of an ongoing deal to use the facilities, ALOMO chose to record *Goodnight Sweetheart* at Teddington Studios in Teddington, Middlesex. The studios had a long and rich film and television history. Before they existed, wealthy stockbroker and cinematograph fan Henry Chinnery owned and lived in Weir House next to the River Thames in Teddington. During the early 1910s, Henry allowed a group of amateur filmmakers to use his greenhouse for filming. Ec-Ko Films were then given permission to make short silent comedy films at the location; and later Master Films arrived, built a modest stage and went into production with a string of feature-length films.

In 1931, the studios were renamed Teddington Film Studios and the filmmaker E. G. Norman, and the silent-screen actor Henry Edwards, made considerable improvements to the studio buildings and the equipment. Warner Bros. then took a lease on the studios the same year to make 'quota quickies' and eventually purchased the site lock, stock and barrel. During the 1930s, the stars to make films at the studios included Rex Harrison, Ida Lupino, and 'the cheeky chappy' Max Miller. After Errol Flynn played the lead role in the crime thriller *Murder at Monte Carol*, the film's producer Irving Asher contacted Warner Bros. executives in Hollywood and recommended they sign Flynn. They agreed and the rest, as they say, is history – film history.

In the 1940s, the stars of the day to make their way to the studios included James Mason, Florence Desmond and John Gielgud. However, on 5 July 1944, a direct hit from a V1 flying bomb caused considerable damage to the studios and the untimely death of three employees. After the war, rebuilding work took place and the studio was finally reopened by the comedian Danny Kaye in January 1948.

Stars who were ushered onto the studio floor during Teddington Studios' final years as film studios included Richard Burton, Joan Greenwood and Kenneth More. For a time, Hawker Aircraft company even used the site for storage.

The late 1950s saw ABC remodel the studios for television production. Programmes the company made there included the drama anthology series *Armchair Theatre*, the first three series of the espionage series *The Avengers* and *The Eammon Andrews Show* for their Midland and Northern ITV franchises and the ITV network during the 1960s.

Following ABC's merger with Rediffusion in 1968, Teddington Studios became the long-time home of Thames Television. The company held the ITV franchise for London and the surrounding areas from 30 July 1968 until 31 December 1992. During this period, Thames made a rich assortment of programmes at the site. They included comedy shows starring Benny Hill, Tommy Cooper and Morecambe and Wise, sitcoms such as *Bless this House*, *George and Mildred* and *Men Behaving Badly*, dramas ranging from *Rumpole of the Bailey* to *Armchair Theatre* and *Jennie: Lady Randolph Churchill*, and much-loved children's programmes as varied as *The Sooty Show*, *Magpie* and *Rainbow*.

Interestingly, it was a popular children's science-fiction series that first brought Nicholas Lyndhurst to the studios. 'I played Karl Brandt in two episodes of *The Tomorrow People* in 1978. It was a magical place,' Nicholas said.

By 1993, Thames were not only operating as an independent production company, but were hiring their studio facilities to high-profile broadcasters and independent production companies. The complex was dominated by the large Studio 1, which boasted audience seating for five hundred people, together with a spacious three-section control gallery overlooking the studio. Studio 1 was set to be used for the majority of the studio-based pre-recorded scenes and all the studio audience recordings of the fifty-eight episodes of the original six-series run of *Goodnight Sweetheart*.

Allan McKeown is said to have once considered buying Teddington Studios because he thought it made more economical sense due to the number of productions that ALOMO were making at the complex, but for some reason this never went beyond the idea stage.

Thames Television was bought by Pearson plc in 1993, and eventually the studios passed into the hands of Barnes Trust Media in 1997 after the company decided to move Thames to their office block, which included two small studio spaces, on Stephen Street, just off the Tottenham Court Road in London. However, Barnes Trust Media sold the site to Howard Holdings in 1999, and continued to lease areas such as the studios, dressing rooms, scenery stores and restaurant block. Plans by Howard Holdings to create a media village, including flats and a restaurant on part of the site, did not come to fruition.

Despite all the changes, the nineties saw sitcoms including *Birds of a Feather*, *My Hero* and *Babes in the Wood* made at the studios. Thames continued to tape their light entertainment programmes including *Des O'Connor Tonight*, *This is Your Life* and *Take Your Pick* there.

There were further changes in 2004 when Howard Holdings sold the complex to Haymarket Publishing. Then in April 2005 the studio areas became part of the Pinewood-Shepperton Group.

In the first decade of the 2000s, the sitcoms that were made at the studios included *Coupling*, *As Time Goes By* and *After You've Gone*. Ricky Gervais and Stephen Merchant also used office space at the studios to make their sitcom, *The Office*. Other light entertainment series made at the studios include *The Brian Conley Show*, *Today with Des and Mel* and *Harry Hill's TV Burp*.

The 2010s saw recordings of sitcoms including *Reggie Perrin*, *Not Going Out* and *Still Open All Hours*. Comedy, chat and music was the order of the day when *The Rob Brydon Show* was recorded at the studios. Also, editions of the panel show *A League of Their Own* and the game show *The Chase* were made there.

The last programme to be recorded at Teddington Studios was an episode of *Still Open All Hours*, which starred David Jason, in Studio 1 on Friday 21 November 2014. Pinewood handed the keys to Haymarket Publishing on 19 December 2014. The company then sold the studios to the Singaporean firm City Developers, who demolished the complex and built a large residential development on the land. This sadly ended a century of film and television production at the site on Broom Road in Teddington.

Meanwhile, Roger Andrews was engaged as the production designer on *Goodnight Sweetheart*. 'Laurence and Maurice first met Roger when he designed *The New Statesman* at Yorkshire Television,' explained Claire Hinson. 'He was a real artist and hard taskmaster whose team would do anything to deliver what he wanted. He refused to cut corners and was endlessly inventive in finding ways of recreating scenes from the 1940s on what was essentially a sitcom budget. No small challenge, and sometimes it got a bit tense! But Roger always pulled it off and what he achieved – sometimes just for a single episode – was quite breathtaking. In this he was brilliantly supported by lighting director Christopher Clayton.'

In addition to designing forty-eight episodes of *Goodnight Sweetheart*, Roger's credits included the Galton and Simpson sitcom *Steptoe and Son*, the sketch comedy *The Dick Emery Show* and the variety series *The Val Doonican Show*. He also designed episodes of the sitcom *Yes, Honestly*, the period drama *Flambards* and the sitcom *My Family*.

The original version of the song 'Goodnight Sweetheart' was written by the songwriting team of Ray Noble, Jimmy Campbell and Reg Connelly in 1931. Several vocalists have performed the song over the years, including Al Bowlly, Bing Crosby, Connie Francis and Dean Martin. For this series, the song was arranged by Anthony Sadler and Gaynor Sadler. The recording of the number for the opening and end titles of series one to six took place on Tuesday 14 September 1993 at Logorhythm Music Studios, which were owned and run by Anthony and Gaynor, on Lexington Street in Soho, London. 'Two singers, Bob Segar and Nick Curtis, were auditioned to perform the title song,' explained Gaynor. 'However, Nick was chosen. He was not only a lovely singer, but a wonderful person. He died very suddenly in the mid-nineties. Everyone who knew him was shocked and deeply saddened to hear of his passing and he was greatly missed by all of us who had the pleasure of working with him.'

The full list of musicians for the recording was as follows:

Trumpet:	Kenny Baker
Violin:	Johnny Van Derrick

Alto sax:	Ray Swinfield
Tenor sax:	Roy Willox
Baritone sax:	Martin Dobson
Guitar:	Judd Proctor
Piano:	Trevor Brown
Double bass:	Malcolm Creese
Drums:	Paul Robinson

Playing the piano on the recording for the *Goodnight Sweetheart* theme tune was not the first time Trevor Brown had met Anthony and Gaynor. 'I well remember them as I worked several times at Logoryhthm in Lexington Street,' he said. 'The trumpeter on the recording session was Kenny Baker. There was never another one quite like him! Dear old Johnny Van Derrick, the violinist, was such fun to be with. I lived in Uxbridge at the time and he lived nearby in Denham. Paul Robinson was Tony and Gaynor's usual choice of drummer. Sadly, Ray Swinfield, the alto sax player, and Roy Willox, who was on tenor sax, are no longer with us.

'I had huge admiration for Nick Curtis, who sang "Goodnight Sweetheart". I used him as my "lead" boy singer whenever I arranged television music involving any combination of "backing singer". He had a beautifully focused and compassionate way of working as well as being a wonderful musician and he really knew how to get the very best out of a group of singers. His death was both unexpected and appalling.'

Trevor's music career started at the age of eight, playing the accordion in summer season variety shows in the Thanet area. In 1966, he moved to London to study chemistry at University College but at weekends was regularly playing in dance bands and writing music arrangements for various cabaret artists. On leaving college in 1971, Trevor entered the music profession on a full-time basis and has since worked extensively in many areas. He joined the Victor Silvester Orchestra in 1972, and was subsequently part of Bob Miller's band The Millermen and spent twenty years as pianist with the Joe Loss Orchestra.

Music arranging has always been of great interest to Trevor. 'I was fortunate enough to work closely with musical director Alyn Ainsworth from 1978 during which time I contributed to many television shows including several editions of *The Royal Variety Performance, Night of 100 Stars* and BAFTA award shows,' he recalled. 'I also had a hand in shaping and arranging music for many television series such as *Wednesday at Eight, Live from the Palladium, Summertime Special, Russ Abbot's Madhouse, The Cannon and Ball Show, The Paul Daniels Magic Show* and many more. *Stars in Their Eyes* occupied me almost continuously between 1990 and 2006, and I also worked on *Soapstar Superstar* and the first two series of *Pop Idol*.'

The original opening title sequence for *Goodnight Sweetheart* was used in all six series. The responsibility of making the initial vision a reality was given to Paul Peppiate. 'I was commissioned directly by John Bartlett at ALOMO,' he said. 'I'd produced several title sequences and graphics for John during my time as a designer at Yorkshire Television. I had just left the ITV franchise-holder and had joined a graphics and post-production agency called The Look. They were part of the Leeds-based advertising agency, Poulters. *Goodnight Sweetheart* would have been one of the first projects we worked on there.'

The scenario for the opening sequence came from the production team at ALOMO. John Bartlett remembered that it was him, Robin Nash and Roger Andrews that came up with the idea and pitched it to Laurence and Maurice. 'It was my job to design the poster and I was given the creative freedom to do that,' said Paul. 'I remember researching the look of period film posters and creating a visual style to match (although with many years' hindsight I don't think the typography was that brilliant!). The searchlights were the key visual – a very quick and recognisable visual reference of London during wartime Britain. The viewer doesn't get long to register detail, so something iconic was required. It was also important to hide the identity of Gary Sparrow's female partner on the poster.

'The design and editing will have taken place in Leeds, but I attended initial meetings with ALOMO at Teddington Studios along with my producer at The Look, David McKendrick.'

The footage of Nicholas Lyndhurst, as Gary Sparrow, approaching the cinema poster in the title sequence was filmed at the Odeon Cinema in Wimbledon, South West London. The cinema was built and operated by County Cinemas chain and opened as the Regal Cinema on 20 November 1933. In the early days, the cinema's programme used to include variety acts as well as films. At the start of the Second World War, the cinema became part of Oscar Deutsch's chain of Odeon Theatres. The Regal was renamed Gaumont in November 1949 and later Odeon in September 1962 after another Odeon located nearby was closed. In November 1972, the Odeon became a triple-screen cinema. The cinema was finally closed in December 2002 when a new Odeon multiplex was opened in Wimbledon. The former cinema building was demolished the following year and an office block was built in its place.

'For the titles shoot, I had two posters printed,' recalled Paul. 'You only just see a glimpse of the first one. My current company, Works, were also involved in the original sequence as they employed an incredibly talented scenic artist at the time called Rick Duffield. He painted the poster artwork without the text, which I then scanned to work on in the edit – adding the animated text. We then had a composite of the poster with text printed off for the shoot.

'I cannot remember what software I used, but the first version was relatively easy to create, so it may have been done in an online edit suite – nothing fancy from a graphics point of view. All we had to do was "fly" the text into position to create the poster and then edit the sequence together with the shots of Nicholas Lyndhurst walking past the poster.

'The individual episode titles were added in the programme online edits. We designed the poster frame so that "TONIGHT" could be replaced with the episode title.'

When there were cast changes, videotape editor Chris Wadsworth had to alter the poster to reflect the name changes. 'I can remember that taking some considerable time,' he admitted. 'It's easier today, of course, but then quite a battle with travelling mattes and graphics. If you look closely and freeze the frame you can just see the join. And, I had to do it more than once, so further cast changes were met with a large groan from me. At least with digital technology, which had just come in, the quality was maintained.'

The rehearsals, location filming, pre-records and studio audience recordings for series one of *Goodnight Sweetheart* took place between Monday 16 August 1993 and Thursday 14 October 1993.

As this was the first series, an extra read-through for the first-ever episode of *Goodnight Sweetheart*, entitled 'Rites of Passage', was arranged and took place at Teddington Studios on Monday 16 August 1993. 'It's always very nerve-wracking,' Dervla Kirwan once said about the rehearsing process. 'It's like the first day of school and you walk in and just hope that you're going to be good and that no one is going to fire you when you have your first initial reading of the script – and fortunately, they didn't!'

The dates of the location filming for the first series were Friday 20 August 1993, Monday 23 August 1993, Tuesday 24 August 1993, Wednesday 25 August 1993, Thursday 26 August 1993 and Friday 27 August 1993.

It was location manager Julia Morpeth who was responsible for finding the locations for the first four series of *Goodnight Sweetheart*. Julia can still remember the work that was required to make the pub and the nearby shops ready for filming. 'When we first found the Royal Oak, I seem to recall all the brickwork had been painted a horrible red,' she said. It took six days of high-powered pressure washing to strip all the paint and reveal the brickwork and the original signage. The original production designer, Roger Andrews, was passionate about detail. We had to repaint and dress every shop and house on both sides of the street and remove and reroute all the television aerials. It wasn't the best way to introduce ourselves into the neighbourhood, but we won them around eventually!'

Julia's other credits as a location manager included the final series of the drama *Howards' Way*. Thereafter, she mainly worked in the same capacity on sitcoms including *My Hero*, *The Green Green Grass* and *Not Going Out*.

Assistant director Simon Haveland was engaged as a first assistant director on the first five episodes of *Goodnight Sweetheart*. Simon still has good memories of his time on the sitcom. 'It was a very happy series to work on,' he recalled. 'I had not worked with ALOMO before, but I later worked as a location manager on a series of *Birds of a Feather*. The very nature of my role as first assistant director meant that I had to work very closely with the director, Robin Nash. After Robin introduced himself to you, he would ask you what your role was and what that entailed. I believe that this was because at the BBC the role of certain positions was not the same as that in the commercial sector. Robin would make these enquiries with the delivery of a teacher welcoming a small child to his or her first day at school. He was over six feet tall, a good head of grey hair and always wore a bow tie. It was very endearing. I remember walking around Teddington Studios with him one day during pre-production and I noted that in a noticeably short time he had got to know everyone's name. For instance, the receptionist, cleaners and dinner ladies etc. I remarked on this one day and he explained that he had acquired this skill/habit at the BBC and that he felt it was an important tool to bring both harmony and unity to a workplace. It was a trait that I took with me.'

Prior to any location filming taking place for *Goodnight Sweetheart*, there would be what was called a technical recce. This meant that Simon took part in these visits during the making of the first series. 'It was my job to visit all the locations required for the filming with Robin, and the other heads of department, to discuss his plan for shooting the sequences,' he said. 'Obviously, we were combining "present day" locations with 1940s London and, of course, the latter restricts your choices. We used Columbia Road, which is famous for its flower market, for the area leading up to the pub, as it still retains a "period" setting. After collating all the information, I produced a shooting schedule and call sheet for each of the day and night sequences.'

Simon's other television credits include the children's science-fiction series *The Tomorrow People*, the sketch show *Tracey Ullman: A Class Act* and more recently the BAFTA-winning sitcom *Stath Sells Flats*. He has also worked as an assistant director in the film industry. This led him to work on productions including the fourteenth James Bond film *A View to a Kill*, Jim Henson's musical fantasy *Labyrinth* and the biting satire *Whoops Apocalypse*.

Nicholas still has vivid memories of the challenges that filming on location for *Goodnight Sweetheart* presented. 'Ezra Street and Columbia Road were difficult locations to work at,' he remembers. 'There was nowhere to park the vans or the generator for the lights. For the first few years, the make-up and wardrobe departments used to be based upstairs at the Royal Oak on Columbia Road. This made it quicker than going back to the unit base, which was a couple of miles away.

'I didn't realise just how noisy the East End of London could be. We spent ages waiting for things to quieten down. The noise used to range from jets and pneumatic drills to music coming from the kebab shop across the road.'

Laurence was left feeling more than a little shaken while attending the first location shoot for *Goodnight Sweetheart* in the East End. 'I was walking down the Columbia Road with Nicholas,' said the writer. 'He was very quiet and reserved but we got talking. We were suddenly besieged by fans of *Only Fools and Horses* shouting "Rodney!" I thought, is this how it's going to be?! They were screaming and eventually started chasing us down the road. I told Nicholas to follow me and we sought refuge in the Royal Oak pub, which of course we were using for filming. I was so grateful that I decided there and then that we would change the name of the pub in the script from the Duke of Marlborough to the Royal Oak!'

While being recognised in public, especially when you're filming on location, can have its drawbacks, Nicholas isn't fazed by the attention. 'It's part of the job,' he admits. 'It's flattering. If you're lucky to get recognition it means you must be doing something right.

'People that used to come and watch the filming would get bored quite quickly. They used to ask if it always took so long, and I would tell them that most of the time it's ninety per cent waiting and ten per cent filming.'

John Bartlett explained how well Nicholas coped with the process of filming, especially on location. 'Nick is such a professional,' he remarked. 'For example, when we were filming on location, his continuity was superb. He gave the exact same performance on master shots and close-ups.'

There was, however, a problem that had to be rectified during the location shoot for the first episode. 'We were filming a scene where Nick was supposed to drive down Shipton Street in Bethnal Green and park near Ezra Street, an alley that we were using as Duckett's Passage,' recalled John. 'I had wrongly presumed that Nick had a driving licence, but he didn't – he only had a provisional licence. I asked why he hadn't taken his test and he told me he always had a driver. In the end, we managed to get someone to crouch in the car just out of shot in order to help Nick drive the car for just a short distance.'

Simon also remembers how the crew managed to improvise when it came to the scenes where Nicholas was required to drive. 'We pushed the van into shot or asked Nick to drive the last few feet,' he said. 'Inevitably, he would hit the brakes too hard as often happens when you're driving an unfamiliar vehicle and have the whole crew watching!'

As Nicholas didn't have a full driving licence, it was down to Malcolm Marks, Laurence Marks's brother, to drive Nicholas to and from the rehearsals, locations and studio recordings. Interestingly, he drove Linda Robson to the rehearsals and recordings for *Birds of a Feather*.

With the location filming complete for the first series, it was time to rehearse and tape the interiors for each episode. The studio recording dates took place in Studio 1 at Teddington Studios each Thursday between Thursday 9 September 1993 and Thursday 14 October 1993.

Apart from the Christmas special in the third series and the special in 2016, the rehearsal process tended to follow the same pattern. Christopher Ettridge remembers this well. 'We would do a read-through of an episode first thing on Friday mornings, having recorded an episode the night before,' he said. 'There would then be a discussion about the new script and what we thought did and didn't work. Laurence and Maurice, or the other writers, would then go to another room to make any necessary changes. In the meantime, the director and the cast would start working through what we could. There would be a break for lunch, and we would receive rewrites as appropriate. We never worked on Saturdays, but we would rehearse on Sundays, Mondays, Tuesdays and Wednesdays.'

John Bartlett proved particularly invaluable to Robin Nash and the cast each Friday. 'Robin once admitted to me that he wasn't overly confident with actors and actresses,' he revealed. 'So, to help him, I used to do the blocking at the Friday rehearsals, which I loved.'

Nicholas had his own routine for committing each script to memory. 'I used to learn my lines each Saturday in the attic of where I was living at the time,' he said. 'In fact, when you appear in a sitcom you must learn everyone's lines, not just your own. You had to have a good foundation for when you start rehearsals because otherwise people notice and make comment. Also, they used to put a stopwatch on the episode early in the week. We had to make sure the episode didn't run over because it had to finish on time for the next programme.'

To use boxing parlance, Laurence noticed that Nicholas never left the fight in the gym. 'When he was rehearsing, Nick was almost unintelligible,' he remembered. He would sit in his baseball cap and mumble his lines. It was fascinating to watch him learning Gary Sparrow, as it were. But no one doubted Nicholas's ability, of course. We never thought, he won't be able to do it. Rik Mayall filled the room at the read-throughs for *The New Statesman*, but Nick was the complete opposite.'

The experience Nicholas had gained over the years had certainly prepared him for playing the role of Gary Sparrow. 'I had a fairly shallow exposure to the world of sitcom to begin with,' he pointed out. 'Appearing in *Going Straight* gave me the opportunity to be in the presence of the genius Ronnie Barker and watch him at work. I then appeared with Geoffrey Palmer and Wendy Craig in *Butterflies* where all I had to do was say the odd funny line and wear a funny T-shirt. I was still finding my feet and serving my apprenticeship. In the early days of my career, I can remember standing in a studio and listening to some of the technicians who were talking and not understanding a word they were saying. That's why I made a point of learning about all the different departments that work on a series. All this meant I felt ready by the time I joined the cast of *Only Fools and Horses*. If I had gone straight into *Goodnight Sweetheart* at the very start, it would have been a very different story!'

Ironically, Victor McGuire's abiding memory of the rehearsal period was not about the rehearsals themselves. 'The main thing I remember is all the venues we used,' he said, reminiscing. 'They varied from a hall in the Chelsea Barracks to a small scout hut in Kingston!'

Mia Jupp was engaged by ALOMO for several years prior to *Goodnight Sweetheart*. 'I worked my way up the ranks from production secretary to production manager,' she said. 'This meant I had a couple of positions on *Goodnight Sweetheart*. For the first two series, I was the production co-ordinator, which basically means that along with the rest of the production team we were responsible for making sure everyone got the right information to be on set, on location or at rehearsals at the right time. It involved booking crew, setting up recces with Julia Morpeth and so much more. Even though it was an office-based job, we all helped during the location shoots and were part of the studio recording days.

'Nick Lyndhurst and Vic McGuire (and, of course, the rest of the talented cast!) were amazing to watch perform. Even in rehearsals, you'd get comedy gold from them every time, and their timings were spot on; they were such fun to work with.'

Mia's other credits included being a producer on the sitcom *A Many Splintered Thing*, the children's drama *The Story of Tracy Beaker* and the children's horror-comedy, *Young Dracula*. She was also the executive producer on the animated version of Judith Kerr's classic children's story, *The Tiger Who Came to Tea*. Mia died in 2021, not long after sharing her recollections for this book. Echoing the thoughts of her family, friends and colleagues at her untimely death, Maurice said, 'We were all shocked and saddened.'

Among the other production team members who worked on *Goodnight Sweetheart* was the lighting director, Christopher Clayton. 'The smooth running of *Goodnight Sweetheart* behind the scenes owed a great deal to the hard work and diligence of the production team,' he said. 'The heads of departments who deemed it necessary would attend the Friday read-through. We would have visited a producer's run on the Tuesday morning and discussed the following week's sets and floor plan. I would design the lighting Tuesday afternoon, order equipment and draw a lighting plot. All heads of departments, except the designer and lighting director, would attend the producer's and tech run on Wednesdays at 11.30am.

'Also on Wednesday mornings, the lighting crew of six to eight electricians would check the delivery and rig the lights, working safely with the scenic crew, carpenters and painters, who again would be unloading and building the sets. To an outsider it would appear a noisy chaos, but everyone would know exactly what they had to do. They were a good team. As the sets arrived and were assembled and the different departments worked around the studio, the sets would be propped and finished. After lunch I would start to "fine light", adjusting every individual lamp and building "set files". Other departments would arrive from the morning's "outside rehearsal" and conduct their own rigs and preparations. By 7.00pm, everything would be ready for the tech run. It was the first opportunity for the cast to work in the sets, for the director and others to check the camera script and for those in all the departments who had not seen a rehearsal to understand the following day's requirements. Under some circumstances that did change, and we did some pre-recordings on the Wednesday evening; but that was usually if the script was heavy studio-wise rather than having location content.'

Christopher started his career at Yorkshire Television. During his time there, he worked on programmes including the sitcom *That's My Boy*, the game show *3-2-1*, and the comedy drama *A Bit of a Do*. Later he became a freelancer and his subsequent credits have included the sketch series *Little Britain*, the stand-up special *Peter Kay: Live at the Top of the Tower* and the sitcom *My Family*.

The Thursday recording days for *Goodnight Sweetheart* were long and demanding for the cast, especially Nicholas. 'We would invariably have an early start on studio days because we would often have to pre-record scenes that had complicated set-ups. If we were called any later than 7.30am, it was luxury!' he joked. 'Timing lines for an audience to watch eight hours ahead was quite difficult to do. Once we had finished the pre-recorded scenes we had to go and rehearse other scenes on the other sets to the sounds of the other sets being struck, which was always noisy. We did a basic tech that involved taking each scene step by step, line by line about eight to ten times so that everyone, including the cameras, lighting and sound, knew what they were doing. There would then be a break for lunch before finishing the tech and then doing a dress rehearsal.'

The writers' presence on the day of recordings was crucial to the overall success of the various episodes. 'We'd do a run-through for Laurence and

Maurice who would give some notes,' recalled Christopher Clayton. 'These sometimes required scary changes!'

Despite starting early in the morning, time was always an important factor on the studio days. 'We were always having to watch the clock, and quite often one or two scenes would not have been finished in time before dinner and the audience arriving,' said Nicholas. 'The break before the evening recording was an important one but was equally nerve-wracking.'

Christopher Ettridge concurred. 'The cast and production team would have something to eat; then we'd start to panic,' he said. 'Then we'd record the episode in front of a live audience, which was thrilling and scary.'

If things became stressful, Nicholas would seek time alone. 'I sometimes used to go down to the river to get a breath of fresh air when it got a bit much,' he admitted. 'Then we recorded the episode in the evening in front of an audience, and had to be finished by 10.00pm. I used to get tired by this time, but fortunately adrenalin always kicked in for the main recording. I used to get nervous, and even now I still get a knot in my stomach when I hear the theme tune to *Goodnight Sweetheart, Only Fools and Horses* or *After You've Gone!*'

By the time Victor McGuire came to work on *Goodnight Sweetheart*, he was also used to busy studio days. 'The experience of working on other sitcoms such as *Bread* meant I felt at home working on a multi-camera series,' he said. 'I have always found working in the studio less stressful as you can always do another take if you make a mistake. The only time I did get stressed on the series was when we were filming on location and time was short.

'When you are working on a series, you are just in the moment. It became a routine of rehearse, tech, dress rehearsal and then record. The thing I most loved about working at Teddington Studios was being in the bar that overlooked the river. It was great to socialise there with the cast and crew.'

Once the audience, who had queued patiently at the front of Teddington Studios, was seated in Studio 1 ready for the recording, they were greeted by one of the warm-up artists.

Denny Hodge was a warm-up artist on the first two series of *Goodnight Sweetheart*, including the first-ever episode. 'Until I decided to become an actor in 1998, I was one of the country's top warm-up comedians,' he said. 'I worked on hundreds of programmes from *Birds of a Feather* to *Only Fools and Horses*, *Red Dwarf* to *University Challenge* and *Telly Addicts*. At the time, I had a company that also booked television studio audiences, so my wife and I found the audiences for these shows as well. I remember it as being a very happy time.'

Ted Robbins is the brother of the actresses Kate and Amy Robbins and a first cousin once removed of Paul McCartney. He is best known for playing Den Perry in the Peter Kay sitcom, *Phoenix Nights*. His other acting credits on television include playing Terry in the comedy drama *Mount Pleasant*, Barry Quid, founder of discount chain World of Quid, in an episode of *Birds of a Feather* in 2014, and Victor St James in the comedy *Benidorm*. As well as being a respected actor, comedian and radio presenter, Ted has also worked as a warm-up artist and was no stranger to Teddington Studios. As a warm-up artist, he worked on sitcoms there including *Birds of a Feather* and *Men Behaving Badly*, and other light entertainment programmes including *This is Your Life* and *Des O'Connor Tonight*. This made him the perfect choice to work on *Goodnight Sweetheart*. 'I got on great with all the cast and we became good friends,' said Ted proudly. 'Nick is a smashing bloke, as well as a good actor. He has a lovely wife called Lucy, who used to be a ballet dancer. I used to tease Nick by telling him he was punching above his weight! When we were in the bar, he would tell me all the things he and David Jason used to get up to when they were making *Only Fools and Horses*. He's a very private person, so I respected him for taking the time to talk to me.

'I always used to attend the dress rehearsals and would sit with Marks and Gran in the audience. I made sure I always got a script for each episode in advance, so I could remind the audience of what was happening in the story as well as in the studio. If there was a pause of, say, ten minutes in the recording, they would tell me and I'd get up and do a few gags with members of the cast and crew or the audience. Everybody on the series was kind and it was a very happy time for me.'

When it came to the evening recordings, Laurence and Maurice did not sit in the studio audience. 'We always sat in the producer's box,' recalled Laurence.

After each recording, the de-rig would begin. 'Everything would be cleared by midnight,' Christopher Clayton said, 'so that whatever show followed us in on the Friday could start to paint the floors, just as we had done early Wednesday morning.'

After the recording was finished, the cast could finally unwind. 'Then there would be a chance for a complimentary drink in the studio bar,' said Nicholas. 'That was before going home around 10.30pm to rest before starting the read-through and blocking for the next episode at 10.00am the following morning.'

After each studio audience recording took place, the episode would be edited. As previously mentioned, Chris Wadsworth was one of the editors who worked on *Goodnight Sweetheart*. 'I joined the "Beeb" as a videotape engineer in 1976, in the Television Recording Department at BBC Television Centre in London,' said Chris. ' I was promoted to senior recording engineer in 1978 and editor in 1980. As a junior editor I was allocated all sorts of work like *Match of the Day*,

Top of the Pops, *Play School*, *Rugby Special*, *Film '80*, *Nationwide* and trailers for BBC One and BBC Two.

'Within a year, I started to concentrate on light entertainment programmes. They included *Blankety Blank*, *Only Fools and Horses*, *Not the Nine O'Clock News*, *Terry and June*, *Just Good Friends*, *Blackadder*, *Brush Strokes*, *Hi-de-Hi!*, *KYTV*, *On the Up*, *Saturday Night Clive*, *One Foot in the Grave*, *Absolutely Fabulous*, *As Time Goes By* and *French and Saunders*. I left the BBC to go it alone in 1998 and continued to work freelance on programmes including *Parkinson*, *Mirrorball*, *The Catherine Tate Show*, *The Green Green Grass*, *Mock the Week* and *Still Open All Hours*. I am now semi-retired.

'All my episodes of *Goodnight Sweetheart* were edited in the post-production area at BBC Television Centre the Wednesday after each Thursday recording. This grew out of what was called the Television Recording Department. By 1993, we had moved out of the basement to new areas, including eleven new online suites on the fourth floor in the Spur.

'The various takes, retakes, pick-ups and the shown location material, now with audience reaction, came back to an edit suite and I started to assemble the bits into a complete programme of twenty-nine minutes. From studio notes and timecodes, material was found, judged, compared and a best selection made and recorded on a new tape, which was to become the transmission master. The pictures and sound also had to comply with and fall inside defined technical limits, so this had to be addressed as well with the help of scopes and meters. The process took a day (usually from 8.00am to 7.00pm) in an online suite, to edit the programme. We edited to D3 at that time. D3 was an uncompressed PAL-encoded digital format designed by Panasonic, and widely adopted by the BBC at that time. Sony's Digi Beta was launched in 1993, the year of the first series, and we eventually moved over to Digi instead of D3. Digi Beta eventually took over for transmission too, but the BBC would have wanted D3 for at least the 1993 series. An online suite consisted of three D3 machines, one recorder and two playbacks. Signals passed from the playback machines to the recorder via vision and sound mixers. In a comedy, the sound was always the hardest thing to get right, because you were not only editing the dialogue, but you were also editing the laughter of the studio audience and trying to make it sound real while going from take to take. Any music cues recorded after the edit and composed to fit the edit are added in a dub.

'The editing time for the location material varied according to the amount shot. This was single- or two-camera shooting using, at least to start with, Beta SP cameras. You could produce five to ten minutes of completed material in a day. The "rushes", or more accurately tapes, came back to me and I would edit the shots together to best cover the action. I had to make allowance for where the audience that would eventually see the footage might laugh. This I did by delaying the next dialogue to leave a gap that hopefully would be filled with laughter. This was an inexact science, but if a ninety per cent success rate was achieved then you were doing quite well.

'The location material for the first series was edited from Beta SP, a medium-quality analogue tape format. This would have been simple tape-to-tape editing, presumably editing to D3, a digital tape format, using a Sony 900 controller. From series two onwards, for the location edits, I have references in my diary to Lightworks, one of the first non-linear systems. This became the norm for a while: location single-camera material was edited on a non-linear system, and studio edits straight to online.

'When Robin Nash was directing, he would pop into the location edits to keep an eye on how they were going, but I was mostly left alone. Robin would not alter much, but when he did, it was usually for a good reason; he was the boss after all. We had worked together for several years before that and had achieved a good working relationship.

'Sometimes there was a need for what is called a pre-record in the studio. They were usually recorded in the morning or afternoon of the main studio recording on Thursdays, and were designed to get a scene, or shot, out of the way, that would have been difficult to do in front of an audience. Any editing that this required was undertaken by Howard Denyer at Teddington Studios. Howard was the recording engineer, an ex-Thames guy of many years' experience, who could do these assemblies very well. That, along with the location material, was played in to the audience in between the live scenes, to present the audience with as complete a programme as possible. We needed their laughter on the pre-recorded material as well.

Chris was keen to pay tribute to the professionalism of Nicholas Lyndhurst. 'I have known Nick from the earliest days on *Only Fools and Horses*, and indeed *Butterflies*,' he recalled. 'He is probably the most consistent actor I have ever worked with. Contrary to most perceptions of editing, continuity is not the overriding consideration, as pace and timing a gag would, in my opinion, be more important; but with Nick you never had to worry as you darted between takes, as he was always so accurate with his actions, matching perfectly with the words every time.

'Robin would have been too busy with the current week's programme to be at the edit suite all day. I was given the PA's notes and any thoughts from Robin and John Bartlett, the producer, and I would put the show together with these notes beside me, going between takes, tightening and tweaking as I thought fit.

Robin would appear in the afternoon and we would finish off for John to review it with us before close of play. If there was anything that was not liked, we would correct the edit, or bounce to another tape and re-edit. This was rare.

'Working with Robin was one of my happiest memories. He could get quite fiery in the gallery, in the heat of battle as it were, but always the gentleman after the show, over a drink in the bar. In the edit suite he was happy to relax and watch the show as we put it together. If we were over length, I would look to Robin about a suggested cut, and he would accept or reject in an instant with no mucking about. With online (which was expensive) you just had to get it right on the day.'

As 'Rites of Passage', the first episode of series one, begins, television repairman Gary Sparrow is seen enduring a lacklustre birthday party organised by his assertive wife, Yvonne, at their Cricklewood home in 1993. The only upside to this depressing celebration for Gary is that this is where he meets eloquent artisan Ron Wheatcroft, the husband of Yvonne's best friend, Stella, for the first time.

Ron enters the living room to find Gary sitting on the settee accompanied only by the pounding beat of 2 Unlimited's 'There's No Limit'. 'I reckon this is the worst party since Charles and Di's tenth wedding anniversary,' comments Ron, not realising it's Gary's party! With the rest of the guests in the kitchen, Gary and Ron get to know each other and exchange what will become their trademark banter. After revealing it's his birthday, and Yvonne is his wife, Gary admits that since his other half started doing a psychological course, she's been so adept at manipulation he can't get a thought in edgewise, which explains why the choice of music and food at his party is not to his liking.

After the disappointing party, Gary's attempts to initiate lovemaking with Yvonne in their marital bedroom are thwarted because she's watching an Open University course programme on video. 'So, Open University and closed legs, is it?' Gary says with witty brashness. Fortunately for Gary, the video breaks down and his request for a 'leg-over' is finally met.

Back at work, Gary finds himself asking a police constable for directions to Hugh Gaitskell House in the East End of London, where he's due to fix a television set, after becoming lost. After listening to the police constable rambling, Gary manages to get him to focus and give directions. However, they are delivered at such speed that Gary manages to just about make out that he should head for Duckett's Passage, and ask at a pub called the Royal Oak if he gets lost again.

Gary drives and parks at the entrance to Duckett's Passage and wanders down the alleyway. Without realising it, Gary time-travels back to the East End during war-torn 1940. He then makes his way to the Royal Oak to ask for further directions. There, he meets attractive barmaid Phoebe Bamford for the very first time.

When Gary asks for directions, Phoebe, not surprisingly, has never heard of Hugh Gaitskell House. She then asks her landlord dad, Eric Elward, who's in the cellar, to come up. Again, he's never even heard of any Hugh Gaitskell, let alone a tower block called Hugh Gaitskell House. He's more concerned as to why Gary is asking. 'Careless talk costs lives,' the landlord reminds him. Gary smiles, believing the overbearing landlord is keeping in character as he believes it's a theme pub. The television repairman still doesn't realise that he's been bestowed with the gift of time travel. Therefore, when he's questioned by Eric as to why he's not in uniform, he decides to play along again. 'I'm not at liberty to divulge that information,' he tells the landlord.

However, when Phoebe charges Gary tuppence farthing for a quick half, he excuses himself so he can go outside. Looking around, he's shocked to see the nearby bomb damage. Gary experiences further confusion when PC Reg Deadman arrives at the pub. He is the grandad of the police constable who he met earlier. As they look alike, Gary addresses him as if they had met, something which PC Deadman, of course, denies. Gary concludes that he's dreaming and thinking out loud to himself wonders whether he will get a chance to get his 'leg over' with the barmaid, Phoebe.

After going back inside the pub, Eric reminds Gary that he owes tuppence farthing for his drink. Gary, believing he's in a dream, tells him he's come out without any coppers on him. He then takes out his German Montblanc fountain pen, the birthday present from Yvonne, and offers to pay by cheque or write him an IOU. Noticing the pen, Eric asks where he acquired it and is concerned to see it was made in Germany. Gary's explanation that he was given the pen as a birthday present doesn't wash with the landlord, who accuses him of being a spy. Phoebe argues this is nonsense due to Gary bringing so much attention to himself.

Gary manages to prove he's English by reading the words 'Worcestershire beat Warwickshire by ten wickets' written down for him by Eric. While not fully convinced of his innocence, Eric concedes. He then outbids PC Deadman in an impromptu auction to buy Gary's new pen, less the cost of the drink he ordered.

Noticing a piano, Gary can't help walking over to it and tinkling the ivories. At first, he accompanies himself as he sings a few words of 'Your Song'. When Phoebe shows approval, Gary tells her he wrote it. Asked if he's written any other songs, Gary plays and sings a line from 'My Way'. The latter causes Eric to complain, saying he doesn't want any defeatist songs in his pub. After Eric goes, Phoebe asks Gary's name. He then makes the mistake of telling her he's a television repairman, before quickly telling her he's switched to other things such as radar. Sensing a rapport between his daughter and the relative stranger, Eric reminds Phoebe that she's a married woman.

Phoebe goes on to reveal her husband, Donald, is away due to the war and the last she heard he was in Tunisia. Gary, still believing he's dreaming, offers to take her dancing. Still unsure of Gary, Eric becomes concerned that he doesn't have a gas mask and ponders as to whether he has any ID papers. Fortunately, Gary is saved by an air raid and before long finds himself joining everyone in the pub in sheltering in the cellar, which brings on his claustrophobia.

When Gary comes round after passing out in the cellar, he's disappointed to discover that he's not having a dream and really is in 1940. Later, to help boost morale, Phoebe encourages Gary to teach everyone one of his songs. Before long, they're all singing 'Your Song' in a wartime style. That is, apart from Eric.

When Eric realises the till tray, including the evening's takings, is still upstairs in the bar, he climbs out of the cellar. At the same time, Gary's claustrophobia gets the better of him and he follows Eric. There is a large explosion and rubble falls down the entrance into the cellar.

When Phoebe and Reg finally manage to make their way up to the bar, they discover Gary giving mouth-to-mouth resuscitation to Eric who has been knocked out by the till tray. Not realising that Gary is attempting to safe his life, PC Deadman tries to pull Gary off Eric. Gary informs him that he learnt the technique in America, and Phoebe begs Gary not to let her father die. When he comes around, Eric changes his tune about Gary when he discovers he's saved his life.

Realising he needs to try and get back home to 1993, Gary leaves the Royal Oak and begins to make his way to Duckett's Passage, followed by Phoebe. Gary persuades her to go back to her father and the others at the pub. She gives him a kiss and turns and heads home. Gary then makes his way towards Duckett's Passage.

Back at home in 1993, in a state of shock and with his overalls covered in dirt, Gary is asked by a worried Yvonne, already in bed, where he's been. Gary tries to explain that he visited a pub and that, when the landlord tripped and fell down an open trapdoor into the cellar, he banged his head and stopped breathing. Not convinced, Yvonne sarcastically asks whether he gave him the kiss of life. When Gary tells her he did, she doesn't believe him. She thinks it's an excuse for him staying out drinking with his mates and tells him he doesn't need to lie to her as she's not his mother. Gary heads to the bathroom and as Yvonne says 'goodnight', Gary replies, 'Goodnight sweetheart,' as he stares into a mirror and reflects on the evening's events.

The main read-through, together with the blocking, for the first-ever episode of *Goodnight Sweetheart* took place at the London Welsh Rugby Club, 187, Kew Road, Richmond, TW9, on Friday 3 September 1993.

On Thursday 9 September 1993, Laurence and Maurice watched the recording of the first episode in the producer's box. It was the same one in which they had sat through the recordings of the sitcoms *Birds of a Feather* and *Get Back*. Also present in the box were a myriad of people including Martin Fisher and David Lilley from the BBC, and Allan McKeown and Claire Hinson from ALOMO. In his diary, Laurence noted:

> We are heartened as Denny Hodge introduces to a packed audience Nicholas Lyndhurst, and judging by the reception he receives from the audience we know that we have chosen a star (as if we ever had any doubts) and that the audience will be with his new character from the word go.

Despite *Goodnight Sweetheart* being a sitcom that really was a break from the norm, ironically the first episode started in the typical living room of a suburban part of London, which is often seen as cliché territory in the world of sitcom. However, right from the opening scene, the first episode is full of Marks and Gran's trademark witty and clever dialogue and style. All the main characters, complete with the various strengths and weaknesses, are quickly established. For instance, it becomes clear straight away that Yvonne is the more dominant and ambitious partner in Gary and Yvonne's marriage. Although Gary is clearly frustrated by the status quo, it's clearly a marriage that would have continued without him seriously considering straying from the marital leash, if fate hadn't had other ideas.

Equally pleasing is that the rapport that had first been spotted between Nicholas and Victor at the latter's audition is very much in evidence in the opening scene set at Gary's lacklustre party. However, on reflection, Laurence feels that while the opening scene is important, it doesn't actually move the story along. 'The episode, in my opinion, really gets going when Gary wanders down Duckett's Passage and into the 1940s,' he said. 'Yet we realised it was important to meet Yvonne and get some indication of their marriage, their relationship, what kept them together or what would pull Gary apart.'

Maurice also has mixed feelings about the opening scene. 'These days it seems too long,' he said. 'But on the other hand, it sets up three of our characters rather well. I'm ashamed to say the only reason Gary and Ron didn't know each other was so that Ron could comment on Yvonne's bum, not knowing she's married to Gary.'

The onscreen chemistry between Nicholas and Dervla was also very clear to see in the first episode. 'Chemistry is very rare to find, and I think it's very hard to generate chemistry if it doesn't naturally exist,' said Dervla. 'I certainly couldn't put my finger on why it was there. I think it was all down to the casting and we were very good together. I really enjoyed working with Nicholas. He's a very sweet, private, kind man. He could see I was very green, very inexperienced, and was very caring with me. But I think chemistry is in the luck of the draw. There are times when I've done jobs where you think there's going to be chemistry and it just isn't there.'

For Dervla, making the first episode of *Goodnight Sweetheart* was particularly nerve-wracking. 'I was like a robot because the fear that I experienced was just terrifying, it was absolutely terrifying,' she admitted.

When writing the first episode, Laurence and Maurice decided that not being too specific about Gary's wartime duties meant that they could justify why a young able-bodied man in civilian clothes was in the East End of London in 1940 and not away fighting for his country. One of the reasons why they made Gary a television repairman was so he could wear green overalls that wouldn't draw too much attention. However, it would not be long before they would have to make changes to his attire.

The idea of Gary pretending to have written songs that hadn't even been composed yet would, of course, become a regular feature of *Goodnight Sweetheart*. 'Your Song' was chosen by Laurence and Maurice because they realised it was a good morale-boosting party song and one Gary could teach everyone to sing while sheltering in the cellar from the air raid. Even though this was the first time Gary claimed to have written an established song from the future, they were delighted that the audience immediately got the joke, even when Gary had just sung and played a few bars of the song and then 'My Way'.

'John Bartlett bought me a large keyboard so I could be given lessons,' recalled Nicholas. 'However, there simply wasn't enough time what with learning the script and rehearsing the episodes. If I knew that my hand or hands were going to be in shot, then I learned enough to make it look as though I knew what I was doing. But anything over three notes and you could forget it! Although I wanted to make it look as though I knew what I was doing: I was a pretty good faker.'

On the subject of music, one of the cues Anthony and Gaynor Sadler composed for the first episode was originally intended to be played over the footage where Gary walked down Duckett's Passage for the very first time. 'It was an attractive electronic motif rather like a "mystery chord",' explained Gaynor. 'However, it was decided not to use this cue because they didn't want to pre-empt the secret of the time travel. Looking at the episode in retrospect, they were undoubtedly correct.'

The scene set in the cellar of the Royal Oak where Phoebe, Eric and PC Deadman crowd around Gary in the 'death of Nelson' inspired tableau was a stroke of genius. However, this idea wasn't down to the writers. 'All credit must therefore go to the director, Robin Nash,' said Laurence.

Voicing the role of the OU lecturer heard on the video Yvonne was watching for her coursework in this episode was Pete Drummond. A former radio DJ and television presenter turned voice-over artist, Pete's varied credits include being part of the original Radio 1 line-up in September 1967. He can be spotted in the famous photo featuring all the DJs taken outside All Saints Church in London.

This episode saw the first of a handful of appearances of the old codger in the Royal Oak. Laurence and Maurice admit they only invented the character, later named Stan in series two, and played by the character actor John Rapley, to try and establish a catchphrase – 'Oi, ladies present!' – for the series.

John's other television roles included Dunwoody in the drama series *The Onedin Line*, Colonel Chapman in an adaptation of Tom Sharpe's comic novel *Blott on the Landscape* and Crompton in the sitcom *Land of Hope and Gloria*, with Sheila Ferguson and Joan Sanderson. Meanwhile, his film credits included the pantomime King in the biographical drama *The Elephant Man*, a gun-shop salesman in the Clint Eastwood drama *White Hunter Black Heart*, and Dr Schell in the adventure comedy *Jane and the Lost City*, with Jasper Carrott. John died on his birthday on 18 April 2016, aged eighty-one.

Locations-wise in the first episode, the scene where PC Deadman's grandson gives Gary directions was shot outside a shop that at the time was a shoe shop located at 77 Hackney Road, London; while the road on which Gary parks his van, near to the fictionally named Duckett's Passage, is Shipton Street, close to Horatio Street, in Shoreditch, East London. The passage that leads off Shipton Street and doubles for Duckett's Passage and the nearby street is in fact Ezra Street in Shoreditch, East London; while the Royal Oak public house is located at nearby 73 Columbia Road, Shoreditch, East London.

After the recording of the first episode, Laurence wrote the following thoughts in his diary:

> Without going into the specific details of the show, I can say quite categorically that it is a huge success; we even finished recording at half-past nine, with a show of immense quality in the can. Robin shoots all the sequences twice, doesn't use the ISO camera for he prefers to shoot pick-ups, and doesn't care much for dubbing either; thus the first scene is played over a background of monotonous rock music, but that doesn't distract from the fine performances of Nicholas Lyndhurst and Vic McGuire.
>
> David Ryall is the only performer who is a little larger than life, but I put that down to nerves; but Christopher Ettridge, Dervla Kirwan, and Michelle Holmes, particularly Michelle, are all superb, and we leave the box having consumed many bottles of champagne accompanied by peanuts and raisins. Maurice and I are fairly confident that we have just written another hit show...

After viewing the first episode, Laurence felt there was something not quite right about the scenes set in the forties. 'In the early days, to make the 1940s footage look different, I remember, at Laurence's request, experimenting with a colour corrector on the vision mixer in the edit suite,' explained the editor Chris Wadsworth. 'We eventually arrived at a small amount of desaturation, and a drift towards a brownish, sepia-like look. But any colour adjustment was slight. We did this less and less over the years. Some of this look was generated in the studio by lighting and cameras, and later in a separate grading session.'

In 'Fools Rush In', the second episode of series one, Gary admits to Yvonne that he didn't buy a suit for his impending promotion interview at work. He explains that he's not willing to fork out the best part of forty quid for a suit that he will only wear once. When Yvonne sarcastically asks if he's going to go to his interview wearing jeans and a sweatshirt, Gary explains that it will be a new sweatshirt. He argues that if he's going to get the job it will be because of his technical know-how and innate charisma, not his gentleman's apparel.

As Yvonne works at the same company, he attempts to find out if he's in with a serious chance of getting the job, as several other people have already been seen. Although she claims she hasn't heard any gossip in the photocopying room as to who is most likely to be given the position, Yvonne does mention that the other applicants wore suits.

Over dinner, Yvonne gets her first real indication of Gary's increasing interest in the Second World War as he quotes from a book about the period and then plays her part of a cassette in which Al Bowlly sings 'The Very Thought of You'.

Realising he cannot tell Yvonne about his experiences in war-torn London, Gary finds himself calling Marty Harty's phone-in show on the radio. Marty invites listeners to call in if the mystical or inexplicable has ever happened to them. Unable to resist the temptation and wanting to make sense of his time-travelling experiences, Gary rings the show and gives his name as Angelo Garibaldi. However, Gary is cut off and branded 'looney of the week' after telling Marty he had time-travelled to the East End of London in 1940 and found himself sheltering from an air raid.

Unfortunately for Gary, Ron overhears the interview on his car radio while driving home from his art class. Ron heads over to Gary's home and, after initially sending him up about his call to the radio station, the two men go on to discuss the subject of time travel. Gary quickly senses that Ron is becoming suspicious that he may have really discovered a time portal and inadvertently wandered back into wartime yesteryear.

After Gary has his interview for a promotion at work, an argument ensues when he discovers Yvonne telling Stella, Ron's wife, on the phone that he didn't get the job. This is, as Yvonne predicted, predominantly because he wore jeans and a sweatshirt to his interview instead of a suit like the other applicants. Gary storms out of the house with the intention of buying a suit. However, he finds himself at a collectables and bric-a-brac fair in a local church hall where he purchases a 1940s hat, suit, coat and pair of shoes from Edna, one of the stallholders. She also directs him to Cissy, a fellow stallholder, who sells period money.

Gary then drives to Duckett's Passage again, now dressed in his 1940s clothes and armed with wartime currency. He travels back in time to the war and makes for the Royal Oak. After further ingratiating himself with Phoebe by presenting her with a bunch of bananas, something Eric is afraid will start a riot, despite the pub being practically empty, Gary convinces Phoebe to go dancing with him, much to her father's disapproval.

After Gary makes a fool of himself on the dance floor, he buys Phoebe a Gin and It, and they sit down for a heart-to-heart. Phoebe tells Gary more about her husband, Donald, and Gary admits he once dated a woman called Marilyn Monroe, until a correspondence course she was taking came between them.

After spending the evening together, Gary accompanies Phoebe back to the pub while singing a couple of lines of 'On the Street Where You Live' from *My Fair Lady*, another song he claims to have written.

Back at the pub entrance, Gary goes to give Phoebe an affectionate goodnight kiss. Although she admits to being tempted, she refuses as she's married. As the barmaid goes to enter the pub, Donald, unexpectedly home on leave, opens the door and, seeing the couple together, hits Gary in the face, sending him falling backwards onto the cobbles.

Back at home in 1993, Gary is forced to make an excuse for why he has a black eye. Obviously unable to admit to being hit by Donald, Gary claims to have fallen down a trapdoor into the cellar while helping behind the bar at the theme pub he previously told her he'd visited. Although Yvonne tries to get herself back in Gary's good books with an offer of giving him the kiss of life, the time traveller declines the offer as he's still sulking about her not telling him he didn't get his promotion. Gary reminds her that she should have told him. Yvonne agrees and says she's seriously considering resigning, something Gary doesn't agree with. But she is adamant because they should haven't put her in such an awkward position. Yvonne tells Gary that he was the best man for job, despite his 'crap dress sense', and invites him to go and do what he does best. Jokingly, Gary refuses to erect a satellite dish at that time of night. They hug, but it's clear from his expression that Gary's mind is back in 1940.

It quickly becomes apparent in the second episode that Gary's continuing references to America are a euphemism for 1993. He cleverly realises that all Phoebe, Eric and Reg know about America is what they see at the cinema. It means he can safely make claims about the food, drink and technology that the country and its troops have access to.

This episode is a prime example of arguably one of the biggest challenges Michelle Holmes faced when playing the role of Yvonne: to give Gary a hard enough time to make him stray from the marital leash, but still be appealing enough to make him stay with her. 'That was always my main concern when we were taping the series,' the actress once said. 'He had to love them both. If he didn't love them both, it would be over and we would never believe it, even though it was comedy. I hope that came across.'

As would become the norm with *Goodnight Sweetheart*, the main cast received great support in this episode. Roger Kitter played the voice of the no-nonsense radio presenter Marty Harty. Roger is best remembered for taking over the role of Captain Alberto Bertorelli in the seventh series of the Jeremy Lloyd/David Croft wartime sitcom, *'Allo 'Allo!* A popular comedian, he appeared weekly with Lulu throughout her 1973 BBC One series *It's Lulu* and was a regular on the ITV show, *Who Do You Do?* His other credits included playing an Ugly Sister opposite Dave Lee in two versions of Jim Davidson's adult pantomime *Sinderella* on stage, DVD and video. Roger died on 3 January 2015, aged sixty-five. Paying tribute, Maurice said, 'He was an old friend, and one of the first we made in the industry. He also played Mr Blackbird in an episode of our sitcom *Get Back*.'

Also lending her voice in the radio programme scene was Karen Frawley. The actress was cast as Marty's other radio show caller, Alice. Karen's other television credits include Vicky in the 1980s daytime fashion drama *Gems*, Venetia in the firefighting drama *London's Burning*, and Claire Carter in lavish period drama *Bramwell*.

Pamela Cundell gave a spirited performance in this episode as stallholder, Edna. Pamela was a performer for all seasons. Her theatre roles included playing the friendly witch in the Robert Nesbitt pantomime *Little Old King Cole*, with a cast including Charlie Drake and Janette Scott, at the London Palladium; the maid in the Ray Cooney farce *Out of Order*, with Donald Sinden and Michael Williams, at the Shaftesbury Theatre, London; and Mrs Orlock in the Ben Travers farce *Plunder* at the Savoy Theatre, London, and on tour. Pamela's other television credits included Mrs Fox in the Jimmy Perry/David Croft sitcom *Dad's Army*, Vi Box in the Ray Brooks comedy drama *Big Deal* and Mrs Monk in the miniseries *The Choir*. Her film parts included Ruby in the saucy comedy *On the Buses*, a coach passenger in the Michael Winner drama *The Wicked Lady* and a war widow in the big-screen version of Ray Cooney's farce, *Run for Your Wife*. Pamela, who was once married to the actor Bill Fraser, best known for appearing in the sitcom *The Army Game*, died on 14 February 2015, aged ninety-five.

Playing a barman in the dance hall was the supporting actor, Freddie Stuart. His other television credits include playing a taxi driver in the sitcom *May to December*, which saw Anton Rodgers play solicitor Alec Callender, Olawa's chauffeur in the crime series *Bodyguards*, which starred Sean Pertwee and Louise Lombard, and Stan in the minicab comedy drama *Roger*, which was written by the *Only Fools and Horses* writer, John Sullivan.

Interestingly, Ben Lobb played Phoebe's husband Donald Bamford in this episode. Ben was the first of two actors to play the character. His fleeting appearance saw him deliver just one line before hitting Gary outside the Royal Oak; whereas Ralph Ineson would go on to play Donald with far more screen time in an episode called 'There's Something About a Soldier' in series three. Ben's other television roles include a policeman in the sitcom *The Detectives*, a van driver in the comedy drama *An Independent Man*, with George Cole, and as a police constable in selected episodes of the soap opera *EastEnders* in the nineties.

The best sequences in this episode are undoubtedly those set in the dance hall. The impressive set was built at Teddington Studios, complete with a bar, dance floor and small stage. Adding to the authenticity were Les Brown and His Music, who performed extracts from the songs 'Anything Goes' and 'Love is the Sweetest Thing'.

The Thursday studio schedule for the second episode of series one was particularly intensive. Here is a copy, which was printed in the camera script:

Studio Schedule	
Make-Up and Costume	07.30 – 09.00
Breakfast/Line-Up	08.00 – 09.00
Rehearse/Record (Sc.13)	09.00 – 10.30
Camera Rehearsal	10.30 – 13.00
Lunch Break	13.00 – 14.00
Rig and Record Voice Overs	14.00 – 14.30
Camera Rehearsal	14.30 – 16.15
Make-Up and Costume	16.15 – 17.00
Dress Run	17.00 – 18.00
Supper Break	18.00 – 19.00
Audience in/Warm-Up	19.00 – 19.30
VTR – Episode 2	19.30 – 21.30
Technical Clear	21.30

After the recording of the dance hall scene was completed, the dance hall set was 'struck' and the audience seating and other sets were built for camera rehearsals, the dress rehearsal and that evening's recording. Although it has been previously claimed that the dance hall scene was taped in Studio 2, the lighting director Christopher Clayton remembers otherwise. 'The dance hall set was definitely Studio 1,' he confirmed. 'In those early episodes the audience seating was widthwise in the studio, under the control rooms. That is where the dance hall set was pre-recorded. I remember standing on the walkway outside the control rooms with Lo and Mo looking down on it. They were delighted with how their show was developing.'

According to the call sheet, a total of thirty-nine supporting artists (seven males and thirty-two females) were called for the dance hall scene, which was choreographed by Mandy Demetriou, a Zimbabwean choreographer and movement director who has worked in a wide variety of styles and methods. 'I first came to choreograph an episode of *Goodnight Sweetheart* by serendipity,' said Mandy. 'I bumped into someone working on the production at Teddington Studios while I was there on another project. I think just having seen me, I was in the forefront of his mind and luckily for me they contacted my agent. I was asked to meet the wonderful Robin Nash, who I knew only by repute but had not worked for. We got on well and I was given the job.

'I remember going to a rehearsal to choreograph the foxtrot with Nicholas and Dervla. I was given maybe an hour out of their rehearsal day, and for non-dancers that's very little time. Dervla was easy with dancing but Nick, who's not a natural dancer, was very anxious about it. I remember keeping it very basic for them but when he saw the dancers on the shooting day, Nick was a little nonplussed. It was great that his character was not a great dancer, so it was easy for him to make that aspect real!'

Additional locations used in this episode included the shop window and the alleyway that supposedly led to the church hall where Gary purchased his 1940s clothes. They were both located on Broad Street, Teddington, not far from the studios; while the scene inside the church hall was filmed at Ham Christian Centre on Lock Road, Ham, Richmond, Surrey.

At the beginning of 'Is Your Journey Really Necessary?', the third episode of series one, Gary discovers while reading a book on the war that enemy action was considerably greater than of late on 25 October 1940, that day's date fifty-three years ago, when heavy bombing started earlier in the evening than normal in the East End. Realising that he needs to warn Phoebe, Gary tells Yvonne that he's left his best circuit tester in Holborn. This not only gives him an excuse to visit Phoebe, but gets him out of visiting Alison, his sister-in-law, and her new baby boy.

After Phoebe informs Gary, who's calling from a nearby phone box, that Donald is no longer at home on leave, he goes to the Royal Oak to tell her, together with Eric and PC Deadman, about the planned enemy action. He recommends Phoebe shelter in an Underground station, preferably in the West End. Gary's news, which he claims was sourced from one of his contacts, makes the local ARP warden, Manny, suspicious.

Although far from happy, Eric allows Phoebe to head for a shelter. However, when she discovers that Gary wants her to go on her own, she refuses. Without thinking, he mentions that he needs to get back to Yvonne. When Phoebe asks who she is, Gary panics and tells her that Yvonne Goolagong is his boss.

After returning to 1993 and being unable to call Yvonne from a phone box at the end of Duckett's Passage due to it being vandalised, Gary rushes back to 1940 and accompanies Phoebe on a bus journey to the Underground. When they arrive at Holborn (Kingsway) Underground Station, Gary buys two shelter tickets from a spiv after a station mistress explains that two return tickets to Whitechapel would not give them the right to shelter there.

After climbing onto their top bunks, Phoebe admits that she would do anything for a bar of chocolate. Quick as a flash, Gary produces a large bar of Dairy Milk, which he claims to have bought from a sweet shop at the American Embassy. Disappointingly for Gary, his only reward is a peck on the cheek!

Meanwhile, in the East End, Eric, PC Deadman and Manny are sheltering in the cellar of the Royal Oak while the air raid takes place. By now, Manny is curious as to how Gary predicted the enemy action with such accuracy.

Back at the Underground station, Phoebe admits that she is not in love with Donald, her husband. Gary tells her that things will be different after the war and that people will no longer have to stay married to people they don't love. Their subsequent first kiss is interrupted by the accordion player The Great Alfonso launching into 'Roll Out the Barrel'.

In 1993, Yvonne is getting worried as to Gary's whereabouts and relates her concerns to Craig, one of Gary's friends, on the phone. The call is interrupted by the arrival of Ron who informs her that he has found no sign of Gary while driving around the neighbourhood. He later suggests that Gary might have stumbled through a hole in the space-time continuum and found himself in a parallel universe in a different point in history. Yvonne rejects this theory, believing he could be having an affair.

While Phoebe is asleep, Gary attempts to think of a believable excuse as to where he's been all evening. Suddenly a lady in a nearby bunk goes into labour.

When a nurse arrives, she instantly dismisses Gary's advanced knowledge of giving birth, which he learned on the American drama series *Thirtysomething*, and tells him to go and boil a kettle.

When Gary and Phoebe return to the East End, it's clear that enemy action has inflicted a great deal of damage on buildings close to the Royal Oak. However, there's a bigger shock in store for Gary at the pub in the form of DI Howard and DS Martin, two detectives who wish to interview him after Manny has brought the time traveller to their attention.

At the same time as Gary is being taken away for a formal chat, Yvonne is watching a news report about a bomb that has been detonated in modern-day Holborn. Although no one has been hurt, she is concerned that Gary might still be in the area.

During Gary's interview, DI Howard calls Derek Milton, one of the intelligence boys, to see if anyone is aware of Gary's claimed involvement in the secret service. When Derek responds in the negative, Gary quickly tells DI Howard that Winston Churchill and President Roosevelt have just concluded a secret arms deal to equip ten British divisions. This is a fact he read in a history book, but he claims he would only know if he was a secret agent. When Derek confirms this news, Gary is freed. He returns home to Yvonne and, by way of an excuse, tells her he had been helping to deliver a baby.

By now, Laurence and Maurice had really got into their stride with the series. Their confidence in their new work was showing, not only with their dialogue and the development of the various characters, but with the invention of the situations they found themselves in.

The scenes set in Holborn (Kingsway) Underground Station in this episode were a veritable triumph for the production designer, Roger Andrews. Due to their complexity, including the number of supporting artists required, these scenes were pre-recorded during the Thursday recording day before the audience arrived later that evening.

This episode saw Harry Landis play Emanuel 'Manny' Solomons for the first time. Harry's journey onto the series to play Manny was an easy one. 'I think the casting director must have seen me in something else I appeared in,' he recalled. 'Because they cast me right away without an audition.'

During his eight-decade career, Harry's theatre appearances included playing Private Albert Huggins in the Anthony Kimmins comedy *The Amorous Prawn* at the Saville Theatre, London, Private Mason in the R. C. Sherriff drama *Journey's End* at the Cambridge Theatre, London, and Melter Moss in the Tom Taylor melodrama *The Ticket-of-Leave Man* at the National Theatre, London. A talented theatre director, Harry's credits included directing forty plays and two pantomimes while he was the artistic director of the Marlowe Theatre, Canterbury. On television, viewers also saw him play Bloom in the action drama *The Saint*, barber Felix Kowalski in the soap opera *EastEnders* and Mr Morris in the sitcom about the gloriously idiosyncratic Goodman family, *Friday Night Dinner*. His film credits included a modicum of war films; for example, he played Dr Levy in *Dunkirk*, Lance Corporal Lamb in *Private Potter* and a soldier in *The Longest Day*. Harry died on 11 September 2022, aged ninety-five.

For this, her one and only appearance in *Goodnight Sweetheart*, Maggie Guess was given the role of the officious station mistress who gives Gary and Phoebe a hard time when they try to take shelter at the Underground station. A hard-working actress, Maggie's stage roles included Truvy in Robert Harling's beloved play *Steel Magnolias* at the Lyric Theatre, London, a court clerk in Brian Clark's hospital drama *Whose Life Is It Anyway?*, which starred Kim Cattrall, at the Comedy Theatre (since renamed the Harold Pinter Theatre), London, and Dr Elizabeth Woolley in the Frederick Knott mystery play *Write Me a Murder* at Vienna's English Theatre in Vienna, Austria. Her other television credits included Mrs Parker in the comedy drama *Father Matthew's Daughter*, with James Bolam as Father Matthew Fitzstanton, a Tory woman in the drama *Mosley* and a customer in the comedy drama *How Do You Want Me?*, which featured Dylan Moran, Charlotte Coleman and Emma Chambers. Maggie died on 16 August 2014, aged sixty-eight.

Another stroke of genius casting in this episode came in the form of Peter Cellier, whose performance as 'The Spiv' bubbled with enthused grandeur. A remarkable character actor, Peter's theatre credits have included Eric Skelding in the Ronald Millar drama *The Case in Question* at the Theatre Royal Haymarket, London, William Collyer in Terence Rattigan's devastating masterpiece *The Deep Blue Sea* at the Greenwich Theatre, London, and Gerald Wentworth in Nöel Coward's wickedly funny and final play *Star Quality* at the Apollo Theatre, London, and on tour. Peter's other television roles include Henry Pritchett in the award-winning costume drama *Upstairs, Downstairs*, Andrews in the *Doctor Who* story 'Time-Flight', and Sir Frank Gordon in the political satire sitcom, *Yes, Prime Minister*. The character actor's film parts have included Morris Pluthero in the big-screen version of the sitcom *Man About the House*, a head waiter in Colin Welland's Oscar-winning sports drama *Chariots of Fire* and Sir Leonard Bax in the compelling drama *The Remains of the Day*, with Anthony Hopkins and Emma Thompson.

Maria Gough, meanwhile, was cast in the role of the pregnant girl sheltering from the Blitz in the Tube station. 'All the cast were very polite and professional,' she said. 'I was young and quiet and had a sense of wanting to let them get on with things without interruption. However, I remember Victor McGuire being friendly and chatty to me.

'The thing that struck me the most about the read-through and the rehearsals was that I could barely hear anyone. It seemed strange, coming from a theatre background, as I did, where projection is king, that scenes could be rehearsed across the room and be barely audible, therefore seeming underpowered and under-energised. However, once picked up on camera they were brilliantly nuanced and timed with all the distilled and economic acting television requires. I quickly realised that the cast really understood their medium.'

After first being seen begging Gary for a piece of chocolate, Maria's character becomes a focus of one scene when she goes into labour in the bunk directly below Gary. 'I wore a pregnancy bump that was skilfully crafted and weighted to look and feel real,' she said.

Although not required, Maria was invited to stay for the evening. 'After the recording, I was asked to stand and take a bow,' she said. 'I was a little sheepish about doing this as I felt I was pretty insignificant compared to the main cast. However, I sensed that it would be highly unprofessional and churlish of me not to do so.'

Maria continues to work in the acting profession. Her theatre work has included Edna Baker in the George S. Kaufman and Ring Lardner comedy *June Moon* at the Hampstead Theatre, London, and Vaudeville Theatre, London, Jane in the Alan Ayckbourn comic masterpiece *Absurd Person Singular* at the Birmingham Rep, and Miss Prism in the Oscar Wilde comedy *The Importance of Being Earnest* at the Stephen Joseph Theatre, Scarborough. Her other roles on television include Teresa Dalton in the crime drama *Silent Witness*, Nurse Ryan in the sitcom *Boy Meets Girl* and DCI Peet in the soap opera *Hollyoaks*.

The nurse who comes to the pregnant girl's aid after she goes into labour in the Tube station was played by Jean Challis. Jean was once married to the late actor John Challis, who played Boycie in the sitcom *Only Fools and Horses*. Her stage roles include playing Widow Corney in the Lionel Bart musical *Oliver!* at the Crucible Theatre, Sheffield, Ivanova in Ivan Turgenev's savagely funny play *Fortune's Fool* at the Chichester Festival Theatre, and Ethel Chauvenet and Betty Chumley in Mary Chase's gentle family comedy *Harvey* at the Royal Exchange Theatre, Manchester. Best known for playing Mrs Arnott in the John Sullivan sitcom *Dear John*, Jean's many other television appearances include Hilda Bryers in the drama *Love Story* and Nancy Platt in the medical drama *Casualty*.

Anthony Pedley, who played DI Howard, one of the two detectives who interview Gary in this episode, remembers being quite nervous when taping his two scenes. 'The pressure is always on, no matter how experienced you are,' said the actor. 'Funnily enough, I was looking back through old videos a year or two ago, and thought it wasn't a bad performance considering my nerves!'

A character actor of high repute, Anthony's long list of theatre appearances includes Cool in the Dion Boucicault comedy *London Assurance*, with Donald Sinden and Judi Dench, at the New Theatre, London, and the Palace Theatre, New York. He also played Big Jule in the Frank Loesser, Jo Swerling and Abe Burrows musical *Guys and Dolls* at the National Theatre, Bristol Hippodrome, and Prince of Wales Theatre, London. Anthony also took on the roles of Harry Clamacraft and Lofty in Adam Faith's production of the Bill Naughton play *Alfie* at the Queen's Theatre, London, and on tour. Anthony's other television roles include Sir Percy in the sitcom *Two's Company*, alongside Elaine Stritch and Donald Sinden, Agrippa in Jonathan Miller's production of *Antony and Cleopatra*, and Rodrigues in the comedy drama *Legacy of Murder*, which starred Dick Emery. For the big screen, his credits include two John Cleese comedies. He played an irate driver in the comedy *A Fish Called Wanda* and a sea-lion spectator in the spiritual successor, *Fierce Creatures*.

Michael Garner was cast as the second detective, DS Martin. 'It was the standard sitcom format of a few days' rehearsal, then a technical and dress run-through and finally the recording,' recalled Michael. 'A lot of drama and comedy used to be rehearsed and then recorded in studios in my early days as an actor; but I think *Goodnight Sweetheart* was the last time I personally did this.

'I had a day off from rehearsals to attend the big press launch of my first series of *London's Burning*, which I had finished filming a couple of months before. If you watch the beginning of my next series of *London's Burning*, you will notice I still have the remnants of my 1940s haircut from *Goodnight Sweetheart*!

'The director Robin Nash was an affable chap, very relaxed and experienced, and managed to laugh encouragingly at lines he had heard many times before. Nicholas was similarly low key and relaxed. It was the first series, so the premise of time travelling was a fun element that had to be explained to us occasionally. You never know if a show is going to be a success, and I did not really consider that – you just try to make a good contribution to your episode.

'Recording a comedy with an audience is a bit of a strange hybrid, but I enjoyed it. The recording day is like a mini first night in the theatre, and the build-up does get your adrenaline going in a way that single-camera filming rarely does. I remember that although the interview scene seemed to go well, Nicholas asked if we could do it again, which was fair enough, and we did. I've no idea which version they finally used. What is strange is that even when you repeat a scene the audience usually laugh a second time at jokes they've already heard!'

Michael's theatre roles include Jimmy Beales in Arnold Wesker's kitchen-sink drama *Roots* at the National Theatre, London, Bill in the Arthur Smith and Chris England football comedy *An Evening with Gary Lineker* at the Duchess Theatre, London, and Thomas Killigrew in Jessica Swale's rollicking Restoration play *Nell Gwynn* at the Apollo Theatre, London, which included fellow cast members Gemma Arterton and Michele Dotrice. Best known for playing Geoff 'Poison' Pearce in the long-running firefighter series *London's Burning*, his other television credits include Inspector Dekker in the crime drama *Van der Valk* and Michael Portland in the thriller *Slow Horses*. Michael's film credits have included Alec Sims in the drama *Rogue Traders*, Master Page in the William Shakespeare comedy *The Merry Wives of Windsor* and the man kissed by Issy, played by Ellie Goulding, in the romantic short *Tom and Issy*.

Completing the supporting cast in this episode was Tanveer Ghani, who played the television newscaster who gives an update on the detonating of the bomb in Holborn. Tanveer continues to add to his impressive body of work. On the stage, his credits have included Lennox in the William Shakespeare tragedy *Macbeth*, which featured Helen McCrory as Lady Macbeth, at the Tricycle Theatre, London, Ali Mahmood in John Steinberg and Ray Kilby's political farce *In the Balance* at the New End Theatre, London, and village elder, Gandhi and Justice Teja Singh in the premiere of the Howard Brenton play *Drawing the Line* at the Hampstead Theatre, London. On television, the actor's other characters include Bapu Ram in the much-lauded drama *The Jewel in the Crown*, Rezaul Kabir in the soap opera *EastEnders*, and Crenshaw in *The Royals*, a drama starring Elizabeth Hurley about a fictional British royal family in modern-day London. Meanwhile, Tanveer's film roles have included Balbir in Gurinder Chadha and Meera Syal's comedy drama *Bhaji on the Beach*, the video man in the sports comedy drama *Bend it Like Beckham*, which featured Parminder Nagra and Keira Knightley, and Jawaharlal Nehru in the biographical drama, *Viceroy's House*.

At the start of 'The More I See You', the fourth episode of series one, Gary is seen looking through a book of wallpaper samples as Yvonne gets home from work. He claims he's planning to paper their bedroom while she's away on her Open University course residential weekend at the University of Huddersfield. In reality, he's secretly planning to visit Phoebe instead.

Later, Gary visits Ron and asks him to print an authentic set of identification papers and a ration book that would pass muster in the Second World War. This, he claims, is so that his cousin Jilly can use them as props in an amateur production of the Lionel Bart musical, *Blitz!* However, Ron tells Gary he believes he was telling the truth when he called Marty Harty's radio show. Gary then admits that he has been going back to 1940 and has met a girl called Phoebe. He also mentions he was nearly thrown in jail for not having the right identification. After being convinced, Ron agrees to print the documents – but on one condition.

While looking for a suitcase to use for her weekend away, Yvonne finds one in the loft in which Gary has hidden his 1940s suit and stashed presents that he plans to give to Phoebe. When quizzed by Yvonne as to why he has the items, Gary claims he was organising a surprise 1940s birthday party for her. Although not entirely convinced, she lets him off the hook – for now.

Ron's side of the bargain for printing Gary's documentation is to accompany Gary on one of his jaunts to war-torn London. Dressed in clothes of the period, Ron drives them both to the East End in his car. After being accosted by a boy asking him for a penny for the Guy, Gary leads Ron towards Duckett's Passage. Ron stops to tie his shoelace and when Gary arrives in 1940, he finds that the printer is no longer with him. However, he continues his way to the Royal Oak. Meanwhile, Ron emerges from the other end of Duckett's Passage in 1993. Feeling somewhat conspicuous, Ron asks a mechanic if he's seen a man dressed in 1940s clothes. When he is told no, he thinks Gary is playing a prank on him.

After Gary arrives at the Royal Oak and proudly shows Eric his full set of documents, the landlord tells him that Phoebe has gone to live with his sister-in-law, Dot. When Eric refuses to give him the address, Gary bribes Eric with a large bar of chocolate and is instantly rewarded with the answer. At that moment, Phoebe walks into the pub and announces that Aunty Dot's house was bombed while she was at the market. With Dot in hospital and her house gone, Eric asks Phoebe to come to live back home, but she isn't keen.

During a walk in a local churchyard, Phoebe asks Gary to take her back with him. At first, Gary thinks she means 1993; and then realises she means Cricklewood, which he tells her is not possible. Phoebe then tells him that Donald has sent her a letter in which he has revealed nothing of importance, such as his feelings for her.

Back in 1993, Ron drives to Gary and Yvonne's house for a showdown. When no one answers the door, he leaves a message on their answer machine asking why Gary is making a mug out of him and threatens to drive to Huddersfield to ask Yvonne what she thinks of his strange behaviour. He also reminds Gary that he owes him seventy-five pounds for printing the documentation.

After entering a small church to shelter from the rain, Phoebe tells Gary that she believes her dad is afraid of her being independent. Gary then tells her his marital problems mostly started due to his wife getting a job she thought was more important than his. Phoebe is shocked to hear that Gary was in fact

Goodnight Sweetheart: A Guide to the Classic Sitcom

married to Marilyn Monroe. Gary admits they got married but he doesn't like talking about it. When Phoebe suggests she rent a room in his house in Cricklewood, Gary declines. He claims that Marilyn has followed him over from America and they're still living together. This upsets Phoebe who slaps Gary after he offers her some money so she can rent a flat.

Back in 1993, Gary drives up to Huddersfield to see Yvonne after he hears Ron's answering-machine message. Thanks to a security guard giving him directions, Gary finds Yvonne in the bar and dancing with a man he nicknames Mr Leather Elbow-Patches. When Yvonne confirms that Ron hasn't been to see her, Gary relaxes. However, when she questions his unexpected long journey, Gary quickly has to deflect from the situation by moaning about her being 'off-hand and snotty' when she found the suitcase. He also admits he wondered if she had another man in Huddersfield, something she denies. Friends again, Yvonne offers to take Gary back to her room for a 'good seeing to', which he readily accepts. However, he suddenly stops as he recalls Phoebe asking him to take her back with him. Rather than dwell on this flashback, Gary asks Yvonne for a dance and insists upon the foxtrot.

One of the biggest pivotal moments in this episode, and indeed the first series, was Gary finally telling Ron the secret of his duplicitous behaviour. 'We knew that Gary needed someone in whom he could confide what was to be his incredible secret,' said Laurence. Marks and Gran also realised pretty quickly that Gary would need recourse to a paleoprinter and chose Ron's job accordingly.

Increasingly, viewers were getting to see just how quickly Gary could get himself tied up in knots and how the fallout affects everyone around him in both periods. As the wartime saying goes, 'Loose lips sink ships;' and he proves the point after accidentally forgetting his 'story' and revealing to Phoebe he's supposedly married to Marilyn Monroe, causing her to storm out, almost losing her for good in the process. This scene was just one of many that proved that, like the writers Perry and Croft before them, Marks and Gran were capable with their sitcoms of making you laugh one moment and cry the next.

There were three actors who supported the main cast in this episode. The small boy who asked for a penny for the Guy near to modern-day Duckett's Passage was played by Bobby Coombes. His other television roles include Phil Dillon in Lynda La Plante's ensemble drama *Civvies*, Craig in the firefighter series *London's Burning* and Michael Spence in the wartime drama *No Bananas*.

Also appearing was Nirjay Mahindru as the car mechanic. Nirjay's other television roles include Staff Nurse Langdon in the drama series *Children's Ward*, Selim in the comedy drama *Making Out* and PC Tandon in the comedy drama *The Locksmith*. Nirjay has since become a playwright and producer and was one of the founder members of Conspirators' Kitchen, which is devoted to producing new writing.

Making a small, but pleasing, cameo as a sarcastic security guard, complete with guard dog, at the University of Huddersfield, was Martyn Whitby. A highlight of the scene sees Gary dive for cover when someone lets off a firework near to the university campus, forgetting that he's in 1993 and not back in 1940. Martyn's other roles on television include an SPG Inspector in an episode of the crime drama *The Sweeney*, which also featured an appearance by Morecambe and Wise in the cast; David Hughes, the ex-husband of Kate Sugden and father of Rachel and Mark Hughes, in the soap opera *Emmerdale*; and Aldridge in the comedy drama *Minder*.

The location of Ezra Street was used for scenes set in both 1940 and 1993 in this episode. This was the only time that the street was used in *Goodnight Sweetheart* for a modern-day scene. Also in this episode, the scene where Gary and Phoebe were walking in the cemetery was filmed in Weybridge Cemetery, which is located on Brooklands Lane, Weybridge; while Ron could be seen driving to Gary and Yvonne's Cricklewood house, which is actually located on Thamesgate Close, Richmond, London. The car park at the University of Huddersfield was in fact one of the car parks at Teddington Studios. Finally, the university bar was the Thames Club Bar at Teddington Studios.

As 'I Get Along Without You Very Well', the fifth episode of series one, begins, Gary is busily pretending to play Stevie Wonder's 'Superstition' on a keyboard as Hazel, a charity worker, rings the front doorbell. She's there to collect any old clothes that he may wish to donate. Believing his time-travelling days are over, Gary sees this as the ideal time to give away his wartime suit. However, Hazel is not impressed and leaves empty-handed.

Just then, Yvonne arrives home and is full of her weekend away on her Open University course. She questions why Gary is cuddling his spiv suit, and he tells her he was trying to get rid of it. When Yvonne asks if this means he has cancelled the surprise 1940s theme party he was planning, Gary pretends he has, saying it wouldn't be much of a surprise now. Yvonne promises to make amends and also suggests they learn to dance.

When Gary visits Ron, he's still sulking. To convince him of his time-travelling abilities, Gary presents him with an edition of a 1940 newspaper in pristine condition. Although he now believes Gary, Ron can't understand why he couldn't go back, and admits he wants to try again. However, Gary tells him he won't be going back due to Phoebe walking out on him. He also tells him that he wants to

Goodnight Sweetheart: A Guide to the Classic Sitcom

try and make his marriage work and spend more time with his mates. However, when Ron offers to share a bevvy with him that night, Gary has to take a rain check because he and Yvonne are starting ballroom-dancing classes.

After attempting to learn to dance while watching an instruction video, Yvonne shows Gary that she has bought a 'marital arts' video. While Yvonne goes upstairs to slip into something more comfortable, Gary takes the other video out of the machine just as a newsreader is explaining how a plucky eighty-year-old pensioner from Bethnal Green called Phoebe Sparrow had recently fought off two raiders.

The following day, Gary tells Ron he believes this news report is evidence that he and Phoebe must have got married. He's concerned that if he doesn't go back, he risks changing the course of history. Ron suggests he visit the 'battling granny' but Gary is worried the shock could kill her. He then asks Ron to cover for him so he can go back to 1940. When Ron asks if this is so he can marry Phoebe, Gary tells him that she already thinks he's married – to Marilyn Monroe. Ron, while laughing, gives him a photo of Marilyn in the iconic subway grating scene from *The Seven Year Itch*, which he signs 'All my love, Marilyn'. Gary then tells Ron he plans to go back to see Phoebe the following day when England are playing football in Lithuania. He suggests telling Yvonne they have been given tickets. Ron agrees to cover for him until Gary tells him he will have to go to Lithuania in case Stella says something to Yvonne. However, Ron changes his mind again when Gary offers to pay his airfare.

After Yvonne reluctantly agrees to let him go on the football trip with Ron, Gary makes for the Royal Oak. It is a dark and foggy night and he's knocked down by an ambulance just outside the pub. Gary comes round in hospital with Phoebe and PC Deadman at his bedside. After PC Deadman heads off to the mortuary to have a cup of tea with his friend Cyril, Gary and Phoebe share a heart to heart. Phoebe tells Gary how concerned she was when she found out about the accident. Gary tells her he didn't know she cared, given she walked out on him the last time they met. Phoebe tells him she acted hastily and has had time to reflect on their situation.

PC Deadman returns with Gary's personal belongings, including his 'signed' photo of Marilyn Monroe and a pair of illustrated boxer shorts. When he offers to inform Gary's wife about his accident, Gary isn't keen as in reality the woman at the address is his grandma. However, Reg insists on paying a visit. Eric then arrives and demands that Phoebe return to the pub to prepare the bar for opening. He then accuses Gary of staging the accident in order to win Phoebe back.

Not realising that Gary has had an accident, Ron pops around to his Cricklewood home to see if he fancies going for drink. Confused as to why Ron isn't with Gary, Yvonne demands to know why they have been parted. In a desperate panic, Ron concocts a story in which he says Gary is probably awaiting trial in a Lithuanian prison due to being chased naked through the street by seventeen armed gendarmes after a regrettable incident in a small museum.

Phoebe returns to see Gary at the hospital just after he's been discharged. While they talk, Eric arrives and reminds Phoebe that he forbade her to ever see Gary again. Just as things begin to get heated, PC Deadman arrives to tell Gary that he visited Marilyn and she appears to have moved in another man. Gary realises that the couple are his grandparents. He pretends to be upset at this convenient development. When Gary and Phoebe are alone, they share another kiss but are interrupted by Eric calling for his daughter.

When Gary returns home, Yvonne questions him about his behaviour in Lithuania. Although unaware of Ron's cover story, he manages to bluff his way out of the situation before Yvonne goes to see her sister so she can calm down.

Unable to resist any longer, Gary looks up Phoebe Sparrow's address in the phone book. When he goes to the address, an old lady opens the door. Believing this is his Phoebe, Gary tells her he believes they might have got married. A West Indian lady then comes to the door to see who their visitor is. Her friend tells her that this 'crackhead' think he's her husband. She then tells the West Indian lady – whom she addresses as Phoebe Sparrow – to get her gun as she closes the door. Gary smiles with relief as he realises that he's made a mistake.

Although Yvonne had proved herself to be adept at manipulating Gary from the get-go, this episode really showed that her time-travelling husband was now himself becoming pretty adept at manipulating Yvonne with his lies in order to cover for his new-found double life.

This episode featured what would obviously become a recurring theme over the full run of the series: Gary Sparrow being torn. Torn between concentrating on making his marriage succeed with Yvonne or trying to further his relationship with Phoebe in the relative tranquillity of the Blitz. Also, trying to maintain a friendship with Ron without pushing him too far as a result of the fallout from his two-timing life and the need for his help, and not even hiding the fact that he's using him and his business for the benefit of his lust life.

One of Anthony and Gaynor Sadler's music cues was used as part of the opening joke in this episode. 'The track of "Superstition" that Gary mimed playing on his home keyboard was pre-recorded at our studio, Logorhythm Music,' revealed Gaynor. 'Anthony played the music on a Clavinet.'

A number of the scenes in this episode were situated in a London hospital in 1940. Once again, this large set, built in Studio 1 at Teddington Studios, was the brainchild of the production designer, Roger Andrews.

In the final scene of this episode, in which Gary goes to what he believes might be Phoebe Sparrow's house in 1993, Nicholas can be seen wearing the same cap that he wore when he arrived for his first meeting with Marks and Gran at Orso's Italian restaurant in Covent Garden.

This time, there were four actresses offering strong support to the main cast. The first was Rachael Weaver, who played the charity collector, Hazel. Rachael's various other television roles include Janine in the period drama *Nanny*, which starred Wendy Craig in the title role, Molly in the fashion-based costume drama *The House of Eliott*, with a cast including Stella Gonet and Louise Lombard, and Mrs Banks in the remake of the 1960s private detective series with a spiritual twist, *Randall and Hopkirk (Deceased)*.

The second actress was Claire Williamson, who played the television newsreader who reveals the story about the mugging of a pensioner called Phoebe Sparrow. Claire's other work on the small screen includes playing Verity Barraclough in the veterinary drama *All Creatures Great and Small*, Effie Rowlandson in the mystery series *Campion* and Alice Meadows in the crime drama *Shadow of the Noose*. In more recent years, Claire has worked as both an actress and acting teacher in America under the name of Claire Jacobs.

The third actress was the veteran performer Hilda Fenemore, who played the old lady that Gary first suspects might be Phoebe after he arrives at the address of a Phoebe Sparrow in 1993. Hilda became an actress in the 1940s. Her theatre credits included Mary Roberts in the Philip King thriller *How Are You, Johnnie?*, which included Ian McShane and Derek Fowlds in the cast, at the Vaudeville Theatre, London; Violet in the Terence Rattigan drama *The Winslow Boy*, with Kenneth More and Annette Crosbie, at the New Theatre, London, and on tour; and Mrs Pearce in George Bernard Shaw's most popular play *Pygmalion*, with a cast including Diana Rigg, Alec McCowen and Bob Hoskins, at the Albery Theatre, London. Meanwhile, on television, Hilda played, amongst many other roles, Queenie Beal in the sitcom *Dad's Army*, Miss Pringle in the comedy drama *Gone to Seed* and an old lady in the sketch show, *Harry Enfield and Chums*. Hilda's film appearances included playing Mrs Rhoda Bray in the comedy *Carry On Nurse*, Mrs Thompson in the courtroom drama *The Boys* and Mrs Hoskins in the thriller *Absolution*. Hilda died on 13 April 2004, aged eighty-nine, after an acting career lasting over sixty years.

Finally, there was a great cameo from Peggy Phango, a South African actress and singer who was blessed with an infectious laugh. Peggy, who came to live in England during the 1960s, played the feisty mugging victim, Phoebe Sparrow. Her many theatre roles included Joyce in the Harry Bloom, Todd Matshikiza and Pat Williams pioneering South African musical *King Kong* at the Prince's

Theatre, London. Peggy was also a member of the ensemble in a production of the Jerome Kern and Oscar Hammerstein II musical *Showboat*, which included Cleo Laine and Derek Royle in the cast, at the Adelphi Theatre, London. The performer also returned to the West End in 1988 with the revival of *Showboat* at the Prince of Wales Theatre. Peggy's other stage roles included Rose in the Richard Harris comedy *Stepping Out* at the Duke of York's Theatre, London, and on tour. In addition to *Goodnight Sweetheart*, her other television credits included Mrs Lamb in the detective crime drama *C.A.T.S. Eyes*, Mrs Riley in the sitcom *The Upper Hand* and Mrs Wald in the Lynda La Plante crime drama *Trial and Retribution*. Peggy died on 7 August 1998, aged sixty-nine.

At the beginning of 'In the Mood', the sixth and final episode of the first series, Phoebe is seen giving her father, Eric, a piece of her mind just as Gary walks into the Royal Oak. After emerging from the cellar, Eric attempts to give Phoebe a dressing-down for her outburst but notices Gary. PC Deadman then arrives to inform everyone that the King is set to make a visit to the borough. Phoebe and Eric's enthusiastic reaction bemuses Gary. Phoebe tells him that she'd hate to miss an opportunity to see the King and Queen in the flesh. When Gary points out that the royal family will probably one day end up showing Japanese tourists around Buckingham Palace for eight quid a throw, Eric bars him from the pub for his lack of respect.

If Gary was hoping for a better reception at home, he is wrong. A bunch of flowers does not stop Yvonne from ironing while simmering with anger. She then shows him two pages of their recent bank statement, proof of his spending on 1940s memorabilia. Gary promises to cut back on his spending and make the dinner, but this doesn't improve her mood. Besides, there is no dinner because the machine rejected her credit card in the supermarket – another symptom of Gary's spending spree. Yvonne then gives him the choice: get rid of either the memorabilia, or her.

Ron turns down Gary's offer to buy his memorabilia, telling him he doesn't need his own Imperial War Museum. Although Gary says he wants to concentrate on the here and now, Ron realises he is besotted with Phoebe and that she haunts his every waking moment. He reminds him that he's in the unique position of having an untraceable 'bit on the side'. Gary realises that Ron's empathy has an underlying subtext. He then admits he wants Gary to do him a small favour: take two hundred and fifty pounds in period fivers which he has printed, and invest it in a company called Arbuthnot Brothers Radio Ltd who have gone on to become Eurotronics plc. Gary is not convinced it's a good idea as he believes this would be meddling with history.

Later, while packing up his memorabilia, Gary finds a videocassette featuring old newsreels. He puts it in the machine and the announcer explains the King and Queen visited the London Hospital in the Whitechapel Road in 1940. He realises this is the visit PC Deadman was referring to. Before he can watch any more, Yvonne comes home, and he quickly stops the machine. She asks what he is going to do with all the stuff he has packed up, and he tells her he plans to sell it at a 1940s memorabilia fair in Runcorn.

Although he is banned from the Royal Oak, Gary pays a flying visit to tell Phoebe, Eric, PC Deadman and Manny that the King and Queen will be visiting the London Hospital at 1.30pm. Gary suggests they borrow some white coats to pass themselves off as doctors so they can tag on to the reception party. PC Deadman says he will borrow some from his friend, Cyril, at the mortuary. He assures them they will be clean.

Gary then tells Manny, who is reading the financial section of his paper, that he has come into a small inheritance and thinks he should invest in some shares because prices are bound to go up when Britain wins the war, as they surely will. He tells him the company he wants to invest in, and Manny says he will ask his brother-in-law, who dabbles in the market, for some advice.

At the London Hospital, Gary, Phoebe, Eric and PC Deadman arrive for the King and Queen's visit but are soon challenged by one of the doctors. Gary informs him that he is Professor Gareth Sparrow of the Department of Experimental Plastic Surgery and his colleagues are members of his team. This is just as the royal couple arrive. The King is introduced to Gary, who in return introduces him to Dr Phoebe Bamford – who faints on the spot.

Back at the Royal Oak, Gary announces that he wants to celebrate by taking Phoebe to supper at the Savoy. He then announces that he's going back to Hollywood to work on a musical version of George Bernard Shaw's play, *Pygmalion*. Manny arrives and tells Gary his brother-in-law will introduce him to his stockbroker the following morning.

When an air raid sounds while Gary and Phoebe are dining at their table in the Savoy's restaurant, seventy feet below ground level, the head waiter assures all the diners they're in one of the safest places in London. When Phoebe admits she doesn't fancy travelling home in the air raid, Gary discreetly asks the head waiter if he could arrange a room for the night. When he's told they're very busy, Gary presents him with a white fiver, and he's informed the Imperial Suite is available. As they have brought no night attire or toothbrushes, the head waiter tells him that his friend is the manager of Andrews and Errington of Jermyn Street and they always keep some items of lingerie in stock for their more important patrons. Gary pays another six pounds for his help and writes a card to go with the lingerie for Phoebe.

Meanwhile, back in 1993, Ron is drooling over a car magazine. Presently the security guard buzzes through and tells Ron that Yvonne is there to see him. On arriving, she tells Ron that she's worried about Gary and thinks she may have been a bit hard on him, despite him almost bankrupting them with his 1940s fixation. When she asks Ron what he thinks she wants and needs, he mistakenly believes she is coming on to him. She tells him she'd rather go to bed with Sid Vicious, even though he's dead! After Yvonne leaves, a car dealer calls Ron and he reserves the car of his dreams that he plans to buy with the return on his shares investment.

Back at the Savoy, Phoebe is hanging onto Gary's every word as he describes his ideas for *My Fair Lady*. The head waiter returns, tells Gary the Imperial Suite is now available and hands him his purchases in a bag. When Gary tells Phoebe he's booked a suite, she is concerned as to what she will tell her dad. He suggests she tell him they spent the night sheltering in the restaurant. However, before they get the chance to go to their suite, Eric arrives with a telegram for Phoebe. She asks Gary to read it out and he tells her that Donald has been taken a prisoner of war by the Italians. Gary is surprised when Eric and Phoebe are relieved by this news. Phoebe points out that he could have been killed. Eric then tells her he has come to take her home. As they leave, Gary and Phoebe bid each other farewell from a distance.

Yvonne is watching the tape that Gary left in the video as he arrives home still dressed in the dinner jacket that PC Deadman lent him. By way of an excuse, Gary claims he bought it from one of the stalls in Runcorn and someone stole his jeans and sweatshirt while he was trying the suit on. Gary then cheekily gives Yvonne the lingerie he bought for Phoebe as a present. He tells her a story that, while it doesn't give anything away to Yvonne, contains references to him and Phoebe. She reads the card, which is a line from the song 'Tonight' from *West Side Story*. Genuinely touched, she tells Gary that he can be sentimental. In an attempt to change the subject, Gary asks Yvonne what she's watching. When she plays the tape, we see that Gary has changed history. He can now clearly be seen in the footage being introduced to the King. Without realising it, Yvonne is looking at Phoebe, who stands next to Gary and her dad. Blissfully unaware, she points out Gary's resemblance to the doctor and he tells her he would probably have looked like that – had he been around back then.

The final episode of the first series was particularly strong and continued to deliver a clever mixture of laughter and tears right until the end credits. Although one could argue the story was tied up and could have ended on this sixth episode, Laurence and Maurice had left themselves with somewhere to go with the series. For instance, there was the investment that Gary had made with the help of Manny and his brother-in-law in Arbuthnot Brothers Radio Ltd. Most of all, there was temptation for Gary. Could he really carry on living knowing that Phoebe and the ability to travel back in time were available just by taking a short walk down Duckett's Passage? Could he really stay with Yvonne knowing that real, deeper love in a more innocent time was just waiting for him, despite the various obstacles such as Phoebe's husband, Donald, and her interfering father, Eric. Yes, things finally seemed better with Yvonne by the end of this episode. She had suddenly become gentler and more understanding. But would that really last? She was an ambitious, impatient go-getter and wanted everything and more – and all yesterday! This was at odds with Gary's more laid-back view of life and his job.

Laurence and Maurice are justifiably proud of the final episode of series one. 'It is one of the most beautifully constructed half-hours we have ever written,' said Laurence proudly. 'It was the perfect conclusion to a series that we didn't at the time know would be recommissioned.'

Maurice was in full agreement. 'We often show "In the Mood" to students and I'm always amazed how much we packed in, and how well,' he said. 'Most writers would have the King George story and the Savoy Hotel story as quite separate episodes. It again showcases the brilliance of the production design by the late and great Roger Andrews.'

In one scene set in the bar of the Royal Oak, Manny, played by Harry Landis, had to quote an old-fashioned expression to Gary. However, the line made the director curious. 'I remember Robin Nash said to me during rehearsals, "Harry, is the phrase 'From your mouth to God's ears' a real Jewish expression?" I assured him that it was.'

Also appearing in this episode was Jerome Willis, who played the doctor that suddenly found himself introducing Gary to the King. Jerome became a highly respected actor during his six-decade career. His theatre roles included Master Hammon in the Thomas Dekker comedy *The Shoemaker's Holiday* at the Old Vic, London, Creon in Euripides' ancient Greek tragedy *Medea* at the Lyric Hammersmith, London, and Octavius in the Albert Camus play *Caligula*, translated by David Greig, at the Donmar Warehouse, London. Jerome's other television credits included Lovelock in the crime drama *Redcap*, starring John Thaw, Inspector Thornton in the *Return of the Saint*, with Ian Ogilvy playing Simon Templar, and Captain Rexton Podly in Gerry Anderson's series *Space Precinct*, which combined science fiction and crime drama. He was also a busy film actor, with appearances including Lieutenant Commander Tavener in the horror thriller *Doomwatch*, a translator in biographical drama *Orlando*, and the older board member in the Ray Winstone comedy, *The Sea Change*. Jerome died on 11 January 2014, aged eighty-five.

There was also wonderful support in this episode from Roger Brierley as the head waiter at the Savoy who is not averse to taking a friendly bribe from dinner guests – including Gary. Roger achieved considerable success in all the mediums he worked in. On stage, his credits included Captain Lesgate in the Frederick Knott suspense thriller *Dial 'M' for Murder* at the Queen's Theatre, Hornchurch, Admiral Juddy in the Ben Travers farce *Rookery Nook* at the Colchester Repertory Theatre and Digby Trumpington in the Robert Bolt play for children *The Thwarting of Baron Bolligrew*, with a cast including Roy Kinnear and Roger Lloyd-Pack, at the Aldwych Theatre, London. For television, his other roles included Julian in the much-loved Clement and La Frenais sitcom *The Likely Lads*, starring James Bolam and Rodney Bewes, Mr Compton, Stanley's new headmaster, in *Shine on Harvey Moon*, and Chief Superintendent Rivers in the Morecambe and Wise comedy *Night Train to Murder*. Meanwhile, his feature film appearances included a terrorist in the action adventure *Superman II*, with Christopher Reeve, a town hall official in the comedy *Ali G Indahouse*, alongside Sacha Baron Cohen, and Mr Chalmers in the romantic comedy *About a Boy*, which cast Hugh Grant as Will, a cynical and selfish thirty-something bachelor. Roger died on 23 September 2005, aged seventy.

Incidentally, although the end credits claim that Aaron Aardvark voiced the newsreel commentator in this episode, this was actually a temporary pseudonym for the series producer John Bartlett who, as previously mentioned, occasionally lent his voice to the series.

After the final recording of the first series on Thursday 14 October 1993, ALOMO organised an end of recording party for the series' cast and production team aboard the boat *Sir Thomas More*, which was moored at the side of Teddington Studios at Teddington Lock until 1999. The party started just after the recording wrapped at 10.00pm.

To herald the arrival of the first series of *Goodnight Sweetheart*, the *TV Times* featured Nicholas Lyndhurst on the front cover dressed as Gary Sparrow for their edition dated 13-19 November 1993.

The first episode of *Goodnight Sweetheart* was broadcast by BBC One on Thursday 18 November 1993 at 8.30pm, just five days before the thirtieth anniversary of the first episode of *Doctor Who*, which, of course, also featured a lead character with the gift of time travel! That night, Laurence and Maurice and Allan McKeown were at Teddington Studios for a recording of an episode of *Birds of a Feather*. Laurence and Alan excused themselves from the gallery and went to watch the first episode being broadcast in a nearby room.

The episode received a more than respectable ten million viewers. 'At the time we were used to getting ten to fifteen million viewers for *Birds of a Feather*,' said Laurence. 'So there was no great euphoria, but it has held its own.'

The remaining five episodes of the first series were originally broadcast by BBC One on Thursday 25 November 1993, Thursday 2 December 1993, Thursday 9 December 1993, Thursday 16 December 1993 and Thursday 23 December 1993 at 8.30pm.

During the production of series one, presenter Judi Spiers travelled down to Teddington Studios to interview Nicholas for an edition of *Pebble Mill* on the set of the Royal Oak to help promote the new sitcom. This interview was broadcast by BBC One at lunchtime on Tuesday 23 November 1993.

A second series of *Goodnight Sweetheart* was duly commissioned by the BBC. However, not all of the cast members from the first series were set to return.

2
The Singing Spy

ALTHOUGH THE CHARACTER OF Phoebe's father, Eric Elward, had appeared in all six episodes of the first series, Laurence and Maurice realised by episode three that they had gone as far as they could with writing his character. They also decided that the character of Emanuel 'Manny' Solomons, who appeared in two episodes in the first series, would not return for the same reason. Harry Landis could see the writing was on the wall for Manny. 'I would have liked to have appeared in more episodes,' he admitted. 'But I think my character was seen as superfluous, and one of us had to go.'

There was better news, however, for Christopher Ettridge who played PC Deadman. Despite being a peripheral character in the beginning, PC Deadman, or just Reg as he would mostly be called from series two onwards, was set to become a central figure in all future episodes. 'In series one, there were three older characters: Reg, Eric and Manny,' said Christopher. 'I think they realised there wasn't room for us all. I got the long straw. I also think Lo and Mo were responding to the way things developed.'

One of the other main changes to series two was the increase in the number of episodes from six to ten. 'We proposed an extension of the series,' said Maurice. 'We proved we could do longer runs and that was our strength. We were fairly confident of running the story all the way through the war.'

Laurence and Maurice wrote their episodes for the remaining five series in the former's office, which was a converted cattle shed in the grounds of his then home, a barn conversion, situated close to the Cotswolds town of Burford. Due to the increased number of episodes, they decided to initiate a programme of hiring other writers. However, this was by no means a new way of working for the duo. 'The first time we brought other writers onto one of our shows was when we wrote *Relative Strangers*,' recalled Maurice. 'This sitcom went out on Channel 4 in 1985 and 1987. They commissioned a first run of twelve episodes at a time when we were writing *Shine on Harvey Moon* too, so we saw the need for, and value of, a writing team.

'*Relative Strangers* was made for Channel 4 by Humphrey Barclay Productions, so Humphrey introduced us to some promising writers whose work had "crossed his desk", including Gary Lawson and John Phelps, and Geoff Rowley. We also brought in Paul Makin, who was with our agent.'

For series two of *Goodnight Sweetheart*, Paul Makin and the writing partnership of Gary Lawson and John Phelps were contracted. However, their engagement wasn't merely to lighten the workload. 'We enjoy working with other writers as they help to keep things fresh,' said Maurice.

Micheál Jacob, a good friend of Laurence and Maurice, worked in public relations and journalism before joining ALOMO as a script editor to work on *Birds of a Feather*. He became head of development and was involved in programmes across the company. Having acted as a script associate on the first series of *Goodnight Sweetheart*, Micheál returned for the second series as script editor.

To the uninitiated, the exact role of a script editor might be a mystery. 'In essence, their main responsibility is to analyse scripts in relation to what the writer is seeking to achieve, whether the script is delivering that, and whether the script is structurally sound,' said Micheál. 'The basis of dramatic structure goes back to ancient Greece and deals with how stories are organised. The convention is one of three acts. The short first act establishes the main characters and the basis of the story. The second act develops the story and complicates it. The short third act resolves it in a satisfying way.

'Story is the first consideration, but then there is character. Questions script editors ask are whether characters are consistent through a script and through the episodes of a series? Are the characters rounded and human, with human emotions that the audience can feel sympathy with, or are they just people in a script? And in comedy, do the characters have some flaw that makes them funny?

'And then, where is the source of conflict? Drama comes from conflict – not from people having arguments, but from people with different views of the world butting up against one another. Yvonne wants Gary to have more get up and go. Gary wants Yvonne to get off his back. Reg wants Phoebe to remember she's a married woman. Phoebe wants Reg to allow her to live her life.'

Before *Goodnight Sweetheart*, Micheál had been script editing the sitcom *Birds of a Feather*, which had introduced a British style of team writing. 'In America, shows were written by writers sitting together in a room, led by the creator or creators and working collectively,' he said. 'In Britain, until *My Family*, which was created by an American writer and had an American-style writers' room, the Marks and Gran model involved writers as individual contractors who would come together at the beginning to discuss possible stories, talk them through in headlines and then be allocated episodes to write, with the approval of the creators. The writers would then deliver storylines – stories presented in scenes – on which they would receive notes before they went on to write a script.'

Micheál went on to combine working as a company script editor on *Birds of a Feather* with working on *Goodnight Sweetheart*. 'I had several roles in this process,' he said. 'At the beginning, Marks and Gran, the writers and I would get together over two or three days. Laurence and Maurice would outline their overall idea of the series, and then there would be general discussion before talking about ideas for individual episodes. My role was to keep notes on the discussion, write promising ideas on a whiteboard, and keep track of what everyone was saying, where the discussion was leading, and who might be allocated which episode. After that, I produced a summary document, discussed it with Marks and Gran, and contacted the writers to say which episode they were allocated, and deadlines for story submissions.

'As the stories came in, I analysed them and did notes for Laurence and Maurice, who would agree with my notes, disagree with their notes, and add their own, which I turned into a document and sent to the writers, who were then given a script delivery deadline.

'When the scripts came in, we followed the same process, which led to one or two further drafts, until all the scripts were ready to feed into the production process.

An additional responsibility was to check every script for historical accuracy. If a song was mentioned, or a historical event, did it align to the right year? Accuracy was essential, and writers sometimes prefer poetic truth.

There was, however, one hard and fast rule that Micheál and the writers understood: Laurence and Maurice would always write the first and last episode of each series.

The increase in episodes was obviously set to be a challenge to the cast. 'I had to put myself in a marathon mentality,' said Nicholas Lyndhurst. 'I lived and breathed the job and there was no time for any kind of social life, let alone flying, which is one of my passions. However, as hoped, the clever mix of comedy and drama made the character of Gary Sparrow more interesting to play as a performer.'

The rehearsals, location filming, pre-records and studio audience recordings for series two took place between Wednesday 10 August 1994 and Thursday 17 November 1994.

Because series two was extended from six to ten episodes, the production process had to change to facilitate the increase. The location filming and studio recordings were separated into blocks. The first location block took place between Wednesday 10 August 1994 and Tuesday 16 August 1994, while the first block of studio audience recordings took place between Thursday 25 August 1994 and Thursday 22 September 1994.

The second block of location filming took place between Wednesday 5 October 1994 and Wednesday 12 October 1994, with the second block of studio audience recordings taking place between Thursday 20 October 1994 and Thursday 17 November 1994.

Goodnight Sweetheart: A Guide to the Classic Sitcom

Prior to the location filming for series two of *Goodnight Sweetheart*, Harry 'Aitch' Fielder received a request from a friend on the production team asking for his help. 'I got a call from Chris D'Oyly-John, the location manager,' explained Harry. 'He asked me to help him out for a week in the East End doing some public liaison work on the series. I got on well with both cast and crew and the week soon passed with only the occasional altercation from a couple of drunks. As lorries and cars were passing by, the drivers would see Nicholas and shout out, "Rodders, you plonker!" as they thought we were making *Only Fools and Horses*.'

After he worked on the series, Harry received the following letter from Chris:

Dear Aitch,

Re: Goodnight Sweetheart – Series B

Now that filming has been successfully completed, a quick line to say thank you very much for your major contribution in making the filming go smoothly – I know that John Bartlett, the producer, was very pleased, particularly with the diplomatic way in which you dealt with certain inebriated characters!

Many thanks for location 2A and 3B – I hope we work together again soon. The programme will be transmitted in the autumn or winter and I hope you get a chance to see it.

Yours sincerely,
Chris D'Oyly-John
Location Manager

Harry spent the majority of his adult life working as a supporting actor and background artist, a career that ran from the 1960s until the 1990s. His television credits included playing Mike Pratt's double and also a passer-by in the action television series *Randall and Hopkirk (Deceased)*, a laundry man in the sitcom *Fawlty Towers* and a jury member in the courtroom drama, *Kavanagh QC*. For the big screen, Harry's roles included a Burpa in the saucy comedy *Carry On Up the Khyber*, a lorry driver in the Alfred Hitchcock thriller *Frenzy* and a Death Star Trooper in George Lucas's space opera film, *Star Wars Episode IV: A New Hope*. Harry, who loved regaling people with anecdotes about his time in the 'business', died on 6 February 2021, aged eighty.

At the start of 'Don't Get Around Much Anymore', the first episode of series two, Gary and Yvonne are coming to the end of a hard-going evening with Josephine and her mortgage broker husband, Magnus. The upshot from picking Magnus's brains is that the couple cannot afford to buy their dream home on

Maple Avenue. The conversation soon turns to Gary's friends – or rather the lack of them! Yvonne is curious to know why he doesn't mention Ron, who she suggests probably has a few thousand he could lend them. However, Gary refuses to go cap in hand to Ron after they had a serious parting of the ways on a matter of principle.

Unfortunately for Gary, Yvonne suspends all carnal activity until he agrees to make things up with Ron. As expected, Ron is not best pleased to see Gary arrive on the doorstep of his office at Nostradamus Printing. He's still sulking because Gary didn't invest the white fivers following his break-up with Phoebe. Greed gets the better of Ron who suggests that he go back in time to make an investment for him or, indeed, both of them. However, Gary is reluctant as he couldn't face the idea of going back and seeing Phoebe again. Ron reminds him that he wouldn't have to go to the Royal Oak. All he has to do is to go back to 1941, invest a modest amount and then come back so they can cash in the enormous pile that would have accumulated in the interim. With Gary still not convinced, Ron points out that this is the only way he will ever raise the money to buy his dream home, because he won't lend him any.

During a break from work, Gary goes in search of a bank in the East End of London. Standing outside a likely target for his investment, PC Deadman's grandson, still a police constable, confirms that the bank was there during the war.

Gary later makes for 1941 via Duckett's Passage and heads in the direction of the bank. As he passes the Royal Oak, he bumps into Reg Deadman. Reg tells him that a lot has changed since he went to America and invites him inside, realising he obviously wants to see Phoebe. Gary is shocked to discover that Phoebe has changed. She is more feisty, tougher and stronger. After initially greeting Gary warmly, she admonishes him by using unladylike language for not writing to her. It's then that Gary discovers Eric was killed in an air raid four months previously. Phoebe admits to missing him, even though he was 'a terrible nag'. Gary also discovers that Phoebe is now running the Royal Oak with Reg's help – if you can call that help! She is confused as to why Gary has come all the way from Hollywood to Stepney to look her up despite the beautiful weather in Hollywood and the fact that he was able to hobnob with many of the film stars. He tells her he didn't fit in and wanted to see her again.

While Phoebe is serving two customers, Reg comes over for a chat and tells Gary how hard it's been for Phoebe since her dad died and begs him, 'Don't go breaking her heart.' Gary replies, 'I couldn't if I tried' – wittily completing a lyric from the Elton John and Bernie Taupin song, 'Don't Go Breaking My Heart'. He points out that Phoebe has now become as tough as nails.

Goodnight Sweetheart: A Guide to the Classic Sitcom

When Gary arrives at the bank to make his investment, he comes face to face with a bank manager by the name of Mainwaring and his chief clerk who goes by the name of Wilson. By strange coincidence, both men display similarities to their namesakes in the sitcom *Dad's Army*. This amuses Gary and he starts singing the *Dad's Army* theme tune until he remembers where he is.

Gary tells Mainwaring that he wishes to make an investment, but the latter is suspicious as to where he has earned such a large amount of sterling. When Gary tells the po-faced bank manager he earned the money from working as a songwriter in Hollywood, he doesn't believe him. However, he gives him the opportunity to prove himself by singing a few bars of Handel's *Agrippina*, an opera he, naturally, once had a leading role in. When offered a copy of the libretto, Gary explains that he can't read music. This arouses further suspicion in Mainwaring, who calls Wilson back into the office. Sensing he's about to be shown the door, Gary points out that lots of songwriters can't read music, including Irving Berlin who wrote 'Alexander's Ragtime Band'. When Wilson arrives, he also tells the same story about Irving Berlin. He then suggests that Gary sing one of his own compositions. Mainwaring agrees, and Gary sings a line from the song 'Get Me to the Church on Time' from *My Fair Lady*, which he, of course, claims to have written. With the unorthodox test successfully over, Gary is allowed to make his investment, but not before a clumsy Private Pike lookalike called Major arrives and makes a mess of serving tea.

Before Gary returns to 1994, he decides to pay Phoebe another visit at the pub. There he gives her a present of a brooch and tells her he's going back to America again. Gary claims the film company making his musical *My Fair Lady* are keen to cast Judy Garland in the role of Eliza Doolittle, and his producer wants him to meet her. Gary tells Phoebe she doesn't need him around confusing things as she has Donald to think about. Phoebe reminds him that it's not fair to come back and stir up all the feelings she thought she had got over. Before parting, she presents him with a lipstick-imprinted handkerchief to remember her by, and kisses him passionately.

Gary returns to 1994 to see Ron and presents him with a share certificate receipt. Ron is keen to celebrate with a high alcohol content bevvy, after he realises that their Eurotronics plc shares are currently worth four hundred and fifty thousand pounds. Gary, however, is far from happy, something which Ron can't understand given he's boosted both his finances and his 'nookie rating' both sides of the space-time continuum in just one morning! Phoebe keeps playing on Gary's mind. He realises she's still going to be waiting for him back in 1941.

When Gary casually waltzes into the lounge, Yvonne is curious to know where he has been. Now an old hand at making up excuses, Gary tells her he's been arranging them a mortgage with a bank that Ron suggested. Yvonne is delighted – until she realises it's from an Arab bank. However, her eyes light up when he claims they've offered him a low interest five per cent fixed rate. Furthermore, she's delighted to hear that Gary has made it up with Ron.

As Ron is desperate to get his hands on the cash from the shares, Gary arranges an interview for them with the modern-day bank manager, Mr Thursfield. Their plan is to claim that they're the grandsons of Gary Sparrow who purchased twenty thousand shares in Arbuthnot of Ealing Ltd, which became Eurotronics plc in 1973. Gary claims he's the sole beneficiary of his will and thus entitled to the shares. When Thursfield questions why their grandad never returned for his share certificate, Ron, with rather unsubtle prompting from Gary, explains he suffered a serious concussion in an air raid in 1941 which caused loss of memory.

All is going well; that is, until Thursfield is called out of the office and Gary and Ron start to look through the files. Gary discovers a memo written by the then bank manager in 1957, which explains that the Arbuthnot brothers, Cecil and Harold, who owned the business, had a vicious bust-up when Harold found Cecil in bed with his wife. The partnership was dissolved and both brothers then set up rival companies. Harold started Arbuthnot of Ealing Ltd and Cecil, Arbuthnot Electronics Ltd. Since the then bank manager was unable to trace Gary, he chose to invest with Harold's company, which went out of business – thus rendering the share certificate worthless. When Thursfield returns to the office, he realises what has happened. This is a hard pill for Gary and Ron to swallow, made worse when Thursfield reveals that the 1957 bank manager was formerly the clumsy tea boy, Major.

A second series of any successful sitcom always brings with it the worry of whether it will be as good as the first. However, from the opening episode it was clear the standard of performances and writing were going to be maintained. If anything, this series proved to be even better than the first.

The dramatic change in Phoebe's character from the very start of series two was welcomed by Dervla Kirwan. 'I was very grateful that there was a strength there and emotional strength and a development,' she said. 'I think it made Phoebe much more interesting for me to play. I think one of the main difficulties I had as an actress was trying to sustain the sense of naivety and the greenness without her coming across as completely stupid and ignorant all the time. It was understandable as here you had this character from the future who was dashing and funny, smart and witty and amazed her continuously with his insight into what was going to happen next. If there hadn't been that emotional development in series two, it would have become very one-dimensional.'

During a discussion about the first episode of series two, Laurence suddenly found himself becoming inspired by another wartime sitcom. 'We decided that Gary would have to visit the bank,' he recalled. 'I said to Maurice, "What if it was managed by a bank manager called Mainwaring and his chief clerk was someone called Wilson?" John Bartlett thought it was a good idea, but he said we would need permission from David Croft and Jimmy Perry, the writers and creators of *Dad's Army*, first. I asked if he could contact David. We were working on the third episode of series two in the cattle shed at my home in the Cotswolds when the phone rang. It was David Croft. We discussed our desire to use two of their character names and he gave us his blessing because he knew we would do so with care and diligence. We added a character that was just like Pike, but we called him Major. The real Pike would come later!'

Alec Linstead was inspired casting for the role of bank manager, Mainwaring, in this episode. In an accomplished career, Alec's theatre roles have included Oscar Nelson in the Jean Kerr comedy *Mary, Mary* at the Castle Theatre, Farnham, Stephen Hench in Simon Gray's bleakly comic play *Otherwise Engaged* at the Lyceum Theatre, Edinburgh, and Dr Hastie Lanyon in the David Edgar drama *Dr Jekyll and Mr Hyde*, based on the Robert Louis Stevenson story, at the Barbican Theatre, London. His other television work includes Sergeant Osgood, Jellicoe and Head of Stengos in the science-fiction series *Doctor Who*. Away from time travel, Alec played a doctor in the drama *Anna Karenina*, which starred Nicola Pagett in the lead role, and a registrar in the pulsating 1960s comedy drama, *Sex, Chips and Rock n' Roll*. His film roles have included a hotel desk clerk in the drama *Richard's Things*, Fincham's brother in Stephen Poliakoff's romantic comedy *Food of Love* and Prete in the Italian-British romantic comedy *South Kensington*, with a cast including Rupert Everett, Elle Macpherson and Sienna Miller, in her first screen role.

There was also the skilful casting of Terrence Hardiman as Mainwaring's clerk, Wilson. 'I remember it was a relaxed and pleasant rehearsal week, followed by the usual nervous tension of performing before a studio audience,' he said. 'Not that it was the first time for me, but it doesn't get easier.

'I didn't audition for Wilson; so, I suppose my build and type had enough to suggest an echo of John Le Mesurier! Alec and I had just the one scene to play, and it was unnecessary to use more than some brush strokes to suggest the characters. Alec had enough of a physical resemblance to Arthur Lowe's Mainwaring, while I wafted my arm and stroked my brow in what I hoped was a Wilson-like fashion. Fortunately, the audience caught on to the conceit quickly enough.

'I was a child during the war, living in London where my father was a policeman, so a few nostalgic nerves were touched. Al Bowlly singing "Goodnight Sweetheart" has always been a favourite song!'

Terrence's list of acting credits proves what a prodigious career he had as an actor. In the theatre, his roles included Lucio in William Shakespeare's powerful and darkly comic play *Measure for Measure* at the Royal Shakespeare Theatre, Stratford-upon-Avon, Professor Steiner in the Ken Hill play *The Curse of the Werewolf*, at the Theatre Royal, Stratford East, and Neville Chamberlain in the Howard Brenton play *Never So Good*, which portrays the life and career of Harold Macmillan, at the National Theatre, London. His other television appearances included Frank Crawley in the drama *Rebecca*, based on the Gothic romance novel by Daphne Du Maurier, the title role in the children's drama *The Demon Headmaster* and Doctor Evans in the award-winning drama, *The Crown*. Terrence also played characters on film including a doctor in the action adventure *Running Scared*, with a cast including Robert Powell and Gayle Hunnicutt, David in the heist crime *Loophole* and Ramsay MacDonald in Richard Attenborough's biographical drama, *Gandhi*. Terrence died on 8 May 2023, aged eighty-six.

Also in the cast was Max Digby as the clumsy tea boy, Major. Since appearing in *Goodnight Sweetheart*, Max's theatre roles have included Barnette Lloyd in Beth Henley's dark comedy *Crimes of the Heart* at the King's Head Theatre, London, Prince Yeletsky in the John Clifford play *Tchaikovsky and the Queen of Spades* at the Nuffield Theatre, Southampton, and Phipps in the Oscar Wilde comedy *An Ideal Husband* at the Vaudeville Theatre, London. Meanwhile, his other television work has included playing Grigori Rostov in the drama *Bugs*, Mr Pugh in an episode of the children's series *The Story of Tracy Beaker*, and a blind date in the Jessica Hynes sitcom, *According to Bex*. Additionally, Max's film credits include Carl in the horror *Artefacts*, an MI5 agent in the crime drama *Shoot on Sight*, and Angelo in the drama *Acts of Godfrey*.

Finally, Eamonn Walker was cast as the outspoken bank manager, Thursfield. Eamonn made his acting debut playing the role of Tarquin in the rock musical *Labelled with Love*, which was based on the songs of Chris Difford and Glen Tilbrook of Squeeze, at the Albany Empire in Lewisham, London. His high-profile theatre credits include Mark Antony in the William Shakespeare tragedy *Julius Caesar*, which starred Denzel Washington in the role of Brutus, at the Belasco Theatre on Broadway in New York, and the titular role in *Othello* at Shakespeare's Globe, London. Many viewers will remember him for playing Winston in the 1980s sitcom, *In Sickness and in Health*. Another of Eamonn's early television roles saw him play hairstylist Floyd alongside Nicholas Lyndhurst and Sharon Maiden (who is best remembered for playing Laura Wisely in the John Cleese film comedy *Clockwise*) in an episode of the first series of the sitcom *The Two of Us* called 'Cracks in the Pavement'. In more recent years, Eamonn has worked on American television where his roles have included Walter Lutulu in the action thriller *Strike Back* and Wallace Boden in the drama *Chicago Fire*. As well as acting on stage and television, Eamonn has appeared in films playing roles such as James in the action drama *Blood and Bone* and Danny in the drama *The Company Men*, which starred Ben Affleck, and Andy in the thriller, *A Lonely Place to Die*.

The building used in this episode for the exterior of the bank featured in scenes set in both 1941 and 1994 has since been replaced by Penhurst House. This state-of-the-art business centre, complete with serviced office units and full conference facilities, is located at 352–356 Battersea Park Road, Wandsworth, London.

As 'I Got it Bad and That Ain't Good', the second episode of series two, begins, Yvonne is seen sitting up in bed and doing a spot of creative writing on an advert for selling the house. Her focus suddenly changes, and she demands that Gary get his shorts off and get into bed. Rather taken aback by this request, Gary questions if she learned her seduction technique from the Gestapo. His spouse then reveals that it is the most fertile day of her cycle – a fact that Gary admits is not in his Letts Boy Scout Diary – and that she's keen that they should have a baby. However, the pressure of moving, her desire for a child and his working in the remorseless world of television repair is preventing Gary from feeling anything south of the navel.

To get away from the stresses and strains of the bedroom, Gary spends the afternoon with Ron on a boating lake. But with things on his mind, the two attractive ladies amusing Ron by struggling to handle their oars correctly in a nearby boat fail to interest Gary.

Afterwards, in a nearby café, Ron reveals his theory as to why Gary is unable to keep Yvonne satisfied. He believes that while he may love Yvonne, his loins are crying out for Phoebe. Ron advises that Gary go back to 1941 and see Phoebe again, believing that this is his destiny and that he can't close the book until he finishes the story.

Returning home, Gary realises he has forgotten that a couple have come to look round the house with a view to possibly buying the property. The tension between him and Yvonne is palpable, and the gay couple, Frederick and Joe, decide to withdraw to the spare bedroom to 'measure something'. Yvonne then questions if they're really serious sellers, which Gary admits he's been trying to tell her all along. When the couple return, it becomes clear that Joe is jealous of the friendship that is developing between Frederick and Gary over their mutual interest in jazz.

After the couple leave, Gary and Yvonne exchange words over the time traveller's recent inability to procreate. This line of questioning touches a nerve and Gary leaves in a sulk, but not before he notices Yvonne's blouse hanging in the hallway. He pauses to take it, then leaves the house and heads off in the direction of the past.

Upon returning to the war-torn East End, Gary spots Phoebe at a market stall arguing with a woman over a blouse. Gary tells her to leave it. Annoyed, Phoebe questions Gary about why he's not making his *My Fair Lady* back in Hollywood. He tells her the film has fallen through as they're only making war films now. Also, that his house in Cricklewood has been bombed out, blowing his Bechstein piano to pieces. Phoebe mistakenly believes his Bechstein is a type of dog!

Back at the Royal Oak, Phoebe asks why Gary stopped her from buying the blouse in the market. He then presents her with Yvonne's silk blouse all wrapped up in modern wrapping paper. As much as she likes it, she tells him that bringing her presents won't impress her or turn her head that easily. When Reg turns up, Phoebe even slates Gary's songwriting skills, remarking that everyone should be doing their bit to beat Hitler. Reg asks where their morale would be without Gary's songs such as 'I Can't Get No Satisfaction'. Desperate to impress Phoebe, Gary goes to the piano to play 'If You Leave Me Now', which he, of course, claims to have written. While singing, he notes that a dapper young man in uniform has come into the bar and embraces Phoebe. When a jealous Gary questions Reg as to how long 'Rudolph Valentino' has been hanging around Phoebe, Reg explains that he's called Ludo, like the board game, and he has been making a real fuss of her every day he's visited for the last fortnight.

There's instant tension between Gary and Ludo when they're introduced by Phoebe, especially when Ludo tells Gary that Phoebe described him as a long streak of dishwater who writes songs! Although Reg attempts to come to Gary's defence, Ludo is neither impressed nor convinced and further annoys him by inviting Phoebe to go for a walk so he can put a little proposition to her.

Back in 1994, Yvonne confesses to her friend, Stella, on the phone that she believed that the row she had with Gary would result in them having a night of raunch. That is, until she realised that he'd taken her best silk blouse.

On Phoebe's return to the Royal Oak, Gary asks her whether she feels anything for him any more. Phoebe admits she would be lying if she said she didn't. However, his lack of reliability means that she is unwilling to have a proper relationship with him. Attempts to impress her again with presents of tea, coffee, sugar, butter, biscuits and steak don't work and she even insists on paying him for his outlay.

When Ludo, who at Phoebe's suggestion now calls himself Robert for when he becomes a naturalised Englishman, arrives back at the Royal Oak, he tries to persuade Phoebe in Gary and Reg's presence to invest her dad's savings and pension money, amounting to two hundred pounds, in Argentinian beef. This instantly makes Gary suspicious. To try and find out more, Gary tells Ludo that he has three thousand pounds he's thinking of investing. Suddenly Ludo changes his attitude towards Gary. That is, until Gary starts asking a few leading questions about the scheme, including how and when the returns would be paid. Realising that Gary has put doubt in Phoebe's mind about the validity of his investment scheme, Ludo leaves, somewhat flustered. Despite now accepting that Ludo is a con man, Phoebe remains upset with Gary and storms out of the bar. Gary then drowns his sorrows with Reg.

By the time Gary gets back to 1994, he is well over the limit. After breaking into his own van, he gets arrested by Reg's grandson for being drunk in charge of a vehicle. Gary then calls Yvonne who asks if his arrest is anything to do with him taking her silk blouse.

This episode felt like a defining moment for Gary and Phoebe. Both of them clearly realise that their feelings for each other are still there and there's a desire to go forward, despite the fear of being hurt. Yet somehow Gary, as ever, seems still willing to fight for his marriage to Yvonne back in 1994. It showed yet again how Gary's behaviour in one era could affect his life in the other. After all, he may have got drunk back in 1941, where there was no such thing as the breathalyser, but a quick walk, or stumble, along Duckett's Passage back to 1994 and his past soon caught up with him.

Despite not having any lines, Alison Beattie was credited in this episode as Girl in Boat. However, the actress lists the character's name as Jane on her biography. When Jane accidentally drops one of the oars into the boating lake, Ron characteristically interprets this as flirting. Alison's other television credits include Mrs Barnett in the soap opera *EastEnders*.

Also appearing was Paul Shearer, who was cast as jazz-loving Frederick. Paul first worked with Nicholas Lyndhurst back in 1982 on an *Arena* documentary called *A Genius Like Us: A Portrait of Joe Orton*. Scenes from the Orton play *Loot* were filmed for the programme at Ealing Studios, which were owned by the BBC at the time. In these extracts, Paul played Hal while Nicholas took on the role of Dennis. 'I found Nicholas to be a lovely, quiet man,' said Paul, summarising his time of working with the actor. 'He was very talented but never showed off.'

Paul began his career as a sketch comedy actor in a national stage tour with the Cambridge Footlights, appearing alongside Stephen Fry, Emma Thompson, Hugh Laurie, Tony Slattery and Penny Dwyer in *The Cellar Tapes*. This show won the first ever Perrier comedy award at the Edinburgh Festival Fringe in 1981. His stage credits also include appearing alongside Marti Caine and the then future *Goodnight Sweetheart* actress Emma Amos in *Snow White and the Seven Dwarfs* at the Cambridge Arts Theatre. Paul also played Cinna, second poet and Volumnius in Deborah Warner's production of the William Shakespeare play *Julius Caesar*, which starred Ralph Fiennes and Simon Russell Beale, at the Barbican Theatre, London. For television, Paul's other appearances include playing various characters on the sketch show *The Russ Abbot Show*, an ethics board official in the news channel sitcom *Drop the Dead Donkey* and Mr Truman in the period medical drama, *The Royal*; while his film roles include a reporter in the comedy *The Man Who Knew Too Little*, which starred Bill Murray, and Reverend Flynn in the Zara Turner thriller, *The Blind Date*.

The role of Frederick's partner Joe was played by Patrick Pearson. Patrick remembers working on this episode of *Goodnight Sweetheart* as being a positive experience. 'It was a very nice and happy job to work on,' he recalled. 'Sitcom is not normally the type of programme I appear in, although I have been acting for many years. I remember it felt really strange being introduced to the audience before the recording by the warm-up man. He went through all the actors and actresses one by one and then came to me and said, "And this is Patrick Pearson, he's playing Joe." It was a bit of an unnerving process as I was used to just playing a character!

'These days you don't have many opportunities to rehearse. For things to be funny, they have to be truthful and that's what gets the laughs – and that's what you get from the rehearsal process.'

An esteemed actor, Patrick's theatre roles have included Gerald Forbes in the J. B. Priestley comedy *When We Are Married* at the Whitehall Theatre, London, Henry Dundas in Alan Bennett's multi-award-winning drama *The Madness of George III* at the National Theatre, London, and Paravicini in the Agatha Christie murder mystery *The Mousetrap* at St Martin's Theatre, London. His other television credits also include PC Naylor in the courtroom drama *Crown Court*, Captain Richard Mortlock in the airline comedy drama *Mile High* and Patrick Lamb in Peter Kosminsky's powerful factual drama, *The Government Inspector*. Patrick's film appearances include playing Stephen Flowers in the comedy *Privates on Parade*, an adaptation of Peter Nichols' play of the same name, Clara's father in the musical fantasy *The IMAX Nutcracker* and Giles in the ensemble comedy drama, *The Best Exotic Marigold Hotel*.

This episode also saw Duncan Faber appear as the stallholder. Duncan's other television credits include playing a sailor in the biographical comedy-drama *The Naked Civil Servant*, a man in the market in the *Only Fools and Horses* Christmas special *The Frog's Legacy*, and Ken in the sitcom *Barbara*.

Also cast in this episode was Louise Tomkins as the lady in the market competing with Phoebe to buy a blouse. Away from the small screen, Louise's theatre credits include playing Maisie in the Denis King, Benny Green and David William musical *Valentine's Day*, adapted from the play *You Never Can Tell* by George Bernard Shaw, at the Globe Theatre, London. She has also played Emily Wardle in the Wolf Mankowitz, Cyril Ornadel and Leslie Bricusse musical *Pickwick* at venues including the Chichester Festival Theatre, the Sadler's Wells Theatre, London, the Alexandra Theatre, Birmingham, and the Lyceum Theatre, Sheffield. Louise has also played Annette in the Martin Charnin, Thomas Meehan and Charles Strouse musical *Annie* at the Victoria Palace Theatre, London, and the Churchill Theatre, Bromley. Her other television credits include the sitcom *Get Well Soon*, written by John Antrobus and Ray Galton. Louise was also a dancer in the DVD and video version of the Tim Rice and Andrew Lloyd Webber musical *Joseph and the Amazing Technicolor Dreamcoat*.

Finally, there was an appearance from Jonathan Cake who played the prickly con man, Ludo. The actor and director's theatre roles have included Coriolanus in the William Shakespeare tragedy *Coriolanus* at Shakespeare's Globe, Romain Tournel in the Feydeau farce *A Flea in Her Ear* at the Old Vic Theatre, London, and Frank in Jordi Galceran's *The Grönholm Method*, translated by Anne García-Romero and Mark St Germain, at the Menier Chocolate Factory, London. Jonathan's other television credits include playing the title role in the Marks and Gran drama *Mosley*, Reg in the boundary-pushing mystery comedy drama *Desperate Housewives* and Griffin Ford in the medical drama *Grey's Anatomy*. His various film parts include Sonny in the romantic drama *The One and Only*, Rex Mottram in the poignant romantic drama *Brideshead Revisited* and Jonas in the drama *Entangled*.

This episode included two locations not seen before in the sitcom. Gary and Ron could be seen in a boat on a boating lake, and then in a café, in reality La Gondola Al Parco, which are both located at Battersea Park, Battersea, London.

As 'Just One More Chance', the third episode of series two, starts, Ron arrives to accompany Gary to court where he has been summoned to appear after being arrested while being drunk in charge of a vehicle. Yvonne is angry because she realises that Gary is going to lose his licence and his job.

Ever-supportive Ron bets Yvonne that Gary will walk from the court without a stain on his character. However, when they emerge from the court, Ron hands over his money to Yvonne as Gary has indeed lost his driving licence – despite his desperate attempts to plead 'extenuating circumstances'.

Back at home, Gary pours himself and Ron a libation and announces he intends to get 'rat-arsed'. Still upset by the outcome of his court appearance, Yvonne pours Gary's drink on his trousers and puts the glass in the sink. Just when Gary thinks his day can't get any worse, his boss calls and sacks him after hearing the outcome of his brush with the law.

By way of rest and recuperation, Ron suggests that Gary visit Phoebe in wartime London. Tempted, Gary reminds him that Yvonne will expect him to look for a new job. Realising his predicament, Ron suggests Gary tell Yvonne that he's going to work for him. Gary is over the moon at the offer from his best mate. Well, that is until Ron clarifies that it isn't a serious job offer. It's merely a ruse to keep Yvonne off his back while he takes stock.

Gary tries to keep the peace by scouring the jobs page in the paper that night and making out his lack of employment could open up a whole new world of exciting possibilities for them. When Yvonne asks for an example, he reluctantly points out that someone is needed to collect the trolleys in the car park at Tesco. At her wits' end, Yvonne suggests that maybe they shouldn't try to keep going. After skirting the issue, Yvonne asks whether Gary wants them to split up. She goes on to suggest that maybe they go to Relate for some marriage guidance. Gary is quick to rule this out as he's not keen on discussing their intimate personal 'doodahs' with a stranger. Not that there's been any intimate personal 'doodahs' for the past month, which, confirms Yvonne, is part of the problem. Gary aborts the conversation and says they will talk about it in the morning. Yvonne is not convinced he will keep his promise, but is keen for him to face up to their problems and not run away from them forever. Gary says he isn't running away. Besides, where has he got to run away to?

The following morning Gary takes Ron's advice and makes a visit back in time to the Royal Oak. The fact that he has indeed gone against his promise and run away leaves Yvonne fuming. Once at the pub, the time traveller amuses Phoebe and Reg by presenting the barmaid with a pair of tights, something she has never seen before as she wears stockings. Reg offers to take them off her hands if she doesn't like them in order to store his onions. Now in a sulky mood, Gary moans that he had visited with the hope of being cheered up. Phoebe gets upset and reminds him that what with her dad dying and with running the pub, she doesn't have the strength to help improve his low morale.

Gary heads to Ron's print works and explains that he's facing another crisis and feels lost. In typical fashion, Ron does his best to cheer up Gary – this time with a boxing match analogy about his situation, which fails miserably. He reminds him that he still has Yvonne. Not that Gary is convinced after walking out on her earlier that morning. He realises he's been selfish, not least because Phoebe and everyone else back in 1941 are really up against it with shortages. He leaves promising to be more positive but fails to confirm which of the two women he wishes to commit to.

The unemployed time traveller returns home and comes face to face with one of Yvonne's friends from college, Jenny, who turns out to be a marriage counsellor. Gary gets annoyed when he realises he's being railroaded into discussing their marital problems. Gary agrees to share his innermost thoughts when Yvonne says this is their chance to make their marriage work. However, very soon it's Yvonne and Jenny that need pulling apart when they start arguing about their old flames, much to Gary's amusement. It appears Yvonne had a failed romance at college with a sensible shoes-wearing student called Trevor Harrison. This leads to Jenny's private life, which is littered with failed romances, including one with a mother's boy called Tony Price. To top it all, Yvonne reveals that Jenny is so unlucky in love that she had three unused wedding dresses made.

In bed later that night, Gary reflects on the very adult and grown-up evening they've just shared in which Yvonne ended up throwing a flowerpot at Jenny as she hastily retreated from the house. They agree to give things another go and end up kissing, despite Gary's worry that it could lead to Yvonne being with child. Not that she is convinced it will happen tonight.

The following day, Gary, having checked his history books for what was happening during the war on the same date, heads off to see Phoebe, who is feeling down. She explains that she's not angry after their falling-out the other day. She reminds him that everyone gets 'out of sorts' from time to time due to the war. Gary comforts her and assures her that things are going to get better. He mentions that Hitler has just made the mistake of his life and bitten off more than he can chew. He's just about to tell her that Hitler has invaded Russia when Reg comes in and tells her, stealing his thunder. After being admonished by Gary, Reg returns and tells Phoebe that Yvonne is here. Fortunately, the Yvonne in question is in fact Phoebe's auntie, much to Gary's relief!

Looking at the last two episodes closely, one can see that Laurence and Maurice were gradually guiding the story to a point where a change in Gary's professional circumstances would be necessary. Gary being a television repairman was simply too restricting. After all, he couldn't continue to spend all his days in the past and still hold down a job repairing television sets. Giving the character more freedom to come and go would also ultimately give the writers inspiration for more plots.

This episode was particularly noteworthy for being the first not to have been written by Laurence and Maurice. This honour went to West Midlander, Paul Makin. His other writing credits included the sitcoms *A Kind of Living*, *Nightingales* and *Grown-Ups*. Paul, who wrote a total of seven episodes of *Goodnight Sweetheart*, died on 4 July 2008, aged just fifty-four.

The Northern Ireland actress Clare Cathcart was cast as wedding-dress-obsessed marriage counsellor Jenny in this episode. In a relatively short but successful acting career, Clare's theatre roles included Rachel in the Arthur Miller tragedy *The Crucible* at the National Theatre, London, the nurse in the Rona Munro play *The Indian Boy* at the Royal Shakespeare Theatre, Stratford-upon-Avon, and Luce in William Shakespeare's farcical comedy *A Comedy of Errors* at the National Theatre, London. Her other television credits included Shona Temple in the drama *Psychos*, Liz Tufnell in the mystery drama *Afterlife* and Mrs Torpy in the period drama *Call the Midwife*. Clare's film parts included Angela in the musical *Up on the Roof*, Lorraine Bull in the dark comedy *Hotel Splendide*, with a cast that included Toni Collette and Daniel Craig, and a schoolteacher in the action drama *The Healer*.

Tragically, Clare passed away in her Brighton home on 4 September 2014, aged just forty-eight, following an asthma attack. The comedienne Miranda Hart said at the time, 'I am reeling from the news of Clare's death. I had the privilege of some serious laughing together with her in *Call the Midwife*. She was a ball of joy.'

There was one additional exterior location in this episode. The building used as the exterior of the court was Lavender Hill Magistrates Court, Magistrates Court House, 176A Lavender Hill, London.

Gary is seen looking reflective while eating his breakfast as 'Who's Taking You Home Tonight?', the fourth episode of series two, begins. Ron presently arrives wearing a badly ironed shirt to announce that he's getting grief at home from Stella because Yvonne has moaned about the hours Gary is supposedly working for him. For a quieter home life, Ron asks his pretend employee to make it clear that his hours are at his own discretion. When Yvonne appears, she moans that Ron doesn't give his staff much downtime. To try and placate their wives, Gary agrees with Ron that he will travel to Reading by train and come home early that night. However, Yvonne tells him that she won't be in as she's going to a cheese and wine evening.

Back in wartime London, Phoebe offers to cook Gary a meal that night in the flat above the Royal Oak, by way of thanks for a lovely afternoon together. This

Goodnight Sweetheart: A Guide to the Classic Sitcom

surprises the time traveller as normally Phoebe is concerned about what people would think. She brushes these concerns aside, admitting that people already suspect that they're an item.

Thinking he's alone back at home, Gary decides to have a quick bath before popping back to Phoebe's to share their romantic evening together. He checks his history book to see if there will be an air raid that evening and discovers there will be one at 9.00pm. This means they could end up sharing their pudding with the locals down a nearby air-raid shelter! Yvonne unexpectedly walks in and sits on the settee. After wrongly assuming her downbeat mood is due to PMT, Gary deduces that she's upset about all the hours that he's been pretending to work. Realising that he's backed himself into a corner again, Gary cheekily blames Ron. To try and make amends, Gary offers to take her out for a meal. Yvonne seizes upon the opportunity and says they should go out that evening. When Gary tries to suggest another night after making out he's seeing Ron, Yvonne insists.

Gary races over to Nostradamus Printing to tell Ron of his latest predicament. Then Gary is struck by a brainwave. He could attend both meal dates if he and Yvonne go to a restaurant close to Duckett's Passage, and if he wears a green suit that would pass muster in both eras.

Gary and Yvonne arrive at their restaurant and Gary quickly enquires about the whereabouts of the toilet. This is important as it will form part of his excuse for disappearing throughout the evening. When Sanjay, the restaurant owner, apologies for how quiet his establishment is, despite being open for eighteen months, Yvonne encourages Gary to give him a quote for some leaflets. However, his mind is on Phoebe. Faking an upset stomach, he heads off in search of the gents' toilet.

Leaving his Walkman and speakers playing a recording of him singing to make people believe he's still in the cubicle, Gary climbs out of the small window and stops off at Ron's car to collect the wine. He then goes to Phoebe's who complains about his tardiness. She becomes visibly irritated when Gary tells her he will have to keep phoning in to the Ministry via a public call box as it's more secure. When Phoebe discovers that the wine he has brought is German, Gary is for once justifiable in blaming Ron. After taking a few sips of the soup Phoebe has served for the first course, Gary runs off back in the direction of 1994.

Gary goes to Ron's car and tackles him about the wine. Ron tells Gary it came from Threshers, but Gary reminds him it came from Germany. Presently they hear a Cliff Richard track blaring out into the evening air. Gary realises that his tape has run out and charges back to the restaurant where he climbs back in through the window and stops the tape. He then realises he has accidentally put one of his feet in the toilet bowl.

Back with Yvonne, Gary begins to hurry his next course and she tells him to slow down. She then begins to play footsie with him and questions why one of his feet is soaking wet. He claims his foot slipped into the sink while he was tying his shoelace. Yvonne then reminds Gary to prepare a quote for Sanjay. Put on the spot, Gary dreams up a figure for the printing. When Sanjay appears to question the amount, Gary drops the price by fifty pounds only to be told by Sanjay that he was happy with the previous quote. He then insists on one of his waiters serving Gary with more Chicken Tikka to thank him, further adding to Gary's digestive woes. Sensing his reluctance, Yvonne wittily tells him not to look a gift course in the mouth.

Gary is understandably struggling with his second course back at Phoebe's flat. She reminds him that the character Potato Pete says that wasting food is as good as giving it to Adolf. Out of patriotism, Gary reluctantly attempts another mouthful of lamb chops, potatoes and peas.

Back in the restaurant, Gary is understandably wishing that he'd never thought of the idea of having two meals with two women as he tucks into yet another course. Yvonne is struggling to work out whether her other half is bulimic or pregnant because he's bolting his food one moment, then can't face it – and in between he's rushing to the toilet. Gary tries to convince her that he's fine until a loud rumble emits from his stomach. This makes her question if the noise came from him or if they're on top of the Underground!

Not surprisingly, the suet pudding Gary is attempting to eat back at the Royal Oak is not going down well. Gary tries to raise a smile when Phoebe comments that she wishes every night could be the same!

Ron has fallen asleep in his car listening to cricket highlights as Gary makes a pit stop on his way back to see Yvonne. Gary admits that he's being a total embarrassment. He then confides that he's either having chronic ingestion or in the middle of a major coronary. Gary then suggests a plan to get him away from the restaurant and asks Ron to walk into the restaurant in five minutes' time. Without going into details, he leaves the printer with a handful of suet pudding by way of his revenge for the wine debacle.

When Ron finally makes it to the restaurant, Gary stages a fake argument and Yvonne calls his pretend boss a tyrant. Gary tells Yvonne and Sanjay that he and Ron are going to air their differences outside the restaurant. At first, Ron is impressed with Gary's cunning plan. That is, until he realises how bad it makes him look.

Back in 1941, Phoebe vents her frustration for the way the evening has gone and admits she wanted them to spend the night together. Ever resourceful, Gary explains the reason he had to keep checking in with the Ministry is because they're expecting an air raid and they suspect the Germans will be using a different type of bomb. When Phoebe asks when they can expect this air raid, her clock chimes nine o'clock and he tells her any second now. Presently, an air-raid siren sounds to back up his claim.

Although Ron congratulates him on his achievement, Gary feels far from proud about lying to and deceiving the two most important women in his life. Ron points out that's the price you pay for being married with a bit on the side. However, he reminds him that his actions have saved the evening from ending with three shattered lives. Presently, Stella rings Ron on his mobile phone and we hear him getting an extreme ear-bashing for supposedly disturbing Gary and Yvonne's evening together.

The inspired script for this episode, which cleverly showcased Nicholas's skills as a comedy actor, was written by Gary Lawson and John Phelps, who first met when they were at school. Although it was the first script the writing partners had written for *Goodnight Sweetheart*, they had been working with Laurence and Maurice for a number of years. 'We first worked on *Relative Strangers*, then they executive-produced our series *Young, Gifted and Broke* for ITV,' said John. 'We'd also been writing episodes for *Birds of a Feather* from series two. So it was probably natural for them to ask us when *Goodnight Sweetheart* was commissioned for more episodes than they could handle.

'Laurence and Maurice were always generous enough to give everyone free rein to come up with their own ideas for scripts. Before every series, all the writers got together to talk it through. What generally happened was that we all arrived with our own ideas which we'd kick around; and nine times out of ten writers would go off and work up their own, amended ideas into full storylines. We don't ever remember anyone being disappointed at not getting a particular episode.'

In this episode, Phoebe had decided that this was going to be the first time that she wanted her and Gary to make love, but this didn't happen. 'I think we did decide it would be fun to make Gary wait,' recalled John. 'Also, we had to remember that due to the morals of the time, this would have been a massive step for Phoebe, not something she would rush into.'

Gary's ongoing dislike of George Formby began in this episode and was the idea of Lawson and Phelps. 'Neither of us ever got why George was as big a star as he was,' said John. 'If Ken Dodd had been around in wartime, we'd have made Gary hate him as well!'

As with all writing partnerships, Gary and John have their own way of writing scripts. 'Mostly we each work on different scenes, sometimes we get together to write a scene,' said John. 'When that happens Gary usually does the typing.'

Although it was their first episode of *Goodnight Sweetheart*, Gary and John received one of their best reviews. 'The *Daily Mail* called it "Pinteresque",' said John proudly.

Their other writing credits include contributing episodes to the comedy dramas *Minder* and *Shine on Harvey Moon*, the sitcoms *The House That Jack Built*, *My Hero* and *The Green Green Grass* and the daytime medical drama, *Doctors*. They have also written children's comedies including *The Story of Tracy Beaker*, *The Revenge Files* of *Alistair Fury* and the comedy horror and drama series, *Young Dracula*.

When it came to the writing of the series, Nicholas was always happy with the material. 'I never suggested ideas to the writers,' he clarified. 'I did have ideas, but I didn't need to suggest them as every plot was really clever. With some writers you have to change lines as their scripts can be really clunky and you realise that they don't read them out loud. But ninety-nine per cent of the time we never had to change any of the scripts that were delivered to us.'

The restaurant owner, Sanjay, in this episode was played by Raj Patel. Raj was very nervous to begin with at the recording. Proving yet again what a generous actor he is, Nicholas deliberately fluffed a line to make Raj feel better and relax. Nicholas is said to have done this on more than one occasion to help actors and actresses who found it daunting coming into a successful show and having to perform in front of a live audience.

Raj's other roles on television include Farrukh Azzam in the sitcom *Mind Your Language*, Mr Rashim in the children's drama *Grange Hill* and Dr Mirchandani in the drama *Kavanagh QC*. He has also appeared in the romantic comedy film *The Butterfly Effect*.

Nimmy March would go on to be seen playing Ron's wife, Stella, in three episodes in the third series of *Goodnight Sweetheart*. However, in this episode she could only be heard ranting to her husband on the phone.

When she was a child, Nimmy was adopted by the Earl and Countess of March and Kinrara, who later became the Duke and Duchess of Richmond. On 30 April 2004, a Royal Warrant decreed that any children adopted by peers now had a right to any noble or courtesy title. This meant that Nimmy (Naomi) instantly became the Lady Naomi Gordon-Lennox.

Nimmy's theatre credits include the title role in John Webster's Jacobean revenge tragedy *The Duchess of Malfi* at the Duke of Cambridge Theatre, London, Titania and Hippolyta in the William Shakespeare comedy *A Midsummer Night's Dream* at the Library Theatre, Manchester, and Mary in a tour of Ged McKenna's moving love story, *The Farmer's Bride*. Her other television roles include Claudette in the sitcom *The Lenny Henry Show*, Denise in the comedy drama

Goodnight Sweetheart: A Guide to the Classic Sitcom

Common as Muck and Ottilie Dubois in the crime comedy drama, *Death in Paradise*; while Nimmy's film work includes playing Mrs Darling in the romantic drama *Summerland*, which starred Gemma Arterton, Gugu Mbatha-Raw and Penelope Wilton.

This episode featured Gary climbing out of a window, which was supposedly part of the restaurant. The window Gary climbed out of is part of a property on Shipton Street, close to Horatio Street, in Shoreditch, East London. Ron was parked across the same street close to the entrance to Ezra Street, used as Duckett's Passage.

At the start of 'Wish Me Luck…', the fifth episode of series two, Yvonne is seen cracking open a bottle of champagne just after Gary arrives home. The time traveller instantly jumps to the worrying conclusion that she's pregnant. Sharing this thought rather kills the moment, but after some coaxing, Yvonne tells him that she's been promoted at work to assistant personnel manager. Gary suggests they go to a little Malaysian restaurant to celebrate. But just as he's getting ready, the phone rings and Stella leaves a message on their answering machine telling Yvonne that she hopes Gary doesn't mind that the new job is in Cheshire – Macclesfield to be exact. This obviously upsets Gary who is dead against moving out of the capital. She tells him that if they move there, he could have a career. However, in a bid to persuade her to change her mind, Gary tells her that Ron is looking to make him head of marketing development, which Yvonne finds amusing, given that there is supposedly only one person – him – in the department. Yvonne mentions that she has got to travel to Macclesfield for a few days before she finally accepts the job, but he refuses to accompany her on the trip.

Gary later tells Ron that he couldn't face the idea of not seeing Phoebe whenever he wanted, even though he knows he should be supporting Yvonne. Gary admits that he can't go on like this and that he needs to commit to one girl. He tells Ron that when Yvonne's in Macclesfield he's going to leave his clothes on a bridge, fake his own suicide and disappear. He believes this will allow Yvonne to get on with making a success of her life and in turn will mean he can move in with Phoebe, get married and run the pub together. He tells Ron it will be a clean and final break, and although he won't be able to stop him with his plan, he will need his help.

Back at home, Gary is seen finishing a spot of DIY in the kitchen as Yvonne enters. The time traveller tells Yvonne he loves her while giving her a meaningful hug. He then reveals that he has prepared them both a spot of lunch. Gary then hugs Yvonne again and she begins to wonder if he's had some kind of premonition. Before she leaves, Yvonne starts to question if Gary is okay. He tells her he will be going to Scotland to see if he can crack the Celtic market for Ron – who, after all, has never been very big north of the border. Not that he's ever been very big south of it, according to Stella!

Ron drives Gary to Southwark Bridge where he plans to leave his clothes and a suicide note. Gary tells Ron to keep an eye on Yvonne. But Ron tells him to stop being a pillock and come home and look after her himself. Gary reminds him that they've already discussed this. When Gary goes to hug Ron, he is reluctant. He agrees to a manly, but not excessively demonstrative, handshake instead. Ron tells him to have a good death. As Ron drives away, Gary realises that he doesn't have any change for the bus as he only has the white fivers that Ron gave him.

Gary has to walk all the way to Duckett's Passage, and thus 1941, from Southwark. When Phoebe enters and spots Gary with a suitcase in the bar of the Royal Oak, she suspects the worst and asks him what's going on. He confirms that he's moved on from Cricklewood forever and is planning to live in the area, much to her and Reg's delight. Although she says he can rent her spare room, Reg says he thinks that would be unseemly and suggests he rent a flat above a hat shop run by a lady friend of his who occasionally buffs up his helmet!

Phoebe later calls at Gary's new flat above Maison Bloss, a hat shop, which belongs to Mrs Bloss. Gary is keen to prove that the room has a good blackout, but Phoebe is not in favour, fearing she will get a reputation as people will think they're indulging in a spot of 'hanky panky'. Just before they share a kiss, Mrs Bloss starts to bang on the door to remind Gary of the rule about women being in her rooms. He replies that he already has one!

When Gary, Phoebe and Reg go to the cinema, they discover, much to Gary's dismay, that they're showing the George Formby comedy *Turned Out Nice Again* instead of the historical drama *Lady Hamilton*. This gives Gary the hump and he leaves halfway through, telling Phoebe he is far from amused. Phoebe returns to watch the film and Gary storms off home.

Back at his new abode, it soon becomes clear that Gary's missing all the comforts of living in 1994. Phoebe arrives telling him she doesn't want them to say goodnight while they're on bad terms. They both acknowledge the difficulties of seeing each other, including the ever-vigilant Mrs Bloss. Having spotted her going into the cinema and realising that she will be out for hours, they decide to get a little closer. Just as things are beginning to hot up, Reg arrives. Phoebe is worried about what he will say, and Gary suggests she hides under his bed until he gets rid of him. Having declined Reg's kind invite to go dancing with him and his wife and sister, who apparently isn't bad looking from a distance, Gary reluctantly lets Reg in. He then proceeds to bore Gary with his problems. Fortunately, an air-raid siren sounds. Gary tells him not to worry as intelligence has led him to believe that the docks will get it tonight, apart from one bomb that will fall on Gibbons' furniture warehouse. When Reg questions where that is, Phoebe emerges from under the bed to tell them it's just around the corner! When a bomb drops, Reg dives under the bed with Phoebe.

In 1994, Yvonne arrives at Nostradamus Printing to see Ron. This is the moment the printer has been dreading. He's afraid she has discovered that Gary has taken his own life. After initially getting their wires crossed, it becomes clear that Yvonne doesn't know that Gary has decided to live permanently in the past. Her low morale is in fact caused by her potential new job not being what she hoped for. She asks for a contact number for Gary in Scotland, but Ron explains that she cannot phone him where he is. When Ron offers a shoulder to cry on, she mistakes this for him making a move on her and threatens to tell Stella.

Meanwhile in 1941, Gary is facing the realities of the Blitz as he helps with the injuries of those hurt in the air raid at the Royal Oak. He can't get his head around all the pain and suffering from just one bomb. One of the injured men, Sid, was up on the roof fire-watching – something that Reg reminds Gary he's going to be doing the following night!

Looking at this and the following episode written by Gary Lawson and John Phelps, it could be argued that they're a two-parter. 'In our heads, yes, it is definitely a two-parter,' agreed John. 'But we also had to make sure that each individual episode had its own story, beginning, middle and end, so each could be watched as a standalone episode.

'We felt that we'd got to the stage where Gary would feel he'd have to make a choice between Yvonne and Phoebe. Once he'd made that choice and realised he couldn't live full-time in the past and neither could he give up Phoebe, it put that feeling to bed, and the fact no one rumbled his pretend suicide was God giving him permission to carry on leading a double life.

'All sitcom plots are usually circular, a descent into the unknown and then a return. In other words, no matter what happens during the episode, you have to bring things back to how they were at the start. Otherwise you destroy the "sit" and the show will fall apart. So yes, by the end of the second episode we had to have Gary back living his double life.

'This episode and the next were great to write early on as it meant we had to do lots of research into life during the war, which came in very useful in future series. We read lots of books, obviously, but a big help was the Britain at War Experience, an interactive museum that used to be on Tooley Street next to the London Dungeon. Another big help was the *Chronicle of the Second World War*, which gives a week-by-week account of what was happening at home and on the front line.'

This was the first of four episodes in which Yvonne D'Alpra played the hat shop owner, Mrs Bloss. Yvonne was originally due to appear in Hélène Cixous's play *Black Sail, White Sail*, which was translated by Donald Watson, at the Gate Theatre in Notting Hill. During the rehearsal period, the actress developed appendicitis and had to go to hospital to have her appendix removed. This understandably meant she was unable to take part in the theatre production. While she was recovering, Yvonne was asked to play the role of Mrs Bloss in *Goodnight Sweetheart* for the first time. She was told all her dialogue in the scene would just be a voice-over. 'I got quite a shock when I arrived at Teddington Studios,' she said. 'Normally you record a voice-over in a booth, but they wanted me to perform my dialogue out of sight during the studio recording while there was an audience present.'

The character of Mrs Bloss was devised by Gary Lawson and John Phelps and named after someone Phelps worked with in the Civil Service. 'The name just seemed to fit,' said John.

Away from playing Mrs Bloss, Yvonne's theatre roles have included Madame La Falourdelle in the Ken Hill play *The Hunchback of Notre Dame* at the National Theatre, London, Mrs Brown in the Stephen Fagan comedy *The Hard Shoulder* at the Hampstead Theatre, London, and the Aldwych Theatre, London, and Mrs Jackson in the John Arden drama *Live Like Pigs* at the Royal Court Theatre, London. Her other television credits include Annie Kettle in the drama *The Gentle Touch*, Joan in Ricky Gervais and Stephen Merchant's mockumentary sitcom *The Office* and Jean in the talent agency comedy, *Ten Percent*. Yvonne's film work has included playing Muriel in the romantic comedy *Swinging with the Finkels*, Pest's nan in the comedy horror *Attack the Block* and Mavis in the crime drama, *Trespass Against Us*.

Also appearing in this episode was Colin Spaull. Colin played Sid, the one-legged man who Gary helps when he's brought into the Royal Oak during an air raid. 'Although my involvement in this episode of *Goodnight Sweetheart* was brief, it was a pleasure to do and they were all lovely people to work with,' Colin confirmed.

Colin's theatre credits include playing Otto in Frank Wedekind's seminal play *Spring Awakening* at the Royal Court Theatre, London, Eric in the Alan Ayckbourn comedy *Ten Times Table* at the Yvonne Arnaud Theatre, Guildford, and on tour, and Fred in the Noël Coward comic play *Present Laughter*, which starred Donald Sinden and Dinah Sheridan, at the Greenwich Theatre, London, and the Vaudeville Theatre, London. His other television roles include Fred in a televising of the production of *Present Laughter* at the Vaudeville Theatre, London, Lilt and Mr Crane in the science-fiction series *Doctor Who*, and Roy in the coming-of-age teen sitcom, *The Inbetweeners*. Colin's film appearances include Alf in J. Lee Thompson's comedy drama *Before Winter Comes*, with a cast that included David Niven and Topol, an uncredited part in the Alfred Hitchcock thriller *Frenzy*, and Arthur in the comedy drama *Redemption Road*.

As mentioned earlier, Southwark Bridge was used as the location where Ron drops off Gary before he fakes his own suicide. The arch bridge on Southwark Bridge Road, London, was opened on 6 June 1921 and links the district of Southwark and the City across the River Thames.

At the beginning of '…As You Wave Me Goodbye', the sixth episode of series two, Gary wakes up and wonders what time and era it is. When he opens the blackout blind, he realises it's 1941. As he prepares to boil some hot water, he admonishes himself for faking his own suicide so he could go back to live in the land of bombs, air raids and shortages. Presently, Phoebe arrives to tell him that there's no water as a bomb damaged the mains. She adds that Reg has collected water from a stand pipe and there's water for him over at the pub if he needs it. This does little to improve Gary's mood and neither does the arrival of Mrs Bloss, who sneaks into his room for a nose around. When he wishes her a good morning, this startles her, and she makes an obvious excuse to justify her presence in his room without an invitation.

After Phoebe leaves, Mrs Bloss tells Gary that one of the fire-watchers had his head blown clear off the previous night, and can't help but take pleasure in reminding him that he will be fire-watching that evening. In a fit of pique, Gary tells her to feel free to give away his hat if the same happens to him. She then asks if Phoebe is his next of kin. Gary tells that she's not and that they're lovers who are sharing sexual aerobics morning, noon and night. This shocks Mrs Bloss, who is presently thrown out by the would-be secret agent.

Gary later adopts a fake limp and hobbles around to the Royal Oak, desperate to try and get out of his fire-watching stint that evening. When Reg says they will find him a chair on the roof, Gary wonders if he has to open a vein to get out of it! Phoebe tells Gary that Mrs Bloss has been spreading malicious gossip about them in the meat queue at the fishmonger's. She's concerned that if the brewery hears the gossip, she could lose her licence. Gary apologises for not thinking.

While Phoebe and Reg share a cheese sandwich, they talk about old times including the Coronation. Gary isn't interested and moans about their desire to wander down memory lane. Phoebe tells him off and asks why he's become some a gloomy-guts recently. She mentions that he was always a ray of sunshine, and the rationing and shortages never bothered him before. He notes that nothing has changed – and that's the problem!

Ron isn't in the least bit surprised to put down his paper in a local greasy spoon to find Gary staring at him from across the table. He knew this is what would happen and that Gary would miss his wife, friends, and the comforts of modern living. Gary is concerned that he has made a big mess of his life. Fortunately for him, Ron tells him that no one found his suicide note and that he's in the clear. Ron goes on to mention that Yvonne accused him of propositioning her while he was away and asks Gary to straighten things with her at the earliest opportunity. Relieved to be back to his old life, Gary orders a large breakfast to celebrate.

Gary takes Ron back to his Cricklewood home and finds Yvonne having a party for some of the girls from work and far from distraught at Gary's absence, despite being bored of sitting alone each night.

Later that evening, Gary and Yvonne discover Ron and her friend Wendy cosying up together under a pile of coats that had been placed on their bed. The following morning, Ron begs Yvonne not to tell Stella that he became a mite more friendly with Wendy than he should. She gets him to make an apology to her and briefly tricks the printer into thinking that Stella is listening to his desperate apology in the lounge.

When Gary returns to the Royal Oak, he gets the cold shoulder from Phoebe, Reg and the customers in the bar because he didn't turn up for his stint on fire-watching duty. Phoebe believes he was too afraid and that's why he was limping around the day before like Long John Silver! Not wanting to appear afraid, Gary reluctantly agrees to go fire-watching that night.

Left alone to fire-watch on the top of a warehouse roof, Gary and Phoebe soon find themselves in the thick of it when an air raid begins, and a host of incendiaries begin to fall on the roof. They manage to put them out with buckets of sand. Satisfied by his heroic efforts, Gary quips that the experience is better than sex! The bombing becomes much worse and they go and hide in the corner of the roof. At Phoebe's request, Gary begins to sing to keep her morale up. His choice of song is appropriately 'Up On the Roof' by The Drifters.

When the all-clear sounds, Gary goes back home and claims to be suffering from the flu, even though he's clearly afflicted with shell shock. Yvonne assures Gary that domestic bliss has returned to the Wheatcroft home after she's put Stella right, and advises he get some sleep.

Although Gary returned to his old routine of commuting between eras in this episode after the reality of living in the past was proving difficult to cope with, he soon realised that he would continue to risk losing the respect he had gained from

Phoebe, Reg and the regulars of the Royal Oak unless he at least appeared to be doing his bit for the war effort. But, for a wartime novice, fire-watching during a heavy air raid was always going to be a tall order. It's no wonder, therefore, that he began to experience shell shock once he was safely back in 1994.

Having previously just provided the dulcet tones of Mrs Bloss, this episode marked Yvonne D'Alpra's first onscreen appearance as the hat-shop owner. 'I was told I would have to wear a wig as they didn't want me to have dark hair,' she admitted. 'Hair and make-up really were painstaking with their efforts on the series. In my case, it took ages for the wig to be fitted and removed afterwards.'

Although Gary and John were given free rein to create supporting characters, such as Mrs Bloss, in their episodes of *Goodnight Sweetheart* to make their storylines work, there was a condition. 'They had to earn their keep: the characters had to be vital to the plot and/or help the comedy,' said John.

There were two supporting actresses who made their one and only appearances in this episode. The first was Maria Pastel as the café waitress. Maria's other television credits include June in the comedy drama *Shine on Harvey Moon*, Yvonne Cooper in the soap opera *EastEnders* and Maureen Barden and Mrs Rhodes in the police drama, *The Bill*. Her film roles, meanwhile, include Vicky in the John Godber rugby comedy, *Up 'n' Under*.

The second actress was Amanda Richardson. Amanda played Yvonne's friend, Wendy, who takes an interest in Ron at Gary and Phoebe's spontaneous party. Her other television roles include a barmaid in the sitcom *The Detectives*, Mrs Franklin and Sue Ford in the drama *The Bill* and a cashier and Valerie in the sitcom *Birds of a Feather*.

Incidentally, this episode was the first time in which the old codger, who was played by John Rapley, was referred to by his first name of Stan.

The late Ted Scott was a sound supervisor on the first two series of *Goodnight Sweetheart*. In his career in sound, Ted worked on television programmes including Bing Crosby's last special *Bing Crosby's Merrie Olde Christmas*, in which Bing famously duetted with David Bowie on 'Peace on Earth'/'Little Drummer Boy', the sketch comedy series *The Muppet Show* and the sitcom *Birds of a Feather*. He died in 2020.

In 1976, Nicholas played Tootles in a production of *Peter Pan* made by ATV. Ted also worked in the sound department on this live-action musical version of the well-known play. 'Nick was delighted when I was able to provide him with a VHS of that show,' Ted once explained.

This episode called for a large rooftop set to be built in Studio 1 for the air raid sequence. 'I got to Teddington Studios at 6.00am that morning,' Ted once recalled. 'This was so I could make up recordings of about twenty minutes of air-raid sirens, bombs and gunfire. The lengthy sequence was shot in one take and at one point I was rolling three tape machines and several spot effects machines, so the explosions coincided with the script.'

Given the size of the set and its technical requirements, the scene was recorded in studio on the morning of the studio audience recording. Seeing their ambitious ideas realised on videotape was quite overwhelming for writers Lawson and Phelps. 'When we came in later in the day, we couldn't believe what the director Robin Nash and the guys had achieved in the studio,' John admitted. 'It was outstanding. Even now when we watch it, it amazes us that it's not a location sequence. Robin was brilliant. Roger Andrews, our fantastic designer, also deserves a lot of kudos for his contribution.'

In 'Would You Like to Swing on a Star', the seventh episode of series two, Gary reveals that pretending to work for Ron at Nostradamus Printing is all well and good – until it comes to pay day! When Gary tells Ron that Yvonne is going to expect to see some wages, the penny drops, and Ron immediately tells him not to come looking to him for a loan. However, after Gary rings directory enquiries and asks for the number of the nearest hostel for the homeless, Ron gives in and writes him a cheque for a modest amount that will get him through until he's in work again. In return, Ron asks Gary to take him for a drink that evening. However, he and Yvonne have a prior engagement with the Willesden Wildeans, an amateur dramatics company who are Cricklewood's answer to the Royal Shakespeare Company – and not a good one, according to Ron. Their sudden interest in amateur dramatics started after they rented a video of the film *Evita* and Yvonne claimed she could be a better actress than Madonna, something Ron says he could be too!

Later that evening, Yvonne auditions for the lead role in a new play, which is a searing melange on marriage strife set in the 1950s. Impressed, the director, Gregory, whose play it is, gives her the role on the spot. But when Gary expects to audition for the male lead role of Justin, he's disappointed as professional actor Lance will be handling Greg's big part. In an attempt to placate him, Gary is saddled with one line as a policeman and doing men's wardrobe. Worse still, he's not happy at the idea of the lovemaking scene that Yvonne will be doing. In an act of desperation, Gary suggests the group do *Annie Get Your Gun* instead!

Gary persuades Ron to accompany him on his quest to find costumes for the play at a collectors' fair being held at a local hall. While there, he picks up a moth-eaten suit for Lance and a couple of 1940s suits for himself. Ron notices a stall selling old money. When Gary asks how much a pound note is, he's somewhat shocked when he's told thirty pounds by the female stallholder. Ron jokingly says that Gary would be better off getting the banknotes from the 1940s and selling them in the present. Ron's shaft of wit instantly inspires Gary as to how to earn a living. Gary then asks the price of the most expensive 78rpm record she has. She responds that she has a first pressing of 'See You Later Alligator' by Bill Haley, but couldn't accept less than a hundred pounds for it. Sensing a huge profit, Gary asks how much a Frank Sinatra waxing would be worth. When she tells him it could go to a couple of thousand pounds at auction, the time traveller quickly heads for war-torn London.

After meeting Phoebe at the Royal Oak, they make for a record store where they listen to a Frank Sinatra record. Gary asks to purchase two copies – one for himself and Phoebe – and then presents the assistant with a list of other records he wishes to buy. Of course, he intends to sell them in the future. As Phoebe doesn't own a gramophone player, she suggests Gary enter a local talent contest at the Rivoli Picture Palace that evening to try and win one. Gary is reluctant, citing that becoming a famous singer wouldn't be compatible with his secret war. He says he might as well call himself 'Gary Sparrow the Singing Spy'!

Back with the stallholder, she questions where the records came from. Gary claims that an old aunt died, and he found them in the loft. She checks in with another dealer and offers to pay seven hundred pounds for the three records. Gary readily accepts and asks her to make the cheque payable to Ron in order to help pay back his temporary wages loan.

Gary returns home and sees Yvonne trying on a pair of stockings, required for her character, for that evening's run of the play, which more than concerns Gary. He then shows her his pay cheque from Ron. However, Yvonne is displeased, pointing out that he was paid more when he was blue-collar. Gary reminds her it's a hard world out there and he's on commission and that takes time to come through. Gary isn't keen to go to rehearsals for his one line but is persuaded when Yvonne promises to keep the stockings on when they return home!

At rehearsals, Yvonne is greeted by Greg, the director, who dismisses Gary as it's only a main cast rehearsal. When he's told he can make the coffee, Gary is upset and storms off.

Back in 1941, Phoebe and Reg are queuing to see impresario Sidney Wix at the Rivoli Picture Palace with the aim of entering Reg into the talent contest. When he reaches the front of the queue, Reg enters himself as Biffo 'you can't help loving him' Bloggs, despite not being entirely sure what act he intends to perform. Presently, Gary arrives and tells those 'tutting' in the queue that Phoebe has been keeping his place while he gave blood, which he quietly admits is a lie. The time traveller then enters the contest as a singer/songwriter.

After Reg dies a death on stage with his attempt at stand-up comedy and a George Formby impression, Gary is introduced to the stage wrongly as Barry Sparrow and sits down at the piano. As he launches into 'All the Way', Gary begins to daydream that he's a Frank Sinatra-type crooner singing the same number. As he ends the song, Gary realises the audience is giving him a standing ovation.

Never one to miss out on an opportunity to make money, Sidney Wix quickly dismisses the audience members trying to get autographs from Gary, who has won the competition, before attempting sign him up for a series of twice-nightly variety concerts. After Phoebe helps to secure him a better deal, Gary agrees to perform in a tour of the outer suburbs of London that will climax at Ponders End, which Gary jokes is north London's answer to Las Vegas.

When Gary returns home, Yvonne is in bed learning her lines. Although he's desperate to reveal he won a talent competition, Gary has to settle for telling her he won a karaoke contest. As usual with his achievements, Yvonne is not impressed. She's also unhappy that the suit Gary bought for Lance was infested, and he was bitten half to death the moment he tried it on. After ripping the suit off he resigned from the Willesden Wildeans and left. As a result, Greg has no choice but to offer Gary the lead role of Justin in order to save the play because Yvonne told him she wouldn't appear opposite anyone other than her husband.

With this episode, which again has a two-parter feel about it, Laurence and Maurice wrote a script that was clever, funny and full of invention. It also presented Michelle Holmes with an opportunity to come to the forefront a little more with the character of Yvonne being cast in a leading role in Gregory's play for the Willesden Wildeans.

This episode was important in the grand scheme of things because Gary had finally found a new way to make a living, thanks to a throwaway comment by Ron. The idea of selling old wartime memorabilia back in the 1990s would remain the former's primary source of income until the end of the original six-series run of the time-travelling comedy. In due course, Gary's ability to sell items would be taken to a whole new level.

The role of the playwright and theatre director Gregory in this episode was played by the critically acclaimed character actor, Peter Blythe. In 1963, Peter toured west Africa with Judi Dench. Both appeared in William Shakespeare's comedy *Twelfth Night*. At one performance, Judi fell ill with malaria. 'I passed out and Peter had to carry me off,' recalled the actress. 'There was thunderous applause. They thought it was part of the play.'

Peter's other theatre roles included Michael Quince MP in Howard Brenton and David Hare's satirical play *Pravda*, with Bill Nighy and Tim McInnerny, at the National Theatre, London, David Bliss in the Noël Coward comedy *Hay

Fever at the Savoy Theatre, London, and on tour, and Gilbert Marshall in the George S. Kaufman and Edna Ferber comedy *The Royal Family*, which starred Judi Dench, Julia McKenzie and Emily Blunt, at the Theatre Royal Haymarket, London. His other small-screen credits included Samuel 'Soapy Sam' Ballard in the classic legal drama *Rumpole of the Bailey* and Tom King in the comedy drama *The Alan Clark Diaries*. In addition, Peter's film parts included Roger de Courtenay in the adventure *A Challenge for Robin Hood*, Anton in the Hammer horror *Frankenstein Created Woman*, with Peter Cushing and Susan Denberg, and Phillip Morrell in the biographical drama *Carrington*, which featured Emma Thompson and Jonathan Pryce. Peter died on 27 June 2004, aged sixty-nine, shortly after being diagnosed with lung cancer.

Gregory's partner, Lance, was played by Robin Lermitte. Robin's other television credits included playing Dickie Metcalfe in the Perry and Croft sitcom *You Rang, M'Lord?*, Dr Jeremy Atherton in the period drama *Call the Midwife* and Justice Trehearne in the costume drama, *Poldark*. His film roles included Alexander 'Alex' Snivelroe in the comedy *The Princess Academy*, Ronnie Collins in the action drama *The Zero Option* and a manager in the crime drama, *B. Monkey*.

Robin entered and won a competition on the daytime programme *This Morning* in 2002 to become ITV's newest weather presenter. This led to him presenting the weather nationally and in some local ITV regions. Robin, who returned to acting in 2015, using the name Robin McCallum, died in October 2022.

The cast of this episode also included Nicola Redmond as Ellie, the stall holder who helps to sell Gary's records. Nicola continues to work as an actress. Her stage roles include playing Belinda Blair in the Michael Frayn farce *Noises Off* at the Pitlochry Festival Theatre, Imogen Parrott in Arthur Wing Pinero's comic play *Trelawny of the Wells*, with Betty Marsden and Helen McCrory, at the National Theatre, London, and Julia in the John Webster play *The Duchess of Malfi* at the Theatre Royal, Bury St Edmunds and Wyndham's Theatre, London. Her other television credits include Amelia in the children's adventure series *The Phoenix and the Carpet*, Miranda Myles in the drama *Bad Girls* and an estate agent in the Warwick Davis, Ricky Gervais and Stephen Merchant sitcom, *Life's Too Short*.

The role of Dick, the stallholder who Gary buys suits from at the collectors' fair, was played by Len Howe. The actor and comedian was once in a double act with his wife, Audrey Maye, who died on 3 September 2017. Len and Audrey appeared in summer seasons, music halls and pantomimes together. Len's other television credits included a coach driver in the sitcom *Oh No, It's Selwyn*

Froggitt, Old Adam in the drama *Dick Turpin* and Mr Watson in the sitcom *Hi-de-Hi!* Len died on 20 October 2013, aged ninety-four.

In the record shop scene in this episode, the role of the record assistant was played by Natasha Gardiner. 'My audition was with John Bartlett, Robin Nash and Susie Parriss in an office at Teddington Studios,' she recalled. 'The rehearsal period was very straightforward. I was nervous because it was my first time working on a sitcom. But everyone was friendly, and I was immediately put at ease. I remember chatting with Nicholas about where he trained and with Dervla about acting in general. Dervla and I kept in touch for a while afterwards because we were of a similar age.

'During rehearsals, I remember there was an issue with one of my lines not making sense with the way it rolled off the tongue. I ended up mentioning it after a few days, and the producer John Bartlett changed the line slightly to make it work.'

Natasha's scene, which was set in the record shop, was not taped in front of an audience. 'My call was early one morning,' she said. 'I remember being in hair and make-up and costume for far longer than I had expected, and my hair being coiffured really nicely in a 1940s style.

'Not really knowing the ropes with television, I had no idea where to walk off after my scene, having performed in theatre for all my acting career up until then. I then realised it didn't matter at all because of the cameras! It all went smoothly, and I remember going home and patiently waiting for the date of the recording. When the evening finally arrived, I went with my mother and some friends by train. I still remember the excitement on the long walk from the railway station at Teddington to the studios by the river with other members of the audience of people who were going to the recording.'

At the age of twenty-nine, Natasha, who attended the University of Cambridge and was a member of the Cambridge Footlights with performers including Alexander Armstrong, David Mitchell, Sue Perkins and Mel Giedroyc, realised she'd had enough of all the rejections that are part of being an actress. 'I opted to go behind the camera and try my luck at another career,' she revealed. 'I did work experience on the daytime chat-show series *Kilroy*, which was originally made at Teddington Studios. I ended up working on the programme full time and eventually moved with the production out to BBC Elstree Centre in north London. We had a lot of fun meeting the production staff and talent from other programmes in the bar. It was the most bizarre place. There were cast and crew members from *EastEnders* and *Holby City* all having a drink together with those of us from *Kilroy* and the stars who had just been appearing on *Top of the Pops*. In fact, I met my husband there as he was working as a sound engineer for the BBC at the time.

Goodnight Sweetheart: A Guide to the Classic Sitcom

'I then worked for the BBC World Service Trust, an NGO at Bush House, where I made a television documentary about leprosy for BBC World with Jenny Barraclough. I then went to work at Endemol on programmes including the health and fitness series *Fighting Fit*, the cookery show *The Best* and in the early production stages of the first series of talent show *Fame Academy*. I then relocated to BBC Television Centre to become a senior researcher and assistant producer on the programmes *Crimewatch* with Nick Ross and Fiona Bruce and *Watchdog* with Nicky Campbell and Julia Bradbury.

'I still occasionally work as a researcher on programmes such as the *Pride of Britain Awards*. I am half-Italian and bilingual, so I sometimes get asked to do specific research work for productions by former colleagues. My husband and I now run an outside broadcasting sound company, which specialises in live broadcasts. I also teach Spanish to primary school children part time during term time in Surrey.

'I loved working at Teddington Studios. There was such history there. The greats had walked those corridors and performed in those hallowed studios. It was so sad when they ended up knocking them down to build flats. In a strange coincidence, we ended up living in Teddington when our children were young, just a stone's throw from the studios that had had such a significant impact on my professional life: firstly in my appearance in *Goodnight Sweetheart*, and secondly working in television on the production side.'

Also joining the cast of this episode was the veteran actor Ronnie Stevens, who made the first of three appearances in the sitcom as Sidney Wix, the impresario with short arms and long pockets. Whether it was in dramatic or comedic parts, Ronnie gave a faultless performance every time. After appearing in successful revues in London, with performers including Cyril Ritchard and Joan Sims, he went on to play various other roles in the theatre. They included Launcelot Gobbo in the William Shakespeare comedy *The Merchant of Venice* at the Regent's Park Open Air Theatre, London, and Colonel Whittaker in the Nöel Coward comedy *Easy Virtue* at the King's Head Theatre, London, and the Garrick Theatre, London. He is still remembered for his many television credits including several sitcom appearances. They included a hypermarket sales assistant in *Fresh Fields*, Zoe's father in *May to December* and Eric, the mature boyfriend of Judith, in *As Times Goes By*. Ronnie's films included various comedies, which continue to be shown and released. His parts included a waiter in *Doctor at Large*, Brian Dexter in *Dentist on the* Job, which also starred Bob Monkhouse, Shirley Eaton and Kenneth Connor, and a drunken passenger in *Carry On Cruising*. Still much missed, Ronnie died on 11 November 2006, aged eighty-one.

Also appearing in a supporting role in this episode was Michelle Cattini as an autograph seeker. Her other television credits include playing Joanna Sweet in the sitcom *Get Back*, Chloe in the medical drama *Casualty* and Iris in the comedy drama, *Shine on Harvey Moon*.

Thanks to the sequence in which Gary is seen daydreaming at the talent contest, Nicholas found himself having to sing 'All the Way'. The recording session took place on 3 November 1994. 'This was an interesting and challenging cue,' admitted Gaynor Sadler. 'ALOMO delivered to us Nick's vocal and piano accompaniment, with the real accompanist being unknown to us, from which we were asked to create a Nelson Riddle-style arrangement for the dream sequence that was part of his talent competition scene. The problem we were faced with was that the budget only ran to covering three session musicians!' The three musicians Gaynor and Anthony booked for the recording were as follows:

Trumpet:	Dave Pluse
Violin:	Gavin Wright
Flute:	Andy Findon

'The rest we handled ourselves, with a real harp played by me, and Anthony blocking out the full orchestral arrangement himself on samples. The other tricky situation was to organise a "click" to the already-recorded track so the musicians could play to it. This involved matching the tempo to Nick's vocal and piano track, which had been done freestyle, which then enabled me to be able to conduct the musicians in perfect time with the pre-recorded track. We were very pleased with the result and think it sounds truly Riddle-esque!'

Once again, there were additional locations not seen before in this episode. For instance, the scenes set inside the Willesden Wildeans' Cricklewood-based theatre were filmed at the Mary Wallace Theatre, which is located on the Embankment in Twickenham, Middlesex. The theatre is the base of the Richmond Shakespeare Society, a highly respected amateur dramatic society. Founded in 1934 to perform Shakespeare's plays annually in the open air, they have grown to have a programme of eight productions a year by vastly differing playwrights of all eras, from ancient Greece to the modern day. Meanwhile, the scenes set at the collectors' fair were filmed at Hampton School on Hanworth Road, Hampton, Middlesex.

As 'Nice Work if You Can Get It', the eighth episode of series two, gets under way, Gary proves that he's taking his pretend job far too seriously by making up a convoluted excuse about being in the midst of clinching a quarter-million-pound printing contract with Sashimi Oil plc in Aberdeen. All this to cover his secret double life. Concerned at his behaviour, Ron hints to Gary that he might be rather overdoing it. The two-timing time traveller, however, claims to be on top of everything – including Yvonne!

After returning to 1941, Gary plays 'Love is the Greatest Thing' in the bar of the Royal Oak before he and Phoebe are picked up by Sidney Wix in a charabanc to take them to tonight's venue.

After wowing them on stage in Palmers Green, Gary, who desperately wants to party into the early hours, heads to Ron's house back in 1994. Unfortunately for Gary, Ron is not best pleased to see him as he was asleep and begs him to keep the noise down to avoid waking Stella. As Ron has work in the morning, he refuses to go and hang out with Gary and the likes of Lionel Blair and Bonnie Langford in Joe Allen's in the West End.

Back at home, and in the early stages of a hangover, Gary stands in the dark of his lounge. Yvonne comes downstairs and turns on the light and is shocked to see Gary standing there dressed like a head waiter. Gary bluffs his way out of the situation by claiming that his formal attire was at the request of a certain Mr Yakimoto of Sashimi Oil plc, the Japanese company Gary claims he's attempting to do business with. While concerned whether he will get the printing contract, Yvonne is rather more interested in them rehearsing their parts in the play for the rehearsal the following evening.

After making his excuses to Phoebe for his lack of presence at the Royal Oak the previous night, a gramophone, Gary's prize for winning the talent competition, is delivered by Sidney Wix with Reg doing the hard work. Sidney then asks Gary to move up the bill for his appearance at the Plaistow Astoria as the fire-eater has gone sick with a septic toe. He agrees, and Phoebe negotiates him an extra ten bob a night pay rise. Sidney then tries to persuade Gary to sign a songwriting contract. Realising that he could change the course of history by having well-known songs he claimed he wrote published before they were officially written, Gary refuses, much to Phoebe's annoyance.

Later, at rehearsals back in 1994, Gary is showing signs of stress and forgetting his lines as a result. Gregory loses his temper, worried that his play will be a disaster if Gary doesn't pull himself together.

At Yvonne's urging, he visits family physician Dr Jakowitz to find out why he's been suffering from fatigue, inexplicable spates of déjà vu, panic attacks and manic-depressive episodes, not to mention an unusually high build-up of earwax. In the end, stage fright is what the doctor diagnoses, and a course of tablets is prescribed. In return for his help, Gary offers him a couple of tickets for the first night of the play.

The Singing Spy

In the wings of the Plaistow Astoria, Gary is popping pills for his nerves while Phoebe and Sidney watch. Phoebe reminds Gary that if he took up Sidney's offer to get all his songs published, he could make his fortune and give up performing. Before Gary's spot at the piano, Phil McCavity, a stand-up comedian, takes to the stage. He dies on his feet and is heckled as he attempts to gain laughs with jokes that could have easily come out of the ark! To try and get the audience back on side, Sidney quickly introduces Gary. Pausing only to down another round of pills, Gary nervously walks on stage – and is delighted to hear an air-raid siren sound.

Under the stage, the cast gather to shelter from the air raid. Gary is feeling no nerves due to taking the pills. At Sidney's request to sing a song, Gary performs a slightly spaced-out version of the Beatles' 'I Am the Walrus'. Although everyone is initially shocked by what they've just heard, Gary shares his pills and they proceed to become equally high as they learn and sing the song.

Meanwhile, back in 1994, Yvonne is concerned as to why Gary isn't at the theatre and calls Ron to find out his whereabouts. She threatens to turn his spleen into a hot-water bottle if Gary has gone to Aberdeen today of all days. Just then, Gary turns up at Nostradamus Printing, flying as high as a kite. Ron then assures Yvonne he will get him to the theatre.

By now, Gary is no fit state to perambulate let alone perform. Ron arrives at the theatre and practically has to carry Gary into the back of the theatre. Although Yvonne and Gregory are pleased to see him arrive, they're concerned about his incoherent state.

When the curtain rises, Yvonne has time to deliver just one line from the play before Gary passes out on stage. Ron then walks onto the stage to make his apologies for Gary, followed by an angry Gregory. This leads Dr Jakowitz, who's sitting in the audience with his wife, to comment that it's all a bit avant-garde for his liking!

In this episode, Nicholas gave another tour de force as the overstretched time-traveller-come-salesman and sometime performer on the verge of a nervous breakdown. Once again, there was solid and admirable support from the main and supporting cast. Ronnie Stevens and Peter Blythe both returned to play Sidney and Gregory respectively.

Joining the cast for the first time was the seasoned actor and narrator, David de Keyser. David, who was once described as having a 'honeyed, dark caramel voice' due to narrating Pathé Pictorial cinema newsreels and television adverts, played mild-mannered Dr Jakowitz. On stage, his roles included Sandor Horvath in Robert Ardrey's final play *Shadow of Heroes* at the Piccadilly Theatre, London; Mr Maraczek in the Jerry Bock, Sheldon Harnick and Joe Masteroff musical *She Loves Me*, which starred John Gordon Sinclair and Ruthie

Henshall, at the Savoy Theatre, London; and Howard in Wallace Shawn's harsh and poetic play *The Designated Mourner* at the National Theatre, London. His other television appearances included a doctor in the crime drama *Interpol Calling*, Leon Crouzil in the drama *Bergerac* and Gaston Beaujeu in the mystery drama *Poirot*. Meanwhile, David's film credits included Zissell in the comedy drama *Having a Wild Weekend*, which featured the Dave Clark Five, a doctor in the James Bond title *Diamonds Are Forever* and Doctor Alvarez in the romantic comedy *A Touch of Class*, starring George Segal and Glenda Jackson. David died on 20 February 2021, aged ninety-three.

Also appearing in this episode was Steven Speirs, who played the role of would-be comedian, Phil McCavity. The actor recalls that playing the role was a big learning curve. 'I was in my twenties at the time,' he said. 'I was quite nervous as it was my first audition for a studio-based sitcom, and it was with the legendary Robin Nash. The casting director said they wanted a northern accent in the casting breakdown, but as a lad from the South Wales valleys it meant I had to do a bit of practice to land the job!

'Sitcom was a totally new way of working in television for me as I'd only done single-camera productions before. It's like rehearsing a short play for a live performance. Where you stand and knowing what you're supposed to say is therefore key. There's no time to "find" a performance. You have to hit the ground running.

'Robin, the director, trusted the people he'd given the job to. You very much got the sense that he was the boss and was in charge. These days there seems to be a lot of people in charge!

'All my scenes ended up being pre-records and I was really gutted. I envied those who went out in front of the audience and were able to receive a reaction from the audience after all the hard week's rehearsals. Comedy actors love and need that response with this form of comedy.

'Since then, I've gone on to do various studio-based sitcoms, like *Keeping Mum*, *Miranda*, and various series and Christmas specials of *Upstart Crow*. But I learned an invaluable lesson from Nick Lyndhurst during my first week there on *Goodnight Sweetheart*. We rehearsed hard all week and got all the timings right, chiselling moments, crafting the beats where we expected the gags to land and keeping the pacing etc. Then, you do what is called the "tech run". This is where all the heads of departments come into the rehearsal room and stand around as you perform that week's episode. They aren't really looking at your performance. The camera department are looking at the floor plan for their camera shots and movements and the sound boys are sizing up where they can get the boom in. Meanwhile, the costume and make-up departments are making notes. So, when we started our run to total silence, and with no experience of this whatsoever, I must have looked pretty crestfallen. That's when Nick sidled up to me and whispered, "Don't worry, this is the bit where they all stand around and make you think you're the unfunniest person in the world. You'll get used to it." He was right. Thankfully, I have got used to it!'

Steven's theatre credits include Tommy Cooper in the Garry Lyons play *Frankie and Tommy* at theatres including the Lyric Hammersmith, London; Mr Waldo and voice of the guide in the Dylan Thomas play for voices *Under Milk Wood* at the National Theatre, London; and Richard Burbage in the Ben Elton comedy *The Upstart Crow* at the Gielgud Theatre, London. His other television work includes playing Bernard Bresslaw in the comedy drama *Cor, Blimey!*, Mr Davis in the Ricky Gervais comedy drama *After Life*, and Glyn Tucker in *The Tuckers*, a sitcom about a family of chancers in the Welsh valleys, which he also writes. Steven's film parts include Captain Tarpals in the George Lucas blockbuster *Star Wars: Episode I – The Phantom Menace*, Sloan in the action fantasy *Eragon*, and Bob in the crime thriller *Concrete Plans*.

This episode was a triumph not only for the writers, Marks and Gran, but for the designer Roger Andrews and his team. For example, the backstage, stage and auditorium areas set in the fictitious Plaistow Astoria were sets built in Studio 1 at Teddington Studios. Thanks to clever positioning of the cameras and scenery, the theatre not only looks realistic but much bigger than in reality. At one point you can see one of the studio's green walls and the stairs behind Dervla Kirwan and Ronnie Stevens that led up to the control room in the background.

The Mary Wallace Theatre, on the Embankment in Twickenham, Middlesex, once again doubled for the Willesden Wildeans' Cricklewood-based theatre.

At the start of 'Let Yourself Go', the ninth episode of the second series, Gary tells Yvonne that he is thinking of going into work that day for a couple of hours to see how he copes. This is because he believes he's all but recovered from his recent 'illness', which Yvonne feels he has been dragging out. Their discussion concludes with Yvonne revealing that she is 'late' – and not just for work!

When Gary goes to see Ron, he reveals that Yvonne might be expecting a child, although he's not sure. Although Ron is pleased, Gary admits to being 'freakin' petrified'. He admits that while they were trying for a child, now is not the best time, not least because he has Phoebe to consider.

Sitting at home watching the sport on television is not doing enough to help Gary relax. He considers whether he could get to see Phoebe and be back in time before Yvonne comes home from a night out. He decides to chance it.

It's just before closing in the Royal Oak when Gary arrives and is pulled a pint by Reg, who is 'helping' behind the bar. When Phoebe arrives, she announces that she is going to Buckinghamshire for a couple of days to see her orphaned cousins, Peter and Sally, who have been evacuated. Having never been to the countryside before, she isn't keen, being a city girl, and asks Gary to come with her. She suggests that they could pretend to be a married couple and take advantage of being alone. Although not enthusiastic, because he realises it could be tricky to get away from Yvonne, he eventually hints that he will accompany her on the trip, which gets Phoebe a little hot under the collar.

After racing home at breakneck speed, Gary finds time to make the lounge look as though he's spent the whole evening as a couch potato in front of the television watching a football match, complete with the contents of a crisp packet being thrown everywhere. Yvonne presently arrives home and declares that she is excited at the prospect of being with child. Not for the first time that evening, Gary struggles to show any enthusiasm. Yvonne then tells him that she's going to spend a couple of days with her mother and encourages him to go for a walk in the country instead of just watching television. Gary takes this as justification to accompany Phoebe on her jaunt to Buckinghamshire.

Having finally found the farm where Peter and Sally live with their guardian Mrs French, Gary and Phoebe struggle to be convincing as a married couple. However, Mrs French is still willing to let them share the same room. After Phoebe greets the children, she encourages Gary to do the same, but he is too formal. When he asks how he's supposed to address them, he instantly receives a lesson from New-York-born Harry Meadows, who the children call Uncle Harry, who's popped in to see if Mrs French has any eggs. When Harry meets Phoebe, there is an instant attraction between them, much to Gary's annoyance. A flight navigator with one of the bomber crews at the nearby airbase, Harry invites them all to a children's party at the NAAFI the following day.

On their way to the NAAFI, there is tension between Gary and Phoebe because Gary turned away from her in bed the previous night and she can't understand why. It's obvious that Yvonne and her possible pregnancy are playing on his mind.

At the NAAFI, all the children are tucking into their food and drink apart from Sally who is oddly withdrawn. Phoebe's attempts to bring her out of her shell don't work; and then Gary suddenly finds a way of cheering her up by pretending to be a French waiter. She comes round and when Harry, acting as the official camp photographer for a shilling shot for the kids, takes a photo of them both she asks him to take one of just Gary for her as well.

Later, at the bar, Harry and Phoebe have a heart-to-heart. Although she is tempted by Harry, she makes it clear that she's married to Gary. When Gary arrives, Phoebe indiscreetly tells him that Harry has said how much he fancies her but that she told him she was in love with Gary.

When the kids are being entertained, Phoebe encourages Gary to go up and perform a number at the piano. After finally being persuaded, Gary makes his way to the stage and Harry introduces him. Gary invites Sally onto the stage while he sings the Beatles song 'Here, There and Everywhere' with one eye on Phoebe.

Later Gary and Phoebe consummate their relationship in the haystack of a barn. During the afterglow, Gary admits the reason he changed his mind was that he loves her. The only thing that spoils the moment is a German bomber dropping a bomb on the barn. Fortunately, the damage is small and other than a sprinkling of dust, they escape without any injury.

Gary is feeling thoughtful when he returns home. When Yvonne returns from visiting her mother, she spots the photo of Sally, which Gary claims he bought from a bric-a-brac shop in the country. Gary tells her that she is right and having a baby would be a good idea. Yvonne then breaks down and tells him that it was a false alarm and that she isn't pregnant. Gary says they will try again and admits that, if they have a baby, he would like a little girl.

This episode proved a pivotal point in the relationship of Gary and Phoebe. It featured some expert playing, especially by Nicholas, Dervla and Michelle, in what was a well-constructed and emotionally charged episode by Paul Makin.

Making the first of three appearances as Mrs French in this episode was the actress Jeannie Crowther. Jeannie can still remember how she first came to appear in *Goodnight Sweetheart*. 'I had to audition for Robin Nash at Susie Parriss's office on Regent Street in London,' she recalled. 'According to my diary, it was on Tuesday 20 September 1994 at 6.30pm. They offered me the role of Mrs French there and then. She was a farmer's wife who looked after Phoebe's young cousins, Peter and Sally, who were billeted with her in the country as their parents had been sadly killed in the war. My first episode was made in 1994, the second in 1995 and the third in 1997, so my three appearances were quite spread out! All my scenes in the first two episodes were with Nicholas and Dervla, who were lovely to work with.

'The read-through for my first episode, "Let Yourself Go", took place on Friday 4 November 1994 at a rehearsal room in Kingston-Upon-Thames. On Thursday 10 November 1994, I was picked up by a car at 7.00am for an 8.30am make-up call at Teddington Studios. I noted in my diary that I was given a nice dressing room.

'My scenes in the farmhouse kitchen and the NAAFI, which included children as extras, were not taped in front of a studio audience. I remember I had lunch with Dervla. The NAAFI scenes took ages to record and we finally finished at 3.30pm. I wasn't needed for the evening recording, so I got the train home early.'

Jeannie's theatre credits include Florrie Lack in the Falkland Cary and Philip King comedy *Sailor, Beware!* at the Gateway Theatre, Chester, Rebecca Huntley-Pike in Alan Ayckbourn's dramatic comedy *A Chorus of Disapproval* at the Theatre Royal, York, and Mrs Jeffcote in the Stanley Houghton play *Hindle Wakes* at the St Edmund's Hall, Southwold. Her other television roles include Hazel Edwards in the much-loved 1980s children's programme *No.73*, Margaret Porcher in the mystery thriller *The Woman in White* and Mrs Kirkby in the feel-good comedy drama, *All Creatures Great and Small*. Jeannie has also played Brenda in the short comedy film, *Do Not Disturb*.

This episode saw the first of three appearances of Phoebe's orphaned cousins Peter and Sally. Peter was played by Chase Marks, whose other television roles include Ronnie Beale in the drama *CivvyStreet*, which told the story of life in Albert Square during the Second World War, Adam Burridge in the sitcom *One Foot in the Grave* and Tommy Poyser in the comedy drama *Adam Bede*, part of the *Screen One* strand.

The role of Peter's sister, Sally, was played by Kate Donnison, whose other television credits include Joanna Matlock in the miniseries *The Politician's Wife*, Lucy in the children's series *The Demon Headmaster* and Vicki Marsham in the lavish period drama, *Bramwell*.

Also joining the main cast was Adam Henderson, who played Harry. 'I felt very privileged to be working with Robin Nash,' said Adam proudly. 'I was aware of his experience and he was clearly a master craftsman. Very gentlemanly and quite flashy. He was funny too. Nicholas was charming, hard-working, focused and unassuming. Dervla was delightful and very kind to me. She was open and willing to flirt and engage with me as the scenes required.

'Working on the show was a civilised process. It was more like rehearsing a play. We went beat by beat through long continuous scenes, adding layers of depth and refining the dialogue each day. I thought at the time, this is why British sitcoms are better than American ones. In America we would rehearse and shoot, rehearse and shoot without time spent massaging each gag to perfection. This process allowed a leisurely examination and development of the script. Then they trusted the actors and actresses to deliver a single polished but alive performance.

'For sitcom acting, a complete belief in the need of the moment is required. Emotions must turn on a dime without doubt. My character, Harry, had to be everything that Gary was failing to be: an unceasingly lustful, courageous man of action. Harry was everything the wartime English loved and loathed about

Americans. For me, that is a fun joke to play: lucky but unaware, charming but arrogant, unashamed but entitled, free but selfish, brave but egocentric, good but ignorant.

'There was something about that nostalgic gloss that was rehearsed into the behaviour of the characters. It wonderfully offsets an otherwise morally questionable set of characters, who are unfaithful and promiscuous despite mild-mannered shy Englishness.

'I remember on the recording day feeling breezy, not nervy. The detailed exploration we had done allowed a light playing style. When you know what you mean, you do not need to act. There was no pushing for laughs. A thoroughly lovely experience.

'I am struck, watching it now, that it completely predicts the movie *Yesterday* with Gary's performance of a Beatles song.'

Born in New York, Adam worked as an actor in London before moving to Vancouver in Canada where, as well as being an actor, he is a director, dialect coach and audiobook narrator. He teaches at the Vancouver Film School and at the University of British Columbia. For the theatre, Adam's various credits have included playing a producer and English DJ in the Alan Janes musical *Buddy – The Buddy Holly Story* at the Theatre Royal, Plymouth, and Victoria Palace Theatre, London; Menelaus in the Euripides play *Women of Troy* at the National Theatre, London; and Lucky in Samuel Beckett's tragicomedy *Waiting for Godot* at the Vancouver East Cultural Centre, Vancouver, Canada. His other television roles include Lowell Thomas in the action adventure series *Highlander*, a medical examiner in the drama series *John Doe* and an attorney in the science-fiction drama *Second Chance*. Meanwhile, Adam's film parts include Franck in the French drama *La Neige et le Feu*, Fuppie in the science-fiction action movie *Judge Dredd*, which starred Sylvester Stallone in the title role, and Charles Dennison in the drama *Unknown Things*.

There was also an appearance in this episode from Steve Rider as a television presenter. Steve is an experienced sports presenter and journalist. His television credits include the sports programmes *Sportsnight*, *Grandstand* and *Sports Personality of the Year*.

Also, John Motson appropriately played a football commentator. Over the years, John, who was the BBC's voice of football for nearly half a century with an encyclopaedic knowledge of the game, commentated on over two thousand football games on television and radio. He died on 23 February 2023, aged seventy-seven.

The location used for the exteriors of Mrs French's farm in Buckinghamshire in this episode was Roaring House Farm in Fetcham Downs, Leatherhead, Surrey.

As well as using the exterior of the Grade II listed farmhouse for the scene where Gary and Phoebe arrive at the farm, the production used the interior of a barn at the site to film the scene where the couple are sitting up in the hayloft.

At the beginning of 'Don't Fence Me In', the tenth and final episode of series two, Gary is just getting dressed in his flat above Maison Bloss when Phoebe arrives in a state. She informs him she has received a letter from the brewery in which they say the tenancy agreement was with her dad and they had only been letting Phoebe stay on *pro tem*, which, as Gary explains, is Latin for 'for the time being'. She asks him to help, saying she couldn't bear it if she couldn't see him.

On arriving back in 1994, we discover that Duckett's Passage and the surrounding buildings are in the process of being pulled down. Appearing from out of nowhere, Gary not surprisingly causes some shock to the builders.

Back at home, Gary attempts to wrestle with an old typewriter in order to write a letter to the brewery. He gets the ribbon jammed up and ink all over his hands. When Yvonne arrives home and questions why he's not using his expensive computer, Gary explains he's making a stand for Britain's dying industry by buying the old machine.

A story comes on the television news explaining that the builders working on the Duckett's Passage development claim to have seen a ghostly figure wearing 1940s clothes who, when challenged, sang a chorus of 'There'll Be Bluebirds Over the White Cliffs of Dover'; in reality, of course, they spotted Gary coming through the time portal. Yvonne says Gary is gullible for thinking their story may be true as there's no such thing as a ghost. After hugging Yvonne, he realises he has left two print marks in the shape of his hands on the back of her new and expensive coat.

In order to make his next visit to war-torn London, Gary pretends to be Gary Compton, a safety officer from Tower Hamlets council, when he visits the demolition site. After winding up one of the builders, he drifts into the past. One of the other builders tells his colleague that he's remembered where he's seen Gary before – he's the ghost they spotted.

In the Royal Oak, Phoebe introduces Gary to George Harrison – not *the* George Harrison, but the area manager for Hanbury Truman, the brewery. Gary hands over his letter, which was not completed due to Gary's ribbon breaking. After hearing Gary's plea on behalf of Phoebe, he takes her aside and proposes a private and mutually convenient arrangement that is far from legal or moral. Phoebe begs Gary to use his contacts to try and resolve the situation she finds herself in.

In 1994, the ringleader of a gang of youths is trying to persuade them to join him in breaking into the demolition site in order to steal a compressor. However, they soon run away when Gary appears from 1941 and greets them.

Back at home over dinner, Gary answers a call from Mary Cunningham, a typist from Yvonne's workplace, who claims she's been harassed by a man called Duncan Grainger from accounts who's sitting in his car outside her flat. Although reluctant, as she thinks she's making it up, Yvonne takes the call and tells Mary she's not alone and she will be there for her. When she suggests they could record one of the conversations between Duncan and Mary, this inspires Gary to do the same for a conversation between George and Phoebe.

Gary takes a small and modern tape recorder to the Royal Oak, which impresses Phoebe and Reg, and asks Phoebe to put it behind the bar. George duly arrives and metaphorically puts his cards on the table; and the tape recorder catches all of his devious plan. With Reg present in uniform, Gary plays the evidence back and sends George packing – but not before he has agreed to give Phoebe a couple of free barrels of beer each month in return for buying their silence.

After Phoebe goes upstairs, relieved that her ordeal is over, Reg tells Gary that it will be her birthday on the Saturday, and she'd be heartbroken if he forgets to visit. Gary rashly promises to be there.

Yvonne later explains that they recorded Duncan sexually harassing her colleague at work. In return, she explains that she has taken to their marital bed early because she wants to show her gratitude to her husband for inspiring her plan to catch Duncan out.

The following morning, Gary persuades Ron to help petition passers-by at the old Duckett's Passage site in an attempt to stop the development. Unfortunately, a senior citizen fails to agree with him. A female television reporter and a cameraman from the BBC then arrive and attempt to interview Gary about his quest to stop the rebuilding work. Gary makes a fool of himself using the excuse of dark powers being at work. The reporter cuts short the interview and leaves with the cameraman in tow. Gary then quietly admits to Ron that he doesn't know what he will do if he can't go back to see Phoebe.

After returning home, Yvonne shows Gary the interview on video and questions why he wanted to protest about the development instead of staying in bed that morning to celebrate his marriage.

In an attempt to aid his return to 1941, Ron helps Gary break into the building site early one morning, despite a security guard with a dog being hot on their tail. Gary manages to jump from the first floor of a site office building and disappear into the past. This is the first proof Ron has had that Gary can go back. He then attempts to do the same but ends up lying on the dusty ground.

Gary makes his way to the Royal Oak and surprises Phoebe, who is taken aback to see him there so early, with a small birthday cake, complete with candle.

As already proved in the first two series, Gary's life in the present could help his life back in the past and vice versa. In this episode it was the former, with the subplot about Yvonne's colleague, Mary, being sexually harassed inspiring Gary to find a solution to Phoebe's problems with George. Yes, a television storyline involving secretly recording a conversation to help bring someone to justice is, admittedly, far from original; but in a wartime sitcom, the protagonist's ability to take modern technology back to catch a character out adds a unique twist.

Written by Laurence and Maurice, 'Don't Fence Me In' marked the final episode of series two. Each series of *Goodnight Sweetheart* had a strong cliffhanger, which, to be fair, is not a prerequisite for most sitcoms. However, it was definitely a must in *Goodnight Sweetheart*, which was story-driven. That said, each episode was written and crafted in such a way that they can be watched and enjoyed as stand-alone episodes. This final episode of series two certainly had an important cliffhanger. With the demolition and planned development of the site that included Duckett's Passage, there were obvious questions for the viewers as well as Gary. What would be built on the site? Would Gary be able to continue to come and go as he pleased between the two eras if a private building was constructed on Duckett's Passage? More importantly, would the time portal survive the redevelopment plans?

In this episode, Jonathan Stratt played the annoyed foreman who gives Gary a hard time on the building site when he tells him he's a safety officer from the council. Jonathan's other television credits include Arthur in the sitcom *Up the Elephant and Round the Castle*, with Jim Davidson; a Christmas-tree seller in the comedy *Merry Christmas Mr Bean*; and a robber in the flatshare sitcom, *Game On*. In addition, his film appearances include playing a policeman in the comedy *Eat the Rich*, and a taxi driver in both the comedy drama *Love and Death on Long Island* and the crime drama, *Bodywork*.

Glen Davies, meanwhile, played a worker on the site who realises where he's seen Gary before and claims he's the ghost. Glen's other television roles have included a porter in the sitcom *Second Thoughts*, a shopkeeper in the period drama *Call the Midwife* and Roy in Stan Lee's action crime drama, *Lucky Man*. His film credits include playing a pub barman in the crime drama *Swimming Pool*, a taxi driver in romantic comedy drama *The Best Exotic Marigold Hotel* and a coalman in the comedy drama *The Personal History of David Copperfield*.

The role of George Harrison was memorably played by Michael Troughton, son of the late *Doctor Who* actor, Patrick Troughton. This episode of *Goodnight Sweetheart* was not the first time that Michael appeared in a sitcom penned by the same writers. 'I had worked with Laurence and Maurice before, playing Piers Fletcher-Dervish in *The New Statesman*,' said Michael. 'So that's why I was cast as the slimy district manager. They told me it was a great character, but rather sleazy! When I read the script I saw what they meant. It was something to really get my teeth into. The characters that Lo and Mo write are pretty clear from the start. Anyway, you always find out at the read-through if you are way off the mark with the character. This time everyone was laughing so I guessed it was okay.'

Michael still remembers how he managed to amuse Laurence and Maurice on the recording day. 'When I walked onto the studio floor for a dress rehearsal in the afternoon at Teddington Studios, Lo and Mo came over to me in fits of laughter,' he recalled. 'I asked them what they thought was so funny? They both said that the huge moustache I had decided to wear made me look like Lech Wałęsa, the Polish labour activist! I have to admit it was a very good moustache and made the creepy character even more detestable.'

The actor's experience of working on *Goodnight Sweetheart* was made all the more enjoyable by the fact that he had worked with two of the lead actors before. 'I had worked with Nick a couple of times before, so we got on very well,' Michael revealed. 'He's a thoroughly good chap, and what a professional. He deserves all the success he has achieved. Nick also got to know my dad, Patrick Troughton, during the making of the first series of *The Two of Us*. And although we didn't have scenes together this time, I had worked with the lovely Vic McGuire before when we did two series of the late Sean Hughes's sitcom, *Sean's Show*.'

During his summer holidays in 1971, Michael got a job at the London Palladium as a crew member. At the time, a variety show called *To See Such Fun*, with a cast including Tommy Cooper, Clive Dunn, Anita Harris and Russ Conway, was being staged at the famous theatre. 'Those few weeks, spent in what I think is the most wonderful of all the London theatres, filled me with a craving to step on stage and into those lights and become an actor,' he admitted.

Michael's theatre credits include playing Simon Bliss in the Nöel Coward comedy *Hay Fever*, with a cast including John Le Mesurier and Glynis Johns, at the Yvonne Arnaud Theatre, Guildford, and on tour; Christopher Sly in a tour of William Shakespeare's fierce, energetic comedy of gender and materialism *The Taming of the Shrew*; and Jimmy Dexter in a tour of the Kurt Weill, Elisabeth Hauptmann and Bertolt Brecht musical comedy *Happy End*. The actor's other television roles include Melish in the comedy drama *Minder*, Mr Barstow in the sitcom *2point4 Children* and a therapist in the comedy drama *Cold Feet*. Michael's film parts, meanwhile, include Mr Mermagen in the espionage thriller *Enigma*. Also a writer, Michael wrote a well-received biography of his father, appropriately entitled *Patrick Troughton: The Biography*.

The gang of youths who were trying to break into the site when Gary emerges from the time portal include Pete, who was played by Wayne Goddard. Wayne's other television roles have included Buddy Clark in the drama *Buddy*, an armed robber in a reconstruction in the crime documentary *Crimewatch UK* and Michael Cleary in an edition of the highly regarded documentary series, *Trial and Error*. His film appearances including playing Louis in the drama *Lionheart*, a bus driver in the comedy drama *Night Bus* and Francis in the sports drama *90 Minutes*.

The gang also included Mike, who was played by Scott Mitchell. Despite rumours to the contrary, this is not the same Scott Mitchell who was married to the late actress Barbara Windsor. Scott's other television credits include playing a youth in the firefighter drama *London's Burning*, Xavier in the sitcom *Nelson's Column* and Ian Taylor in the legal drama, *Kavanagh QC*.

The old woman who tells Gary in no uncertain terms she is in favour of the Duckett's Passage site being developed was played by the veteran actress Fanny Carby. On stage, Fanny's credits included playing Lily Dolly in the Stephen Lewis play *Sparrers Can't Sing*, with Brian Murphy and Bob Grant, at the Theatre Royal, Stratford East, and Wyndham's Theatre, London; Minnie in Alan Cullen, Roderick Horn and Jonathan Hainsworth's play with music *The Stirrings in Sheffield on Saturday Night* at the Crucible Theatre, Sheffield; and Mistress Overdone in William Shakespeare's dark comedy *Measure for Measure* at the Royal Exchange, Manchester. Her other television appearances included Polly in the drama *The Newcomers*, Gladys in the saucy sitcom *On the Buses* and Mrs Kell in the costume drama *Middlemarch*. Fanny's roles on film included Lil in the comedy drama *Sparrows Can't Sing*, Dolly in the musical comedy *What a Crazy World* and Mrs Kendal's dresser in the biographical drama *The Elephant Man*, which starred John Hurt. Fanny died on 20 September 2002, aged seventy-seven.

Suzy Aitchison, the daughter of the much-missed actress June Whitfield, also made a welcome appearance in this episode. 'I decided to base my reporter on Moira Stuart for some reason,' said Suzy. 'I admired her and loved her voice, and watching my episode again I remembered that my slightly staccato delivery was based on her. I believe the director allowed me to give my nod to Moira in my characterisation – not that anyone would have known! I also played a reporter in *EastEnders* the same year, so I began to wonder if that year was to be one of journalist roles!'

Suzy's theatre credits include Sorel Bliss in the Nöel Coward comedy *Hay Fever* at the Redgrave Theatre, Farnham, and on tour, Maeve in the premiere of Ben Brown's funny and touching play *Larkin with Women* at the Stephen Joseph Theatre, Scarborough, and Kate in the Alan Ayckbourn comedy *Bedroom Farce*, with Richard Briers and June Whitfield, at the Aldwych Theatre, London. Her other television work includes playing Susan in the last episode of the sitcom *Are You Being Served?*, a murder victim in the sketch series *French and Saunders* and Susie in the sitcom *Jam and Jerusalem*. Suzy's film roles include Lesley in the supernatural horror *Bloody New Year* and Polly in the drama *Innocent*.

As Duckett's Passage and some of the nearby buildings had to appear in this episode to be in the process of being demolished, and a building site to take its place, another location had to be found to replace the usual locations on Ezra Street and Shipton Street. The solution was found at a location in Hammersmith where a new Tesco supermarket and residential properties were set to be constructed. The production team adapted the side of an old house at the building site to make it look more like the entrance to Duckett's Passage, complete with signs and phone boxes, and the remainder to appear like a busy building site. The part of the site that the programme used was situated on Lena Gardens in Hammersmith, opposite the since-closed Lena Gardens Primary School. During the development work, a gated access road was built next to the old house used as the entrance to Duckett's Passage in this episode and remains to this day.

When the BBC repeated the first series back to back with the start of the second series, it meant viewers had *Goodnight Sweetheart* on their screens for a total of sixteen weeks, and that's when the sitcom really became a big hit for ALOMO and the BBC. Indeed, episode two of the second series, 'I Got it Bad and That Ain't Good', saw the highest ratings figure for any episode of *Goodnight Sweetheart* with 13.45 million viewers tuning in to see the latest exploits of Gary Sparrow.

The second series was first broadcast by BBC One on Monday 20 February 1995, Monday 27 February 1995, Monday 6 March 1995, Monday 13 March 1995, Monday 20 March 1995, Monday 27 March 1995, Monday 3 April 1995, Monday 10 April 1995, Monday 24 April 1995 and Monday 1 May 1995 at 8.30pm. No episode was broadcast on Easter Monday (17 April) due to a film being shown instead.

Although she realised that the sitcom had all the right ingredients, Dervla Kirwan was actually surprised by the show's success. 'Contrary to what people think, I am actually deeply insecure, and I always question what I am doing,' the actress admitted. 'There was an enormous amount of people writing in and being so warm and appreciative and I had never really experienced that. I had never been regularly once a week on television in something that had struck such a chord with all generations because it wasn't just geared at people who had survived the war. It was geared at their grandchildren who could sit there with them knowing that they were going to get a very slightly sugary lesson on that period of British history. But nevertheless, it gave them some insight as to what their grandparents suffered and went through. I thought the series handled that very well. I think it had that nostalgia and a sentimentality about it that the public really liked. It was easy viewing and it was entertaining.'

David Jason remains thrilled with the success that Nicholas Lyndhurst achieved with *Goodnight Sweetheart*. 'Working with Nick was one of the most enjoyable phases of my career,' said David. 'Del and Rodney became one of the most famous sets of brothers in modern-day history in *Only Fools and Horses*. It was therefore a delight to hear that Nick had gone on to pastures new in *Goodnight Sweetheart*. It was an unusual and appealing storyline that Nick's character, Gary Sparrow, could travel back in time and reflect some of the scenarios and atmosphere of the Second World War and life in the 1990s. Nick has a great ability to not only be extremely funny, but he has tremendous pathos and a vulnerability which led to the huge success of the show. The writers, including Marks and Gran, played on this tremendous range and Nick was perfect in the role which led him into all kinds of capers and heartfelt and comedic moments over six series.

'Despite the fact that we used to wander nervously round the back of the *Only Fools and Horses* sets before a live audience asking ourselves, "Why do we do this? Why do we put ourselves through it every week?", I would give anything to have the time portal that Gary Sparrow found and go back in time to our glory days together: Del and Rodney, brothers united and having a great deal of fun in the process. However, like a big brother, I am so pleased and proud for Nick that he had such an award-winning success with his own show.'

With the second series broadcast, viewers would have to wait until Boxing Day 1995 for another episode of the time-travelling sitcom.

3
Blitz and Pieces

THE THIRD SERIES OF *Goodnight Sweetheart* finally saw Claire Hinson receive an onscreen credit as an executive producer alongside Allan McKeown. 'Executive producers take on different roles depending on the company and production,' explained Claire. 'In my case, I acted as executive producer on most of ALOMO's shows after I became managing director, including *Birds of a Feather*, *The New Statesman* (MEP version) and *Unfinished Business* etc. I also produced *Men of the World*, a massively underrated series starring John Simm and David Threlfall, which was written by Danny Peacock.

'The executive producing role meant overseeing deals with actors, actresses, writers, producers and directors, signing off the production budget and taking responsibility for the production coming in on budget. I would liaise with the broadcaster, in this case the BBC, and be involved in both financial and creative negotiations. I worked closely with Laurence and Maurice, Micheál Jacob, our head of script development and the script editor on *Goodnight Sweetheart*, as well as the individual producers and production managers on each production. I also had input at script meetings, read all the scripts in development and worked with writers. We were a very tight-knit little team with writers like Gary Lawson and John Phelps very much part of the "family".'

On 5 July 1995, producer John Bartlett wrote to the production team. Here is an extract from his witty letter:

> Welcome to Series C
>
> Firstly, hearty congratulations to everyone who worked on Series B. Thanks to all your efforts we had a splendid series which was both critically well-received and the earner of mammoth ratings. Thank you. We're all looking forward to getting the family back together again.
>
> Well, here we go again, immersing ourselves happily into another series of life in strife-torn London, a time of shortages, desperation and the constant threat of living under the iron jackboot of a maniac (punctuated only by regular visits to the 1940s) and if the first drafts we have so far are typical of what we may expect, we're on for another cracker.

The location filming, rehearsals, pre-records and studio audience recordings for series three took place between Thursday 11 August 1995 and Friday 1 December 1995. However, not all the episodes were made in the order that they were broadcast. The first episode, 'Between the Devil and the Deep Blue Sea', was made after all the other episodes were recorded, while episode five wasn't made in order.

Filming for the first location block took place on Friday 11 August 1995, Saturday 12 August 1995, Sunday 13 August 1995, Monday 14 August 1995, Tuesday 15 August 1995 and Wednesday 16 August 1995. This block included all the Duckett's Passage and Royal Oak exterior scenes for each episode from episode two until episode eleven.

Filming for the second location block took place on Wednesday 4 October 1995 until Tuesday 10 October 1995 for all other exterior scenes including episode one, the Christmas special, apart from the Duckett's Passage and Royal Oak exterior scenes which had been filmed in block one.

The following list includes the dates of the studio recordings for series three. This confirms that episode one and episode five were not recorded in order.

Episode 1	Thursday 30 November & Friday 1 December 1995	Block 2
Episode 2	Thursday 24 August 1995	Block 1
Episode 3	Thursday 31 August 1995	Block 1
Episode 4	Thursday 7 September 1995	Block 1
Episode 5	Thursday 19 October 1995	Block 2
Episode 6	Thursday 14 September 1995	Block 1
Episode 7	Thursday 21 September 1995	Block 1
Episode 8	Thursday 26 October 1995	Block 2
Episode 9	Thursday 2 November 1995	Block 2
Episode 10	Thursday 9 November 1995	Block 2
Episode 11	Thursday 16 November 1995	Block 2

During the first scene of 'Between the Devil and the Deep Blue Sea', the first episode of series three, Phoebe is seen listening to the news on the wireless with Reg. Although the news is bad, Phoebe is more concerned as to why Gary, who is supposedly out East, has not contacted her.

At his Cricklewood home, Gary is complaining that his local Chinese takeaway has given him the wrong order. An attempt at complaining on the phone is met with confusion. In fact, quoting numbers to the takeaway makes them mistakenly believe they have won a prize on the National Lottery!

Meanwhile, Yvonne is feeling down. Gary, however, refuses to show any compassion, reminding her that she's only been redundant from her job a fortnight. He suggests they cancel their skiing holiday, but she says she will be even more depressed if they have to stay in England. Their discussion ends with Gary managing to burn his hand on a plate warmer.

Although he now has a bandaged hand with a protective covering, there's better news for Gary when he and Rob drive to Duckett's Plaza, a new development that has been built on the site of Duckett's Passage and the nearby area. Realising that the only way he can regularly come and go is via the time portal, Gary has come up with the ingenious idea of opening a shop for his memorabilia and arranges to meet an estate agent with Ron in order to view the units with the hope of finding one that has the time portal in its yard. To Ron's amusement, the attractive estate agent is called Jayne Mansfield.

Ron attempts to use charm and wit to keep Jayne amused while Gary seeks out 1941. However, he has to view three units before he finds the one with the time portal, during which time Jayne is becoming more and more flirty with Gary. However, when Jayne calls in to reserve unit number three for the time traveller, she discovers that the owner of a Chinese takeaway has already reserved it because three is his lucky number.

Gary returns home disappointed and finds Yvonne in an equally bad mood due to being unable to find a job with her experience and salary requirements at the Job Centre and having been involved in a trolley rage incident at her local supermarket. When Gary points out that his hand still hurts, Yvonne tells him his hand will get better; her life won't. Just when all seems lost, Jayne calls Gary and tells him that he can now have unit number three. However, this news does not go down well with Yvonne who up until now has not been aware of Gary's plan to open a shop.

It turns out that Mr Ming-Lee from the Chinese takeaway has agreed to change his mind on which unit to have after Jayne told him the adjacent unit was being rented by a pet-shop owner specialising in insects and if any escaped the health inspector would be most displeased! As three is his favourite number the landlord has no objection to the units being numbered from the other end.

When it comes to the paperwork, Jayne suggests they either squat down on the dusty concrete floor of Gary's new shop or discuss it over a cosy drink in pleasant surroundings at a nearby pub called the Royal Oak. Gary makes an excuse and Jayne agrees to take a rain check on the drink, leaving Gary to change into his period clothes before heading for 1941.

When Gary walks into the Royal Oak, he surprises Phoebe by asking for a light ale while she is serving another customer with a drink. When asked where he's been drinking, Gary tells Phoebe the Rising Sun in Tokyo and convinces her that he really has been in Japan by producing a silk kimono robe for her as a present, which amuses another customer at the bar. However, Phoebe is confused by the other present, a bottle of sake, which she thinks is a bottle of perfume.

Reg then spots Gary and comes over to enthusiastically shake him by the hand – the hand with the new-fangled burn dressing.

During a chat over a drink, Gary tells Phoebe she won't have him home for Christmas as he has to go away again (narrowly avoiding telling her he's going skiing) to Singapore. However, he promises that they can celebrate Christmas early and they won't go without a turkey and all the trimmings.

Back in the shop, Gary tells Ron he's having an identity crisis, because in ten days' time the Japanese will attack Pearl Harbour, the Americans will declare war and London will start to fill up with GIs who might start asking awkward questions about the time Gary claims to have spent in America. He asks Ron to ask him some questions from one of the library books he's borrowed, including *Prelude to War: US Politics 1936-1941*. After teasing Gary with a joke question about Franklin D. Roosevelt's shoe size, Ron reads aloud an interesting fact that he's found in the book. It mentions that while the Japanese dealt a savage blow to the American Pacific fleet, none of their aircraft carriers were damaged as they put to sea a few days before the attack on Pearl Harbour for exercises. When Gary claims it was a bit of luck, Ron jokes that maybe it was down to secret agent Gary Sparrow tipping them off. However, Gary suddenly realises that he may have really told the Americans that the Japanese were going to attack Pearl Harbour. Ron points out that this is verging on megalomania and that he is only a common or garden time traveller. As their discussion becomes more heated, Jayne arrives to remind Gary that he hasn't completed the paperwork for the shop. She provocatively tells Gary that he needs taking in hand and offers to help him, suggesting they complete the papers over dinner. When Gary reminds her that he's hardly dressed for a restaurant, she invites him to her place. Although he reminds Jayne that he's a married man, she continues to make it clear she has more on her mind than paperwork and her commission. Gary reluctantly agrees to go to dinner with her that Thursday. Ron warns him that he'd be safer at Pearl Harbour!

In preparation for going on their skiing holiday, Gary and Yvonne visit a dry ski slope to get some practice. As they take the ski lift to the top of the slope, she agrees to him trying to make the shop work. However, when he tells her he will have to go on trips to find memorabilia, she offers to go with him. Quick as a flash, Gary makes an excuse, and this upsets an already prickly Yvonne. He pushes in front of her at the top of the ski slope and proceeds to fall as he attempts to ski. Gary asks Yvonne for help, but she skies off down the slope in a huff, leaving him to struggle to his feet on his own.

After Gary hears Ed Murrow on the radio in Phoebe's flat at the Royal Oak, he makes for Broadcasting House to try and talk to him, in the process coming almost face to face with Winston Churchill. Although tired, Murrow allows Gary to buy him a coffee. After ordering lunch from a rude waitress, Gary attempts to tell Ed about a vivid dream he's been having. By now Ed is starting to believe he's playing a joke on him. But Gary perseveres, telling him that in his dream the Japanese air force was attacking American warships in a sort of a harbour and there was something about pearls and a newspaper that said 7 December. However, Ed is not impressed and is ready to skip his lunch and leave. In desperation, Gary tells him that he's had dreams come true before: for instance, that the Germans were going to invade Russia. By now, Ed is growing tired of what he considers are Gary's flights of fantasy and prepares to leave. In a last-ditch attempt to get Ed to take him seriously, Gary writes down the Royal Oak's phone number and asks him to call him if he wants to hear more about his vivid dreams. At first Ed screws up the card with the number, but then puts it in his pocket before walking out.

After considering Gary's lurid dreams, Ed leaves a phone message with Reg at the Royal Oak inviting Gary to a cocktail party at the Dorchester Hotel. After Reg finally manages to make sense of his own handwriting, he reads the message to Gary. When Phoebe overhears, she insists on attending with him.

At the cocktail party, Ed asks Gary how he really knew the Italians were going to surrender and Gary informs him that he used his intelligence, which is what Ed thought it would boil down to. Ed introduces him to a friend who works for the BBC who also takes a great interest in matters of intelligence. The man in question is curious to know which department Gary is with. Having asked who his contacts are, he begins to suspect that Gary might be a spy for a country that doesn't have English as its first language. Gary shows a reluctance to speak, but Ed's friend encourages him to stay and continue the conversation by showing him that he's carrying a gun. When Gary reminds Ed that he gave him the information in complete confidence, Ed reveals he trusts his friend more than him. However, the friend turns out to be a certain Guy Burgess. Gary then shocks Guy by subtly making it clear that he's aware of his Russian connections. Realising that he knows a little bit too much about him for comfort, Guy informs Ed that he can trust Gary before swiftly departing to have a word with T. S. Eliot. Gary then asks Ed who he's going to tell about Pearl Harbour. He agrees to tell a pal in Washington who's reasonably connected and who just happens to go by the name of Eisenhower.

While decorating Gary's new shop, Ron asks Gary what would happen if Guy had been frightened into given up spying for the Russians. Gary assures him that he didn't, having checked in his reference books as soon as he got back. After pointing out the burden of responsibility he has in the past, and knowing that his slightest action could change history, Ron suggests that Gary change his name to God by deed poll!

Jayne breaks up their chat by arriving all dressed for her date with Gary, which he has forgotten due to more important things – such as Pearl Harbour! Gary tells her to wait in the car while he gets changed. Pleased, Jayne reminds him that they have a long night ahead of them and, more importantly, she's wearing stockings! This nugget of information causes Ron to fall off his ladder. Gary tells Ron he has no choice but to go on the date. However, Ron suggests he go and hide back in 1941 to avoid the evening ending in tears.

Realising that Gary has stood her up, Jayne makes her way over to Cricklewood to see him. After Yvonne tells her he's not there, she decides to exact revenge by making a false confession.

When Gary arrives home, Yvonne summons him to the living room and proceeds to tell him about Jayne's visit. It appears that she accused Gary of coming on to her and that they went out together, not realising that he was married. Gary strenuously denies the allegations and tells her that *she* has been coming on to *him* ever since he clapped eyes on Duckett's Plaza. He finally convinces her by saying that he would swear on a stack of bibles that there isn't a woman anywhere in the world – today at least – that he would even give a second glance to. Eventually, Gary placates her.

As promised, Gary arrives at the Royal Oak with a turkey, all the trimmings and plenty besides, which he claims to have got from the Yanks, for an early Christmas celebration. Although Gary is keen to be alone with Phoebe, she has promised that Reg can share their dinner due to his wife telling him he shouldn't expect anything out of the ordinary come Christmas Day!

Meanwhile, in a bid to get revenge on Jayne, Yvonne pops around to her office and tells her to stay away from Gary because he's a one-woman man. Her parting shot is to pour a hot drink on Jayne's computer screen causing it to blow a fuse.

Early the next morning, Gary, who has stayed over at the Royal Oak, rises to listen to the news on the radio. Wilfred Pickles announces that the Japanese have launched an unprovoked air attack on the United States Naval Base at Pearl Harbour; heavy damage and loss of life has been reported in Honolulu and several battleships have been reported on fire in the harbour. However, all the aircraft carriers in the Pacific fleet had put to sea for manoeuvres. This confirms to Gary that Ed has indeed taken his advice and spoken to Eisenhower. When he tells Phoebe that the Americans are now in the war and she asks if this will be over by the next Christmas, he tells her it may take another three or four years. When she asks what will happen to them, he tells her they should live one day at a time. Before he leaves, he gives her a present to open on Christmas Day. When she admits having not bought him anything as yet, he tells her that having her to come back to is present enough.

The Christmas special, written by Laurence and Maurice, was not only the longest episode of *Goodnight Sweetheart* ever made, running at fifty minutes, but also one of the most plot-driven. 'In general, we've always looked for a big story when writing a special, otherwise it isn't that special,' said Maurice. 'Because of the way that *Goodnight Sweetheart* follows the chronology of the war, Pearl Harbour was as tempting a target for us as it was to the Japanese. However, we also used the special to deal with the problem Gary had been set at the end of series two, when Duckett's Passage was zoned for redevelopment and Gary lost his access to the past.'

Without doubt, the Christmas special is one of the best episodes of the entire run of *Goodnight Sweetheart*. The ingenious plot, including the introduction of Gary's new shop, Blitz and Pieces, and the inspired use of actual historic figures Ed Murrow and Guy Burgess, and not forgetting the stalker subplot featuring estate agent Jayne Mansfield, certainly rewards viewers with an engaging fifty minutes. What remains a mystery is why another Christmas special wasn't commissioned. However, it wouldn't be the last time that the subject of Christmas would be part of a plot in the sitcom.

This episode was the first time that the row of properties housing Gary's shop, Blitz and Pieces, was seen. For obvious reasons it was a different location to Shipton Street and Ezra Street, which, of course, were not really knocked down. The shop used for Blitz and Pieces until the end of the fifth series is situated at 18B Pitfield Street, Shoreditch, London.

The location of the ski slope, which Gary and Yvonne visited to get some practice in before their ski trip, was Bracknell Ski Centre. It was part of the John Nike Leisuresport Complex, on John Nike Way, Bracknell. Filming took place on Tuesday 10 October 1995. As the scenes on the ski slope were set at night, filming took place from 7.00pm onwards. During the filming, Nicholas's skiing double was Jamie Edgell and Michelle's was Emma Toose. Sadly, the John Nike Leisuresport Complex closed in March 2020 when coronavirus restrictions were imposed and was later demolished in 2022.

The rehearsal and studio recording schedule for the Christmas special went as follows:

Tuesday 21 November 1995:

    10.30am: Read-through BBC Rehearsal Rooms, Acton

Wednesday 22 November 1995:

    Rehearsal at BBC Rehearsal Rooms, Acton

Thursday 23 November 1995:

    Rehearsal at BBC Rehearsal Rooms, Acton

Friday 24 November 1995:

    Rehearsal at BBC Rehearsal Rooms, Acton

Monday 27 November 1995:

    Rehearsal at BBC Rehearsal Rooms, Acton

Tuesday 28 November 1995:

    Run-through for Designer and Lighting Director

Wednesday 29 November 1995:

    12.00pm: Tech Run

    Set built and lighting rig

Thursday 30 November 1995:

    Christmas Special Studio Recording (Episode 1) (no audience present)

    On Camera 9.30am – 12.30pm

        Sc.22 Int. Gary's Shop (State B)
        Sc.19 Int. Lyon's Corner House
        Sc.30 Int. Estate Agency

    12.30pm – 1.30pm Lunch

    On Camera 1.30pm – 7.00pm

        Sc.4 to 10 Gary's Shop (State A)
        Sc.21 Int. Hotel Reception
        (Sc.17) Phoebe's Sitting Room
        (Sc.29) Phoebe's Sitting Room
        (Record above two scenes if time)
        Sc.31 Phoebe's Bedroom

    5.00pm – 10.00pm: Edit Inserts at BBC Television Centre

Friday 1 December 1995:

Christmas Special Studio Recording (Episode 1) (audience present in evening)

On Camera 9.30pm – 10.00pm

(Please note the dress rehearsal will be at 4.00pm)

Block and rehearse the remaining scenes:

Sc.1 Royal Oak
Sc.2 Sparrow's Kitchen
Sc.11 Sparrow's Lounge
Sc.12 Int. Gary's Shop (State A)
Sc.14 Int. Royal Oak
Sc.15 Int. Gary's Shop (Stage A)
Sc.20 Royal Oak
Sc.23 to 27 Sparrow's Hall/Kitchen/Lounge
Sc.28 Royal Oak

Diana Kent, who played Jayne Mansfield in this special, was one of only two guest performers to have their name displayed in the opening title sequence. The other cast member to receive the same accolade was Timothy West in his two episodes in series five.

'It was the first sitcom I'd appeared in,' said Diana, 'although I'd already done quite a bit of television. I didn't get offered many comedy parts in those days and Jayne Mansfield was a gift for any actress, so I was really pleased to get the role.

'My chief memory is of how nice everyone involved was and what a good team they were to work with – not just Nicholas, Victor and Michelle, but the director, producer and the writers, Laurence and Maurice, who were present throughout and very much part of the process. Their attention to detail was meticulous and they honed the script during the rehearsal process. However, at no time was anyone prescriptive; everyone was very open and accepting of ideas. For example, I suggested the line, "Lou or Elvis?" (referring to the dress designer Costello) that Victor says to me and it was written into the script.

'Recording in front of a studio audience didn't bother me a bit. I like the frisson a live audience gives you. I was also thrilled to have the chance to rehearse the scenes and get them solid – not an opportunity you often get with television work.

'The "stockings" line has stayed with me and I still get complimentary email about it, especially when the episode is repeated!'

Diana's theatre credits have included Sheila Birling in the J. B. Priestley drama *An Inspector Calls* at the National Theatre, London, Caesonia in the Albert Camus play *Caligula*, with Michael Sheen, at the Donmar Warehouse, London, and Caroline in James Rushbrooke's debut play *Tomcat* at the Southwark Playhouse, London. Meanwhile, her other television roles include Mrs Lamb in the wartime drama *Band of Brothers*, Lady Rose in *Father Brown*, which features Mark Williams and Sorcha Cusack, and the Duchess of Richmond in the drama *Belgravia*. Diana's appearances on film include playing Hilda Hume in the Peter Jackson crime drama *Heavenly Creatures*, Rachel Petkoff in the comedy *How to Lose Friends and Alienate People* and the older Jennifer Stirling in the romantic drama, *The Last Letter from Your Lover*.

Also appearing in this episode was Winston Churchill lookalike, John Evans. He appeared in a scene set outside BBC Broadcasting House where Gary spots him while waiting for Ed Murrow.

Playing Ed, meanwhile, was Michael J. Shannon. The actor and playwright has worked in both the UK and America. In the theatre, his roles have included Ralph Austin in Leonard Gershe's funny, touching and emotional play *Butterflies Are Free*, opposite Gloria Swanson and Dirk Benedict, at the Booth Theater, New York. Michael has also appeared as Charles Bradford in the Frank Harvey drama adapted from Thomas Hardy's story *The Day After the Fair*, with Deborah Kerr, in the Eisenhower Theater at the John F. Kennedy Center for the Performing Arts in Washington, D.C, and on tour. He has also played President Kennedy in *JFK on JFK*, a one-man show he wrote about the late president, at the Stella Adler Theatre, Los Angeles. Michael's other television credits include Major James Kiley in the wartime drama *We'll Meet Again*, Randy Anderson in the action series *The A-Team* and Avery Wilson in the comedy drama *Boston Legal*; while his film parts include playing the president's aide in the action adventure *Superman II*, Jerry in the crime drama *American Gun* and Dr Morgan in the crime thriller, *The Raven*.

Josie Kidd also made a memorable cameo as the feisty 'Nippy' (an affectionate term used to describe a waitress at one of the restaurants of J. Lyons & Co. Ltd). Josie was a character actress who had a diverse and prolific acting career. Her theatre credits included Julia Price in Arnold Ridley's comedy thriller *The Ghost Train* on tour, Dorothy in the Peter Quilter comedy *Glorious!*, which starred Maureen Lipman, at the Duchess Theatre, London, and on tour, and Mrs Coade in J. M. Barrie's fantasy play *Dear Brutus* at the Southwark Playhouse, London. Josie's other television roles included Staff Nurse Olive Carr in the medical soap *Emergency-Ward 10*, Janet in the sitcom *Dear Mother... ...Love Albert*, with Rodney Bewes, and Ada in the period drama *Call the Midwife*. She also played Susan's mother in the film crime drama, *Shoot on Sight*. Josie died on 4 June 2018, aged eighty.

This episode also featured Tim Dutton as Guy Burgess, who Gary meets at the cocktail party. Tim is a talented and versatile actor. His theatre roles have included Jack, Spadge and Squire in the Laurie Lee drama *Cider with Rosie*, alongside Vicki Pepperdine, at the Birmingham Rep Theatre and on tour; O'Brien in Robert Icke and Duncan MacMillan's production of *1984*, adapted from George Orwell's novel, at the Almeida Theatre, London, Playhouse Theatre, London, and on an international tour; and Douglas in Stephen Bill's dramatic comedy *Curtains* at the Rose Theatre, Kingston. His other television credits include Brian Selig in the comedy drama *Ally McBeal*, alongside Calista Flockhart, Aidan Carmichael in *Vera*, which starred Brenda Blethyn, and Klaas Gilbert in the crime drama *Van der Valk*, featuring Marc Warren. Meanwhile, the film parts he has played include Maurice Haigh-Wood in the romantic drama *Tom and Viv*, Eamon in the action thriller *The Bourne Identity* and Ian Howard in the crime drama *The Infiltrator*.

It was down to Jon Glover to provide the voice of the actor and radio presenter Wilfred Pickles in this special. Wilfrid spent time as an occasional radio newsreader on the BBC Home Service during the Second World War. He was the first newsreader to not speak with Received Pronunciation, which was a deliberate attempt to make it more difficult for Nazis to impersonate BBC broadcasters. This would be the first of two engagements for Jon in series three. He would later appear in person as Doctor Stone in the same series in an episode called 'Someone to Watch Over Me'. 'It's likely that I was asked to voice the role of Wilfred Pickles because of my work with Harry Enfield as Mr Cholmondley-Warner,' said Jon. 'I had cornered the market in period voices and I still do a lot of that kind of ADR today.'

Jon is a well-known actor and voice performer. His stage credits include playing Barry Gillis and Ettore Santangelo in the premiere of the Larry Belling family drama with a dash of dark comedy, *Stroke of Luck*, at the Park Theatre, London; Sir Gregory Pitkin in the Brian Cooke comedy *The Men from the Ministry… Reloaded*, adapted from two episodes from the original BBC radio series, at the White Bear Theatre, London; and Robin Day, Michael Heseltine and various others including Boris Johnson in the Michael McManus play *Maggie and Ted* at the White Bear Theatre, London, the Garrick Theatre, London, and the Yvonne Arnaud Theatre, Guilford. Jon's other television roles include a management consultant in the science-fiction comedy *The Hitchhiker's Guide to the Galaxy* and playing the Duke of Edinburgh, Melvyn Bragg, Steve Davis, Oliver Reed and various others in the satirical puppet series *Spitting Image*, and Jacob Rothstein in the crime drama, *Father Brown*.

*

Goodnight Sweetheart: A Guide to the Classic Sitcom

After Gary and Yvonne return home from their skiing trip at the beginning of 'It Ain't Necessarily So', the second episode of series three, the former discovers that he has caught the sun. Yvonne can't resist nicknaming him Rudolph! However, the novelty of going on holiday soon wears off. Being driven home at breakneck speed from the airport by Ron who's depressed over the state of his marriage and the lack of a New Year's Eve party to go didn't help matters! The situation is made worse for Gary when he discovers that they've been invited to a New Year's party being organised by Stella – and Ron hasn't been invited! Worse still, a waiting bank statement reveals that the holiday cost all of Yvonne's redundancy payout.

Keen to see Phoebe, Gary makes the excuse of needing to cycle to the all-night chemist to get something for his shiny nose. On arrival at the Royal Oak, Gary finds her wiping a table in the snug. The reunion is a happy one until Gary discovers that Betty Harding, Phoebe's friend from school, is staying with her. However, Gary suggests while Betty is enjoying her regulation five inches in the bath that they make the most of their time together. Unfortunately, Betty is Donald's cousin. However, that doesn't stop them from creeping off to his flat above Mrs Bloss's shop to make up for lost time.

After Gary tries to sneak Phoebe out of his flat and the shop, Mrs Bloss, dressed in her most unflattering night attire, appears in the doorway to complain about their 'fragrant act of immorality'. After a bitter exchange of words, Mrs Bloss tells Gary she wants him to leave her house by the end of the week or she'll have the police to him – and she means a proper policeman, not PC Deadman!

Back at home, Gary has to devise yet another excuse for where he was all night. Gary claims he spent the night speaking to Mike, of Mike and Audrey, who had sent them a Christmas card. His convoluted story soon bores Yvonne. When he tells her he's keen to get to the shop to put all the stock on the shelves, Yvonne offers to accompany him as she's currently devoid of job prospects.

Once at the shop, Blitz and Pieces, it doesn't take long for Yvonne to lose interest. When Ron arrives, she realises this is her cue to leave, but not before she drops a subtle hint to Gary about not telling Ron about Stella's New Year's Eve party. However, Ron has discovered about the party from his postman – who has been given an invite. He asks Gary to persuade Yvonne to interpose with Stella and plead his case. Gary agrees to try in return for Ron looking after the shop during his lunch hours while he goes to see Phoebe. The prospect doesn't appeal until Gary bribes him with an extra Christmas present – a pocket watch. Ron notices that the watch is running an hour fast. Gary explains that back in 1941 they had British Summer Time all year round, which as well as preventing road accidents in the blackout will sneakily enable him to see the New Year in with both Phoebe and Yvonne.

Back at the Royal Oak, Phoebe tells Gary he's got her into trouble with her local Labour Exchange. Mrs Bloss's brother-in-law turns out to be the deputy manager and because Gary was so cheeky to her, Mrs Bloss has decided to get revenge by telling him about their relationship. Mr Bloss has warned Phoebe that if they carry on carrying on, he will see to it that she gets conscripted to the ack-ack battery in Grimsby. Gary points out that he can't make her do that even though he says he has discretion under the King's regulations. However, if they stop seeing each other, he will lose her file in the pending tray. Gary promises to go and talk to Mrs Bloss but Reg points out that as he mocked her Cyril, she won't want to help. He also points out that she's a proud woman, and hasn't claimed a ha'penny of her war widow's pension, which Reg thinks is strange as she hates taking in lodgers – a revelation that intrigues Gary.

With his mind still processing Reg's piece of gossip, Gary and Ron go to the Imperial War Museum. There, they meet a hard-of-hearing and elderly curator who looks up Cyril Bloss, Mrs Bloss's husband, on the computer records. He discovers two Bloss brothers – Henry and Cyril – who both joined the army on the same day. However, it transpires that both brothers survived the war. Henry went back to Whitechapel and Cyril to live in Luton. The curator remembers Cyril at one of their reunions with a chic young French lady, whom he claimed was his wife!

Back at home, Gary walks into his bedroom to discover Yvonne and Ron's wife Stella decorating. When Gary points out to Stella that Ron is depressed, she isn't impressed, saying that Ron has a lot to hate himself about, not least his increased weight.

While packing his belongings back at his flat, Gary reveals to Mrs Bloss that he has discovered that her husband, Cyril, is still alive. He tells her to inform her brother-in-law to leave Phoebe alone. Realising that Gary will blackmail her if she doesn't cooperate, she confesses that she knows Cyril went to live bigamously with a 'French tart' in Luton. She also tells Gary that him spreading the news would do no more to hurt her than the life she's had to live the last twenty years. She also admits to feeling jealous when she hears Gary and Phoebe canoodling in his flat while she has got nothing to keep her warm apart from memories and a hot-water bottle. He points out that that's no reason to be so vindictive, and that her brother-in-law was jeopardising his job and pension by abusing his position in this way. Mrs Bloss begs Gary not to tell anyone about Cyril as she couldn't cope with people feeling sorry for her. She then flirtily tells her time-travelling lodger he doesn't have to go and that it's nice having a young man about the house.

As midnight approaches on New Year's Eve 1941, Gary arrives at the Royal Oak to tell Phoebe that everything is now 'tickety-boo'. Although he can't accept her kind offer to go upstairs for a New Year's cuddle after they close, Gary agrees to see in the New Year in the public bar with her and the pub regulars. Gary then sings and plays the Beatles song 'All My Loving' just before the clock strikes twelve. As the clock chimes, Gary and Phoebe embrace but Reg interrupts and persuades them to take part in singing 'Auld Lang Syne'.

Back in the present, Gary takes some money out of a cash machine across the road from Blitz and Pieces before catching a minicab to Harrow for Stella's New Year's Eve party. When he arrives, Yvonne questions where he's been, and he tells her to Wincanton on business and shows her the money he took out from the machine. Although Stella's ban on Ron attending the party has been lifted, he is absent without leave. He eventually turns up and apologises for being late to Stella, explaining that the pocket watch, which Gary gave him, had stopped!

The episode, written by Laurence and Maurice, marked the start of an increase in the marital difficulties between Ron and Stella. On balance, their marital problems were usually connected to Ron covering up for Gary's double life, although his own inadequacies as a husband became a popular theme. Either way, they would both end up making Ron's marriage like a war zone in the coming episodes.

This episode marked Terry Kinane's first as a director on *Goodnight Sweetheart*. 'The episodic workload was such that Lo and Mo felt that a second director was needed to be planning upcoming episodes, working with the writers on those scripts, and location hunting for the exterior scenes,' he explained. 'I was directing *Birds of a Feather* for ALOMO at the time and had directed Nick on his LWT sitcom, *The Two of Us*. I was, therefore, the obvious choice for the job.'

Terry, who directed a total of seventeen episodes of the sitcom, including the last episode of the final series, now lives in the northern suburbs of Atlanta in America, and no longer works as a director. More recently, however, he penned the script for a new American television film called *Christmas on the Ranch*. He still looks back with affection at his involvement with the time-travelling comedy. '*Goodnight Sweetheart* had a fantastic cast, and we all had a lot of fun making the show,' he said. 'One particular memory I have is of Nick doing an impression of Richard Burton in the movie *Where Eagles Dare*. He would quote the line, "Broadsword calling Danny Boy" to me whenever he had a problem with a scene. It was a code that only he and I understood. It still makes me smile. In fact, Nick and his wife Lucy were once walking past a bookstore in London, and Nick saw that someone had written a book about the making of *Where Eagles Dare* and the author had named the book *Broadsword Calling Danny Boy*. It made him laugh, and he sent me a copy of the book!'

Terry's other television directing credits included the light entertainment series *Surprise Surprise* and the game show *Blind Date*, along with the comedy shows *Cannon and Ball* and *The World According to Smith and Jones*. His other sitcoms include *Trouble in Mind*, *Get Back* and *Men of the World*.

The sound supervisor Bob Newton regards working on *Goodnight Sweetheart* as a career highlight. 'My principal memory of the location shooting is that they were happy shoots,' he said. 'The cast and Terry Kinane were a pleasure to work with. Coming from a vision-mixing background, Terry had the whole location element of the scripts already edited in his head and only shot precisely what he needed to make any given sequence work.'

Since working on *Goodnight Sweetheart*, Bob's credits have included the sitcoms *I'm Alan Partridge*, *Coupling* and *Kate and Koji*, while his film work includes the comedies *In the Loop*, *Alan Partridge: Alpha Papa* and *The Inbetweeners 2*.

Yvonne D'Alpra, who played Mrs Bloss again in this episode, remembers working with Nicholas with a mixture of affection and amusement. 'Nick is a lovely man,' she said. 'On this episode, I remember we struggled to get through the scene where I had to tell him, "You don't have to go, Mr Sparrow. It's rather nice having a young man about the house," without laughing!'

Also appearing in this episode was Charles Simon as the hard-of-hearing museum curator. A one-time friend of George Bernard Shaw, Charles's theatre roles included the presiding judge in the Salvato Cappelli play *The Devil Peter* at the Arts Theatre, London, Charles in the Jim Cartwright drama *Bed* at the National Theatre, London, and Escalus in the William Shakespeare play *Measure for Measure* at the Lyric Hammersmith, London, and on tour. His other television credits included Gower in the action drama *The Saint*, George Adams in Dennis Potter's miniseries *The Singing Detective* and Father Jim in the sitcom *Father Ted*. Meanwhile, on film, he played a night clerk in the spy comedy *The Man Who Knew Too Little*, Lord Carnivore in the crime comedy *102 Dalmatians*, which starred Glenn Close as Cruella de Vil, and Ralph Stein in the comedy drama *Paradise Grove*. Charles died of pneumonia on 16 May 2002, aged ninety-three, after a career that lasted nearly eighty years.

The actor who played the taxi driver in this episode was Malcolm McFee. Malcolm directed and appeared in various theatre productions, including pantomimes. His credits included the club page in the George Bernard Shaw social satire *The Philanderer* at the Mermaid Theatre, London, Tom in the Ann Jellicoe comedy *The Knack* at the Theatre Royal, Stratford East, London, and Ivor in Peter Nichols's bittersweet play *Forgot-Me-Not Lane*, with a cast including Anton Rodgers and Joan Hickson, at the Greenwich Theatre, London, and the Apollo Theatre, London. Best known for playing Peter Craven in the school-based sitcom *Please, Sir!* and in all but one series of the spin-off, *The Fenn Street Gang*, his other television roles included Norman in the sitcom *Bless this House* and Lukey Sparrow in the action drama *The Sweeney*. On film, Malcolm played Frederick Percy 'Freddie' Smith in the Richard Attenborough comedy musical *Oh! What a Lovely War* and Peter Craven in the big-screen version of the sitcom *Please, Sir!* Malcolm died suddenly on 18 November 2001 at his home in Braintree, Essex, aged just fifty-two. He had been due to play the dame in the pantomime *Beauty and the Beast* at the Elgiva Theatre in Chesham that Christmas.

Finally, this episode saw Nimmy March making the first of her three in-vision appearances as Stella Wheatcroft.

At the start of 'One O'Clock Jump', the third episode of series three, it would be fair to say that Yvonne's get-up-and-go has got up and gone! The post is yet again full of job rejection letters – that is, until Gary shows her that she has a letter from Simyung Electronics, a Korean firm that has opened a new factory in Hatfield. Yvonne is over the moon and says it's a miracle because she never applied for a job with the company. Gary then admits he persuaded Ron to print up a few 'improved' CVs, which he sent out on her behalf.

Later, when the brewery try and deliver Phoebe's order for the week, they're literally left out in the cold as she doesn't answer the door. They leave the barrels on the pavement outside and depart. This is due to her and Gary being otherwise occupied sharing a spot of afternoon delight upstairs.

Afterwards, Gary and Phoebe listen to the wireless while basking in the afterglow of their lovemaking. Gary admits to being in a state of mild shock as he only popped around for a cup of tea! Phoebe then asks Gary whether he's ever thought about having children. Although he dismisses this as being physically impossible, it's clear Phoebe is serious. Gary points out that it's the wrong time to bring children into the world. She agrees but asks: if she could get a divorce from Donald, would he like them to have a baby after the war? Hearing the bad news on the radio, Gary reminds her that they've got to win the war first.

Back at the shop, Gary discovers Ron waiting impatiently outside with a box of catalogues. Once inside, Ron admits that it's all quiet on the bedroom front at home – although the rows that he and Stella are having are far from quiet. Unfortunately, Ron's eloquence about his marital problems puts Gary to sleep. Once awake, their conversation is interrupted by the arrival of Reg Deadman's grandson who previously gave him directions for Duckett's Passage and later arrested him for drink-driving. This time, he's there in his capacity as a crime prevention officer. Taking off his helmet, Gary and Ron are treated to the sight of his rather obvious wig. He soon realises that Gary is not taking the matter seriously even though it's a high crime neighbourhood. In passing, he mentions that the whole area used to be safer in his grandad's day.

Back at home, Yvonne offers Gary a glass of champagne as he walks through the door. She tells him she went to Simyung Electronics for an interview and it went really well. Gary is not impressed and questions her decision to work for a Japanese company, as living back in the 1940s has reminded him of their war record. However, Yvonne tells him she will accept the job if offered and then informs him that Mr Shik wants to meet Gary. This is because Simyung is a very family-oriented business and he has invited them for dinner at a Japanese restaurant, which doesn't go down well with Gary.

Back in the pub, Phoebe is on the phone to the brewery complaining that her order hasn't arrived. When they tell her it was delivered, she realises it has been stolen.

Over a drink at the bar, Reg tells Gary that he hasn't got any children. But having met his grandson, who is the spitting image of Reg, this confuses Gary and he takes him aside to dig a little deeper. Reg admits he had a brief fling with a bus conductor called Margie Hook. Margie later moved to Streatham, which Reg mistakenly calls St Reatham, with a bus driver after they patched things up.

Determined that Reg should meet his child, Gary goes to the bus depot in Streatham and board's Margie's bus. During the brief journey, Gary pretends he's from the Secret Service and tells Margie that Reg would be as 'pleased as punch' about the baby. She eventually agrees to take their son to the Royal Oak that evening.

Back in the shop, Ron is still in a low state of morale, and is cynical at the prospect of Margie turning up to present Reg with the fruit of his loins. The reason for his mood is that Stella has told him that she can't go on living with a fat, boring, flatulent, badly dressed Scouse know-all. When Gary suggests that Ron make some changes to himself, Ron points out that he wouldn't be the man Stella married. In response, Gary reminds him that she doesn't want the man she married!

To keep Reg from going on duty, Gary plies him with drink and, out of desperation, pretends he has a lead on what happened to the barrels of bitter that were stolen. As they talk, a small boy runs into the bar and is caught by Reg. He is followed by Margie who tells him she wanted him to meet little Frankie. He soon realises that the boy is his son and they hug.

Although Phoebe thinks what Gary did was wonderful, she doesn't believe for a second that he didn't know that Reg had a son. She admits that it sends shivers down her spine knowing that there's this little organisation that knows all your secrets. Once again, she brings up the subject of children and asks if he would like a son that he could play football with or teach to play the piano.

At the restaurant, Gary becomes quite touchy with Mr Shik as he still mistakenly believes that Simyung Electronics are Japanese. Gary's attitude upsets Yvonne who is afraid that he will lose her the job. Mr Shik, however, is on Gary's side with regard to how the Japanese behaved during the war and assures him that he, as with Simyung, is Korean and hires Yvonne on the spot. Gary then asks why Mr Shik's wife doesn't seem to talk. He tells him it's because she doesn't speak English, because she's Japanese!

Gary could always quite rightly be accused by Yvonne of not being totally invested in his marriage. If that was the symptom of his marital difficulties, then having an affair with a woman who was born during the First World War was definitely the cause. However, it was the crafty streak that Gary possesses in abundance that would constantly buy himself out of Yvonne's bad books. A prime example in this episode was when Gary admits to getting Ron to print off a few enhanced CVs for Yvonne, which ultimately helps her to get a new well-paid job. Of course, this was not entirely selfless on Gary's part. With Yvonne's mind distracted by her new job, Gary realised that she won't be as fixated on his comings and goings.

This episode saw Christopher Ettridge working with a member of his real family. 'I remember the scene where my little boy Alfie played little Frankie,' he said. 'He'd been told to hit me on the nose – and he did, hard! Bloody hell, it hurt. No acting was required on my part when I had to react!'

The storyline that introduced Margie and little Frankie gave Christopher yet another chance to play opposite Nicholas in a scene on their own, which he more than welcomed. 'I loved working with Nick. He was so generous,' Chris recalled. 'If I tried something out in rehearsal that he thought was funny, he would laugh like a drain and say, "Yes, let's do that." Often, he'd say, "Chris, why don't you try such and such; I think there's a laugh there." He never cared who got the laugh; he wanted laughs. It never mattered to him whose they were. But it wasn't all about laughs as Nick has great integrity, which was an inspiration to me.'

Making the first of seven appearances in *Goodnight Sweetheart* in this episode was Eve Bland, who played Margie Hook. In addition to appearing in the sitcom, Eve's theatre credits included playing Platinum Sue in the Claire Luckham play *Trafford Tanzi* at the Lyric Hammersmith, London, and on tour, Josie in a tour of the Nell Dunn comedy *Steaming* and Griselda in Julia Schofield's morality play *Love on the Plastic* at the Half Moon Theatre, London. Her other television roles included Dora in the sitcom *All in Good Faith*, Heather Dunn in the crime drama *She's Out* and Moira in the sitcom *15 Storeys High*. A talented comedy and dramatic actress, Eve died in 2016.

Nick Bayly joined the cast of this episode to play a cheerless bus inspector. Nick's stage roles include Brassett in a tour of the Brandon Thomas farce *Charley's Aunt*, with Frank Windsor and Gabrielle Drake, Inspector Evans in *Are You There, Moriarty?* at the Palace Theatre, Southend, and Sam Henderson in a tour of the Frederick Knott thriller, *Wait Until Dark*. Meanwhile, his other television credits include playing Toby in the comedy drama *An Independent Man*, Ben Harrow in the crime drama *Hetty Wainthropp Investigates* and Danny Green in the soap opera *Emmerdale*. Nick also played Arthur in the horror film *The Haunted*.

David Aldous, meanwhile, played the small role of Margie's husband, Mr Hook. He was the first of two actors to play the role. Gordon Winter was later cast as Jackie Hook in the sixth episode of series four. David's other television credits have included playing a coach driver in the sitcom *The Legacy of Reginald Perrin*, a driver in the drama *Peak Practice* and a fairground announcer in the medical drama *Casualty*. Meanwhile, his film roles include John in the drama *Boston Kickout* and a guard in the biographical drama *Monarch*.

Malaysian-born actor Eddie Yeoh was also cast as Mr Shik, Yvonne's new boss. Eddie's other television credits included Mr Wu in the sitcom *Desmond's*, a Chinese restaurant manager in the comedy drama *Perfect Scoundrels*, which starred Peter Bowles and Bryan Murray, and Mr Kim Tae Woo in the comedy drama *Ballykissangel*. His film roles included Mr Chow in the action comedy *Eat the Rich*, a Korean bidder in Michael Winner's crime comedy *Bullseye!* and General Hun Chea in the crime thriller *Spy Game*. Eddie died in 2016.

Finally, the non-speaking role of Mrs Shik in this episode was played by Nana Takahashi. Her other credits include playing a girl on the phone in the horror film, *I, Zombie: The Chronicles of Pain*.

On Monday 14 August 1995, location filming took place for two location scenes in this episode. The first location was Kingston Bus Garage, Cromwell Road, Kingston, London. The interior of the bus garage was used to film the scene where Gary asks the bus inspector if Margie Hook works there. When he mentions that she is the conductor of a bus just leaving, Gary quickly hops aboard her bus, which her husband is driving.

The second location was Building 22, Royal Arsenal West, Woolwich, London. Here, the scene set on the moving bus with Gary and Margie was filmed. An exterior shot of the bus at a bus stop in the same scene was also filmed at the same location.

As 'It's a Sin to Tell a Lie', the fourth episode of the third series, begins, Ron is silently practising his chat-up technique in the mirror as Gary arrives in the living room. He is confused as to why Gary is dressed casually as he's hoping the two of them might pick up two ladies in the King's Head as it's the hottest vibe in Cricklewood come the sabbath. Unfortunately for Ron, Yvonne is gatecrashing their trip to the pub as it might be her last chance before she goes on a course, so his chances of getting some extramarital fun have to be put on hold. As a result, Ron changes his mind about going to the pub and decides to go home.

It's a busy night in the Royal Oak back in 1942 as Gary sings and plays the song 'Delilah' to the regulars. After playing the number, Gary speaks to a new customer, Owen Jones – a salesman from Wales who sells brushes. Phoebe then forces Gary to go and speak to Reg who is not in a good mood as he suspects that the Welshman in question has become a little too close to his wife, Minnie. He confirms he's also upset because there's been a report of counterfeit currency in the area. This worries Gary, believing that he's been rumbled. When it comes to paying for his round, he tells Phoebe to put it on the slate, afraid that the white fivers he's carrying might also be slush.

Gary goes to see Ron in a desperate panic, and they argue, and a fight ensues when he accuses Ron of being the printing equivalent of Mr Bean. He suspects him of 'cocking up' on purpose because he's jealous of his love life. Ron spots one of the low-quality banknotes that Gary got in his change, which he sees as proof that there's a spy at work. To back up his claim, Ron explains that in 1943 the Germans launched Operation Bernhard and flooded the country with false currency that almost wrecked the economy; until this point, their attempts were 'dead crude'. They were only used to pay off Nazi agents who were too greedy to know the difference. Gary apologises and says that he will be there for him with whatever problems he's having with Stella. They agree to go for a drink and chat that evening, but Ron warns Gary that he should call for him given Stella's current highly jaundiced view of the male population!

Ron duly turns up to meet Gary, but the time traveller is still not back from 1942. Yvonne suggests to Ron that he talk to Stella about their marital problems, including her request for the occasional bout of sex outside the bedroom. However, Ron is not keen. When Gary finally arrives, he is all pumped up and, while Yvonne makes him a cup of decaffeinated coffee, Ron complains that he's late. Insensitively, Gary replies that it's not as though they're married, and tells him he's caught the spy. Ron reminds him that their planned conversation was important to him, and that it's a real pain when your mates aren't there for you. Upset, Ron leaves despite Gary's attempts to get him to stay.

Yvonne then tells Gary that she has to write a story for her course to test her 'creative abilities and resourcefulness'. This gives Gary an opportunity to tell her how he caught the spy, while pretending it's a story he heard at a memorabilia fair. The reality of what happened in 1942 is then shown in flashback.

Gary is seen setting a trap at Maison Bloss. He and Phoebe wait around hoping for a result while Reg takes the idea of 'going undercover' literally by hiding under a ladies' hat. Eventually, Mrs Bloss is handed a fake note. Not thinking straight, Reg accuses a vicar's wife of the crime, but it turns out that it was Phoebe who tried to buy a scarf with a note that Reg gave to her earlier that day. This confuses Reg who is worried that this makes him a spy! When Gary asks where Reg got the money from, he tells him that it was given to him by Minnie, who had been handed it by Owen – not that Reg wanted to ask why!

Gary, Phoebe and Reg then make their way to Owen's flat and break in using one of Gary's Visa cards. (Gary explains that Visa stands for Very Important Security Article!) The room is in a state and it's clear Owen has left in a hurry. Phoebe finds more false notes and some photos of the anti-aircraft batteries, with their exact locations written on the back. It turns out that Reg is in front of one of the photos. He explains he was trying to keep an eye on Owen and his Minnie. Reg finds a notebook, and using a pencil Gary reveals a secret message that says: Vic. 16.55. Gary deduces that Owen has gone to catch a train from Victoria Station at 16.55. Gary, Phoebe and Reg then leave in the direction of the station.

On the train, which is packed with servicemen and women as well as other passengers, Gary comes across a guard who is singing 'Delilah', which proves that he has met Owen. He tells him that Owen claimed he was feeling queasy and gave him five pounds to let him sit in his guard's van. Gary tells the guard to go and get Constable Deadman and not to spend the note as it's fake.

When Gary enters the guard's van, Owen panics and pulls a gun on him. Owen then reveals that he's spying for the Nazis for money. When Gary asks why he became a spy, he explains that poverty and unemployment were all he came home to after the First World War – not to mention having lost his private parts. Owen then tells Gary to move across to the other side of the carriage and tie his legs up with rope. At that moment, Reg knocks on the door. Gary tells him not to come in and to keep away from the door, but Reg does the opposite and knocks Owen out cold in the process. Gary congratulates Reg for catching a Nazi spy. He then tells Reg that nothing happened between Owen and Minnie and whispers why. Reg states that he doesn't think losing your penis is any excuse for betraying your country, leaving Phoebe somewhat speechless.

Back at their Cricklewood home, Yvonne is amazed at Gary's ability for storytelling and how he brought the characters to life. She then goes to make a start on writing up the story for her course. Ron arrives; Gary apologises, and Ron says he overreacted. They agree to go to the Anglers pub for a drink and a chat. After telling Yvonne, who's busy writing the story down, she comes out into the hall to ask what the name of the pub was that Phoebe worked in. Not realising the story Gary has told Yvonne, Ron is concerned that the time traveller has revealed everything behind his double life.

Later, over a glass of wine with Gary, Yvonne reveals she got the impression from the way he talked that something about Phoebe turned him on. She asks if he would like her to pretend to be Phoebe the next time they make love. But he says no. She dares him and says he can pretend to be Reg!

Looking back on the process of coming up with the ideas for this episode, John Phelps reveals that he and his writing partner Gary Lawson decided they wanted Gary to do something 'spy-like' and 'have a bit of an adventure'.

It wasn't just the performances that impressed John when they reached the studio with this episode. 'I was astonished at the set for Maison Bloss hat shop,' he said. 'I couldn't believe how good it was, considering it was only used for a couple of episodes.'

Equally impressive were the railway carriage sets. 'The carriage scenes were taped on the morning of the recording day, as they would have been too problematic in front of an audience,' explained John. 'But the final showdown scene in the guard's van was recorded in front of the audience, as we wanted to get the maximum reaction.

'We remember that Reg's line, "Losing your penis is no excuse for betraying your country" was put onto a badge and handed out at the series wrap party – except that the printer got it wrong and printed, "Losing your pen is no excuse for betraying your country." They all went into the bin!'

In addition to the return of Yvonne D'Alpra as hat-shop owner and busybody Mrs Bloss, this episode featured other guest performers. First, Ken Jones was cast as the duplicitous Welsh salesman and spy, Owen Jones. John Phelps reveals that he and Gary Lawson approved of his casting. 'We liked Ken Jones a lot and always thought he was funny,' said John. 'But casting was always left to Paddy, Susie and John Bartlett – they never let us down.'

An accomplished character actor, Ken's theatre roles included George Bland in the Donald Howarth play *A Lily in Little India*, with Ian McKellen and Jill Bennett, at Hampstead Theatre, Hampstead, and the St Martin's Theatre, London; and Syd in the Willy Russell comedy *Breezeblock Park*, which also starred Wendy Craig and Julie Walters, at the Mermaid Theatre, London. Ken also attracted further critical acclaim for playing Jim Bloggs in Raymond Briggs' dramatic comedy *When the Wind Blows*, co-starring Patricia Routledge, at the Little Theatre, Bristol, and the Whitehall Theatre, London. Best known for playing 'Horrible' Ives in the sitcom *Porridge*, his other television credits included Henderson in the crime drama *Softly, Softly*, and Jotham in the award-winning drama *Jesus of Nazareth*. Ken's film parts, meanwhile, included Mr Dicks in Alan Parker's comedy drama *Melody*, a dock guard in the crime thriller *Murder by Decree* and 'Horrible' Ives in the big-screen version of the sitcom *Porridge*. Ken died on 13 February 2014, aged eighty-three.

Also making a guest appearance in this episode was Charmaine Parsons as the snotty rail passenger who berates Gary when he complains at the conditions on the railways, forgetting that back in the war the railway and its workers were much admired. Charmaine's theatre credits include Margaret in the William Shakespeare play *Much Ado About Nothing*, Camilla in Ray Cooney and Royce Ryton's comedy *Her Royal Highness…?* at the Palace Theatre, London, and on tour, and Lydia in the Arthur Miller drama *All My Sons* at the Royal Theatre, Northampton. On television, her roles have included Stephanie in the sitcom *Don't Wait Up*, Ellie in the last series of the action drama *Bergerac*, with John Nettles in the title role, and a shop assistant in the comedy drama, *The Hello Girls*.

Finally, John Bardon played the guard on the train. In an illustrious career, John's theatre roles included Private Walker in Perry and Croft's *Dad's Army* stage show on tour and at the Shaftesbury Theatre, London, and Max Miller in his successful one-man show *Here's a Funny Thing* at the Edinburgh Fringe and the Fortune Theatre, London, which was also televised. The veteran actor also won a Laurence Olivier Award for Best Actor in a Musical for his performance as Max ('Hands') O'Hagan in Bella and Sam Spewack and Cole Porter's musical *Kiss Me, Kate* at the Old Vic, London, and the Savoy Theatre, London. Best remembered for playing Jim Branning in the soap opera *EastEnders*, his other television credits included Harold Forster in the sitcom *Dad's Army* and Doc Boyd in the action drama *The Sweeney*. Meanwhile, John's film work included playing a bookmaker in the family comedy *One of Our Dinosaurs is Missing*, the ticket collector in the comedy *Clockwise* and Mr Moorhouse in the comedy drama *East is East*. John died on 12 September 2014, aged seventy-five.

At the start of 'Change Partners', the fifth episode of series three, Ron, during one of his many visits to Blitz and Pieces, admits that there's not much wrong with Gary's life. The time traveller agrees. Ron, meanwhile, is drinking from a hip flask at 9.30am! He points out that personal tragedy has no timetable. Ron's marriage is still a war zone. In fact, he's expecting Kate Adie any day now. He comments that he's so desperate he's even thinking of asking Gary for advice. Gary considers himself an expert due to keeping two women happy, which is why he is holding a mug with 'World's Greatest Lover' printed on the side. Arrogant, maybe, but he refuses to apologise. He is rather pleased with himself.

Goodnight Sweetheart: A Guide to the Classic Sitcom

After all, he has the gift of time travel, a lucrative business and the love of two terrific women. Unable to disagree, Ron asks for Gary's advice. He tells him to stay out all night and get Stella guessing as to his whereabouts. He believes this will make her realise how much she misses Ron.

However, Gary's perfect world soon begins to crumble when he returns to the Royal Oak. There, he finds Phoebe has been spending the evening chatting to Violet Bigby, who goes out with a tank driver, a submariner, a Canadian sergeant, an ack-ack gunner and an able seaman. Gary starts to get the feeling that all is not well as Phoebe is being a little cold with him. Meanwhile, Reg is in the cellar, building a model for his little boy's birthday. However, Gary advises he abandon his plans to build a scale model of Buckingham Palace and Phoebe suggests he build a fort instead.

After Reg and Violet have gone, Phoebe complains that Gary used to bring her presents and take her out and court her; now he treats her as a convenience and the only reason he bothers to show up here is 'for a bit of the other'. He tries to wriggle his way out of the argument, but it becomes clear that not only was that his intention, but he has brought his own breakfast as well! In order to teach him a lesson, Phoebe tells him the hotel is closed for the evening and she goes to bed leaving Gary standing in the dark.

With no real reason to stay in 1942 for the night, Gary goes back home to present-day Cricklewood and surprises Yvonne who thinks he's a burglar. After she gets over the shock, which caused her to try and defend herself with a can of polish, Gary discovers that she isn't happy with their relationship either. It appears that Yvonne has her own life away from the marriage and goes clubbing with friends from work, something he didn't even know about. To try and get things back on track, Gary proposes they have a party to celebrate 'the new us'. She reluctantly agrees on the condition that he doesn't play any of his records.

The next morning, Gary goes to Nostradamus Printing and hands Ron an invite to the forthcoming party. It's clear that Ron is in a better mood. He predicts an upturn in the state of his marriage after he took Gary's advice, which amazes and worries the time traveller. Unfortunately, this backfires and Stella storms in and asks where Ron has been all night. When Ron asks if she missed him, she tells him she missed him as much as the nation misses smallpox. She ends her tirade by slapping Ron and storming out. As usual, Gary tries to make it all about him and tries to deflect by saying that they're both in the same boat now.

In an attempt to fix things with Phoebe, Gary goes to the Royal Oak to take her out but finds she's gone to the Palais de Danse with Violet 'flirty something' Bigby. On his arrival at the dance hall, Gary discovers Phoebe and Violet with Tom and Harry. Phoebe takes Gary aside and tells him he doesn't have any right to follow her. When Gary asks if Phoebe's 'blowing him out', she tells him they're just two fly boys who want some company before they go on their next mission. Phoebe, Violet and the two men then proceed to dance the palais glide. Not to be left out, Gary dances, or does the best he can, with a woman he meets on the dance floor.

Later, Gary looks on as one of the men, Tom, treats Phoebe and Violet to a made-up story about a dangerous bombing mission. When the two women go off to the ladies', Gary tells the men that he's aware they're two RAF erks, leading aircraftmen, because of the insignia on their uniforms. Tom gets defensive and asks him not to broadcast it. Gary says he's sure their CO would take a dim view if he knew. Tom promises they will leave if he keeps quiet. When Phoebe and Violet return, Gary tells the former that Tom and Harry had to get back to base. However, she realises that he's given them their marching orders.

After Gary and Phoebe dance, they sit and talk. Phoebe tells him she only went out with Tom and Harry to teach him that he's not the only man on God's earth. He tells her he had the evening all planned out, complete with a movie and then supper in a West End hotel. She moans he'd want to follow this up as usual with a few hours under the eiderdown before he has to dash off again. But he tells her he thought after supper they could have taken a taxi and a bottle of champagne to the top of Highgate Hill to watch the dawn come up – even though it's the winter! He admits having been complacent towards the women in his life. When Phoebe picks up on this, he points out he means he had forgotten his aunt's birthday. When the palais glide starts again, Phoebe begs him to join her on the dance floor. However, Gary complains he looks like a dying duck in a storm when he attempts the popular dance!

Gary and Phoebe go back to the Royal Oak where they discover that Reg has completed the fort for little Frank – and it's surprisingly good. Reg gives back the superglue Gary lent him to aid with the build. Phoebe then invites Gary to keep her company for a few hours. He smiles but his attempt to follow her is hampered by the arm of his trench coat being stuck to the bar where Reg has been careless with the superglue!

Back at their home in the present, Gary and Yvonne's fancy-dress party is under way. Yvonne and Stella are impressed with the effort some people have made – apart from a rather inebriated Ron who just looks like he's dressed normally! He explains that he's come as Saddam Hussein, but admits his ensemble has lost some of its mystique since his false moustache fell down the toilet!

Gary enters the lounge dressed as Maid Marian. He chose the costume after mistakenly believing that Yvonne was going to be dressed as Robin Hood when in actual fact she's dressed as Peter Pan!

Goodnight Sweetheart: A Guide to the Classic Sitcom

Stella's boss Ken (who Ron describes as a 'tree hugger') walks over with his 'life partner', Gillian, and Ron introduces them to Gary. Stella, dressed in a witch's costume, returns and takes Gillian away to meet Yvonne.

Gary and Yvonne dance and chat until Ron starts doing a mock strip. Yvonne tells Gary to take him outside before he throws up all over the Axminster. Obediently, he guides Ron into the garden where Ron sees what appears to be Ken kissing Stella. He goes over and punches Ken and then discovers that Stella and Gillian changed costumes because Stella's was too tight! Out of revenge, Stella knees Ron in the groin, causing Gary, still dressed as Maid Marian, to quip with mock disapproval, 'Men!'

When Gary Lawson and John Phelps wrote this episode, it had a different title. Originally they named it 'Don't Get Around Much Anymore', which of course was the title of the first episode of series two. However, the producer, John Bartlett, fortunately noticed this and it was subsequently changed to 'Change Partners' before it was broadcast. It's interesting to note, though, that the original title had not been changed by the time copies of the scripts were being sent out to the cast.

Ron and Stella were, of course, not the only couple having problems with their relationship in this episode. Phoebe deciding to remind Gary that he wasn't God's gift to women was further proof of how much stronger her character was becoming. For once, she was in control and made it clear who was calling the shots when it came to Gary staying over.

This episode arguably holds the record for including the most ever extras for an episode of a UK sitcom! But if you were thinking that the writers, Gary and John, were nervous about including two such highly populated settings as the dance hall and the fancy-dress party, you would be wrong. 'Our attitude is always that it's our job to let our imagination run riot and push for as much as we want (within reason), and the producer's job is either to make it happen or tell us we can't do it,' explained John. 'That's the advice Humphrey Barclay gave us right at the start of our career.'

As mentioned earlier in this chapter, this episode was not made in the order it was broadcast. It was also made in conjunction with episode eight of series three, which was entitled 'There's Something About a Soldier'. This meant that a studio recording without an audience took place for selected scenes in both episodes on Thursday 19 October 1995, and a studio recording *with* an audience for the remaining scenes of both episodes on Thursday 26 October 1995. Due to this schedule, it was decided to cancel the first rehearsal, originally scheduled for Friday 13 October 1995, and go straight into blocking the scenes that were set to be recorded on Thursday 19 October 1995. The rehearsals took place at the BBC Rehearsal Rooms in North Acton, London, between Sunday 15 October 1995 and Wednesday 18 October 1995.

On Wednesday 18 October 1995, a music recording session for the Palais de Danse scenes took place in Studio 2 at Teddington Studios. Then the following day, Thursday 19 October 1995, the schedule in Studio 1 went as follows:

On camera rehearse/record	09.00
Lunch	12.30
On camera rehearse/record	13.30
Supper	19.00
On camera rehearse/record	20.00
Wrap	22.00

During this time the following scenes were taped:

1.	Ron's office	Ep.5 / Sc.6
2.	Sparrows' bedroom	Ep.8 / Sc.3
3.	Phoebe's bedroom	Ep.8 / Sc.12
4.	Newsagent's	Ep.8 / Sc.2
5.	Sparrows' lounge Lunch	Ep.8 / Sc.13
6.	Palais de Dance Hall	Ep.5 / Sc.8, 9, 10
7.	Sparrows' lounge Supper	Ep.8 / Sc.6; Ep.5 / Sc.2, 5
8.	Sparrows' lounge/garden	Ep.5 / Sc.12, 13, 14

All the scenes in the dance hall were choreographed by Mandy Demetriou, who had, of course, worked on *Goodnight Sweetheart* back in series one. 'We had no rehearsal time before the recording day with the dancers,' she said. 'The dancers were all brilliant professionals and as such were used to picking up steps really quickly. If they had not been so accomplished, we would not have been able to do it in the time. We did the palais glide, social foxtrot and waltz. I did have time with the principals who were to do a simple social foxtrot. The dancers were fitted for costumes prior to the recording and the men had to agree to period haircuts. I had to make that clear to them when I engaged them. I remember making so many phone calls to dancers I knew asking the men if they would agree to have their hair cut if necessary. It was great fun researching the palais glide, and we were able to get some fabulous wartime footage of the palais glide as reference.

'Robin Nash and I quickly realised that we didn't have enough dancers to fill the huge space, so we got the camera to keep quite a tight angle and as the dancers went past the camera and out of shot they ran around and danced back into shot thus giving the impression of a crowded wartime dance hall. It was a very relaxed and enjoyable day with the dancers bringing such energy and verve to the shooting. The palais glide was a huge success and even the crew were dancing it along with us out of shot. I was delighted and relieved that it had all gone so well and remember Robin, who was a good dancer himself, whisking me into a bit of a celebration waltz around after filming. My memory was of a wonderfully enjoyable, energetic day and a great atmosphere on set.

'Robin was such a great character, a real true gentleman, and I feel very fortunate to have worked with him; and when I saw the finished version I was thrilled as you could not tell there was more space than dancers to fill it!'

This episode saw Regina Freedman join the cast to play Violet Bigby for the first of three episodes over three series. 'I had first worked with Robin Nash and John Bartlett in 1995 on an ITV sitcom written by Carla Lane called *Searching*,' said Regina. 'They then invited me to read for the part of Violet. I was delighted as *Goodnight Sweetheart* was such a great success. She was a funny, flirtatious character and I was very pleased to be offered the role! The writing was so perfect that it was immediately clear who Violet was and how she should be played.

'I remember the rehearsals were so enjoyable and the cast were welcoming and friendly. Having worked with Robin and John before, I felt very relaxed and "at home". The recordings were great fun. It's always nerve-wracking recording in front of a live audience, but the characters were so loved that the atmosphere was wonderful. I enjoyed playing the part of Violet and would have loved it if she had appeared more. It would have been very interesting to see how the character would have developed. I'm sure she would have got up to lots more mischief!'

Although Nicholas was not very keen on having to dance again in this episode, Regina was more enthusiastic. 'Learning to dance was great fun,' she said. 'I was quite nervous as I didn't want to trip my partner up when we were recording! There were quite a few extras in the scene, and I remember it being rather magical.'

During her acting career, Regina's theatre credits included playing Flora in Jon Pope's *The Turn of the Screw*, adapted from a book by Henry James, at the Crown Theatre, Edinburgh, Violet in the Tennessee Williams drama *Sweet Bird of Youth* at the National Theatre, London, and Helen in the Neil Simon comedy *Laughter on the 23rd Floor* at the Queen's Theatre, London, and on tour. Her other television credits included Inspector Murray in the comedy drama *Love Hurts*, Theresa in the comedy drama *Marion and Geoff*, which starred Rob Brydon, and Marion Taylor in the drama series *Primeval*.

Joining the cast for just this episode was the actor Bryan Lawrence. His audition for the role of Tom took place on Tuesday 26 September 1995 at 91 Regent Street in London with Robin Nash and the casting directors, Paddy Stern and Susie Parriss. 'I remember at my audition sitting across the desk from the director, Robin, with his big booming voice and spotted bow tie,' said Bryan. 'I was in awe of him because I knew he had directed programmes like *Top of the Pops* and was a legend in light entertainment.'

According to his diary, Bryan found out he had been cast in the role on Friday 29 September 1995. Just a few weeks later, he found himself rehearsing his scenes at the BBC Rehearsal Rooms at North Acton. 'I loved rehearsing there,' said Bryan. 'You could go for a wander and have a peek into other rooms to see who else was rehearsing in the building.

'Nicholas and Dervla were great, and Michelle was lovely to me. In fact, when I lost my wallet on one of the rehearsal days, she lent me twenty pounds to get home.'

Reflecting on his recording day in Studio 1, Bryan said, 'I remember thinking how amazing the huge set was and how much money they had spent on all the extras and the musicians considering it was for a sitcom.'

'I played Tom, and my friend Harry was played by Darren Bancroft. The characters were two RAF erks (members of the ground crew) who were a bit drunk and lairy. They were desperately trying to impress Phoebe and her friend Violet. As an actor, you always want to do more, and I would have loved to have appeared in more episodes.'

Bryan's other television work includes playing Luke in the sitcom *2point4 Children*, David Mason in the crime drama *Thief Takers*, Mike in the soap opera *Hollyoaks* and Bob Mellish in the comedy drama *Stonehouse*. He also has over four hundred television commercial credits to his name. In addition, Bryan's film roles include Perry in the drama *AKA*, Bryan Clayton in the sports drama *Khido Khundi*, Matt in the short drama *Shielding Sheila* and Mr Rand in the drama *Shrimati Umbrella*.

Playing the role of Harry was extra important to Darren Bancroft because it was one of his first television appearances. 'I remember being extremely nervous and a bit starstruck towards the cast,' he admitted. 'I needn't have been nervous because everyone was so nice. We had plenty of laughs, especially rehearsing the dance. From what I recall, Robin didn't offer too much direction on the character. He allowed me and Bryan to just get on with it and create what you saw on screen. As a young inexperienced actor just starting out, eager to learn, I would arrive early for my "call" and spend as much time as possible watching Nicholas, Dervla, Michelle, Victor, Regina and Nimmy rehearse. I still do that now, whenever the opportunity arises, on a set. I've learnt much watching my peers and you never stop learning.

'I can remember having lunch with Nicholas during rehearsals. I was a massive fan of *Only Fools and Horses* and he was more than happy to talk about the series. He told me how excited he used to get when he received the scripts in the post.

'I vividly recollect having my hair cut (I miss those days!) in a 1940s style at Teddington Studios. It was my first experience of working in a studio in front of a number of cameras. It was quite unnerving to begin with, but I soon relaxed into it. The director Robin and the producer John were up in the gantry and I remember recording the dance required a number of takes.'

In his career to date, Darren's theatre credits have included PC Williams in a rehearsed reading of the Mufaro Makubika drama *Shebeen* at the Nottingham Playhouse, Jim in the Paul Allen play *Brassed Off*, based on Mark Herman's film screenplay, at Derby Theatre, and Carlson in a tour of the John Steinbeck drama *Of Mice and Men*. Additionally, his other television roles have included Rob Doolan in the sitcom *The Job Lot*, DC Holden in the soap opera *Coronation Street* and Stu in the comedy drama *The Larkins*. Meanwhile, Darren's film work includes playing a corporal in the drama *Titanic Town*, Detective Constable Worth in the thriller *Endgame* and Gareth in the drama *Wounded*.

Angus Kennedy, who was cast as Stella's boss, Ken, was called for a couple of days' rehearsal prior to recording the party sequences. 'I had made an episode of *Birds of a Feather* in the same studio a couple of years before,' he recalled. 'On that occasion, my scenes were recorded in front of a studio audience, but this time they were pre-recorded without an audience. I played Harriet Thorpe's life partner, Ken, and we got on well. The scene where we had to be dressed as Druids was great fun to do.

'There was a bit of hanging around and I do remember having long chats with Nicholas and Nimmy in the studio canteen while waiting to record the fancy-dress party scenes. When it was our turn, both Harriet and I were absolutely sweltering under the studio lights in our heavy costumes!

'In the garden scene, I had to have a bit of a cuddle with Gillian (Harriet), and Ron (Victor) thought I was kissing his wife, Stella (Nimmy). Harriet was kind and jolly when we did it. We had spent a bit of time with a fight director in the rehearsal room as Vic had to pretend to punch me. If I remember rightly, the punch went off without a hitch and I think we may have even done it in one take.

'The atmosphere was very relaxed, and I didn't feel any pressure doing the episode. I think it had got into a steady routine of rehearsing and studio week by week by the time I arrived.

'I think there were a few more lines in the main party scene. Nicholas and I had had a bit more banter about the football references and we had a moment of embarrassed silence after Harriet got dragged away by Michelle. But when the episode was transmitted, I noticed a couple of those lines had been edited out.

'I worked with Victor again a couple of years later in the comedy series *Health and Efficiency* at BBC Television Centre.'

Angus has had a prolific and varied life as an actor. On stage, he has played roles including Giles Ralston in a tour of Agatha Christie's classic murder mystery *The Mousetrap*, Hendricks in the John Willard melodrama *The Cat and the Canary* at the Haymarket Theatre, Basingstoke, and Tom in Chaucer's bawdy romp *Canterbury Tales*, adapted by Richard Hope, at the Lawrence Batley Theatre, Huddersfield. For television, Angus's other parts have included Mr Brindley in the historical drama *North and South*, Max Baxter in the children's series *Genie in the House* and the tavern landlord in the fantasy drama *The Sandman*. Also, his film credits include Jeffrey in the romantic war drama *Allied*, Chief Inspector Mort in crime drama *Intrigo: Death of an Author* and Pete in the horror *Alive*.

Harriet Thorpe, who played Gillian in this episode, believes the cast of *Goodnight Sweetheart* were like a family. 'It was the same with the casts of *The Brittas Empire* and *Absolutely Fabulous*, which I also appeared in,' she said. 'The rehearsals were enjoyable, but for me rehearsals are always fun because they are the best way to get to meet and know everybody.

'The high production values that *Goodnight Sweetheart* had were a luxury of the time. You always imagine how a programme will look, but it's always a thrill to see everything come to life on the day of the recording.

'I think the reason why the series is still so popular is because the premise of someone going back into the past and finding love in an unexpected way is magical and compelling.'

A talented and prolific actress, Harriet's theatre roles have so far included Brigitte Aigreville in the Peter Tilbury comedy *Under the Doctor* at the Churchill Theatre, Bromley and the Comedy Theatre, London, Tanya in the Benny Andersson and Björn Ulvaeus musical *Mamma Mia!* at the Prince of Wales Theatre, London, and Her Ladyship in the Ronald Harwood play *The Dresser* at the Duke of York's Theatre, London. On television, she has played various characters in the sketch series *French and Saunders*, while her other credits have included Cat Rogers in the comedy *Mirrorball*, which also starred Jennifer Saunders, Joanna Lumley and Julia Sawalha, and Flora Marshall in the drama *The Madame Blanc Mysteries*. Harriet has also played characters on film including Brenda Mooney in the comedy *Calendar Girls*, a customer in Alan Bennett's *The Lady in the Van* and Fleur in the Jennifer Saunders comedy, *Absolutely Fabulous: The Movie*.

The following day, Friday 20 October 1995, rehearsals began at the BBC Rehearsal Rooms in North Acton to read through and block the remaining scenes for episodes five and eight, which were to be recorded on Thursday 26 October 1995. On the studio audience recording day, the audience were also shown the scenes that had been recorded the previous week. The scenes recorded on the day were as follows:

Episode 5:

The Royal Oak	Sc.1
Gary's shop	Sc.3
The Royal Oak	Sc.4
The Royal Oak	Sc.7
The Royal Oak	Sc.11

Episode 8:

Gary's shop	Sc.1
Gary's shop	Sc.4
The Royal Oak	Sc.5
Gary's shop	Sc.7
The Royal Oak	Sc.9
Phoebe's flat	Sc.10
The Royal Oak	Sc.11

*

A relaxing evening at home is ruined for Gary and Yvonne when Ron arrives with a suitcase during 'Goodnight Children Everywhere', the sixth episode of series three. Stella has thrown Ron out due to her getting the sack for him hitting her boss. Given all the little white lies, not to mention the whopping great big ones, Gary has no choice but to offer Ron a roof over his head for a day or two – much to Yvonne's disapproval.

Sensing that Yvonne is not overly happy about his presence in their marital abode, Ron goes on a charm offensive and presents her with a bunch of flowers – from the vase in the living room. Despite her reluctance, Yvonne tells Ron he's welcome. After she leaves for work, Ron criticises Gary for seemingly having it all in the present and yet still wanting to sneak off back to 1942 to get his leg over to the sound of George Formby. It is starting to become clear that Ron is in the early stages of developing a crush on Yvonne.

Meanwhile, on arriving back in 1942 through the time portal, Gary slips and falls on his back in the ice and snow. He then makes for the Royal Oak and discovers Phoebe's cousin Peter being bullied by a group of local children.

Arriving at the Royal Oak, Gary is given a warm welcome by Phoebe's other cousin, Sally. After sending the children upstairs, Phoebe tells Gary she had to take the children in as the parents are dead and she's the only family they've got. When Reg senses a tear, he panics because he's not too handy with tearful situations at present – something which Minnie has been taking full advantage of. Phoebe tells Gary that having the children there will be practice for when they have their own! Gary has a feeling that things are going to change and that the chances of him and Phoebe being able to be alone will become less and less. His point is proved when Sally calls down and asks Gary to play the piano.

Having had no success so far, Reg is again struggling to fix one of the beer pumps in the public bar of the Royal Oak and seems to be doing more damage than good. He promises to return in the morning to have another go. Meanwhile in the snug, Gary is helping Peter and Sally to catch up with their lessons. He is shocked to discover they haven't been to school for over a year. Reg comments that Gary appears to have started a school all of his own. Phoebe, Reg and Mrs Cooper, who has dropped in to ask Reg to do a plumbing job for her, suggest that he start teaching in the snug for children in the area out of hours, including her little Henry. Gary reluctantly agrees.

After returning home, Gary tells Yvonne he has tried to persuade Ron to move in with his brother in Dunstable, which he doesn't feel Ron deserves. He asks her to speak to Stella to see if she will take him back. Yvonne tells him that she rang her this afternoon only to find out she was in bed. When Gary asks if she's picked something up, she explain that she has – Ron's paper supplier, Frank. This despite the fact that she's only just finished an affair with her boss. Apparently there's been at least three other affairs in the last month. All this talk of cheating makes Gary uneasy and a little guilty and he suggests that Ron should move out the next day and stay with his brother in Dunstable after all. However, Yvonne refuses to throw poor Ron out and instead says he can stay.

Ron is suddenly feeling guilty about lying to Yvonne about Gary's double life. He asks Gary not to make him lie to Yvonne any more as he considers her a friend. Gary gets angry and reminds him that he's put a roof over his head and allowed him to ram-raid the fridge-freezer. The argument soon has to end, however, as Gary has to go back to wartime London to teach a lesson to the children.

Gary is happily teaching the children their times tables when Reg (who has put his uniform on specially for his quest) and Mrs Cooper enter the pub. Mrs Cooper has made a complaint about what Gary is teaching the children. For instance, he's told them that in years to come we'll all be driving German cars and listening to Japanese wireless sets. When Gary starts to teach the children the Bob Dylan song 'The Times They Are a-Changin'', Mrs Cooper removes her son from his lessons.

Later, Phoebe tells Gary that she thinks she's being a lousy mother and she's struggling to cope, not least because she can't entertain Peter and Sally in the same way that he can. Also, they complain that the food in London isn't as good as in the country. She thinks she's dragged them back from the country for all the wrong reasons. Gary devises a plan to resolve the situation and gives it the codename 'Operation Dunkirk'. While sounding impressive, it merely involves him calling in at the local post office.

Back at home, Gary is preparing memorabilia to sell in his shop. Ron asks Yvonne where she thinks all this memorabilia comes from. It's obvious that he's trying to wind Gary up by dropping hints to his wife about his other life. After Yvonne goes to bed, Gary uses a clever analogy to explain that there would be no winners if he tells Yvonne the truth about his misdemeanours back in the past.

It's not long before Mrs French is giving all the latest gossip to Peter and Sally at the Royal Oak. At first Phoebe tells Mrs French her timing is perfect, and she must be a mind reader. However, she reveals she's actually a telegram reader instead. When she asks what telegram, Gary enters and reminds her about 'Operation Dunkirk'. He thought a visit from Mrs French would be a sort of present for the children – although he admits he hoped once she saw them that she'd like to take them back with her as they're no longer happy in London. Mrs French openly admits that she would like to take them back to the country as the place is as quiet as the grave. Realising it would be for the best, Phoebe takes the kids upstairs to pack. Gary then surprises Mrs French with some money for anything they will need in the coming months, together with some clothing coupons.

Reg comes back in and Phoebe says it's drinks all round. When Reg says he could do serious damage to a pint, it becomes clear he already has as the beer-pump handle comes off!

Keeping his double life a secret was always a problem for Gary. But as long as Ron was there to back him up with excuses for his absence and his seemingly odd behaviour, he was safe. However, in this episode, Ron's guilt about lying to Yvonne was obviously starting to concern him. While it could have been down to him discovering he had a conscience after all, it was more likely due to him being in the early stages of developing a crush on Gary's other half. That is to say, his other half in 1996. With Gary realising that Ron was now having trouble keeping his love life back in the war a secret, and that he was using it almost as a hold over him to ensure he could continue to stay, it therefore came as no surprise when Gary lost his temper with the artisan during one scene. However, with Ron able to blow his life in the present apart at any moment, he had no choice but to hold his temper. It's no wonder that the time traveller found the strength to stop himself from telling Ron about Stella's secret rampant behaviour with other men.

This episode saw the return of Chase Marks and Katie Donnison as orphans Peter and Sally, respectively. Meanwhile, making her one and only appearance in the series was Kim Clifford as the outspoken local resident Mrs Cooper who had an issue with the lessons her son, Henry, and some of the local children were being taught by Gary in the Royal Oak. Best known for having played Sandra Hallam in the firefighter drama *London's Burning*, Kim's other television credits included Medusa in the *Grange Hill* drama spin-off *Tucker's Luck* and Mandy in the sitcom *Colin's Sandwich*, which starred Mel Smith and Louisa Rix. Her film roles included Barbara Evans in the children's adventure *The Copter Kids*, Sybil's maid in Colin Welland's biographical drama *Chariots of Fire* and Dingy in the Jack Rosenthal comedy, *The Chain*. Kim died in 2019, aged fifty-eight.

Having made a successful appearance in series two, it was inevitable that Jeannie Crowther would be asked to appear as Mrs French again in series three. It wasn't just Jeannie who was pleased that she was back on set, as the actress recalled. 'Nick is very shy, but he gave me a big hug when he first saw me at rehearsals for this episode,' she said.

What most surprised Jeannie, however, on her return to the sitcom was that the original script she had been sent was different to what was finally recorded. 'I was sent a second draft of the script for this episode on 1 September 1995,' she said. 'It had been radically altered. Originally, there was to be a conspiracy between Gary and Mrs French and she would have known that the white fivers and clothing coupons he gave her were fake. However, there must have been a meeting in which it was decided to change this so that Gary remained looking a hero and Mrs French the innocent.'

According to Jeannie's diary, 'Goodnight Children Everywhere' was taped on Thursday 14 September 1995 at Teddington Studios. 'I was picked up at 11.00am and called for 12.00pm,' said the actress. 'I got on the floor to rehearse just after lunch. There was a dress run at 4.00pm and it overran, and I got a chance to do my scene in the Royal Oak quickly at 6.15pm. We only had about an hour's break for dinner before the audience came in for that evening's recording.

'As my dress rehearsal was a bit rushed, I had a nerve-wracking wait for my scene that evening. After the recording, I remember having a very nice chat with Nick and Kim, who played Mrs Cooper, in the bar.'

At the start of 'Turned Out Nice Again', the seventh episode of series three, Ron attempts to prove he's a 'new man', by saying he will be out of Gary and Yvonne's space that weekend as he's enrolled in a manhood workshop! Gary later points out to Yvonne that Ron is merely trying to raise his chances of getting his leg over. He begs Yvonne to ring Stella and persuade her to take him back. She refuses, saying she sees it from Ron's side now too, and anyway she hasn't spoken to Stella since her sudden sexual liberation.

After time-travelling back to 1942, Gary realises he's forgotten to bring the chocolate for Royal Oak regular Lil's birthday. Phoebe insists that he sing Lil a song instead. As she's sixty-three, Gary decides to sing her the Beatles song 'When I'm Sixty Four' as it's close enough. He finishes playing just as Sidney Wix enters the bar and tells Gary that with a few more choruses that could be perfect for George Formby whom he's presenting at the Hackney Empire on Saturday 14 February 1942. Sidney tells him he could bring George to the pub to meet him the next day. Although Phoebe is thrilled and Reg promises police presence at all times, Gary realises the potential consequences of selling him the song and is somewhat troubled by the prospect.

Back at Blitz and Pieces, Ron announces to Gary that he's cancelled his manhood workshop. He notes the George Formby poster and Gary explains about his meeting the next day. Ron reminds Gary that continuing to claim he wrote 'When I'm Sixty Four' would be deception, copyright theft and fraud. As their discussion reaches its crescendo, a man comes into the shop and asks how much the poster is. Gary isn't sure as you don't see many of them around. The man then explains that their rarity is due to George Formby never actually having played the Hackney Empire.

Later in Cricklewood, Gary points out to Yvonne that Ron's flirting with her is getting a little bit much. When she says that she will call Stella when he's gone, Gary quickly leaves. She calls up Stella who breaks down crying on the other end of the line and Yvonne agrees to talk.

When Gary reluctantly turns up at the Royal Oak for his meeting, Phoebe tells him to behave himself when George and Sidney arrive, reminding him that his career could take a step forward. Presently, Sidney arrives and introduces George Formby, only for a woman – George's wife Beryl – to enter instead and politely shake their hands. George then arrives and greets them with a cheery 'Turned out nice again!' much to the delight of Phoebe and Reg. Beryl hurries George away from the bar and starts laying down the law. Reg tells Gary to play his song loudly on the piano in order to drown her out.

Eventually, Gary and George sing and play together. Beryl agrees that the number is just what George needs for 'the old ones'. Panicking, Gary tells George that he might want to change a few things. George concurs and says he wants to change some of the words. Gary suggests he work on the song and present it again at a later date pointing out that he's not even written the song down. George tells him that it's too late as he's already memorised the song and he never forgets a lyric unless he's had a few. Quick as a flash, Gary suggests they sneak out for a swift half, but George tells him that Beryl wouldn't allow it. Just then a vehicle crashes into George's new Bentley outside the pub. While everyone goes to see the damage, Gary encourages George to follow him out through the side entrance.

In a local wine bar in the present, Yvonne greets Stella as she arrives. She admits that all the stories of sleeping with other partners were made up and she got carried away. However, she does admit that she nearly had an affair with her boss's brother who used to be their area manager; but he got transferred away to another office. She admits she lost track as she is a lousy liar.

Meanwhile, Gary is getting George gradually drunk in a London pub in 1942, watched by some of George's admiring fans. There, he tells Gary how possessive Beryl is.

Also becoming merrier are Yvonne and Stella while they talk about the downsides to men, especially their partners.

Heading back towards the Royal Oak, George is now very much the worse for wear; but, as was his intention, Gary isn't. George admits that he can no longer remember the lyrics to 'When I'm Sixty Four' and treats him to a chorus of 'Chinese Laundry Blues' instead.

Reg and Sidney, who have been out looking for Gary and George, emerge from Duckett's Passage and spot the two men. Seeing the state George is in, Sidney comments that Beryl will kill not only George, but all of them!

Back in the future, Yvonne and Stella are laughing over a glass of wine as Ron arrives back at the Sparrows' Cricklewood home. He's surprised to see Stella not only there, but looking happy. Ron and Stella then literally kiss and make up before heading off to the Star of Bengal, leaving Yvonne asleep on the settee.

Understandably, when George, Gary and Reg arrive back at the Royal Oak, Beryl is not best pleased to see how inebriated George is. She demands Sidney get them a cab so they can leave. But Sidney doesn't want her to be hasty and Phoebe reminds her about the song. Gary apologises for any upset and tells Beryl he would understand if she wanted to leave. Sidney tries to persuade Beryl that they don't have to meet and reminds her that good material is hard to come by.

In a last-ditch bid to destroy the deal, Gary tells Beryl while sitting together at a table in the corner that he's concerned about the bad publicity if it should ever come out about his 'convictions'. Although Reg tries to steady George, he is becoming increasing unruly and jealous of Gary talking to his wife. He goes to hit Gary but misses and hits his hand on another table near the fireplace, damaging his strumming hand in the process. With matters getting more and more out of hand, Phoebe tells Reg to throw them all out – but not before Reg attempts to get an autograph from George, who's nursing his hand. Sidney leaves the pub broken-hearted, realising that the show tomorrow won't take place; while Gary realises that is why George Formby never played the Hackney Empire.

Given his ongoing dislike of George Formby, it was inevitable that Gary was going to come face to face with the popular entertainer sooner or later. However, despite the time traveller's animosity being the invention of writers Gary Lawson and John Phelps, it was Geoff Rowley who penned this episode. It was obvious that if Gary came into contact with Formby, then sooner or later the idea of him writing a song for the film star would be raised. Therefore, realising that selling him an established song could change the course of history, Gary had no choice but to scupper the deal. So sadly, as the storyline in this episode proved, George never did get to release 'When I'm Sixty Four' – or any other Beatles song for that matter! This was a disappointment for Ron who, in a light-hearted way, asked Gary in this episode whether he could persuade George to perform 'Strawberry Fields Forever'!

The location scenes for 'Turned out Nice Again' were filmed between Monday 14 August 1995 and Wednesday 16 August 1995 during one of the hottest weeks of the year. 'My abiding memory of filming on location was of when it was hot,' said Nicholas. 'I tended to be wearing a 1940s suit, trench coat, hat, brogues and carrying a leather case. I was usually sweating cobs by 11.00am. I felt like I was suffering from heat exhaustion!'

Producer John Bartlett remembered only too well how the hot weather affected the location unit. 'The camera crew were all wearing shorts, while the actors, actresses and background artists, including my daughter, Lucy Bartlett, were all in big overcoats,' he said. 'I thought, if this doesn't put her off acting, nothing will!'

This episode was rehearsed in a hall within Cavalry House, Duke of York's HQ, just off the King's Road in London. The read-through and blocking took place on Friday 15 September 1995 while the remaining rehearsals took place between Sunday 17 September 1995 and Wednesday 20 September 1995. Finally, the studio audience recording took place in Studio 1 at Teddington Studios on Thursday 21 September 1995.

This episode saw the return of Ronnie Stevens as the impresario Sidney Wix. This would sadly turn out to be Ronnie's last appearance in the sitcom.

It was Polly Hemingway who was cast as Beryl, the wife of George Formby. The actress has pleasant memories of her brief time on the series. 'Working on the episode was an extremely enjoyable experience with lots of fun and laughter as well as a serious approach to the work in hand,' said Polly. 'I loved playing Beryl. She was such a strong, overbearing, domineering character and I particularly remember the attention to detail with regards to the costume and make-up. Beryl wore a superbly elegant and expensive outfit, with beautifully coiffed hair, which juxtaposed against the rather shabby appearance of poor henpecked George!'

Polly's theatre credits have included Lady Macbeth in the William Shakespeare tragedy *Macbeth* at the Riverside Studios, Hammersmith, London, Clara Soppitt in the J. B. Priestley comedy *When We Were Married* at the West Yorkshire Playhouse, Leeds, and the Liverpool Playhouse, Liverpool, and the grandmother in the D. H. Lawrence play *The Widowing of Mrs Holroyd*. Her other television roles, meanwhile, have included Gracie Fields in the drama *Pride of Our Alley*, Nelly in the costume drama *Wuthering Heights* and Gertrude in the crime drama *Wallander*. In addition, Polly's film parts have included playing the casting director in the comedy drama *ChickLit*.

Also appearing in this episode was Phil Nice as George Formby. 'I was told by the director that I did not have to do a spot-on impression, more of an interpretation,' he said. 'I looked at tapes and listened to recordings of Formby's to help with my performance. I did wonder why they cast me as I was a little on the plump side compared to George when he was young!

'I remember having to go for a fitting for the large prosthetic teeth I wore for playing George. I kept them after the recording, and I have since worn them for live comedy performances, to play a joke on friends and more recently when I hosted an online quiz.'

Phil also has memories of the hot days on which they filmed the location scenes for this episode. 'It was ironic,' he said. 'They had fake snow on the ground, and I was dressed as George, complete with hat, scarf and coat. It was difficult to look cold when it was incredibly hot!'

The studio recording was far more comfortable for the actor. 'The audience responded well to me and laughed at all the gags,' Phil recalled. 'I sang "When I'm Sixty Four" live and Nick and I mimed playing the music to a backing track. I am never nervous of acting in front of a studio audience as it is something I have always enjoyed.'

Performers are often known for keeping souvenirs of their time on a series and Phil has kept two items from his appearance on the time-travelling sitcom. 'The character of Sidney Wix was supposedly producing George's show at the Hackney Empire. Gary took a copy of the poster to sell in his shop. It featured a photo of me as George. After the recording was over, I was given this poster and I still have it to this day along with my copy of the script!'

Phil's stage work includes playing Emerson in the children's show *Dogman* at Brighton Festival, the Edinburgh Festival Fringe and the Riverside Studios, Hammersmith, Geoffrey in Richard Harris's tap-dancing play *Stepping Out* at the West Yorkshire Playhouse, Leeds, and the Theatre Royal, Bath, and Reverend Canon Chasuble in the Oscar Wilde comedy *The Importance of Being Earnest* at the Bristol Old Vic. His other television credits have included playing Ted in the comedy *Love Soup*, with Tamsin Greig, Mr Henderson in the sitcom *Outnumbered* and Andrew Darlington in the crime drama *Broadchurch*, which starred David Tennant and Olivia Colman. On film, Phil appeared as a customer in the comedy film *Magicians*, which featured Robert Webb and David Mitchell.

Completing the cast for this episode was Nimmy March who was making her last appearance as Stella, Ron's wife.

In one of his more provocative moods, Ron asks Gary at the start of 'There's Something About a Soldier', the eighth episode of series three, if he ever has any qualms of conscience of going back to World War Two to bulk-buy newspapers to sell for an extortionate profit in his shop, thus arguably making money out of other people's misery at the same time. Gary tells him that what happened in the Second World War wasn't his fault and that he's just the messenger who's forging a link with the past and keeping it alive. At the same time he reminds Ron that he needs to make a profit with the shop because Yvonne is still keen on him getting a job at Simyung Electronics where she, of course, now works.

On his next visit to wartime London, Gary goes straight to see his regular newsagent who has put aside the usual number of papers he needs due to the surrender of Java. The newsagent then asks if he would be interested in a copy of the *Hackney Gazette* as they've been selling like hot cakes due to page three – but not the page three Gary was thinking of! The story in question is about Phoebe's husband, Donald Bamford, escaping from the Italians. Gary picks up a copy and then rushes out of the shop without taking his other papers or change.

Back in the shop, Gary tells Ron that Donald has returned. He explains that while Donald was being transferred from the prisoner-of-war camp to one of the islands, his ship got torpedoed and the Royal Navy picked him up. Despite agreeing with Ron that he's a hero, Gary comments that he wishes he'd stayed in the prisoner-of-war camp – something he admits was a terrible thing to say. He tells Ron he loves Phoebe so much and, now it's all gone, it's over. Ron in his unique way tries to remind Gary that it's only a glitch that Donald has come back and will want to resume married life and that they can get around that with a plan. Unfortunately, Ron hasn't got a plan and awkwardly leaves the shop.

Back at home in their bedroom, Yvonne reminds Gary that she has got him an interview for 9.30am the following morning at Simyung Electronics. Gary confesses to being reluctant to attend the interview at Hatfield as the shop is doing well, despite admitting that it will never be the M&S of the memorabilia world. But Yvonne is keen that they both earn enough money to have a baby. In an attempt to deflect from the seriousness of the situation, Gary asks how much babies cost these days. Never short of an answer, Yvonne reminds Gary the stuff he sells in the shop isn't going to last for ever. After all, it's not as though he can just pop back and buy some more when he needs it! Gary admits that it's best to think of the future and that it's no good living in the past.

Back at the Royal Oak, Donald comes into the bar and there's an evident awkwardness between him and Phoebe as they kiss. Phoebe has been preparing a banner and flags for the bar for his party that night. It soon becomes clear that although they've been apart for a long time, intimacy has not taken place between them. However, Donald tries to put on a show when Reg comes up from the cellar and starts joking with him. After Donald goes for a bath, Phoebe sends Reg to get some more ales from the cellar.

When Gary arrives, Phoebe tells him how confused she is about the situation. Gary tells her it would be all wrong for them to see each other now Donald has come home. With Reg finished in the cellar and boys off the ack-ack arriving, they realise it isn't the best time to say goodbye. Gary agrees to come back that evening instead.

Later that day, Gary is watching an old weepy on television and is almost oblivious as Yvonne rushes in, chats about her day, tells him how to prepare his dinner and leaves again in a rush to go to her gym class. However, realising she's had no reaction, Yvonne comes back to see if Gary's okay. He says he was just sitting there thinking about life, including the future. Yvonne assures him it's going to be a good future for the two of them and begs him not to let her down at this job interview the next morning as she went to a lot of effort to set it up.

Prior to taking one last trip back to 1942, Gary tells Ron he's going to sell the shop and that he plans to burn all the stock. He tells Ron he cannot expect Gary to sit in the shop every day knowing Phoebe is just a hundred yards away.

In the Royal Oak, Donald is telling some of the customers who have come to his party about the times he spent in the camp playing sport. Reg keeps interjecting and trying to point out that those days are behind him.

When Gary arrives, Reg isn't pleased to see him, reminding him that it's Donald's night, not his. Gary tells him he's not stopping and that he's going away again. Reg assures him that it's for the best and says he's been a good friend to him and Phoebe.

Gary goes to say goodbye to Phoebe up in the flat. He tells her he's going to miss her so much. Phoebe says there must be a way around this, and can't she come and see him? But Gary tells her it would be impossible. Phoebe tells him to take care and look after himself, to send a letter or a postcard and to remember the time they had together. She then reveals that she doesn't love Donald and he doesn't love her. If only his auntie, who kept chickens in her back yard where Phoebe went to buy eggs, hadn't introduced them, they would never have got married. His family thought they would make a good match. Realising this was an opportunity to get away from her dad, she warmed more and more to the idea and before either of them knew it they were walking down the aisle together. Had the war not come along, Phoebe admits she would have stayed with Donald and made the best of marital life.

Gary and Phoebe end up kissing and, without them realising, Donald has entered the room and caught them. Donald orders Phoebe to get out of the room. Thinking that Donald is going to beat him up, Gary goes on the defensive. He tells Donald that they love each other and there is nothing he can do about that. Donald begins to pack his bag and says he can't bring himself to fight Gary. He also proceeds to tell Gary about his auntie – the one who kept chickens – and that they didn't have any say in the matter. He then says he had plans before he had to get married. He and his friend Steve were going to go to Australia to work on one of the farms. They could have stayed there for the rest of their lives. It becomes clear from the way he is speaking that Donald and Steve were more than just friends. Steve's mum wrote Donald a letter while he was in the POW camp to tell him that he had been killed during the north Africa campaign. Donald explains that his death took a lot of getting over.

Donald goes on to ask Gary if he loves Phoebe, and he says he does. Donald makes it clear that he would come back and kill him if he's not serious about her. He then says he's going back to his regiment early because he can't get the hang of civvy street and marriage. Gary tells him to take care and they hug just as Phoebe bursts into the room accompanied by Reg. Gary and Reg leave the room and Donald tells Phoebe that Gary will take proper care of her. She is surprised, but Donald opens up and admits their marriage was never going to work out. They have always been more like brother and sister, he says.

Gary is waiting in the bar downstairs when Phoebe arrives to tell him that Donald has gone. She asks if Donald has someone else, but he assures her that if ever he loved a woman, it was her. Gary assures Phoebe that their current situation won't be like this forever. However, he needs to go as he has to be in

Hatfield the following morning at 9.30am for a very important briefing. She asks him to stay with her that night and, with some reservation, he agrees.

The following morning, Gary wakes up in Phoebe's bed at 10.00am and realises he's overslept and missed his interview. Meanwhile in Cricklewood, Yvonne is looking very angry as she stares out at the garden. She walks over to a photo of them together and slams the frame down. She then picks it up and we see the glass is broken.

Although Gary only briefly met Phoebe's husband, Donald Bamford, in the second episode of series one, it was inevitable that their paths would cross again. Although Phoebe had talked about Donald and that their marriage had not been a happy one, it wasn't until the character returned that we knew the full extent and the background as to why they had married and very quickly started to drift apart. As well as revealing more details to the viewers, it also helped the story to move forward.

The newsagent in this episode was played by Arthur White, who is the older brother of David Jason. His other television credits include George Tyldesley in the medical soap opera *Emergency-Ward 10*, Kinano in the science fiction series *Space: 1999* and the collator (police archivist) Ernie Trigg in the crime drama *A Touch of Frost*.

Also joining the cast for this episode was Ralph Ineson who played Donald Bamford. As previously mentioned, Ralph was the second of two actors to take on the role, with Ben Lobb having played him briefly in the first series. Ralph played the role with great sensitivity; and the fact that he opened up to Gary in a way that he couldn't to Phoebe, leading them to have an understanding of their respective situations, was a welcome piece of writing from Paul Makin.

Famous for his deep, rumbling, Yorkshire-accented voice, Ralph's other television roles have included Chris Finch in the sitcom *The Office*, Connor Nutley in the period drama *Peaky Blinders* and Commander Bregman in the bomb disposal thriller *Trigger Point*. Meanwhile, his film credits include playing Mr Kelly in the drama *Is Anybody There?*, Wayne New in the coming-of-age musical comedy drama *Everybody's Talking About Jamie* and Dean Possey in the thriller *Misanthrope*. Ralph has also worked on various commercials, trailers and documentaries as a voice-over artist.

Gary is lying in bed pretending to be ill as Yvonne comes home from work at the beginning of 'Someone to Watch Over Me', the ninth episode of series three. She asks how her poorly soldier is. He lists a variety of flu-like symptoms but she is unconvinced, telling him to get up as he's been there for three days now.

Goodnight Sweetheart: A Guide to the Classic Sitcom

Gary tries to persuade her that he fell ill at Ron's house and had to be put to bed. He wanted to go to the interview, but Ron said he wasn't up to it. When he asks what there is for tea, Yvonne offers a bowl of Scotch broth as the only option; but Gary isn't keen, commenting it looks like something you see on a pavement outside an Indian restaurant. She reminds him it's her gym night – the one night where she can get away from this remake of *The Secret Garden*. She tells him Ron is coming around to look after him and keep him company. When Gary asks if Ron said anything about him being 'ill', Yvonne says no because she was too busy telling him off for getting Gary drunk and making him miss his interview. Although not true, her version of the events at least gets him off the hook once again.

Later, Ron knocks at the door and Gary comes down to answer. Without any proper greeting, Ron pushes in carrying an Indian and Chinese takeaway and demands a plate. He asks what he's supposed to have done to warrant yet another telling off from Yvonne. Gary explains that he was with Phoebe.

Sensing what is about to happen, Gary asks Ron if he's really going to eat an Indian meal and a Chinese meal at the same time and on the same plate? Ron confirms that it can be done! Announcing that he's on a diet, he tells Gary to strangle the git who invented lettuce if he meets them on his time travels and save the world from salad. Ron proceeds to open a can of lager and switches the television on. Gary then subtly moans that he's had to exist on soup and semolina all week due to pretending to be 'ill'. Realising that he's hinting that he wants to share his food, Ron tells him to eat if he wants to eat. He begins to help himself just as the doorbell goes. Ron casually informs him that it's a pizza being delivered and that it will be about a tenner.

After ending his spell of pretend illness, Gary returns to the past and the Royal Oak. There he is told by Reg that Phoebe is in bed with 'a touch of the sniffles'. After a mind-numbing conversation with Reg, Gary goes to see her and, discovering that she is unwell with flu-like symptoms, he tricks her into taking some horrible medicine. Gary then apologies for his recent absence due to a 'cold' and promises he can bring her things to make her better.

The following morning while Yvonne is preparing to leave, Gary walks in with a paper bag that contains bottles of tablets and has to pretend that he's throwing them away. With a slightly guilty air about her, Yvonne tells Gary that she will be late tonight as she will be at the gym again as Terry, her personal trainer, thinks she might benefit from a more 'intensive workout'. It's clear that she wants to say more, but Gary, who has Phoebe on his mind, reminds her she's going to be late for work. When she leaves the house, Gary retrieves the bag from the bin with a view to taking them to Phoebe.

When Gary visits Phoebe again, she's in bed and being attended to by her family physician, Dr Stone. Phoebe introduces Gary as a 'friend of the family'. After the doctor leaves the room, Gary follows him and asks what her illness is. When he says it might be pneumonia, Gary, not thinking, tells him it's treatable and says that she needs penicillin, which he has read up about and knows was invented by 1942. The doctor points out that as far as he's aware it's currently only an experimental drug used by the army to treat certain 'social diseases'. Gary asks if it's possible to prescribe her any, but he reminds him that there's a war on and there's a shortage of everything.

While Yvonne is in the bath, Gary wanders into the bathroom. After turning down her invitation join her, Gary makes an excuse and crosses to a cabinet. He begins to root around inside, looking for penicillin. Yvonne tells him that Terry, her personal trainer, says she has very well-developed calves. Gary's mind, however, is miles away. He finds a bottle of penicillin from when Yvonne had an infection. He enthusiastically reminds her she was really ill but got better. He then finds a pregnancy testing kit, which Yvonne says she's planning to take onto the *Antiques Roadshow*! After Gary refuses to stay in for a romantic night because he's seeing Ron, she says she'll go to the gym, pulls the shower curtain across and goes into a sulk.

Gary is then seen looking troubled while sitting at his counter at Blitz and Pieces. Presently, Ron arrives with a bottle of penicillin, which was originally prescribed for his late red setter, Sheba. Gary points out that the health service back in 1942 was in a bad way. No proper drugs, no hospital beds, and cutbacks. Ron then sarcastically thanks God that we've moved on since then. Gary puts all of the tablets into the bottle Ron brought. In return for his help, Gary gives Ron a large milkshake, double order of French fries and triple quarter pounder. As promised, he asked them to hold the lettuce.

On his arrival back at the Royal Oak, Gary comes face to face with Reg, who's fresh from whitewashing the cellar. He tells Gary that Phoebe has taken a turn for the worse and been taken to the German Hospital in Dalston. To get around the problem of visiting out of hours, Gary persuades Reg to lend him a white coat like his so they can both go to the hospital pretending to be doctors.

Reg is finding the whole cloak-and-dagger world of Gary's hard to handle as they furtively walk around a hospital ward where Phoebe has been admitted. Gary tells Reg that Phoebe needs the pills but that he's not going to be there to give them to her so Reg will need to help. When Nurse Williams, on her first day, arrives to speak to them, Gary introduces himself as Dr Sparrow and Reg as Dr P. C. Deadman. This amuses the nurse who feels his surname will hardly give patients any confidence! Reg then tells her off and almost gives himself away when he tells her 'Mind how you go'. But there's worse to come when Dr Stone arrives. Reg goes and hides and leaves Gary to bluff his way out of the situation. Fortunately, Dr Stone believes the reason Gary displayed a knowledge of penicillin is because he's a doctor. After convincing him that he trained at the Spielberg Institute in Vienna, where, by coincidence, Dr Stone also trained, Gary sneaks off to find Phoebe leaving the doctor standing and reminiscing about his training days to himself. When he finds Phoebe he quickly offers her some pills just as Dr Stone walks in. He proceeds to lecture Gary about how highly unethical it is to treat someone else's patient. Gary tells him he doesn't want her to die. Stone agrees to ensure she takes the tablets.

Gary is rushing his meal so he can go and see Phoebe, but Yvonne tells him she wants to talk. She admits that she's been seeing someone else. Gary gets upsets when he realises she's having an affair and has the cheek to ask, 'Yvonne, how could you?' Yvonne explains she couldn't help it and clarifies that all they've really done is to hold hands in a restaurant. Gary realises that it's with her personal trainer, Terry. She points out that he shows an interest in her, which is more than Gary does. In spite of his romantic interest in her, Yvonne told Terry it was over the previous night; but she wanted to confess and say that she's sorry. She's surprised to find that Gary's more understanding than she might have expected. To calm the situation, Gary agrees to Yvonne's suggestion that they go away for a couple of days.

Back at the hospital, Phoebe is much better thanks to the pills which Dr Stone managed to give her – once he learned how to get the lid off the bottle! However, Phoebe is concerned as to who Sheba is as her name is on the bottle. Gary relaxes and assures her that she is not his 'bit on the side'. As Phoebe settles down to rest, Gary begins to confess he's a time traveller and he has a wife called Yvonne. But when Gary turns around, he sees she has fallen asleep and not heard anything he said.

With Donald and Phoebe now separated for good, Gary must have thought life would become simpler. However, this episode proved otherwise with Phoebe falling ill to the point where Gary could have lost her. Again, this episode gave the writer Paul Makin, and thus Gary, the opportunity for part of the modern day to help resolve a situation in the past; in this case, a ready supply of modern-day penicillin – even if some of the supply had originally been intended for Ron's late dog!

Gary's admission to Phoebe, although she turned out to be asleep, at the end of this episode was yet again proof that the character did have some conscience about his double life. Yet, although part of him was desperate to admit everything, he was more than acutely aware that he would lose Phoebe forever if she thought he had been two-timing her. Then there was the small matter of the time travelling. How in reality could he have made Phoebe comprehend that he was from the future?

This episode featured Jon Glover's first and only in-vision role in *Goodnight Sweetheart*. As mentioned earlier in this chapter, Glover had impersonated Wilfred Pickles in a radio broadcast heard in the Christmas special. 'I got the part of Dr Stone because I was appearing in a lot of radio and television comedies at the time and the casting directors, Susie Parriss and Paddy Stern, were both fans of my work,' he said. 'I wasn't worried about appearing in the sitcom as I was very experienced by this stage and I only had a couple of scenes, so I wasn't under pressure like Nicholas Lyndhurst! By now they were on series three and the brilliant cast were a well-oiled team. Robin Nash, who reminded me of Frank Muir, was always immaculately turned out in his trademark bow tie. He epitomised the urbane English gent and was a really superb director. My only disappointment in appearing in the episode was that, due to room required for the sets, I had to pre-record my scenes earlier on the recording day without an audience.'

Also making an appearance was Helena Calvert as Nurse Williams. 'I do remember feeling terrified at the thought of stepping on set with Nicholas Lyndhurst and Dervla Kirwan,' admitted Helena. 'I was straight out of drama school with little, if any, experience and *Goodnight Sweetheart* was one of my first jobs. Nick, however, was utterly charming and put me at ease immediately with his playful and relaxed approach to acting. It was an absolute privilege to start my career working with such skilled actors.'

Helen's other television credits include Faye Clarke in the soap opera *Emmerdale*, Isobel in the sitcom *Barbara* and Jeannie's mum in the biographical drama *Pistol*.

Nicholas was quick to praise Robin Nash for creating a breeding ground for new talent on *Goodnight Sweetheart*. 'Robin was always keen to give youngsters a try, even if they hadn't acted on television before,' he said. 'There's a lot to take in. You have to dodge the boom mic, try not to shadow anyone, remember precise positioning and make sure you're not in anyone's shot. I used to think, bless their hearts, they don't know what's going on. They needed a friend, so I used to gently guide them when we were on set. Because you're all in it together, there should be no form of hierarchy.'

When Gary arrives at the Royal Oak at the beginning of 'The Yanks Are Coming', the tenth episode of the third series, he finds it busy. Rather disconcertingly, he's suddenly no longer the novelty he once was due to the arrival of the Americans. A little bit of Hollywood has come to Bethnal Green and all the men are six-footers with toothpaste advert smiles. In an attempt to get her attention, Gary gives Phoebe some chocolate. But he's too late: the Yanks have brought in lots of candy.

Billy Joe McCarthy from Braintree, Alabama, US of A, arrives and offers to buy drinks all round. This puts Gary Sparrow of Whitechapel, East 13, United Kingdom's nose further out of joint. He's then introduced to Corporal Zeffirelli who proceeds to ask embarrassing questions about where Gary stayed when he was supposedly in LA. He gives Phoebe a pair of stockings she wanted, like those Betty Grable wears, which does little for Gary's morale. When Zeffirelli offers to get Gary anything he needs, he tells him that this is one Brit that doesn't need anything from Uncle Sam.

Back in the future, Ron asks Gary for parts for a US Army jeep, despite driving a Saab. His brother Nelson has a World War Two jeep chassis stored in his lock-up. He's been meaning to do it up for ages but can't get the parts. Ron's brother sacrificed his youth to bring him up when their mum and dad died. Ron feels this would be the ideal way to repay him for moulding him into the man he is today. Gary responds by asking if he couldn't just get him a pair of socks instead. When Gary refuses to do business with Zeffirelli due to the way he belittled this country, Ron tells Gary that his problem with the Yanks is that they have stolen his thunder. As their discussion descends into childish quarrelling, Yvonne arrives home and begins to make fun of their behaviour. Ron tells her that Gary has some American contacts who can get US war memorabilia but he won't get him any parts for his brother's jeep. In retaliation, Gary informs her that he won't do business with these particular Americans because are arrogant and condescending. Yvonne points out that people go big on Americana and says she could get him some business at work, including from her boss. When Ron mentions that her boss is likely to be 'double chuffed' if Gary could get him a genuine leather jacket as worn by bomber pilots, Yvonne insists that he acquire one for her boss. In an attempt to deflect from the situation, Gary tells Yvonne that that would be 'blatant brown-nosing', but she still insists.

On his next visit to the Royal Oak, Gary decides to approach Zeffirelli regarding the jeep parts. Phoebe warns him to be careful as he's 'a bit of an operator'. But Gary claims to have something up his sleeve when it comes to deals. However, his attempt to sell the American keyrings that bleep when you whistle fails to impress and he ends up having to pay cold hard cash for the leather jackets and the jeep parts.

Reg is rather surprised to see two 'coloured chaps', Niles and James T, come into the bar while he's serving. Gary and Phoebe are quick to try and defuse a potential situation in case they felt he was being deliberately rude. Phoebe explains that they haven't seen black people before. However, they realise this and, after ordering two beers, explain that they're from Chicago. They're in the area because James T's ancestors came from nearby. His great grandad left there for the states in 1821 and he's hoping to still have relatives in the area. In turns out his name was Deadman, or as he was better known, 'Daft Jack Deadman'. Instantly making the connection, Gary calls Reg over to give him a surprise.

Over a pint, Reg and James celebrate discovering that they're cousins. It turns out that the reason Daft Jack ending up emigrating to America was that he went down to the docks and got on the wrong boat having originally intended to go to Woolwich! James T soon proves that he's equally as lacking in intelligence as his cousin Reg by asking why they called Jack 'Daft Jack Deadman'!

While Gary and Niles order another drink at the bar, Billy Joe McCarthy enters and asks why Niles is in the Royal Oak, calling it a 'white man's bar'. Sensing trouble, Phoebe tells Billy Joe to behave himself. She reminds him that everyone is welcome at the pub. He then has the cheek to say he's going to have his beer at the other bar 'where the air is just a little bit cleaner'. Gary is shocked and sarcastically comments that good old southern charm gets you right in the heart.

In Ron's brother's lock-up in Dunstable, Gary apologies to Ron for losing the plot because he was jealous about Phoebe paying attention to the Americans. Just then, Yvonne rushes in and, in her unique way, attempts to apologise and asks if Gary can get any more leather jackets for selling in his shop. Mr Shik showed his jacket to his cousin who 'went potty about it'. He has an Americana shop in Seoul and says he can sell them by the crateload, and has ordered two dozen for starters. This is the reason for her apology. Before this, she dismissed his shop as 'a childish indulgence' and 'a sort of premature mid-life crisis', but now she believes this idea has potential and even suggests he move out of his 'tacky little shop'. Gary realises she's having one of her 'ambition attacks', and asks if he has any say in the matter. But Yvonne reminds him that he will be grateful when they're turning over millions. After Yvonne leaves on the crest of an ambition wave, Gary admits to Ron that thanks to his jacket idea, he's now going to end up spending so much time buying memorabilia he won't have time to see Phoebe. Worse still, he won't be able to travel back in time to see Phoebe at all if Yvonne makes him sell the shop. Ron suggests the radical solution that he tell her no, but Gary reminds him that like something from *Alien*, Yvonne gets stronger the more you go against her!

On his next visit to the Royal Oak, Gary can't resist performing the song 'I Heard it Through the Grapevine' at the piano. Naturally, he claims to have written the song. Impressed, Zeffirelli offers to manage him if he ever comes back to the stage. But Gary admits he's too wise to take him up on his offer.

Ron then announces that Cousin James is going to play a tune at the piano. Thinking he's going to treat the regulars to a rendition of a blues number, Gary is shocked to hear him play 'When I'm Cleaning Windows', the song made famous by George Formby. Gary tells Reg this must be his doing and he replies that he just wanted to teach his cousin a Deadman family favourite! Niles stops James T as soon as Gary informs him that George is, in his opinion, 'Britain's own war crime'.

The bar then falls silent as Billy Joe arrives flanked by two military policemen from the American army. Phoebe is quick to tell Billy Joe that she hopes he's going to behave himself. Billy tells her he's brought the two MPs to keep things 'nice and peaceful'. He points out that the American army is a segregated army and that Captain Lawson feels that to avoid any friction there should be separate recreational arrangements for those who are non-Caucasian. He's spoken with the pastor who's willing to allow them to use the local church hall until around ten o'clock each night. Phoebe tells him that no one uses that hall as it's dirty and cold. Billy Joe makes it clear that he believes it's fine for 'them'. He then announces that the pub will be for whites only from the following day. Phoebe reminds him that this is her pub and she says who she serves, not him or Captain Lawson. Billy Joe says the MPs will remove the black members of the army in the pub by force if she doesn't ban them. This prompts Zeffirelli and two of his friends to leave the pub saying they don't want to be a party to his ruling. Gary then proceeds to give Billy Joe a piece of his mind about his attitude towards people he doesn't rate. This causes Billy Joe to ask him to step outside, which Gary isn't keen on doing. Wishing to avoid trouble, Niles and James T make to leave; but Reg, in police uniform, takes matters into his own hands. He reminds Billy Joe that he has the authority in this area and not the MPs. He then asks Phoebe if she would like anyone to leave the pub. She indicates that she would like Billy Joe and his colleagues to leave. Realising he's beaten, Billy Joe and the MPs leave the pub, but he claims they haven't heard the last of the matter. This prompts Gary and Phoebe to congratulate Reg for his professionalism and bravery. Although Phoebe offers him a drink on the house by way of a thank you, Reg asks for James T to give another rendition of 'When I'm Cleaning Windows' on the piano instead.

Later, just after Reg leaves and the pub is closed, Billy Joe returns to the pub a little worse for wear and swigging from a bottle. He offers Phoebe a bottle of whisky by way of making amends. However, he is far from a changed man. He quickly reveals that Captain Lawson has put all pubs off limits to non-Caucasians in the American army. Phoebe questions his parentage by way of a retort. Gary, however, decides to play it clever and, by way of smoking the pipe of peace, gets Billy Joe drunk enough so he can get away with knocking him out cold.

Another visit to the lock-up in Dunstable finds Ron has completed the restoration of his brother's jeep. Gary is impressed and promises to take his hat off to him the next time he's wearing one! By way of thanking him, Ron tells Gary he's devised a cunning ploy to help rid Yvonne of her plans for world domination. With that he calls for Vanessa to enter the lock-up. The plan is for the slightly dizzy chip-shop worker with a difficult grasp of names – she calls Gary Mr Rook instead of Mr Sparrow – to pretend to be Gary's secretary on his business trips in order to make Yvonne jealous. When Yvonne arrives at the lock-up, Ron starts to pile the plan on thickly. However, Yvonne soon sees through the wind-up and takes the point and agrees to abandon her plans to interfere with Gary's business.

With normality resumed, Ron suggests they all go for a spin in the jeep. Unfortunately, Ron and Gary discover the hard way that bollards placed in front of the doors of the lock-up mean the jeep isn't going to be moved any time soon.

With *The Yanks Are Coming*, Gary Lawson and John Phelps wrote an episode that was pivotal for Gary Sparrow and his time in the Second World War as it featured the arrival of the Americans. 'As soon as we read in *Chronicle of the Second World War* that we'd hit the point the Yanks came in, we knew we had to write "The Yanks Are Coming",' explained John. 'Short of Lennon and McCartney walking into the Royal Oak, it was Gary's worst nightmare. Not only did they steal his thunder, as he wasn't the most exciting guy in Phoebe's life for once, they threatened to expose his whole Hollywood fantasy life as a fraud.'

As mentioned, Gary purchases parts for Ron's brother's US Army jeep from Zeffirelli in this episode. If you thought you might have seen this idea in another series before, you'd be right! 'This gag was inspired from the American war comedy-drama *M*A*S*H* when the character of Radar was sending a jeep home bit by bit,' admitted John.

As well as comedy, Gary and John skilfully dealt with the darker subject of racism while still making it appropriate for the timeslot and genre. 'On the whole, we were satisfied with our finished script,' said John. 'It was tricky, and our main hope was that it wouldn't come across as patronising, but we're not sure we were entirely successful in that regard. When it came to the American characters, we did lots of reading and researching; there was plenty of anecdotal stuff to base them on.'

For Matt Rippy, who played Dino Zeffirelli, appearing in this episode made a lasting impression. 'I can't say I was nervous going into *Goodnight Sweetheart*, but I certainly was excited,' he remarked. 'I hadn't been in England for very long and it was my first ever television gig. I had always wanted to try my hand at acting on screen, but theatre was my background and I hadn't a clue what to do in front of a camera. I started asking around about the series and discovered that everybody, and I mean everybody, loves Nicholas Lyndhurst. We didn't get many British television programmes in the States when I was growing up. We had three: *The Benny Hill Show*, *Monty Python's Flying Circus* and *EastEnders* with subtitles – no joke – so I wasn't familiar with *Only Fools and Horses*. I was about to guest on a hugely popular sitcom starring legend Nicholas Lyndhurst!

'Shooting live in front of a studio audience, of course, means rehearsing and I love rehearsing. It's the phase of the creative process that John Cleese calls the "open mode" where being playful is crucial. Everybody on the series, cast and crew, was very playful and relaxed, which allowed me to also relax and enjoy the process. This was their third season, so the regulars knew the ropes well and they really helped me find my footing. Literally! Having never worked in television before, I kept planting myself directly in between my fellow actors and the camera and so was constantly being gently nudged over by Robin Nash, the director.

'Taping live for a studio audience offers the same excitement as an opening night in the theatre. Will they love it? Will they laugh? Or will they sit sombre and stony-faced? Will I remember my lines? Sure, unlike theatre, if I fluff a line I can always go back. But I wanted to nail everything right the first time to get an honest audience reaction. And the stakes are higher in a live studio taping, because in theatre you can try again tomorrow night – not so here! The performance will be recorded and can never ever be changed. Best not to think about such things! However, in the end, the audience were fantastic, and we had great fun playing for them. There was a great vibe in the room. I haven't felt anything like it since.

'I remember being well impressed on the first day when Nicholas budged up next to me and the other guest actors at lunch. I never really have any predetermined ideas or expectations about actors, but I'm never surprised if someone super famous turns out to be somehow socially impaired – or just plain rude. Nicholas, on the other hand, turned out to be such a nice and easygoing chilled-out dude who loved getting to know the new guys on the series. I remember for some reason we talked a great deal about ghosts. I think Dervla, or maybe Michelle, had recently seen a ghost and so we all took turns sharing stories of sightings. Did we talk about the script or scenes? Not really. I suppose we didn't feel the need as the scenes just seemed to flow naturally in rehearsals.

'It was an amazing feeling walking around the Royal Oak set during the taping. The cast all looked fabulous in their World War Two garb. Everything outside the bar set just faded to black. I couldn't see the audience in the dark and if I just squinted my brain slightly I could totally feel what it was like to actually be in a pub in wartime London.

'I fondly remember the make-up and hair department gathered around my chair to say farewell to my hair. It was long, below my shoulders and curly, prior to shooting. I had this notion that I would become known as the actor with that hair. My new headshot showed me in my long glorious locks. I looked very much akin to Michael Hutchence from INXS. Not at all a US military cut from 1942, so it had to go. Sadly, I've not had long hair since!'

Matt moved to England in 1994. Since then, his theatre credits have included being a member of the company of the Reduced Shakespeare Company's productions of *The Bible: The Complete Word of God (Abridged)* at the Gielgud Theatre, London, and *The Complete Works of William Shakespeare (Abridged)* at the Criterion Theatre, London. He has also played Sidney Bruhl in Ira Levin's comedy thriller *Deathtrap* at the Frinton Summer Theatre. Matt's other roles on television include the 'real' Captain Jack Harkness in the science-fiction series *Torchwood*, John F. Kennedy in the drama-documentary *A Very British Deterrent* and James Wilson in the historical thriller *Glória*. Meanwhile, his characters in films include Dr Logan in the horror *Day of the Dead*, Corporal Rostok in the epic adventure *Rogue One: A Star Wars Story* and Henry Gordon in the family drama *Black Beauty*.

Playing the role of Niles in this episode was Tommie Earl Jenkins but credited as Tee Jaye. An all-round performer, Tommie's stage roles have included Four-Eyed Moe in the Clarke Peters musical *Five Guys Named Moe* at the Albery Theatre, London, Rum Tum Tugger in the Andrew Lloyd Webber musical *CATS* at the New London Theatre, and Michael in the London premiere of the Jonathan Larson musical *Tick, Tick...Boom!* at the Menier Chocolate Factory, London. His other television credits include Donald in the crime drama *How To Get Away with Murder*, Dean Paulson in the soap opera *General Hospital* and Ellison Pevney in the action drama *Pandora*. Tommie's film work, meanwhile, includes playing Chuck Rydell in the romantic comedy *The Callback Queen*, Tom in the comedy drama *Papi Chulo* and Bob in the thriller *Paradise Highway*, with a cast including Juliette Binoche and Frank Grillo.

Niles' friend, James T, was played by Rhashan Stone. Another talented all-rounder, Rhashan's theatre credits include Jesse B. Semple in the Langston Hughes and David Martin musical comedy *Simply Heavenly* at the Young Vic, London, and the Trafalgar Studios, London, and Hero in the Stephen Sondheim, Burt Shevelove and Larry Gelbart musical comedy *A Funny Thing Happened on the Way to the Forum* at the Regent's Park Open Air Theatre, London. He has also played Yakov in the Anton Chekov play *The Seagull*, which starred Ian McKellen, at the West Yorkshire Playhouse, Leeds. Rhashan's other television work includes Bernie in the sitcom *Desmond's*, Jez Bloxby in the detective series *Agatha Raisin* and Benjamin in the drama *Baptiste*; while his film roles include Ash in the comedy *A Deal is a Deal*, Hubert Harrison in the biographical drama *The Marcus Garvey Story* and Sergeant Ed Graham in the thriller *Eve*.

For any actor, playing the role of Billy Joe McCarthy was always going to be a challenge. In the event, that challenge fell to Sam Douglas. 'At the time, one has to admit that, being a liberal white American, it was particularly hard to approach this part, I'm happy to say, but still necessary.

'As a professional actor, one must hold back on any judgement call when approaching a role, be it gay, overweight, non-Caucasian or in direct conflict with one's own political or religious views, but rather approached openly and with full heart, fully and completely. Anything less would not be doing justice to the role or to the author's intent.

'I have an African American actor friend whom I've known over many years and we have worked on many projects together. I have joked with him over the years as he always plays the typical typecast black bellboy or similar roles, and he has returned the comment as I always seem to play the redneck racist sheriff or similar roles. As this has bothered us both in the clichéd casting, I had come to realise that it is good and best to fulfil these type of roles as best I can and be hated as best I can and to draw up this type of character to the public for right and just reasons. This has given me motivation and justification, if you will, to tackle these types of parts in order for the good. The part of Billy Joe McCarthy was one such role.

'Nicholas is amazing. He can hold the moment in a scene and use his straight or deadpan look, knowing full well the next moment was going to be hilarious. He did this with such focus, concentration and involvement on my episode that it was a credit to his acting ability. I have never seen it performed as well before or since, for that matter, in my career.

'Just before Nicholas had to punch me, I was so focused on him that I forgot my line and we had to stop and do another take. I couldn't match his concentration and a few times I had to bite my lip to stop myself from laughing, even when we had rehearsed this scene many times.

'It was such a joy to be on board and to trade acting punches (metaphorically) with him and be involved with this series. The added bonus was this particular episode dealt with significant social and racial issues that needed and wanted airing, so it felt good and right.'

Observant viewers of *Goodnight Sweetheart* may have noticed that the character of Billy Joe McCarthy refers to a Captain Lawson during one of the scenes in the Royal Oak. What they won't realise is that neither Gary Lawson nor John Phelps added this name into the original script as they have a golden rule that they never put either of their own names into their scripts. However, Gary knew Sam Douglas via a mutual friend and so he added the name Lawson as a bit of an in-joke.

A busy actor with many UK and American credits to his name, Sam's theatre roles have include playing the chaplain in David Mamet's one-act play *Edmond*, which starred Connie Booth and Miranda Richardson, at the Royal Court Theatre, London, Steve and Mitch in Tennessee Williams' masterpiece *A Streetcar Named Desire* at the National Theatre, London, and a detective in Trevor Nunn's production of George and Ira Gershwin's musical opera *Porgy and Bess* at the Savoy Theatre, London. Meanwhile, the other characters he has played on television include Brick Eagleburger in the comedy *Adrian Mole: The Cappuccino Years*, a bouncer in the sitcom *Red Dwarf* and Mr Fielding in the comedy drama *Bounty Hunters*. On film, Sam's credits have included Moe in Stanley Kubrick's erotic mystery psychological drama *Eyes Wide Shut*, Saul Goldstein in Guy Ritchie's spy action comedy *Operation Fortune: Ruse De Guerre* and Henry Burke in George Clooney's drama *The Boys in the Boat*.

Actress Belinda Stewart-Wilson believes it was playing Dilys Perkins in two episodes of the 1995 version of *Shine on Harvey Moon* that saw her cast in the small role of Vanessa Masterson in 'The Yanks Are Coming'. 'I was only twenty-four at the time and had only just left drama school a couple of years before,' she recalled. 'I hadn't done very much acting work at that stage.

'Although I only had two lines, I was required to attend rehearsals at the BBC Rehearsal Rooms in North Acton for the whole week. I have very fond memories of that place. It was a very fun episode to do although I only had a small part. However, as I was told at drama school, "There are no small parts, only small actors!" I decided to make as much out of the part as possible because I wanted to make an impact. But as there was little to go on, I decided to make up a character for her and decided she should chew gum. When I watched the episode back a few years ago, I thought I had overacted!

'I had lunch with Nicholas at the studio and he was very sweet to me because I was the new girl. Dervla was lovely and very professional, and Michelle gave me a lift back home to south London. I admired Dervla and Michelle and was deeply impressed by them both. My abiding memory of Victor is of him making me laugh!

'Although my pink top came from wardrobe, the short black skirt I wore was mine and the boots used to be my mum's! She wore them back in the 1960s. I loved them and used to wear them when I went clubbing in the 1990s until I wore them out!

'My scene set in a garage was recorded in front of an audience. The crew on the series were so professional and slick.'

Belinda's theatre credits have included Jackie in the Arnold Wesker play *The Kitchen* at the Royal Court Theatre, London, and Tania in the Robin Hawdon comedy *Shady Business* at the Mill at Sonning, Reading. She also collaborated on the play *Punched* at the Criterion Theatre, London. Directed by Jude Kelly CBE, it supported the annual global initiative '16 Days to End Global Violence Against Women' and raised money for The Circle, Refuge and Southall Black Sisters. Belinda's other television roles include Polly McKenzie in the sitcom *The Inbetweeners*, Mrs Quint in the crime drama *Ripper Street* and Bellender Bojangles in the comedy *Toast of Tinseltown*, with Matt Berry. Meanwhile, the characters she has played on film have included Camilla in the comedy thriller *Kiss Kiss Bang Bang*, Polly McKenzie in both the comedies *The Inbetweeners Movie* and *The Inbetweeners 2*, and Eve in the drama *Everything I Ever Wanted to Tell My Daughter About Men*.

In 'Let's Get Away from it All', the eleventh episode of series three, Yvonne, in an attempt to move her and Gary further up the social ladder, arranges for them to see a new apartment. Gary isn't keen, even though they'd have use of a swimming pool and gym – and Yvonne isn't keen on going to the viewing with him dressed in his 1940s clothes ready for going to the shop afterwards.

Having changed to prevent Yvonne being ashamed of him, Gary dutifully goes to view the apartment. Standing by the swimming pool, Gary makes it clear that he thinks it's an elephants' graveyard where old yuppies come to die. However, he shows more interest when Yvonne points out that its location is nearer to his shop than their present home.

In higher spirits, Gary returns to the past and the Royal Oak. There he discovers Reg is writing to the prime minister because someone has stolen his allotment. In reality the ARP has placed a shed on top of it. This means his bumper crop will be ruined and the Women's Institute won't be able to admire his marrow this year.

Meanwhile, upstairs the sheep's heart Phoebe had for her tea last night hasn't agreed with her and she's feeling decidedly queasy. But there's more shocking news for Gary when Phoebe admits she's been thinking of moving. Although she would still run the pub, she feels that it would be better for them to live somewhere else where they could be more of a family. Despite the hint, the penny doesn't drop with Gary.

Yvonne is prematurely going through some old bits and pieces belonging to Gary with a view to throwing things out prior to moving. She begs Gary to go on yet another drive by the apartment even though their offer has still to be accepted. Then, of course, there's the small problem of selling their Cricklewood home as well! Anyway, going out together is a non-starter as Gary is due to play football with Ron and friends on Wormwood Scrubs Pitch 137. Or at least that's what he thought his excuse was for visiting Phoebe. In the event, Ron turns up in cricketing apparel. Fortunately, Ron covers for him by saying Gary will be having a trial for the Dog and Trumpet's Second Eleven cricket team afterwards. While Gary and Ron get over yet another tricky moment, Yvonne goes to answer the phone. She then returns with the news that their offer on the apartment has been accepted and the move is on.

Having escaped Yvonne and her moving plans in Cricklewood, Gary has made his way back to 1942. There, he and Phoebe go for a walk in the nearby churchyard. Again, she attempts to drop hints that she's expecting more than the brewery to deliver. It's only when they end up viewing a house that an old lady is renting that Phoebe admits that she's pregnant. They agree to rent the house, complete with its walk-in larder, which Phoebe has long coveted.

Having kept a low profile for a few days, Ron turns up at the shop to see what the problem is. It's then that Gary admits Phoebe is pregnant. At first, Ron concludes that the baby is Donald's and that it was conceived on his brief return to London. However, Gary explains that the baby is his and that it can't be Donald's because he's gay. Not only is Ron shocked but he's also concerned at Gary's plans to spend more and more time with Phoebe. Gary tries to justify his actions by saying she will need him more now and Yvonne will need him less because she'll have her new yuppy friends.

On his return to wartime London, Gary discovers that Reg has had a letter from Mr Churchill himself. Although he's over the moon and has committed the letter to memory, it's clear that Reg is not getting his allotment back.

Gary quickly surmises that Phoebe has something on her mind. She has changed her mind about moving out of the Royal Oak. She was born there and it's all she knows. Phoebe is relieved that he doesn't mind her wanting to stay put, or that they've wasted nine pounds on a month's rent. Gary smiles and says, 'Hang the expense.'

In Cricklewood, Gary discovers Yvonne is unpacking and that the move is off. She has changed her mind and called the estate agent to take their house off the market. She claims it's because the apartment was too small. What worries her more is that he'd be upset because they've wasted over five hundred pounds on surveys and solicitor's fees. As with Phoebe, he tells her to 'hang the expense'. That is, until he realises the reality of how much has been spent. Yvonne promises to make it up to him and starts by saying they should go to a restaurant called San Marco's as her treat. This is to help cushion the blow of her wasting another eight hundred and ninety-nine pounds on a new three-piece suite – oh, and the fact that she's pregnant!

In this episode, the final part of series three, Maggie Jones played a forthright battleaxe who persuades Gary and Phoebe to rent her home, complete with walk-in larder. A consummate character actress, Maggie's theatre work included Amy, Countess of Gosswill, in the Jean-Paul Sartre play *Kean*, originally written by Alexandre Dumas, at the Globe Theatre, London, and Mrs Elton in the Terence Rattigan drama *The Deep Blue Sea* at the Ashcroft Theatre, Croydon, and the Cambridge Arts Theatre. Her stage credits also included a saleswoman in Clare Boothe Luce's comedy of manners *The Women* at the Yvonne Arnaud Theatre, Guildford, and the Old Vic, London. On television, Maggie's other roles included Smither in the costume drama *The Forsyte Saga*, Mrs Peake in the sitcom *Lucky Feller*, which starred David Jason and Cheryl Hall, and Deirdre Barlow's interfering mother, Blanche Hunt, in the soap opera *Coronation Street*. Although she tended to appear on the stage and television, she did play Hetty Soames in the uproariously risqué film comedy *Every Home Should Have One*. Maggie died on 2 December 2009, aged seventy-five.

The gym and swimming pool locations used in this episode were based at Bracknell Ski Centre on John Nike Way, Bracknell, Berkshire. This was the same complex where the ski-lift and ski-slope scenes were filmed. Indeed, the scenes were filmed in the afternoon of Tuesday 10 October 1995, which, as previously mentioned, was the same date that the ski-slope scenes were filmed.

The third series of *Goodnight Sweetheart* was broadcast by BBC One starting with the Christmas special on Tuesday 26 December 1995 at 8.00pm. The remaining episodes of the series were shown on Monday 1 January 1996, Monday 8 January 1996, Monday 15 January 1996, Monday 22 January 1996, Monday 29 January 1996, Monday 5 February 1996, Monday 12 February 1996, Monday 19 February 1996, Monday 26 February 1996 and Monday 4 March 1996 at 8.30pm.

The *Radio Times* dated 30 December 1995 to 5 January 1996 promoted the third series of *Goodnight Sweetheart* as being part of a new season of programmes. Photos of both Nicholas Lyndhurst and Penelope Keith, appearing in the second series of a sitcom called *Next of Kin*, adorned the front cover.

After the third series, the script editor Micheál Jacob wrote *Goodnight Sweetheart: The Sparrow Diaries*. Published in October 1996, the book drew on scripts from the first three series of *Goodnight Sweetheart*. While Micheál filled in some blanks, and invented some material, the publication largely represented the broadcast programmes up until that point.

With high ratings continuing for *Goodnight Sweetheart*, a fourth series was always going to be on the cards. Once again, the series was ending with a cliffhanger: in this case, with both Phoebe and Yvonne announcing that they were pregnant. However, arguably the biggest cliffhanger of the end of this particular series related to events behind the scenes. To put it succinctly, it was announced that Dervla Kirwan and Michelle Holmes were both set to leave the series. When the news was released, confirmation of who would replace the actresses became eagerly anticipated.

4
A New Dimension

IN MARCH 1996, ALLAN MCKEOWN left ALOMO when Pearson Television, the then owners of Thames Television, acquired SelecTV, of which, as previously mentioned, ALOMO was a subsidiary. This ended Allan's involvement with *Goodnight Sweetheart*.

Allan's departure meant Claire Hinson would now be credited as the sole executive producer on the sitcom from series four until the end of its original run.

As pre-production work began on series four of *Goodnight Sweetheart*, one of Claire's biggest concerns was recasting the roles of Phoebe and Yvonne after the departures of both Dervla Kirwan and Michelle Holmes. 'It was a slightly anxious time,' said Claire. 'They had fitted the roles so perfectly, and viewers become very attached to characters.'

In 2006, Dervla openly explained in an interview why she decided not to return to the sitcom for the fourth series. 'It was a really hard decision to leave,' she said. 'It was a decision that, upon reflection, I regret. It was a decision that I was forced into by many external voices, let's put it that way. I was getting a lot of chatter telling me to do things at that time. Also, *Ballykissangel* had also really taken off and was a massive hit, but it was a completely different character. Agents and friends and lots of people, who really didn't have, and shouldn't have, any influence in a career, were telling me to move on. I listened and made that decision.'

While viewers may have initially been concerned about the future of the sitcom, Laurence and Maurice were not. 'The only reason we would have ended the series after Dervla and Michelle left is if Nick had not wanted to carry on,' said Laurence. 'But he wanted to make more episodes as he liked playing the character of Gary Sparrow.'

One of the actresses being seen for the role of Phoebe was Elizabeth Carling. 'I had to audition for the role of Phoebe, but I didn't have to do a screen test,' Elizabeth recalled. 'It was one of several interviews I was doing at the time. But it was weird as I had just finished playing an East End barmaid in the 1940s in a tour of the Noël Coward play *Peace in Our Time*. I thought, this is odd, I've already been doing the East End accent for seven months!

'Because I was always working, I hadn't seen *Goodnight Sweetheart* before. I called Dervla Kirwan, who I was seeing lots of socially at the time, and told her that I was auditioning for the role of Phoebe and she was thrilled for me. I asked her if I could borrow one of her videos of the series and she had it sent around by bike. I watched fifteen minutes and I thought, right, I don't want to watch any more because I want to make the part my own.

'I had a couple of meetings with Susie Parriss and Lo and Mo and then one with Nick and I am pleased to say we got on like a house on fire. I found out that I had got the part of Phoebe in August 1996.'

Elizabeth, who was born in Middlesbrough, Teesside, became an actress in her teens. 'I joined the National Youth Theatre when I was eighteen and appeared in a musical version of *Macbeth*,' she said. 'I was taken on by an agent who suggested looking at other avenues of work other than just singing.' An early acting role on television was playing Laura Marsh in *Boon* for Central Television. 'I learned a lot from working with Michael Elphick and all the fantastic technical crew,' the actress revealed.

Elizabeth's other theatre roles include Eustasia in a tour of the Ken Hill play *The Hunchback of Notre Dame*, Janet in a tour of the Richard O'Brien musical *The Rocky Horror Show*, and Eva Jackson in the Alan Ayckbourn comedy *Absurd Person Singular*. She has also played Steffy in the Neil Simon comedy drama *I Ought to be in Pictures* at the Library Theatre, Manchester, Chelsea Thayer in a tour of the Ernest Thompson play *On Golden Pond*, and Maggie Deakin in the gritty but humorous John Godber play *Muddy Cows* at the Stephen Joseph Theatre, Scarborough. Elizabeth's other television credits include Carol in the sitcom *Men Behaving Badly*, Wendy in the drama *Crocodile Shoes*, which starred Jimmy Nail, and Charlotte in the comedy drama *Border Café*. She has also played the characters of Linda Pond in the sitcom *Barbara*, with a cast including Gwen Taylor and Sam Kelly, Selena Donovan in the medical drama *Casualty* and Betty Scanlon in the glamorous period drama *Hotel Portofino*, which also starred Natascha McElhone and Lucy Akhurst. Elizabeth's film work, meanwhile, includes playing Barbara Clough in the Tom Hooper sports drama *The Damned United*, with Michael Sheen, Carol in the drama *Almost Saw the Sunshine* and Jean in Jo Brand's dark comedy, *The More You Ignore Me*.

Having originally auditioned to play Phoebe before the first series started, Emma Amos found herself being invited back to audition for the role of Yvonne. 'I had two auditions for Yvonne,' said Emma. 'The first was to go on tape with Susie Parriss. The second was a recall with Lo and Mo, the director Robin Nash and producer John Bartlett. Susie and Nick were there too. I had to read with Nick, and I remember it clearly as they were all so supportive.

'I wasn't nervous at all joining the series. It was a popular well-written sitcom and the writers made it clear I could put my own stamp on the role. I had seen a few episodes, but I didn't watch any more as I wanted to approach it with fresh eyes.

'It was special for me and Elizabeth because we both started at the same time. We used to cling together for support. The rest of the cast welcomed us with open arms. They were the kindest guys to work with. Nick, Vic and Chris were all wonderfully welcoming.'

Emma's theatre credits include playing Snow White in the pantomime *Snow White and the Seven Dwarfs*, which starred Marti Caine, at the Cambridge Arts Theatre, Fanchette in the Pierre Beaumarchais comedy *The Marriage of Figaro* at the Watford Palace Theatre, and Myra Arundel in the Noël Coward comedy *Hay Fever*, in a cast including Maggie Steed and Philip Bretherton, at the West Yorkshire Playhouse, Leeds. The actress has also played Miss Lucy in the Tennessee Williams play *Sweet Bird of Youth* at the Chichester Festival Theatre, Pauline in the Alan Bennett comedy drama *The Lady in the Van*, with William Gaunt and Sara Kestelman, at the Theatre Royal, Bath, and Martha Babakina in Anton Chekhov's drama *Ivanov* at the Chichester Festival Theatre and the National Theatre, London. Emma's other television roles include Mandy in the sitcom *Men Behaving Badly*, Miss Fleming in the dark and twisted comedy *Murder Most Horrid* and Cathy in the romantic comedy drama *Rescue Me*, with Sally Phillips. She has also played Julie Davies in the comedy crime drama *The Last Detective*, which also starred Peter Davison and Sean Hughes, Mrs Machin in the sitcom *Still Open All Hours* and Agatha Higgins in the comedy drama *Doc Martin*. In addition, the film parts the actress has played include Dawn in the comedy drama *Buddy's Song*, Paula in the comedy drama *Bridget Jones's Diary* and Kimberly in the absorbing, funny and poignant drama, *The Football Monologues*.

'Elizabeth Carling and Emma Amos were both excellent and different enough to bring their own special qualities to the parts,' said Claire Hinson. 'So the transition was seamless. They were also a joy to work with.'

Series four saw the return of Mia Jupp to the production team. Having worked as the production co-ordinator in series one and two, Mia was now back in the position of production manager. 'I was now looking after the budget mainly but was still very involved with all aspects of filming,' she recalled. 'However, I was very much in charge of the purse strings, making sure each department kept to their budget and doing cost reports.'

Also joining the production team was Julie Sykes, who is the daughter of the late actor, writer and comedian, Eric Sykes, as the first assistant director. 'I have fond memories of *Goodnight Sweetheart*,' she said. 'I forged many relationships because of it. The recordings were always a great night of entertainment. I have never laughed quite so much.

'Part of my job to book the supporting artists who would be in the background, especially in the pub. I decided that there would always be the same two gentlemen, and one lady, sitting together in a corner of the pub every time we were in there. They also became part of the *Goodnight Sweetheart* family, and they thoroughly enjoyed sitting in period costume, occasionally playing draughts, or reading the paper. The cast and crew knew their names as time went by, and it was always a delight to see them. Indeed, over the three series that I worked on, we saw them nearly every week. I can still see them sitting in their corner. The two gents always doffed their hats on meeting. Happy memories.'

Julie's other television credits have included the sitcoms *Coupling*, *My Hero* and *Not Going Out*. She has also worked on programmes as varied as the sketch series *French and Saunders*, the children's programme *In the Night Garden* and the soap opera *EastEnders*.

From series four, the searchlights on the opening titles began to move whereas they had not previously been animated. 'It was Terry Kinane's idea,' said Paul Peppiate. 'It proved to be quite difficult to do, as we had no access to the original footage or edit so had to amend the existing "baked" titles. Designer Mike Flower at The Look helped me create this version using the Quantel HAL graphics editing system. We moved both the searchlights and the planes flying over the glowing cityscape.'

Following the initial location filming, the rehearsals, pre-records, studio audience recordings and extra location filming for this series took place between Friday 10 January 1997 and Thursday 10 April 1997.

On a visit to see Dr Jakowitz with Gary in 'You're Driving Me Crazy', the first episode of the fourth series, Yvonne says that while she's been fit and healthy during her pregnancy so far, it's Gary who's feeling sickly and run down. He's off his food, he's not sleeping and worse still his libido has gone absent without leave! Understandably, Gary is not keen on Yvonne sharing this information with their family physician. The doctor informs Yvonne that he's spoken to the midwife about home delivery and she will be in touch. At first, Gary is pleased until he discovers he's referring to the delivery of the baby and not nappies from the local supermarket.

At home, Gary admits he will struggle to see their bed as a place to share intimacy again after it's been used as an outhouse of the maternity unit. In an attempt to cheer him up, Yvonne attempts to instigate lovemaking on the settee, but yet again he's not able to rise to the occasion due to things playing on this mind. Rather than set his mind at rest, Yvonne adds to his worries by announcing she's going to give up work when the baby is born. But Gary claims that if she does this he'll have to stay away more, going to collectors' fairs to stock up the shop. Yvonne suggests she help get him a job at her company again, but he says he doesn't want to go back to being blue-collar. Besides, her help would shift the balance of power in their marriage and be the final nail in the coffin of their sex life to boot. Realising time is getting on, Gary tells Yvonne he needs to get to the shop. He turns down her offer of having lunch together, saying he will get a pie and a pint in the Royal Oak instead. This makes Yvonne wonder what the Royal Oak has got that she hasn't.

Shortly after arriving back in war-torn London, Gary has to help Reg to the Royal Oak after he sprains his ankle on point duty when he's run over by two small children in a home-made go-kart. Worse still, Phoebe is suffering from morning sickness. Although Gary is able to persuade her to take the multi-vitamins he's brought her, she refuses his plea for her to give up smoking. Gary tells her that smoking doesn't have to be her only pleasure. However, Phoebe makes it clear again that making love is well and truly off the menu until after the baby is born. Her friends have tipped her the wink that it would be a bad idea and could harm the baby.

Gary later confesses to Ron in the shop that he's in a weird situation. Phoebe has gone right off sex and he fancies her more than ever, while Yvonne is rampant but she doesn't turn him on. Ron, meanwhile, is more concerned as to what sort of mind dreams up pork and prune pie filling. After all, Ron is finding it hard to raise an interest in Gary's sexual problems as he gets his leg over about as often as Long John Silver in the high hurdles! Gary then admits that money, or a lack of it, is bothering him. Ron suggests that he buy and sell old watches as it could prove very lucrative.

On his return to the East End in wartime, Gary decides to call *The Times* to place an advertisement making it known that he will pay instant cash for top-quality Swiss watches. The newspaper agrees, but not before passing judgment on his proposed vulgar insertion in their publication. Upon hearing his call, Reg offers his pocket watch even though it's not reliable, Swiss or valuable. Not that Reg wants to sell it anyway. He was just offering it to Gary because he's a patriot. Gary comments that the word should be 'pillock' instead! Gary tries to cover his tracks by telling Reg they're looking for watches to equip their agents when dropping them behind enemy lines. Reg, being Reg, swallows the story.

In an attempt to cheer Phoebe (and himself) up, Gary gives her some sexy undergarments bought back from the future. However, this doesn't tempt her to model them for him and she continues to uphold her nookie ban. While breaking his own rule about smoking, Gary quips that they'll be lucky if they 'do

Michelle Holmes, Nicholas Lyndhurst and Dervla Kirwan pose as their characters for a publicity photo to promote the time-travelling comedy, then still in its infancy.

Gary Sparrow (Nicholas Lyndhurst) and Phoebe Bamford (Dervla Kirwan) have a heart-to-heart in the dance hall in 'Fools Rush In', the second episode of the first series of *Goodnight Sweetheart*.

Gary Sparrow (Nicholas Lyndhurst) and Yvonne Sparrow (Michelle Holmes) discuss Gary's dress sense, or lack of it, in the episode 'Fools Rush In'.

Nicholas Lyndhurst, as Gary Sparrow, entertains Phoebe Bamford (Dervla Kirwan) and Reg Deadman (Christopher Ettridge) and some of the patrons of the Royal Oak with his rendition of the Beatles' song 'All My Loving', which he claims to have written. This scene is from 'It Ain't Necessarily So', the second episode of the third series of *Goodnight Sweetheart*.

A photograph of Christopher Ettridge, Emma Amos, Nicholas Lyndhurst, Elizabeth Carling and Victor McGuire taken in the late 1990s to promote the sitcom.

Dr Jakowitz (David de Keyser), Yvonne Sparrow (Emma Amos) and Gary Sparrow (Nicholas Lyndhurst) in the opening scene from 'You're Driving Me Crazy', the first episode of the fourth series.

Elizabeth Carling and Nicholas Lyndhurst pose in character on the set of the Royal Oak at Teddington Studios for a publicity photo for *Goodnight Sweetheart*.

Phoebe Bamford (Elizabeth Carling) and Gary Sparrow (Nicholas Lyndhurst) in the engagement scene from 'And Mother Came Too', the fourth episode of the fourth series of *Goodnight Sweetheart*.

it' again this side of D-Day. Naturally, Phoebe questions what D-Day is and Gary tells her to forget he spoke as it was just a spot of careless talk.

Later that day, Gary returns home and discovers Yvonne has already started turning the spare room into a nursery. He apologies for his mood that morning and Yvonne questions whether he's trying to sweet-talk his way into her good books. Into her underwear, he admits, to be precise. A promising kiss and a cuddle is soon aborted when Yvonne smells cigarettes on his breath. When she mentions it, Gary doesn't deny it – after all, he's a grown-up. Pointing out that he's been drinking doesn't go down well either. Gary blames being under a lot of pressure due to her announcing her pregnancy, giving up work, and telling him he has an interview and has to give up the shop. She announces that the interview is on Thursday at 2.30pm. Gary tells her to stop trying to run his life. Not thinking, he attempts to light up a cigarette from a packet he bought back in the war. Yvonne stops him and is shocked to discover he's trying to smoke some of what she believes is his stock. She mentions that the unborn child can suffer from passive smoking too. Given Yvonne's attitude towards his smoking habit, Gary quickly surmises that a 'bunk up' is going to be out of the question that night.

Gary is given a better welcome when he goes back to the Royal Oak, although he's expected to help behind the bar. The fact that Phoebe is wearing the push-up bra that Gary gave her has not gone unnoticed by some of the male customers. Their approval rating is proved by the number of drinks she has been bought and are waiting for attention.

While Gary is serving behind the bar, a man called Clifford arrives, orders a pint and asks if Gary Sparrow is around. At the same time, another man arrives with a couple of friends, orders from Phoebe and offers her a drink. Clifford, who saw Gary's advertisement in *The Times*, is a little perturbed as he finds it hard to believe that a barman would have the wherewithal to buy a fine Swiss timepiece. Gary, however, explains that he's been saving up. Although Clifford tries to convince Gary of his sob story about his auntie losing her life in the Blitz and his wife being in poor health, it's clear that he's a fence looking to make a quick buck – seventy-five quid to be exact! Gary gives him fifty pounds on account and Clifford leaves to go and fetch the watch out of his safe in Pimlico, claiming he will return before closing time. Phoebe admonishes him for parting with the cash and says he will never see it again, but Gary thinks Clifford is on the level. Phoebe wagers ten bob he'll never see his money again; but, never one to give up trying, Gary hints at a prize of a more physical nature instead. Just when he starts to go into detail, Clifford arrives back in record time with a suitcase.

Gary and Clifford retire to a nearby table as Reg rushes in. Upon noticing Phoebe's enhanced cleavage, Reg quickly becomes like a rabbit caught in the headlights of a car. Reg then recognises a man at the bar as Tommy Kingdom. At the same time, Gary is handing over the remaining twenty-five pounds to Clifford. Realising he can trust Gary, Clifford opens a secret compartment in his suitcase to reveal he has more watches in stock. Gary can't help saying with his tongue firmly in his cheek, 'Well, you've suffered more than your fair share of family tragedy.'

Not realising that Tommy and his pals are on undercover reconnaissance, Reg loudly tells Phoebe that they were former police cadets together and he's just been made chief inspector at Scotland Yard. Reg then goes over to Gary to invite him to meet his old oppo, Chief Inspector Tommy Kingdom. This revelation scares Clifford who grabs his case and bolts for the door. Tommy orders his colleagues to chase after him. But it's not long before they discover he's got away. Not best pleased, Tommy reveals they've been after the fence for months. The penny drops and Reg realises that he's ruined an operation. Tommy then tries to feel Gary's collar due as he was trying to buy from the suspect, but Reg tells him that he can't arrest him as he's a member of the secret service. Gary then proves his position by showing his identification to Tommy. Confused, he asks Gary what the secret service want with 'dodgy' watches. Reg butts in and tells them the excuse that Gary told him earlier. Gary tells Tommy he couldn't reveal the real reason. Tommy then asks for the white gold Patek Philippe watch believed to have been stolen from the London flat of the Lord St Oswald, which Gary bought from Clifford, as evidence. Gary tries to make an excuse, but Tommy saw him put it in his jacket pocket. To Gary's surprise it has disappeared, and it appears that Clifford has pickpocketed the watch from him. Realising it's not his day, Tommy tries to save face by asking poor Reg to accompany him down to Stepney Green police station to talk to his station commander. Tommy points out that Constable Deadman is an apt name. Reg then limps off with his old colleague.

Gary is none too pleased. He lights up a cigarette and moans about not having any money, the watch or any nookie. Phoebe instantly cheers him up by producing the stolen watch from her ample cleavage.

The subject of smoking was featured heavily in this episode, something that arguably wouldn't be allowed if the episode was made today. However, Nicholas feels it was justified. 'I used to smoke a packet of cigarettes on each recording day,' he said. 'At the time, the BBC were trying to cut smoking from as many programmes as possible. I said, "Well, you will have to cut it from another series because most people smoked during the war, especially when they were in the pub with a pint in their hand." It was one of the battles we had with the BBC that we actually won. The irony is I later gave up smoking in 2005.'

Elizabeth Carling and Emma Amos hit the ground running when they joined the series. What helped all concerned was the respective actresses' decisions to play the roles their way. This certainly paid off and the transition was seamless, and very quickly it became obvious that the future of the sitcom was secure as a result. In time, it would become clear that the recastings would also allow writers to take the characters and storylines in directions that they couldn't have gone before.

Emma was grateful for the guidance and support she was given during the making of the series. 'Although I had done live sitcom episodes previously, Nick was very helpful with advice regarding multi-camera recordings,' she said. 'It's not like theatre where you are visible for the whole time. I had to remember to save good comedy moments we had rehearsed in the week until the camera was actually on me.

'We all loved the days at Teddington Studios as it was a wonderful studio. I must admit Lizzie and I clung to each other on studio recording days. Our first few were quite scary! The adrenalin was always pumping. It's quite an art to get the performance level right, not too theatrical but not too filmic. No matter how prepared we were, those studio evenings never got any easier. The bar afterwards was fun!'

Elizabeth also has fond memories of Teddington Studios. 'The feeling of the building was so wonderful, and the history was palpable,' she enthused. 'I can't believe they're not there any more.

'The recordings days were always very busy and stressful. I would keep myself to myself in order to stay in the zone. I would spend all the time I wasn't needed on set in my dressing room as I prefer to be on my own when I feel anxious or nervous.

'I would get very nervous before every recording and it took a couple of takes before I would relax. *Men Behaving Badly* was the only multi-camera sitcom I had appeared in before *Goodnight Sweetheart*. I hadn't had a lot of experience of recording with a live audience. I used to hide behind the bar during the Royal Oak scenes between takes when the lovely Ted Robbins was talking to the audience. I was afraid he would ask me questions and I didn't want the audience to hear my Middlesbrough accent while I was in character.

'When I was being directed by Robin Nash, he used to say to me, "I like the way you do the same thing each time",' which was actually a compliment as he said it made it easy to edit my scenes.'

There was, of course, more to worry about than just learning lines when working on a series partially set during the Second World War, as Elizabeth soon discovered. 'I was asked to have a perm to make it easier for me to set my hair in the 1940s style,' she recalled. 'However, I was mortified by the outcome of what was supposed to be a loose perm so it would take a curler easily. To make things easier, I wore a hairpiece from series five, which I still have.'

The supporting cast of the first episode of series four of *Goodnight Sweetheart* included the return of David de Keyser as the friendly family physician, Dr Jakowitz.

Also appearing was Danny Swanson as a young soldier. 'I had been appearing in sitcoms such as *2point4 Children*, *Waiting for God*, *Second Thoughts* and *Game On* when I got a call to read for the small role of a solider in this episode,' said Danny. 'I remember it being a very quick reading!'

Despite only sharing a few lines with both Nicholas and Elizabeth in the Royal Oak, Danny was surprisingly asked to attend the whole week of rehearsals. 'That's how it tended to be in those days,' he recalled. 'It created a good atmosphere. The cast were a very friendly bunch. They were very confident with what they were doing. Although it was clear who was in charge, it didn't feel like there was any hierarchy within the cast. Everyone was easygoing and I was made to feel part of the team.

'The recording day was quite long and tiring,' noted Danny. 'Although we were doing okay for time when we started the main recording, we later came under pressure to speed up as we had to be finished by 10.00pm. I believe this was to avoid anyone having to be paid overtime. I think we only got behind because there were a few retakes needed due to technical reasons.'

Working on the series for just a week was to benefit Danny far more than he realised two years later. 'I only recently discovered that Laurence and Maurice decided to cast me in the role of Steve Gadney in their sitcom *Starting Out* due to my brief appearance in *Goodnight Sweetheart*.'

Danny's stage credits have included Zapo in the Fernando Arrabal drama *Picnic on the Battlefield* at the Gate Theatre, Notting Hill, Bailey in Glyn Maxwell's critically acclaimed play *The Best Man* at the Underbelly Theatre, Edinburgh, and Billy in Mike Packer's dark comedy *The Dysfunkshonalz!* at the Hen and Chickens Theatre, Islington; while his other television roles include playing a lager lout in the sitcom *Second Thoughts*, Dean in the comedy *Every Silver Lining*, which starred Frances de la Tour and Andrew Sachs, and Giles in the flatshare sitcom *Game On*.

Also appearing was Tim Stern, who played the fence, Clifford. Tim was the husband of the casting director Paddy Stern who, of course, worked on the sitcom. While working as an actor, his theatre credits included playing Laurence in the Mike Leigh comedy *Abigail's Party*, with Alison Steadman and John Salthouse, at the Hampstead Theatre, London, Miguel Estete in the Peter Shaffer play *The Royal Hunt of the Sun*, with Denis Quilley and Rufus Sewell, at the

Theatre Royal, Bath, and Martin in Stewart Permutt's scathingly funny comedy *Many Roads to Paradise* at the Jermyn Street Theatre, London. His other television roles included Barry Snatch in the sitcom *You're Only Young Twice*, Lew in the drama *Spender*, and Mr Gifford in the sitcom *All Along the Watchtower*. Tim's film characters included Boog in the heart-warming fantasy *Santa Claus: The Movie*, a hypnotist in the comedy drama *Just Like a Woman*, and Panfield in the crime comedy *Shooting Fish*. Tim has now retired from acting.

This episode also saw Nick Stringer play the part of Tommy Kingdom. However, had things been different, Nick might have ended up being cast as one of the main characters instead. 'I had been considered for the part of Reg in the original casting sessions,' he explained. 'I was called in for a meeting with Robin, Susie, Laurence and Maurice. I knew Marks and Gran because of working on *The New Statesman* with Rik Mayall. Television is a small world!

'Rehearsals on sitcoms are pretty intense affairs because of the short amount of time. It's not just rehearsing the lines; as time is also taken up with studio rehearsals plus all the costume calls and suchlike, but Teddington was always a lovely place to work; being located by the river gave it an aura of almost Hollywood-like sophistication.

'I'd first worked with Nicholas Lyndhurst on *Butterflies*; then, of course, on *Only Fools and Horses*. Chris Ettridge and I were old friends having worked in theatre together and although I didn't get the part of Reg, I was pleased that a chum had got the part. I already knew Tim Stern, and enjoyed working with him. I hadn't met Elizabeth Carling before, but she seemed very pleasant and professional.'

Nick's theatre work includes playing Sergeant Harry Asquith in the Mike Stott comedy *Funny Peculiar*, with a cast including Bill Nighy and Julie Walters, at the Everyman Playhouse, Liverpool, Ken in the Shane Connaughton play *Forever Young* at the Nottingham Playhouse, and Luddy Beddoes in Timothy Findley's gleefully rude comedy *Elizabeth Rex*, alongside George Costigan and James Dreyfus, at the Birmingham Repertory Theatre. A familiar face on television, his other roles include a cabbie in the Jack Rosenthal comedy drama *The Knowledge*, PC Ron Smollett in the police drama *The Bill* and Max Derwin in the soap opera *Family Affairs*. Meanwhile, Nick's film credits include Billy in the crime drama *The Long Good Friday*, Detective Sergeant Rice in the comedy *Clockwise* and Inspector Blather in an adaptation of the classic Dickens tale *Oliver Twist*.

At the start of 'In the Mood', the second episode of the fourth series, Gary is reading a list of Korean foods to Yvonne. However, his efforts are doing very little to help her look forward to her forthcoming business trip to Korea. It's also not helping her nausea, which she proves by rushing to the downstairs loo during Gary's monologue. However, in an attempt to be sympathetic, Gary assures her there's bound to be a McDonald's somewhere in Korea. In response, Yvonne complains to Gary from the loo that she's not very well and it was sex with him that caused it!

As ever, Ron has picked the wrong time to arrive at the Sparrows' door. He explains that he's a refugee from the tireless wrath of Stella and enquires if this is by way of being a safe house. Gary tells him that Yvonne is throwing up and she blames him; also, sex is a cruel plot, pregnancy is hell and all men are bastards. Ron dismisses that as mild banter by Stella's standards.

Gary explains to Ron that Simyung want Yvonne to go to Korea to do a stint at their head office on a three-week trip. Ron doesn't believe that there's a reason for sickness during pregnancy, which doesn't go down well with Yvonne. To try and lighten the mood, Ron does the 'I hear you're planning a wise Korea move' joke. This doesn't go down either. It doesn't help that he's the twenty-seventh person to crack that joke. Yvonne announces that she's going to bed and, when Gary asks if he can bring her anything, she requests P. D. James and a Cumberland sausage. Her parting shot to Ron is to mention that Stella called earlier to tell him she will be home very late and not to call the police out again. Ron explains to Gary after Yvonne departs that he called the police out last time because Stella is having an affair and he wanted to embarrass her. He's convinced of this because she walks around with the faint but unmistakeable smile of a woman that's recently had a thorough seeing-to and is expecting more in the not too distant future. Sadly, Ron is not responsible for the look of satisfaction on his spouse's face, hence his bitter streak.

Later in bed, while Yvonne chews on a large Cumberland sausage, Gary begs her not to go on her business trip. He tells her its obvious that she's not very enthusiastic about the prospect. It's not just his unique male intuition: he heard her on the phone earlier admitting to her friend Wendy that she'd rather go nude bungee jumping in Rhyl. Gary moves in for a tender kiss but is greeted with her sausage instead as she announces she's going to be sick.

On his trip back into the past, Gary announces to Phoebe that he has a fortnight off work. Although she's pleased, the news makes her cry. Reg explains that this has been the status quo for a couple of days. One minute sunshine, the next the waterworks. Gary explains that's due to mood swings. Not the brightest spanner in the toolbox, Reg thinks he's referring to Glen Miller, not realising it's connected to her pregnancy. But when it comes to having babies, Reg has very little knowledge. He admits to Gary he's never understood how they come out of a woman's belly button! Gary realises trying to explain the reality would be a waste of time.

Up in the flat, Phoebe tells Gary that she's far from happy about having to pretend that their baby is Donald's. Gary points out this won't sit well with Donald either. He asks if she has written to tell him the news about her being pregnant, but she admits she hasn't got around to it yet. She says she was feeling well until the last couple of days, but now it's all tears and dry retching. Gary sarcastically comments he's come at the right time. Phoebe asks Gary to give Reg a hand downstairs as she's starting to feel queasy because the faggot she had earlier hasn't agreed with her. As Gary goes to leave, Phoebe admits to feeling nervous and a bit sad about everything with the baby, including Donald having to know and Gary being away such a lot of the time. Gary offers to hold her hand every step of the way, including at the birth – something Phoebe is not keen on. She reminds him that the baby is supposed to be Donald's, something that Gary isn't happy with. Phoebe reminds him that she'd soon start losing her regulars if they knew the real situation.

In an attempt to keep Yvonne happy, Gary picks up the iron and does his best with her laundry when next at home. While reciting her list of orders, Yvonne mentions that little Arthur is arriving in the morning. Gary quickly backtracks and asks who little Arthur is. Yvonne realises she forgot to tell him that his nephew (who is also his godson) is coming to stay while his parents, Alison and Craig, go away for the weekend.

The following Saturday proves to be very busy at Blitz and Pieces. Yvonne calls Gary to tell him her morning sickness has returned with a vengeance and right now she's not best placed to play Mary Poppins to little Arthur. 'At present, "spit spot" has taken on an entirely different connotation for me,' Yvonne tells Gary. Gary tells her to call Astro Cabs and ask Dave to bring little Arthur over to the shop where he can look after him.

Dave duly brings little Arthur over to the shop. Gary tells Arthur there's a train set out the back that he can play with. Although Dave is captain of Gary's darts team, the taxi fare and tip is still important to him. Having finally prised a decent tip out of the time traveller, he goes on his merry way, passing Ron on his way out of the door. The troubled artisan has arrived bearing board-mounted posters. Gary is more concerned about the proofs of his new catalogue that Ron has printed. He questions whether he was sober when he put them together. Although initially offended, Ron admits he was drunk, and he will be drunk again due to being sad, confused and tense thanks to his ongoing marital difficulties. Ron then ponders whether his marriage would be in rude health if he had acceded to Stella's request to make love in unlikely domestic locations.

Gary eventually tells Ron to keep his voice down because of the kid. Confused, Ron asks what kid as there's no child to be seen. Unable to find him, Gary starts to panic and mentions he's looking after, or rather not looking after, his nephew, Arthur. Ron mentions that he can't have gone out of the front door or they'd have seen him. They go outside to look at the yard. Gary dismisses Ron's idea that he got through the gate. When Ron asks what he looks like, Gary realises he doesn't know as he hasn't seen him for two years. The thought suddenly occurs to Ron that little Arthur has 'gone back'. Gary isn't convinced, believing only he can 'go back'. Ron questions where he is, if not back in the past. Just in case, Gary decides to make a trip back to the past. After all, if he doesn't find him, by the time Arthur comes to be born he'll be fifty-four! In an attempt to see if he too can go back, Ron makes his way to the security gates after Gary disappears through them with ease. However, he just crashes into them and ends up regretting it.

Little Arthur, meanwhile, is safe and well. He is hiding under one of the cloth-covered tables inside the shop. Realising that Gary and Ron are no longer in the shop, he makes a break for freedom out of the front door.

In a desperate bid to find his nephew, Gary is searching the area near to Duckett's Passage. He goes over to a nearby woman and asks if she's seen a little boy wearing strange clothing – a Power Rangers T-shirt, Junior Wranglers and Reeboks.

Another small but grubby boy in wartime clothing then walks into the Royal Oak and asks Reg for a pint of old and mild. Phoebe takes pity on him and offers to give him some sausage and mash and a ginger beer, as well as a bath in the sink. This disappoints Reg who was intent on arresting him. After all, it would have been his first arrest for seven months.

Gary's search for little Arthur has taken him to a small yard where a group of young boys are playing football. He asks them if they have seen a boy wearing 'American clothes'. One boy asks what the information is worth and when he produced a couple of coins, the boy lies and sends him on yet another wild goose chase while the boys argue over the money.

Eventually, Gary ends up in the Royal Oak to ask Reg if he's seen the boy. After giving a description, Reg explains that he's in the sink being given a scrub down by Phoebe. Gary runs upstairs and finds the boy wearing one of Eric's old shirts and eating sausage and mash. Not realising it isn't little Arthur, he drags him off with a view to taking him back to the future, explaining that he's Mrs Bloss's neighbour's nephew who he was looking after. Gary promises to return later, especially when Phoebe hints that she's feeling better enough for a little romance.

On arriving back at Duckett's Passage, Gary attempts to carry the boy through the time portal but obviously fails. He tries this twice before the boy complains he doesn't like this game and runs off, hotly pursued by Gary.

After the boy gives him the slip, Gary returns to Phoebe in the flat in the hope that he has returned there. When Phoebe asks if he's lost him again, Gary, to save face, says the boy lost some money he gave him. When he says it was two pounds by mistake, Phoebe gets on her hands and knees and tries to find the cash while Gary goes in desperate search of the boy again.

Having failed to find little Arthur, and after explaining his predicament to Ron back at the shop, Gary returns to Cricklewood wondering what to say to Yvonne, let alone Craig and Alison. When he gets to his front door, Yvonne opens it and slaps him across the face. On entering the lounge he sees the real little Arthur sitting with Reg Deadman's police constable grandson, complete with his rather obvious toupee. Yvonne explains that the police constable found him wandering around the street in the East End. Knowing what a pillock Gary can be, she took the precaution of putting their contact details in little Arthur's pocket. She points out that this doesn't bode well for when they have their own child. After giving Gary a thorough dressing-down, she explains that she and Wendy are going out to the wine bar for a drink and that he's on childcare duties again. This doesn't appeal to Gary who had planned to spend a romantic evening in with Phoebe. The police constable mentions that Yvonne gave the boy a hamburger and a strawberry milkshake, which, after he leaves, little Arthur explains has made him feel sick.

This episode in series four of *Goodnight Sweetheart* was not the first to be titled 'In the Mood'. The sixth episode of the first series had also been given the same title. It's said that the duplication was due to an administrative error.

Although Ron's drinking, due to his marital problems, and morning sickness both sides of the time portal were important subplots in this episode, the possibility that Gary's godson, Arthur, was capable of time travelling was obviously the overriding plotline. Although it was discovered to be a false alarm, the idea that another character could time travel and lead to even more problems for Gary, in either the past or present, was not only tantalising for the viewers, but as it turned out hinted at plotlines that were set to follow.

'In the Mood' was the first of nine episodes to be written by Sam Lawrence. 'I first worked for Laurence and Maurice when I wrote episodes of *Love Hurts*, *Shine on Harvey Moon* and *Birds of a Feather*,' he said. 'It was a real pleasure to work with two such masters of comic writing. Prior to writing my first episode of *Goodnight Sweetheart*, I was sent tapes of previous episodes so I could get a notion of all the characters and their relationships. As an average, it took me anywhere from three or four days to a week to write an episode. Sometimes writing comes easily and you want to get your head down and finish an episode; whereas sometimes you feel like having a break to relax with a whisky! Either way usually worked for me!

'Sitcom is so difficult to do well, though. You have to keep the narrative going, keep the integrity intact and yet still try to get laughs in each episode. I remember a piece of advice Laurence and Maurice once gave me: "Humour must come from character, not from jokes".

'I always went to rehearsals and usually someone in the cast or production team would spot me arriving and would joke, "Oh God, the writer's here, put it all back the way it was!" Although to be serious, if one of the actors or actresses came up with a suggestion to get a laugh with a line or even with just a look, it was usually a good note. I was never precious about my scripts.

'I always enjoyed going to Teddington Studios for the recording days of my episodes as it was a good day out! Lo and Mo and I would sit in the gallery, and there were usually boxes or packets of sweets sitting on the vision mixing desk that we could share. Before the recording, we'd go to the Anglers pub next door for a drink. When we'd go back to the studio, we would walk past the audience queuing for that evening's recording and I loved that!'

Sam's other television credits include writing selected episodes of the comedy drama *Shine on Harvey Moon*, the drama *Noah's Ark* and the sitcom *Birds of a Feather*.

Julie Sykes recalls that a spell of inclement weather became a problem while filming one of the scenes for this episode. 'We staged a football game with some young boys on a derelict patch of ground,' she explained. 'They were all dressed in the appropriate costumes of the time. That included shorts, as it was meant to be summer. However, snow was forecast, and we had to organise warm blankets for hypothermia, hot water bottles and hot drinks. We did try to get the game going, but as fast as the props men were sweeping the snow away, it was falling on the ground behind them. They also had to spray dead lilac flowers purple, to try and make it look like summer. It was completely impossible. Those poor shivering little mites! So, we transferred the game to a nearby empty garage, and the boys thoroughly enjoyed the next couple of hours kicking the old leather football around.'

Playing the role of the cabbie who takes little Arthur to Gary's shop was Richard Albrecht. Richard's theatre credits include Ron in John Godber's black comedy *Perfect Pitch* at the Derby Playhouse, Marley's Ghost in Adrian Berry's reworking of Charles Dickens' tale *A Christmas Carol* at Jacksons Lane Arts Centre, London, and Clarence and Uncle Billy in a tour of a radio version of the iconic Frank Capra film, *It's a Wonderful Life*. His other television work includes playing a reporter in the comedy *The Gravy Train*; Derek Heavey, Maxine Peacock's truck-driving father, in the soap opera *Coronation Street*; and Bob Forsyth in the thriller *The Escape Artist*. On film, Richard's roles include Peter Mason in the period drama *Jude*, Rabbi Cohen in the action drama *Walking with the Enemy* and Al in the family adventure *Paddington*.

Also appearing in this episode was Elliot Henderson-Boyle as Arthur. As a baby, Elliot appeared in commercials and in an episode of *Mr Bean* appropriately entitled 'Mind the Baby, Mr Bean'. His other television credits include voicing the character of Pipkin in the animated series *Watership Down*, and playing Boyd Payne in the crime drama *Judge John Deed* and James Mee in the comedy drama *Life Begins*. Elliot has also played the role of Young Lancelot in the historical adventure *King Arthur*.

The role of George in this episode was played by Zak Maguire. Zak's other roles on television include Jonathan in the sitcom *Men Behaving Badly*, young Sid in the soap opera *EastEnders* and Jason Masters in the medical drama *Casualty*. In addition to playing Noah Home in the short *The Cross of Joshua Home*, Zak's film credits include Alex in the thriller *Botched* and Andrew Osbourne in the comedy *Lady Godiva: Back in the Saddle*.

Finally, for the supporting cast of this episode, the part of the 'big kid' was taken by James Craise.

Phoebe is busily extolling the virtues to Gary of Mrs Carter's farm that they're both going to stay at for their holiday at the beginning of 'Out of Town', the third episode of series four. This holiday is, of course, only possible due to Yvonne being away on her business trip to Korea. Reg is jealous as the nearest he's ever got to the country is Hyde Park after the Coronation where ducks, pigeons and a bit of mud and some brawn that had gone off were the highlight of his day. Gary looks concerned as he studies the letter of confirmation from Mrs Carter, leading Phoebe to fear there will be a problem. However, Gary promises there won't be a flap on to spoil their romantic trip away to a farmhouse surrounded by cows, sheep, pigs, geese and chickens.

After arriving back home in the future, Yvonne greets Gary in the hall by complaining that he's half an hour late to help her prepare for her trip. Annoyed, her time-travelling other half points out that she'd still have time to check into the airport early if she went there by milk float. This conjures up recollections of how she arrived at the church for their wedding not only before Gary but before the congregation too – and half-way through the previous wedding!

Realising they're going to be parted, Gary suggests they say their farewells while being horizontal during the ten-minute wait for the taxi. She tells him they don't have enough time and to save it for when she's back from Korea. Like a dutiful duplicitous time traveller, he tells Yvonne he couldn't be unfaithful to her – well, not in her lifetime.

To get around the problem of Yvonne phoning home each night at 11.00pm GMT, Gary has devised a plan that will allow him to go away with Phoebe and, as usual, to tie Ron up in knots. Over a cheeky Indian warmed up by Gary's own fair hands, Ron demands to know what favour he's after now. The plan is for Ron to move in and answer the phone each night and make out that Gary has laryngitis and he will pass on her messages, including the embarrassing ones, and make up his replies. In return for help, Ron demands that Gary gift him his signed copy of *The Beatles' Hits*, their very first EP, which is practically a Sparrow family heirloom. Not that Ron covets the record: he plans to swap it for a limited-edition photo of Sharon Stone signed across the bottom, so to speak.

However, the best laid plans of mice and time travellers often go wrong. This is proved when Gary's father, George, turns up on the doorstep for a visit. He's in London for a philatelists' convention at Olympia and naturally assumes he can stay at Gary and Yvonne's house. He's got the time off work, and Gary's mum has agreed to do her own ironing for a change. Unable to refuse, Gary agrees he can stay there. Due to the shock, Gary has forgotten he's supposed to have lost his voice and it's only Ron's timely arrival home that reminds him to get back on track with his story. Gary tries to explain that he's going away for a week the following day on a buying trip for the shop. George tries to persuade him to delay the trip, but Gary realises what's at stake, and he, along with Ron's input, tries to explain how important the journey to the Hebrides will be. Despite telling his father it's great to see him as he makes for the spare room, George is far from convinced.

Over a glass of wine, Gary and Ron try to work out what to do next. Gary suggests he postpone the trip and tries to role-play his speech with Ron playing Phoebe. Ron throws the wine in his face, making Gary realise he's on a hiding to nothing. Instead, he decides to retire for the night with Ron insisting he sleep on the sofa while Ron takes the marital bed.

On his next visit to the Royal Oak, Gary, with Reg's support, tries to persuade Phoebe that he has it on the best authority that the meteorological boys believe weather for Kent is likely to be less than clement. As a result he suggests they postpone their holiday until the following week. However, Phoebe is not having it. After all, she's rearranged the brewery and Reg has taken a week's leave to look after the pub and the farm's booked. More importantly, she's borrowed Violet's turquoise gaberdine with the rabbit trim. Gary then tries to use the excuse that there might be a flap on at work, something he backtracks on when Phoebe threatens to pour a drink over his head.

Back in the nineties, Gary goes out for a drink in an East End pub with his father. There, George buys him a rum and blackcurrant, believing the story about his laryngitis. Due to feeling guilty about his trip, Gary presents George with a ticket for the Three Tenors, which is about all he got out of a hundred pounds when he bought it! George is thrilled. George then proceeds to tell Gary he hardly recognises the East End since he was there in the 1960s. He then tells him that when he was odd-jobbing he got a call-out to a house and, after he got lost, asked a policeman for directions. He ended up walking down a small alleyway and by a pub and and everything looked different. Almost that it wasn't the 1960s and more the 1860s and that he was in the Victorian age. Instantly, Gary starts to believe that time travelling is in their case hereditary. He starts to ask if he met anyone and started going back to have another life. George is soon confused by his son's strange line of questioning. But to Gary's disappointment, George explains that it was just how it felt, not that he had actually gone back in time. There was dirt and poverty and children had no shoes, and had it not been for Billy J. Kramer on the wireless and aerials on the chimneys it could have almost been the 1860s.

Back at the Royal Oak, Phoebe drops a bombshell over dinner. She has come around to Gary's way of thinking and due to the met boys' advice has decided to change all the arrangements so they can go away the week after next. Reg later admits to having a hand in persuading her to change her mind.

Over a can of lager, Gary explains to Ron that he's told his father that due to the weather in the Hebrides he's had to change his plans. Also, that he's going to have a sudden recovery from his laryngitis and have a relapse the next week. Ron declares his admiration at his best friend's resourcefulness while living a double life. Unfortunately, fate is about to throw an Yvonne-type spanner in the time-travelling works. She calls and explains that she's missing Gary, and raw fish makes her want to throw up so much she plans to come back early. This sends Gary and Ron into a sudden panic, and Gary's mood is not improved by the arrival of his father back from the Royal Albert Hall and attempting to impersonate Pavarotti performing 'Nessun Dorma'.

Overnight, Gary comes up with a new plan and asks Ron to print him a new weather report to show Phoebe. It confirms that freak weather conditions now make it impossible to go away the following week.

Having shown Phoebe the weather report on his return to the Royal Oak, Gary says he will call Mrs Carter and tell her they're on their way, that Reg can deal with the brewer's men and to go and get packed.

To make up for taking his business trip early after all, Gary leaves his father a note and a whole book of assorted wartime stamps in pristine condition. Over the moon, George tells Ron he plans to sell so he can take his wife on holiday to the West Indies.

The following morning Ron wakes up on the settee in Gary and Yvonne's living room, surrounded by champagne bottles. He turns on the answering machine and discovers that Yvonne has left a number of messages wondering why Gary and Ron weren't there the previous night to take her call. She also mentions Simyung have asked her to stay on another week. Ron realises that they're both in trouble but realises it will be Gary who will get it in the neck. He looks out of the window and notes that at least the weather is good. Ironically, after all the chopping and changing, we discover that Gary and Phoebe are sat inside the farmhouse due to heavy rain.

This episode featured the one and only appearance of George Sparrow, Gary's father, in the present. The character would, however, later appear as a younger man in the 2016 special. George does his fair share of inadvertently causing nightmares for Gary and Ron in this episode, so it's surprising that he wasn't brought back again to cause more problems for his time-travelling son.

The role of George was played by Roger Sloman. 'I wasn't nervous about making the episode as I had been appearing in sitcoms for a long time,' he said. 'But it was still a nice challenge for me. I realised that I was in safe hands as Robin was a wonderful director. He was very much an old-school director. He was a charming man and generous. In fact, it was a nice group of people to work with.

'The series was run incredibly well. We had a good script by Sam Lawrence, and a lot of time to work on the scenes. The characters of George and Gary had a proper father-and-son relationship – although it did feel like Gary behaved more like the father and George the son!

'The whole experience was very relaxed, and I had no anxiety. Teddington Studios was one of my favourite places to work. I was able to cycle there and back on the recording day because I lived nearby.'

Roger is a skilled and accomplished character actor. His theatre credits include Tom Browne in the Howard Brenton and David Hare satirical play *Brassneck* at Nottingham Playhouse, Bernie in Kevin Elyot's bittersweet comedy *My Night with Reg* at the Criterion Theatre, London, and the Playhouse Theatre, London, and the colonel and the lieutenant in Tony Kushner's inventive and vigorous translation of Bertolt Brecht's play *Mother Courage and her Children* at the National Theatre, London. His other television roles have included Keith Pratt in the comedy drama *Nuts in May*, Trevor in the comedy drama *Shameless* and George in the sitcom *Still Open All Hours*. Roger's film parts include Midge in the comedy *Beautiful People*, Geoffrey in the black comedy *Chunky Monkey* and Frank Gilmont in the comedy *Lady Godiva Back in the Saddle*.

During a chat at the beginning of 'And Mother Came Too', the fourth episode of series four, Ron asks Gary if he became a little more friendly with Samantha Hickey at his school reunion. He says no, but arrogantly points out that while he could have done, it would be inappropriate as both his wife Yvonne and girlfriend Phoebe are expecting his baby. Downhearted at Gary's response, Ron tells him his marriage is over – again! Ron ventured home and discovered Stella and her boyfriend making love on the living-room carpet in time to Ron's Luther Vandross CD. Fortunately, Ron explains that he was cool and dignified. Or to clarify, he was cool and dignified all the time he was hitting Stella's lover. His revengeful actions duly bring the police to Gary's door.

Gary arrives back at the Royal Oak to discover that Phoebe's husband, Donald, has been killed by a sniper who fell out of a tree and hit Donald on the head! Worse still, his mother, Dolly, is staying at the pub. Despite it not being the ideal time, Phoebe accepts Gary's ill-timed marriage proposal. Gary explains that he knows Donald would have wanted Phoebe to be happy.

Back in the present, Gary goes to visit Ron who is in custody for beating up Stella's lover. Ron is pleased to see Gary, thinking he's going to get him out. But as usual, Gary selfishly puts himself first and announces that he and Phoebe are going to get married as Donald has been killed. This doesn't impress Ron who reminds his time-travelling mate that he's in the nick.

Phoebe and the Reverend Timms are discussing Donald's memorial service as Gary arrives. He incorrectly assumes Phoebe is discussing their plans to get married and embarrasses both of them as well as himself. Fortunately, he redeems himself by giving the Reverend a box of Ferrero Rocher. When the Reverend asks if Gary got them via his embassy contacts, Gary, with his tongue firmly in his cheek, explains that the ambassador has them at all his receptions.

Gary arrives late at court with Ron's bail money and realises that he only has wartime currency on him. He's told to get back quickly with modern currency or Ron will face another night in the cells. He rushes back to the Royal Oak to retrieve his wallet and ends up coming face to face with Donald's mother, Dolly. She is keen to have her say as she's heard all the local tittle-tattle about Gary and Phoebe. During a heated exchange between Phoebe, Gary and Dolly, the news comes out about Phoebe being pregnant with Gary's child. By way of a parting shot, Dolly calls Phoebe a 'whore' as she and her friends and relatives leave the pub.

Later that afternoon, Gary and Phoebe go for a walk in the local churchyard. Phoebe announces that she wants them both to get married as soon as possible now Dolly knows everything. Phoebe shows Gary a small tree that they have planted in Donald's memory. When Phoebe says they will be old and grey by the time it's fully grown, Gary remarks that she should speak for herself.

Suddenly realising that it is getting late, Gary rushes Phoebe back to the Royal Oak so he can head to Duckett's Passage, the present and Ron at the court. On his arrival he discovers that Ron is waiting outside. Stella has agreed to drop all charges in exchange for a divorce. To cheer Ron up, Gary takes him to a local hostelry to drown his sorrows and then Donald's tree, which is now fully grown.

The episode ends with Gary presenting Phoebe not only with a pram for their baby and earrings, but an engagement ring. Despite being happy, this makes Phoebe cry, much to Reg's confusion.

Despite the fact that this was the one and only episode in the entire run of *Goodnight Sweetheart* that did not include an appearance by Yvonne, it certainly did not disappoint in terms of plot and laughter. But given that the character of Donald dies, his mother, Dolly, arrives at the Royal Oak and finds out that Phoebe is pregnant, Ron ends up being arrested and Gary and Phoebe get engaged, one would imagine that most writers would have found writing this episode a daunting task. However, Gary Lawson and John Phelps didn't see it that way. 'It might seem like there's lots of stories,' said John, 'but for us this episode was about just one thing: Gary being an utterly selfish bastard. The second he realises he and Phoebe can get engaged now, it's all about what he wants. Each subsequent action is a consequence of that: not appreciating the gravity of Ron's situation when he's in the cell, embarrassing Phoebe in front of the vicar, failing to ensure he's got the right cash to bail out Ron which meant he had to turn up at the wake when Phoebe had asked him to stay away, blurting out the news of the pregnancy… All of which results in him failing to be there for Ron when he needed him – again.'

Victor remembers a particular scene in which Ron ended up in a prison cell after assaulting Stella's lover. 'Gary arrived to see Ron and began selfishly telling him that he and Phoebe were getting married,' he said. 'Ron just said, "I'm in the nick!" Not only did it get a big laugh, but for me the exchange summed up their friendship and just how much Gary used Ron.'

John agrees with Victor about Gary's selfishness. 'Gary was very much the centre of his own universe,' he said. 'But it was poor old Ron that suffered most – and Vic played the part brilliantly.'

Nicholas also has frank views on the time traveller. 'Gary Sparrow was a pretty selfish character,' he said. 'But Vic was always adept at getting the audience back on side.'

The policeman who allowed Gary to visit Ron in his police cell in this episode was played by Martin Beaumont. Martin entered the business by appearing in films when he was just eleven. He has continued to be an actor and in 1995 also became a stand-up comedian, who has performed all over the world, and a comedy writer. As an actor, Martin's other television credits include playing a security guard in the police drama *Between the Lines*, Bob Adams in the sports drama *Dream Time* and Desmond in the comedy drama *William and Mary*. His film roles as a boy included Hunter in the Lindsay Anderson satirical drama *If…*, Kolnay in the drama *The Boys of Paul Street*, based on a 1906 Hungarian children's novel by Ferenc Molnár, and Martin in the family drama *Cry Wolf*.

Also appearing in this episode was Kerry Angus in the non-speaking role of a transvestite who ends up sharing the police cell with Ron. Kerry's other television credits include Debbie in the comedy *Ain't Misbehavin'*, Sister Steadman in the soap opera *Coronation Street* and Marian in the children's drama *Byker Grove*.

Welsh actor Peter Halliday made the first of his three appearances in this episode as the vicar, Reverend Timms. The character was, incidentally, named after the vicar in the children's series *Postman Pat*. Peter's stage roles included Campbell in the Terence Feely thriller *Who Killed Santa Claus?*, which starred Honor Blackman and Maurice Kaufmann, at the Theatre Royal, Windsor, Lieutenant Joy in the Alec Coppel melodrama *The Joshua Tree* at the Duke of York's Theatre, London, and Jack Taylor in Jeffrey Archer's second play *Exclusive*, with Paul Scofield and Eileen Atkins at the Theatre Royal, Bath, and Strand Theatre, London. On television, the actor played a variety of parts including Dr John Fleming in *A for Andromeda*, Vargas in the action drama *The Saint* and Mr Perkins in the drama *Yesterday's Dreams*, which starred Paul Freeman and Judy Loe. Peter's film credits included a rowing husband in the John Schlesinger drama *Sunday Bloody Sunday*, a club manager in the notorious horror *Virgin Witch* and a customs officer in the spy thriller *The Black Windmill*. Peter died on 18 February 2012, aged eighty-seven.

The golf-mad magistrate in this episode was played by Jane Briers, who is the real-life younger sister of the late actor Richard Briers. Jane is also the aunt of the actress Lucy Briers, and the first cousin, once removed, of the actor Terry-Thomas. The character actress always brings a unique and engaging delivery to every character she plays. In the theatre, Jane has played characters including Mrs Manningham in the Patrick Hamilton play *Gaslight* at the Theatre Royal, Lincoln, Beryl in the Charles Laurence comedy *Snap!*, which starred Ray Brooks and Maggie Smith, at the Vaudeville Theatre, London, and Mrs Foran in Sean O'Casey's powerful anti-war play *The Silver Tassie* at the Theatre Royal, Stratford East. Her other television credits have included Mrs Faye in the children's drama *The Swish of the Curtain*, the feisty receptionist Rose in the sitcom *Close to Home*, with Paul Nicholas and Angharad Rees, and a counsellor in the comedy drama *Cold Feet*. Although the actress has concentrated more on stage and television roles, Jane has appeared in film roles include Mrs Tulip in the drama *Just Inès*.

Playing the role of Ron's solicitor in this episode was Sebastian Abineri. Sebastian started work as an actor at the age of just seventeen and appeared in repertory productions at Bexhill, Eastbourne, Folkestone and Southwold. His other theatre credits include playing a taxi driver in the Ben Travers comedy *The Bed Before Yesterday*, with a cast including Helen Mirren and Jim Broadbent, at the Lyric Theatre, London, Sergeant Mitchem in a tour of the critically acclaimed Willis Hall play *The Long and the Short and the Tall*, and Papa Gonzales in the Tennessee Williams drama *Summer and Smoke* at the Apollo Theatre, London. His other television roles include Dick, the groom, in the drama *Flambards*, Detective Sergeant Dick Maltby in the police drama *Juliet Bravo*, and Ron Williams in the soap opera *Coronation Street*. Sebastian's film appearances have included playing Sergeant Treadwell in the Richard Attenborough war drama *A Bridge Too Far*, William Roye in the biographical drama *God's Outlaw* and a coach driver in the Guy Ritchie period drama *Sherlock Holmes*.

The role of the prosecuting barrister was played by Ellen O'Grady. 'I really enjoyed playing my scene with Nicholas, Victor, Jane and Sebastian,' said Ellen. 'It was my very first television job and I remember being nervous. My mouth was dry, and Jane gave me a piece of chewing gum and smiled and said, "This should do the trick". I thought that was very lovely!'

Ellen's theatre roles have included Velma Kelly in the Kander and Ebb musical *Chicago* at the English Theatre Frankfurt, Germany, Helen Alving in the Henrik Ibsen play *Ghosts* at The Other Palace, London, and Morgelyn in the April de Angelis and KT Tunstall musical *Saving Grace* at the Riverside Studios, London. Meanwhile, her other television credits have included Nadine Woods in the medical drama *Holby City*, Mrs Pearson in the drama *Daddy's Girl* and Margie Flynn in the medical soap opera *Doctors*.

The part of Donald Bamford's interfering mother Dolly Bamford in this episode was played by Rowena Cooper, the widow of Terrence Hardiman who, as previously mentioned, played Wilson in the first episode of the second series. 'I didn't audition for the role of Dolly as I'd stopped doing auditions by that time,' said Rowena. 'I just had a meeting with the director Robin Nash instead. The cast were lovely people, and it was a joy to be with them and to be part of the episode. It was a very pleasant job altogether. I thought *Goodnight Sweetheart* was a wonderfully mad idea. It was brilliantly cast, and all the actors and actresses played it for real, which made it easy for the viewers to accept and go along with the crazy plots.'

Rowena's theatre roles have included Martha in the Edward Albee play *Who's Afraid of Virginia Woolf?* at the Little Theatre, Bristol, Marion in the John Osborne drama *Watch it Come Down* at the Old Vic, London, and National Theatre, London, and Kathleen in David Storey's haunting, elegiac play *Home*, which starred Paul Eddington and Richard Briers, at Wyndham's Theatre, London, and on tour. Her other television credits include Mrs Fenner in the sitcom *The Rag Trade*, with a cast including Peter Jones and Miriam Karlin, Connie White in the historical drama *The Jewel in the Crown*, and Angela Price in the science-fiction series *The Sarah Jane Adventures*, with Elisabeth Sladen. In addition, her film parts have included Maryson in the comedy *Dentist in the Chair*, Jez's teacher in the romantic crime comedy *Shooting Fish* and Lady Willingdon in the drama *Jinnah*.

This episode saw Hoffman Square in London double as the exterior of the court for this one and only time. As the scene begins, Ron can be seen waiting for Gary who is late with his bail money. The Grade II listed building, which was built in 1825, is situated on Chart Street. Set within gated grounds, the site features forty apartments, surrounded by communal green space in the heart of Hoxton, just minutes' walk from Old Street Station. At one stage in its history the building was owned by the London College of Furniture.

As 'The Leaving of Liverpool', the fifth episode of series four, begins, we discover that Ron is still being allowed to stay in Gary's spare room due to the fair Yvonne having not yet returned from Korea. However, if Ron was hoping for some quality time downing a few pints with his best pal, he's to be disappointed as Gary has agreed to accompany Phoebe on a trip to Liverpool to visit her gran to tell her about the baby. Ron explains that his grandad Albert Wheatcroft lived in the same area during the war. Indeed, he was elevated to hero status fifty-four years ago that week, as witnessed by the *Liverpool Echo*, when he saved a child from a blazing building. He asks Gary to buy him a drink and give him one of Melton Mowbray's finest pork pies. Gary refuses to do the latter explaining that no one goes time travelling with a pork pie!

Having left Reg in charge of the Royal Oak, Gary and Phoebe make for Liverpool by train. After meeting Phoebe's gran, and being told he will have to stay with a nearby Scoutmaster, Gary and Phoebe take gran for a drink in her local pub. There, Gary meets Albert Wheatcroft (who steals his wallet) and fails to impress the publican or the locals, including John Lennon's father, with his rendition of 'Penny Lane' at the piano. When he hears that Albert has been caught and locked up, Gary realises that this will change the course of history.

He decides to go back to London, the present and to see Ron. When he reaches the present he discovers that history has been changed. Yvonne has married a different husband; President Thatcher is in office and Ron has become a man of the clergy. Gary returns to wartime Liverpool realising that all he has now is Phoebe, and sensing the only way he can change history back is to spring Albert from prison and ensure that he saves the child from the burning building. The plan goes well until Albert refuses to enter the blazing building. Instead, Gary does the brave deed and then passes the child to Albert. In doing so, the crowd of onlookers, including Phoebe's gran, mistakenly believe that Albert is responsible. Phoebe points this out to Gary, but he's just relieved that everything is back on track. Although Phoebe hasn't found the right time to tell her gran about the baby, she has guessed that she is pregnant.

Gary and Phoebe return to war-torn London and discover that Reg has turned the Royal Oak into a temperance bar, much to the delight of the Salvation Army, because he forgot to make an order to the brewery. Gary then returns home to find all is back to normal and, with Ron having always looked up to his grandad, somehow finds it in his heart to tell him that Albert was a hero.

This episode allowed writer Geoff Rowley to show an example of what would happen if the course of history is changed. However, Victor primarily recalls this episode not because he played two roles (three, if you include his brief appearance as a vicar), but because of an idea he suggested. 'I never had any input with the writing or plots on the series as we had a great team of writers headed by Laurence and Maurice,' he confirmed. 'Although I did suggest bits of physical business, which the writers and directors sometimes accepted, the only other contribution I made was to the end credits of "The Leaving of Liverpool". I played both Ron and Ron's grandad, Albert Wheatcroft, in that episode. However, you will notice that Vic Noir is credited as playing Albert. My wife once mentioned that someone had called and mistakenly asked to speak to Vic Noir instead of Vic McGuire. I told that story to Nick and we thought it would be fun to use the name on the credits – and the director, Robin Nash, agreed!'

This episode reunited Nicholas with Dublin-born Carmel McSharry. 'Carmel was a superb actress,' he recalled. 'We worked together on the play *Straight and Narrow* by Jimmy Chinn on tour and then in the West End.' As you may recall, this was the play Nicholas was appearing in when he first met Laurence and Maurice to discuss the possibility of appearing in what would go on to become *Goodnight Sweetheart*. Carmel played Phoebe's breathtakingly outspoken gran for just this episode.

A prolific stage actress, Carmel made her West End debut as Edith Westmore in the J. B. Priestley play *The Linden Tree* at the Duchess Theatre,

London. Her other West End roles included Miss Tipdale in the John Chapman and Ray Cooney farce *Not Now, Darling*, with a cast including Donald Sinden and Bernard Cribbins, at the Strand Theatre, London, and on tour; and Mrs Bedwin in the Lionel Bart musical *Oliver!* at the London Palladium. On television, her credits included Nancy in an adaptation of the Charles Dickens novel *Oliver Twist*, the title role in the comedy drama *Beryl's Lot*, and Mrs Hollingbery in the sitcom *In Sickness and in Health*, with Warren Mitchell and Arthur English. Carmel could be seen playing parts in films including Mrs Ashley in the crime drama *Life in Danger*, Mrs Dowsett in the horror title *The Witches*, and Mrs Briggs in the drama *All Coppers Are?* Carmel died on 4 March 2018, aged ninety-one.

Kenneth Cope admitted that he was 'up to [his] old tricks of ad-libbing' when he played the landlord in this episode. During their first encounter in the landlord's pub in Liverpool, Gary tells him that he is after souvenirs from the area. The landlord shows him a programme from the last football match he'd been to see. Being a 'manic lifelong Everton supporter', Kenneth ensured that it was Everton that 'hammered' Liverpool by one-nil in the first leg at Anfield of the War Cup.

Before retiring from acting, Kenneth garnered an abundance of memorable credits. His other television roles included Jed Stone in the soap opera *Coronation Street*, Marty Hopkirk in the private detective series *Randall and Hopkirk (Deceased)*, and Ray Hilton in the Liverpool-based soap opera *Brookside*. His film roles included two *Carry On* comedies: he played the disruptive shop steward Vic Spanner in *Carry On at Your Convenience*, and the failed first-time thief Cyril Carter in *Carry On Matron*. In a similar vein, Kenneth played hitman Harvey in the spin-off to the sitcom *George and Mildred*, alongside Brian Murphy and Yootha Joyce.

As 'How Long Has This Been Going On', the sixth episode of series four, begins, Gary is speaking on the phone to Yvonne, who will shortly be returning to the country, Gary and their marital abode. As a result, Gary is clearing up and attempting to persuade Ron to get his act together and move out. Ron, however, is more interested in playing computer games than looking for a flat.

Back in war-torn London, Gary and Phoebe have gone out to the cinema for the evening to see the film *Mrs Miniver*. On returning to the Royal Oak, they discover that stand-in barman Stanley has taken charge of the bar as Reg is absent without leave. He soon returns and explains that Margie's husband, Jackie, has been knocking her about and unfairly accusing her of flirting with the passengers

Goodnight Sweetheart: A Guide to the Classic Sitcom

on their bus. Gary advises that Reg leave his wife Minnie and move in with Margie and little Frankie. But neither Phoebe nor Reg are convinced that this would be the right thing to do.

On his return home, Gary discovers that Ron has cleaned the house and will be 'dossing at his office' until he finds a flat. Through a business called Empathy, Ron is planning to meet a surrogate, a professional lady who helps to improve a man's sexual performance. Gary is less than impressed, however, when the penny drops that the lady in question will be visiting Ron at Gary's house. But before he can argue, the phone rings with the devastating news that Yvonne has had a miscarriage.

At the hospital, Gary attempts to comfort his wife while a debonair doctor fawns over his wife and Helen, his abrupt mother-in-law, arrives to take charge of the situation. Realising that Gary has left the house without bringing anything that Yvonne needs, she demands the keys to the house and sets off to get her a nightie, bedsocks, hairdryer and one of Catherine Cookson's novels.

On Helen's arrival at Gary and Yvonne's house, Ron answers the door and mistakenly believes she is his surrogate and chases after her up the stairs when she goes to get her daughter's belongings.

Back in the Royal Oak, Margie, sporting a black eye, is telling Phoebe about her problems with her husband when Reg arrives. Asking what happened to her face, Phoebe bitterly tells him she got hit by a bus driver. Meanwhile, little Frankie is playing dominoes with Stanley at a nearby table. Reg tells Margie that she and little Frankie are his responsibility now and he will ask Mrs Bloss about the flat above Maison Bloss – although, for official purposes, he will still be living with his wife, Minnie. Unfortunately, Margie's 'old man' knows about Reg and she tells him that he intends to come and sort him out after his shift ends.

Meanwhile, Helen returns to the hospital and encourages Gary to go and reopen his shop. This is so she can privately reveal to Yvonne what happened between her and Ron. Rather than open the shop, Gary heads for the Royal Oak in the hope that a bunch of flowers will make up for his recent absence. With him being unable to explain the real reason, Phoebe is upset, especially as he wasn't there to accompany her to a doctor's appointment.

Hearing raised voices brings Margie into the bar thinking that it might be Jackie. Presently, little Frankie comes into the bar as he's unable to sleep. She explains to Gary that she can't take it any more. To help settle Frankie, Gary plays the song 'That's What Friends Are For'. Unfortunately, Jackie arrives and mistakes Gary for Reg. Despite Gary's attempts to calm him down, Jackie is about to hit him until Reg arrives in full uniform and knocks Jackie out cold with his trusty truncheon.

Back at home, and with Yvonne still in hospital, Gary finds Ron has decided to stay to keep him company. When Gary asks how his appointment with the surrogate went, Ron reveals he mistook Helen for the other lady but says gentlemen may kiss but never tell. He does, however, point out that if he plays his cards right he could end up being Gary's father-in-law!

At Christmas 1996, the BBC broadcast three high-rating episodes of *Only Fools and Horses*, which culminated in Del and Rodney finally becoming millionaires. The second episode saw Rodney's wife, Cassandra, played by Gwyneth Strong, suffering a miscarriage. This called upon Nicholas and Gwyneth to play emotionally charged scenes. This episode of *Goodnight Sweetheart* called upon Nicholas to do the same when Yvonne returned home having suffered a miscarriage on the plane. Despite the subject matter, Laurence and Maurice managed to write scenes which not only dealt sensitively with the situation but also managed to include humour.

This episode saw Doug Fisher playing the part of the some-time cockney barman, Stanley. Doug had an impressive resumé. His theatre credits included Bernard in a highly successful tour of the Marc Camoletti farce *Boeing-Boeing*, with a cast that also included Richard O'Sullivan, Yootha Joyce and Sally Thomsett. Doug also directed and appeared in the same farce with Richard O'Sullivan in a tour of Australia. His other stage work included Edmund in a tour of the Don Taylor play *The Exorcism*, starring Norman Eshley and Kate O'Mara, and various roles in a tour of the Keith Waterhouse comedy *Jeffrey Bernard is Unwell*, based on the writings of its subject, which also starred Dennis Waterman and Judy Buxton. For the small screen, Doug's other roles included Larry Simmonds in the popular sitcom *Man About the House*, Jim Medhurst in the firefighter drama *London's Burning* and Ted in the sitcom *Close to Home*. His film parts included Larry Simmonds in the big-screen spin-off of *Man About the House* and Sammy in the dramas *The Stud* and *The Bitch*, with Joan Collins. Doug died of a heart attack on 9 July 2000, aged fifty-eight.

Dr Obote, whose devotion to Yvonne is arguably motivated by the fact that she is a private patient and not an NHS patient, was played by Nigerian-born Cyril Nri. A gifted actor, his theatre roles have included Ajibala Morrison in Caryl Churchill's satirical play *Serious Money* at Wyndham's Theatre, London, Moyo in Anders Lustgarten's political drama *Black Jesus* at the Finborough Theatre, London, and Sheldon in the Alice Childress drama *Trouble in Mind* at the National Theatre, London. Cyril's other television credits include Graham in the quintessential British nineties drama series *This Life*, Mayor Jeremy Richards in the comedy drama *Death in Paradise* and Seun in the sitcom *Holier Than Thou*. Additionally, his film parts have included Dr Wilson in the horror

Long Time Dead, Adam Hale in the drama *Jellyfish* and the chief doorman in the Robert Zemeckis supernatural comedy *The Witches*.

The role of Helen Shackleton in this episode was played by Susan Tracy. 'I had a pleasant few days working on the episode,' said Susan. 'It was very well written as I recall. It was a lovely cast and director. Helen was a good rounded character and it was a pity she didn't return in another episode.'

Susan's prolific number of theatre credits have included Marquise de Merteuil in the Christopher Hampton play *Les Liaisons Dangereuses* at the Ambassadors Theatre, London, Rebecca Huntley-Pike in the Alan Ayckbourn comedy drama *A Chorus of Disapproval* at the Harold Pinter Theatre, London, and Mary in the Kevin Kautzman drama *Dream of Perfect Sleep* at the Finborough Theatre, London. Her other roles on television include Fran in the action drama *The Sweeney*, Emily in an episode of the drama series *Tales of the Unexpected* and Maureen in the crime drama *Manhunt*. Susan can also be briefly seen playing Edith Collier in the comedy film *The Likely Lads*, which was inspired by the sitcom of the same name and the follow-up series, *Whatever Happened to the Likely Lads?*

With Ron already parted from his wife, Stella, this episode saw the turn of Reg in having a change in his personal life. The return of the character of Margie Hook also meant the welcome return of Eve Bland as Margie.

Gordon Winter became the second of two actors to play the role of Margie's bus-driving husband. This time the character was given the name of Jackie Hook. 'I'd previously appeared (as a plumber) in an episode of *Birds of a Feather*, called "Getting a Grip", which was also written by Marks and Gran,' said Gordon. 'Coincidentally, Eve Bland was also in this episode (as another plumber).

'The cast were very welcoming. It can be daunting as a supporting actor, arriving on a job where everyone else knows each other. The advantage of a sitcom rehearsal period is the opportunity to bond with the other actors and actresses. Nicholas Lyndhurst and Elizabeth Carling were charming. I thought Christopher Ettridge was a comedy genius! It was great to work again with Eve Bland, one of the kindest and most generous souls I've ever met. We became friends for a while. I was very sorry to hear that she passed away.'

Gordon believes it was the quality of the writing that made it easy for him to develop his characterisation of the role of Jackie. 'Sitcom comes out of variety and is rooted in tradition,' he said. 'So I was the big, scary baddie; they built me up in the script before I appeared. It was great to have a reputation preceding my appearance!

'It's about giving one's own individuality to a stereotype; I'm a big guy and it's a lot of fun to be scary! In real life, one is often working hard to overcome other people's wariness about one's size, but sitcom, like panto, gives one full rein to be a believable stereotype!

'*Goodnight Sweetheart* was a great series and I was proud to be a part of it.'

As an actor, Gordon's theatre work has included Flaubert in the Paul Godfrey play *The Candidate*, inspired by an unfinished script by Gustave Flaubert, at the Royal Exchange, Manchester, Lucky Eric in a tour of the John Godber nightclub comedy *Bouncers* and Mephistopheles in the Christopher Marlowe Elizabethan tragedy *Doctor Faustus: The Imaginarium* at the Happy Cell, Hove. For television, his credits include Ron Rumsby in the comedy drama *Frank Stubbs Promotes*, Stuart in the medical drama *Casualty* and Eddie Blood in the sitcom *Friday Night Dinner*. He has also appeared in over one hundred commercials, including the award-winning Guinness advert, *Anticipation*. On film, Gordon can lay claim to appearing as a laughing man in the Mike Leigh comedy drama *Secrets and Lies*.

At the very beginning of 'Easy Living', the seventh episode of series four, Ron is showing Gary around the costly and spacious apartment in an old East End warehouse he's moved into. Cheque by cheque and direct debit by direct debit, Ron intends to fill it up with black goods as far as the eye can see. After all, things are so serious that even his solicitor has started to tell the truth. Stella is going to get half of the lot, so he's decided to make sure the lot is very little.

Meanwhile, in an attempt to look after her mental and physical health, Yvonne, who has parted company with Simyung with the help of a lump sum to speed her exit, is getting into a range of therapies. She has read about someone who had a shamanic experience in her kitchen. Gary quips that will serve them right for leaving their back door open! On a serious note, Gary is worrying about the costly pills and potions she's taking. For instance, if you take Cat's Claw followed by Devil's Claw, which one wins?! This is why Yvonne is keen to go on a course to learn more. Realising that Yvonne being away could give him the opportunity to go and see Phoebe, he encourages Yvonne to book.

Reg, meanwhile, is concerned about being talked about. He has a new sergeant at the station who is keen that all his officers should be properly married and not living in sin like him and Margie.

Having been away for over a week, Gary is in Phoebe's bad books for missing the meeting with the vicar without the courtesy of sending even a note to say why. Once again he uses the department as an excuse.

At Gary's suggestion, Yvonne has booked a weekend away on a course. The problem is Gary hadn't realised she meant that they both go away. Gary then

Goodnight Sweetheart: A Guide to the Classic Sitcom

manipulates her into cancelling, making her believe that stocktaking in his shop is more important. Unfortunately, she wants to help out.

As the time traveller has to be at All Saints' Church by twelve, Gary, as usual, asks Ron to help him out. Desperate to persuade Yvonne to leave the shop so he can make a timely exit to the past, Gary asks her to go to a local sandwich bar for coffee and sandwiches. She's not keen until Ron mentions that there is a Chinese herbalist next door. This works and Yvonne goes off in search of alternative remedies and sandwiches.

Gary and Phoebe make their appointment with the vicar on time, but the organist rehearsing rather ruins the occasion. On their return to the pub, Phoebe complains that Gary is not taking the wedding seriously and storms off, while Reg is hiding from his new sergeant in the bar and Gary walks out leaving him in a panic.

Back at Blitz and Pieces, Ron is attempting to calm Yvonne down after she becomes annoyed at Gary disappearing and leaving her to finish the stocktaking on her own. On his return, Gary receives an earbashing from Yvonne before she storms out. Gary then tells Ron that there is no making women happy. Ron asks if he's ever tried. In the heat of the moment, Gary insensitively retaliates by reminding Ron that he's on the verge of a divorce. Ron is about to walk out on him before Gary apologises.

Gary returns to the past determined to make amends. He first convinces Reg's sergeant that Margie is not living in sin with Reg but under house arrest and has assigned Reg to guard her. Gary then apologises to Phoebe and assures her that he loves her as much as he ever did and that he wants her wedding to be the best day of her life. He tells her he's determined that his best man will not be any ordinary friend, but a British serviceman. This doesn't convince Phoebe who says she's worried that she'll be standing at the altar at the church while he's outside trying to pick up a sailor!

As described, Gary was by now failing to make anyone happy – least of all himself. For example, although Gary and Ron had often had a frank exchange of views about their respective personal lives, none had ever been so frank as in this episode, written by Geoff Rowley. It's not surprising when you consider that Ron's life was gradually taking more and more of a downward turn, and as a result of his loyalty to Gary and his double life. And although Gary was more than aware of the harm he was causing him, his selfish desire to keep both Yvonne and Phoebe happy and unaware of his philandering was more important to him than helping his best friend. In a fit of pique, Ron in this episode was actually on the verge of walking out on him and their friendship for good. Whether Gary realised in that moment that he'd really pushed Ron too far, or he was merely worried about where the next bunch of white fivers was coming from, is hard to say. But based on Gary's ongoing behaviour, it could be argued that it was a combination of both. Either way, it wouldn't be the last time Gary would cross the line with Ron and risk losing him as a friend and co-conspirator. Gary's selfish behaviour was also risking his friendship with Reg who didn't know where to turn trying to keep his new-found status with Margie a secret from his police sergeant. In real life, of course, people would have deserted Gary weeks before. What the writers of the series continued to do was cunningly devise ways, including playing on Gary's charming and devious handling of situations, to keep him from losing everything. As Laurence and Maurice realised right from the start, only Nicholas Lyndhurst could have negotiated his way through the minefield of situations that Gary found himself in and still make him believable and likeable. Also, with Ron moving to the East End, this made it easier for the various writers to pen scenes that would take full advantage of his new residence being closer to Gary's shop. Previously, of course, Ron had resided in Harrow, north London, until Stella evicted him from his marital abode.

There were just two supporting actors in this episode. The first saw the return of Peter Halliday as the Reverend Timms, while the second saw Jonathan Hackett play the police sergeant with high moral values. Amongst his various theatre credits, Jonathan played Robert and Guy in the Mark Bunyan comedy *Dinner* at the Warehouse Theatre, Croydon; Master Richard Rich in the Robert Bolt play *A Man for All Seasons*, with a cast including Charlton Heston and Roy Kinnear, at the Chichester Festival Theatre, Savoy Theatre, London, and on tour; and Eddie Carbone in the Arthur Miller drama *A View from the Bridge* at the Royal Exchange Theatre, Manchester. His other television work includes playing Julian in the sitcom *Watching*, Joshua Rigg in the costume drama *Middlemarch* and a doctor in the crime drama *Foyle's War*. On film, Jonathan's roles have included a glider pilot in the war drama *A Bridge Too Far*, a dining-car waiter in the comedy mystery *The Lady Vanishes* and a priest in the drama *Breaking the Waves*.

While preparing to get married – for the second time – as 'Come Fly with Me', the eighth episode of series four, unfolds, Gary is playing the Beatles song 'Love Me Do' in the bar of the Royal Oak. He then fails again to tempt Phoebe to change her mind about waiting until after their baby is before indulging in carnal pursuits. Worse still, Reg is dropping hints about the fun they're going to have on Gary's stag night.

Later that evening, Gary and Phoebe chat in their room. Phoebe tells Gary she realises that some brides are making do with a curtain ring until times are a

Goodnight Sweetheart: A Guide to the Classic Sitcom

little easier. However, Gary assures her she will have a ring with their names engraved on. Phoebe then asks if it can also have the word 'forever' and two hearts entwined. Gary tells her she can have anything she wants.

On Gary's next visit to Ron's apartment, the printer is busily compiling a list of likely new employments. Gary is not happy about him giving up the print works. Who's going to print his updated ration books, MI5 identity papers and white fivers? After all, he has a wedding breakfast to pay for.

Meanwhile Yvonne has had a vision – a vision of quids rolling into hers and Gary's bank account as she wants to bring together alternative therapy practitioners and organise them. Basically, a business with a printable income which is actually a force for good in the world.

While Phoebe goes to the King's Head for her hen party with some friends, Gary has a stag night at both Ron's apartment and at the Royal Oak. At the former, Ron has ordered a stripper dressed in RAF uniform. Sadly, Ron passes out from the effects of alcohol and Gary declines to watch the stripper complete her routine – much to her disappointment.

Back at the Royal Oak, Gary takes part in a drinking contest with a Canadian airman called Joe, which Gary wins. Later, Reg passes out behind the bar after performing an enthused version of the song 'Knees Up Mother Brown'. Gary goes to rest against the bar but realises the bar flap is up. He puts the flap down, taps his nose and gives a knowing look to another airman he's been talking to called Steve. Gary then passes out on the floor.

Gary later wakes up in a Lancaster bomber with Steve, and they end up bailing out and floating on a rubber dinghy in the English Channel. Fortunately, Gary is rescued by a British submarine and arrives back at Cricklewood at quarter to seven in the morning. He sets his alarm and sneaks into bed next to Yvonne in the hope of getting some sleep before his wedding later that day.

Yvonne awakes from a wonderful night's sleep and prepares for a business meeting – with a man with wooden balls. Seeing that Gary is fast asleep, she turns off his alarm to give him an uninterrupted lie-in.

In this episode, Gary didn't even attempt to hide his selfishness when Ron announced that he was planning to give up his print works and take on new employment. Without the print works, Gary could see that his life would be seriously curtailed back in the Second World War. But if Ron wasn't sure about his future, we saw early signs of Yvonne planting the seeds of hope that would in time launch her into the world of big business. Reg, meanwhile, for all his bitterness about the lustful antics of his ex-wife Minnie, seemed content that this was all in the past and he now had a new family.

As previously mentioned, many of the cast members of *Goodnight Sweetheart* loved the BBC Rehearsal Rooms at North Acton. This particular episode was just one of several rehearsed there during the sitcom's run. Nicholas still remembers them with great affection. 'I grew up at the "Acton Hilton",' he said. 'I first rehearsed there in the early 1970s and have many happy memories. It was crammed with the cream of British talent. I met John Gielgud, saw Morecambe and Wise coming out of a lift and sat opposite Judi Dench. I never knew who I was going to meet while queuing for lunch! When you had finished rehearsals, you could go back home on the Central Line. It was a wonderful place, especially given where it was in London! The area used to be full of warehouses and bricklayers and merchants. It was glorious up there. It was a beacon of North Acton. Now student accommodation stands in its place.'

Elizabeth has a particular memory of rehearsing at the 'Acton Hilton'. 'I once met Judi Dench in the lift there when she was rehearsing *As Times Goes By*,' she said. 'I noticed how beautiful her nails were and they made me feel bad about mine!'

The easy-going Canadian airman, Mike, in this episode was played by John Fitzgerald-Jay. The actor's theatre roles include Ronnie Shaughnessy in the John Guare farce *The House of Blue Leaves*, which starred Denis Quilley and Nicola McAuliffe, at the Lilian Baylis Theatre, London, and various characters in the Arthur Miller memory play *After the Fall*, with Henry Goodman and Josette Simon, at the National Theatre, London. John's stage work also includes Mr Perry in the Jay Presson Allen comedy drama *The Prime of Miss Jean Brodie*, with Patricia Hodge in the titular role, at the Theatre Royal, Bath, and the Strand Theatre, London. For television, John's other credits include Mathieu in the astrological crime drama *Moon and Son*, Rocky in the comedy *Jeeves and Wooster*, with Stephen Fry and Hugh Laurie, and Peter Guthrie in the crime drama *Murdoch Mysteries*.

Playing the role of the stripper that Ron booked for Gary's stag night in the present was Danielle Tarento. 'I remember laughing a lot during rehearsals!' said Danielle. 'I was only in one scene (with Nicholas and Victor), so I was not around for the whole rehearsal period, but it was so much fun.

'As far as I remember, I did not work with a choreographer. I had a fair bit of input which, as a non-dancer, was interesting, but I don't think she was meant to be a huge pro! It was lovely to work on and the boys were so gracious.

'We got the strip (very tasteful I might add!) in one take which, from a professional point of view, I was delighted about. One of the boys (I genuinely cannot remember which!) turned to the audience and apologised that they would not get to see me strip again and called me a one-take wonder! The audience whooped – I was very proud!'

Asked why she believes *Goodnight Sweetheart* remains popular, Danielle said, 'Because of its gentleness. It is a proper British sitcom, in the old tradition.

Also, and maybe most importantly, because of its humanity and truth. It was incredibly moving as well as being gorgeously funny.'

Several years later, Danielle came face to face with Nicholas again. 'I saw him at the press night after-party of *Carousel*, which he was appearing in, at the ENO,' she recalled. 'We got chatting and I said I was sure he wouldn't remember but that in a past life I was an actress and had stripped at Gary's stag do; and he said he absolutely did remember, and we had a good laugh! Of course, he could have just been being polite, but I am taking it!'

Danielle's other television credits during her acting career included Mia in the drama *This Life*, a receptionist in the techno-espionage series *Bugs* and Lisa Gerard in the sports drama *Dream Team*. Danielle has since changed career paths and has become an award-winning producer and casting director. She also co-founded the award-winning studio theatre the Menier Chocolate Factory in 2004.

The music for 'We'll Meet Again'/'The Stripper', which Danielle danced to at Gary's stag do, was arranged by Anthony and Gaynor Sadler. It was recorded at Logorhythm Music Studios, Lexington Street, Soho, London, on 13 March 1997. The musicians taking part in the recording session were as follows:

Bb clarinet:	Jamie Talbot
Trumpet:	Colin Smith
Trombone:	Pete Thoms
Tenor sax:	Martin Dobson
Piano:	Cliff Hall
Double bass:	Don Richardson
Drums:	Paul Robinson

The role of the aggressive Canadian airman, Joe, was played by the actor, writer and director Jay Simon. 'I had recently returned from living in Canada for a year,' he recalled. 'My agent thought I'd be able to play the part with a convincing accent. Nevertheless, I thought I'd play Canadian throughout the entire rehearsal process. I did this as I felt that people might think I was bad for putting on an accent and I wanted the character to be believable. I felt quite pleased with myself that no one busted me – or perhaps they did but were nice enough not to embarrass me by saying anything!

'I was quite nervous the day the episode was taped as it was to be in front of a live audience, so we had to get it right. The atmosphere that night was amazing, and the audience responded to everything. I remember we only had a couple of stops, which were mainly due to technical issues.

'The one thing I did unscripted in the drinking contest on the day was spit the cork out before pouring the shots. It seemed fitting with the aggressive, macho style of the character.

'Nick landed right on top of me on the floor when he finally passed out on the first take. We were both literally trying not to corpse. Luckily, we went again on that without the ensuing laughter. The drink was apple juice, by the way, just in case you were wondering!'

On stage, Jay's credits include Lysander and Quince in the William Shakespeare comedy *A Midsummer Night's Dream* at the Edmonton Festival in Canada, the sadistic dentist Orin Scrivello in the Alan Menken and Howard Ashman musical *Little Shop of Horrors* at the De Montfort Hall, Leicester, and Sky Masterson in Pimlico Opera Company's production of the Frank Loesser, Jo Swerling and Abe Burrows musical *Guys and Dolls* at the Wormwood Scrubs Prison in London. His other television roles include Jan Lund in the crime drama *The Knock*, Lionel Symon in the comedy drama *Perfect Strangers* and heart surgeon Dr John Petersen in the medical soap opera *Shortland Street*. Meanwhile, Jay's film parts include playing Matt Malloy in the thriller *Empty Mirror*, William Horris in the romantic drama *Older* and Doug in the Netflix romantic comedy *The Royal Treatment*. In 2012, Jay moved to Wanaka, Central Otago, on the South Island, New Zealand, and continues to write, perform and direct.

The writer of this episode, Sam Lawrence, remembers how Nicholas suggested an addition to the script. 'When we were rehearsing the drinking scene in the Royal Oak where Gary, Reg and the airman get drunk at his stag party, Nick suggested the bar flap gag,' recalled Sam. 'This consisted of Gary Sparrow almost making the same mistake David Jason as Del Boy made in an episode of *Only Fools and Horses* called 'Yuppy Love' by going to lean on where the flap would have been when, in fact, it was up, then noticed, put it down, leaned on it and tapped his nose knowingly. I thought it was a funny idea but some of the team said the BBC won't like it because it will be too referential. Nicholas was adamant it would be fine and in the end the joke was added to the script.'

David Jason is pleased that Nicholas suggested this visual gag. 'Nick's reference was a creative nod to his old stomping ground,' he said proudly. 'But he made it his own and got a tremendous reaction from the audience.'

It seems that actor Chris Humphreys was almost fated to play the role of Steve. 'I was born in Canada, left when I was two and lived in LA from the age of two until six, when I was moved to London,' explained Chris. Later, because I had a Canadian passport, I decided to visit Vancouver for a summer – and stayed five years! When I finally got back to London, it was hard to get my acting career going again. I couldn't get an agent, so I was looking for work in something called PCR – Professional Casting Report, which came out every week. I saw an advert for genuine Canadians. Now, even though I considered myself more English, I had been playing Canadian in Canada, so I thought I'd throw my hat into the ring. Susie Parriss had forgotten about me and wanted to see me read. She then invited me to meet the producer and director of this episode. By then, I'd had a chance to look at the script and thought I could do something a bit different with the character who was written a bit straight. So, I said to them, "How about I do it like he's maybe flown 'one mission too many'?" And I read the role for them in that burnt-out Vietnam vet voice and with drug-addled eyes. They loved it, and arranged for the part to be rewritten based on my audition, changed me from Steve to "Crazy Horse" and wrote me into an extra episode. I was in the front row at the wedding! *Goodnight Sweetheart* really relaunched my British career – and my British bank account!

'I really remember the read-through for this episode. None of the actors, of course, had heard me read and so when I came out with my deranged "Crazy Horse" voice, people really started cracking up! I then thought: wouldn't it be cool if I had a toothpick? I asked for one and they gave me this big period dark brown one. It became pretty central to my character!'

Chris's theatre roles have included Fortinbras and alternate Hamlet in the William Shakespeare tragedy *Hamlet* at the Theatre Calgary, Lord Mountbatten in the William May and Jason Sprague musical *Always*, which starred Shani Wallis and Sheila Ferguson, at the Victoria Palace, London, and Krapp in Samuel Beckett's one-act melodrama *Krapp's Last Tape* at the Frederick Wood Theatre, Vancouver. The actor's characters on television include Mr Brooks in the crime drama *South of the Border*, Clive Parnell in the soap opera *Coronation Street* and Dr Martin in the drama *A Million Little Things*. Also, Chris's film credits include Clive in the Profumo affair drama *Scandal*, with John Hurt and Joanne Whalley, a reporter in science fiction film *The Core*, and Detective Inspector Amer in the psychological thriller *Out of Bounds*, with a cast that included Michael Elphick and Celia Imrie. Furthermore, Chris is a writer and playwright. His plays have been produced in Calgary, Vancouver and London.

The Lancaster bomber sequence in this episode was filmed in a genuine Lancaster out at the Imperial War Museum Duxford, which is in Cambridgeshire. 'Nick is a pilot and my dad was a Battle of Britain fighter pilot, so the two of us were like kids in a candy store!' said Chris, who played Steve. 'We loved filming in there although I don't think the cameraman was quite so happy as it was very cramped. It was very sobering to think of all those amazing airmen going out in these tiny machines risking their lives every night!'

Nicholas also shares similar views. 'How the hell they got out of a Lancaster bomber in an emergency, I don't know,' he said. 'They're so cramped. I have so much respect for the crews that flew in them, let alone having to bomb the enemy at the same time.'

In addition, Frensham Great Pond, which is situated between Farnham and Hindhead on either side of the A287 in Surrey, doubled as the English Channel in this episode when Gary and Steve found themselves having to bail out of the Lancaster and are left drifting on a rubber dinghy.

'Heartaches', the ninth episode of series four, commences with Gary waking up after the stag night from hell and, for a time, failing to remember what he has to do that day. He takes some tablets for his hangover. Meanwhile Phoebe is standing at the altar with Reg and Reverend Timms, with the wedding guests looking on, waiting for Gary to arrive. Presently, Gary's memory comes back with a vengeance and he rushes to get ready, aided by Ron at the shop. He tries to explain to Ron why he slept in while he shaves. Gary's advice: never have two stag nights in two different time zones fifty-four years apart – advice that Ron takes on board and duly discards. On finally arriving at the church very late, Gary bursts in and apologises, only to find there's now a funeral taking place. Embarrassed, Gary pretends to be upset and makes a hasty departure.

Gary heads to the Royal Oak, but Reg tells Gary that Phoebe isn't there. Reg admonishes Gary for having cold feet and not turning up, leaving Phoebe standing at the altar seven months pregnant.

Back at the shop, Ron fails to cheer Gary up with one of his famous 'as I see it' speeches and points out that maybe psychologically he didn't want to get married for a second time because he left without the wedding ring that morning.

Gary attempts to see Phoebe at the Royal Oak again, but this time he doesn't believe Reg when he says she's not there as he smells the Jean Paul Gaultier perfume he gave her. He goes to the flat to see her; she at first throws an assortment of ornaments at him, and is about to throw a large vase until she remembers it cost one-and-sixpence. She then tells him she wasn't surprised based on all his excuses in the past. Gary attempts to explain the events of his stag night but, despite being true, they sound more and more unlikely. But she tells him he should have told her that he had cold feet.

Having finally convinced Phoebe that they should still get married, Gary ensures he is awake on time to get ready to make for 1942 and the church. However, he manages to wake Yvonne in the process as the furniture has been moved around in the lounge due to her new obsession with feng shui. A half-asleep Yvonne asks where Gary is going so early in the morning; he makes an excuse about wanting to see the sun come up. Only mildly convinced, she suggests he come back to bed when he returns. However, he quickly reminds her that he has a trip booked to Swansea that day to go to yet another trade fair.

With that he makes for the shop where Ron is waiting to assist with the last-minute arrangements – such as remembering the cake. Once back in the past, Gary finds that it's him that is left waiting at the altar. The reason? Phoebe is sitting outside in the churchyard due to having cold feet – and not because of the weather. After reassuring her that everything will be okay, they finally exchange their wedding vows.

Gary and Phoebe and several of the wedding guests then make their way to the Royal Oak to witness Reg giving the worst best man's speech. Gary then replies with a speech consisting of some of the lyrics from the song 'We've Only Just Begun' by The Carpenters.

With a complicated double life that requires precision timing, it can only take a single curve ball to throw an important schedule out of synch. In this case it was, of course, Yvonne turning off Gary's alarm on his second wedding day, which, if one was to be pedantic, officially makes it his first wedding day due to it taking place in the past. The writer, Paul Makin, as with the writers on many other episodes of *Goodnight Sweetheart*, did not take the easy way out when writing this episode. He could have easily confined the plot to the fallout of what happens when events conspire to cause a wedding to be cancelled. Instead, we not only saw Gary negotiating his way through the difficulties of convincing everyone that he overslept, but persuading Phoebe to give him another chance and the wedding actually taking place.

With all the ups and downs faced by the characters revolving around the difficulties Gary and Phoebe were to experience with their nuptials, it's easy to forget that this, despite how long the series had been running, was the first episode in which Gary showed Ron a photo of Phoebe. It's hard to imagine why Ron hadn't asked to see a photo as far back as the first series, but the moment came in this series and despite being late, it was still a moving scene.

While the wedding may have been both funny and moving for the viewers, Elizabeth has one abiding memory of the cold location shoot. 'I remember being kept warm by the pregnancy bump when we were filming the wedding scenes,' she said.

The wedding scenes were the perfect excuse for some of the past characters to return to the series. This meant Peter Halliday returned as the vicar, Chris Humphreys as Steve, Jeannie Crowther as Mrs French, Chase Marks as Peter, Katie Donnison as Sally, Yvonne D'Alpra as Mrs Bloss, Eve Bland as Margie and Regina Freedman as Violet Bigby. Doug Fisher also made his second and final appearance as Stanley at the wedding reception. Although not credited, Christopher Ettridge's son Alfie Ettridge Rogers also made an appearance as Reg and Margie's son, little Frankie.

For Jeannie Crowther, her involvement in the location filming brought about a mixture of highs and lows. 'The church was not far from my agent's house,' she recalled. 'So I stayed there the night before we shot the wedding scenes. I was called for 9.00am. I didn't have any dialogue, so I spent most of the day talking to Yvonne, who played Mrs Bloss, and Eve, who played Margie, between takes. Sadly, it was my final episode of the three I appeared in. I realised the petrol tank on my car was leaking and I had to limp home after the filming.'

Gary and Phoebe's wedding scenes and the funeral scene were all filmed at St Lawrence Church, Church Street, Effingham, Surrey, on Monday 3 March 1997. In 2018, St Lawrence Church became one parish with All Saints Church, Little Bookham. Sir Barnes Wallis, who is best known for inventing the bouncing bomb used by the Royal Air Force in Operation Chastise to attack the dams of the Ruhr Valley during the Second World War, used to live in Effingham. When he died in 1979, Wallis was buried in the churchyard at St Lawrence Church.

In 'Careless Talk…', the tenth episode of series four, Phoebe reminds Gary that he has responsibilities now they are married. In reply, the time traveller with two wives reaffirms that being a spy isn't a nine-to-five job. But due to his schedule, and a lack of available local tradesmen, Gary has no choice but to pay Reg to paint the nursery for their as yet unborn baby. Worse still, Gary has to explain to Phoebe why she can't accompany him to Mothercare to buy new things for their baby. In a moment of overconfidence, Gary says he will take her to Harrods instead, as well as pay Reg ten quid for his work on the nursery. Then he realises that he's getting short of wartime currency.

Back in the future, Yvonne is bringing her journalist friend Kate, who works on the *Salford Evening Argus*, up to date on her new business ideas when Gary returns. Ron then turns up with a bottle of wine, which annoys Yvonne and Kate as he's been around five times since Gary was away as he has the 'raging hots' for Kate, who finds him boring. Yvonne and Kate head for the door and a local wine bar when Ron is in the kitchen looking for some glasses. Ron has become used to the sound of members of the opposite sex stampeding to the door of late. Worse still for Gary, Ron has lost the will to print due to losing his wife, home and half the value of his business due to his impending divorce. This means Gary will remain short of wartime funds. However, Ron offers Gary a deal – if he asks Kate out and she says yes, he will print his money; if not, he will have to consult the *Yellow Pages* for a new forger!

Back in wartime London, Gary admits his current shortage of funds, which is awkward as Reg has already spent his own money (which he saved up for

Goodnight Sweetheart: A Guide to the Classic Sitcom

Margie's birthday present) on the paint and wallpaper for the nursery. However, Gary promises to replace it in time. If the worst comes to the worst, Reg says, he can always wrap up a tin of paint. Mind you, that won't go down well as Margie was hoping for a new handbag.

Gary later leaves Ron and Kate alone in the hope that she might change her opinion of him and go on a date. When Ron realises he is boring her, he decides to try and impress her by saying that Gary is a time traveller. Later Yvonne and Kate tell Gary of Ron's last-minute bid to endear himself. Gary is furious and later pays him a visit at his warehouse apartment to give him a dressing-down. He reminds Ron that Kate is a journalist, and not only that but one that believes in crop circles. Consequently this could tempt her to set a trap for him. He points out that he might have been a headline in the *Sunday Sport* along with 'Budgie Eats Nun'. With no date on the horizon, Ron reminds Gary that no Kate, no date, no dosh.

As predicted, Kate has become suspicious, not least because of Gary's reaction to them telling him Ron's story. She persuades Yvonne to hide out in Gary's shop to see if he really is a time traveller. Realising that Yvonne and Kate must be in the shop because of Kate's car being outside, he hides in a crate in the yard and surprises them. Gary claims that the whole idea of making them think he was a time traveller and luring them there was Ron's idea. Yvonne is devastated that she has been made a fool of by Ron. However, Kate is impressed and agrees to Gary's suggestion of her going out on a date with Ron. She makes for the phone in the shop while Gary dissuades her from trying to change her mind with the threat that he might just tell everyone they know what happened!

Ron keeps his side of the bargain and prints Gary's money. Gary, Phoebe and Reg, now paid, head to Harrods. There, Reg finds himself torn between buying Margie a handbag or a coconut. To thank him for doing such a good job on the nursery, Gary gives Reg some extra money, meaning he can now buy both. Meanwhile, in a scene reminiscent of the film *Pretty Woman*, Gary bribes a rather rude shop assistant with obscene amounts of money on the condition that Phoebe is fawned over, grovelled at and generally made to feel like the lady she is.

Feeling smug about the way he has handled things; Gary almost talks himself into buying a mobile phone while chatting to Yvonne, something she says would be useful. He manages to evade the issue and reminds himself what happens when he gets cocky.

The ability by the various writers working on *Goodnight Sweetheart* to devise characters that could cause major upsets for Gary in the past and present was certainly evident in this episode, which was written by Gary Lawson and John Phelps. John explained why he and his co-writer created the character of crop circle and alien-loving journalist Kate. 'Jeopardy is really good for comedy,' he said. 'And an inquisitive journalist poking her nose into Gary's life was a good way to threaten his secret being exposed and put him on the back foot. We really enjoyed the fact it gave us the opportunity for Yvonne to scare Gary by pretending she knew all about his double life, and it was also a rare chance for Ron to have the upper hand on Gary.'

So did the writers ever consider bringing the character of Kate back as a girlfriend for Ron in any of the future episodes? 'No,' confirmed John. 'We doubted their relationship would survive more than one more date!'

Playing the role of Kate in this episode was Allie Byrne. 'Although I had previously appeared in individual episodes of the sitcoms *So Haunt Me* and *Men Behaving Badly*, I was more experienced at television drama,' she said. 'However, it was hugely exhilarating, if a little nerve-wracking, to do a sitcom. It's like a marriage of television and theatre and requires a different muscle and technique. Your performance must be heightened and truthful for the cameras, but you need to entertain the studio audience as well. You learn something different on each acting job and when you worked on *Goodnight Sweetheart* you got to learn about a different period too. It was like you were getting a history lesson!

'They were a warm and welcoming company. Although Nick has done so much sitcom, and is a master, he was very gracious, friendly and modest. Liz and Emma and the rest of the cast were also hugely talented and very friendly. I felt there was a bonding of the cast and they seemed almost as nervous as me before the recording. Everyone cared and was watching out for each other. The audience really helps in the studio and thanks to Ted Robbins, the warm-up artist, there was a really fun and electric atmosphere. I loved Kate's storyline and I loved that she did end up giving Ron a chance.'

While she was working as an actress, Allie's theatre roles included Olivia in William Shakespeare's romantic comedy *Twelfth Night* at the Richmond Theatre, Second Witch in Shakespeare's tragedy *Macbeth* at the Theatre Royal, Bath, and Richmond Theatre, and various roles in the Christopher Marlowe Elizabethan tragedy *Dr Faustus* at the Greenwich Theatre. Her other television credits included Cynthia Murdoch in the crime drama *Poirot*, Lucy in the comedy drama *Minder* and Alyson Butler in the action drama *Call Red*. In addition, her film parts included playing Kate in the thriller *Safe Haven*. Allie stopped acting in 1999 and since then, under her married name of Allie Esiri, has become an award-winning anthologist and curator and host of live poetry events including a yearly show at London's National Theatre, at the Bridge Theatre, and at major literary festivals.

Also appearing in this episode was Peter Hughes as the rather snotty Harrods floorwalker who Gary finally wins over thanks to a spot of bribery.

During an acting career that spanned over six decades, Peter's theatre credits included George Charles in the Mawby Green and Ed Feilbert farce *Pyjama Tops*, based on the French comedy by Jean de Letraz, at the Whitehall Theatre, London, Baxter in the Alan Drury play *An Empty Desk* at the Royal Court Theatre, London, and Charles Brinton in the Alfred Shaughnessy thriller *Double Cut* at The Mill at Sonning, Reading. On television, his characters included Earnshaw in the police drama *Z Cars*, Alderman W. Gale in the comedy drama *Mrs Thursday*, with Kathleen Harrison and Hugh Manning, and a party guest in the sitcom *Steptoe and Son*. Peter's film roles included Maître D in the Jim Henson musical heist comedy *The Great Muppet Caper*, the P&O manager in the historical drama *A Passage to India* and Franco in the Tim Rice and Andrew Lloyd Webber musical *Evita*, which featured Madonna and Jonathan Pryce. Peter retired from acting in 1999 and died on 5 February 2019, aged ninety-six.

In 'The Bells Are Ringing', the eleventh episode of the fourth series, Yvonne's plans for world domination now appear to include selling a vile health food drink and working with a new business partner called Clive La Zouche who, to Gary's dismay, has a ponytail. According to Yvonne, Clive is a man who's not afraid to trample over anyone to get what he wants – but in a caring way. Gary, however, has bigger things to worry about – namely the imminent arrival of his and Phoebe's new baby. Ron, however, is facing a trip to the bank to discuss a tiny blip in the Wheatcroft finances with his bank manager over a plastic cup of coffee. Although he's putting on a brave face, it's clear there are worrying times ahead for the financially stretched artisan.

Gary arrives at the Royal Oak to discover that Phoebe is with an officious local midwife called Miss Weatherell. Said midwife comes into the bar to discover Reg being less than complimentary about her to the time traveller. Fortunately, a drop of brandy and splash of soda placates her. Despite politely introducing himself to Miss Weatherell, Gary receives the cold shoulder – especially when he explains he wants to be present when Phoebe gives birth.

Gary goes upstairs to see Phoebe who hints at her frustration at not seeing him recently. He tells her he's been involved in the north Africa campaign and quickly tries to make amends by being attentive, not that his fussing is being appreciated by Phoebe. Nor is his desire to be present at the birth with a sea sponge to mop her brow. This causes Gary to go into a sulk and Phoebe to softly chastise him for behaving like a little boy. However, he prematurely ends his sulky behaviour when Phoebe begins to feel some discomfort. He quickly goes for Miss Weatherell for help.

While they wait for news, Gary introduces Reg to the questionable joys of smoking. Not that Margie, who is keeping an eye on the bar, is impressed. In an attempt to pass the time, Gary then offers to show Reg his sponge. Not that it's the jam or chocolate sponge poor Reg was expecting!

Eventually, Miss Weatherell comes back into the bar and once again catches Reg talking about her behind her back. Again, a drop of brandy helps to prevent a row. The midwife then diagnoses Phoebe's pains as a false alarm and that she doesn't believe she will have the birth until the next Thursday. Not that Gary is convinced. After all, he points out she's not Mystic Meg – a reference that is, not surprisingly, lost on a confused-looking Reg, Margie and Miss Weatherell.

As if impending fatherhood isn't enough for Gary to worry about, Yvonne reveals over a quiet dinner for two that she has invested all of their savings in her business venture with Clive 'ponytail' La Zouche. Although Yvonne dismisses Gary's concerns, he's not convinced.

Gary turns up at the Royal Oak to discover that far from taking things easy, Phoebe is down at the greengrocer's and, on her return, reveals she has been standing in a queue for two hours. Again, Phoebe admonishes Gary for fussing over her; although, after being given some concerning reports about childbirth, Phoebe drops a hint that she would like Gary to be there at the birth of their baby after all.

The following morning, Yvonne is on the phone, desperately trying to arrange a meeting with Clive who has been somewhat elusive. Apparently he has been 'astral travelling' – not that this impresses Yvonne who is keen he leaves his answer machine on next time. Their heated conversation is aborted when Gary comes downstairs as Yvonne doesn't want Gary to know that she has concerns about her business relationship with Clive. For once, both Gary and Yvonne are keeping secrets and not doing their best to hide their worries. Just as Gary goes to leave, he asks Yvonne if she has seen his sea sponge. Unfortunately, she reveals she has used it to wipe down the sink. With Gary heading for the shop, Yvonne tries to call Clive again only to get his answer machine.

Ron turns up at the shop desperate for Gary's advice only to discover his time-travelling friend is stressed about D-Day – or rather B-Day. And not only that, he no longer has his reassuring sea sponge. For once, Ron is succinct and reassures Gary that in just a couple of hours he will be a father. With that, Gary heads to wartime London leaving a financially bereft Ron to mind the shop.

Gary arrives back at the pub to discover that Phoebe has already gone into labour. The problem is that, although Miss Weatherell is there, she's drunk. In a desperate panic, Gary and Reg attempt to sober her up leaving Margie to look after Phoebe.

Back in the present, Yvonne arrives at Blitz and Pieces to find Ron looking after the shop and getting drunk – despite it only being eleven o'clock in the morning! Feeling equally jaded, Yvonne decides to join him.

With Miss Weatherell out for the count, Margie has had no choice but to take complete charge and asks Gary to comfort Phoebe who is now in a painful labour. She then dismisses Reg who is clearly not keen on being involved.

Yvonne admits to Ron that she believes Clive has done a runner with all their savings. Ron admits he can top that, having lost his business as the receivers have been called in. Nostradamus Print is no more; who would have predicted that, Ron painfully remarks.

Margie confesses to Gary back in the past that she doesn't think the baby is coming out right and, in a last-minute attempt to get Miss Weatherell to help, Gary goes downstairs and asks Reg to help him sober her up again. However, they hear the baby crying and realise the birth is all over.

Now somewhat intoxicated, Ron makes a half-hearted attempt to make a pass at Yvonne. When she calls him out, they both burst out laughing. That said, Ron tells her they have so much in common. He reminds her they're both free spirits and both drunk. In return, she reminds him they're both broke. Although she wasn't keen on Gary opening the shop, Yvonne, concerned at what Gary will say when he discovers what's happened, admits to Ron it's all they have left.

Still somewhat inebriated, Miss Weatherell tells Gary and Phoebe she doesn't know what they needed her for as they seem to have managed all on their own. Gary sarcastically reminds her they didn't have much choice! She departs, but not before turning down Reg's kind offer of a drink – claiming she never drinks on duty!

When the church bells begin to ring, Phoebe says they're ringing for the Battle of El Alamein. But Gary says they're ringing for their baby, who they name Michael Montgomery Sparrow, even though Phoebe was keen on naming him Eric after her late father.

Although the last episode of series four finally saw the arrival of Gary and Phoebe's son, there were the usual cliffhangers. Gary was blissfully unaware as he celebrated with his other wife that Yvonne had lost all her and Gary's savings to a rather elusive man with a ponytail, and Ron was facing up to life without Nostradamus Print.

For Elizabeth, this episode, written by Laurence and Maurice, brought about the challenge of pretending to give birth. 'I had to use my imagination when I was acting in the labour scenes,' the actress recalled. 'I remember getting a sore throat because of all the screaming. I must have been doing something right as all the men in the room, including the director, Terry, were wincing at the horrible noises I was making!'

The episode saw another appearance by Eve Bland as Margie, who comes to Gary and Phoebe's aid after Miss Weatherell helps herself to the brandy.

The grumpy midwife was played by Brenda Cowling. The veteran actress attended the drama school RADA with Lionel Jeffries, Warren Mitchell and Jimmy Perry. In the theatre, she played roles including Miss Helen Browne in the Graham Greene melodrama *The Living Room* at the Leas Pavilion, Folkestone, Nurse Libby in the Emlyn Williams psychological thriller *Night Must Fall* at the Greenwich Theatre, and Violet in the Terence Rattigan drama *The Winslow Boy* on tour and at the Globe Theatre, London. Her other television credits included the hospital sister in the infamous episode of *Fawlty Towers* entitled 'The Germans', Mrs Margaret Billington in the light-hearted detective series *Shoestring*, with Trevor Eve, and Mrs Blanche Lipton in the Perry and Croft sitcom *You Rang, M'Lord?* Brenda also played film parts. While at RADA, she made her debut in a small role in the Alfred Hitchcock film noir *Stage Fright*. The actress also played Mrs Viney in the family drama *The Railway Children*, a hospital matron in the saucy comedy *Carry On Girls* and Alice in the drama *International Velvet*. Brenda retired in 2006 after suffering a stroke, and died on 2 October 2010, aged eighty-five.

The eleventh episode marked the final episode of series four. The series had pleasingly seen both Elizabeth and Emma quickly settle down into the roles of Phoebe and Yvonne. A continuing high standard of writing saw a host of comedic and dramatic storylines ranging from the death of Donald, the engagement and marriage of Phoebe and Gary and the birth of their son, Michael.

The series was broadcast by BBC One on Monday 3 March 1997, Monday 10 March 1997, Monday 17 March 1997, Monday 24 March 1997, Tuesday 8 April 1997, Tuesday 15 April 1997, Tuesday 22 April 1997, Tuesday 29 April 1997, Tuesday 6 May 1997, Tuesday 13 May 1997 and Tuesday 20 May 1997 at 8.30pm. In addition to the BBC deciding to switch to showing each episode on Tuesdays during the run, there was once again a break for Easter.

Planning soon began on series five for 1998, which would see Gary and Phoebe move out of the Royal Oak and unexpectedly become friends with 'The Master' himself, Noël Coward.

5
West End Living

SERIES FIVE OF *Goodnight Sweetheart* would bring a host of new challenges for Gary Sparrow and the various other characters both sides of the time portal. As with the past four series, Laurence and Maurice and the other writers recognised there would be a need for some changes to keep the series fresh and inspire new storylines.

After some initial location work, rehearsals, additional location work, pre-records and studio audience recordings for series five took place between Friday 16 January 1998 and Thursday 9 April 1998.

Time has moved on and it's now 21 January 1944 in 'A Room with a View', the first episode of series five. Gary and Phoebe are listening to a version of Noël Coward's play *Private Lives* on the wireless in the flat above the Royal Oak. Phoebe remarks that there's nothing funny about being on your honeymoon and getting off with your ex-wife. She remarks that some men are nothing but animals. This makes Gary feel guilty and by way of a deflection he asks if she can hear Michael crying.

Phoebe persuades Gary to take Michael out for a walk in his pram. In an attempt to stop him crying, Gary sings 'Space Oddity' by David Bowie. After chatting to Reg who is on duty in the area, Gary gets caught up in an air raid. A bomb lands near to Duckett's Passage and sends both Gary and Michael into present-day London. Not realising what's happened, Reg and Phoebe, who arrive on the scene, think that they're both buried under the rubble.

Having attempted to settle Michael by bribing him with chocolate, Gary takes him round to Ron's who is surprised to be introduced to Gary's son. Suffering with shock, Gary promptly faints. While he's out cold, Ron uses his first-aid experience, gained because St John Ambulance get into football matches for free, on Michael to check he's okay.

Yvonne later pops around to Ron's apartment to look at some printing work that Ron is doing for her. She promptly comes face to face with Gary, who is supposed to be at a memorabilia fair in Blackburn, and his son, despite him trying to hide behind a wall. He quickly deflects her question by reminding her she's supposed to be at a ginseng symposium in Zurich. She tells him she got a lift back in Sting's private plane. This is the first hint of Yvonne's new-found success. Struggling for an excuse, Ron tells Yvonne that Gary got a lift back on a dustcart. With Yvonne noticing that the baby reminds her of someone, Gary and Ron between them come up with the excuse that he's looking after him for Mrs Chowdhury, a saree-shop owner based in Whitechapel, who looks after foster children.

Ron attempts to divert Yvonne's attention with the layout he's designed for one of Yvonne's new brochures. As Gary attempts to make his way outside to wait for an ordered taxi back to his shop, Michael says 'Daddy' to Gary and attracts the attention of Yvonne. Fortunately, this still does not cause her to put two and two together and come up with Gary as being the father.

Gary heads back to the shop and is relieved to find he and Michael can time-travel back to 1944. After emerging from the rubble to Reg, Phoebe and the rescue workers, Gary pretends he and Michael took cover in an Anderson shelter and he had to dig them both out. The shock allows Gary to convince Phoebe that they should move from the East End to somewhere safer and take a flat up West. At first she suggests somewhere in the country in Cornwall, but Gary reminds her that he has to live in London as he's on twenty-four-hour call due to his war work.

Despite having been nearly blown to Smithfield Market, Gary manages to convince Phoebe he has to go back to Headquarters that night. Not that she's best pleased. However, the prospect of some 'debriefing' back at home with Yvonne is obviously playing on his mind.

Back at the shop, the time traveller finds himself with yet more explaining to do when Yvonne arrives. For extra privacy, he's changed the locks so Yvonne can't get in. She's clearly still suspicious as to who the baby she saw earlier belongs to, and Gary has to launch into a painful and convoluted excuse. He convinces her that the child belongs to a less than responsible mother who left him in a buggy outside a theme pub called the Fly in the Ointment.

Yvonne convinces herself that Gary's supposed caring for the baby was his way of dealing with them losing their baby. She tells him her way was to throw herself into her work. Gary reminds her that it was 'a bloody good throw' given that she has become a millionairess in less than eighteen months; thus proving that Clive, her business partner with a ponytail, did not disappear with their savings after all, and that her stumbling into holistic medicine was in fact the right thing to do.

With Sting's plane still at her disposal until the following lunchtime, Yvonne then convinces Gary that they should fly to Paris for the night.

Still tired from his all-night antics with Yvonne in Paris, Gary takes Phoebe to look at an apartment, once owned by a spy, up West. While being shown around the flat by the estate agent, Mr Rutley, there's an air raid and they make for the private shelter available to residents. Unfortunately, George, the commissionaire, is not happy about them sheltering there; but Noël Coward, already resident in the block, comes to their rescue. Asking if they live there, Gary wittily mentions that they've just bought a room with a view, a reference to one of Coward's songs.

Proving that *Goodnight Sweetheart* still had the power to surprise as well as create laughter, the first episode of series five did both in abundance. The bombing near Duckett's Passage, the revelation that Yvonne had become a millionairess, and Gary and Phoebe deciding to move to a flat in the same block as Noël Coward were all ingeniously intertwined in this episode, which was written by Laurence and Maurice.

The timid rescue worker in the episode was played by Alan Turner. Alan's other television credits include playing a policeman in the crime drama *Jemima Shore Investigates*, a waiter in the sitcom *Life Without George* and Andrew Wheeler in the soap opera *EastEnders*. His film roles include Vigil in the crime thriller *Captive*.

The affable estate agent Mr Rutley, who troubled Gary for tuppence for the phone in this episode, was played by James Grout. This was the first of two appearances that James, who was once described as 'a supporting actor of authority and distinction' by the *Guardian,* would make in the sitcom.

On stage, James's roles included Harry Chitterlow in the David Heneker and Beverley Cross musical *Half a Sixpence*, which was based on the novel *Kipps* by H. G. Wells, starring Tommy Steele, at the Cambridge Theatre, London, and at the Broadhurst Theatre on Broadway; Alderman Helliwell in the J. B. Priestley comedy *When We Are Married*, alongside Brian Murphy and Prunella Scales, at the Churchill Theatre, Bromley, and the Whitehall Theatre, London; and Boss Finley in *Sweet Bird of Youth*, with Lauren Bacall, on tour and at the Theatre Royal Haymarket, London. The actor's other television work included playing Chief Superintendent Strange in the crime drama *Inspector Morse*, Olli Olliphant in the John Mortimer courtroom drama *Rumpole of the Bailey*, and George Batt in the drama *Mother Love*, which starred Diana Rigg and James Wilby. James's film credits included a sergeant in the dark comedy horror *The Abominable Dr Phibes*, Fairbrother in the heist drama *Loophole*, with Albert Finney and Susannah York, and Mr Watkins in the rock 'n' roll drama *Julie and the Cadillacs*. James, who used to write a column for his local newspaper when he lived in Malmesbury, Wiltshire, died after a long illness on 24 June 2012, aged eighty-four.

The commissionaire George, who could have easily inspired the phrase 'jobsworth', was played with vim and vigour by Richard Syms, who would make two appearances in the sitcom. An esteemed actor, Richard's theatre credits include a Swedish tourist in the Niccolò Machiavelli comedy *Mandragola* at the National Theatre, London, Sam Shipley in the J. B. Priestley play *I Have Been Here Before*, which featured a cast including George Costigan and Jenna Russell, and Stephen Spettigue in the Brandon Thomas farce *Charley's Aunt* at the Theatre Royal, Bath, and the Richmond Theatre. As well as appearing on stage, Richard has directed over a hundred shows ranging from Greek tragedy to Pinter and from Shakespeare to American musicals. The actor's television roles have included Mr Banks in the sitcom *Bless Me Father*, a delivery man in the sitcom *As Time Goes By*, and Lord Hailsham in the historical drama *The Crown*. His film work has seen him play characters such as Symonds in Anthony Minghella's fantasy drama *Truly Madly Deeply*, which starred Juliet Stevenson and Alan Rickman, a Drunken Repeater in Martin Scorsese's historical drama *Gangs of New York*, and a reverend in a chronicle of John Lennon's formative years, *Nowhere Boy*. Somehow, Richard has also found the time to be a priest.

The first episode of series five saw David Benson join the cast as Noël Coward. This would be the first of six episodes he would appear in across the last two series of the original run of the sitcom. The story of how David came to play 'The Master' begins in Scotland. 'I was performing my first one-man show, *Think No Evil of Us: My Life with Kenneth Williams*, at the Edinburgh Festival Fringe in 1997,' he said. 'While having a huge hit with the show, I also spent that August ending a four-year relationship, a deeply painful process for both of us. On this particular morning, having said our last goodbyes to each other, I had an 11.45am show to do at the Assembly Rooms. At the Edinburgh Fringe, you take the best timeslot you can get, and I was on the morning shift.

'I was very upset and feeling wretched when I arrived at the venue. I was sharing a dressing room with Bob Kingdom who was appearing in his one-man show about Elsa Maxwell, the 1930s party hostess and social power-broker. I was stood there being comforted by Bob dressed in his full Elsa Maxwell drag when Hannah Campagna, my stage manager, came to say good morning. I told her what had happened earlier and how I wasn't sure I could face the performance. She told me I could cancel if I wanted, but the show was totally sold out and there was a queue around the block for returns. "I'll leave it to you," she said.

'I thought of Judy Garland in *I Could Go On Singing*, leaving her troubles at the Palladium stage door, as she had done so often in real life, throwing down her fur and walking onto the stage to triumph. Amazingly, the same thing happened to me. I did go on and perform the show to the most astonishingly receptive and enthusiastic audience I had ever played to. It was as if they sensed my emotional rawness and embraced me.

'I used to jump off the stage at the end and sign programmes after each show. When I went into the foyer that day, this very tall, elegant lady came over, handed me a business card with a name I recognised on it and spoke, in a sexy German accent. "We very much enjoyed your show," she said. "My husband, Laurence, would like to meet you." The couple had been in the audience with Maurice Gran and his wife. They invited me to go and have dinner later with them at the George Hotel, where the Edinburgh Television Festival was in full swing. I thought, "Wow, this is the sort of thing you dream about happening to you!" Only a year before, I was a totally unknown outsider, but the success of my solo show had changed everything.

'At the hotel that evening, Laurence and Maurice told me they were working on the next series of *Goodnight Sweetheart* and wanted to find something for me to do in it. I had heard about the series, but I must admit I had never watched a minute of it; my attention was elsewhere at the time. This was in a period when they were looking to bring some other characters into the series and add some new blood.'

It would not be an exaggeration to say that Laurence and Maurice were inspired by seeing David's one-man show. 'We never had an intention of including Noël Coward in *Goodnight Sweetheart*,' said Laurence. 'However, when we realised that the bombing would have been getting heavier, it was obviously getting dangerous and Gary, knowing this, would have moved. We thought, why don't we move Gary and Phoebe to the West End and have Noël Coward living upstairs or next door?'

It wasn't long before David discovered their plan. 'Word later reached me that they wanted me to play the role of Noël Coward in the next series,' he said. 'In my solo show, there is a bit where I impersonate Kenneth Williams impersonating Noël Coward, so I think that must have put the idea in their minds of introducing Noël as a character.

'I was invited to a meeting with the series casting director Susie Parriss, the producer John Bartlett and the director Terry Kinane. However, I didn't have to audition as Marks and Gran wanted me to play Noël; they said Susie would not be seeing any other actors for the role. This was a very rare privilege for me as an actor and a huge honour. I knew the character of Noël inside out as I had been a fan of Coward since I was twelve years old and was well versed in his music, plays and persona.'

David went to Chelsea Barracks to rehearse with the cast for his first episode. 'I was rather nervous about meeting Nicholas Lyndhurst,' he admitted. 'But he was absolutely charming and welcoming to me from the start. There was no edge about him at all. In fact, I was made to feel welcome by all the cast and crew, even though I was coming in as an outsider and had never done television before other than just interviews.

'I did let rip with a Kenneth Williams impression on one of my lines at the script read-through. I can't remember which line it was, but I knew Laurence and Maurice were dying for me to "do the voice". It got a huge laugh and helped establish me with the company. They knew who I was after that.'

David can still remember his first recording day at Teddington Studios. 'I was allowed and encouraged to look at all the various sets in order to familiarise myself with the working environment,' he said. 'It was a such a great thrill for me to be there as a professional and not just as a visitor.

'My first scene, which was at the end of the episode, was a pre-record without an audience. I remember standing at the top of some steps behind a flat waiting for my cue. I was handed a lit cigarette by Hayden Buckingham-Jones, one of the props team on the series, who became a pal, and I entered on cue and managed to walk down to the bottom of the steps at the right time. This was tricky since, unlike on a theatre stage, I could not see or hear the actors before I entered and so had to learn to judge my entrances from indirect cues: a light, or a technical person mouthing, "Go!" Unfortunately, I took a draw on the cigarette during the scene and manged to obscure my face with smoke. We did another take and this time everyone seemed happy.'

With his scene recorded, David was then free for the rest of the day. 'I was able to relax and enjoy myself while all the cast were nervously preparing for the recording,' he disclosed. 'Later, I watched Ted Robbins' warm-up. I loved his humour and his impression of Les Dawson. Ted had appeared with Kenneth Williams on various game shows and he loved hearing me impersonate him; like a lot of people then, they missed Kenneth's voice and were glad to hear my approximation of it. We had a good rapport and he often got me up to speak to the audience. In fact, I got most of my biggest laughs on *Goodnight Sweetheart* with him in the warm-ups. Ted was always the life and soul of the party in the bar after the recordings and a wonderful man – getting to know Ted was one of the great pleasures of *Goodnight Sweetheart* for me.

'I remember going up to the gallery and pausing to stand on the walkway to look down onto the audience. I later watched the recording of the episode, which included a playback of my scene, in the gallery thanks to the director Terry Kinane, who was very happy for me to wander about during the taping and never made me feel like I was an imposter.

'My first episode was broadcast on the very same night I premiered *Think No Evil of Us* in the West End at the Vaudeville Theatre. I realised later that this one episode had been watched by more people in one go than would ever see my show if I toured it for the rest of my life!'

In addition to *Think No Evil of Us*, David has appeared in several other stage productions. They include the award-winning one-man show *Lockerbie: Unfinished Business*, Gareth in the National Theatre's smash-hit comedy *One Man, Two Guvnors* with James Corden, which clocked up over a thousand performances, and *The Dad's Army Radio Show*, in which he and Jack Lane played twenty-five characters between them. He and Jack have also performed together a two-man version of *A Christmas Carol* by Charles Dickens at the Capitol Theatre, Horsham. David played the character of Ebenezer Scrooge while Jack played the remaining characters. More recently, David joined the tour of the jukebox musical *Dreamboats and Petticoats – Bringing on Back the Good Times!* by Laurence Marks and Maurice Gran. During the production, David's roles included a cameo as Kenneth Williams. Away from the stage, David portrayed the Liberace hologram in the neo-noir science-fiction film, *Blade Runner 2049*.

Due to the nature of the explosion and stunts required in this episode, Roger Andrews was required to design a set that was a replica of Duckett's Passage and the surrounding buildings as they would have looked in 1944. The sets were then built at Shepperton Studios. Now part of the Pinewood Studios Group, the studios are located in Shepperton, Surrey, just eighteen miles from central London.

Like most film studios, Shepperton has learned to embrace television over the years. Programmes made there have included the game show *You Bet!*, the classic sitcoms *Red Dwarf* and *Last of the Summer Wine*, the panel show *8 Out Of 10 Cats*, which is hosted by Jimmy Carr, and the topical comedy *Russell Howard's Good News*.

The films that have graced Shepperton Studios over the years include Carol Reed's film noir *The Third Man*, the black comedy *Dr Strangelove*, which starred Peter Sellers, the musical *Oliver!*, based on Lionel Bart's 1960 stage show of the same name, Stanley Kubrick's dystopian crime drama *A Clockwork Orange*, the big-screen version of *Dad's Army*, the supernatural horror *The Omen*, Richard Curtis's romantic comedy *Four Weddings and a Funeral*, and Dennis Kelly and Tim Minchin's *Matilda the Musical*, an adaptation of their Tony and Olivier award-winning theatre musical, which is based on the Roald Dahl novel.

Another location not used in the series before was the exterior of 50 Sloane Street, Knightsbridge, London. The front entrance can be seen in the scene where Gary and Phoebe enter the building to view a new flat. The interior of the flat and the entrance hallway were built in Studio 1 at Teddington Studios.

*

Having moved into their new apartment in the West End, Phoebe is quick to acquaint herself with her new surroundings in 'London Pride', the second episode of series five. When she visits the local butcher's, he snottily refuses to add her as an account customer because he clearly thinks she's too common, despite them having bought their apartment for cash. Worse still, one of the snooty local nannies thinks Michael's eyes are too close together. Phoebe tells Gary that she doesn't like living in the West End any more because she doesn't fit in. In Stepney people think she's posh. Gary offers to give her elocution lessons. He reminds her that he's been trained to fit into any stratum of society!

Reg proves to be a tonic to Phoebe when he turns up to visit, but bores Gary by revealing the full name he was christened with due to his father being a fanatical Spurs supporter. Reg was conceived in 1901 following a post-Cup Final outburst of marital passion after Spurs beat Sheffield United. He reveals his full name as Reginald Clawley Erentz Tait Jones Hughes Morris Smith Cameron Brown Copeland Kirwan Deadman.

Back in the present, Ron has kindly recorded Yvonne's appearance on a Channel 5 show called *Breaking Out, Breaking In*. They watch it on a television in Gary's shop. Unfortunately, the tape runs out before the end of the interview, leaving Gary unable to find out what Yvonne meant when she said her business partner, Clive, has '... always been on hand to give me a damn good...'

Yvonne reveals she has plans designed for the building of a large new seven-bedroom house with an acre of garden. Gary, however, is more concerned as to why she was singing Clive's praises in the interview. Yvonne reminds him that she owes Clive everything. When Gary brings up the phrase that is bothering him, Yvonne protests that she can't remember what she says in every interview. The discussion at an unsatisfactory end, the millionairess makes for her waiting limo, which is about to take her to the airport and a plane bound for Brazil (where, she reminds Gary, the nuts come from) for the weekend.

Back in 1944, Noël Coward is kindly giving Phoebe some elocution lessons. When Noël mentions Eliza Doolittle in *Pygmalion*, Phoebe proudly tells Noël that Gary wrote a musical based on the play and that he used to court her with songs he had written for the production. Noël admits he never realised Gary was so 'enormously endowed... with talent'.

Back in the present, after Gary sells Mr Hornby some original model trains for twelve hundred pounds cash, Yvonne arrives in the shop having returned from her trip to Brazil and informs Gary she's going to the Mansion House for the Woman of the Year dinner. Gary says it's a bit short notice as he has a darts match that night. She tell him he's not invited as it's ladies only, but he is invited to the drinks party at No. 10 afterwards and that she'll leave his name on the gate. Gary is interested but still wants to know the answer to what she said in the interview. Yvonne is insulted by his lack of faith in her. However, she has seen a tape of the interview and explains that she said Clive is always on hand to give her 'a damn good kick up the backside whenever I'm feeling sorry for myself'. This leaves Gary embarrassed.

Returning to wartime London, Gary discovers that Noël has transformed Phoebe into a well-spoken lady and she is walking around like a character in a Coward play. Phoebe encourages Gary to perform one of his songs. Worried that he might impress 'The Master', he deliberately sings The Smiths' song 'Heaven Knows I'm Miserable Now' badly. This fails to impress Noël who tells him not to give up his day job. Phoebe is annoyed, believing he has done it deliberately as he doesn't want to be a famous songwriter.

Gary heads back to the nineties and No. 10 Downing Street. He informs a female police officer that he's come for the party. When she asks Gary for his invite, he says he doesn't have one but that his name is on her clipboard. She doesn't believe Yvonne is his wife as everyone knows she's married to the hippy-looking chap with the ponytail.

Not best pleased, Gary returns to 1944, goes back to the flat and tells Phoebe that he should have been attending a meeting at No. 10, but the prime minister forget to put his name on the gate. Phoebe is confused, and Gary quickly remembers there wasn't a gate at the entrance to Downing Street back then.

The following day, Gary and Phoebe decide to take revenge on their local butcher for how he treated Phoebe. Gary pretends to be from the Ministry of Food, there to impound his venison stolen from Windsor Great Park due to the fact that he refused to register Gary's wife as a customer simply because she was posing as a member of the lower orders. Phoebe also informs him that her husband had received complaints about his unpatriotically superior attitude to people of humble origins and that she had been sent to test him out. Gary explains that the only reason they're not taking further action is that Noël Coward spoke up for him; apparently, he particularly esteems his Cumberland sausage. Finally convinced, the butcher agrees to give them what's left of the illicit venison from the shop, which they plan to transport back to the flat on Michael's pram.

Laurence and Maurice were quick to take advantage of the changes that had been made to Gary and Phoebe's living arrangements and Yvonne's new status as a millionairess. Whereas Gary had often felt like a fish out of water being a time traveller in a strange time, Phoebe now felt the same living in the West End and dealing with a different class of people. Despite the butcher and some of the locals she encountered giving her a hard time, fortunately Noël Coward wasn't judgemental and, like Gary, found Phoebe's realness endearing.

Earlier in the run of *Goodnight Sweetheart*, it was revealed that Reg's name was Reginald Horatio Deadman. As mentioned, the police constable announced a much longer set of names and his initials would easily fill an eye chart! It's noticeable, however, that for some reason Horatio has now disappeared from his full name.

The snotty-nosed butcher in this episode was played by Lloyd McGuire in his one and only appearance in the series. Early in his career, Lloyd's theatre credits included playing William Gladstone in William Francis's remarkable play *Portrait of a Queen* at the Redgrave Theatre, Farnham, Sam Grundy in the Walter Greenwood and Ronald Gow drama *Love on the Dole* at the Wyvern Theatre, Swindon, and Autolycus in William Shakespeare's romantic comedy *The Winter's Tale* at the Bristol Old Vic. Best known for playing Bob Porter in the comedy drama *Teachers*, his other television roles have included Tommy Butler in the police drama *Between the Lines*, which starred Neil Pearson, and Martin Shell in the supermarket sitcom *Trollied*. Lloyd's film parts, meanwhile, include playing the Midlands rep in the footballing comedy *Mike Bassett: England Manager*, with Ricky Tomlinson, John in the comedy *Ali G Indahouse* and a master of ceremonies in the short comedy *Bad Night for the Blues*.

The role of Mrs Greig, a customer in the butcher's shop, was played by Toni Palmer, whose credits on stage, television and film would be the envy of any actor or actress. Toni's many theatre appearances have ranged from playing Betty in the Lionel Bart musical *Fings Ain't Wot They Used T'Be*, with Barbara Windsor, at the Theatre Royal, Stratford East, and the Garrick Theatre, London, a lead performer in the revue *Danny La Rue at the Palace* at the Palace Theatre, London, and Mrs Hall in the Ken Hill musical *The Invisible Man* at the Theatre Royal, Stratford East, Vaudeville Theatre, London, and the Comedy Theatre, London. Her other television credits are innumerable and include Edi Driscoll in the action drama *The Sweeney*, Mrs Delaney in the period drama *The Duchess of Duke Street*, and Mrs Barlow in the sitcom *Hi-de-Hi!* Toni's film roles, meanwhile, include a Buttercup Girl in the First World War-based comedy *Up the Front*, which starred Frankie Howerd, Mrs Endicott in the romantic drama *The French Lieutenant's Woman*, and Aunt Winnie in the comedy drama *Personal Services*, with Julie Walters.

The presenter who interviewed Yvonne on the fictional Channel 5 series *Breaking Out, Breaking In* was Esther McVey. Before beginning a high-profile career in politics, Esther worked as a broadcaster and a journalist, presenting and producing programmes. She worked as a presenter on programmes including *GMTV*, *5's Company* and *The Heaven and Earth Show*. More recently, Esther and her husband Philip Davies have co-hosted a programme called *Friday Morning with Esther and Philip* on the news channel, GB News.

There was also a nice cameo in this episode for Nick Lucas as Mr Hornby. Nicholas Lyndhurst clearly relished delivering the name Hornby as he sold the character the model trains during the scene in question. Nick's stage work includes playing the Porter in the Edmond Rostand play *Cyrano de Bergerac*, with Robert Lindsay, at the Theatre Royal Haymarket, London, Bobo in the Brendan Behan absurdist tragi-comedy *The Hostage* at the Barbican Theatre, London, and Professor Metz in Moss Hart and George S. Kaufman's comedy *The Man Who Came to Dinner* at the Chichester Festival Theatre, which starred Richard Griffiths and Eve Matheson. On television, his other credits include playing a police sergeant in the crime drama *Maigret*, Mr Winstanley in the light-hearted 1960s drama *Heartbeat*, and Mr Huss in the period drama *Fingersmith*. Additionally, Nick's film roles have included Hubert Cleggie in the dark comedy *Gentlemen Don't Eat Poets*, Gerard in the short comedy *On the Roof* and Justiciar in the action adventure *Robin Hood*.

Returning for this episode was David Benson as Noël Coward. 'David was fabulous as Noël Coward and I loved working him,' said Elizabeth. 'I particularly liked the scene we did together in this episode when he was teaching Phoebe to speak properly à la Eliza Doolittle in *My Fair Lady*.'

Having never acted on television before, let alone in a sitcom, working on *Goodnight Sweetheart* was certainly a learning curve for David Benson. This was especially the case when it came to recording scenes in front of an audience. Fortunately, he was able to seek advice from his fellow cast members, including Christopher Ettridge. 'I was talking to Chris about timing and how you time your laughs with a studio audience,' recalled David. 'He said, "You play to the laughs that you're getting. You don't really know where they're going to come until the audience are there and laughing." It's a strange thing when you're recording a sitcom as you can't really see the audience. Studio 1 at Teddington was so long that sometimes the audience could see you straight on, but other times we could be miles away and they could only see us on a monitor above their heads, and thus the audience feels very remote compared to theatre. I could be talking to Nicholas Lyndhurst or Liz Carling in a scene, and I could hear this strange and distant laughter coming from a parallel universe. Chris gave me some other great advice: he said, "It's much better to pause at the end of a line, even if there isn't a laugh from the studio audience, than to talk over a laugh, because they can't edit that. You must think about the editing. They can always tinker with it later and make a little cut or boost the laughter." That was one of the key things I learned from working on the series.'

Penelope Solomon played not one but two different characters in series five of *Goodnight Sweetheart*. Her first role, in this episode, was playing a policewoman who caused Gary to miss out on the opportunity of partying at No. 10. 'They sent a taxi to pick me up and transport me to the location,' she explained. 'The scene was filmed pretty quickly outside the gates of Downing Street on Whitehall. When I arrived and got out of the car I saw everyone setting up; it was so exciting. I was really pleased that it was just Nicholas and me in the scene. He was very professional. But I was a bit confused about the macadamia nut body scrub line because I didn't know what a macadamia nut actually was as Google didn't exist then!'

Amongst her theatre work, Penelope has staged productions at the Edinburgh Fringe with her company, Laffa Jaffa. They include *Smashing Shakespeare: Romeo and Juliet*, which she adapted and performed. On television, Penelope's credits include the Stewart Lee and Richard Herring sketch show *Fist of Fun* and the comedy *Cuts*, which was written by the late David Nobbs.

Gary arrives at the shop with Yvonne, who's giving one of her employees a piece of her mind on her mobile phone, after a successful trip away as 'When Two Worlds Collide', the third episode of series five, begins. After taking care of business, Yvonne presents Gary with a present – a palmtop computer in a customised antique silver case. The time traveller is very pleased and comments that it must have cost a lot of money. Yvonne tells him that she thinks he's worth it.

Ron duly arrives and tells Gary and Yvonne that he's going on a date. Yvonne cheekily asks if he's 'bought a tart'. However, Ron explains that he's joined a dating agency. He then asks the couple for brutal advice to help his chances with his love life. Knowing him as she does, Yvonne suggests he spend much and say little.

Back at the Royal Oak, Reg arrives with some worrying news. Everyone has got to evacuate to the local school hall because they've found an unexploded bomb in Duckett's Passage. Gary panics, realising this could seriously affect his chances of getting back to the present.

Gary and Phoebe later go to Duckett's Passage and find Reg on guard duty. Selfishly, Gary asks Reg to ask the sappers how long it's going to be before they've finished making the bomb safe. Reg reluctantly agrees and, while he goes to check, the bomb goes off and the force of the blast throws poor Reg into the air. He then falls against a wall. In normal circumstances, such an accident might cause memory loss or worse. However, in Reg's case it causes him to 'turn bright'. Gary jests that this miracle could make this place more popular than Lourdes!

With Reg recovering, Gary manages to find the time portal and get back to present-day London. Relieved, he promises himself the biggest double brandy. Just then Phoebe walks into the shop via the back door and renders Gary into a deep shock. Phoebe says he looks as though he's seen a ghost. After clambering over rubble in Duckett's Passage, she's been propelled into present-day London. Gary says this can't be happening and Phoebe begins to suspect that he's shell-shocked. When his better half asks where they are, quick as a flash Gary says that it's his secret headquarters and the reason she's never seen it before is that the bomb has caused damage to the nearby walls. Although impressed, Phoebe comments that it looks like a shop.

Realising that he needs to get his wartime wife back to the past as quickly as possible, Gary blindfolds her and tries to lead her back to the time portal in the yard. Each time he tries to guide Phoebe through the time portal, she just hurts herself on the gates. Gary realises that the time portal has closed, possibly due to the explosion back in wartime London. By way of an excuse, Gary tells her the security gates are on a time lock and they will have to wait until they open.

Curious, Phoebe starts to look around the stock in the shop. After she starts asking difficult questions, Gary realises he needs to quickly conceal anything that is post-war. He sends his wife to the toilet while he tidies up. While in the cubicle she asks what a Toilet Duck is, and Gary quickly retrieves it.

Gary goes to check if the time portal has opened again and is upset to find it's still closed. He returns to the shop and pulls the blinds down, so Phoebe won't see anything out of the windows, such as modern cars.

When Phoebe comes back into the shop, she asks why they have to wait for the time lock and can't just go out of the front door instead. Thinking on his feet again, Gary tells her of an expected air raid and then uses a tape recording of an air raid to persuade Phoebe it's too dangerous to leave.

Gary and Phoebe then take cover in a small Morrison shelter in the shop. Officially called the 'table shelter', it was nicknamed after Herbert Morrison, the then Minister of Home Defence.

As Phoebe is hungry, Gary looks for some mints in his jacket. While doing so, Phoebe spots Gary's new palmtop computer. After Gary tells her it's an old cigarette case, Phoebe breaks it while killing a spider.

The phone rings. Although it's an old-style phone, Gary still has to explain what an answering machine is. Yvonne begins to leave a message and Gary quickly answers the phone. After she offers to come to meet him at the shop, Gary tells her he will see her at home in about an hour instead.

Gary calls Ron on his mobile for help. He is standing in Piccadilly Circus holding a rose and waiting for his date to turn up. When Gary explains why he wants him to drop everything and come to the shop, Ron is shocked and instantly agrees to come. He drops the rose and makes his way. Just after he leaves, his very attractive date turns up and looks disappointed as she picks up the rose and can't find Ron.

Once Ron arrives at the shop, Gary tells him he'll be back as quick as he can, and Ron agrees to keep Phoebe, who is making the most of a lull in the 'air raid' to visit the toilet again, entertained. He tells Ron about the air-raid tape and reassures him that Michael is back at home being looked after by Noël Coward. As a cover story, he tells Ron to say he works with him in the Secret Service. But because Phoebe met his grandad, Albert Wheatcroft, Gary tells Ron he needs to change his name. Ron suggests Bond. Concerned, Gary tells him not to go over the top.

After coping with Ron and Phoebe meeting at the shop, a rather hyped-up Gary goes back home to Cricklewood where his behaviour concerns Yvonne. Gary pretends that he's left his wallet in the shop and that he's going to need it in the morning. Yvonne offers to come back to the shop. Unable to come up with an excuse as to why she shouldn't accompany him, Gary is faced with no alternative than to return with his spouse.

On arriving at the shop in Yvonne's car, Gary tells her that he's allowed Ron to use his shop because his date has a fetish about the war. They both spot that Ron is casting shadows on the window and the effect is reminiscent of the opening sequence of a James Bond film.

When Gary enters the shop he discovers that Ron has bored Phoebe to sleep with made-up stories of his James Bond-type missions. Gary tells him that Yvonne is outside in the car. Ron tells him that the two can't meet as it would be like matter meeting antimatter.

Gary goes outside into the yard and checks the time portal. To his relief, he discovers that it is open again – although, in testing the portal, one of Gary's arms appears back in the war and scares an ARP warden on duty in Duckett's Passage. Gary goes back into the shop and wakes Phoebe, telling her that the all-clear has sounded, the time lock on the gates has opened and they can go home. Just then, the inevitable happens: Yvonne enters the shop and Gary's two wives come face to face for the very first time. Gary stands looking shocked. Fortunately, neither woman realises the truth of the situation and Gary accompanies Phoebe home while Yvonne waits in the car.

On returning to the Royal Oak, Phoebe tells Reg an excuse about where they have been. Just when Gary is starting to relax, he turns around and comes to face to face with Ron who says, 'Finally made it, mate.'

The storylines in this episode featured some of the worst things that could happen to Gary. Phoebe coming into the present, the time portal closing and both of his partners meeting in his presence. So was this a difficult episode for Gary Lawson and John Phelps to write? 'Tricky, but a lot of fun,' said John. 'A bit of a farce, like 'Who's Taking You Home Tonight?' in series two. The one thing we were determined to engineer was a meeting between Yvonne and Phoebe: Gary's worst nightmare.'

At no stage did the storylines ever allow for the character of Yvonne Sparrow to venture back into the Second World War. Michelle, the first Yvonne, was once asked whether she would have liked to have appeared with the other series regulars in the scenes set in the past. 'Yes,' she replied. 'I love the forties, especially the clothes, hair and make-up! But the cast always worked together anyway as we rehearsed all week, then taped each episode in front of a live studio audience.'

However, Emma was less convinced. 'I don't think it would've worked,' she said. 'It would have been far too complicated to explain that one! So this was a great episode as it was lovely to actually do a scene with Lizzie!'

The stunt in which Reg Deadman was seen to fly through the air was co-ordinated and performed by Lee Sheward. 'I knew Julie Sykes who was a first assistant director on this particular series,' said Lee. 'She recommended me to the producer, John Bartlett, and the director, Terry Kinane. I went to Shepperton Studios and had a meeting on the Duckett's Passage set. We talked about the stunt and the angle of the shot they wanted. I also had a costume fitting. When I arrived on the day of the filming, I set up the air ram, which I used to throw me into the air. You press the button on the ram and/or step on it to fire it; I used the button. It's pressurised with nitrogen gas and when you press a button the gas is released, and the ram fires the performer – in this case me – through the air before landing on a crash mat. On this occasion, I did the stunt backwards. I was meant to be thrown about twenty feet through the air, but I went a little high on take-off and so did not make that distance. However, the extra height worked out far better and I only had to do the stunt once.'

Lee is a stunt co-ordinator, performer and second unit director, and has worked across all forms of media globally for over thirty-five years. For television, Lee has contributed his skills to the science-fiction series *Doctor Who*, the motoring programme *Top Gear* and the historic drama *The Crown*. Lee's many film credits, meanwhile, have included the action thriller *Mission: Impossible*, with Tom Cruise, James Cameron's *Titanic* and *Wonder Woman*, starring Gal Gadot and Chris Pine.

Realising that he would be a loose cannon in war-torn London, Gary quickly brings Ron back to present-day London at the start of 'Mairzy Doats', the fourth episode of series five. He tells Ron he has no knowledge of the period and could end up giving both of them away. For example, he points out that wearing an Echo and the Bunnymen 1998 jacket was not the best of ideas.

Yvonne enters the shop and reminds Gary that she's been waiting in the car for fifteen minutes. At first she wonders where Ron's date is but quickly decides she doesn't want to know after Gary had said she had a fetish about the war. Besides, she has an early start the following morning at Stamford Bridge to do a one-day consultancy on healing injuries for the Chelsea football players. In an attempt to divert Ron's mind away from 1944, Gary asks Yvonne to see if she can get them tickets for the big European game the following night. She reluctantly says she will ask if the subject of tickets crops up.

Gary tells Yvonne he will catch a taxi home as he realises he's going to need extra time to settle Ron's desire to go time travelling. Yvonne leaves and, as expected, the promise of tickets isn't enough to keep Ron happy. More eager than ever, he promises to return the following morning with the right clothes and papers. He reveals that he printed ID papers for himself ages ago in case this 'miracle' should arise.

Realising that the time portal is currently a two-way street, and people and objects can go both ways, Gary decides to dress in an army uniform and keep guard in the yard in case anyone comes through. Thankfully, the only thing that comes through is a football. Predictably, Gary scares the children the other side of the time portal when he throws it back.

When Ron returns the next morning still insistent on experiencing life in the war, Gary becomes desperate and tells him that the portal has closed to all traffic both ways. Given that Gary doesn't appear to be very upset, Ron is unconvinced and tries it for himself again. He goes through and makes for the Royal Oak pursued by a desperate Gary, afraid of what he might say. Once there, Ron, or rather Commander Bond, meets Phoebe again along with Reg, now seconded to Scotland Yard because he's solved all the crime in the area, and Margie for the first time. However, it's not long before Reg, still in intelligent mode, tells Gary he thinks that Ron is somehow out of place. To placate him, Gary tells Reg that Ron is eccentric. Ron then decides to splash out and take everyone up West to a nightclub to celebrate Reg's new position at Scotland Yard.

Back at the shop, Yvonne leaves a message on Gary's answering machine telling him she's got tickets for her, Gary and Ron in the VIP lounge at Stamford Bridge at 6.00pm. Free drinks and a chance to meet the players are also on the cards. Unfortunately, Gary isn't there to pick up the message as he's coping with Ron's many faux pas back in 1944.

Because five is an uneven number, Phoebe suggests that they find someone to accompany Ron as his date at the nightclub. Gary suggests her friend, Violet Bigby. Phoebe approves of the idea: after all, Violet's never been out with a commander before. Gary quips that they've found a rank she's missed!

Once they reach the nightclub it's not long before Ron begins to embarrass himself and everyone else. His sense of humour and suggestive remarks to Violet don't help either. He also upsets the nightclub's flamboyant owner, Peter Strangefellow.

After an evening of mixed success, Gary and Phoebe take Ron back to their flat. Violet, still coping with bruised feet due to Ron's pitiful dancing, has limped home accompanied by Reg. When an air raid sounds, they head to the shelter, complete with little Michael who has been looked after by a neighbour. Ron soon admits to being bored and Gary asks what the 'moron' expected. Ron comments that he shouldn't be talking to a commanding officer in such a fashion. George, the jobsworth commissionaire, overhears and agrees, much to Gary's annoyance.

Ron then stirs up trouble and before long Gary finds himself tied to a chair, which amuses the new time traveller. Even Reg's arrival in his official capacity does nothing to help Gary. Then Ron ignores the wartime admonition that 'loose lips sink ships' and he finds himself hoist by his own petard. He ends up being overthrown by some of those in the shelter and handcuffed to Gary, who reminds everyone not to spread any of the mad things that Ron has been saying.

When the all-clear sounds, Gary manages to drag Ron back to the present. Yvonne arrives at the shop, and asks Gary and Ron where they were the previous evening. Gary tells her they were at a friend's stag party. Yvonne mentions that they missed out on the VIP evening she arranged at the football match.

Now angrier than ever, Ron decides he can no longer put up with life in the nineties and heads for the gates in the yard and 1944. Worried that Yvonne will see Ron go back in time, Gary tries to make her look away. To his relief, Ron can no longer get through the gates and hurts himself in the process. This amuses Yvonne who asks why she wasn't allowed to enjoy Ron's discomfort.

This episode certainly proved just how much extra trouble and stress Gary would have faced if Ron could have travelled back in time on a regular basis. Although Gary would often make mistakes, he at least mastered the basic rudiments of day-to-day living in wartime London, which Ron would probably never have got to grips with – especially etiquette when dating a member of the opposite sex!

Back to give support in this episode were Eve Bland as Margie and Regina Freedman in her last appearance as Violet. Also, Richard Syms made the second of his two appearances as George the jobsworth commissionaire at the block of flats where Gary and Phoebe live. Richard happily revealed his favourite moment from making this episode. 'Nick and the director were discussing how to get the "extras", as they were then called, to mob him savagely,' he said. 'Nick suggested that he filled all his pockets with sandwiches!'

There was also a brilliantly performed cameo from David Simeon, who in real life is married to the *Brush Strokes* actress Elizabeth Counsell, as nightclub owner Peter Strangefellow. The name was a simple but amusing play on the name of the real and legendary one-time owner of Stringfellows nightclub in London, Peter Stringfellow, who died on 7 June 2018.

David's many stage appearances include playing Ronald Hawes in the Agatha Christie play *Murder at the Vicarage* at the Salisbury Playhouse, Patrice Bombelles in the comedy *Ring Round the Moon* at the Theatre Royal, Windsor, and Trevor Farrington in a tour of *Theft*, a fast-paced comedy by Eric Chappell, the creator of *Rising Damp*. His other television roles have included playing Jumbo in the wartime drama series *A Family at War*; Mr Mackenzie, one half of a young couple who didn't get their alarm call, in the episode of *Fawlty Towers* called 'A Touch of Class'; and Priestley in the crime drama *Silent Witness*. Although David's list of film credits is small, he did find himself being reunited with John Cleese when he played the court clerk in the farcical comedy *A Fish Called Wanda*.

In 'Pennies from Heaven', the fifth episode of series five, we soon discover that Ron is far from happy. His new-found ability to commute to 1944 has ended, while Gary still comes and goes as he pleases. In an attempt to get Ron in a good mood, because he needs yet another favour, Gary offers to take him out for a drink. While Ron gets his coat, Kate Flanagan, Ron's new boss, arrives and instantly begins flirting with Gary, only going back to her office when Ron returns. Ron asks Gary what favour he needs. He asks Ron if he's printed him some more white fivers as promised, as he's down to just twenty pounds. Ron hasn't and makes it clear he's not in a generous mood, but that a visit to a local hostelry will help as once there he can become as generous as a newt.

Gary and Ron later return to Blitz and Pieces and Gary asks again about the wartime currency. Ron still says no, the reason being it's more difficult to print them now because he's no longer his own boss. The rest of the staff at the print works also have fiddles on the go, or at least would have if Mrs Flanagan was out of the office long enough. Ron suggest Gary give in to his boss's flirting and ask her out. Gary is far from keen and reminds him that he's got two wives and, despite how complicated his life is, he's a happily married man. At that moment Yvonne arrives at the shop and, having heard Gary, innocently asks him if he's got a secret wife somewhere. Shocked by her unexpected arrival, Gary asks why she's not at Newmarket talking to the racing fraternity as planned. She explains that their 'closed minds' made the trip a waste of time. However, someone felt sorry for her wasted journey and gave her a couple of betting tips, so she asks

Goodnight Sweetheart: A Guide to the Classic Sitcom

Gary to place fifty pounds on each horse. Ron's eyes light up and he admits there's something about a woman being reckless that turns him on. Yvonne thanks him for the warning.

After Yvonne leaves for Paris, Ron suggests that placing bets in the past might be a good way for Gary to make some money. Better still, researching the results in old newspapers would make the bets dead certs. Although Gary is not comfortable with the idea at first, he soon realises it would, as Ron reminds him, be highly profitable.

When Phoebe discovers that Gary has been asking Reg if he knows of any bookies who trade illegally, she becomes angry and upset. She reveals that her dad's gambling drove her mum to an early grave.

Reg tells Gary about a chancer from up north who's operating an illegal bookie's on Mo Green's old patch. Desperate for wartime money, Gary suggests they visit him. He can win some money and Reg can observe, take notes and collect evidence with a view to raiding him the following week. This appeals to Reg and they decide to make a secret visit to the bookie in question.

Naturally, Reg decides to visit the bookie, based in a dusty garage, in a poor disguise, wearing strange glasses and a wig. On arriving, Gary tells the cocky bookie that he's one of Mo Green's old credit customers, but that he doesn't expect credit. This is just as well as the bookie does not offer any.

With Gary having placed his bets, Phoebe turns up and causes a scene. After failing to win his first two bets, Gary realises that the bookie is lying about the winners. Worse still, in an attempt to deflect from the situation, the bookie accuses Gary of being a race fixer. After refusing to pay his winnings, the bookie punches Gary. When Reg protests at Gary's mistreatment, one of the bookie's henchmen hits him on the head. This causes Reg to return to his 'normal self'.

After giving Phoebe the remainder of his money for some outstanding bills back at the Royal Oak, Gary is left broke and wondering what to do.

Meanwhile, back in the present, Ron reminds Gary that he can only print more wartime notes if he has three hours, and his boss is never out of the office that long. Given that Kate couldn't make it clearer that she's attracted to Gary if she tried, asking her out on a date seems to be the best possible solution. As her heels are heard clattering down the corridor, Ron begs Gary to do his best to lure her out of the office. He mentions that the whole of the print works are behind him.

Kate suggests she and Gary go for a drink at the Theatre Royal Stratford East's bar. Gary reluctantly agrees and turns around to see Ron and some of the other print workers showing their approval behind the window of an adjoining print room.

In an attempt to keep Kate out of the office a bit longer, Gary takes her back to his closed shop to play for time. At first she is confused as to why he's brought her back to this strange museum, which isn't on the tourist map, but then begins to wonder if he has a fetish for the war and dressing up. When he invites her into the yard, she suspects making love outside might be his 'thing'. The reality is he intends to use the time portal as a way of making Kate think she is having some kind of breakdown. It works. After Gary disappears and reappears, she thinks she's ill and asks him to take her back to the print works.

Back at the office, the police are in the middle of carrying out a raid. DS Bruce of Obscene Publications informs Kate that two of her staff have been arrested for producing pornographic material and Ron for forgery – despite him producing only 1940s fivers.

Later, at Gary's shop, Ron moans to the time traveller about not getting him legal representation, but Gary points out that he didn't need any. But although Ron has been released, the police are not happy with him. In fact they want him to visit a psychiatrist!

Yvonne pulls up outside the shop, fresh from Paris. It's then that Gary remembers he forgot to put her bets on. Ron laughs and exacts revenge by telling her that Gary got better odds. This means he will have to pay his millionairess wife six hundred pounds. But it's not all doom and gloom for Gary, as Ron points out that the police let him keep the six hundred pounds in white wartime fivers and hands them over to him.

Although Phoebe's father Eric had not been seen since the last episode of the first series, he was still referred to during the remainder of *Goodnight Sweetheart*'s run. In this episode it was, of course, discovered that he had a gambling habit. Basically, this subplot is proof of how the writers, in this case Geoff Rowley, could introduce new character traits, even to characters who were no longer in the series, to aid plot devices.

One of the most memorable guest performers in this sitcom has to be Pippa Haywood. She played Ron's long-suffering and somewhat frustrated boss, Mrs Flanagan. Described by Pippa as 'more the captain of a hockey team than a sex symbol', still waters ran deep with the character as Gary soon found out. Her marriage was far from happy. Her husband was an organ donor, but, as the character revealed, he rarely donated to her. *Goodnight Sweetheart* was not the first time Nicholas and Pippa had worked together. 'I had worked with Nicholas before on a five-month tour of the Peter Shaffer one-act plays *The Private Ear and Black Comedy*,' she explained. Matthew Kelly was also in both casts. It was the first acting job I had done with well-known performers, and I got to know Nick well. We even did a charity performance at the Theatre Royal, Windsor, in the presence of Prince Edward. After the tour ended, Nick and I continued to see each other when we were rehearsing separate comedies at the BBC Rehearsal Rooms in North Acton.

'I was really thrilled to be asked to play Mrs Flanagan. In addition to knowing Nick, I was at the same drama school as Victor and knew Elizabeth from when we appeared in episodes of *Boon* together. I had also met Emma before because I knew her husband, Jonathan Coy. So not only did I have a cracking part to play, but I had lots of mates who I was looking forward to seeing again.

'I played the character of Mrs Flanagan as a sort of head of the hockey team type who moved and behaved quite awkwardly. This was so there would be an obvious contrast to the very overtly sexual way she behaved with Gary during the rest of the episode.

'I get asked a lot to do one-day cameos on television, but I find them stressful. With *Goodnight Sweetheart* you had almost a week to rehearse and that gave you time to settle. It was a lovely atmosphere and it was great fun when Marks and Gran and John Bartlett popped into the rehearsal room.

'I guess cutting my sitcom teeth in *The Brittas Empire* prepared me for appearing in comedies like *Goodnight Sweetheart*. It meant I was used to acting in front of a studio audience. What I also learned was it's best to nail a scene the first time and treat the recordings like they are a live stage performance.

'Although I enjoyed working on the sitcom in the big studio at Teddington Studios, I loved going on to the balcony just outside the bar that overlooked the River Thames after the recording. It helped reacquaint me with nature after what was a busy day.

'I have fond and joyful memories of making the show. It would have been great to play Mrs Flanagan again. She could easily have come back in other episodes as she was Ron's boss.

'I think the great cast, writing and the ingenious idea of time travel made the series stand out from other sitcoms of the period.'

The award-winning actress has achieved many plaudits during her career. Her theatre roles have included Amanda Prynne in the Noël Coward comedy *Private Lives* at the Redgrave Theatre, Farnham, Ross in the Joe Penhall drama *Landscape with Weapon* at the National Theatre, London, and the Duchess and Red Queen in *Alice*, Laura Wad's adaptation of Lewis Carroll's novel *Alice in Wonderland*, at the Crucible Theatre, Sheffield. Her other television credits include playing the hot-tempered, sex-mad human resources director Joanna Clore in the sitcom *Green Wing*, for which she took the Best Comedy Female Performance award at the 2005 Rose d'Or Television Festival in Switzerland, the Duke of Hastings' housekeeper Mrs Colson in the historical fiction-romance

Bridgerton, and Dr McAndrew in the crime thriller *Trigger Point*. In addition, Pippa's film parts have included a bookshop owner in the family fantasy *Four Kids and It*, based on the book *Four Children and It*, Lilly in the romantic drama *Supernova*, which also starred Colin Firth and Stanley Tucci, and Tanya in the short drama *Reaching Four*.

Also in the supporting cast for this episode was David Ross, who played the bookie of dubious repute. David's work on the stage has included playing Lenny Anderson in the Alan Bleasdale adult comedy *Having a Ball* at the Comedy Theatre, London, Metcalfe in the George S. Kaufman comedy *The Solid Gold Cadillac*, with Roy Hudd and Patricia Routledge, at the Yvonne Arnaud Theatre, Guilford, and the Garrick Theatre, London, and William Blore in the Agatha Christie dark thriller *And Then There Were None* at the Gielgud Theatre, London. Best known for playing the first Kryten and the second Talkie Toaster in the science-fiction comedy *Red Dwarf*, his other television credits have included Mr Sedley in a 1998 adaptation of the romantic drama *Vanity Fair* and Elgin Sparrowhawk in the sitcom *The Green Green Grass*. David's film roles include playing an officer in the crime drama *Vice Squad*, Sergeant Richardson in the comedy *Splitting Heirs*, which starred Eric Idle and Rick Moranis, and Joe in the action adventure *She*.

Nick Carpenter was also cast as the 'punter' who checks Reg is all right after he receives a knock on the head. His other television work includes playing a character called Monk in the long-running police drama, *The Bill*.

Finally, Robert Perkins played DS Bruce of Obscene Publications. Robert's theatre credits include playing Gerry Evans in the Brian Friel memory play *Dancing at Lughnasa* at the Library Theatre, Manchester, John Malcolm and Major Pollock in Terence Rattigan's two one-act plays under the title of *Separate Tables* at Salisbury Playhouse, and Captain Lestrange in a tour of the Frederick Knott mid-century melodrama *Dial 'M' for Murder*. On television he has played characters including Flood in the techno-espionage series *Bugs*, Lyle Goodson in the crime drama *Rosemary and Thyme* and Dr Joshua Phipps in the soap opera *EastEnders*. Robert's film roles include Richard in the short drama *Close Encounter*, with Lindsay Carr, the town car man in the comedy drama *The Upside of Anger* and Nick in the short drama *Gone*, with Suranne Jones.

Yvonne departs on yet another high-powered business trip at the start of 'We Don't Want to Lose You…', the sixth episode of series five. This time it's to Paris, Milan and Madrid. Her busy life of non-stop glamour is starting to make Gary jealous. Selfishly forgetting for a moment that he has two wives and the gift of time travel, he tells Ron that no one knows who he is and that he feels like Mr Anonymous.

After sharing dinner with Phoebe at the Café Royal in London's West End, Gary is ordered by intelligence chief Tufty McDuff to get into his car, which is waiting outside. He is driven back to MI5 headquarters where Tufty reveals that he knows Gary has been falsely claiming to work as a secret agent and possessing fake wartime identity papers. However, in return for buying his silence, Tufty wants him to go on a secret mission posing as Colonel Henri Dupont, of whom Gary is an exact double apart from not having a Ronald Colman moustache, to the Isle of Wight. In return for helping his country, he will get legitimate papers, full MI5 cover and a chance to pick up his life where he left off. If he refuses, he faces being shot by a firing squad in the basement in five minutes' time. Realising that he has no choice if he wants to save both his lives, Gary agrees.

Back at the flat, Gary plays it cool and tries to make out to Phoebe that being forced to get in Tufty's car at gunpoint didn't bother him one bit. Phoebe isn't convinced and asks why he was crying. Gary chooses not to reply, his manly pride hurt. He does, however, want to know why Phoebe was happy to sit outside the room having a cup of tea and a Garibaldi biscuit despite being unsure as to whether he was being tortured or not! That said, she admits to apparently not having enjoyed it very much. Phoebe bolsters his ego by saying how proud she is of him, especially as he faces certain danger on his forthcoming mission. This begins to worry the two-timing time traveller.

Ron tries to talk him out of his mission for McDuff as there's sure to be danger. After all, the whole point of a decoy is to deflect flak from the real target. Gary reminds Ron that his mission is on the Isle of Wight where he will impersonate Colonel Henri Dupont, to make the Germans believe Dupont is at a loose end while in reality the colonel is attending briefings on the upcoming D-Day landings. Ron isn't convinced at Gary's safety and fears he will come eyeball to eyeball with the Grim Reaper.

After Ron plants seeds of doubt in his mind, Gary speaks to Tufty about the possibilities of danger, including capture and interrogation, during the mission. Tufty assures him none of this will happen. Just then, Colonel Henri Dupont enters the room and the two men come face to face for the first time.

To solve the problem of Gary's lack of moustache, McDuff calls the Deceit, Dirty Tricks and Disguises department for their help. He then gives Gary a briefing of his schedule once he arrives at the Isle of Wight. On the face of it the plan seems straightforward. However, Ron was right to be concerned for Gary.

Gary returns to the Royal Oak now wearing his new Ronald Colman moustache, which he can't get off because of the special MI5 glue. Reg starts to share his concerns about what might happen if Gary should get captured and interrogated. Irritated, Gary orders a drink and then catches up with Phoebe, who enters the bar. While she might be impressed with his new moustache, she is already bored with the prospect of his impending mission; a mission, she reminds him, which just amounts to spending a few days on the Isle of Wight. Gary isn't pleased and admits he realises everyone would be much happier if he was captured and given a manicure with a pair of pliers.

Back in the present, Gary discovers that Yvonne is planning to catch a later plane to Madrid. She asks if he will do her a favour and collect the model Simone Sutherland from her hotel and take her to the venue for Yvonne's new product range launch event the following Saturday, and help to ensure she knows her lines. Remembering that he will be in the Isle of Wight pretending to be Colonel Henri Dupont, Gary uses the excuse that he has the shop to look after. This doesn't convince Yvonne who reminds him that they can forgo the low profits from the sale of the odd ration book and ARP warden's helmet. He reluctantly agrees.

By postponing her flight, this has created a window in Yvonne's schedule for her and Gary to make love. Gary readily accepts the invite once he's established that they won't be disturbed. After making love, Yvonne expresses her gratitude and notes his new moustache, which she believes must have grown so fast due to all his testosterone being on red alert.

Before travelling back in time for his date with destiny, Gary goes to the shop where he's presented with a bulletproof vest by Ron. Gary says he won't need it, believing he will be safe, but accepts the gift so as not, he claims, to appear ungrateful.

Gary is given a uniform to wear, identical to the colonel's. But if warning bells aren't ringing yet for the time traveller, they should be. Tufty announces that Gary will be departing from a boat in Dover. He claims it's all part of the ruse, but it's not long before Gary realises he is the duck and not the decoy after all as he finds himself not in the Isle of Wight, but Nazi-occupied France.

The first of an ambitious two-part story saw Gary discovering that you should be careful what you wish for. He wanted to be somebody but, as Ron pointed out, it was a chance for Gary to be somebody else. Fate always had a nasty way of making Gary pay for his duplicitous ways and on this occasion it seemed that Gary was going to pay with his life.

Nicholas's performance, added to some clever editing by Graham Carr and the use of a double, ensured that the scene in which both Gary and Colonel Henri Dupont shared dialogue worked seamlessly.

Without doubt, one of the highest-profile guest performers in the entire run of *Goodnight Sweetheart* was Timothy West, who played Tufty McDuff in this and the following episode. Married since 1963 to the *Fawlty Towers* actress Prunella Scales, alongside whom he's often worked, Timothy has enjoyed an outstanding career. In the theatre, his roles have included Roger Mortimer of Wigmore in the Christopher Marlowe historical tragedy *Edward II* at the Piccadilly Theatre, London, Professor Serebryakov in the Anton Chekhov drama *Uncle Vanya*, translated by Michael Frayn, with Dervla Kirwan and Maggie Steed, at the Chichester Festival Theatre, and the title role in the William Shakespeare tragedy *King Lear* at Bristol Old Vic. Best known for playing Bradley Hardacre in three series of the sitcom *Brass*, the actor's television credits have also included playing Horatio Bottomley in the historical drama *The Edwardians*; Winston Churchill in *Churchill and the Generals*, a drama set in the Cabinet Office and War Rooms between 1940 and 1945; and Councillor Albert Parker in the comedy *When We Are Married*. Timothy has played parts on film including Prof. Karl Gebhardt in the biographical drama *Hitler: The Last Ten Days*, Porton in the 1978 remake of *The Thirty Nine Steps*, based on the novel of the same name by John Buchan, and Captain De Wet in Richard Attenborough's epic apartheid drama, *Cry Freedom*.

As a recap at the beginning of '…But We Think You Have to Go', the seventh episode of series five, intelligence chief Tufty McDuff is giving an update to the prime minister Winston Churchill. He explains that Gary fell for the ruse and that the likeness between him and Colonel Henri Dupont is amazing: he's a perfect double and is bound to be spotted and shot by the Gestapo, making them think they've killed a vital Allied officer. Meanwhile, the real Dupont is back in England helping to make the plans for D-Day. McDuff confirms that Gary is in France now – condition green. The sparrow has landed.

Meanwhile, Gary is hiding from the Gestapo who are on patrol in the area. A woman called Celeste, a member of the French Resistance, comes over and introduces herself. She tells Gary to take off his cap and adds that she is confused as to why he's in uniform. She tells him they're going to walk across to a nearby café, and that if they see any German soldiers he is to kiss her passionately to make them think they are lovers. This duly happens and Gary questions whether he's having a dream or a nightmare!

When he walks into the café, Gary is greeted warmly by some of the locals. He sits at a table with Celeste and points out that everyone seems pleased to see him. She mentions that they were expecting Colonel Henri Dupont and they think he's really him. They believe the end of the war is in sight. Celeste assures him that she is there to help him. Just then Weiss and a number of German soldiers storm into the café and make for Gary. To save his life, he tries to convince them it's a case of mistaken identity and tells them to ask Celeste. However, when he turns around, he finds that she has left the café.

Back in the East End of London, the real Colonel Dupont is told by Tufty McDuff to pose as Gary Sparrow and to stay at the Royal Oak in order to keep up the deception, something that Phoebe is not happy about.

Gary is now ensconced in a prison cell and is presently visited by Weiss. Gary attempts to point out again that he is not Colonel Dupont and merely looks like him. He apologies for any inconvenience and tells him he's prepared to make his own way home! Weiss is not convinced by his protestations, especially as they're in English. However, he says he will play along and also speak in English. He introduces himself and Holz. He tells him that the following evening they will take Gary to Berlin where he will be interrogated. He admits to being disappointed that they can't interrogate him there as it's a dull little town and they have to make their own amusements. Out of increasing desperation, Gary admits to having been sent to France as Dupont's double, but Weiss points out that it makes no difference. Whether he's Dupont or not, Gary will still be tortured to find out the reason for his presence in France.

Back in England, Yvonne is having a crisis. She's called Ron over to Cricklewood and tells him that Gary is missing, despite promising he would help her with her launch the following day. Once she has finished letting off steam, Ron also does the same. As she's not convinced Gary will be back in time, because he's never there when she needs him, she tells Ron he will have to accompany Simone Sutherland to the launch. Ron reminds her that it's Saturday tomorrow and that he will be on time and a half. Yvonne tells him to phone in sick and she will give him two hundred pounds. He agrees. She gives him a file with all the details and tells him that Simone will be at the Hambleton Hotel. The millionairess points out that men faint as she walks by so he will not have trouble recognising her. She asks him to ensure she gets her lines right for the launch. Realising the trouble involved, Ron ups his fee to three hundred and then four hundred. However, Yvonne tells him not to push his luck. She mentions the hired car will be a stretch limo. Also, she suggests that as Simone is bulimic, he should take a snack and a sick bag.

Gary presently receives a visit from Celeste in his cell. He says he should have known. However, she claims that the Germans are wrong to trust her as she's a double agent. Celeste confirms his suspicions that she's there to offer him a night of passion in return for secret information. For once, Gary says that is the last thing on his mind. Celeste, however, has a plan. When they take him tomorrow to Germany he should make a scene in the square to upset the Germans. The villagers will join in and help to make a diversion so he can escape as there will be a boat and men standing by to help him. Although Gary is initially concerned about being shot by the Germans, he remembers that he's wearing the bulletproof vest that Ron gave him before he left.

To keep up the pretence, Colonel Dupont is sitting up in Gary and Phoebe's bed back in London. He is keen to share a night of passion with Phoebe who is not in the least interested in his patter and romantic advances. Instead, she decides to stay with Margie. Meanwhile Reg sleeps in the same bed as the colonel back at the pub.

Celeste tells Gary she will inform the Germans that he didn't tell her anything, despite her offer to make love. Gary apologises but says that as it could be his last night on earth, he plans to remain faithful – if not to one, then one or two!

Ron picks up Simone in the car and they quickly establish a bond. It turns out the model likes a man in a man's job. She decides she would rather skip the launch and spend time making love with Ron, who, not surprisingly, thinks all his birthdays have come at once.

Back in France, Gary is taken under guard at gunpoint into the village square. Both he and the villagers begin to whistle an insulting song about Hitler's missing testicle and Weiss calls for silence. Gary makes a run for it but is shot by a German soldier. Fortunately, his bulletproof vest has done its job. A German soldier goes to Gary but is hit by a gun carried by a member of the French Resistance. Gary picks up the soldier's gun and points it at Weiss who stands there with Celeste at gunpoint. He tells Gary to drop his gun or he will shoot her. Gary tells Weiss to drop his gun or he will shoot him. They both start to count to ten, but Gary suddenly quickens the count and a member of the Resistance takes Weiss away at gunpoint. Celeste thanks Gary for saving her life and they part. Gary gets on the boat and is taken back to England.

Ron and Simone arrive back at the hotel in the limousine and Ron asks when he can see her again. However, it becomes clear that Simone wanted this to be a one-off, not least because they live separate lives.

Back in Blighty, Gary comes face to face with intelligence chief Tufty McDuff. He commends Gary for a job well done, saying that the Germans now think that the big push will be Pas De Calais. Gary isn't so pleased, as Tufty knew that Gary faced certain torture and death. The time traveller pulls a gun on him. In an attempt to be spared, Tufty offers Gary a George medal for outstanding bravery and fifty-six pounds in cash. He tells Gary he should receive it from His Majesty, but officially Gary doesn't exist! Gary takes the medal but when he puts the gun down on the desk, Tutfy picks it up and claims he didn't think Gary was really going to shoot him. Tufty then accidentally shoots himself in the foot – not for the first time!

Phoebe is far from impressed at Gary's exploits; after all, Gary goes on secret missions all the time. She's also upset that her husband doesn't seem bothered that she nearly ended up as another of Colonel Henri Dupont's conquests.

Back in the present day, Ron is more interested in his own adventures than those Gary faced in Nazi-occupied France. Indeed, Gary thinks he's sending him up when Ron tells him he made love to Simone Sutherland.

In a desperate bid to get someone to listen, Gary later tries to recount his exploits to his son, Michael. However, he's asleep in his cot and shows even less interest than Phoebe.

This episode saw the return of Timothy West as Tufty McDuff. There was also excellent support from Sally Dexter, who played the role of Celeste. 'Appearing in the series left a lasting impression on me,' she said. 'There was a friendly atmosphere from the moment we all got together at the first read-through all the way to the "we're all in it together" camaraderie of the live recording.

'Sam Lawrence had written a smashing script and a strong independent character for me, which made it very enjoyable to play, although I remember wishing I'd allowed myself a bit more fun with it – there was certainly plenty of scope for that – especially when playing opposite the fabulous Nick Lyndhurst, who was a delight throughout! His timing and inventiveness really impressed me; I think he took us all by surprise with his uber-speedy counting from six to ten as I was having a gun held to my head by the handsome Peter Czajkowski!

'This series had just the right balance of humour and humanity while giving a genuine nod to some of the dangers faced by some extraordinarily brave people in the Second World War.'

Sally's theatre work has included playing Nancy in Sam Mendes's revival of the Lionel Bart musical *Oliver!* at the London Palladium, opposite Jonathan Pryce; Anna, the married photographer in Patrick Marber's original production of *Closer* at the National Theatre, London; and the White Witch in Rupert Goold's adaptation of *The Lion, the Witch and the Wardrobe* at the Sadler's Wells Theatre, London. For television, her credits include playing DS Lawson in *A Touch of Frost*, Sam in the comedy *Sugartown* and Faith Dingle in the soap opera *Emmerdale*. Meanwhile, her film roles include Molly Holland in the period romance *Firelight*, Linda in the black comedy *The Final Curtain* and Bridget in the comedy drama *Gloves Off*.

Also appearing in this episode was Peter Czajkowski as Weiss. 'I could see immediately that the script was great,' he said. 'Really funny, with a great plotline. Weiss was a lovely character too. I relished the chance to read for it and as we read it flew off the page. It must have gone well because I got the part. I was lucky, I suppose: I was a good fit for the part physically, and I had already played roles with accents and felt comfortable with the German accent and language.

'I was excited and enthusiastic because when I get a good script, an interesting part and a lovely director, I know I will enjoy the work. Of course, the series had been running for a while and was very successful, but as an actor you always want to work on the best productions, with the best cast, and this was an example of that. It has also endured in popularity, showing it is still held in high regard. I have had people telling me they saw it when it came out or recently in a repeat and they absolutely love it.'

With Weiss, Peter was allowed the freedom to interpret the role and how the character was written. 'I don't remember any specific direction,' he recalled. 'I am sure there were suggestions from the director, but it all seemed to flow along nicely. It was all there in the writing. The beauty is that we had rehearsal time before we went onto the set to record. The comedy Nazi is a classic trope and I remember seeing those characterisations when I was growing up, watching shows and films like *Hogan's Heroes*, Mel Brooks' *The Producers* and *To Have and Have Not*; but I also recalled the somewhat more realistic Nazi interpretations, such as Marlon Brando in *The Young Lions* or Derren Nesbitt and Anton Diffring in *Where Eagles Dare*, which fed into my characterisation.'

Given his accent and delivery of the dialogue and song lyrics in German was so exemplary, it was obvious that Peter had some experience of the language. 'I hadn't studied the language formally,' he explained. 'But I had worked in Germany a lot doing commercials and corporate presentations so had picked up some phrases and the feel of the language. I had also played Polish parts because I speak a little of the language as I am half Polish, and had learnt Russian for a part in *Doctor Who* and used a Russian accent in *Love Hurts*. I had also tackled Czech in another role. So I guess I sort of specialised in accents and languages for a while. It is challenging working in another language but also immensely enjoyable. My agent knew I was able to do certain accents and bits of language. "Oh, you can do that, can't you darling?" she'd say. If I thought I could do it, I'd go for it. I would get a part and then quickly have some lessons to perfect the language. Luckily, my father spoke Polish and Russian fluently so helped me. Or I would seek out friends or translators to help me by recording the lines and writing it out phonetically, so I could practise at home. A friend of mine who was a fluent German speaker helped me for this part. But it was also a fabulous piece of writing to use the absurdity of a Nazi singing "Hitler has only got one ball" in German at a really scary moment in the plot – and I really enjoyed doing it – with a straight-ish face! I think it works because of the danger and the absurdity. The character had to enjoy it but at the same time be terrified of the taboo. By the way, actually ball is translated as "ei" in German, which means egg. Germans don't say balls for testicles, they say eggs (sometimes nuts I believe). In Polish it's little eggs – "ja-ja" – but don't ask for that in a restaurant as a real egg is "jajko" and you'd get some funny looks asking for boiled testicles!'

For Peter, the fun of making the episode wasn't confined to the recording of the scenes. 'I remember it being a good cast and a lovely director and we rehearsed in the old Chelsea Barracks near Sloane Square,' he said. 'I travelled over on the Tube as did most of us but remember Sally whizzing in with great gusto on her bicycle. We sat around in the green room waiting to go in and rehearse, chatting, reading, practising a little; it was all very easy-going. I was thrilled to be in the same team as Timothy West, who I had seen on stage giving a fabulous performance in O'Neill's *Long Day's Journey into Night*. But all the cast were great. We went off in groups to work with Nicholas, who was pretty much in every scene. The rehearsals seemed to go well. The brilliant thing about these types of sitcom is that you work like a mini play, so you have some rehearsal before the recording.'

Once again, Roger Andrews' wonderful set designs deserve a mention, particularly those for the scenes set in France. Without doubt, they were some of the best sets that have ever been seen in a British sitcom. Given the high production values on this series, it was no surprise to discover how impressed the actor was with the sets. 'I remember walking into the studio and seeing a huge film-like set and thought, "Hey, this is a bit different," said Peter. 'We realised the importance of these episodes, as this time Gary was in real danger – it brought it home. We all upped our game, I think. It was marvellous to work on. Later, as we were recording the studio scenes, we could see the other actors' scenes, with the live audience reactions. Watching it all come together with the audience reactions was quite special. At the end, we all had a bit of a drink and a celebration. It was a very civilised way of working.'

Some twelve years later, Peter was given a reminder of the episode by a colleague. 'I was working in a school and I met a twenty-two-year-old teacher, who said to me, "I saw you in *Goodnight Sweetheart*, it's my favourite series!" It was one of his favourite series as a child, which made me feel pretty old, but I realised that he had a real and enduring affection for the programme. He said it was different from any other comedy because of the time travel and the danger element as well as the history lessons!'

As well as working as an actor and teacher, Peter is a presenter and the founder and artistic director of Brit-Pol Theatre Company. Over the years, his theatre roles have included Ventidius in the William Shakespeare tragedy *Antony and Cleopatra* at the Chichester Festival Theatre, Nick in the Alan

Ayckbourn comedy *Bedroom Farce* at the Redgrave Theatre, Farnham, and an officer in the controversial John Osborne play *A Patriot for Me*, based on the true story of Alfred Redl, at the Barbican Theatre, London. His television credits have included Sergeant Prozorov in the classic science-fiction programme *Doctor Who*, Lord Nicholas Beacon in the action adventure series *The New Adventures of Robin Hood*, and Martin Waller in the medical drama *Holby City*. Peter has also played a German admirer in the biographical film drama *Hilary and Jackie*.

The role of Holz in this episode was played by Jason Hall. 'I remember Timothy West being very nice,' he said. 'He used to sit in the corner and read his paper until it was time to do his scenes. I already knew Sally Dexter, and funnily enough I later cast her in the soap opera *Night and Day* when I had a spell of working as a casting director.

'They built the huge and amazing village set in Studio 1 at Teddington Studios. We recorded all the village scenes, apart from the scenes at the harbour's edge, without an audience. The cell scenes were recorded in front of a studio audience. I was pleased when I watched the episode back to see that one of my lines got a big laugh from the audience!

'There are many reasons why I think *Goodnight Sweetheart* was so successful. For instance, there was a good cast. I remember Nicholas was a good company member. Also, Laurence and Maurice and John Bartlett kept a tight rein on everything. John would always say exactly what he felt and was very hands-on. I think one of the other reasons was Paddy and Susie's casting of the characters.'

Jason's other television roles during his career have included playing PC Mooney in the crime drama *Maisie Raine*, Stevens in the adventure drama *Horatio Hornblower: The Wrong War* and Arnold Greenhalgh in the period drama *Call the Midwife*.

Also appearing in the supporting cast was Rae Baker as the model Simone Sutherland. Rae received a personal bursary from Cameron Mackintosh to train at the Central School of Speech and Drama. Her theatre credits include Anna Bagalucci in Denis King and Dick Vosburgh's pastiche of Hollywood film musicals, *A Saint She Ain't*, at the King's Head Theatre, London, and the Apollo Theatre, London, Madge Allen in the Andrew Rattenbury thriller *The Postman Always Rings Twice*, based on the novel by James M. Cain, and which starred Val Kilmer, at the Playhouse Theatre, London, and as Vivian in the Eleanor Bergstein musical *Dirty Dancing* at the Aldwych Theatre, London. Best known for playing Detective Constable Juliet Becker in the long-running police drama *The Bill*, her other television roles include playing Emily in the sitcom *Birds of a Feather* and Mimi in the crime drama *Father Brown*, starring Mark Williams.

Rae's film work includes playing Julie in the crime drama *Shadow Run*, which starred Michael Caine, which was based on the novel by Desmond Lowden.

Simone's hotel in this episode was in reality the Lensbury, which was called the Lensbury Club at the time of filming. A conference centre, hotel and leisure facility based on Broom Road in Teddington, Middlesex, its history dates back to 1920, when it was a club for Shell employees. Now under the ownership of London and Regional Hotels, the future of the Lensbury has been secured for generations to come. Before they were demolished, Teddington Studios were situated just next door. Indeed, during the period in which Thames Television owned the studios, programmes including *The Benny Hill Show* used the Lensbury Club as a location.

'Have You Ever Seen a Dream Walking', the eighth episode of series five, finds Gary still on a high from his not-so-secret mission to France. Ron, however, is feeling down because his belongings have been repossessed. A pencil is about all he has left – and Gary accidentally snaps it due to his restless behaviour. Gary is keen to talk through his experiences with the Nazis one more time, to help get it out of his system, because Phoebe is bored of hearing about it, and he can't exactly tell Yvonne. Ron is also keen to talk about his problems, including his divorce. Realising that he will have to listen to Ron's issues in return puts Gary off and he selfishly makes his excuses and quickly leaves his apartment.

Worse still for Gary, he's started experiencing odd dreams that are leaving him unsettled and afraid to go to sleep. One such dream involved Phoebe turning up at Yvonne's home in Cricklewood with a pram containing a bomb.

After a bad night's sleep Gary wakes up back at the West End apartment and walks into the lounge to see Reg and Phoebe listening to the radio about D-Day. Irritable, Gary snaps at them both and says he's fed up hearing about D-Day and that frankly he's OD'd on D-Day! He decides to close his eyes for a few minutes to try and clear his head, and ends up having a nightmare in which he's accompanying himself on the piano while singing 'Two Little Boys' and Rolf Harris suddenly appears and joins in, before reminding Gary in front of Phoebe that he didn't write the song.

Phoebe wakes up Gary and he appears to be back in reality and still in the West End flat. He admits to not feeling right at all.

Meanwhile at Ron's apartment pretty much everything but a deckchair has been repossessed. Ron's bank has given him a thumbs-down on the loan he needed. He offers Gary a coffee as they're not turning the water off until 4.00pm. After falling asleep in the deckchair, Gary has a dream in which he's seeing a sexy female therapist. She admits to wanting him and is just about to take off her blouse when Ron wakes him up, worried he is having a nightmare. Gary goes back to sleep and the dream continues from where he left off before he was woken up. It's just getting interesting again when the therapist suddenly turns into Reg – dressed in her blouse!

Gary wakes up and asks Ron why he didn't wake him up. After all, Reg can be pretty persistent! Ron is more concerned about his living accommodation. He's going to lose his flat and although he could afford a bedsit, he has no need. After all, he has a best friend with a West End flat. Gary points out that was in 1944 and he has no idea what he's done with it since. Ron asks if he can check it out and, if it's all okay, whether he can live there. Gary isn't sure. After all, it's a prime piece of real estate that could be bringing in a lot of money in the 1990s. Ron reminds Gary of how he bought the flat in the first place. This, of course, was with the white fivers that Ron printed for him.

Back at home, Gary has another strange dream. This time it is of Ron dressed in a wartime uniform while Yvonne hits him with a kipper. Upon waking up, Gary declares that he's never sleeping again!

Ron moves into the flat and is soon settled in as he only has one dustbin liner of belongings. Ron confirms that Gary still owns the flat. The management company have assured him that rates and maintenance charges are settled annually from an investment fund Gary set up. The time traveller can't get over how weird it is as he was in the flat only two hours ago. Then he realises the whole flat is a potential minefield as there could be all sorts of clues as to what Gary did in the past. But Ron assures him the whole flat is empty and there are none of his or Phoebe's personal effects anywhere.

Given his distress, Ron offers Gary some sleeping tablets, aware that he's not getting proper sleep. But Gary refuses to take them as sleeping has become too scary. Gary suddenly feels funny and Ron goes out of focus. It's no wonder as Gary hasn't slept properly for thirty-six hours. Ron has a flask of malt whisky and suggests they both drink some; after all, it will help Gary to relax. Gary agrees to just a small one as he's struggling to hold on to reality as it is. Gary takes a sip and wonders what the bitter aftertaste is. Ron admits to having slipped a sleeping tablet into his drink.

Very soon, Gary is falling asleep again and experiencing his worst nightmare yet. Both Yvonne and Phoebe are sitting on the settee in the flat and Ron in an armchair. 'Welcome to your nightmare,' says Ron, and all hell lets loose. Both women argue about Gary and their respective relationships with him while the time traveller tries to stop them. Then Ron, now in a 1940s suit and hat, joins in and complains about how Gary uses him to get him out of his various scrapes.

Reg also turns up and complains about being the butt of his jokes and tells him he's a con man with a pocket full of counterfeit fivers. Reg says that if he wasn't an exceptionally stupid policeman, he would have run Gary in years ago. Then Yvonne tells him he has to choose between the two women. He refuses, saying as it's just a dream he doesn't have to, and tries to wake himself up. At first we think Gary has woken up, but Yvonne and Phoebe suddenly appear from behind the settee and begin to nag him into a decision. Gary initially chooses Phoebe because Yvonne is successful and doesn't need him. Phoebe takes exception to this and refuses him. So he chooses Yvonne who also refuses, saying she's no one's second choice. When Gary tells Ron he can't win, Ron points out that's bigamy for you!

Awake again, Gary is initially unsure which era he's in. The flat is dark, save for some burning candles, and no one is around. When he finds a mobile phone that isn't working, he wonders why everything is mixed up and if he's awake or asleep. Or whether he's stuck between the two time zones in a twilight nether world. 'Oh my God, I'm in *X Files* hell,' he comments. Then Ron appears, having been to the toilet. Gary hugs him and tells him he was scared. Ron points out they've had a power cut, and his mobile doesn't work because they cancelled his line rental due to his financial situation. Gary tells him about his nightmare. When he says he's concerned about how to stop the dreams, Ron suggests he go on the holiday he had previously mentioned. After all, he reminds him that Eastbourne is nice at this time of year.

Gary agrees to Ron's suggestion and is seen waiting in the dining room of a small bed and breakfast. Presently, the landlady, Mrs Hardcore, arrives to confirm his breakfast order. An elderly couple have just arrived and sat down. They instantly look recognisable. Gary looks shocked as he realises that it's him and Phoebe as they would look now. It soon becomes apparent that this was another bad dream and Gary has fallen asleep at the breakfast table. The same landlady wakes him up and asks if he's all right. Gary confirms that he will be staying for another week!

After the wartime heroics of the previous episode, the writers Gary Lawson and John Phelps were keen to bring Gary back down to earth with a bang in this episode. 'It was an opportunity to make Gary face up to the consequences of his double life,' explained John. 'We enjoyed making him pay the price for his extraordinary life!'

Elizabeth has two particular reasons for remembering this episode. 'It was very funny recording the dream sequences,' she said. 'It was one of only two occasions that I got to work on screen with Emma. The only problem was I had laryngitis and so the only time I was able to speak that day was when I said my lines!'

The decision to move Ron into Gary's flat was a collective one taken at the writers' conference. It meant that the flat could be utilised for stories set in the late nineties and give Gary and Ron some extra storylines together. In time, Yvonne would also visit the flat.

This episode featured Penelope Solomon's second role in series five. This time she played the therapist in two of Gary's strange dreams. 'I was absolutely thrilled when they asked me to appear in the dream sequences,' she said. 'This episode was my favourite of the two I appeared in. I was asked to go shopping with the costume designer to source my outfit.

'On the studio day, I remember the make-up team put my hair in rollers, as they wanted it curled. I thought to myself, "I've made it." The two short scenes were pre-recorded in the afternoon. Other than the producer John Bartlett giving me a small note about putting emphasis on a certain word, it was fairly event-free. It was great fun and very liberating to be able to take out my hair clip and flick my hair in such a ridiculous way!'

Although Penelope had obviously read the script, she hadn't quite visualised how the dream sequence would end. 'I didn't realise that I was going to begin to unbutton my blouse and then suddenly turn into Reg until I saw the video at the recording in the evening,' she explained.

As mentioned in the episode description, Australian entertainer and painter Rolf Harris played himself in one of the dream sequences. This sequence now tends to be edited out of reruns of this episode. Harris died on 10 May 2023, aged ninety-three.

The role of the landlady Mrs Hardcore in this episode was played by Anna Karen. 'The director Robin Nash rang me up and told me he wanted to take me out to dinner,' she recalled. 'I thought, how sweet of him. It was certainly the first time a director had ever done that! Robin told me he wanted me to play the role of Mrs Hardcore, who was a landlady of a bed and breakfast, because he knew I would be able to play the twist in the two scenes well. I did go to a rehearsal, but I wasn't there the whole time as I only had a small part. I remember being happy with the episode when I first watched it being shown. It was a pleasant and joyous experience.'

The much-loved actress's theatre roles included Nurse Olive Butler in the Sam Cree farce *Stop It Nurse!* at the Windmill Theatre, Great Yarmouth, Deirdre in a tour of the Ray Galton and John Antrobus farce *When Did You Last See Your Trousers?*, and Emma Hornett in the Philip King and Falkland Cary comedy *Sailor, Beware!* at the Gaiety Theatre, Douglas. Best known for playing Olive Rudge in the sitcom *On the Buses*, Anna's other television credits included playing Olive Rudge in *The Rag Trade*, and Aunt Sal in the soap opera

EastEnders, often alongside her friend Barbara Windsor as Peggy Mitchell. Her film credits included two *Carry On* comedies: she played a schoolgirl in *Carry On Camping* and a wife in *Carry On Loving*. She also played Olive Rudge in the three *On the Buses* spin-off films: *On the Buses*, *Mutiny on the Buses* and *Holiday on the Buses*. Tragically, Anna died in a house fire on 22 February 2022, aged eighty-five.

In 'Love the One You're With', the ninth episode of series five, we discover that Margie's fortieth birthday is coming up, not that Gary has remembered. Phoebe reminds him to be there with some biscuits and tells him that Reg and Margie will be upset if he isn't there as they think the world of him.

Back in the present, Reg's police constable grandson is trying to give Gary security advice for his shop again. He tells Gary he's going to be on *Crimewatch UK* on an item detailing a post-office raid security video – not courageously foiling the crime, but buying a postal order! He notices a blackout torch in the shop and tells Gary his grandad was in the force and will be ninety-seven at his next birthday. Gary is amazed to hear he's still alive. Reg is in a care home in Cuthbert Street but his memory isn't what it was, and his mind has gone back to the Second World War.

As Reg's grandson leaves, Yvonne arrives and presents Gary with a copy of her new autobiography. Gary feels a mixture of pride and guilt as he reads the dedication out loud:

To Gary,
   Who was always there for me and who I love more than words can say.

Amongst the photos of Yvonne, including one with her and Cherie Blair when she won the New Businesswoman of the Year Award, is a photo of her and Gary on their wedding day. Well, Gary's hand on Yvonne's hand on the cake knife. It turns out that her ghostwriter helped her write the book, which Gary, even with a few glances, can tell is a tissue of lies – a box of man-sized tissues of lies, to be exact. Yvonne points out that they will sell as a result.

During a visit to see Ron in the West End flat in present-day London, Gary is asked by the grumpy porter to move his car, otherwise he will have it clamped. During the conversation he reveals that Gary's grandfather (in reality Gary) was killed in an accident on Tuesday 23 July 1944. He had nightmares for months and his mother was sick to the stomach. His grandfather was crossing the street just outside when a bus skidded and knocked him down, leaving his head like an overripe watermelon that had been dropped from a high building. With the anniversary of the accident set to be the following Tuesday, Gary realises that he was that watermelon and thinks he might be dead.

To try and understand what happened, Gary goes to see Reg in his care home in the present to see if he can remember. Sadly, he is too confused and has no recollection.

Gary then goes to see Phoebe to tell her he can't go to Margie's fortieth birthday because he will be in Brussels. This does not go down well as she reminds Gary he promised to be there.

Back at home, Yvonne is complaining that she is tired. After all, it's not easy being the most sought-after new author in Britain! When she says she wishes Gary would come to one of her book signings, Gary says he is at a loose end on Tuesday 23 July. This pleases Yvonne, who mentions she will be doing a big book signing in Piccadilly and suggests they stay over at the Ritz hotel afterwards. Gary agrees, thinking it might just save his life as well as please his wife.

Ron, however, isn't convinced that Gary's plan will work. After all, the porter was trying to remember something that happened over fifty years ago; how can they be sure he's right? But given that the porter was sure it was the man who lived in the flat who died, then the obvious thing to do would be to sell the flat before the next Tuesday.

Gary meets with the same estate agent that sold him the flat, but he tells him the market is not exactly ideal for a quick sale at present. Gary says he's not concerned with the price and just wants to get rid of it by next Monday, which he explains by claiming that matters of national security are involved. In desperation, Gary says that he wants no money at all. The estate agent remarks that he does have a professional associate who's looking to rent a pied-à-terre, and asks if he can use Gary's telephone to make a local call. Gary replies that he can fax the pope for all he cares!

All is agreed; however, the idea of them having to leave the flat for a few days does not go down well with Phoebe. Telling her the reason is top secret doesn't help matters either. So Gary tells her he thinks the Germans will be dropping a new type of bomb in the area; its code name is 'Watermelon'. To placate Phoebe, he says he can now come to Margie's party at the Royal Oak.

All seems well, until Gary uncharacteristically has a pang of guilt about having potentially sentenced the flat's new tenant to death. He tells Ron he will have to go back the next day to warn him – despite it being Tuesday 23 July 1944.

Acting like a dutiful husband for once, Gary goes to Yvonne's book signing. Unfortunately, Yvonne is so preoccupied with signing books that Gary ends up slipping away, knowing he has some important business to take care of back in 1944.

Gary goes back to the flat in 1944 and discovers that the professional associate the estate agent was referring to was actually himself. When a woman's voice is heard calling from his bedroom, Gary asks if it's his wife. At first he says it is, but then admits it's his lover. He says he loves both his wife, who is ill, and his lover and just wants them to be happy. Gary realises he's found a kindred spirit, given the ups and downs he faces trying to keep two partners happy. Gary is just about to warn him about the bus accident when they hear the screeching of a bus's brakes outside. They both go to the window and are met with the sight of a man, who the estate agent says is Mr Foster from Flat 16, who has been fatally injured. Gary asks how he can tell, given the serious head injuries the man has endured. The agent tells him they both go to the same lodge and he recognises his socks.

Later that day, Gary heads to the Royal Oak where Noël Coward is performing 'London Pride' at the piano for Margie's fortieth birthday party. Margie is over the moon and thanks Phoebe for organising the party and making her feel part of the family.

After Gary apologises for not consulting Phoebe about moving out of the flat, they make up. Before Gary shoots off again, Noël insists he stay to watch Phoebe perform a song they have been rehearsing in secret. After showing some last-minute nerves, we see Phoebe perform part of the song 'I'll See You Again'.

Later, Yvonne is home alone watching *Crimewatch UK* on television. Gary presently arrives and uses claustrophobia as an excuse for suddenly running out on her in the bookshop. Having made up with his second wife, Gary quickly turns up the TV sound so he can watch a report on *Crimewatch UK* in which the presenter is showing a photofit of Reg's grandson whom the police suspect of being an accomplice. This causes Gary to laugh but, having been eating nuts, he starts to choke until Yvonne comes to his aid with the Heimlich manoeuvre.

In this episode, written by Laurence and Maurice, Gary was once again not around long enough to watch Yvonne bask in the glow of her success. With life becoming ever busier in the past, he was finding it increasingly difficult to be there for Yvonne – not that she always noticed. The fact that Gary attended the book signing in the first place was only because he thought it would save his life!

The main cast of this episode were once again joined by James Grout as the estate agent Mr Rutley, David Benson as Noël Coward and Eve Bland as Margie.

Also appearing for just this episode was the actor, director and playwright Brian Rawlinson as the bad-tempered porter. In a diverse career, Brian's theatre credits include playing Dr Michael Emerson in the Brian Clark play *Whose Life is it Anyway?* at the Churchill Theatre, Bromley, Sir Anthony Absolute in Richard Brinsley Sheridan's comedy of manners *The Rivals* at the Thorndike Theatre, Leatherhead, and Roebuck Ramsden in the George Bernard Shaw drama *Man *and Superman* at the Salisbury Playhouse. His other television roles included playing Sid in the sitcom *Meet the Wife*, which starred Freddie Frinton and Thora Hird, Robert Onedin in the drama *The Onedin Line*, and Parson Thirdly in the romantic drama *Far from the Madding Crowd*. Brian also appeared in films including three *Carry On* comedies: a nervous steward in the comedy *Carry On Cruising*, a hessian driver in *Carry On Cleo* and Burt in *Carry On Cowboy*. Brian died on 23 November 2000, aged sixty-nine.

The actress Liz Whiting also made a one-off appearance in this episode playing the nurse at Reg's care home. Liz's theatre roles have included playing Gabrielle in the Al Frisch, Julian Moore and Bernard Spiro musical *Bordello*, with a stellar cast including Stella Moray and Lynda Bellingham, at the Queen's Theatre, London, Shirley Smith in the Mike Stott play *Funny Peculiar* at the Nottingham Playhouse, and Annie in the Kander and Ebb musical *Chicago* at the Crucible Theatre, Sheffield, and the Cambridge Theatre, London. Liz's other television credits include Wendy in *Open All Hours*, Maggie in the horror fantasy *Chiller* and Sally Harrison in the daytime medical drama *Doctors*.

At the start of 'My Heart Belongs to Daddy', the tenth episode of series five, Gary arrives back at the flat to find Phoebe singing along to a record of 'Smoke Gets in Your Eyes'. He catches her attention by clapping appreciatively, embarrassing her a little as she hadn't heard him entering the room. He hands her a beautiful red dress made by Dolce and Gabbana. She is pleased and says it's just the thing for her to wear while singing in a cocktail lounge. Gary reminds her that, despite Noël Coward saying she has a 'lovely voice', it's a long way from Whitechapel to Tin Pan Alley and that it's a street of broken hearts. She ignores his negative comments and focuses on the positive. She tells him he could write her a song, which instantly makes Gary panic. She teases him, saying he has lost his talent, and Gary reluctantly ends up agreeing to write one for her.

Back in the present, Gary finds Ron trying to work out the minefield that is lonely hearts adverts. Just then, a man clearly down on his luck brings a box of wartime items into the shop in the hope of selling them. Gary offers just a fiver as he has lots of the same things. Then he notices the name Phoebe Sparrow on one of the objects and the man mentions that the items, including a record, belonged to his mum in the war. Gary asks for his name and address, but the man takes offence and tells him the items aren't stolen. Gary says he needs the details for his records. The man confirms his name and address as Michael Sparrow, Paradise Hotel, Slaughterhouse Lane, Hackney. Understandably this amazes Gary and Ron who realise that he's Gary's grown-up son. Ron asks if he has any other items and he confirms he has. Gary expresses an interest in buying them. They arrange to meet again at the shop at 7.00pm the next day. After giving Michael his fiver, Gary starts to ask whether his mum is still alive, but Ron stops him. Instead he asks if she knows he's selling the items. Michael takes offence again, asking if he really thinks he would steal from his own mum.

After Michael leaves, Ron quips that he's a big lad for a two-year-old. Gary says that he was practically dressed in rags and he needs to help him. Ron suggests he slip him a couple of thousand pounds the next time he sees him. But Gary doesn't want to give him a handout; he wants to go back and change his life. Gary asks Ron to follow him when he comes back tomorrow and find out if he really lives at the address he gave. He also wants to find out if Phoebe is still alive. Ron is against the last part of his plan, saying some things should be left alone.

Gary goes home to find Yvonne reading her speech for the forthcoming Millennium Conference. When Gary appears cynical, Yvonne points out it's a chance to help change people's lives and asks, wouldn't he want to do that? Without giving away too many details, he mentions that he has had an upsetting day as someone came into the shop who was really down on his luck and who reminded him of someone he used to know. Yvonne points out that's why we need movers and shakers: to help people. She mentions her speech is called 'We must change the future because we cannot change the past'. Under his breath, Gary says that it depends which way you're travelling.

On his next visit to the past, Gary is shocked to hear that Margie has taken Michael and Frankie to a party at the Kray twins' house. Phoebe is upset that Gary hasn't had time to write her song and so Gary has to lie and say he has. He just needs some words and notes. Despite the poor excuse, this keeps Phoebe happy.

Meanwhile, Ron is getting nowhere on the dating scene. The only reply he's received is from a guy who works on an oil rig. As Gary has two wives, Ron begs him to write an advert for him. Gary finally agrees but only after he's finished copying the words and music to a song called 'One Kiss, One Sigh' by Benny Bingham. Gary explains that the song, published in 1946, never made any money, so he intends to pretend he wrote it for Phoebe because he's not a real songwriter. Just then, Michael, Gary's son, arrives back in the shop with more belongings from the war. When Gary asks if there's anything he wants to keep, he says he can't afford to be sentimental when he doesn't know where the next strong lager is coming from. After being given a hundred pounds for the items, Michael tells Gary that he reminds him of his dad when he was younger and there is quite a resemblance – although he was taller, not so weedy and much better looking. As he leaves, Ron, equipped with binoculars, follows him. After they're gone, Gary opens a box and finds the same red Dolce and Gabbana dress that he gave to Phoebe.

Back in 1944, Phoebe is wearing the dress in the flat while Gary watches her rehearse 'One Kiss, One Sigh' with Noël Coward. Noël is convinced audiences will love the song and says he can arrange for her to perform the song at the Rain Drop Club. Phoebe is keen but Gary is not so sure, fearing that neither she nor the song are ready. Noël disagrees and the subject is closed as he leaves the flat.

Returning to the room after checking on Michael, Phoebe tells Gary she looks at their son in his cot and wonders what he will become and whether he will be happy. Gary tries to reassure her that their son will be fine.

Back at the shop, Ron tells Gary that Michael does live in Hackney. Ron says he thinks Gary should leave everything alone; but Gary refuses to condemn his own son to a life of misery.

Gary goes to see Michael at his hotel. The room is run-down and clearly infested with insects. As an excuse to see him, Gary tells his son that the record he sold him was a rare first pressing and worth far more than he paid him. In fact, five hundred pounds. Michael is clearly delighted and lets him into his less than salubrious room. He commends Gary for owning up about the record as he could have made a good profit. Without an ounce of irony, Gary says that honesty is the best policy as he hands over the money. Michael tells Gary that his father was good at presents but was never any good when he needed him as he was always sloping off somewhere. Indeed, he used to think he had another woman. Gary forgets himself and tells him not to think like that. Michael asks what it has to do with him. Gary says he thinks it's better to think well of someone if you don't really know. When he asks what became of his dad, Michael says that he lost touch as he got into bad company and went to prison.

Gary asks Michael what became of his mum and he's just about to answer when Knacker John, the owner of the hotel, bursts in and demands payment of the rent, grabbing Michael by the T-shirt. Gary pulls them apart and threatens him with violence if he touches him again. Knacker John calls in his hired muscle named Warren and tells him to harm both men. Knowing that Knacker John doesn't have that name for nothing, Michael quickly gives him the five hundred pounds that Gary gave him. It's the rent he owes him plus a month on account. Shocked and surprised, Knacker John calls off Warren and they both leave. Michael thanks Gary and remarks that he was rich for a minute. Gary notes that a minute isn't enough. He goes to ask Michael a question, but thinks better of it as he watches him get stuck into a can of strong lager.

Phoebe is making her debut at the Rain Drop Club watched by a proud Noël Coward in the audience. Gary arrives and sits down at Noël's table. Noël points out that he's not supposed to be there, but Gary reminds him that Reg can't keep a secret. Gary is impressed at Phoebe's performance. Noël tells him that his publisher is keen to publish his song. When Noël tells him there will be royalties, Gary asks if the money could be put in a trust fund for Michael when he's older. Noël replies by saying that nothing would be easier.

Back in the present, history has been changed. A grown-up Michael walks into the shop looking smart and successful. Gary is listening to 'Smoke Gets in Your Eyes' on the gramophone. Michael tells Gary that his mother used to like the song and Gary accidentally says she still does! Michael says that he used to live around the area and has come to look at old haunts. He now lives in New Zealand and is an engineer who builds bridges. He reveals that his dad was a musician and wrote a song once, the royalties for which helped him to get a start in life. Presently he notices the red Dolce and Gabbana dress on the counter and mentions that his mother used to have one just like it. He asks how much it is, but Gary says it's not for sale. Michael says that his wife would look wonderful in the dress and Gary changes his mind. He eventually decides to charge him five pounds. There is an awkward moment as he holds on to his son's hand too long during a handshake as he takes the money.

Michael is about to leave, and Gary asks if he has any children. Michael mentions he has two: a daughter, Phoebe, named after his mum, and a son who, despite Gary being hopeful, is called Dennis. Gary says he too has a son, but he doesn't really know him, which Michael says is a shame. Michael then says Gary reminds him of his dad when he was younger, only he was taller and not quite so slim. Gary suggests that he was also better looking, and Michael says he wasn't going to mention that! Gary hopes they will meet again, but Michael is doubtful as he's flying back to New Zealand the next day.

Back in Cricklewood, Gary is feeling down. Yvonne is conquering the world with her prepacked algae and Phoebe is performing at the Rain Drop Club. But if he hopes Ron is willing to share a takeaway, he's to be disappointed. The brutally honest lonely hearts advert he wrote for Ron has come up trumps and has resulted in twenty-seven responses and climbing; Ron is just off to meet number fourteen. He leaves Gary with a box of lagers to say thank you.

Yvonne returns later that evening just as Gary is catching up on his sleep on the sofa. She's just come home to change before going out to a champagne reception at No. 10 and tells him not to wait up for her.

Feeling left out, he goes back to the Royal Oak to wait for Phoebe. There, Reg is just locking up before going back home to Margie. After Reg goes, Gary starts to play 'One Kiss, One Sigh' on the piano as Phoebe walks in. She tells him that performing isn't the life for her, not least because they'd see even less of each other. She asks Gary to accompany her while she sings the song one last time.

Goodnight Sweetheart: A Guide to the Classic Sitcom

The casting of Ian Lavender as the older Michael Sparrow in this episode was nothing sort of genius; while the script, written by Sam Lawrence, is masterly with many poignant twists and turns. 'I liked breaking the unwritten law of time-travel stories,' he said. 'I did this by allowing Gary to go back to the 1940s and have the royalties from Phoebe's song put in trust for his son so that when Ian Lavender's version of Michael appears again at the end of the episode, he's not an ex-con living in a flophouse, but a successful businessman.

'I didn't write the role of Gary's son with Ian Lavender in mind,' added Sam. 'But I was very glad they did cast him. I didn't have any influence over casting.'

Nicholas was also pleased with the actor being cast as his son. 'It was lovely to work with Ian,' he said. 'He was a very clever actor. I grew up watching *Dad's Army* and I had to do my level best not to bring it up during rehearsals because he must have been fed up talking about it!'

Back once again to play Noël Coward in this episode was David Benson. David was also thrilled to see Ian in the rehearsal room. 'I had met Ian before when we took part in a radio discussion show together,' the actor said. 'We talked about *Dad's Army* and I ran through my various impressions of the cast and he chuckled happily, murmuring, "Ah, dear John," or "Dear Arthur." I remember he would sit in rehearsals and do his crossword, get up when called and do his scene perfectly and then get straight back down to his crossword again.'

Ian successfully played a mixture of comedic and dramatic parts in all of the mediums. However, he will always be remembered for playing a certain scarf-wearing member of the Home Guard in the sitcom *Dad's Army*. An accomplished theatre actor, his roles included Private Pike in *Dad's Army* at the Forum Theatre, Billingham, and the Shaftesbury Theatre, London, and on tour; Solanio in the William Shakespeare comedy *The Merchant of Venice*, with Dustin Hoffman and Geraldine James, at the Phoenix Theatre, London; and Teddy Deakin in a tour of Arnold Ridley's comedy thriller, *The Ghost Train*. Ian's other television credits included Mr Neville in the medical drama *Peak Practice*, Derek Harkinson in the long-running soap opera *EastEnders* and Keith Jackson in the comedy drama, *Stella*. His film parts included Private Pike in *Dad's Army*, Joe Baxter in the saucy comedy *Carry On Behind* and Gerry Buss in the farce *Not Now, Comrade*, which was based on Ray Cooney's West End stage farce *Chase Me, Comrade*. Sadly, Ian passed away on 2 February 2024, aged seventy-seven.

This episode gave Elizabeth another chance to show her vocal talents. 'I enjoyed singing 'One Kiss, One Sigh', the song Gary supposedly wrote for Phoebe,' she said. 'I especially loved the fact that they played it over the end credits of the last episode of series five. It was the only time another song was used over the titles.'

'One Kiss, One Sigh', with lyrics by David Harsent, music by Mark Bastable and an arrangement by Anthony and Gaynor Sadler, was recorded at Logorhythm Music Studios, Lexington Street, Soho, London, on Monday 6 April 1998. Those who took part in the recording session were as follows:

Singer:	Liz Carling
Trumpet:	Paul Spong
Piano:	Cliff Hall
Double bass:	Malcolm Creese
Drums:	Paul Robinson

Although Elizabeth's talent for singing would be invaluable in the sixth series, for now it appeared that the character had lost any interest in performing in front of an audience again.

The part of Knacker John, Michael's landlord in this episode, was played by David Bauckham. David is a highly qualified voice teacher and experienced actor. His theatre credits have included Terry Bailey in Jeffrey Archer's second play *Exclusive* at the Theatre Royal, Bath, and Strand Theatre, London, Henry in Alan Ayckbourn's adaptation of the Will Evans and Arthur Valentine Aldwych farce *Tons of Money* at the Liverpool Playhouse, and as a centurion in the George Bernard Shaw drama *Caesar and Cleopatra* at the Greenwich Theatre, London. His other television work includes playing Jed Wright in the crime drama *Wycliffe*, Trevor in the family sitcom *My Dad's the Prime Minister*, and Graham in the dating comedy *Figg and Dates*. David's film roles include Steve in the crime thriller *The Fruit Machine*, Jack Bradwell in the horror *Hollow* and Stan in the drama *Dom Hemingway*.

The tenth episode marked the end of series five. The series was broadcast by BBC One on Monday 23 February 1998, Monday 2 March 1998, Monday 9 March 1998, Monday 16 March 1998, Monday 23 March 1998, Monday 30 March 1998, Monday 6 April 1998, Monday 13 April 1998, Monday 20 April 1998 and Monday 27 April 1998 at 8.30pm.

Nicholas won the first of his two awards for *Goodnight Sweetheart* in 1998. He was the winner of the Most Popular Comedy Performer at the National Television Awards. The ceremony was held at the Royal Albert Hall on 27 October 1998 and was hosted by Trevor McDonald.

The following year would see the sixth and final series of *Goodnight Sweetheart* being broadcast. Although it would be the last series, there were set to be some important changes to the production team. Additionally, production requirements would see the cast and production team saying goodbye to some familiar exterior locations previously used in the series.

6
Closed for the Duration

IN 1999, JOHN BARTLETT was offered the chance to work on the UK version of the sitcom *That 70s Show*, renamed *Days Like These*, for the Carsey-Werner Company. This meant that he sadly wasn't able to work on series six. 'Looking back, *Goodnight Sweetheart* was my most favourite series to work on,' said John. 'It was the first sitcom I produced, and it was a happy show.'

John's position on the series would be taken by Nic Phillips, who, as well as producing all ten episodes, would also direct the first five. Meanwhile, Robin Nash would direct two episodes and Terry Kinane three episodes.

In 1973, after working through the ranks for five years in commercials and feature films, Nic became a floor manager at LWT and remained working there until 1979. After a spell directing programmes for RTE in Dublin, he returned to London in 1980. Nic then went on to direct episodes of the crime drama *The Gentle Touch* and the children's drama *Grange Hill*, while the sitcoms he directed included *Metal Mickey*, *Hot Metal*, *Roll Over Beethoven*, *Me and My Girl* and *Desmond's*. He also directed editions of the popular Michael Aspel chat show, *Aspel and Company*.

In the late 1980s, Nic became a producer as well as a director. During this period, his sitcom credits included *Square Deal*, *Close to Home* and *Singles*. Between 1990 and 1991, Nic produced and directed two series of the sitcom *Birds of a Feather*. He then became Head of Comedy at Celador Productions and executive producer for all of Jasper Carrott's programmes, including the sitcom *The Detectives*. Nic joined the final series of *Goodnight Sweetheart* after leaving Celador.

Since the start of the 2000s, Nic has directed sitcoms including *Barbara*, *The House That Jack Built* and *My Family*, which won a Golden Rose Palme d'Or in 2009. He has also directed many episodes of the police drama *The Bill* and the medical drama *Casualty*, together with the soap operas *EastEnders* and *Coronation Street*.

The end of series five also marked the end of Micheál Jacob's association with the series, first as script associate in series one and then as script editor from series two to series five. 'I didn't work on the final series because I was producing an ALOMO show called *Cry Wolf*,' he explained. When Micheál left ALOMO, he became an executive producer and creative head of mainstream comedy with BBC Television. The sitcoms he worked on included *Two Pints of Lager and a*

Packet of Crisps, *The Smoking Room* and *My Family*. Since taking early retirement from the BBC he has script-edited many dramas on BBC Radio 3 and BBC Radio 4, has judged writing competitions and mentored new writers.

Taking over as script editor on the final series would be Victoria Grew. Victoria began her career at BBC Films before going to work for ALOMO where she script-edited several series, including the sitcom *Believe Nothing*. After a spell heading up drama development for Talkback Thames, Victoria returned to comedy and worked in the commissioning departments at ITV and UKTV. She also freelanced as a script editor on *Yonderland* for Working Title, and worked for NBCU and several other independent production companies. More recently, Victoria has worked as an executive producer on series including the second series of the sitcom *Timewasters*, series two of *Back*, a sitcom starring David Mitchell and Robert Webb, and the science-fiction comedy *We Are Not Alone*.

Also leaving the series was the production designer Roger Andrews. Taking over his position was David Ferris, who was no stranger to Teddington Studios. During his time at Thames Television, David worked as a production designer on programmes made there including the talent series *Opportunity Knocks*, the sitcoms *Bless this House*, *And Mother Makes Three* and *George and Mildred*, the daytime drama series *Harriet's Back in Town* and the game show *Whodunnit?* He also worked on private detective series *Hazell* and the comedies *The Kenny Everett Video Show* and *The Benny Hill Show*. David's other credits include the police drama *The Bill*, the sitcoms *Birds of a Feather*, *Nighty Night*, *Gavin and Stacey* and *Dad's Army: The Lost Episodes*, and the children's drama *Dodger*.

For series six it was decided, for various reasons, to no longer use Ezra Street and Columbia Road as locations. This meant that the real exteriors of Duckett's Passage, the Royal Oak pub and the surrounding areas would no longer be used. Instead, Duckett's Passage, the market and the exterior as well as the interiors of the Royal Oak were built in Studio 1 at Teddington Studios.

In order to be nearer to Teddington Studios, it was also decided to change the location of Gary's shop Blitz and Pieces from 18B Pitfield Street, Shoreditch, London, to 21 Heath Road, Twickenham.

After some initial location work, rehearsals, additional location work, pre-records and studio audience recordings for series six took place between Friday 19 February 1999 and Thursday 13 May 1999. There was a break of one week for Easter between Friday 26 March 1999 and Thursday 8 April 1999.

*

At the beginning of 'Mine's a Double', the first episode of series six, we discover that Gary and Yvonne have moved to a posh two-storey apartment. Gary has just given Ron a VIP tour and the latter has quickly sensed that all is not well between the couple. To summarise, Yvonne has the hump and Gary, complete with his *Baywatch* pyjamas, has moved into the spare room. Gary explains that it's the usual problem: because he's away a lot, Yvonne is saying that he's not fully committed to the marriage.

After ending her phone call, Yvonne tells Gary that they've been invited to a party tonight by her business partner, Clive. Gary has a problem as he has agreed to go out for a drink with Ron. Ever supportive, Ron says he doesn't mind but Gary is insistent, saying he doesn't want to let his best mate down. This doesn't impress Yvonne who makes the word 'fine' sound exactly the opposite. Ron is confused and says that they can go out for a drink another time. Gary says he isn't going out for a drink with him and it was just an excuse. He needs to go and see Phoebe, who is expecting him. Not impressed, Ron tells Gary there's a nasty side to him and leaves.

After spending time with Phoebe, and almost being rendered incapable of fathering children after Reg operates an umbrella in the vicinity of his groin area by mistake, Gary ventures out into the night and a bad storm. Upon reaching Duckett's Passage, he is struck by lightning. This doesn't just give him a shock but splits him in two; and while one Gary Sparrow lies in the alley in the rain, the other stands looking over him and smiling. It is this version that makes his way back to the present.

Meanwhile, back at the apartment in the present, Yvonne is still decidedly cold when Ron arrives to see Gary. Very soon it becomes clear to Ron that Gary has changed. He even namechecks Ron. The now gum-chewing Gary's banter has become more laddish and Ron questions why he has changed into Jeremy Clarkson! Gary tells him he has just decided to lighten up and there's now a whole new him on the block. He starts by telling Yvonne he wants to make it up to her by taking her on the Eurostar to Paris for a spot of sightseeing and dinner at Maxim's followed by an overnight stay. This instantly defrosts a very cold Yvonne and she agrees to meet him at the apartment at 1.00pm. They kiss and Yvonne departs, leaving Ron in admiration of the new Gary Sparrow. Gary then tells Ron he's off to visit a pub he knows where the beer is tuppence-ha'penny a pint and the landlady fancies him.

At the Royal Oak, Gary is giving Reg the benefit of his sense of humour, which has now become somewhat near the knuckle. After Reg returns to his bar duties, Gary begins to make it clear to Phoebe that he's in the mood for a bit of afternoon delight upstairs. This doesn't impress her as she's busy. Gary starts to get annoyed,

Closed for the Duration

saying he's been waiting all lunchtime. Very quickly Phoebe also begins to notice the change in Gary's personality, including the increase in his alcohol consumption. Not to be discouraged, he decides to go and see Yvonne instead.

On arriving back in the shop, Gary decides to pay a visit to the toilet. There we discover another Gary Sparrow who has been tied up and imprisoned. 'Bad Gary' tells him he's got to decide what he's going to do with him.

Meanwhile, Yvonne is going frantic. Gary is late and they've missed the Eurostar. Yvonne storms upstairs just before the other Gary arrives. Ron questions what he thinks he's doing, and Yvonne says he'd better have a good explanation for missing their trip to Paris. Not knowing about the trip, Gary quickly thinks on his feet and says he had a delivery of gas masks, which doesn't help matters. Yvonne storms out of the apartment. Gary explains to Ron that he now has a double. At first Ron is not convinced that Gary has been cloned. In fact Ron think Gary has time traveller's nut. That is, until Gary's double walks into the apartment, realises what's happened and beats a hasty retreat.

After he finally finishes hyperventilating, Ron tells Gary that he couldn't tell them apart as looks-wise the double is an exact replica. However, there was one difference – he was more fun. Gary points out that his clone left him tied up in a toilet and that he's not fun, he's pathologically evil. He adds that this is the worst time for this to happen what with the state of his marriage, but Ron tells him not to worry as she appears to prefer the other Gary as well.

Back in 1944, the other Gary attempts to make up with Phoebe and persuade her to go upstairs after closing. Phoebe says she will be too tired. Annoyed, Gary starts to look at two women from the munitions factory sitting in the pub. However, before he gets a chance to chat them up, Reg asks him to play one of his songs. He sits down at the piano and begins to play what he says is one of his new numbers – 'Anarchy in the UK' by the Sex Pistols. This, of course, doesn't go down well with the regulars, or Phoebe and Reg.

The following day 'Bad Gary' tries to use his winning ways to get Yvonne into bed, but she makes it clear he has no chance. While she's upstairs, Gary takes cash from her purse and a necklace from her desk. He looks out of the window and notices Ron and the other Gary making their way back to the apartment. He tells Yvonne he's going out and, after she makes it clear she's not interested, he kisses her passionately leaving her almost breathless. He storms out leaving Yvonne almost unable to walk back upstairs.

Presently, the other Gary enters with Ron. Gary is in the middle of telling Ron about his clone's rendition of 'Anarchy in the UK', which he followed up with 'Smack My Bitch Up' before getting drunk and throwing up in the snug. Worse still, he tells him that he innocently walked into the pub that morning and got it in the neck from Phoebe. So now both of his wives aren't talking to him. Gary is concerned that either Phoebe or Yvonne could end up seeing both Garys together, and how would he explain that?! Yvonne comes in and complains that he's returned and spoiled it. She enjoyed the way he kissed her and ran out as it was so macho.

Gary and Ron go off in search of 'Bad Gary' but their mission is aborted when he drives past them in Gary's car.

Back at the pub, Reg comments that the regulars have started to notice that he's become a bit of a card – and also that he was making Phoebe laugh upstairs not long ago. Phoebe comes into the bar and comments that she thought he, who she describes as 'lover boy', had gone. She thanks him again for the necklace (the one that 'Bad Gary' had stolen from Yvonne earlier) and bets he preferred it when she was wearing it with nothing else on fifteen minutes earlier. Gary looks up at the blackboard next to the dartboard and notices a message from 'Bad Gary' to him which reads: 'One down – one to go!'

At the apartment, the proper Gary hides in the kitchen as 'Bad Gary' and Yvonne arrive. He told Yvonne's secretary that their apartment was on fire; but he says there's a fire on his lips and proceeds to kiss her and make love to her, more than aware that the other Gary is in the flat.

Later, in the shop, Ron arrives and comes face to face with Gary pointing a gun at him. Gary apologises, saying he thought the front door was locked. When Ron asks him why he has a gun and what 'Bad Gary' has done now, Gary refuses to tell him. But he does say that's he's taken a few more liberties than a man can tolerate, and forced him to listen to them. Gary tells him he got the gun in 1944 and that they were about the only thing not on the ration back then.

In 1944, 'Bad Gary' arrives at the Royal Oak. Phoebe is expecting him to accompany her to the theatre with Noël Coward, but it was the other Gary who took the invitation from Noël by phone. Hence he is not dressed for the occasion. After giving Gary a piece of her mind about his recent behaviour, she storms off to the theatre alone, telling him to stay and help Reg run the bar instead. Just as he's pouring himself a drink, 'Bad Gary' is shot at by the original Gary; but the bullet narrowly misses, shattering a bottle instead. Reg comes in and sees Gary disappearing through the door. Reg calls out to him and 'Bad Gary' pops up from behind the bar, leaving Reg feeling confused and shaken.

Later at the shop, Gary is explaining to Ron that he has been conned by 'Bad Gary' into thinking he was the real Gary. He tells Ron that guns are hardly his style and he is surprised that he fell for his ploy. Ron hides as the other Gary arrives and pulls a gun on his double. However, he is pinned to the counter by Ron and the gun drops to the floor – where it is picked up by the first Gary, who

Closed for the Duration

reveals he has fooled Ron yet again. He tells them both that he plans do some changing of history: for instance, changing the name of Marks and Spencer to Marks and Sparrow. Alarmed, Gary reminds him of the repercussions.

Then a third incarnation of Gary Sparrow arrives in the shop via the time portal. Ron takes advantage of the distraction to wrestle 'Bad Gary' to the ground and disarm him. Confused, Ron asks whether this is a Gary Sparrow convention! The pipe-smoking version of Gary tells them that when the lightning struck he was formed on the other side of the time portal. He's spent the last three days helping the emergency services after a doodlebug landed just a couple of streets away from where he was formed. He mentions that at the last count he'd rescued six people. Ron comments that he's obviously 'Good Gary'. The original Gary comments that he thought that was him, to which Ron replies that the size of Gary's ego never ceases to amaze him!

Concerned that he might end up spending the rest of his life as one of the Beverley Sisters, the original Gary asks for suggestions as to how they solve this problem. Ron suggests all three versions of Gary go through the time portal together at the same time in the hope they will merge back into one. The idea works and the other replicants disappear.

In 1944, Gary apologises to Phoebe for his recent behaviour and confirms that he has 'pulled himself together'.

Later, in the present, Gary briefly makes it up with Yvonne. However, she is disappointed that he doesn't kiss her as passionately as the psychopathic replica that she seemed to prefer. He says the passionate version has gone for good and this causes Yvonne to put him back in the spare room, both physically and metaphorically.

After playing two characters, Gary Sparrow and Colonel Henri Dupont, in '…But We Think You Have to Go' in series five, this episode gave Nicholas an even bigger challenge – playing an additional two versions of Gary Sparrow. The inspiration for the episode, written by Gary Lawson and John Phelps, came from a 1970 psychological thriller film made at Elstree Studios called *The Man who Haunted Himself*, which starred Roger Moore.

Given the complications that the storyline was going to present, the writers sought advice about what would be possible from a technical point of view. 'We did talk about it with the director, Nic Phillips,' explained John. 'But as the plot hinged on "Good Gary" never being able to pin down "Bad Gary", most of the time they were apart.'

Nicholas can still recall the demands the plot made on him and the team. 'What I most remember about this episode was that I spent most of the day in make-up and wardrobe and changing my clothes,' he said. 'This is because I played three different versions of Gary Sparrow. It was a complicated pre-record and we had to finish it during the daytime. As with all the pre-records we did, as soon as we'd finished, the editor had to at least complete a rough cut so that we could show the scenes to the audience that evening.'

This was the first episode in which we saw the set of the downstairs of Gary and Yvonne's new open-plan luxury penthouse apartment. Also seen in this episode for the first time was the new Duckett's Passage set. As it was built in the studio, a wall flat was built across the alley. The addition of the wall would also be used as a plot device in the final episode. Viewers were given their first chance to see the new sets of the Royal Oak and the market.

In 'All About Yvonne', the second episode of series six, things have gone from bad to worse between Gary and Yvonne. The latter's relationship with New Labour isn't helping. Yvonne admits to being tired of all the arguing they do now. She thought they'd be happier when they decided to move. However, Gary points out that he had no say in the decision. This confuses Yvonne who reminds him that they agreed to the idea of a luxury penthouse by the riverside. Gary childishly replies that she only asked him out of politeness. He says his opinion doesn't count because she's paying for everything. Yvonne thinks his disapproval is because he's jealous of her success, but he claims it's because he doesn't fit in with her whole superficial lifestyle. Given how they've drifted apart, Yvonne says she thinks it would be better if he left. At first Gary thinks she means going to open his shop, but she is referring to them splitting up and him leaving the apartment.

Meanwhile, Ron is having far more luck in his love life. He has started a fling with his new rich neighbour called Flic. They're engaging in some preliminary horseplay as Gary arrives looking for a bed for the night. He tells Ron his marriage might be over; but Ron points out casually that he's got another one. Ron formally introduces Gary to Flic, but is rather tetchy because, as she points out, he was rather hoping to 'put Rover in the kennel about now'. Flic explains that she's a lady of leisure because her father is loaded. He made a fortune from selling fridges in the seventies. Ron wittily quips that he was the original 'fridge magnate'. After Flic goes in search of a glass of champagne, Ron admits he has told her he's a rich self-made man with a business empire. He points out that if she knew he lived in a Mayfair apartment because it was bought in the war for the price of a small Gucci handbag, he'd be chucked quicker than last season's Prada. Gary reminds him that's he living in a house of cards – a house of credit cards. Ron refuses to be judged by a wannabe 007 who claims to have written the Beatles' back catalogue. Keen to spend time alone with Flic, Ron encourages

Gary to ring Yvonne. He does, but despite making out he's talking to her, Ron says he heard her hang up.

Not welcome at home or Ron's, Gary decides to go back to the Royal Oak. Although he gets a warm welcome, Phoebe is keen for him to tell her more about his work as he hasn't done so of late. Gary says he's tired and will do so in the morning.

Gary is keen to leave the pub as quickly as possible in the morning as he has Yvonne on his mind. He tells Phoebe there's a 'flap on', and when he says he can't discuss it, she remarks that it's convenient. The argument escalates and in the heat of the moment, Gary accidentally calls her Yvonne. He quickly corrects himself and leaves. Reg notes that he doesn't seem to tell her any more than he tells everyone else. Phoebe says that he just told her more than he bargained for. Reg reminds her that Yvonne is his boss. She says that he wouldn't be the first person to have an affair with his boss.

Back at the West End flat, Ron confirms that Yvonne hasn't called, and Gary says he's worried that she's thrown him out for good. Ron tries to assure him that she'll get over it. He reminds Gary that women take longer to do everything: like having orgasms, going shopping and appreciating the artistic qualities of the *Daily Sport*. Gary admits that what he said to her was out of order, even though there are bits of her lifestyle that are irritating. He admits that he's sure there are parts of his life that would annoy her; his other wife, as Ron points out, being the obvious candidate. Although Gary is keen to bow and scrape to get Yvonne back, Ron tells him not to lose his dignity as women like a man to behave like a man. However, their conversation has to come to an end when the phone rings as Flic is ready and waiting in a schoolmistress's outfit to give Ron 'detention'.

Gary goes back to the penthouse on the pretext of picking up some clothes and discovers Yvonne is not alone. She has brought in a hunky Italian interior designer called Roberto to help brighten up the place. Realising that Gary is jealous, she tells him that Roberto is accompanying her to a neighbour's drinks party. When Gary declares that will be over his dead body, Yvonne says it could be arranged as Roberto is two times European karate champion and that he'd bone him like a chicken.

Gary creeps back into the Royal Oak late at night, and the following morning Phoebe tells Reg that he's avoiding her and that she's been a fool and believes he's been making excuses to spend time with Yvonne. When Gary is keen to leave due to there being another 'flap on', Phoebe tells him to admit that he's going to see his bit on the side – his boss Yvonne. Gary admits he's been preoccupied at work of late because he has a lot of problems. He says he could be shot for what he's about to tell her but for the sake of their marriage, he's going to trust her. He admits he has been thinking a lot about Yvonne recently because she's been kidnapped. And that she's been held by a particularly nasty renegade Italian agent who goes by the name of Roberto. Gary says she's going to have to trust him in the way he's just trusted her. He says he's going now to try and get her back.

Gary and Ron arrive at an expensive restaurant. Flic is to follow on shortly. Ron is impressed and upon noticing Eric Clapton, greets him, but doesn't quite get the hand gesture he expected in return. Ron looks concerned when he sees the menu and mentions that you could buy a small country for the cost of some of the starters. Gary assures him the meal is on him. When Ron asks him why, Gary tells him he wants to hire his girlfriend while she's in the restaurant. He wants Yvonne to think they're an item and that Flic won't even know. He just has to hold her hand and laugh loudly at her jokes. In return, Flic gets an expensive meal in a flash restaurant with no damage done to Ron's bank account. The aim is to make Yvonne jealous and stop Roberto, the Italian medallion, from walking away with her. Flic arrives and notices Eric Clapton. She asks Ron if he wants to come and say hello, but mentions they have sort of become acquainted. Despite worrying he will feel like a pimp, Ron agrees to Gary's plan. Yvonne arrives and sit at a nearby table. Gary moves his seat up closer to Flic, holds her hand and laughs over the top when she suggests to Ron that they order. Yvonne watches Gary totally unimpressed as he continues his poor attempts at flirting for her benefit. Roberto arrives and impresses Flic with his good looks. He goes over to Yvonne and kisses her before sitting at the table. Ron comments that suddenly he can see the size of Gary's problem. When Ron tells Flic that Yvonne is Gary's wife, she says she will be ex-wife given a month.

Gary goes over to Yvonne and says he's surprised to see her here. But she tells him she knows he called her office to find out where she would be. She tells him that showing off his girlfriend in front of her is childish. When Roberto attempts to get involved in their argument, Gary calls him 'a continental ponce', thinking he doesn't understand English. Yvonne reminds him that the word 'ponce' is universal. Yvonne calls Roberto off to avoid a fight, Roberto walks away and she tells Gary to sit down. He says he wants her back and that he still loves her. Yvonne tells him she's still angry and that the things he said really hurt her. Gary apologises and tells her he was afraid he was losing her. He tells Yvonne that Flic is with Ron. However, she admits she already knew they were dating as she saw their photo in *The Mail* with the headline: 'Who is Flic's mystery date?' They wanted to know who, but Yvonne admits she wants to know why! To make up for his behaviour, Gary agrees to accompany Yvonne to the New Labour 'Movers and Shakers' conference. They leave the restaurant along with Roberto. This leaves poor Ron having to foot the bill for his meal with Flic after all. To try and drastically reduce the cost of the bill, Ron tells her the tomato soup looks nice.

This series more than most would see Gary and Yvonne's marital problems becoming worse. Gary's double life was combining with Yvonne's new successful millionairess lifestyle to create a metaphorical ticking time bomb. Although Gary was obviously very much in love with his wartime bride, he still seemed unable to permanently cut ties with the present and his present-day wife. The challenge for all the writers was to keep making it plausible that Gary and Yvonne would still want to stay together despite leading very separate lives.

This particular episode of *Goodnight Sweetheart* was the last to date written by Gary Lawson and John Phelps and really brought Yvonne to the forefront. So was this intentional? 'Not the main driver,' explained John. 'But it was good to be able to give Yvonne a meatier role. The main driver, as usual, was to make Gary's life as difficult as possible. For obvious reasons, it was always easier to come up with more interesting stories for the past. But the challenge was always to make the scenes in the present just as entertaining.

'Out of all the shows we've worked on, this is the one we miss the most. If there's ever a chance for it to come back, we'll be there.'

The cast of this episode was joined by the actress Sonya Walger in the first of her three appearances as Ron's rich new lover, Flic. Sonya now lives and works as an actress in America. She also curates Bookish, a podcast she created in which she talks to interesting people about the five books that have most shaped who they are. Her other television credits have included Penny Widmore in the drama series *Lost*, Dr Elise Ryan in the comedy drama *Common Law* and Molly Cobb in the science-fiction drama *For All Mankind*. Her film roles, meanwhile, include Lindsay in the comedy drama *Cold Turkey*, Kristen in the science-fiction thriller *Anon*, which starred Clive Owen and Amanda Seyfried, and Jane Wilson in the crime drama *Darkness Falls*.

Making his one and only appearance in this episode as Yvonne's good-looking interior designer, Roberto, was Gavin Abbott. Gavin's theatre roles have included D'Artagnan in the Edmond Rostand play *Cyrano de Bergerac* at the Theatre Royal Haymarket, London, Felix in the Ben Travers comedy *The Bed Before Yesterday* at the Almeida Theatre, London, and Silvius in the William Shakespeare pastoral comedy *As You Like it* at the Albery Theatre, London. His other television credits have included Ginge in the medical drama *Peak Practice*, Andy in the football drama *Playing the Field* and Simon Bentwood in the Catherine Cookson romantic drama *Tilly Trotter*.

*

Goodnight Sweetheart: A Guide to the Classic Sitcom

At the beginning of 'California Dreamin'', the third episode of series six, Gary arrives in the pub looking for Phoebe. Presently a man wearing an eyepatch comes into the bar carrying a crate. He puts it down and looks proudly around the bar.

Meanwhile, Gary has gone upstairs to the flat. He walks into the main bedroom and makes a grab for Phoebe. But it is not Phoebe. He didn't realise who it was as she was bending over while dressing. The lady tells Charlie to stop it as he will be back in a minute. She turns around, sees Gary and screams. The man who was in the bar rushes upstairs to find out what's going on, and throws Gary out of the bedroom. Downstairs in the bar, Phoebe arrives and explains what's happening. The brewery have thrown her out and Fred and Daisy Greengrass are the new tenants. During the row, Gary calls Fred by the name Charlie, thinking that's who Daisy was referring to upstairs. In doing so, the fact that she has been having an affair with his brother is revealed. Gary tries to break up a row between Fred and Daisy and this causes Fred to start fighting with Gary. Reg walks in wearing his police uniform. He hits Fred with his truncheon and admits he really enjoyed it!

Phoebe explains to Gary that her lease at the Royal Oak has finished and, as George Harrison from the brewery has been looking for an excuse to evict her since she turned down his offer of sleeping with him, she will have to leave. Gary thinks that now they have the flat in the West End, it would be good to move on. Phoebe also tells Gary that Reg has been 'retired' from the police force. As she's heard the war will be over soon, Phoebe is keen that they make a move, despite it being a wrench, to California. For obvious reasons, Gary is not keen. However, Phoebe reminds him that there will be nothing to keep them here after Hitler has been beaten.

On arriving back at the flat in the present day, Gary discovers Flic has become imprisoned in one of her own posh frocks. Gary manages to help her get it on just as Ron walks in. However, Ron realises that Gary wasn't up to anything unseemly. Ron then mentions that he and Flic are preparing for the imminent arrival of the team from *Hi!* magazine.

Gary tries to update Ron on his problems in wartime London, but Ron is more concerned with the display box on the table featuring a new work by an exciting up-and-coming artist. Gary thinks it's twenty dead hamsters, but it's called *Tears Before Bedtime*. Gary asks what it is exactly and Ron, unsure, tells him it's twenty dead hamsters. Ron goes on to tell Gary to make Yvonne his priority as he doesn't have to worry about California until VE day.

Yvonne adds to Gary's problems by telling him that she wants to set up Nature Boy in California and for them to move over there. The millionairess

Closed for the Duration

also tells him the Millennium Dome Experience is set to include a tour around a gigantic Perspex sculpture of a man and woman fused together and she has been modelling the female parts. Apparently, visitors will be able to make their way up Yvonne on an educational voyage of discovery via a nonspecific aperture.

Back at the flat, Ron has fallen asleep having been bored with posing for photos with Flic. She wakes him with a kiss and tells him the team from *Hi!* magazine have gone. Ron is glad and moans that he's just spent seven hours posing and with nothing on the table in front of them apart from plastic grouse and some wax fruit. Flic explains that it goes with the territory of being a 'face'; attending parties, gallery openings and film premieres and appearing in glossy magazines is the price you pay for, amongst other things, getting designer discounts. Flic is keen on doing some late-night shopping in Knightsbridge, but Ron wants to, yet again, ring out for a pizza. That is, until she tells Ron that shopping makes her feel sexy. Ron tells her to break the bank as she heads to the door.

Gary arrives and, not for the first time since becoming a time traveller, complains to Ron that things are getting worse in his life. He explains that Phoebe and Yvonne now both want to go to California. He reminds Ron that there's no time portal in downtown LA and commuting is obviously out of the question! Ron tells him to talk them out of it and find a way – offer them an alternative. Gary think he might be on to something. He reaches for an apple and Ron smirks knowing it's made of wax. As it turns out, it's not. However, the apple a hungry Ron then grabs, is!

In a bid to distract Phoebe, Gary takes her to a nightclub which is available to rent. Phoebe notices the small stage where the club's singer performs. The owner tells them there is a singer; she's a terrific girl and they could probably keep her on. Gary tells Phoebe that Noël Coward says he comes here all the time and he couldn't recommend the place highly enough. Gary assures Phoebe they can afford it because they'd be renting it and not buying. The Scottish owner, Angus, says they'd be stealing it from him. He's keen to make a quick agreement on a jazz club in Soho that's up for grabs, otherwise he'd be holding out for more money. Phoebe goes over to the stage and asks if the microphone is turned on. The owners says to give it a try. She tests it by singing an extract from the song 'Blue Moon'. Phoebe asks Gary if they could keep the club on until after the war before they move to California. Gary tells her to think it over. Phoebe suggests that she could be the singer. Gary says he hadn't thought of that… although it's clear this would distract her from thoughts of moving.

While Phoebe is having another look around the club, Gary goes to Reg's leaving do at a small hall in the East End. Sadly, no one has turned up; he's surrounded by uneaten food and drink and a dance record of the era plays on a wind-up gramophone. Reg looks understandably downbeat and presently turns off the music. He explains that he has written a speech but it's a bit of a waste now. The ex-policeman mentions that Margie will be along soon. Gary asks if he would like to share a drop of Scotch from the bottle he's brought, before encouraging Reg to read his speech. They then have a bit of a knees-up on their own accompanied by the gramophone!

Back in the present, Gary arrives home and discovers that Yvonne is packed to go to LA. He says he doesn't want to leave Britain and live in California. She tells him not to worry as she's only going for a recce. In the meantime, she's needed for an emergency modelling session for the Millennium Dome sculpture. Apparently they need to work out where to stick the turnstile.

On arrival back at the flat in 1944, Gary discovers Reg is now working in the reception as Sergeant Commissionaire Reginald Deadman (the stripes come with the uniform!), late of the Metropolitan Police Force. A vacancy occurred as the previous Sergeant Commissionaire retired due to haemorrhoids and worse! Reg tells Gary that Phoebe wants him to meet her at the Blue Door Club at 8.00pm.

Back at home, Gary is still trying to persuade Yvonne to give up the idea of them moving to California. He doesn't want to spend the rest of his life amongst people that have to go into analysis every time they have a bad manicure. He wants to talk but Yvonne can't as the Millennium Dome Think Tank want her to join them for tapas. Apparently there's been an urgent rethink of the Perspex Yvonne. They've had a look at the back elevation, and they're thinking of slipping in a Dunkin' Donut. She's needed to pose for new positions and couldn't possibly think about setting up a new branch of Nature Boy in California – well not for at least a week!

On arriving at the Blue Door Club, Gary is greeted with the sound of Phoebe singing 'Blue Moon' to the audience. He is met by Reg who takes his coat. Reg is now also working as a barman-cum-bouncer at the club.

After finishing her song, Phoebe comes over to Gary. She tells him she is over the moon as the club has lots of customers, all drinking cocktails, who like her singing. Gary tells Reg that she's obviously at home in the club and not missing the Royal Oak too much or mentioning California. Well, that is until she sings her next song (supposedly written by Gary) called 'California Dreamin''!

As well as Sonya Walger returning to play Flic, this episode included three other supporting cast members. Playing Fred, the new publican of the Royal Oak, in this episode was Gary Lammin. He gained the role after some much-appreciated advice from a former *Doctor Who* companion. 'My agent at the time was Wendy Padbury who worked for Evans and Reiss,' he recalled. 'Wendy has previously played Zoe in *Doctor Who* and was a very experienced actress. Wendy told me to use my authentic London accent for my audition with Nic Phillips and Susie Parriss for the role of Fred Greengrass, but to be mindful that *Goodnight Sweetheart* was not a modern-day London accent. It was a valuable tip and I knew exactly what Wendy meant. In fact, I had an ear for the accent because I used to visit people in Hoxton, which is close to Bethnal Green, when I was a child. I always remembered how slightly old-fashioned and rather fascinating the Hoxton accent sounded. So, I based my tonal quality on those early childhood memories. I can still spot a Hoxton accent to this day if I hear an older bloke speaking it! You can never be sure how well an audition has gone, but thankfully I think it was my attention to that Hoxton accent that won them over.'

Once he had been given the part of Fred, Gary was keen to ensure he was doing what was expected of him. 'I remember asking Nick during a rehearsal if what I was "feeding him" was okay,' said the actor. 'He reassured me that it was, adding it had "great energy". He is a gracious man, a real gentleman and I loved working with him. He was very unassuming, despite his status.'

During his costume fitting, Gary was given an unexpected request. 'A lady who worked in the wardrobe department asked if I would consider wearing an eyepatch for my character,' he said. 'I jumped instantly at the idea as it reminded me of an old "geezer" I used to chat to who had a bric-a-brac stall in Brick Lane. He wore an eyepatch. I knew wearing that eyepatch would help add another authentic old-style London flavour to my characterisation of Fred.'

Fast-forward twenty-one years, and Gary found himself being reunited with one of the cast members from the sitcom. 'In March 2020, I was working on the Hat Trick sitcom *Kate and Koji*. One day, during rehearsals, the writer Andy Hamilton said, "Gary, let me introduce you to Victor McGuire." But I already knew him from working on my episode of *Goodnight Sweetheart*, of course! We shook hands and had a good catch-up.'

Gary's other television roles include Jimmy in the soap opera *Family Affairs*, Roger in the drama *Murder in Mind* and a postman in both series of the sitcom *Kate and Koji*. In addition, his film credits have included Ronald in Michael Winner's action comedy *Bullseye*, Mick in Ken Loach's comedy drama *Riff-Raff* and a barman in the action crime drama *The Krays: Dead Man Walking*.

The role of Fred's plucky wife, Daisy, in this episode was played by Tabitha Wady. In the theatre, Tabitha's credits include playing Amy Polegate in the Alan Ayckbourn comedy thriller *It Could Be Any One of Us* at the Chichester Festival Theatre, Rosie Pye in the Charlotte Jones comedy *Humble Boy* at the Northcott Theatre, Exeter, and the Duchess in Thomas Middleton's Jacobean drama *The Revenger's Tragedy* at the Nottingham Playhouse. Best known for playing the receptionist Katrina Bullen in the daytime medical drama *Doctors*, Tabitha's other television roles have included playing Lucy in the sitcom *Holding the Baby* and Lydia Weston in the period drama *Berkeley Square*. Meanwhile, on film, Tabitha memorably played Gemma in the comedy *Kevin and Perry Go Large*, with Harry Enfield and Kathy Burke.

The amiable owner of the Blue Door Club, Angus, was played in this episode by the Scottish actor Donald Douglas. Donald's first professional stage appearance was at the Citizens Theatre, Glasgow. His other roles have included playing Alan in Mart Crowley's *The Boys in the Band* at Wyndham's Theatre, London, General von Shratt in Mikhail Bulgakov's *The White Guard* at the Aldwych Theatre, London, and Aegeus alongside Diana Rigg in Euripides' ancient Greek tragedy *Medea* at the Longacre Theatre on Broadway. On television, Angus's credits have included playing Tony Pringle in the Adam Faith drama *Budgie*, Tony Lloyd in the sitcom *Executive Stress* and Dr Gordon McKendrick in the Scottish drama *Monarch of the Glen*. His film work has included playing a Police Detective in the musical drama *Give My Regards to Broad Street*, Father Rainy in the fantasy action *Highlander: Endgame*, and Admiral Darcy in the Renée Zellweger comedy drama *Bridget Jones's Diary*.

This series saw Phoebe rekindle an interest in singing again thanks to a spot of shifty chicanery by Gary. 'After Phoebe sang in series five, the producers approached me with the idea that Phoebe would become a nightclub singer,' said Elizabeth. 'I was thrilled at the prospect of being able to sing on television again. I felt I really came into my own in the nightclub scenes set in the Blue Door Club.

'I recorded an album called *Goodnight Sweetheart* during a break from making the final series. The one-album deal with Universal Music was a project that I set up. I picked the songs and worked with the wonderful composer and arranger John Altman and we recorded it live at Angel Studios in Islington with an orchestra in just a week! The songs included "Our Love is Here to Stay", "Blue Moon", "I'll Be Seeing You" and "Goodnight Sweetheart".'

Writer Sam Lawrence, who wrote 'California Dreamin'', has a particular memory of this episode. 'When I was watching it back recently, I found the scene featuring Reg's leaving party, where only Gary had turned up, really moving,' he recalled. 'That's even though I wrote it! I thought Chris really got the heartbreak into Reg's leaving speech delivered to an empty room.'

The hall used for Reg's leaving do in this episode was St Mark's Hall, which was located at 23 St Mark's Road, Teddington. Although St Mark's Church remains, the hall that was located next door has been demolished.

*

Closed for the Duration

In 'Grief Encounter', the fourth episode of series six, Gary isn't happy to see that Phoebe is receiving fan mail for her singing in the Blue Door Club. In fact, he comments that one of the letters is from 'a sad old git'. Phoebe suspects that Gary is jealous, but he disagrees. He's annoyed that she spends too much time reading them. She says it's because he doesn't say nice things to her any more.

Noël Coward arrives to offer Phoebe a small role in his new film, *Brief Encounter*. He has written a scene in a nightclub and Phoebe would be given the chance to sing. Phoebe is keen that she chooses the song and Gary also appear in the film. She wants them to perform 'I Just Called to Say I Love You' together. For obvious reasons, Gary isn't keen. Phoebe says that he's too scared to do anything with his talent and too jealous for her to do anything with hers. But she's determined to appear in the film whatever happens – even if she has to be accompanied on the comb and paper by Reg Deadman.

Meanwhile, back in the present, Yvonne is sharing a conference call with her lawyer, Murray. Her business partner Clive is out in California selling her business, Nature Boy, behind her back; and she wants Murray to stop the sale with a court injunction – or if that fails, with a hitman. Gary looks on in shock, thinking at first that she's watching an American soap opera. Yvonne apologises for taking her problems out on Gary. He shrugs them off, saying it goes with the penthouse, the Porsche and the PMT.

While eating a sandwich, Gary and Ron watch the film *Brief Encounter* for their first time on a VHS at the shop. They have reached the part in which Celia Johnson's character runs out of the station buffet and considers ending her life by jumping onto the line and into the path of an oncoming train. The sequence shocks Ron who questions if they're the only two people in the country not to have watched the film. Gary says he tried to the previous Christmas but fell asleep on account of eating two turkey dinners close together. Gary is surprised that so far there hasn't been a nightclub scene. Ron tells Gary that surely if he had appeared in the film, someone would have pointed it out to him by now. Gary reminds him that back in the war they haven't finished filming it yet. Ron questions why they are watching it. Realising his mistake, Gary says, 'just in case'. They reach the end of the film and discover that no nightclub scene made the cut. Ron asks him how he's going to get out of appearing in the film. He doesn't know. He mentions that Phoebe is longing to sing 'I Just Called to Say I Love You' and thinks it's his best song since 'Bohemian Rhapsody'!

On arriving at the Blue Door Club, Gary finds that neither his presence nor his song are required in the film due to his shyness. Instead, Noël has discovered a professional and talented songwriter called Anthony Blair. Presently, Anthony, a wing commander in the RAF, arrives and is introduced to Gary, who is quick

Goodnight Sweetheart: A Guide to the Classic Sitcom

to pick up on the fact that his name makes him Tony Blair. In addition, he and the prime minister Tony Blair back in the present day share many of the same mannerisms. Anthony takes Phoebe over to the piano and Noël tells Gary not to fret, saying she will be safe in Anthony's hands. Anthony accompanies himself on the piano as he sings the song he has composed for Phoebe and the film.

The following morning, Yvonne is back on another conference call. She's telling Murray that she's not selling her company, Nature Boy, which she reminds him was her dream, for a lousy eight million dollars. She announces that she's going to come over to take part in the discussions and tells him to warn Clive to get some body armour. Yvonne then asks Gary what's to stop him joining her in LA? She says she needs someone out there with her she can totally trust. When he asks how long they will need to be out there, she tells him six months tops. This panics him and he accidentally says the war will be over in six months. He then corrects himself, realising he has given away a clue to his double life. She says six months isn't too long to sit by a swimming pool. He tells her she doesn't really want him out there, holding her back. She has a feeling he wants her to go away and says if he's seeing someone then he should just get it out in the open. When he tells her there is no one else for him on this planet, she overreacts by wondering if he's sleeping with an alien. Yvonne goes upstairs and Gary comments that he can't do a thing right. He then discovers that Murray has watched the whole argument.

Over lunch in the shop, Ron tells Gary to look on the bright side. After all, this could be a God-given opportunity to simplify his life, by saying farewell to Yvonne and concentrating his affections on Phoebe. But Gary doesn't think he wants to let Yvonne go.

Back at the flat in 1944, Phoebe arrives home to find Gary has brought her some roses, favourite chocolate, perfume from Paris and some new night attire. She is surprised. Gary asks if she thought they were from Tony Blair. Phoebe tells him to stop bribing her as she didn't have her hair done at Chez Rene to spoil it wrestling with him in the bedroom. She tells Gary she's going out to rehearse her scene with Anthony. Noël has written them some lines now too: lines, she says, Gary could have been performing with her if he hadn't been so 'namby-pamby'.

Reg arrives and sniffs the roses. Sadly, these make him sneeze right into a drink that Gary has just prepared. He does the same again. He mentions he's here to meet with Noël. He takes his hat off and reveals a terrible wig that barely covers his bald spot. On his arrival, Noël comments that it's spectacular and that no one would mistake it for the genuine article!

Noël hands Gary a gramophone record and asks him to play it. They're short of extras for the nightclub scene and a little bird has told him that Reg is a wonderful dancer. In truth, Reg told him this as he'd always wanted to appear in a film. They both proceed to perform a tango. At one point during the song, Noël grabs one of the roses and puts it between his teeth. Getting close makes Reg sneeze again and his wig flies off his head and into Gary's drink.

Back at the shop, Ron once again tells Gary that this might be a God-given opportunity to simplify his life. Basically, go to America with Yvonne and let Phoebe go off with Tony Blair. Gary is quick to point out that this is the exact opposite of the advice he gave him last time. Ron notes that he prides himself on being nothing but inconsistent!

After Gary returns to 1944, Reg tells him that Phoebe has gone to the studios where they're filming the interior scenes for *Brief Encounter*. Gary makes for Denham Studios where Phoebe and Anthony Blair are already on the buffet room set. Anthony is telling Phoebe how much he admires her and mentions that ever since he lost one of his legs, he's despaired of meeting a woman again who sees him as a man and not a cripple. Phoebe tells him she admits she finds him attractive but reminds him she's a married woman. He asks whether Gary loves her. Despite being quieter and not as handsome, or as talented, as him, she's convinced that Gary still loves her. He then admits that he wrote a love letter to her. Their conversation has to end because the director, David Lean, decides to 'go for a take' between Trevor Howard and Celia Johnson.

Just as they're in the middle of the take, Gary rushes in and spots Anthony and Phoebe kissing at the table. He believes this to be real and goes and pulls Anthony up by his coat collar. Noël explains that they were merely filling in with a little background action. Gary apologises, and Anthony comments that he's pleased to see that Gary still feels so passionately about his wife. He limps off leaving Phoebe to remind Gary he only has the one leg. Gary comments that this is hardly his fault. He asks how they could appear in both this scene and the nightclub scene, and Noël explains that that scene has been dropped at Celia's request. He goes off to mollify Anthony while Gary does his best to apologise and make up with Phoebe, who admits that she finds filming boring and wants to go home. Although he has an important meeting, she tells him to phone in sick so they can spend the night together at their flat.

On his return to the penthouse the next day, Gary finds a fax confirming Yvonne's travel details to LA. He rushes to the station to try stopping her from leaving. Dressed in his 1940s clothes, Gary makes for the platform and looks for Yvonne on the Heathrow Express. He begs her to stay, or offers to go with her. But she says it won't work as her world of international capitalism obviously intimidates him. She says he needs a simple home-loving girl who wants to have his babies. An announcement says the train is about to depart and Yvonne gets back on the train leaving Gary running after it as it pulls out of the station. As he does, he trips over a luggage trolley as Yvonne watches. Realising what has happened, she goes to stop the train.

As a result of his accident, Gary has broken his arm. He sits on the settee in the penthouse. The answering machine is activated by a call, and Clive is heard saying he wants to speak to Yvonne and that he is keen to sort everything out and cut the best deal for them both. Gary picks up the phone and decides to take over as the chief negotiator. They eventually agree on fifteen million dollars – but only because Gary has a soft spot for bald men with ponytails! Yvonne is over the moon about the money and promises to speak to her merchant bank about a commission for Gary.

Another of Marks and Gran's very best episodes, 'Grief Encounter' affectionately used the making of *Brief Encounter* to great effect while simultaneously combining the problems Gary was experiencing with his wives both sides of the time portal. The modern take on *Brief Encounter* at the Heathrow Express was particularly inspired.

Proving yet again that not all of the episodes were made in order, 'Grief Encounter' was moved back. The read-through and blocking took place on Friday 9 April 1999 with rehearsals taking place between Sunday 11 April 1999 and Wednesday 14 April 1999. The studio audience recording took place in Studio 1 at Teddington Studios on Thursday 15 April 1999.

For Nicholas, the episode gave him the chance to work with his partner. 'My wife Lucy, who used to be a ballet dancer, played the role of a non-speaking production assistant,' he revealed. 'She can be seen in the background on the film set of *Brief Encounter* sitting next to David Benson, who played Noël Coward. She was petrified and was even getting stress headaches. I said to her, "You've danced at the Royal Albert Hall and all around the world, and yet here you are sitting in a dusty studio in Teddington shaking with nerves!"'

The episode also has fond memories for Elizabeth. 'It was my favourite episode,' she happily admitted. 'The line "He's only got the one leg, you know," which Phoebe said about Anthony Blair while having a row with Gary, still makes me laugh even now!'

Returning to play Noël Coward gave David Benson the opportunity to dance with Christopher as Reg in this episode. 'We rehearsed the choreography a lot to get it right,' David recalled. 'The scene with the dance was a pre-record because of the joke with the wig at the end. I am no Fred Astaire, but this episode did at least give me the chance to dance on television in a nice silk dressing gown.

Astaire has been a hero of mine as long as Coward – in fact, I wrote to him and got his autograph when I was fourteen – so I loved having the chance to do some inept steps as Noël who was a lifelong friend of Fred's.'

The supporting cast in this episode included Rolf Saxon as Yvonne's laid-back American lawyer, Murray. 'I was only briefly called in to rehearse as I had a small and "contained" role,' he explained. 'My scenes were shot separately from Nicholas and Emma on the set and screened on monitors for the audience during the taping, so they felt as if it were a "call" to the States. It was obvious that they both loved what they were doing and it's always fun to be around people who love their work.

'I was lucky enough to also work on episodes of *Love Hurts* and *Birds of a Feather* that were penned by Laurence and Maurice. They possess two of the most important aspects of scriptwriting: they're very clever and very funny.'

Rolf continues to work as an actor in both America and the UK. His theatre work has included playing Eddie Carbone in the Arthur Miller drama *A View from the Bridge* at the Leicester Haymarket Theatre, Johnny in a tour of the Terrence McNally two-hander *Frankie and Johnny in the Clair de Lune*, opposite Kelly McGillis, and Baumann in a tour of the Jerry Herman and Michael Stewart musical *Mack and Mabel*. For television, Rolf's other roles include playing Hudson J. Talbot in the drama *Capital City*, Brian in the sitcom *The Upper Hand* and Art Spellman in the action drama *Ultimate Force*. Meanwhile, the actor's film credits have included CIA analyst William Donloe in the action thriller *Mission: Impossible*, Philip Jones in the Bond movie *Tomorrow Never Dies* and Mikey in the thriller *August Falls*.

The role of Anthony Blair, complete with well-observed Tony Blair-isms, was played by Paul Goodwin. '*Goodnight Sweetheart* was the first and last time to date that I've ever appeared in a sitcom recorded in front of a studio audience,' he explained. 'Because I came from a theatre background I feel I performed more to the audience than I should have. I learned that it's not just about the audience but it's about the cameras. It was also the only time I have ever worked on a television programme that had a rehearsal period.'

Paul continues to work as an actor, teacher and director specialising in classical text, particularly the work of Shakespeare. As an actor he has worked with the National Theatre, Cheek by Jowl, and the Royal Shakespeare Company. In 2008, Paul graduated with an MA in voice studies from the Central School of Speech and Drama, followed by a year with the RSC working in the Text, Voice and Artist Development department. From 2009 to 2017, he was Course Director of MA Acting at Drama Centre London/University of the Arts, leading a forty-five-week intensive postgraduate conservatoire training course, eight weeks of which were spent at the Vakhtangov school in Moscow. Paul continues to teach internationally, leading Shakespeare scene study in English, and is a fellow of the Higher Education Academy. Away from the stage, his other television credits have included playing Martin Adams in the Scottish police drama *Taggart*, SDO Jarvis in the firefighter drama *London's Burning* and Geoffrey Smee in the period drama *Heartbeat*.

Also appearing in this episode was Richard Braine as the director of *Brief Encounter*, David Lean. 'I remember the director Nic Phillips saying that it was important to him to "cast someone with huge ears",' he recalled. 'This is because David Lean had big ears. I have big ears. This probably explains why I got the part!

'Although I had experience of appearing in a situation comedy, having been in *The Brittas Empire* amongst others, I was nervous. But I knew Nicholas Lyndhurst and he immediately put me at my ease. What I remember so vividly about the rehearsal period was that Marks and Gran were there at every moment. Their contribution was so important.'

Richard is an actor, director and playwright. His theatre credits have included playing Peter Sellers in a play he wrote called *Being There with Peter Sellers* at the Pleasance Theatre, London, and on tour, Ratty in Alan Bennett's adaptation of the Kenneth Grahame novel *The Wind in the Willows* at the Bristol Old Vic, and one of the performers in a tour of Patrick Barlow's slick spoof adaptation of John Buchan's novel *The 39 Steps*. His other television appearances include playing Rupert Steggles in the comedy *Jeeves and Wooster*, a vicar in the sitcom *As Time Goes By* and Dr Merivale in the drama *Goodbye, Mr Chips*. His film roles include playing a policeman in the comedy *Calendar Girls*, a vicar in the romantic comedy *Bridget Jones: The Edge of Reason*, with Renée Zellweger, and a black-suited man in the action comedy horror *Pride and Prejudice and Zombies*.

Playing Celia Johnson in this episode was the actress and writer Dolly Wells, who is the daughter of the late comedy actor and writer, John Wells. Dolly's theatre roles have included playing Rosalind in the William Shakespeare pastoral comedy *As You Like it* at the Riverside Studios, London, Alicia in the Kara Miller play *Tamagotchi Heaven* at the Edinburgh Festival, and June in the Wallace Shawn morality play *Aunt Dan and Lemon* at the Almeida Theatre, London. Dolly's television credits include Sister Agatha in the horror drama *Dracula*, Margaret in the comedy drama *The Outlaws* and Janice Fife in the thriller *Inside Man*. Her other television credits include co-writing and appearing in the sitcom *Doll and Em*, with Emily Mortimer, and writing and directing the comedy drama *Good Posture*. Dolly's notable film work includes playing Woney in the romantic comedy *Bridget Jones's Diary*, Sally in the romantic drama *45 Years* and a fur department vendeuse in the love story *I Capture the Castle*.

Also joining the cast for a one-off appearance was Andrew Havill, who played the role of Trevor Howard. 'I mainly worked with Richard Braine and Dolly Wells during the making of the episode,' he said. 'They were both the best company you could wish for. Richard is the most extraordinary raconteur with the funniest stories I've ever heard, while Dolly was just flat-out hilarious. You can, if you listen hard enough, hear her telling us the end of an anecdote about a contortionist during our scene. I have a feeling she came up with that herself, but you'd have to check with the writers!

'My mother came to see the recording and went to the bar afterwards as she was a huge fan of Nicholas because of the sitcoms *Going Straight* and *Butterflies*. *Butterflies* particularly made a huge impression on her and women of her generation. I managed to introduce her to Nicholas, and he was delightful to her.'

Andrew's various theatre credits include Patrice Bombelles in the Christopher Fry comedy *Ring Round the Moon* at the Playhouse Theatre, London, Sir Gilbert Wedgecroft in the Harley Granville-Barker play *Waste* at the National Theatre, London, and Warren Hamilton 'Warnie' Lewis in the William Nicholson drama *Shadowlands* at the Chichester Festival Theatre. On television, his roles have included playing Denis Dawley in the period drama *Call the Midwife*, Douglas Broome in the science-fiction drama *The Nevers* and Sir Robert Fellowes in the historical drama *The Crown*. His film parts include Robert Wood in the drama *The King's Speech*, Henry George Charles Lascelles, 6th Earl of Harewood, in the costume drama *Downton Abbey* and Sir Philip Hendy in the comedy drama *The Duke*, with Jim Broadbent and Helen Mirren.

As with 'Hello, Goodbye', the song Gary supposedly wrote for Phoebe in series five, Anthony Blair's song was specially written for this episode. The lyrics were by David Harsent and the music by Anthony and Gaynor Sadler. Ken Barrie was the singer who provided the guide track and Cliff Hall was the pianist. However, it was the actor Paul Goodwin, who played Anthony Blair, who actually sang it live on the set. The recording of the music took place on Wednesday 10 March 1999 at Logorhythm Music Studios, Lexington Street. Soho, London.

The sequence in which Gary arrived at the station, in an attempt to prevent Yvonne from catching the Heathrow Express to Heathrow Airport and a flight to California, was filmed at Paddington Station in Praed Street, London.

*

In '…The 'Ouses in Between', the fifth episode of series six, Ron arrives at Blitz and Pieces on the scrounge for cash – five hundred pounds to be precise. Gary says he can't finance his lust life with Flic. Ron says it's because he's jealous; not least because they made love in a lift in Claridge's hotel. Gary reminds him that Flic just sees him as a bit of rough, but Ron says a successful bit of rough due to the mountain of lies he's told her. Gary stops their row after hearing a noise in the yard. They go outside and the time traveller remarks on an unusual smell, one he's noticed before. Ron says it's like stale tobacco. Gary points out an object and Ron says it's a cigar butt. He picks it up and it's still hot. Not surprisingly, Gary questions where it has come from.

Yvonne arrives in the shop looking for some memorabilia from her wedding: her husband to be exact. She goes into the yard and explains she had to get out of the penthouse away from all the phone calls and begging letters she's been receiving since she sold her company, Nature Boy. Ron asks whether she has received his begging letter, and she confirms she has. Because, she says, she hasn't ever been particularly nice to him, Yvonne gives him a cheque on the spot to help him get through his current financial problems. Ron says he can live again and leaves the shop shouting 'Claridge's!' in the style of a football chant.

Yvonne invites Gary to attend Phil Collins's party at Madame Tussauds. He remarks that he's made a shrewd choice as it will be packed with celebrities even if no one turns up! Yvonne mentions she's signing some paperwork on the sale of her company but will join him there – his name is on the guest list. Then he realises he might have trouble getting away from 1944.

Gary gets back to his Mayfair flat to find Phoebe is in a flap. He's late to babysit and she needs to get to the Blue Door Club to perform. She reminds him that Michael went to sleep without seeing him again.

Reg arrives as Phoebe sweeps out of the door in a mood. Gary asks whether Reg will be at his post tonight. He confirms he will be there until 2.00am and will see Phoebe in safely. Gary sees this as a way of getting out of babysitting and getting to Phil Collins's party instead. He pretends to call Moneypenny at the Ministry and asks in Reg's presence to speak to 'M' to check on 'the Phil Collins gig'. He pretends they want him there right away for evaluation purposes. Gary tells Reg his country needs him. To be exact, his country needs him to babysit. Reg agrees even though he says it's never wanted him to do that before.

Gary gets a taxi to Duckett's Passage. However, when he gets there, he realises the taxi driver has brought him to the wrong end – the canal bridge end. Gary decides to make his way back through the increasing fog. Very soon he finds himself outside the Royal Oak and goes inside and is shocked to see the regulars are different. In fact, everyone is dressed in Victorian clothes. A pianist is playing on a small stage area while the locals drink and chat. Gary sees a sign mentioning that it is actually the Royal Oak Music Hall, and realises that he's time-travelled the wrong way. He notes a police constable at the bar looking over at him and he is the image of Reg Deadman. In fact, it is clearly one of his relatives.

Presently, the music-hall chairman comes over to Gary and asks why he has come dressed in his stage costume, which is very unprofessional. The chairman has obviously mistaken him for the comedian they've been waiting to arrive. In a moment of panic, Gary says he is and tells him his name. The chairman seems confused but goes on stage and announces him as Champagne Harry Sparrow! Gary reluctantly takes to the stage accompanied by an enthusiastic round of applause. He quickly dies on his feet, and using his cigarette lighter seems to be his only way of getting the gathered regulars to take interest. The time traveller starts to tell a joke about his wife when he realises a woman who looks just like Yvonne is standing in the audience. This throws Gary off his train of thought and he quickly loses his self-confidence. In a bid to redeem himself, he shows the audience his lighter again. Unfortunately, the lighter fuel has run out. The chairman quickly comes on to drag Gary, or should that be Harry, offstage before they're both lynched. The chairman tells the audience they won't book him again. He then introduces the singer Marie Lloyd to the stage who is clearly a relative of Yvonne's.

Meanwhile, at the flat in the West End in 1944, Phoebe comes home to find Reg asleep on the settee. He tells her that Gary had to go as there was a bit of a 'flap on'. She begins to tell Reg her frustrations about Gary always going away when she needs him. Realising that she has shared too much, she is relieved to see that Reg has fallen asleep again.

Back in Victorian times, Marie Lloyd is just in the final throes of singing 'If it Wasn't for the 'Ouses in Between'. After she comes off stage, Gary and Marie meet and realise there is a connection between them. Before either of them can speak, a prostitute screams and comes into the pub to tell everyone that they've found a body in Berners Street and that Jack the Ripper has struck again. As some of the locals head towards the scene of the crime, Gary plucks up the courage to speak to Marie. He tells her he wants to see her again. She agrees to see him the following night at the same time. Gary wonders which time that is exactly! He goes over to Reg's relative, PC Deadman, and introduces himself as Harry Sparrow. Reg's relative, Isambard Randolph Deadman, is quick to criticise Gary's abilities as a comedian. He tells him he can write jokes for him and that usually he writes for Cheeky Charlie Monks but can always spare a page of jokes for anyone in need. Gary asks why he isn't looking for Jack the Ripper. Isambard tells him there's no point as he always gets away and he isn't keen on

Goodnight Sweetheart: A Guide to the Classic Sitcom

looking at the body as he's just had his dinner! He then makes his way over to the prostitute to see if she's working. After a little persuading, they depart together. Gary bids him goodnight and says he hopes to see him again soon. The constable reminds him he will see him the following night.

Back at his West End flat, Gary, dressed more appropriately for Victorian times, is reading a book that details the Jack Ripper murders. He reads out a section to himself that mentions the murders stopped in 1888 as suddenly as they'd started. Phoebe strolls in and berates him for reading a book while poor Reg is in trouble for having left his post while he was babysitting for her and Gary. While he was away, someone came through the front door downstairs and broke into Noël Coward's flat. Gary tells her he'll be back from the Embassy, where he's due to meet General Eisenhower, as soon as he can to sort it out. After Gary leaves, Phoebe decides to take matters into her own hands. She picks up a large ornament and smashes one of the windows in their flat.

Gary makes his way back to the Royal Oak Music Hall in the East End back in 1888. As he walks into the pub, Marie Lloyd is leading a singalong of the song 'The Boy I Love is Up in the Gallery'. Once again, Gary is mesmerised by her and she gives him a wave. At the end of the song, Marie leads Gary, whom she too calls Harry, into the back room at the pub. There is a strong attraction between them. She mentions that she feels like she knows him and has been with him in the past. He comments that maybe it's the future. They begin to kiss passionately.

Back in 1944, a police detective is inspecting the broken window in Gary and Phoebe's flat, while Phoebe looks on with a strong drink in hand. The detective can't understand why she didn't notice the broken window the previous night. She tells him she has been somewhat overwrought of late on account of her husband being away a lot on important war work. She uses the excuse of a hot flush as an excuse for not noticing the broken glass and a gale blowing in the window. She claims the robber broke in through her window instead of entering the main entrance downstairs. Also, that he stole some small objects that Gary supposedly brought back from China. Although the detective isn't convinced, he leaves to consider the story and make his report. Reg has been hiding behind a screen all the time and thanks her for perjuring herself before pouring them both a drink.

Back in 1888, Gary/Harry and Marie are about to make love, but the screams of the same prostitute as the previous night cool Gary's ardour. Jack the Ripper has struck again. As they make their way back into the bar, Isambard questions Gary as to why there is a murder whenever he comes calling. The chairman accuses him of being an imposter and not a comedian. Isambard then asks him exactly who Harry Sparrow is. Marie tells them to leave him alone as she says

Closed for the Duration

he's innocent because they were together. Isambard accuses him of being Jack the Ripper and Marie tells Gary to make a run for it. He goes out to the back of the pub and climbs through the window. Isambard, the chairman and some of the pub regulars pursue him as he runs for his life. Gary finds somewhere to hide and catch his breath. Unfortunately, he comes face to face with Jack the Ripper holding a bloodstained carving knife.

Gary makes a run for it again and ends up back in the yard of his shop in present-day London, closely followed by Jack the Ripper. Gary realises the cigar butts were his and that he's clearly been hiding in his yard. Jack tells him it has been very handy. Gary realises that Jack the Ripper is a time traveller and that's why he was never caught. Jack is surprised to hear this; Gary tells him that he simply disappeared. This worries Jack who says anything could have happened to him. For instance, he could have been murdered. Gary tells him that would have carried a certain poetic justice. Jack is not best pleased at Gary acting as judge and jury and decides to take revenge, not least because he knows too much. He orders him into the back of the shop at knifepoint.

On entering the shop, Jack is surprised to see all the wartime memorabilia that Gary tells him is from the past. However, to Jack it's from the future. He asks Gary to open the front door, but he refuses. Jack tells him he wants to retire in 1999 and buy a little villa in Hastings or Broadstairs. At this point Ron knocks on the door. When Gary lets him in, Jack points the knife at him and tells him to stand away from the door. Gary insists there is no way he's going to let Jack loose on an unsuspecting public, and tells him to take his particular brand of evil back where it belongs. Jack tells Gary to move away from the door otherwise he will make him his next victim. Gary stands alongside Ron while Jack heads out of the shop. Making to cross the road, he runs into the path of an oncoming bus. Gary and Ron run to the door and see that he is dead. Gary tells a disbelieving Ron that it was Jack the Ripper, and realises that's why the deaths stopped so suddenly. Ron says he finds it hard to believe that the nineteenth century's most notorious killer ended his days under the wheels of a number thirty-two bus. Gary goes to find Jack's bag in the back yard. While he's outside, Yvonne comes in dressed as a lady from Victorian times and tells Ron she's due to go to a fancy-dress party and thought she'd surprise Gary. Gary re-enters the shop clutching the bag and catches sight of Yvonne who speaks to him in the accent of the period. He promptly faints.

Until now, Gary had not been able to time travel to any period other than the 1940s and back again to the 1990s. Even if he didn't get to meet Phil Collins at Madame Tussauds, '…The 'Ouses in Between' gave the time traveller the unique opportunity to visit Victorian times and see the Royal Oak in its days as the Royal

Oak Music Hall. Geoff Rowley's inventive script wonderfully tied the three periods in history together. It also gave Emma Amos a chance to abandon the persona of Yvonne and to play not only another character, but Marie Lloyd, who was affectionately called the 'Queen of the Music Hall'. 'This was my favourite episode,' said Emma. 'We were always coming up with ideas and the more the writers got to know us, the more they added to the scripts. In this case, they knew I had trained as a classical singer for four years at the Royal College of Music. So that's why they asked me to play Marie Lloyd and sing in that episode.'

This episode also gave Christopher the chance to play the gag-writing, womanising police constable, Isambard Randolph Deadman. This was, of course, Christopher's third character in the long-running sitcom.

Playing the taxi driver in this episode was Alex Leppard. Early in his acting career, Alex was a member of the Arthur Brough Players. Brenda Cowling, who played Miss Weatherell in series four, was also a member of this repertory company at the same time. Alex played roles for the company including Inspector Bickford in the Monte Doyle thriller *Signpost to Murder*, Henry Hornett in the Philip King and Falkland Cary comedy *Sailor Beware!*, and Speed in Neil Simon's comedy *The Odd Couple* at the Leas Pavilion Theatre, Folkestone. His other television credits include Sid in the police drama *Dixon of Dock Green*, Dorfen in the science-fiction series *The Tripods* and Tommy Rudge in the sitcom *The Detectives*.

Also in this episode was Mike Savage, who played the MC of the Royal Oak Music Hall who mistakenly believed Gary was a comedian there to perform his act. An actor and scriptwriter with umpteen acting credits to his name, Mike's other television work includes playing Ward in the police drama *The Sweeney*, Wendover in the comedy drama *Lovejoy* and Frank Makepeace in the veterinary drama *Noah's Ark*. His film roles have included Kevin's dad in the sex comedy *Confessions from a Holiday Camp*, which starred Robin Askwith, a lorry driver in the David Soul comedy drama *The Stick Up* and a Sergeant in *Dangerous Davies: The Last Detective*, with Bernard Cribbins in the title role.

The role of the heckler who put Gary under pressure at his comedy debut was taken by Terry Bird. On television, Terry's many roles have included Noggsy in the sitcom *Black Books*, Dave in the sitcom *Not Going Out* and a security officer in the comedy crime drama *Jonathan Creek*. His film credits have included playing Dumpy in the horror *Community*, Guv in the crime drama *Abusing Protocol* and Officer Edwards in the horror thriller *Jeepers Creepers: Reborn*.

Also appearing was Sophie-Louise Dann as the woman who rushed into the Royal Oak Music Hall to announce the news of two of Jack the Ripper's deadly deeds. Sophie's theatre credits include Celia in the Gary Barlow and Tim Firth musical *The Girls* at the Phoenix Theatre, London, Madame Thénardier in a UK tour of the Alain Boublil and Claude-Michel Schönberg musical *Les Misérables*, and Madame Morrible in the Stephen Schwartz and Winnie Holzman musical *Wicked* at the Apollo Victoria Theatre, London. Her other television roles include Sally in the comedy drama *My Summer with Des*, Granny in the children's adventure game show *Trapped!* and Lily McCullum in the daytime medical drama *Doctors*. Sophie has also appeared in the film adaptation of Andrew Lloyd-Webber's musical *The Phantom of the Opera*.

The detective who interviewed Phoebe at the flat about the break-in was played by John Harding. During his career, John's theatre appearances included playing Whitaker in the Willis Hall drama *The Long and the Short and the Tall* at the Greenwich Theatre, London, James in the Charles Laurence comedy *My Fat Friend*, with Kenneth Williams and Jennie Linden, at the Globe Theatre, London, and Sir Andrew Aguecheek in the William Shakespeare comedy *Twelfth Night* at the Crucible Theatre, Sheffield. John's other roles on television include Stephen in the Dennis Waterman sitcom *On the Up*, Peter Lime in the comedy drama *The Darling Buds of May* and Barry Metcalfe in the police comedy drama *New Tricks*. On film, John's credits include Ernest in the light-hearted musical drama *Give My Regards to Broad Street*, Lord Bernard Clark in the comedy drama *The Young Visiters* and a cabinet minister in the biographical drama about Margaret Thatcher, *The Iron Lady*. John, who was also a writer and photographer, died on 8 March 2015, aged sixty-six.

Finally, playing the role of Jack the Ripper was Nicholas Day. 'I played the black-cape-with-red-satin-lining-wearing version of Jack the Ripper, complete with Gladstone bag, which I was happy to do,' he recalled. 'However, this, of course, was not the reality of what he would have been like. I can say this with authority as I used to be a tour guide on the Jack the Ripper Tours in Whitechapel.'

As well as the tour, Nicholas presented a two-part *Murder Maps* special for television that re-examined Jack the Ripper's notorious crimes. The programmes revealed how the story we know today was shaped by the sensationalist press of 1888. It stripped back decades of rumour and misinformation to reveal the true lives of the five women slain.

Nicholas's theatre credits have included playing Laurence in the Mike Leigh comedy of manners *Abigail's Party* at the Theatre Royal, Windsor, the headmaster in the Alan Bennett drama *The History Boys* at the Crucible Theatre, Sheffield, and Mr Justice Wainwright in the Agatha Christie courtroom drama *Witness for the Prosecution* at the County Hall, London. On television, he is arguably best known for playing Detective Sergeant Michael Morley in *Minder* from 1991 to 1993. His other credits include playing Sissons in the sitcom

Shelley, Alan Jacobs in the drama *Kavanagh QC*, and Jim Prior in the historical drama *The Crown*. His film roles include Sir William Dolben in the biographical drama *Amazing Grace*, Colonel Montford in the drama *The Wolfman*, which featured Anthony Hopkins and Emily Blunt amongst others, and Charles Jaspar in the thriller *A Dark Reflection*.

The songs 'If it Wasn't for the 'Ouses in Between' and 'The Boy I Love', which, as mentioned, were featured in this episode, were both recorded at Logorhythm Music Studios, Lexington Street, Soho, London, on 22 March 1999. The singer was Emma Amos and the pianist Cliff Hall.

Gary is putting up the decorations in his shop as he prepares for Christmas in 'Just in Time', the sixth episode of series six. Ron is once again on the scrounge for money. He complains that because Flic is spending Christmas in Barbados, he will be spending it alone. He was hoping that Gary and Yvonne would invite him to share the festive season with them. Gary mentions that he's always promised Phoebe a good Christmas and doesn't know what he will tell Yvonne. Ron notes the various goodies in the shop that he's bought in readiness for what he says was a grim Christmas in 1944, not least because of all the shortages.

Their conversation is brought to an abrupt end when a man, Sparks, suddenly appears through the back wall of the shop. He realises he's been seen and disappears again. Gary and Ron go into the yard where Sparks appears and disappears again. Ron comments that he must be a time traveller with a season ticket. However, it's clear from the hi-tech gadgets he's wearing, and the device he's holding, that he's a little more involved in the business of time travel than Gary. Gary realises this could be serious. He mentions to Ron that someone was always going to come along and change things. Ron thinks he's jumping to conclusions as Sparks appears again. Ron tells Gary to confront him and ask what he's doing – after all, it is his yard! Afraid of what he might say, Gary says he hopes they're not putting him off. Sparks assures him that nothing ever puts him off; not even the Battle of Hastings going on via the time portal he's just walked through, despite having an arrow shot at his back. But Sparks points out he has a PX32 to process, which is a job number. He tells Gary he has to check all the frequencies as back at the depot they believe they have a whole epoch vibrating on the wrong frequency. Sparks assures him that nothing will happen unless he gets a DY90, which is an instruction to adjust the frequencies. He confirms to Ron that this does tend to stop people crossing backwards and forwards in time. When Gary explains he has a wife and kid in 1944, Sparks is touched and says, 'Ah, that's nice'. Gary points out it won't be if he closes down

Closed for the Duration

his time portal with him on the wrong side. Sparks assures him it won't be personal. Gary realises that the decision time he was dreading has finally come.

While Gary tries to get his head around what's happening, Ron decides to ask Sparks the age-old question: what is time? Sparks tells Ron to leave him out of it; he's maintenance whereas Ron wants enquiries!

Gary asks how long it will take if the DY90 comes through. Sparks tells him four hours. Gary realises that by six o'clock it could be curtains for his time-travelling days. Sparks tells him to calm down and that he could be worrying about nothing. Unfortunately, a message comes through and Sparks confirms that the instruction has been approved.

After Sparks has left, Gary tells Ron in the shop that now that the moment is here, there's not even a decision to consider. He has to go back and be with Phoebe and Michael. They need him. Ron points out that Yvonne, who has fifteen million dollars in the bank and is friends with Tony and Cherie Blair, is more likely to manage somehow.

Yvonne arrives and tells Gary that's she's feeling high from giving away millions of pounds from the sale of Nature Boy. She and Sting are going to replant the rainforest. Gary tells her he thinks she's been watching too many gardening programmes. She runs out of the shop saying she must go or she'll be towed away. Gary is left wondering if that encounter will be the last time he ever sees Yvonne after all their years together. Life is not a movie, Ron reminds him. There are no grand farewells or famous last words. Gary realises he now simply has to disappear into thin air. Ron promises to make up some excuse to explain his disappearance to Yvonne. He suggests it might even become an alien abduction, depending on how broke he gets. Gary tells Ron he can have the contents of the till as he will only need the wad of white fivers he still has left. He also says he can have the stock as well. The time traveller says Ron will have to sell it for what he can get. But that might not be easy as he's getting too many time-wasters, such as the young guy that has just come into the shop. There's something not right about him and Gary can't put his finger on what it is. He just prices things up and never buys anything. Gary picks up one of the boxes of food he's bought for Christmas and makes his way to the yard followed by Ron. Sparks has returned but says he will go into 1066 while they bid their fond farewells. Gary tells Ron to keep an eye on Yvonne for him. Their brisk and manly handshakes give way to an emotional hug as they realise this is the last time they will meet. After wishing each other the best of luck, Gary fades back into 1944.

Ron heads to the shop and finds the young man still pricing up items in the shop. The new owner tells him to grab what he can as this is by way of a closing-down sale – the difference being that everything is dearer! The man panics and, when he discovers Ron plans to close today, he offers to buy everything. He tells Ron to name his price and Ron plucks the figure of a hundred and forty thousand pounds out of the air. The young guy does some quick sums on his calculator and agrees. They agree on a cash sale, as clearly Ron won't take a cheque, and he says he will be back in about twenty minutes and will start moving it out with the aid of his rucksack. He tells Ron not to worry, he can carry his own weight in non-perishable goods as he's licensed. Ron is now becoming suspicious of the man, not least because some of the words he uses are not of that era. When the man leaves the shop, Ron follows him across the road. He walks down an alley pursued by Ron who keeps hiding to make sure he's not seen. As the man walks towards a wall he suddenly disappears. Ron's suspicions are confirmed – he's another time traveller. However, he's convinced he's from the future and this place is turning into some sort of cosmic Clapham Junction!

Meanwhile, Phoebe is up a ladder at the Blue Door Club attempting to put up Christmas decorations while little Frankie and Michael run around. Margie tells Frankie to take Michael out of the room. Phoebe tells her she's making the extra effort as she's heard this is going to be a bad Christmas. Gary arrives carrying a box of goodies. He announces that he's got a nice long bit of leave and will be around all Christmas and New Year as well, which pleases Phoebe. She tells Michael and Gary picks him up, telling Michael it was him that made the difference, meaning the reason he chose to live in the past. Phoebe suggests they share their Christmas with other people they know. She says that Reg and Margie are chipping in. Margie shows Gary the list of items Reg has said he'll obtain and Gary is impressed with his resourcefulness. Margie and Phoebe are impressed by the contents of the box Gary has brought. Phoebe still has a list of items they need, plus a few things she fancies. Gary notes she has put his name sixth on the list in between Belgian chocolate and pickled walnuts! Then she follows it up with another list. This concerns Gary who reminds her there are massive shortages out there. She says it's never been a problem before, with his contacts. He warns her that some of his contacts have been captured recently, so it's fingers crossed on the pickled walnuts. Phoebe asks Michael to remind Gary what he's been asking for: crackers. She says they're back at his office, and Gary remembers he's left them at the shop. Michael also says he wants a rocking horse and Gary remembers he hasn't picked that up either in the rush to get back to 1944. Gary heads off, saying he has to get in touch with a vital contact.

Back in the shop, Ron's new and best customer arrives back complete with rucksack, fearing the shop has already closed. Ron assures him he was merely protecting his acquisitions. Ron can't resist asking the young time traveller how much all this wartime memorabilia is worth in the future. This shocks him and he attempts to talk his way out of it by laughing it off. Ron tells him that he followed him and saw him walk through a wall in that ever so casual manner that time travellers have. Ron assured him it's okay as he used to have a mate who was a time traveller who went back to the past and that's how all the stock got here. The young man admits he's from 2168 and found a sort of time portal about a fortnight ago. Ron tells him he's an ally in foreign times. Ron formally introduces himself, and the time traveller introduces himself as Brick Beckham. He says there are quite a few of them in the future and they're all named after the prime minister!

Gary heads back to the West End flat and speaks to Reg in reception. He has brought the list Reg has compiled. Gary asks where he's getting everything from. His face drops when Reg says he's expecting to get all the supplies from him. Gary tells Reg that he's on leave at present but come the New Year there are going to be some changes.

It's five o'clock and only an hour until the shutdown. However, Gary decides to chance it and make one final trip back to the present.

In the shop, Ron hands over the last-but-one box of wartime memorabilia into Brick's rucksack. He asks whether Brick's friend, Diogenes, was able to provide the horse-racing results for 1999, the football results 1999 to 2010 and the Lottery results – oh and there's a small matter of whether it snows on the coming Christmas Day. Diogenes needs more time as he doesn't have a research licence, but Brick assures Ron he will find out. He says one more trip should do the trick.

Gary arrives on his flying visit and shocks Ron. Gary is equally shocked at the lack of stock. He picks up some of the boxes he forgot and then remembers he still has to get Michael's rocking horse. Yvonne arrives and tells him that Christmas is off. Comic Relief have asked her to go to one of their famine areas to film a report because Lenny Henry has got food poisoning. She says she will make it up to him in the New Year. Gary keeps looking at his watch, afraid that he will miss the time portal. They kiss and she departs saying she will see him on the twenty-eighth of December. She asks what happened to all the stock. Ron tells her they had a 'Back to the Future' sale and it went very well! As she makes for the door, Gary tells her he will miss her. She obviously doesn't realise he means they won't see each other again.

Gary and Ron go into the yard and find Sparks there. Gary panics and tells him to give him just one more minute. However, he tells him it's too late. Gary walks through the time portal and finds it's still open. He comes back and is confused. The man tells him he wasn't due to close that one, but the one over the road – the one that leads to 2168. Ron panics, realising that Brick won't be able to get back. He explains to Gary that he and Brick had plans: Beckham and Wheatcroft – Time Traders Extraordinaire. Ron tells Gary that Brick was from the future and bought all the stock for a hundred and forty thousand pounds. Gary is amazed until he realises that Ron has lost all his stock and that he gave credit to a time traveller! Gary isn't happy realising he now has to restock the shop all over again. However, he also realises he can, and that he still has both lives again as the time portal is still open.

Over their dinner in the Blue Door Club, Phoebe points out that nobody else will be having a Christmas like them. This makes him feel guilty about Ron, who is back at the West End flat alone wearing a Christmas hat and eating a Pot Noodle while watching Yvonne on television.

Reg gets up and makes a short speech to thank Gary whose contacts have come up trumps again. He points out they even have champagne – vintage 1997! Reg raises a toast to the future and Gary smiles and replies reflectively, 'To the future'.

Thanks to the presence of the character of Sparks, this episode came as close as the series ever did to revealing more about the force or organisation that was responsible for bestowing the lucky chosen few with the gift of time travel. It tantalisingly proved that it wasn't just a game of chance and that there was more behind why it was possible. But if viewers were left hoping to find out more about the mysterious controllers of time, and those who could visit other dimensions, they were to be disappointed. Arguably, that would have spoilt the very essence that made *Goodnight Sweetheart* different to other sitcoms. However, it gave away enough information to prove that there was some kind of organisation behind the time-travelling exploits of Gary and countless others. So many time travellers, in fact, that whoever was responsible saw fit to employ teams of enquiry and maintenance staff to help police the whole process.

The part of Sparks was played by Toby Whithouse (who is listed as 'Toby Whitehouse' on the end credits for this episode). Although Toby initially set out to be a book illustrator, he decided to train to become an actor instead. His theatre roles have included Eugene in the Neil Simon comedy *Brighton Beach Memoirs* at the Salisbury Playhouse, Geoffrey Fitton in the Bill Naughton comedy drama *The Family Way* at the Octagon Theatre, Bolton, and Lucas Brickman in the Neil Simon ensemble comedy *Laughter on the 23rd Floor* at the Queen's Theatre, London, and on tour. The cast of the latter-named play included Gene Wilder and the one-time *Goodnight Sweetheart* cast members, Regina Freedman, who played Phoebe's friend, Violet Bigby, and Rolf Saxon, who played Yvonne's lawyer, Murray. Toby's other television credits include Norman Foss in the period drama *The House of Eliott*, Mr Theakston in the courtroom drama

Kavanagh QC, and Alistair Frith in the comedy drama *Being Human*. On film, Toby has played parts including Frith in the Richard Attenborough drama *Shadowlands*, starring Anthony Hopkins and Debra Winger, Dr Miller in the thriller *Breathtaking*, which featured Joanne Whalley, and Alastair in the romantic comedy *Bridget Jones's Diary*.

Eventually, Toby decided to try and write scripts during breaks from working as an actor. His quest paid off. His first play, *Jump Mr Malinoff, Jump*, an evocative tale of young life, love and fear revisited in a seaside town, was successfully staged at the Soho Theatre, London, and won the prestigious Verity Bargate playwriting award, with *The Office* actor Martin Freeman in the lead role.

His first commissioned television script was an episode of the medical drama *Where the Heart is*. He went on to write episodes of the comedy drama *No Angels*. Since then, Toby's writing credits have included the drama *Hotel Babylon*, the science-fiction series *Doctor Who* and its spin-off, *Torchwood*. He also wrote and created the supernatural comedy drama *Being Human*, and the spy thriller *The Game*, with Tom Hughes and Brian Cox. He was also the showrunner on the drama *Noughts + Crosses*, an adaptation of the Malorie Blackman novel series.

Toby returned to writing for the stage with a razor-sharp media satire called *Blue Eyes and Heels* in 2005 and a one-man comedy about capital punishment, which he also performed, called *Executioner Number One* in 2017. Both plays were staged at the Soho Theatre, London.

Playing the role of time traveller Brick Beckham was Tom Goodman-Hill. 'I was very new to television,' he admitted. 'My only other appearance had been in a wartime drama called *No Bananas*, and I hadn't done any comedy, so I had to audition. At this stage I was nervous about every audition! And I was really excited to be seen for anything at all! My only memory of my audition was thinking how incredibly kind and encouraging Robin Nash and Nic Phillips were.

'I remember being surprised at how relaxed and friendly everybody was. Nick Lyndhurst and Vic Maguire couldn't have been nicer to me. They were both really encouraging, despite the fact I think I was a pretty arrogant little upstart back then!'

Tom's commitment to the episode included filming on location for the scene in which Ron, suspicious that Brick might be from the future, follows him. 'As part of the sequence I had to run "through" a wall, back to 2168,' he recalled. 'The camera crew kept telling me I needed to run really hard at the wall if it was going to look convincing. Of course, when I did that, and failed to pull up, smashing pretty hard into a solid brick wall, I heard the cry of "Cut!" and turned around to see the whole crew killing themselves laughing. You can probably tell when you watch it back; I'm running very fast at that wall!'

After his bruised ego had recovered from filming on location, Tom was called to tape his scenes in the studio. 'The recording day at Teddington Studios was a real thrill for me,' the actor said. 'It was my first time inside a live studio audience recording, and it was a bit like being in the theatre, which was much more familiar to me at the time.

'I was completely clueless about having to be on the right marks for the studio cameras. Vic and Nick both kept me in line and gently reminded me to lean a bit to the right or left so that the camera could see through!

'When we were eating in the canteen before the live recording, I was really stuffing my face, having a huge meal, and Nick looked at me from across the table and asked, "Tom, don't you get nervous?" I replied that I always get nervous before a theatre show but I wasn't at all nervous before this recording. Nick just smiled wryly and said, "Oh right. Okay."

'An hour and a half later, just as the warm-up guy was about to introduce the cast to the audience, Nick turned to me and asked, "Nervous, Tom?" I came clean. "S***ting myself, Nick. Absolutely bricking it."

'I really enjoyed playing Brick and it was great training for me in how television worked, and I realised I really loved doing comedy. It made me very happy over the years to find myself working with Nick quite a few times. He's such a great leading man.'

Tom's career has continued in the ascendant since he appeared in *Goodnight Sweetheart*. In the theatre, his credits have included playing Damis in the Molière comedy *Tartuffe* at the National Theatre, London, Gerardo in the Ariel Dorfman drama *Death and the Maiden* at the Harold Pinter Theatre, London, and David Owen in Steve Waters' quick-paced drama *Limehouse* at the Donmar Warehouse, London. His television roles include Ray in the mockumentary sitcom *The Office*, David Jones in the heart-warming drama *Call the Midwife*, and Mr Grove in the period drama *Mr Selfridge*. Tom's film appearances include playing Kenyon in the romantic drama *In Love and War*, Sergeant Stahl in the historical drama *The Imitation Game*, and Neal Biedleman in the biographical survival adventure *Everest*.

Nicholas and Tom have subsequently worked together on an episode of the sitcom *After Your Gone* and the BBC Radio 4 science-fiction sitcom called *My First Planet*, which also starred Vicki Pepperdine in the cast.

This episode was fated to feature Eve Bland's last-ever appearance as Margie. First seen back in series three, the character Margie had been part of many stories including delivering Phoebe's baby. Most importantly, she saved Reg from his miserable marital life with Minnie.

The location where Ron followed and watched Brick disappear into 2168 is situated on Holly Road, close to 62 Heath Road, Twickenham. This is just a short distance from the shop at 21 Heath Road, Twickenham which doubled for Blitz and Pieces in the sixth series.

At the start of 'How I Won the War', the seventh episode of series six, Yvonne is waiting at the penthouse apartment for the postman. She picks up the post and goes into the living area where Gary startles her with his presence. The phone rings and she quickly runs to answer it, yet again making Gary think her behaviour is becoming suspicious. She says it's rhythmic grunting on the other end of the line. It gets faster and Yvonne is concerned something is about to happen! Gary takes the phone and is about to give the suspected pervert a piece of his mind when he realises it's Ron, who tells Gary he wasn't grunting but merely gasping. He has managed to get his foot stuck in a large ethnic ornamental pot. Gary agrees to come to his aid. It turns out he was hanging a picture, bought as a Christmas present by Flic, on the wall, stepped back to have a better look and put one of his feet in the pot. Gary attempts to get the pot off Ron's foot and fails miserably. He suggests hitting it with a hammer; Ron is not happy at the idea as it's an ethnic antique.

Gary takes Ron to casualty and he's made to wait in a cubicle, lying on a bed with his foot still in the pot. Gary tells him not to worry as they're at a hospital with highly trained staff in pot technology. Yvonne has been very nice to Gary recently and this makes him suspicious that she has a secret lover and is trying to put him off the scent. The time traveller asks Ron to keep an eye on Yvonne's comings and goings because he thinks she's cheating on him. Ron reminds Gary that his lust life has hardly been morally sound for the last few years and so it's a bit hypocritical to worry about what Yvonne may or may not be up to. Gary tells him that his wives exist in different temporal aspects of a four-dimensional space-time continuum. Ron replies that this is a typical bigamist's excuse. Gary reminds him that he's not exactly been honest with the love of his life, Flic. Ron points out that Flic's plane lands at seven-thirty on Wednesday morning and he doesn't intend to be vertical for the next few days! However, he reluctantly agrees to keep an eye out for sleazy types in chauffeur-driven limos – not villains but politicians. Gary tells him he and Phoebe will be in wartime Belgium entertaining the troops with ENSA at Noël Coward's request. With that, a female doctor enters the cubicle and relieves Ron of the pot by hitting it with a hammer.

While travelling along a road in the back of a lorry with the rest of the ENSA party in Belgium, Gary assures Phoebe that they're safe and far from the front line. However, at that point there's an explosion just in front of the lorry and the driver quickly pulls over to the side of the road. Gary tells everyone to get off the lorry immediately. One of the party, a suave actor, refuses, saying it's safer in there. Gary reminds him that it's the lorry the Germans are aiming at. The driver, Bombardier 'Nipper' Smith, admits to having made a cock-up: they have been separated from the rest of the convoy and appear to now be behind German lines. He asks if anyone has any military background, or even some basic training or combat experience. Phoebe whispers in his ear that Gary has. The Bombardier assumes he will want to take charge, but Gary tells him to carry on. Smith goes to look for the other lorries on foot, handing Gary a gun with which to defend himself and the rest of the ENSA party while he's away.

Gary, Phoebe and the others go into a nearby barn. Gary tells them to stay calm, and that they're as safe as houses in the barn. At that moment there is an explosion outside. Phoebe is keen that they go home now as she's forgotten to cancel the milk and left something in the oven on a low light! Gary promises to get Phoebe and the others back home safely. He tells everyone they've got to pool their resources and use their skills. They introduce themselves and their billing: Lariat Annie and the Deptford Kid, a Wild West act featuring knife throwing and lasso twirling; Brian B. Merry, man of a thousand voices, impressionist extraordinaire (his Betty Grable must be seen to be believed, according to the *Bristol Echo!*); and Rock Justice, who just 'stars', not that this impresses Gary. Nancy (Lariat Annie) asks him if he was in a film with Errol Flynn, but Rock points out that Errol was in a film with *him*. He takes Gary aside and says that the best tactical plan would be for Rock to hide in the event of an attack. Gary promises that he will not only reveal his hiding place but tell the Germans he's an undercover agent on a mission to assassinate Hitler. Also, that being a famous film star there to entertain the troops is merely a cover and that he has an incredibly high pain threshold. Having put Rock in a hard place, Gary decides to rally the troops by giving them a rousing speech and even manages to quote some of the lyrics to the theme song from the soap opera *Neighbours*!

In the present, Flic has returned to London. She calls at Ron's flat and he tells her how much he's missed her. However, there is something different about her. She's cooler than usual, and her body language shows that she is no longer interested in Ron's romantic requests. She is keen to talk but he can't help telling her how difficult it has been since she's been away. He attempts to instigate a mad, passionate all-in seconds-out rude bits interface before starting on the *petit déjeuner* he has prepared. As Flic is hungry, they sit and eat instead.

Back in Belgium, Gary is giving his new troops some basic training. Unfortunately, his description of unarmed combat makes Rock sick.

Having not been able to talk to Ron about their 'relationship', Flic tries again while she and Ron are sitting in a car outside Gary and Yvonne's penthouse, keeping an eye on Yvonne's comings and goings. Reg's grandson, PC Deadman, happens to notice them parked where they shouldn't. As Ron is using binoculars, he asks if they're birdwatchers. After making his excuses, Ron starts the engine and manages to run over the policeman's foot as he pulls the car away.

Phoebe confides in Gary and tells him she's worried about what will happen if they can't get back home. She can't stop thinking about Michael. It's clear the same thoughts have been going through Gary's mind, despite his trying to appear relaxed. Phoebe tells him how proud she is that he has taken control with weapons training and pep talks.

Ron and Flic have been arrested. But it's not just the suspicious binocular usage or parking that bothers PC Deadman. Flic isn't happy either and is keen for the matter to be resolved as she wants to get round Harvey Nicks before meeting Tara for a glass of fizz at the Groucho Club. This doesn't impress PC Deadman who is in bad pain with his foot. He begins to remind Ron that he has some past form. Keen that Flic shouldn't know, Ron says he was the one driving, they were his binoculars and that Flic hasn't anything to do with the situation. PC Deadman tells her she is free to go, but Flic doesn't want to leave Ron in his hour of need. PC Deadman reveals that Ron's record includes being arrested for an assault during a martial affray in March 1997 and arrested on suspicion of forging antique bank notes in July 1998.

Back in the past, Gary has concluded that Bombardier Smith isn't coming back and thinks they should make a break for it. He tells them he's going to go outside and recce. He hands the gun to Phoebe and tells her to shoot anyone that comes through that door after he's gone. Gary leaves the barn and Phoebe readies herself and takes aim at the door in case anyone should enter.

Outside, Gary spots a group of armed Germans quickly making their way to the barn. He realises he has to get back to the barn to warn everyone, but, due to nerves, suddenly loses control of his legs and the ability to walk. However, he manages to somehow walk back to the barn. Phoebe pulls the trigger as Gary enters but fortunately the bullet misses him. Gary points out he meant for her to shoot anyone but him! He tells them the Germans are coming their way and to get to their positions, and then asks Brian to help him with their plan to disguise him. The Germans eventually enter, and Gary emerges with a wig and moustache that makes him look like Hitler. This startles them and Gary gives a speech, attempting to sound like the Führer. He tells Brian to pull a rope and a wooden beam comes down, knocking the Germans to the floor. Gary has stolen this trick from the film *Home Alone*. Presently, Bombardier Smith arrives in the barn with reinforcements and is shocked at the sight that meets his eyes. The rest of them congratulate Gary on his resourcefulness and brave plan.

Back in the West End flat, Flic finally gets the chance to break up with Ron. She tells him she's always known he's a bit of rough and she now considers he has passed his use-by date. Ron tells her that he's in love with her, but this doesn't change her mind. She tells him she's going to France for a few weeks and then plans to put her flat up for rent. Flic kisses Ron and tells him not to be sad before leaving him feeling heartbroken.

Back at the penthouse, Gary walks in on Yvonne and a male hugging. He accuses them of something going on. Yvonne says that it's perfectly innocent. The man, Roger, is PA to the PM's PPS. Gary asks what else he is apart from being a monogram. She says he was congratulating her on her new peerage: for services to export, the Millennium Dome, New Labour and for advising on Tony Blair's hair and Cherie's smile. Her title is Baroness Sparrow of Lumbutt. Gary asks if this makes him Baron Sparrow of Lumbutt? Yvonne tells him to not be ridiculous. Besides, what has he ever done for his country?! Gary is about to tell her, but stops himself and gives a wry smile instead.

Baroness Sparrow of Lumbutt had come a long way from being Yvonne Sparrow, née Shackleton, a one-time redundant assistant personnel manager. As much as Gary claimed to have got over her becoming so rich and successful, the feeling of inferiority and jealousy was still there, as was proved again in this episode when he discovered her being congratulated by Roger, the PA to the PM's PPS. Now Yvonne had a peerage, it was inevitable the chasm between her and Gary would become even wider.

Bonnie Langford had been namechecked by Gary and Ron in the second series of *Goodnight Sweetheart*. Therefore, it was somewhat ironic when the actress was cast in this episode as Nancy Potter, one half of the devoted Wild West act, Lariat Annie and the Deptford Kid. Bonnie's career really began when she won the television talent show *Opportunity Knocks*. Since then, there can't be many facets of showbiz that the actress, dancer and singer hasn't tackled, and all with her unique talent and vivaciousness.

Bonnie's innumerable stage roles have included Rumpleteazer in the Andrew Lloyd Webber musical *CATS* at the New London Theatre, Roz Keith in the Dolly Parton musical *9 to 5* at the Savoy Theatre, London, and Evangeline Harcourt in Cole Porter's musical *Anything Goes* at the Barbican, London. Away from the stage, Bonnie has appeared in a multitude of television roles. They have varied from Mel Bush, companion to Colin Baker and Sylvester McCoy's incarnations of the Doctor in the science-fiction series *Doctor Who*, and Betty Johnson in Agatha Christie's *Marple* to Carmel Kazemi in the continuing drama *EastEnders*. Venturing into films gave Bonnie the chance to play Kim Frogmorton in the children's comedy adventure *Wombling Free* and Lena Marelli in Alan Parker's

Bugsy Malone, the classic gangster story of Bugsy Malone told with a cast made up entirely of child performers.

At the time this series was being made, Paul Grunert, who played Sid Potter, was married to Bonnie Langford. Indeed, Bonnie was with Paul when he attended his audition for the episode. Her presence inspired a discussion between the director and the casting director that led to her being cast as Nancy Potter.

Paul's theatre credits have included Officer O'Hara in Joseph Kesselring's uproarious murder farce *Arsenic and Old Lace* at the Richmond Theatre and on tour, Sir Nathaniel in the William Shakespeare comedy *Love's Labour Lost* at the National Theatre, London, and a restorer and shop assistant in the Alan Bennett double bill *Single Spies* at the Chichester Festival Theatre and on tour. His television roles have included playing a television director in the sitcom *Second Thoughts*, Mr Bradshaw in the children's series *There's a Viking in My Bed* and Nicolas Faures in the spy drama *Spooks*. Paul's film work includes playing a barber in Oliver Stone's drama *Wall Street: Money Never Sleeps*.

Playing the vain and conceited actor Rock Justice in this episode was Gary Cady. During his career, Gary has played roles in the theatre such as Sergeant Frank Troy in the Sally Hedges adaptation of Thomas Hardy's *Far from the Madding Crowd* at the Theatre Royal, Bath, and the Swan Theatre, Worcester, Christian in the Edmond Rostand play *Cyrano de Bergerac* at the Theatre Royal Haymarket, London, and Peter Carter in Thomas Morgan and Kevin Metchear's musical *Stairway to Heaven* at the King's Head Theatre, London. On television, he has appeared in a mix of comedies and dramas, with roles including Matthew Fairchild in the comedy drama *Brass*, Gary in the sitcom *As Time Goes By* and William Woodfield in the football drama *Footballers' Wives*. Gary's film parts include a hotel waiter in the crime drama *Mona Lisa*, Keitel Blacksmith in Terry Jones's comedy adventure *Erik the Viking*, and Knut in the comedy drama *Hot Hot Hot*.

Also appearing was Simon Sherlock as Bombardier 'Nipper' Smith. Simon can distinctly remember how he came to appear in this episode of *Goodnight Sweetheart* and his overall experience. 'Susie Parriss, the casting director, was getting me lots of work during the period, including the ITV series *Hornblower*,' he explained. 'She put me forward for the role of "Nipper" Smith.

'I don't usually get starstruck, but I was very starstruck at meeting Nicholas Lyndhurst because of *Only Fools and Horses*. I found Nick to be very quiet and unassuming, given that he was a lead actor.

'It was a hot day when we filmed the location scenes. It didn't help that I was wearing a heavy coat and leather vest as part of my uniform!

'We recorded all the interior barn scenes, including mine, the same week in the studio without an audience.

'After the series ended, Nic Phillips, the producer, asked me to go to the wrap party. He was insistent because he wanted me to meet Laurence and Maurice. This led me to a successful audition for the role of Monty in eight episodes of their series *Starting Out*.'

In his formative years as an actor, Simon appeared in a handful of theatre plays. For instance, he played Richard in the Jonathan Harvey comedy *Babies* at the Royal Court Theatre, London. However, it is for the medium of television that Simon has become best known. His roles include Olroyd in four of the *Horatio Hornblower* historical war dramas, which starred Ioan Gruffudd, Alfie in the comedy drama *Cradle to Grave*, which is based on the memoirs of Danny Baker, and Constable Dwyer in the comedy drama *In the Long Run*, with Idris Elba. The actor has also accumulated various feature film credits. They include playing a soldier in Anthony Minghella's romantic war drama *The English Patient*, Ritchie in the Julian Richards found-footage horror *The Last Horror Movie*, and Dennis in the Cristian Solimeno psychological thriller *The Glass Man*.

Completing the supporting cast was Jim McManus as Brian Merry. In the theatre, his credits included Henry Angell in Agatha Christie's acclaimed thriller *The Unexpected Guest* at the Theatre Royal, Windsor, and Tony Hancock in Heathcote Williams's one-man play *Hancock's Last Half Hour*, in which he toured extensively. His noteworthy panto roles included the Lord Chamberlain in *Cinderella*, with Ronnie Corbett and Janet Brown, at the Church Theatre, Bromley. On television, Jim's other roles included Ron Bateman in the soap opera *Crossroads*, a journalist in Galton and Simpson's classic sitcom *Steptoe and Son*, and an ophthalmologist in the *Doctor Who* serial 'The Invisible Enemy'. He was also a member of Jeremy Beadle's team of actors who helped to set up members of the public in his popular Saturday-night series *Beadle's About*. The actor had previously worked with Nicholas when he played Alex, an out-of-work travel agent, in a 1982 episode of *Only Fools and Horses* called 'It Never Rains...'. Jim's film appearances included playing a detective in the musical drama *Buddy's Song*, with The Who's Roger Daltrey, a chef in the comedy drama *Lawless Heart*, and a barman in the action adventure *Harry Potter and the Order of the Phoenix*. Jim passed away on 11 April 2023, aged eighty-two.

At the beginning of 'Something Fishie', the eighth episode of series six, Yvonne is trying on her new robe, given to her as she's now a peer. She is practising her speech as Gary enters the room. Attracted to her position, Gary suggests some nookie in her new noble robe, but she jokes that it might be treason and they could get sent to the Tower. Despite Gary's attempts to persuade her, Yvonne says she can't as she's due for a photo call for a new Millennium Dome poster.

Now at a loose end, Gary goes to see Ron at the flat. As insensitive as ever, Gary speaks about his problems and gives Ron a bag of presents including VHS copies of the films *Love Story* and *Romeo and Juliet*. This doesn't appeal to Ron who says he's fed up with being humped and dumped. He takes comfort with a bag of pick and mix (mostly wine gums) and Flic's purple wildebeest soft toy, which Gary thinks looks like a colostomy bag. Gary tells Ron that holding on to Flic's things is very unhealthy, but Ron says holding on to Flic's things was what he most liked in life!

In 1945, Reg is performing an enthusiastic version of the song 'Three Little Fishies' while mopping the floor of the Blue Door Club. Just then, he receives an unwelcome visit from two local villains by the names of Smith and Jones, who run a protection racket. After they have broken some glasses, poured a bottle of spirits on the bar and threatened to set fire to it, Reg finally realises they are members of the criminal fraternity. Telling them he's ex-PC Reginald Deadman of the Metropolitan Police, currently holding the rank of Sergeant Commissionaire, doesn't impress them. When they leave saying he won't see them again – emphasising the word 'see' – it's clear they're planning to take revenge for Reg not agreeing to their offer to insure the premises.

That evening, Phoebe is in the middle of performing the song 'Big Noise from Winnetka' to a busy club, when the lights are turned off by Mr Jones. Mr Smith tells Reg it looks like they have a bit of trouble with their electrics. Gary asks what's going on and Reg goes to arrest him, but Jones grabs Reg by his jacket collar and Smith grabs Phoebe. Gary goes to stop him, but Smith warns him not to come any closer or he will break her arm. Jones tells Gary and Phoebe he wants them and their clientele to enjoy the benefits of their fully comprehensive insurance policy. Regular payments are to be made the first of every month, otherwise Phoebe might lose her singing voice permanently. They leave and Gary goes to comfort Phoebe. Poor Reg's voice has somewhat suffered with almost being choked.

In the West End flat in the present, Ron is showing the purple wildebeest some photos he took of Flic. Feeling depressed, the printer takes the soft toy to the window with the aim of climbing onto the roof.

Meanwhile in 1945, Gary and Phoebe are paying a visit to Inspector Priestly to report the intimidation and attempts at extortion they received from Smith and Jones. Very soon it becomes clear that Priestly is involved with the duo. Indeed, he dismisses their complaint without further investigation. Realising that Inspector Priestly is on the take, Gary formulates a plan.

At the West End flat, Yvonne has visited Ron and the purple wildebeest. She questions whether he would really have jumped, and he says no as he has the wildebeest to think of. He explains that he just went outside for some fresh air and decided to stay for a while and think things through. A member of the public saw him and called the police. Yvonne is annoyed that Gary was there but left, despite seeing how upset he was. Ron says Gary wasn't paying him any attention. Yvonne says she plans to take revenge on his behalf. Pleased, Ron tells her to wind him up as he deserves it. She agrees.

Smith and Jones make another visit to the Blue Door Club and tell Phoebe they want a payment of fifty pounds every calendar month. Phoebe tells them they don't keep that sort of money in the till and she doesn't want them coming to the club again as her husband would never agree to pay. She offers to pay them secretly; Smith agrees and tells her to bring the first payment to an address in Greenwich at 1.30pm sharp the following day. They both help themselves to a drink from a bottle of spirits on the bar. After they've each taken a large sip, Phoebe tells them she was taking a stain off the bar and it is liquid paraffin! They both leave dreading the worst. Gary emerges from his hiding place in the club and tells Phoebe all is going to plan.

Reg arrives and, having noticed Smith and Jones leaving in a hurry, asks what they wanted this time. Gary intentionally tells Reg they wanted one hundred pounds – every month. Gary cleverly manipulates Reg into telling Inspector Priestly of their demands, not realising they've already been to visit him.

Carrying out Gary's orders, Reg visits the inspector with his news, and he is understandably angry thinking he has been double-crossed by Smith and Jones.

Back at the penthouse, Yvonne tells Gary that later today she will be hosting a special event at the Millennium Dome. It will be the first foray into Perspex Baroness Sparrow. She will be giving people of prominence tours around the highways and byways of her inner being. 'Up yourself as usual,' Gary comments. She explains that at the grand opening she will be entered simultaneously by the entire Cabinet. Yvonne then tells him that Ron tried to commit suicide while he was away. She tells him she went around to comfort him and the wildebeest because Gary wasn't there. By now quite flustered, Gary tells Yvonne he will go and see him.

Gary races around to the flat and finds a note on the table next to a camera that reads: 'Can't take any more of this, I'm going…'

Gary panics and goes to look out of the window, fearing the worst. Ron emerges from the bedroom with a suitcase and dressed to go away. He tells Gary it wasn't a suicide letter; he just hadn't finished penning the message, which was to tell Gary he was going to stay with his auntie in Liverpool for a few days. Gary

Closed for the Duration

apologises for not taking him seriously and for not being there when he needed him. He tells him he will make it up to him by going for a night out. Ron is pleased until Gary tells him it can't be tonight because he has a spot of trouble with some gangland villains back in 1945. To add insult to injury, he asks to borrow Ron's hi-tech camera that he was preparing to take to Liverpool. As Gary departs, Ron throws a number of empty lager cans at him by way of venting his annoyance.

In 1945, Gary makes for a property in Greenwich. A housewife called Mrs Green opens the door and the time traveller produces a fake ID and says he's from the Secret Military Intelligence Unit. He tells her he believes a number of spies are having a meeting in the house across the road. Gary then asks to take photos from the vantage point of her bedroom window. The housewife tells him to 'bugger off' and slams the door in his face. Gary tries again and says he's from the *News of the World*. He says he's trying to get intimate photos of a sex ring including call girls, a Scoutmaster and the Bishop of Tooting Bec. She instantly lets him in.

Once in the bedroom, the woman tells him she wouldn't normally allow a man into her boudoir, apart from her husband, who comes in to decorate once a year. Gary slips her a white fiver or two to thank her for her cooperation. Gary instantly spots Smith and Jones in the house across the road and begins to take photos of them. Phoebe presently arrives at the house and enters. Gary takes her photo as she meets with Smith and Jones and hands over the money. Meanwhile, the frustrated housewife is getting herself into a lather thinking about what's going on across the road.

After Phoebe departs, Inspector Priestly arrives for his share and to discuss the extra amount they've been charging behind his back. The housewife goes and has a lie down on the bed as the thought of an orgy going on across the road is becoming too much for her. Presently, all three men spot Gary taking photos and make their way over to the house.

Gary is about to leave when Smith, Jones and Priestly come racing in. Priestly accuses him of spying on an officer of the law. He says he must be an enemy agent and is likely to face a firing squad. Just then, a flying bomb is heard overhead. They all dive for cover apart from Gary who runs away; fortunately the bomb doesn't explode.

Ron, meanwhile, is watching the racing when Gary arrives with his camera. He offers to take him out on his promised night on the town, but Ron is more bothered about Flic's Fool, Flic's father's horse that he has a bet on at Towcester. If it wins, he will convalesce in Florida; if not, he will jump out of the window. Presently, the racing is interrupted by a newsflash. A female newsreader reveals that a major explosion has occurred at Greenwich. Early indications are that a wartime bomb has detonated, setting off a chain reaction in the electrical systems of the Millennium Dome. The blast has virtually destroyed the Dome's entire structure. However, the complex was unoccupied at the time and there have been no injuries or loss of life. With that, she returns viewers to the racing. Gary races off in the direction of Greenwich and Ron is about to tell him that no one was hurt when the result of the race is announced. Flic's Fool, a 25-to-1 outsider, has won, meaning Ron will be heading to Florida to help repair his broken heart.

Gary arrives back at the penthouse to find a forlorn Yvonne sitting on the sofa looking at the one remaining part of the Perspex Baroness Sparrow – a finger pointing upwards in a rather insulting way. Gary tells her she is safe and that's the most important thing. But what about the 'mockers and knockers', she wants to know? And the press? What should she say to them? He tells her not to say anything – just give them the finger! She laughs.

Later, Reg arrives at the Blue Door Club in 1945 with a newspaper confirming that Smith, Jones and Priestly have been caught by the police. Phoebe reads the article and notices there's no mention of the unexploded bomb. She tells Gary to inform the authorities. After all, it could lie there for years and years and then suddenly just go off. Gary tells her not to worry and he won't forget to let them know. He gives a sneaky grin.

This episode featured the first of only two visits by Yvonne to the West End flat. Although Ron and Yvonne didn't always see eye to eye, it was good to see Yvonne show her softer side and be there for him in his hour of need; not forgetting helping Ron to take revenge on her absent husband. The visit, of course, came about because Gary wasn't around. In fact, he wasn't even in the same era. Although the time traveller had problems in the past, it was unfortunate timing because yet again it meant him having to walk out on Ron when he needed him.

The read-through and blocking for this episode took place on Friday 23 April 1999 and the rehearsals began on Sunday 25 April 1999 and ran until 28 April 1999. The studio audience recording took place at Teddington Studios on Thursday 29 April 1999.

In *Goodnight Sweetheart*, storylines, however serious, always allowed for plenty of lighter moments. In this case, Ron became the proud owner of one of Flic's former companions. Not that everyone on the production team was happy, as writer Sam Lawrence still recalls. 'Wardrobe weren't at all keen on my idea of there being a purple wildebeest soft toy,' he said. 'They asked if I would settle for an off-the-shelf ordinary teddy bear instead. I refused, saying it had to be a purple wildebeest toy. It wasn't for comic effect – I was just being awkward! In the end, I won. After the episode had been recorded, I walked off with Wildy the purple wildebeest and I gave it to my daughter, Hannah, as a toy. She played with it until eventually the stuffing came out!'

This episode also gave Sam the chance to vent his frustration at one of London's then newest landmarks. 'I liked the fact that I got the opportunity to blow up the Millennium Dome as I thought it was a waste of time and money,' he said.

The supporting cast in this episode were all highly experienced sitcom performers. Playing the role of Mr Smith was Leo Dolan. Leo's theatre roles included the second worker in the David Caute play *The Demonstration* at the Nottingham Playhouse, various characters in the Dylan Thomas drama *The Doctor and the Devils* at the Belgrade Theatre, Coventry, and a soldier in the Romulus Linney play *The Sorrows of Frederick* at the Ashcroft Theatre, Croydon. His television credits included Tinker in the historical drama *By the Sword Divided*, the postman in the Roy Clarke sitcom *Keeping Up Appearances*, and Jack in the bittersweet drama *Grafters*. Leo's film work included playing a milkman in the remake of the thriller *The Thirty Nine Steps*, Tasker in the Leslie Thomas war comedy drama *Stand Up Virgin Soldiers*, in a cast led by Robin Askwith and Nigel Davenport, and Phil in the classic gangster thriller *The Long Good Friday*. Leo died on 19 August 2003, aged sixty.

The character of Mr Jones, meanwhile, was played by Kenneth MacDonald. A popular character actor whose career lasted a quarter of a century, Kenneth enjoyed success in the theatre, playing characters such as Max Miller in Dave Simpson's candid study of the variety star in *The Cheeky Chappie* at the Haymarket Theatre, Basingstoke, and Benny in Kevin Elyot's funny and bittersweet play *My Night with Reg* at the Royal Court Theatre, the Criterion Theatre and Playhouse Theatre in London. Towards the end of his life, he played hardman Eddie in the Terry Johnson comedy play *Cleo, Camping, Emmanuelle and Dick* at the Theatre Royal, Bath, and the National Theatre, London. The actor was best known on television for playing Gunner 'Nobby' Clark in the popular Perry and Croft wartime sitcom *It Ain't Half Hot, Mum* and Mike Fisher, the straight-talking landlord of the Nag's Head, in the sitcom *Only Fools and Horses*. Amongst his other television credits, Kenneth revisited his role of Eddie in the comedy *Cor, Blimey!*, which was an adaptation of the play *Cleo, Camping, Emmanuelle and Dick*. His film roles included playing a security man in the musical drama *Breaking Glass*, which starred Phil Daniels and Hazel O'Connor. Kenneth died on 5 August 2001, while on holiday with his family in Hawaii, aged just fifty. Paying tribute at the time, Nicholas said, 'Anyone who met him will tell you of his sense of fun and almost perpetual laughter, but those of us who were lucky enough to have worked with him knew of his dedication as an actor, his impeccable timing and skilled performances.'

The character of Inspector Priestly, an unscrupulous conspirator of Smith and Jones, was played by Norman Eshley. Returning to Teddington Studios was like coming home for Norman. 'I had previously made episodes of *Man About the House* and *George and Mildred* in Studio 1,' he recalled. 'This was the same studio where *Goodnight Sweetheart* was recorded, of course. It is not always easy to go into a series as a guest, but this was a happy show and I have fond memories of appearing in it. Nicholas made everyone so welcome. He is a lovely man and a consummate professional. It was also nice to be reunited with Kenneth MacDonald as we had been members of the National Youth Theatre together.'

Norman's myriad of theatre roles include Robert Dudley in the Robert Bolt play *Vivat! Vivat Regina!* at the Chichester Festival Theatre, and the Piccadilly Theatre, London, George in Bernard Slade's romantic comedy *Same Time Next Year* at the Yvonne Arnaud Theatre, Guildford, and John Worthing, JP in the Oscar Wilde comedy *The Importance of Being Earnest* at the Birmingham Repertory Theatre. The actor is best known for having played Norman Tripp, his brother Robin Tripp's love rival, in the classic sitcom *Man About the House* and Jeffrey Fourmile in the hugely popular series spin-off, *George and Mildred*. His other television roles include Mike Hales in the supernatural drama *Randall and Hopkirk (Deceased)* and Detective George Caufield in the Ian Ogilvy adventure series *Return of the Saint*. Norman's selection of film appearances include playing Jonathan in the sea-based adventure *The Lost Continent*, Athol in the thriller *Crossplot* and Jeffrey Fourmile in the big screen spin-off to the sitcom *George and Mildred*. A serious car accident in France during 1994 left Norman with multiple injuries including head trauma after being hit head-on by a thirty-eight-tonne lorry. Although lucky to survive, the accident resulted in the end of his stage acting career after he lost the ability to retain lines. However, at the time of writing, he still accepts radio and voice work, as well as continuing to write.

Lynda Baron also appeared in this episode as the feisty housewife, Mrs Green. The year before she died, Lynda reflected on her appearance in *Goodnight Sweetheart*. 'It was a nice relaxed recording, at least it was for me,' she said. 'Nicholas is easy to work with as he lets his fellow actors get on with it. It's good to feel trusted.

'It is a joy to pop into a successful series. You often get to play characters you wouldn't necessarily get to play. What a pleasure. Good memories.'

Lynda came to fame in the West End comedy revue *One Over the Eight*, which was headlined by Kenneth Williams. Her other theatre roles included Simone in the Dave Freeman farce *A Bedful of Foreigners* at the Ashcroft

Theatre, Croydon, Victoria Palace Theatre, London, and the Duke of York's Theatre, London. She also played Sylvia in the Richard Harris comedy *Stepping Out* at the Duke of York's Theatre, London, and Stella Deems in the 1987 London premiere of the Stephen Sondheim musical *Follies* at the Shaftesbury Theatre. She was best known on television for playing Nurse Gladys Emmanuel in the much-loved Roy Clarke sitcom *Open All Hours*, a role she reprised in the follow-up series, *Still Open All Hours*. Lynda's other television work included being nominated for a BAFTA for her portrayal of Violet Carson in the drama *The Road to Coronation Street*; while children came to know her for playing Auntie Mabel in the 1990s series *Come Outside*. Lynda made occasional excursions into films. For instance, she played Long Liz, an ill-fated prostitute, in the Hammer horror *Hands of the Ripper*, which starred Eric Porter and Angharad Rees, Meg in the nautical comedy *Carry On Columbus* and Elsie in the sports comedy drama *Dream Horse*, with a cast including Toni Collette and Owen Teale.

After an accomplished career, Lynda died on 5 March 2022, aged eighty-two.

Finally, playing a newsreader in this episode was Emily Bruni. On stage, Emily's credits include Clare in the Jonathan Lynn comedy *Yes, Prime Minister* at the Trafalgar Studios, London, Goneril in the William Shakespeare tragedy *King Lear* at the Globe, London, and Debby/Deborah in the Donald Margulies black comedy *The Model Apartment* at the Theatre Royal, Bath. Emily really made her mark when she played Sarah in the third series of the comedy drama *Auf Wiedersehen, Pet*. Her television credits have also included Annette de Martignac in the drama *Scarlet Pimpernel*, and Kika Bright in the comedy *Toast of London*, with Matt Berry. Emily's film appearances include Jessica in the domestic farce *Remember Me?*, which boasted a cast including Imelda Staunton and Robert Lindsay, and Janet in the comedy drama *Intimate Affairs*. She could also be seen on the cinema screen playing Caitlin in the Stephen Frears comedy drama *Tamara Drewe* and Goneril in *King Lear: Live from Shakespeare's Globe*.

Anthony and Gaynor Sadler arranged musicians for the scene set in the Blue Door Club where Phoebe is singing 'Big Noise from Winnetka'. They mimed to the music previously recorded at their studio in Soho. The musicians were:

Piano:	Cliff Hall
Double bass:	Bill Brandon
Drums:	Brian Markham

*

At the Blue Door Club in 'Flash, Bang, Wallop', the ninth episode of series six, Gary is encouraging Reg to practise preparing a cocktail as taught by him. Reg is reluctant at first but gives it ago. He proceeds to put a tin helmet on and then performs an impressive routine. Reg asks if this is really going to make people pay more money for their drinks. Gary tells Reg to trust him. However, Reg doesn't think it's natural to be throwing up a drink before you've even swallowed it!

Phoebe arrives at the club and excitedly tells Gary that she's persuaded Noël Coward to come and give them one of his 'turns', or rather a cabaret performance, on Thursday.

Later at the penthouse, Gary is trying to watch the football on television while Yvonne is showing off about having been selected as a judge for a very prestigious book prize: the Hanbury Truman award for non-fiction. Gary is somewhat surprised; after all, he reminds her, the last book she read was *Slapper* by Edwina Currie. Yvonne looks through the box, not sure of which title to read first. She takes a book out on the balcony as Gary lets Ron in. He is still down in the dumps over Flic. Gary hands Ron one of the books Yvonne has been asked to judge. Entitled *Tarzan 2000: How to be a Swinger in the Dating Jungle*, Ron starts to flick through the pages and quickly becomes hooked and asks if he can take it. Meanwhile, Gary starts to look through the Noël Coward biography. He is soon shocked, to say the least, to discover there's a photo in the book of himself with Coward. Ron agrees with Gary that it will be hard to explain. Gary's mind goes into overdrive at the possibilities of what might happen if his modern-day wife sees the photo. More restrained, Ron just tells him to lose the publication. Gary agrees. Besides, she'll never miss one book with so many others to get through. Presently, Yvonne comes inside and says the book she is reading, *The Illustrated History of Pockets*, is really boring. She asks if Gary has seen the Noël Coward book.

After Ron has left, Yvonne settles down and begins to read the Coward biography. She scans the pages as Gary tries to put her off from reading it and ultimately reaching the photos. He persuades Yvonne to warm up the plates for the pizzas she has ordered, which gives him an opportunity to get rid of the book. This he does by unceremoniously throwing it off the balcony. Despite being seen by Yvonne, Gary denies having done it. The doorbell goes and she tells him to find her book while she sees who's at the door. Gary makes an overly dramatic attempt at looking for the book. Yvonne comes back accompanied by Mr Bannister who knows exactly where the book is – it hit him on the head while he was out walking his dog, Freckles. He is confused as to why anyone would throw literature at him, especially as he consider himself to be very popular in this block of flats. Gary is curious as to how he knew it was their book. Yvonne mentions that she has included a sticker with her name on it inside. He leaves threatening that his lawyer will be in touch.

Over lunch, Gary tells Ron the book is possessed. He's tried putting it out with the rubbish, used it as a briquette on the barbecue, and even tied a pork chop to it and left it out for Freckles, who turns out to be a vegetarian, but all to no avail. There are only thirty pages to go and she will see the photo. Ron tells him to tear out the picture, but Gary says she'll know he has something to hide. Ron suggests that Gary ensure the photo doesn't get taken in the first place. After all, he hasn't reached March 1945 when it was taken. If Gary makes sure no one takes a photo of him with Noël in March 1945, he can never appear in the book.

Gary is a little on edge when he finds Noël Coward is sitting with Phoebe in the flat on his next visit back to 1945. And when Phoebe produces a camera, he dives for cover. Phoebe is surprised at his reaction. She tells him that Noël lent her the camera to take some promotional photos for his upcoming appearance at the Blue Door Club. She tries to take one of Gary but he says it wouldn't be a good idea in case it falls into the wrong hands, potentially compromising his effectiveness as a spy. But there's worse news for Gary. Noël has had a wonderful idea for a new play. It's about a young married couple who move into their first flat in Mayfair. He plans to call it *Gary and Phoebe*. To try and put him off, Gary tells him it sounds really boring. Phoebe tells him, as if he didn't know, that it's based on them. He tries to persuade Noël to write one of his films instead, but Noël reminds him he must await the muse. Gary suggests he try penning an action thriller about a man trapped in a building with international terrorists. Noël isn't sold on the idea until he suggests the terrorists have bad manners. The playwright believes it's a provocative subject and says he will leave to start work immediately. He also tells Gary that he agrees that his idea for a play does sound unspeakably boring. This, of course, doesn't go down well with Phoebe who wanted to see their lives portrayed on the stage.

At the Blue Door Club, Noël is accompanying Phoebe at the piano while she sings 'Our Love is Here to Stay'. After performing, Noël admits that one of the benefits of coming to the club is to catch up with his friends. While Gary is lighting a cigarette, he introduces Gary to photographer Cecil Beaton who takes the photo that ended up in the Noël Coward biography.

Gary is quick to regale the story of what happened verbatim to Ron. Not that Ron is that interested as he's preparing to go out. He emerges from the bedroom dressed like a failed superhero, ready to go to the new gym he has joined. According to the book he's reading, the gym is the singles bar of the 1990s. Gary is more concerned as to what to do with the photo. Ron suggests he steal the photo. He agrees, and heads off back to 1945.

After a triumphant evening at the club, Phoebe and Noël return to the flat. There she confides in him that she's concerned that Gary might be losing interest in her and Michael and that he's always going off and missing the best parts of their lives. Noël reassures her that he believes Gary is sane and sighted and therefore can't do anything other than adore her. She asks Noël whether he fancies her, but the most he will commit to is saying she has some very nice shoes. The phone rings; Noël answers and is told that Gary has been arrested.

PC Cotterill is busily and somewhat nervously taking Gary's fingerprints at the police station. The time traveller has been caught stealing the photo and burning the negatives at Cecil Beaton's studio. Reg arrives to see if the news is true. Gary tells him he has very good reasons for what he did. There and then, we discover that there is bad blood between Reg and Cotterill over a matter of lunch. Reg asked him to get cheese and pickle sandwiches and he brought him pilchards.

Cotterill is required to take a photo of Gary for their records. He asks Reg to assist. Cotterill even cuffs them both together, fearing that Gary is violent. Noël arrives and tells Gary not to worry as he knows the police commissioner. At the very moment Cotterill takes the photo, Gary drops out of shot meaning that only Reg and Noël are in the photo. This changes history and therefore it is this new photo that will end up in the Noël Coward biography.

Having seen Ron off on a cheap holiday from Teletext, which turns out to be a trip for swingers over sixty, Gary returns to the penthouse. Relieved that the photo has changed in the book, he is less pleased to discover she has stopped reading it. It turns out that Hanbury Truman have converted the award to a theatre prize as there's more publicity in the arts. She informs Gary she's due at the Playhouse to see the premiere of one of Noël Coward's lesser-known plays called *Gary and Phoebe*. Yvonne comments that it sounds really boring. She leaves; and suddenly the penny drops, causing Gary to race after her.

The read-through and blocking for this episode took place on Friday 30 April 1999 and the rehearsals began on Sunday 2 May 1999 and ran until 5 May 1999. The studio audience recording took place at Teddington Studios on Thursday 6 May 1999.

This episode was the only one that was written by Paul Alexander and Simon Braithwaite. The story of how they came to write it goes back to when they co-wrote, crowdsourced and co-produced a feature film called *Staggered*. The romantic comedy, which featured Martin Clunes (who also directed) and Anna Chancellor, reached number three at the UK box office. 'The same distributor, Entertainment Films, offered to invest part of the budget for the planned follow-up film, a comedy-thriller called *Tourist Trap* that Martin Clunes would again direct, but that would be much bigger scale,' explained Paul. 'We took over a

Closed for the Duration

year to write the script and persuaded an American co-producer to be involved as part of the story was set in America. We flew to LA to meet him and he helped us line up other investors etc. We also engaged Clive Owen and Rosanna Arquette to star, as there was a romcom angle to the script, a bit like *Staggered*, and Christopher Lloyd to play the antagonist. We were a few months away from shooting and just about to launch the film at Cannes when one of the patchwork of investors announced they were pulling their money out and the whole financing structure collapsed like bad Jenga! We went from film to no film in pretty much one phone call – which was horrible.'

While licking their wounds, Paul and Simon asked their then respective agents to try and get them more work writing for sitcoms. 'I'd already worked on a couple of series of *Red Dwarf* by this time,' said Paul. '*Goodnight Sweetheart* partly came out of that. Simon's agents were Seifert-Dench Associates who, at the time, also represented Marks and Gran plus Gary Lawson and John Phelps; so I assume that didn't hurt either. Anyway, ALOMO got in touch with us and asked if we'd like to pitch any ideas for series six.

'One of the trickiest things about coming onto a show six series in is coming up with a story idea, or even a story area, that hasn't already been done. I'm pretty sure we pitched a couple of stories and in fact I've had a look at a disk drive with some ancient back-ups on and found a document dated 7 July 1998 with two stories we presented saved on it. They are "Flash, Bang, Wallop", which was pretty much fully formed, and another one about Gary being asked in the then present day to be a technical advisor on a wartime thriller filming near his shop and getting annoyed with the liberties that Hollywood is taking with the truth. The latter story was, frankly, all over the place – probably because we were so keen for them to pick "Flash, Bang, Wallop" instead!

'Because I'm a big science-fiction nerd, I was extremely keen to do a story that specifically hinged on some aspect of the show's time-travel element, and which we could hopefully make at least somewhat different to how the show had used time travel before. I think as Simon and I talked around it, we got excited by the basic notion of: could there be something utterly innocuous that had happened to Gary in the forties – which ultimately turned out to be standing next to someone while a photo was taken of that person – that would, all of a sudden, have some potentially disastrous effect on his life in the present? A kind of *Twilight Zone* style dilemma that would have to be worked out by the end of the episode. Two other elements influenced us in coming up with that story. One was, in our preliminary discussions about the show, someone, maybe the script editor, described how the character of Yvonne had developed by series six and how she was now a baroness, wealthy, successful, a public figure and the kind of person who's asked to be the celebrity member of public committees or judging panels. That pushed us towards the "MacGuffin" of our story being a photo in a book entered into a competition she was on the panel for.' (For the uninitiated, a MacGuffin is an object, device, or event that is necessary to the plot and the motivation of the characters, but insignificant, unimportant, or irrelevant.)

'The other element was that one of the semi-regulars in the series was Noël Coward and I thought it was cool to have the chance to write Noël Coward as a Noël Coward character,' continued Paul. 'I actually bought and read a compendium of several Coward plays, including *Private Lives* and *Blithe Spirit*, as part of my prep for the series. Therefore the MacGuffin became a photo in a book about Coward.'

Then came the process of beginning to write the episode. 'I've learned over the years that there are as many different ways of co-writing as there are writing partnerships,' he acknowledged. 'With Simon and I, we'd spend a huge amount of time talking about the premise, the story, the plot, the characters, the jokes etc., usually in coffee shops or over lunch at TGI Fridays in Kingston-upon-Thames or another restaurant Simon really liked in Putney. During these sessions we'd take copious handwritten notes and then turn those notes into a detailed step outline – basically a scene-by-scene, beat-by-beat breakdown of the story, including any dialogue and joke ideas that struck us. Once we had that, the bulk of the "work" of writing – the plot, the structure, the arcs – was done and we had just the fun bit – the dialogue – to do. What we'd do then was one of us would go away and write a first draft from that detailed outline. Usually it was me because I type much faster than Simon. I'd write it long – way too long, I'm still prone to overwriting – then send it to Simon who would rewrite – he was always ruthless at trimming down the stuff that bored him – and we'd end up with a joint draft which we'd then go through line by line making further tweaks and trims. Then we'd send it in to the production, who'd get back to us with notes – suggestions for tweaks, extra jokes, ways to improve the plot etc. Depending on the series, and the people involved, the notes process can be a wonderful chance to improve your script by collaboration (television is all about collaboration) or a soul-sucking nightmare! But the notes process on *Goodnight Sweetheart* was fabulous. The notes were actual notes as opposed to notes for the sake of notes, always completely on the money, and the process did exactly what it was supposed to – made the script better!'

Like most writers, Paul and Simon found attending the rehearsals was a useful and rewarding experience. 'It was fun for us to see our story come to life right in front of us,' said Paul. 'This was thanks to a team of actors and actresses at the absolute top of their game who had been playing those characters long enough to completely inhabit them! I think it was also mildly useful for everyone that we were there, so if any questions arose about the script, or if anyone wanted an alternative line, we were there to sort that out. Plus, writers spend so much time on their own, it's always a treat to get out and about and see how the rest of the process works. Also, we got a free lunch every day – and if there's one thing writers love, it's a free lunch!'

It's rare that the cast of a sitcom get to keep props from appearing in a series. However, Paul managed to take a couple of souvenirs away from making this episode. 'I'm pleased to say that the Noël Coward prop book, which was simply entitled *Noël Coward*, has survived,' he said. 'It's in really good condition. Something I didn't realise, until I watched the episode again and then dug out the book, is that the props department actually pasted in a dummy page,' he revealed. 'The book is actually a biography of the actor Peter Finch with the photo of Gary and Noël on page one hundred and thirteen, exactly where we said it occurred in the script, which is very pleasing! I've also got the *Bravo Two Zero – 3D Magic Eye Version* prop book,' he admitted. 'But that's kind of falling apart!'

Paul remembers being 'absolutely delighted' with how the episode turned out. 'In my memory, everyone at ALOMO seemed to be pleased too,' he said proudly. 'I'd have loved to have written more. Not least because when you write an episode of someone else's series, you usually get to the end of the process and it's at that point you think, "I really know how to do that now!" – and it makes you feel very keen to do more. Except our episode was the second to last one ever made of the original run. Weirdly, I'd already had a very similar thing a few years earlier, before I met Simon, when I'd actually written the second to last episode ever of *Lovejoy*. This means I was already an expert on jumping onto the gravy train right before it terminated!'

As writing partners, Paul and Simon wrote selected episodes of the flat-share sitcom *Babes in the Wood*, *2point4 Children* and *My Hero*. They also collaborated on various episodes and specials for the pop group S Club 7. This is, of course, in addition to their romantic comedy film, *Staggered*. Simon gave up writing for television in the early 2000s in order to set up and run a successful publishing business with his wife, Louise, who is a talented artist, to help showcase and sell her work. However, Paul decided to carry on writing both alone and occasionally with other writers.

For the theatre, Paul's writing credits have included revising the book for the Noel Gay musical *Radio Times*. His version then toured with Gary Wilmot and Sara Crowe. Paul also helped to develop and then wrote a musical with Thom

Southerland called *The Smallest Show on Earth*. Based on the Peter Sellers comedy film, the cast included Brian Capron and Liza Goddard, and toured the UK at the end of 2015. The other stage productions Paul has helped to develop include *Henry – A Killer New Musical*, which is about the trial of America's first serial killer.

On his own, Paul's television writing work includes selected episodes of the sitcom *The Green Green Grass*, on which he was also a script editor, the soap opera *Emmerdale* and the sitcom *Life of Riley*.

Paul's film credits have also included co-writing the comedy *S Club Seeing Double* with Kim Fuller; while on his own, he has written films including the romantic comedy *From Me to You*.

At the start of the episode Christopher, as Reg, had to perform an impressive cocktail-shaking routine, which Gary had supposedly taught him. 'I did a huge amount of work on that sequence,' he confirmed. 'I went for a class with someone who worked in a cocktail bar and then, whenever I wasn't needed for a scene, I practised in another room. As I remember, we recorded the scene in front of a live audience and did it in just two takes.' If you listen carefully, you can hear that Christopher was rewarded with a big cheer from the studio audience.

Also appearing in this episode was Robin Meredith as Mr Bannister, who skilfully played the outraged neighbour who catches a glancing blow on the head from the Noël Coward biography Gary sends flying off the balcony. In his time in the acting profession, Robin's theatre roles have included Robert Caplan in the J. B. Priestley psychological mystery *Dangerous Corner* at the Devonshire Park Theatre, Eastbourne, Nixon Trippett in the Walter Ellis farce *A Little Bit of Fluff* at the Churchill Theatre, Bromley, and Cookson in the J. M. Barrie play *Peter Pan* at the Barbican Theatre, London. His other television work has included playing Brush in the period drama *Vanity Fair*, Geoffrey in the sitcom *That's Love* and Eric Bledsoe in the David Renwick comedy drama *Love Soup*. Robin's film credits have included a ruined speculator in Christine Edzard's adaptation of the Charles Dickens novel *Little Dorrit*.

This was the last episode that David Benson appeared in as Noël Coward. 'I will always be grateful to Laurence and Maurice for giving me the opportunity to appear in the series,' he said. 'It was like a gift from God to be working with performers as experienced and generous as Nicholas, Liz and Chris. I often wished at the time that I might have appeared in more episodes – the weeks when I was not needed were dismal ones for me and I longed to be back working with my new friends. Now, I am incredibly grateful to have been asked to join them at all and will always look back on *Goodnight Sweetheart* as one of the great highlights of my career.'

The role of PC Cotterill, the highly-strung enemy of Reg Deadman, was played by Robert Whitelock. Robert still waxes lyrical about appearing in the penultimate episode of series six of the time-travelling sitcom. 'I remember sitting in the foyer of Teddington Studios, waiting to audition for Terry Kinane,' said Robert. 'I'd been at the RSC for two years, so I hadn't done much television. All I recall is that Terry put me at my ease and laughed at everything I did, which was reassuring!

'I was pleasantly shocked at how much time we had to rehearse. I'd been warned at RADA that television was notoriously quick to rehearse, sometimes maybe even just a quick line run before shooting. But this was the complete opposite, being comedy. I think we had five days in the rehearsal room. I recall being nervous about meeting Nick Lyndhurst because I'd been watching him on television since the 1970s and was a bit overawed by him. He seemed very quiet and self-contained, and I didn't want to encroach on his working time. When I eventually gathered up my courage to chat to him, we got on famously.

'Getting into the studio, onto the set and into costume felt very satisfying. At this point, there was no audience in the seats. I had lunch with Nick and Victor, and they asked me if I'd ever done live studio audience before. I said that I hadn't, but that I'd just finished a season with the RSC and that I was very used to a big audience. They very benevolently told me, "That's what they all say; this is different." When the audience came in, I started to understand what they meant. The nerves shot up, as each cast member was introduced and made their entrance. This was a strange, disjointed experience for someone like me, who'd come from the theatre, where we never show "ourselves" to an audience. There was some banter with the audience before we started the recording. I was amazed at the stopping and starting involved, being very new to the medium of television.

'Eventually it was my turn, and I was introduced by the great Ted Robbins, the warm-up man. And warm is a good word to describe Ted. He was very kind to me and presumably must have known how nervous I would be. I remember just before the first take being petrified and thinking, "I can't remember anything!" But I'd experienced this before as an actor and knew that my body (or somatic memory as we call it!) would take over, which thankfully it did! Luckily, I was playing a character who was quite highly-strung and nervy, so I think I got away with it.

'Nick, Christopher and David were so friendly and welcoming that I thoroughly enjoyed doing that scene, although I found it frustrating that I couldn't land a punchline like them. As experienced and consummate performers, they made it seem so effortless. I felt sure that the lines could be funny, and it drove me a bit crazy that I just couldn't find the timing to get the laughs like they did. I now recognise the art and skill of comedy, and that it can't be learned overnight. You also must learn it in the fire of live performance because the audience will let you know if you've timed it right! I became close friends with Dave Benson as a result of working with him on this show. I spent most of the studio day hanging out with David and we watched the recording from backstage. I didn't get to hang out with Chris much, but he was a very kind and warm man. Nick would regale me with hilarious anecdotes, which sadly I can't repeat here. I found him to be an ideal leading man. He was sincere, generous and welcoming to me.

'My overall memories of working on *Goodnight Sweetheart* were of a warm and friendly bunch of people (I haven't even mentioned Emma Amos and Liz Carling who were both lovely to spend time with) and a fun time. I've met Marks and Gran a few times and they were always friendly and engaging. They even put me up for another part in a show they'd written, which I didn't get, but as actors we always appreciate when somebody throws your name into the mix. Having done a lot of television now, I realise that it felt like old-fashioned telly, and I mean that in a good way: lots of rehearsal time, no stress amongst the cast and crew and a director who laughed a lot. Frankly, who could ask for more?'

Although television has been a mainstay of his career, Robert has appeared in several theatre productions. His credits include Richard Hannay in the John Buchan spy thriller *The 39 Steps* at the West Yorkshire Playhouse, Leeds, Andy Maggs in Roy Williams' forceful play *Category B* at the Tricycle Theatre, London, and Bob Mitchell in the Noël Coward drama *This Happy Breed* at the Theatre Royal, Bath. Robert's other television roles are considerable. They include Richard Waterlow in the detective drama *Foyle's War*, Mahler in the science-fiction drama *Doctor Who* and Phil Nightingale in Danny Boyle's biodrama of the Sex Pistols, entitled *Pistol*. His film work includes playing Alfie Hook in the Dick Clement and Ian La Frenais crime thriller *The Bank Job*, an armed officer in the comedy *Alan Partridge: Alpha Papa*, with Steve Coogan, and Malc in the comedy drama *Military Wives*.

Finally, playing the holiday rep who checked in an eager but misguided Ron before he boarded the coach was Dorothea Phillips. In a long-standing career, Dorothea has trod the boards and played roles such as Mrs Ogmore-Pritchard in the Dylan Thomas 'play for voices' *Under Milk Wood* on tour and at the New Theatre, London; Madame Claude, Lady Frederick's dressmaker, in W. Somerset Maugham's comedy *Lady Frederick* at the Theatre Royal, Windsor; and Maggie Jones in the G. A. Thomas comedy *Winter Sunshine* at the Richmond Theatre. As well as her stage work, Dorothea has gained a wealth of other television credits. They include Mrs Edwards in the *Department S* spin-off *Jason King*, Mrs Monroe, the head of first year, in the children's school drama *Grange Hill*, and

Mrs Blenkinsopp in the Jeffrey Archer political drama *First Among Equals*. Dorothea's film parts have included Aunt Beatrice Grubb in the saucy comedy *Carry On Loving*, the first Mrs Dai Bread in the comedy drama *Under Milk Wood*, which starred Richard Burton and Elizabeth Taylor, and Mrs Mirthless in the comedy adventure, *102 Dalmatians*.

At the start of 'Accentuate the Positive', the tenth and final episode of series six, Gary is seen arriving at the West End flat to discover Ron papering over the cracks in his life. Or to be more exact, decorating. Well, choosing which colour paint to use! Gary isn't particularly bothered, he's just keen to collect the rent Ron owes. He needs the money as he has a new Porsche (which Yvonne bought him) to run, and the small matter of paying for the food and drink for the forthcoming VE Day party. Ron points out that, when the war is over, he won't be able to con Phoebe that he's on a secret mission every five minutes. Gary disagrees. He mentions that there will always be convenient conflicts going on in the world that will give him the excuse to get away. Ron admits that even after all this time he's still dumbfounded at Gary's devious resourcefulness.

After singing 'The Last Waltz' to the regulars of the Blue Door Club, Phoebe joins Gary for a drink at the bar. She invites Kenneth, one of the visitors to the club, to join them in a drink. Phoebe ponders whether they should move the tables in the club to make more room for the VE party that is likely to happen soon. Kenneth seems unconvinced and thinks the Germans might suddenly rally like they did in the Battle of the Bulge. Gary says his money is on the eighth of May: the following week. Phoebe tells Gary it will be wonderful to have him home for good and that it was time they started thinking about a little sister for Michael. Gary mentions that although the war might be over in Europe, there's still Japan and Korea to consider. She says that she refuses to have him make a career of being a secret agent – he can think again.

Reg arrives full of excitement. He says the word is that Clement Attlee is going to perform the official reopening of the old Boys' Club. Reg is excited because Attlee helped to set up the club when Reg was a boy, and personally taught Reg to play ping-pong. Reg asks Gary whether Mr Attlee will remember him; Gary sarcastically tells him he probably keeps a picture of him beside his bed! Reg struggles to comprehend where he would have got a picture of him from.

Ron is at home, preparing to do a spot of DIY. The phone rings; it's Yvonne, asking if Gary was in Wigan last night. Ron isn't sure; he might have said Rippon. He tells her he's a bit tied up at the moment as he's rented a stripper until midday and he wants to get his money's worth. Yvonne suspects he means the type that wear tassels, but he means a wallpaper stripper. She mentions there's been a car crash near Wigan and there's footage on television of a Porsche like Gary's all squashed flat. She's concerned it might be Gary. At that point, an unharmed Gary walks through the door and she ends the call. She throws her arms around him and he remarks about the nice welcome. The millionairess tells him she thought he'd been killed. She mentions the report on the television. He admitted he went to Wigan but both he and his car are fine. After he claims to have gone for a walk on Wigan Pier, Yvonne starts to suspect he might not have been in Wigan after all. While Gary goes for a shower, she picks up his wallet. She opens it and finds a photo of Gary and Phoebe together.

On his next return to Blitz and Pieces, Yvonne follows him. She goes around to the back as the front door is locked and asks a workman to give her a lift up on their streetlight repair crane so she can see into the yard. There, she watches Gary, in forties clothes, appear from thin air and walk back into the shop. He has realised he has forgotten to change his watch. The time traveller comes back out into the yard and once again makes for the time portal and vanishes into thin air before Yvonne's eyes.

On coming back to the penthouse, Gary finds Yvonne looking shocked and sipping a glass of something strong. She tells him what she saw at the shop. He tells her he doesn't know what to say. After all, what she has just claimed is impossible. She reminds him it's what she saw. Gary reminds her that he can't walk into walls and proves it, hurting his head in the process. He says she's probably a bit stressed out what with selling the business and becoming a peer, and suggests a week in a health farm. Yvonne tells him she was following him because of the woman in the photo she found in his wallet. She asks if he was with her while he was in Wigan. Thinking on the spot, Gary tells her that he doesn't know who the woman is but it's the only photo he has of his grandad and he knows it's not his grandma.

Gary tells Ron that he managed to get three big brandies down Yvonne and she's now sleeping like a baby. He hopes that when she wakes up in the morning, she will realise that she can't have seen what she thought she saw. Worried, he tells Ron he thinks she's sussed out his double life. Ron tells him he should finally do the right thing and tell the truth. Gary is not convinced. After all, how does he tell Yvonne that the reason she saw him vanish is that he travels back to 1945, where he has a wife and son and a burgeoning reputation as a war hero? Or tell Phoebe that the reason he knows so much about the war is because he's an illegal immigrant from 1999? Ron tells him to think about it.

On his next visit to 1945, Gary takes Michael a small handheld computer game and shows him how it works. In doing so, he accidentally teaches Michael

Closed for the Duration

to say, 'Kick him in the goolies.' Phoebe is not amused and hopes he doesn't say that in front of the babysitter. Phoebe asks Gary if he's okay as he looks down. Gary tells her he has something to tell her. He's about to reveal the truth but thinks better of it. Instead, he tells her that Hitler is dead and that they were up all night at HQ arguing about when to break the news. Emotional, Phoebe tells Michael the war is going to be over and they will have daddy back for good.

At the reopening of the Boys' Club, Clement Attlee makes a moving speech before Reg takes the opportunity to remind him that he once taught him ping-pong. He then asks Clement to play another game with him, which he agrees to do when a press photographer says it will make a good picture. While they have a knock-up, Gary goes to get a drink of juice. At the same time, Kenneth from the Blue Door Club puts something into Attlee's pipe while he thinks no one is looking. He replaces the pipe and walks away. Gary notices that Kenneth seems overly interested in watching Clement preparing to light his pipe. Gary rushes over and grabs the pipe from him and Kenneth goes to run out of the club. Gary tells Reg to stop him, but he is confused as to why. Instead, Phoebe trips him over with her foot. A policeman and a police detective rush over to Kenneth. They search him and discover that he had put cyanide in the pipe. Clement plays down the incident but thanks Gary for probably saving his life. Gary tells him it's his privilege and that he will be the next prime minster and the leader of a great reforming government. Clement is not convinced, failing to believe that the electorate would turn Mr Churchill out of office after all he has done, but Phoebe tells him that Gary is very rarely wrong about these things.

Gary makes his way back to Duckett's Passage trying to work out what to say to Yvonne about his double life. However, when he reaches the passage, he discovers that the time portal has closed, and soon realises that he is stuck back in the past. A drunken Reg, who has had a couple of pints for every year of the war, discovers a very worried Gary sitting on a dustbin at Duckett's Passage wondering what he's going to do. Gary tries to explain to Reg, but he's too drunk to understand. He suddenly realises the time portal has locked because he saved Clement Attlee and that he has fulfilled his destiny. This means he will never see Yvonne, Ron or *Baywatch* ever again!

Back in 1999, three days after Gary disappeared into the past, Yvonne arrives at the West End flat demanding to know where Gary is. Ron tells her he doesn't know and says that is the truth. Yvonne doesn't believe him because Gary always confided in him. She asks if he's got another woman. Ron tells Yvonne this is something for her and Gary to sort out. She knees Ron out of frustration. Ron looks up and spots some writing materialising on one of the walls. The message, from Gary in the past, reads:

Ron,
I hope you find this message. I'm stuck in the past. The time portal's vanished. Tell Yvonne I'm sorry. Tell her everything. Try to explain.

Back in 1945, we see Gary completing the message he has written on the wall. Phoebe tries to get in the room, but he has locked the door and tells her the lock is playing up. This gives him time to paste a sheet of wallpaper over the message.

Returning to 1999, we see that he ended the message as follows:

Tell her I always loved her.

By this point, Ron has told Yvonne everything. Understandably, she sits there in shock. Ron tells her that Gary tried to tell her in the beginning. Yvonne admits the good news is that she's not going mad, and that she did see Gary vanish, but the bad news is that all the accepted laws of physics are 'crap'. She tells Ron she hopes he will understand that she never wants to see him again. He acknowledges her wish and lets her out of the flat.

At a VE Day party, Gary is leading a band in a rousing chorus of 'We Are the Champions' by Queen, a song which he has, of course, told everyone he wrote. Reg is keen for him to sing another number, but Gary is feeling tired. It might be VE Night but he's suffering from a case of anticlimax. Reg admits he used to suffer from that. It turned out his underpants were too tight.

Later that night, Yvonne makes her way to Blitz and Pieces and, standing at the gates in the yard, tries telling Gary how she feels. Ron arrives and Yvonne asks what he's doing there. He tells her he misses Gary too. Yvonne asks what makes him think she misses him. She reminds Ron that she's not speaking to him. Ron reminds her that she's talking to someone who isn't there. He tells her that Gary can't get back and that they've both got to get on with their lives. Yvonne admits that she wishes she could pass through the time warp as she'd give Gary such a slap. She questions whether Gary really loved her and Ron tries to reassure her. He realises she still loves her Gary. He tells Yvonne that because she's been so busy of late, maybe Gary didn't realise. Ron leaves and Yvonne attempts to tell Gary she loves him, misses him and wants him back.

Back in 1945, Gary has his hand placed on the wall in Duckett's Passage. He's talking to himself, expressing how he feels, and doesn't know why he's there. After all, he's not convinced that Yvonne is on the other side. He realises that talking to a brick wall is like a metaphor for the relationship between him and Yvonne. Phoebe and Michael arrive, and she asks who he's talking to. Gary turns around and sees the two of them standing there. Phoebe says that Reg saw him catching a taxi and she was worried. She asks why he's come here. Gary tells her that there's something special about the East End and that this is where they first met. Phoebe reminds him they met at the Royal Oak and not down some smelly alley. Gary explains that he wasn't in the mood for going to the pub, where a big knees-up is taking place. Phoebe tells him she doesn't want to be on her own any more and wants them to be a proper family. He picks up Michael and reassures Phoebe that he won't be going away again; besides, where is there to go?

The end of this series had the ultimate cliffhanger. It seemed that Gary was set to remain trapped in the past and that neither Gary nor the viewers would see him find his way back to celebrate the start of the new millennium. Although Yvonne had been told the full story of Gary's double life, it would appear the idea that she may never see Gary again did finally make her realise just how much she still loved him – even if she was loath to admit it to Ron. It was almost inevitable that Gary would one day end up having to live permanently in the past. That Laurence and Maurice, who wrote this episode, found a way of making it appear that Gary's time-travelling journey had been fated all along so he could save Clement Attlee's life, was an ingenious idea not only for the finale for the sixth series, but for what was planned to be the final episode.

The read-through and blocking for this episode took place on Friday 7 May 1999, and the rehearsals began on Sunday 9 May 1999 and ran until 12 May 1999. The studio audience recording took place at Teddington Studios on Thursday 13 May 1999.

A schedule for the last episode also reveals that pre-recordings took place at Teddington Studios on both Wednesday 12 May 1999 and Thursday 13 May 1999. Here is a copy of part of this schedule:

Wednesday 12 May 1999 (pre-record):
Line-Up   17.30
Rehearse/Record   18.00 – 19.00
Scene 10 Int. Gary's Shop:
    Gary runs into shop and takes off his
    watch and puts on 40s watch.
Scene 26 Ext. Gary's Yard:
    Yvonne and Ron by the time portal.
Thursday 13 May 1999:
Line-Up   09.00
Rehearse/Record   09.30 – 11.00
Scene 16 Int. Gary and Phoebe's Flat:
    Gary shows Michael how to use
    Game Boy; he tells Phoebe that Hitler
    has killed himself.

Scene 22 Int. Gary and Phoebe's Flat:
   Gary locks the door – Phoebe can't get into the flat.
Scene 27 Ext. Duckett's Passage:
   Phoebe and Michael join Gary

Camera Rehearsal	11.00 – 12.00
Rehearse/Record	12.00 – 13.00

Scene 24 Int. Blue Door Club:
   VE Night Party, We Are the Champions finishes, Gary feels homesick – Gary, Reg, Phoebe, musicians and supporting artists.

Lunch	13.00 – 14.00
Camera Rehearsal continued	14.00 – 16.00
Artists to Costume/Make-Up – Tea-Break	16.00 – 16.30
Dress Run of Episode 10	16.30 – 18.00
Playing in VT inserts	
Supper Break	18.00 – 19.00
Doors open/audience in	19.00
Warm-Up (Ted Robbins)	19.15 – 19.30
Record Episode 10	19.30 – 22.00
Playing in VT Inserts	

The end-of-series wrap party then took place after the recording of this episode.

The character of Kenneth, who attempts to assassinate Clement Attlee, was played by the actor and writer Tony Millan. Tony is best known for having played Tucker in the hugely popular John Sullivan sitcom *Citizen Smith*, which starred Robert Lindsay. On television his other appearances have predominantly been in sitcoms. His roles include Maurice in *Lame Ducks*, which starred Brian Murphy and Lorraine Chase, Chalky Smith in *On the Up* and even a gorillagram in *As Time Goes By*. Kenneth also wrote for television with the late *Brush Strokes* actor Mike Walling. Their sitcom credits included *Not with a Bang*, starring Ronald Pickup and Mike Grady, and *The Brittas Empire* and *A Prince Among Men*, both of which starred Chris Barrie.

The part of Clement Attlee, meanwhile, was played by Alan David. The Welsh actor's theatre roles have included the Professor in Jez Butterworth's trailblazing play *Jerusalem* at the Royal Court Theatre, London, the Music Box Theatre on Broadway and the Apollo Theatre, London, and Mr Pritchard and Mr Pugh in Dylan Thomas's poetic masterpiece *Under Milk Wood* at the National Theatre,

London. He has also played Antonio in William Shakespeare's much-loved comedy *Much Ado About Nothing* at the Old Vic, London. Arguably best known for playing Griff in the James Corden and Ruth Jones sitcom *Gavin and Stacey*, Alan's other television work has included playing Maurice 'Granny' Naylor in the drama series *Sam* and Mr Bentinck in the David Jason sitcom *Still Open All Hours*. Also, his film credits include a Welsh teacher in the Sally Potter drama *The Man Who Cried*, Doctor Taylor in the romantic comedy *Wimbledon*, and Mr Higgins in the thriller *The Oxford Murders*.

Claire Hinson, who, as mentioned, was by now the executive producer on the sitcom, had her three-year-old son drafted in to play the voice of Gary and Phoebe's son, Michael. 'I remember sitting in the voice-over booth with him repeatedly exclaiming, "Kick him in the goolies!"' she said. 'And, of course, him repeatedly asking "What are goolies?"'

The backing track of Queen's 'We Are the Champions' for the VE Day party scene was arranged and recorded on 22 March 1999 at Logorhythm Music Studios, Lexington Street, Soho, London. Anthony and Gaynor Sadler arranged for the following musicians to take part in miming playing the instruments in this scene alongside Nicholas at the recording:

    Double bass: Bill Brandon
    Drums: Brian Markham

Reflecting on the recording of this scene, Nicholas admitted to being 'really nervous'.

As with Reg's leaving party in the episode 'California Dreamin'', the location used for the assassination attempt was the since-demolished St Mark's Hall, which was located at 23 St Mark's Road, Teddington.

As mentioned, the last episode of series six was, at the time, meant to be the last-ever episode of *Goodnight Sweetheart*. 'It ought to be said that both Maurice and I knew from the beginning that we would only write six series because we wanted to follow the war's timeline,' said Laurence. 'We felt it had to end on VE Night. There was neither sadness nor joy that this was another series out of the way because we had such a marvellous time either writing or supervising the scripts that made up the whole run. The series was hugely successful and we could ask no more than that – especially as it was thought to be such a "weird idea" when we were describing it to Martin Fisher, BBC's Head of Comedy, before we had written a word.'

Nicholas, however, recalls that future episodes had been considered. 'We had an idea the series was coming to an end because the end of the war was in sight,' he said. 'There was a discussion with Lo and Mo about us doing another series, and maybe go into another period, but I didn't think we could better what we had done. It felt right to end the series with VE Day – as much as I wanted to keep working with everybody.

'The scenery, props and costumes on the series were great. There was a real sense of pride to make sure everything was as authentic as it could be. For instance, the props department would make sure the newspapers had the correct date and headlines if they were in shot. They also made sure the coins always had the right year on them. It got that pedantic!'

In an interview about *Goodnight Sweetheart*, Michelle Holmes once shared her thoughts about the sitcom: 'I thought the scripts were amazing, a really great idea,' she said. 'I knew Nicholas Lyndhurst was playing Gary but I'd no idea at the time how popular the fascination with time travel was. I knew there was a huge fondness and love for the forties, but I had no idea the series would be still talked about and watched today!'

Having played the role of Yvonne for three series, Emma realised that something remarkable was coming to an end. 'I remember the last episode being very emotional for us all, the end of an era,' she said. 'You don't get many long-running television jobs, and this one was very special for us all.'

While aware that the end of the series was a milestone, Victor was sanguine about the sitcom finishing. 'The final episode of a series always feels different to the others when you're making it,' he admitted. 'I felt sentimental when *Goodnight Sweetheart* ended, but I didn't feel any sadness as I knew we would all keep in touch. At the time, I felt the series was ready to end, and it had come to a natural conclusion.'

Chris certainly felt a mix of emotions at the last recording. 'I was so sad. I felt sick and tearful, although I thought there might be more of the same to come,' he said. 'However, it didn't happen in the way I thought it might. That said, I've had lots of lovely work since.

'I think there are many of my generation for whom World War Two was central. I was born in 1948 but my childhood was steeped in my parents' memory of it. The conversations between my parents and their friends were full of war stories. *Goodnight Sweetheart* felt like a tribute to them. It is a sadness to me that they never got to see it.'

Claire Hinson believes *Goodnight Sweetheart* was a unique series. 'It's easy to forget now that the idea of having someone time-travel to another time was really original,' she said. 'I think the only show that had featured time travel at that point was *Quantum Leap*. It felt really fresh and original and "high concept". I remember the writers had such fun coming up with things Gary could whip out of the bag to surprise the residents of the Royal Oak. Of course, music featured heavily with Gary passing off much of the Beatles' back catalogue as his own. But I remember one episode where Gary saved Phoebe's life by taking penicillin back to the 1940s. As the series progressed, and Gary and Phoebe fell in love, the web of deceit became more and more tangled with Gary paying the price for his double life with lots of guilt and a fair number of double dinners! So it was a lovely study of a man who is ordinary (bordering on a failure) in the real world who unexpectedly finds a way to be not only special, but a hero. Nick Lyndhurst just played it beautifully. His ability to move between droll comedy and very touching pathos was perfect for the role and he really suited the 1940s costumes too!'

The final series of *Goodnight Sweetheart* was not to keep the same day or time slot during its run. BBC One broadcast the first three episodes on Sunday 18 April 1999, Sunday 25 April 1999 and Sunday 2 May 1999 at 8.30pm. There was no episode shown a week later on Sunday 9 May 1999. The series recommenced on Sunday 16 May 1999 and then was broadcast on Sunday 23 May 1999 and Sunday 30 May 1999 at 8.30pm. The following episodes were shown on Sunday 6 June 1999 at 8.35pm and Sunday 13 June 1999 at 9.25pm. The final two episodes were moved from a Sunday to a Monday and shown on Monday 21 June 1999 and Monday 28 June 1999 at 8.30pm.

Later that year, Nicholas won the second of his two awards for *Goodnight Sweetheart*. For the second year in a row, he was announced as the winner of the Most Popular Comedy Performer award at the National Television Awards. The ceremony was held at the Royal Albert Hall on 26 October 1999 and was hosted by Sir Trevor McDonald.

By this stage, it did appear to be the end of *Goodnight Sweetheart* – at least on television. However, this was not to be the case – although it would be seventeen years before Gary Sparrow would be able to time-travel once again. In the meantime, repeats of the sitcom would find their way onto the channels BBC One, ITV3, GOLD and Drama.

7
Many Happy Returns

IN MARCH 2016, THE BBC announced a landmark sitcom season to mark sixty years since Galton and Simpson's *Hancock's Half Hour* first began on television. A season of programming across BBC One, BBC Two and BBC Four was set to celebrate the heritage and legacy of BBC comedy by revisiting some of Britain's iconic sitcoms alongside launching brand-new comedy shows. The BBC went on to reveal that there would be revisits to much-loved classics including *Are You Being Served? Porridge, Up Pompeii!* and a special prequel to *Keeping Up Appearances*. However, when the revival of *Up Pompeii!*, which reportedly was set to star Miranda Hart, was put on hold, the BBC needed a replacement.

During this period, Jon Rolph was the managing director of Retort, the FremantleMedia label specialising in scripted comedy. 'I was already working with Laurence and Maurice on *Birds of a Feather* for ITV,' said Jon. 'The BBC indicated that they were looking for celebratory revivals for a special season, so Laurence, Maurice and I discussed it, and we pitched a possible direction to Shane Allen, who, at the time, was in charge of comedy commissioning at the BBC. They were very open to it. I worked on the special as the executive producer from pitch to delivery, and beyond in trying to secure a further revived series.'

Maurice was surprised when Jon got in contact regarding a possible special. 'Out of the blue, Jon told us that the BBC were planning to commission comedy as part of a sitcom season and they were short of a comedy that they wanted to do,' said Maurice. 'He asked if we fancied making a special. We weren't averse to bringing it back, but it wasn't our intention. Our first thought was, where's the jeopardy? Jon said, "Well, it's now 1962." That meant, of course, that the Beatles were about to emerge, and Gary would have huge problems explaining how he knew their songs over twenty years before they wrote them! Laurence also had one major consideration on his mind and told Jon, "Only if we can get the main cast."'

The two writers realised that if they were going to work on a new special, they'd have to work out how to get Gary to the future. 'Because I had read a lot of sci-fi, I knew that you can't be in the same space at the same time,' explained Maurice. 'I said, "Gary needs to come into contact with himself when he is born." This meant we had to cheat and make his birth a year earlier than we'd said in an earlier series. We went from a man in the present coping with the past to a man from the past coping with the present. We made a list of all the things that we had in 2016 that were unimaginable in 1999.

'The reason Gary originally kept going back in time was because he had fallen in love. This time we decided that Yvonne would have got pregnant and that the reason he would want to keep going back to the future was because he was falling in love with his daughter. That gave us the reason to keep coming back if the BBC had commissioned another series.'

So, what of the intervening years between 1945 and 1962? 'Gary never let go of the flat so he would have rented it out in the 1940s, 1950s and 1960s etc.,' said Maurice. 'That would have brought him some money. But Gary would have had to knuckle down as the remaining five years of the forties would have been tough for him.'

Although there was no explanation given as to how Phoebe managed to get a new lease, Marks and Gran decided, quite sensibly given the nostalgia element of the special, to move the couple, along with Michael, back into the Royal Oak. 'By the fifties, the Royal Oak would have been doing well again,' Maurice continued. 'Gary would have had a television and radio repair shop that would have also sold records.

'Reg, who was now retired, would probably have helped Gary in the shop or even been a partner in another series. If a rep had come in offering to sell one Beatles record, Gary would obviously say he'd take twelve or more, knowing they were going to sell. Although he would have had the difficulty of explaining how he had written them back in the war!

'He would have used his knowledge to put bets on the horses and football to make money, and maybe had shares.

'I think Yvonne would have been in *Dragon's Den* for a few years and been like a female Lord Sugar.'

While planning the script for the new special, an idea formulated that would have seen the time traveller get his comeuppance with a certain musical legend. 'We were going to do a scene between Gary Sparrow and Paul McCartney,' said Laurence. 'Paul would have complained about Gary claiming to have written the Beatles' songs. We knew that the warm-up artist Ted Robbins and Paul McCartney were cousins and asked him. Paul said he would have taken part, but he was going to be in New York at the time, so it would have been difficult.'

The *Goodnight Sweetheart* revival was set to be made by the production company Retort. Their credits included the return of the Marks and Gran sitcom *Birds of a Feather* and the then-new sitcoms *Chewing Gum*, featuring Michaela Coel, and *The Rebel*, which starred Simon Callow, Bill Paterson and Anita Dobson.

Humphrey Barclay, who Marks and Gran had worked with in the early part of their career, was set to be the producer. Humphrey is one of the UK's most innovative and award-winning producers of television comedy. As producer and then head of comedy at LWT, he produced classics such as Michael Palin and Terry Jones's comedy sketch show *The Complete and Utter History of Britain* and the sitcoms *Doctor in the House*, which featured actors such as Barry Evans, Robin Nedwell and Geoffrey Davies, and *A Fine Romance*, starring Michael Williams and Judi Dench. He also began Humphrey Barclay Productions, making programmes including the sitcoms *Hot Metal*, with a cast including Robert Hardy, Richard Kane and Geoffrey Palmer, *Surgical Spirit*, which paired Nichola McAuliffe and Duncan Preston, and *Desmond's*, starring Norman Beaton as barber Desmond Ambrose. Humphrey later became a development executive for Celador Productions, and also produced the return of *Birds of a Feather*.

The award-winning television director Martin Dennis was engaged to direct this special. 'I'd worked with producer Humphrey Barclay and Lo and Mo on two series of *Birds of a Feather*, and Humphrey got me on board in May 2016, when the script was still in outline stage.'

As Martin hadn't previously directed any of the episodes of *Goodnight Sweetheart*, he decided to catch up on the sitcom. 'I did watch a couple of episodes to refresh my memory of the show – we were keen to recreate Gary and Phoebe's pub as faithfully as possible.

'It was a happy shoot, as far as I recall; the cast were very pleased to revisit their characters, and the script was very solid, funny and inventive.

'The very high-concept time-travel element was a challenge to get right. I felt we needed to show the "process", especially for viewers new to the show. We engineered some fairly basic green screen "time warp" moments, and were able to generate an extra big laugh with Gary emerges into an occupied toilet cubicle and scares the bejesus out of the occupant!'

Canadian-born director Martin was originally a stage manager with the M6 Theatre Company before joining the BBC as a floor assistant. He later became a production manager before becoming a director. Martin's directing credits include episodes of the Croft and Lloyd sitcom *'Allo 'Allo!* He also adapted the American sitcom *Who's the Boss?* for UK viewers and subsequently directed the first three series of the remake, which was called *The Upper Hand*. Martin also directed every episode of the sitcoms *Men Behaving Badly* and *Coupling*. His other sitcom directing credits include two series and two Christmas specials of *Birds of a Feather*, and five series and a Christmas special of *Friday Night Dinner*.

When contact was made with the main cast, there were some initial concerns regarding scheduling for Emma Amos and Victor McGuire. 'I was doing a play called *The Chekhov Trilogy* at the National Theatre that summer, so I was worried we couldn't work around that,' recalled Emma. 'Thankfully, we did. The recording was on a Sunday so Vic (who was working in the theatre as well) and

I managed to do both.' Indeed, Victor was appearing in *Breakfast at Tiffany's* at the Theatre Royal Haymarket in London with Matt Barber and Pixie Lott.

With negotiations completed, it was confirmed that reprising their roles in the special would be Nicholas Lyndhurst as Gary, Elizabeth Carling as Phoebe, Emma Amos as Yvonne, Victor McGuire as Ron and Christopher Ettridge as Reg.

With Teddington Studios now sadly closed, and the BBC encouraging production outside of London, the new *Goodnight Sweetheart* special was set to be made at dock10 Studios, located at MediaCity in Salford. The studios are owned and managed by dock10, a company that has two major divisions: studios and post-production. The ten purpose-built studios were built on the site of the former Manchester Ship Canal docks. Although ready for production in January 2011, the studios were officially opened by Her Majesty the Queen in March 2012.

The special was to be recorded in studio HQ1. At full capacity, this particular studio can seat an audience of a thousand people. The light entertainment programmes made in this studio include *The Voice UK*, the pilot of *Still Open All Hours*, *The British Soap Awards*, *8 Out of 10 Cats Does Countdown*, *A Question of Sport*, *Alan Carr's Epic Gameshow*, *Who Wants to Be a Millionaire?*, *BBC Children in Need* and *BBC Sports Personality of the Year*.

Given that time had moved on and Gary and Phoebe were now living in 1962, it was decided to give *Goodnight Sweetheart*'s familiar theme song a new arrangement and sound that was more in keeping with the era. This task was awarded to Keith Strachan. 'I was the musical supervisor and later the director of *Dreamboats and Petticoats*, a jukebox musical written by Laurence and Maurice. We have also worked together on the follow-ups called *Dreamboats and Miniskirts*, *Save the Last Dance for Me* and *Dreamboats and Petticoats: Bringing on Back the Good Times*. That explains why they asked me to come up with a Beatles version of the *Goodnight Sweetheart* theme tune. My son, Matthew, also became involved because he helped create the track and we used his studio in Twickenham. It had been my original intention to put together a Beatles group, but the budget didn't stretch that far. So, Matthew and I created a virtual track and I booked Damian Edwards (who I'd worked with on several rock musicals) to sing the song. Matthew and I provided the backing vocals and I played the harmonica – a must-have for an early Beatles pastiche! The song and cues took approximately three days to record.'

Keith has worked extensively in theatre and television as director, musical director, arranger and composer. His theatre credits as director include the West End runs and national tours of *Elvis the Musical* and *Dancing in the Streets* and the national tour of *Laughter in the Rain*. In the eighties, Keith worked in television, as a musical director and arranger on shows such as the variety show *Live from Her Majesty's*, the talent show *New Faces* and the satire series *Spitting Image*. He continues to work in television but principally as a composer. His many credits include the sitcom *The Detectives*, the game show *Talking Telephone Numbers* and the quiz show *Who Wants to Be A Millionaire?* In 2008, the music he composed for the latter was used in the film *Slumdog Millionaire*, which went on to win an Oscar for best film.

The production designer who worked on the special was Anthea Nelson. 'During the summer of 2016, I designed a comedy sitcom pilot called *Split* for Retort,' she said. 'It was written by Roy Clarke and filmed in Harrogate. Shortly afterwards, I was invited to design the *Goodnight Sweetheart* special. I was engaged for about six weeks, which included pre-production and filming in London and Salford.

'As the production designer, my responsibility is always to firstly visualise the script, collaborating with the producer and director. Practical issues that involve team management, budgeting and scheduling also get thrown into the mix.

'The script for the special was very specific, design wise, and the studio sets had to enable the director to accomplish those scenes. As a designer you always try to be as efficient as possible with both budget, time and effort. We built sets as effectively as possible for the script.'

As a production designer, Anthea's other television credits include the teen drama *Girls in Love*, the ninety-minute football drama *Marvellous*, and the family drama *Free Rein*. Meanwhile, as an art director, the programmes she has worked on include the warm-hearted drama series *Where the Heart Is*, the crime drama *Wire in the Blood*, and the critically acclaimed veterinary drama *All Creatures Great and Small*.

Having been involved in the original opening titles sequence back in 1993, Paul Peppiate was asked to help reimagine the cinema poster for the new special. 'I asked the designer Jason Geeves at The Works in Leeds to create a 1960s-style poster, but with a present-day London skyline,' said Paul. 'The World War Two German bombers were replaced with a jet airliner, and we added fireworks as a nod to the explosions that wartime London suffered.

'The poster was created in Adobe Illustrator and Photoshop and animated in After Effects. The completed poster sequence was then sent to the production team to add into the footage of Nicholas Lyndhurst walking past the poster.'

In early July 2016, the news was announced to the media that *Goodnight Sweetheart* was set to return for a special as part of the Landmark Sitcom Season. Laurence and Maurice were quoted as saying:

Gary has been trying for the last seventeen years to find a way back to the present.

Now he's found one, and he's asked us to turn it into a television show, featuring much-loved old *Goodnight Sweetheart* friends and one or two new ones.

Jon Rolph, the new executive producer, added:

I've long been keen to catch up with the life and various times of Gary Sparrow, so it's an absolute delight to see *Goodnight Sweetheart* take its place in the landmark sitcom season.

Shane Allen, the then controller of BBC Comedy Commissioning, said:

The whole sitcom season is geared towards giving comedy royalty their due recognition, and in *Goodnight Sweetheart* we have heavyweight writing and performing talents reunited in this hugely popular and fondly remembered show. The conceptual update is sublime, and it was heart-skipping stuff to read – it's an absolute belter.

The first cast read-through was held at FremantleMedia on Stephen Street, London, on Wednesday 20 July 2016. The first rehearsal then took place at the American International Church on Tottenham Court Road, London, on Friday 5 August 2016 at 10.00am. Rehearsals continued on Saturday 6 August 2016. No rehearsals took place on Sunday 7 August 2016. Rehearsals continued in earnest on Monday 8 August 2016. This included a producer's run at 3.00pm.

The studio get-in at HQ1 at dock10 at MediaCity began on Monday 8 August 2016. The studio was booked for seven days. Anthea, the production manager, remembers this week well. 'We had an art department team in both London and Salford,' she said. 'The props team, brilliantly led by Gary Watson, were dividing up and striking locations in London while "time travelling" to Salford to pre-dress the various studio sets. Terry Jones was my exceptional production buyer who had arranged a magical logistical schedule with prop transport arriving at dock10 and the London locations. The most economical prop hire system was to hire everything from London and transport to Salford. With limited budgets, having a clever team makes all the difference to successful planning. Additional construction in London was organised by art director Siobhan Pemberton who did a great job throughout the show. The corrugated partition at Duckett's Passage and the Duckett's Village CNC gobo arch were made by RDW Scenery. All the location signage cover-ups in London were made by the fabulous M and A Brown Signs Ltd in Manchester.'

The first location filming began in London on Tuesday 9 August 2016. 'The locations were dressed the day before,' explained Anthea. 'There were four locations: Yvonne's flat and the bus stop filmed at Arlington Square, Hoof and Claw and My Ding-a-Ling at Hoxton Market and Duckett's Passage was filmed at Ezra Street.'

The location filming saw Nicholas return to Ezra Street for the first time since series five. 'We didn't get the chance to do many takes on the first scene,' he said. 'This is because the dog who played Ron was getting bored of walking up to the corrugated iron wall. He even sat down at one point. The poor thing obviously didn't understand what filming is about!'

Rehearsals continued at the American International Church on Wednesday 10 August 2016, while the location scenes filmed the previous day were edited.

Meanwhile in HQ1 at MediaCity in Salford, the sets were being completed and dressed. 'The fantastic studio sets were made in Yorkshire by John Thorpe and his team at WRFCS Ltd,' said Anthea. 'They arrived with John's military precision and co-ordination, with Gary Watson ensuring we were as economical with our time and energy working around each other to complete the fit-up and pre-dress.'

There were more rehearsals held at the American International Church on Thursday 11 August 2016; and there was another producer's run at 12.30pm. Martin, the director, and Humphrey, the producer, viewed the edit for the location scenes for changes after rehearsals.

Having performed the night before in their respective theatre productions, Emma and Victor made their way to Salford in readiness for filming the pre-records with Nicholas for the special.

On Friday 12 August 2016, the following scenes were filmed outside HQ1 at dock10 starting at 10.00am:

Sc.11	Ext. *Dragons' Den* Studio	Gary/Ron/Bouncer
Sc.12	Int. Ron's Car	Gary/Ron
Sc.13	Ext. *Dragons' Den* Studio	Gary/Ron/Yvonne

The following scenes were then recorded inside HQ1:

Sc.5	Int. Hospital Maternity Ward	Gary/George/Midwife
Sc.6	Int. Hoof and Claw Gents' Loo	Gary
Sc.17	Int. Hoof and Claw Gents' Loo	Gary
Sc.19	Int. Hoof and Claw Gents' Loo	Gary
Sc.9	Int. *Dragons' Den* Studio	Yvonne
	Opening Titles Cinema Poster/Green Screen	Gary

Sc.8   C/A tight shot of Gary holding Kyle's iPad
Sc.9   Yvonne on *Dragons' Den* Insert

Audio recordings were also made during the day of Gary's mother's screams (the nearest we ever came to the character appearing in an episode) in Scene 5 and Yvonne's voice on the carphone speakers for Scene 12. These would be dubbed over the edited scenes in preparation for showing during the studio audience recording.

After completing their scenes, Victor and Emma travelled back to London early for their evening shows. Elizabeth and Christopher then drove to Salford on the Friday night and stayed in a hotel in preparation for the studio call the following morning.

On the following day, Saturday 13 August 2016, the sets from the previous day were struck. The seating for the studio audience was then set up for the recording the following day. From 11.00am, the cast, apart from Emma and Victor who had to perform in their respective theatre productions back in London, rehearsed on the sets in HQ1. The sets required for the Sunday evening studio audience recording were the Royal Oak, My Ding-a-Ling and Yvonne's flat.

Anthea's memories of the Royal Oak set prove just how much preparation has to go into dressing a set. 'The scenes in the pub included a period 1960s television,' she recalled. 'It was supplied by Golden Age TV, with playback footage and tech support supplied by the brilliant David Williamson at Revolver TV. As additional action props, we organised food and Gary's birthday cake to look edible and authentic for the period. All the graphics (both period and contemporary) including posters and beer labels and any other visual props had to be originally created by the art department for clearance and compliance.'

A technical run took place in HQ1 at 12.30pm with all the heads of department. The pre-records from Friday's filming were then edited for the Sunday recording.

The next day, Sunday 14 August 2016, was to see the first recording of *Goodnight Sweetheart* since the final episode of series six on Thursday 13 May 1999. The schedule for the day was as follows:

9.30am   Camera Rehearsal (5 Cams)
         Sc. 1, 3, 10, 21 (The Royal Oak)
1.00pm   Lunch
2.00pm   Camera Rehearsal cont'd
         Sc. 14 (Yvonne's House)
         Sc. 08 (Phone Shop)

4.00pm	Dress Run
	Inc. Pre-RX Dog shots with Gary
6.00pm	Supper
6.45pm	Audience in
7.00pm	Warm-up (Ted Robbins and Laurence Marks)
	Inc. VT Clip from Last Episode + Intro. Cast
7.15pm	Record
10.00pm	Audience clear then de-rig/Strike

One of Laurence's favourite recollections of the evening was taking part in the warm-up with Ted. 'I introduced the cast at the recording,' he confirmed. 'The place erupted, especially when I announced that Gary Sparrow was now living in 1962.'

Once the recording was completed, the get-out began. The prop hire dressings were logged and prepared for returning to the hirers. The construction team then began to strike the remaining sets. By lunchtime the following day, Monday 15 August 2016, everything in the studio was cleared.

Post-production editing and dubbing took place between Wednesday 17 August 2016 and Friday 19 August 2016. This was followed by another two days on Monday 22 August 2016 and Tuesday 23 August 2016.

As the special begins, we discover it's now October 1962. Gary, Phoebe and Michael are living back in the Royal Oak. Gary is attempting to fix their black-and-white television set, which is sitting on top of the bar. Gary assures them he's nearly finished. Michael is concerned that the world is going to end and they're missing the programme. Phoebe reminds him that war is no laughing matter, especially as there are now atomic bombs. Gary realises that the best way to fix the television will be with 'percussive maintenance' and hits the television set with his hand. This makes the picture come back and they hear an announcer say that Mr Khrushchev has ordered the dismantling of the USSR's nuclear missile bases in Cuba. Phoebe hugs Gary, relieved that the crisis is over. The television set loses its picture again, but Gary says it doesn't matter now. The main thing is the Russians have backed down. He reminds her that he said that normal service would be resumed. Reg remarks that Gary was right about Cuba just like he was about Suez, the Berlin Wall and skiffle. Gary admits he gets lucky.

The crisis being avoided has made Gary hungry. Having discovered that there's rissoles on the menu again, he asks who fancies fish and chips instead. They all agree, and Gary heads off with their dog, Ron, with the intention of giving him a walk on the way to the chippy. He heads towards Duckett's Passage, which is now all boarded up with large pieces of corrugated iron, decorated with posters of the day. Despite loving Phoebe and Michael – and, of course, his dog, Ron – he admits that he's so bored. Even more depressing is that he's missing his future. He speculates that in 2016, people will probably have landed on Mars, cured cancer and achieved European unity. And he's missing out on it all. Not for the first time in the last seventeen years, Gary tries to find the time portal and, with the palms of both hands, push his way through, back into the future. Once again, he fails. While he's doing this, a young couple catch him. Gary tries to explain himself by saying he's a big David Bowie fan. Feeling embarrassed, Gary takes Ron back to the pub.

When Gary returns to the Royal Oak, Phoebe and Michael are confused as to where the fish and chips are. Realising, Gary admits having got sidetracked. Reg, meanwhile, thinks Gary is losing his marbles in his old age. Gary protests that he's only fifty-two – though, as Phoebe reminds him, only until next week.

Michael, his engineering days still in the future, has become a poet – although his efforts don't seem to be impressing Phoebe and Reg. Indeed, Phoebe says she knew they should have apprenticed him to Sid the plumber.

Gary, meanwhile, is concerned as to why he's forgotten his own impending birthday. He wonders if it's delayed brain damage. After all, his mum always said he'd been dropped on his head as a baby. Reg admits the same happened to him. Phoebe tells him not to worry and that he can't turn the clock back. Gary bends down to the dog, Ron, and tells him he doesn't have to turn the clock back, because he needs to be at St Mary's Hospital next Thursday, because that's the day he's being born!

As planned, Gary makes for the hospital. He walks along a corridor and discovers his young father sitting and waiting nervously for Gary's birth. Gary sits next to him and, without realising, they both display some characteristics that make it clear they're father and son. Gary's father, George, introduces himself and Gary replies that his name is Gary Lineker. George mentions that they are going to call the baby Gary if it's a boy. When George takes a snifter from a small bottle, Gary tells him he should be keeping his wits about him. When his last child was born here the midwife nearly dropped him on his head, so this time he's going to be in there with his wife to make sure it doesn't happen. The idea of being in there with his wife makes George feel a little nauseous. Gary points out that having been there at the conception, he should be there at the birth. George's wife, Gladys, starts to call for him from the delivery room and Gary encourages him to go and be with her. He still isn't keen, but Gary guides him in the direction of the delivery room, accidentally telling him to 'make sure they don't drop me on my head'. The sight that meets George's eyes instantly makes him faint. The midwife notes that the excuse for a father has fainted and asks who Gary is; he tells her he must be the excuse for an uncle. She hands Gary as a baby over to Gary as an adult, and this causes a discontinuity in space-time that propels Gary back to the future and the year 2016.

Gary finds himself emerging from a toilet cubicle. It is in an extension of his old shop in the East End. It has now become a restaurant called Hoof and Claw. Gary emerges from the shop and is met with the sight of an eclectic mix of young people, seventeen years after he became trapped in the past. He becomes aware of the obsessive use of mobile phones and selfie sticks. He also notes that Duckett's Plaza has now been pedestrianised and renamed Duckett's Village. He tries to attract the attention of passers-by, but they're too involved with speaking on their phones or listening to music on their headphones. Gary spots a row of three old red phone boxes in the street and heads to them. He opens the first to discover a cash machine, while the second now houses a defibrillator. He moves to the third and discovers it is now a small coffee stall, complete with assistant.

Gary spots a small mobile phone shop called My Ding-a-Ling and heads in its direction. Inside the shop, Gary feels like he's entered another world. The assistant takes a pull on his vape before offering his help. Gary asks what's happened to the phone boxes. The assistant points out that no one uses them any more. After revealing he doesn't have a phone, the assistant offers to sell him a reconditioned smartphone for fifty pounds – or a dumb phone if he only wants to talk to people! He reminds Gary of all the features mobile phones now have. Gary looks flummoxed. The assistant asks where he's been. Gary explains that he's been away for seventeen years, but the assistant thinks he means in prison. But far from judging him, he is impressed at the idea that he's been inside for a long stretch. Gary tells him he needs a phone to call a friend. The assistant offers to lend his phone, but Gary has no idea how to operate it. He tries to tell him Ron's phone number, but barely gets beyond '04…' before the assistant stops him, pointing out that mobile numbers all start with 07. He starts to wonder whether Gary was actually let out or just escaped! The assistant offers to Google Ron's number, but it's not listed. Gary then suggests he search for his wife, Lady Yvonne Sparrow. The assistant is amazed that Gary knows her as he recognises the name from her appearances on *Dragon's Den*. He shows Gary a clip of her on YouTube.

Back at the Royal Oak in 1962, Phoebe, Michael and Reg are concerned as to Gary's whereabouts as it's his birthday. Reg suggests that he might be doing his secret work, like in the war. Michael is confused, believing he was a songwriter, which Reg explains was only a cover story. But Phoebe confirms that Gary did write lovely songs in the war, and she performs a couple of lines from 'Wind Beneath My Wings' as an example. Reg personally preferred 'Hit Me With Your

Rhythm Stick' and attempts to perform part of the chorus. Phoebe explains that Gary gave up writing songs, which Reg says was due to his having been abandoned by his moose, as opposed to his muse. Michael laments that he doesn't have his father's songwriting talents as everyone is starting up groups. He explains he heard a new one on Radio Luxembourg called The Beatles and gives a blast of the song he heard on his mouth organ. Reg recognises it as one of the songs Gary claims to have written called 'Love Me Do'. He mentions they used to sing it down in the air-raid shelter when the doodlebugs were coming over. Michael asks whether his father has finally sold one of his songs. Phoebe says she wouldn't be surprised if it hasn't been stolen from Gary. She mentions that half the songs in *My Fair Lady* were stolen from Michael's father. It's 'I Could Have Danced All Night' all over again, she explains.

Having discovered where *Dragon's Den* is made, Gary goes to the entrance of Studio A and tells a security man he's there to see Lady Sparrow. Gary is amused when the man asks if she's expecting him. He believes she will want to see him as he's her husband. Not convinced, and not just because of the clothes he wears, the security man asks Gary to wait with the other 'husbands'. In reality this is three men waiting to meet her for autographs or selfies. Gary takes one look at them and decides against it. He goes to cross the road and steps in front of an oncoming car. The driver gets out and starts to tell Gary off for almost getting knocked down when they recognise each other – it's Ron. Once his old friend has checked that Gary is not some kind of strange apparition, they give each other a manly hug for the first time in seventeen years. Ron asks when he landed back in the present and Gary tells him today, an hour ago. He asks how, but stops Gary before he can answer, saying it doesn't matter as it never made sense anyway! Ron points out that it's Gary's birthday, and Gary is impressed that he remembered. He mentions that each year he and Yvonne raise a toast to the best man they ever knew. Gary is again impressed until Ron tells him of course they don't and that he's a 'duplicitous egomaniac'. Ron is still upset that he ran out on them. Gary explains that he didn't intend to. Ron tells him to get in the car and tell him everything. They get in and Gary, impressed by the car, comments that it's like something from *Star Wars*!

Ron explains that he's there to collect Yvonne. Gary asks if he and Yvonne are now an item. Ron confirms that they're not, but admits, in his usual eloquent way, that he had hoped for a while that they could have been in order to comfort each other due to the grief at their loss. However, Yvonne put those thoughts out of Ron's mind pretty sharpish! He explains that out of the goodness of her heart Yvonne allows him to live in her basement in return for doing odd jobs, including chauffeuring her around. He asks whether Gary is back in the old routine: two wives, two time zones and lots of lying and deceit and him having to cover for Gary – because he's really missed it! Gary says there will be no more lying. He just wants to apologise to Yvonne for the pain he's caused. Ron isn't sure she will accept his apology.

Yvonne calls Ron to ask if he's outside. Ron replies by impersonating the chauffeur Parker from *Thunderbirds*. She isn't impressed and reminds him he's always doing that and is so predictable. To get his own back, Ron tells Gary to get in the back of the car as he intends to show her he's not predicable. For once, the time traveller does as he's asked.

Yvonne leaves the studio and reluctantly signs an autograph and poses for a selfie and another photo before walking over to the car. Ron asks her how the recording went, and she tells him it was the usual bunch of losers and fantasists. Ron sarcastically tells her she's loved on that show because of her empathy. He then tells her he has a fantastic investment opportunity for her. She says she's not interested after his cat-cloning debacle. He assures her this is different. He has met someone that has discovered the secret of time travel. She laughs as Ron opens the door. Gary looks out and says hello. She looks at Gary and promptly faints sideways onto the ground.

Back at Yvonne's luxury London home, Gary tries to explain to Yvonne how he was able to get to the present and appeared at some trendy burger bar that was once his shop. Ron explains that Hoof and Claw belongs to Yvonne, who tells him there are thirty-five branches and counting. Ron tells Gary his old shop was the first. Proving that his selfish streak is still there, Gary asks if this makes him a partner. Yvonne tells him no as she had to declare him dead, as she needed to move on. He asks if she has remarried. She laughs and tells him once bitten, twice shy. However, she admits that she hasn't lived like a nun. Ron tells him it's true and that he's had to soundproof his living quarters in the basement. She explains to Gary that he broke her heart. He tells her he didn't mean to. She's not convinced and asks sarcastically if someone forced him to be a bigamist. Gary reminds her he got trapped in the past. Yvonne asks if he would still have been stringing two wives along if the time portal had stayed open. Gary tries to assure her that he always loved them both. When she asks if he and Phoebe are still together, he confirms that they are. She then sarcastically checks that he hasn't got a bit on the side tucked away during the Boer War. Gary opens his wallet and shows her a photo of him with Phoebe and Michael. Yvonne tells him she can see why he preferred Phoebe to her. He says he didn't, not exactly. He tells her he kept going back because he always felt inadequate around Yvonne. This is like a red rag to a bull and she is annoyed that he's basically accusing her of being the reason for his actions.

To try and calm things down, Ron asks to look at the photo. He asks if that is Michael, his son, in the photo. Gary confirms it is. Ron notices the dog, which Gary says is a fat lazy old bugger: all he ever does is eat and sleep. Ron asks what they called him, and Gary's expression confirms that he is named Ron. He tells Ron they named him when he was a puppy and they didn't realise he was going to be such a disappointment.

Yvonne sarcastically thanks Gary for coming back from the dead to churn up all the feelings she had for him. He asks what sort of feelings. Angry, vengeful feelings, she replies. Yvonne tells him it's time he went back to his family because with all the will in the world there's nothing for him in 2016. At that moment the front door is heard to be opened and closed. Ron disagrees with Yvonne's remark. Ellie, Yvonne's troublesome sixteen-year-old daughter, then walks in and drops her bag. She is the epitome of a sulky and spoilt teenager. Yvonne questions what she's doing home and is told she ran away from school – again. Ellie makes a jokey remark about the chances of her being expelled from school again, which Yvonne reminds her would be the third time. Ellie complains that her mother only sends her to private school so she can bring weird blokes back to the house. Ron tells her he's not weird and Ellie says that Gary is though. Yvonne tells her he's an old family friend.

A further row, which starts with Ellie asking if she can have a glass of wine, sees Yvonne telling her that in the morning she will drive her back to Cheltenham Ladies' College where she can apologise for her behaviour and beg for mercy. Ron interjects to remind Yvonne that she has the House of Lords committee on child neglect the following morning. She tells Ellie that Ron will drive her back instead. As the row reaches its crescendo, Yvonne sends Ellie to her room, and her daughter dutifully goes while simultaneously having a strop.

Gary takes pleasure that she's Yvonne's daughter. Yvonne tells him not to criticise her as it wasn't her fault she grew up without a father. The penny drops and Gary realises she means him. She tells Gary she didn't find out she was pregnant with Ellie until he disappeared back in time. Gary asks why she never told her about him. Yvonne says she could hardly tell her that her father is an incompetent time traveller. Instead, Yvonne says she told Ellie her father was a 'two-timing bastard' who abandoned them when she was pregnant. She tells him not to tell her otherwise. Gary mentions that he's hardly likely to have the chance to say anything to her now, which is how Yvonne wants things to remain. With that, Gary takes the hint that it's time to leave. Ron says goodbye to him and gives him a big hug. Gary goes to leave but stops to ask if Ron could give him a lift, but Yvonne says he's busy and there's a Tube station down the road. Gary reminds her he only has old money. As he's met with silence, Gary tells them he feels like a walk anyway. Gary departs and Yvonne goes and hugs Ron for comfort. He takes this as an excuse to try and make the hug more intimate, but she repels him.

As Gary walks slowly down the street, he comes across Ellie who is checking her phone while waiting at a bus stop. She sighs as he approaches. He tries to break the ice by asking if they still have buses. Ellie mentions that she's seen one, but never been on one. Gary mentions her mum thinks she's still in her room. He asks how she escaped and is told she's a member of the school's abseiling club. She tells Gary that she's got to get back to school before lights out and she isn't being expelled. She merely had a study day and needed to come home for her tablet. Not realising what a tablet is, Gary is concerned that she's ill. He tries to tell Ellie to cut Yvonne some slack as she's not so bad as she thinks. Ellie tells him he should try living with her and he accidentally tells her that he did. He then covers his tracks by saying they lived together as students in a shared house before she was born. Ellie then asks Gary if he knew her dad. He pauses and says he knew him a bit; they were around at the same time. Gary then tells her that her father was a bit immature and self-centred and a bit of a dreamer, but not the 'tosser' that Yvonne told Ellie he was. By now, Ellie is thawing and displaying a maturity and side that it's clear her mother rarely, if at all, ever sees. She asks why her father walked out on them. Gary explains that maybe he didn't know about her. Ellie tells Gary that although she hasn't told her mum, she plans to go looking for her father when she's eighteen. But she's afraid he won't want to know her. Gary replies that he bets he would.

Ellie's taxi arrives, scaring Gary, who's not used to such quiet cars, in the process. She tells Gary he's okay for a 'weirdo' and 'odd, but interesting'. Gary smiles. She asks if he would like a lift, and he readily accepts. As the car moves off, we hear the Adele song 'Hello' playing on the car's radio. He asks the driver to turn it up.

Gary heads back to Hoof and Claw. Upon reaching the men's toilets, he discovers that someone is using the cubicle that he arrived in. He knocks on the door, saying he needs to 'go', which clearly has a double meaning. The occupant comes out and Gary goes inside and finds the time portal again. To his relief, on passing through he realises he is back in Duckett's Passage in 1962. Deciding to check to see if the portal has remained open, he quickly steps back through and finds himself in the cubicle again, only now with a man trying to go about his 'business'. Gary hastily departs again, leaving the man more than a little shocked.

Back at the Royal Oak, Phoebe is on the phone. She has been ringing around hospitals to try and find out Gary's whereabouts. The publican has prepared food and decorations for his birthday party. She tells Reg and Michael that he's not at the Hackney Hospital. Phoebe is about to ring someone else when Gary comes bursting through the door. He tells them he's been in hospital all day having tests. Reg thinks that means he's been there to apply for a job, but Gary says they were tests on his brain regarding his memory loss. When Phoebe asks what they said, he jokes that he can't remember. They laugh and then he assures them they said everything is fine. He hugs Phoebe and says things couldn't be better. She wishes him many happy returns. Reg and Michael start to sing happy birthday, but she tells them she hasn't lit his candles yet, which his son quips will take all night.

Reg asks Gary to play one of his songs at the piano. He isn't sure he's in the mood. Michael asks him to sing 'Love Me Do'. But Gary says he doesn't know that one. Phoebe reminds him he wrote it! Gary says he will play them a new song he has written. Reg is delighted to discover that Gary has found his moose again! Gary sits down at the piano in the bar and sings 'Hello' by Adele.

One of the best parts of making the new special for Laurence and Maurice was reuniting with their leading actor. 'We got to know Nick more during the making of the special than we did through all the episodes of the past six series,' said Laurence. 'For instance, we went to dinner with him in Manchester.'

For Nicholas, it gave him the unexpected chance to play a cherished role once more. 'I didn't think I would play Gary Sparrow again after the sixth series ended,' he admitted. 'The special was lovely to do, and it was an absolute joy to see everyone. It felt like we hadn't been away. We had kept in touch and had met up at the occasional social event.'

Elizabeth was thrilled to be able to play Phoebe again. 'I was totally surprised when I was told about the special in 2016,' said the actress. 'By strange coincidence, the director was Martin Dennis, who I'd also worked with on *Men Behaving Badly*.

'It took me a while to get back into playing the character. I told Nick to keep an ear out in case I lost the East End accent!

'I thought my hair was a work of art. The hair and make-up artist had a practice run in London during a break from rehearsals. At my costume fitting, I was presented with a selection of dresses. I picked a beautiful pink polyester dress as it reminded me of my favourite dress when I was four years old!

'Everything went really well at the recording and the audience loved it. We certainly crammed a lot in that week!'

Despite being a hectic week, Emma also enjoyed the experience. 'We had the best time rehearsing and recording the episode,' she confirmed. 'The script was so good. Everyone's family came up for the recording in Salford; many of the crew were the same as well.'

Victor was surprised and pleased when Laurence and Maurice announced they were going to record a special. There was one particular moment during the recording that he particularly savoured. 'I don't think it matters how many words or speeches you have in an episode as one good line can be enough to get a big laugh,' he said. 'When Gary showed Ron a photo of his dog and he realised the dog's name was Ron, this got a massive laugh from the audience, which I really loved.'

As with the previous episodes of *Goodnight Sweetheart*, the special included a supporting cast. Gary and Phoebe's son, Michael, was played by Tim Preston. At the time, Tim had not long left drama school, and so the chance to play the role was a welcome early break for the young actor. 'The first audition was held by Susie Parriss at her office,' recalled Tim. 'I then had a second audition at Retort's office at FremantleMedia. Once again, Susie was there as were the writers Laurence and Maurice and the director Martin Dennis.

'*Goodnight Sweetheart* was my first television job. Although I was aware of the sitcom, I must admit I had never watched it before. In order to catch up, I watched a few episodes to get an idea of how Michael fitted into the story.

'It was really scary coming into the read-through as Nicholas, Victor, Elizabeth and Emma were already so familiar with each other and a very close-knit cast. Esme and I were very much the newcomers and it was terrifying and exciting all at the same time! I was in awe of Nick because I had obviously seen him in *Only Fools and Horses*.

'It was nice to have rehearsals because you don't always get the opportunity in television. It meant we could gently ease ourselves into the work. With an old-style sitcom, all the rehearsal and work build to the culmination of a live show in front of a studio audience. This means there isn't the same pressure as a performance in a theatre because you could go again if you made a mistake. However, you still feel the same buzz as a theatre performance. All my scenes were recorded in front of an audience. The best advice I was given was to play to the camera but use the audience as a guide.'

Originally it was suggested that Tim should learn to play the song 'Love Me Do' on the harmonica for one scene in this episode. 'The director soon realised that there wouldn't be enough time for me to learn properly,' admitted Tim. 'So, in the end I mimed playing the song to a track.'

Tim continues to add to his list of credits as an actor. His theatre roles have included Robert in the Mark Hayhurst drama *First Light* at the Chichester Festival Theatre, Slightly in a spellbinding reinvention J. M. Barrie's play *Peter Pan* at the Regent's Park Open Air Theatre, London, and Josh in Katherine Chandler's striking play *Lose Yourself* at the Sherman Theatre, Cardiff. For television, Tim's other credits include Duncan McKenzie in the medical drama Holby City, Charlie in the comedy Warren, which starred Martin Clunes, and George

Allen in the sitcom *Sneakerhead*. His film work includes playing Prince J in a parody of the fantasy drama *Game of Thrones*, entitled *Purge of Thrones*.

Also appearing was Liam Jeavons as Gary's nervous young father, George Sparrow. On stage, his credits have included Passepartout in an adaptation of the Jules Verne adventure novel *Around the World in Eighty Days* at Vienna's English Theatre in Austria; Mitch Ruscitti in the Henry Lewis, Henry Shields and Jonathan Sayer smash-and-grab play *The Comedy About a Bank Robbery* at the Criterion Theatre, London, and on tour; and as a company member in the Daniel Clarkson, Jefferson Turner and Richard Hurst Olivier award-nominated festive celebration *Potted Panto* at the Apollo Theatre, London. Liam's other television roles have included PC Tommy Perkins in the police drama *WPC 56*, Carl in the daytime medical drama *Doctors*, and Young Mickey in the crime drama *Sherwood*.

The unimpressed midwife was played by Angela Murray. Angela has appeared in several high-profile television series. Her other roles have ranged from a pregnant woman in the sitcom *Two Pints of Lager and a Packet of Crisps* to Marchella in the comedy drama *Drop Dead Gorgeous*. She has also played characters including WPC Jones, Joanne Riggs and a paramedic in the soap opera *Coronation Street*.

Also, Khali Best displayed his talents for comic timing and delivery when he played the phone salesman in this special. His actual character name, which didn't appear on the credits, was Kyle. Early in his career, Khali played Anthony Justin 'AJ' James in Tarell Alvin McCraney's coming-of-age play *Choir Boy* at the Royal Court Theatre, London. He then played the regular role of Dexter Hartman in the soap opera *EastEnders*, for which he won Best Newcomer at the National Television Awards 2014, from 2013 until 2015. His other television roles include Mick Hayes in the detective drama *Endeavour*, a policeman in the sitcom *Hold the Sunset*, which starred John Cleese and Alison Steadman, and Khadeem in the crime drama *Top Boy*. Khali's film credits, meanwhile, include Killy/Kiron in the acclaimed crime drama *Blue Story*.

Although he acted as the warm-up artist at many of the recordings of *Goodnight Sweetheart*, including this special, Ted Robbins had never appeared on screen in this sitcom before. Therefore, the role of the bouncer who attempts to keep Yvonne's 'husbands' under control at the studio entrance was the perfect opportunity for him. Julie Sykes, who returned to this special as the first assistant director and floor manager, agreed. 'Ted is a brilliant stand-up comedian,' she said. 'He would talk to the audience whenever we stopped recording. He would remind the audience of the story when we got going again, and he did a brilliant job of bringing the cast, crew and audience all together. When we made the special in 2016, we just had to have Ted back, as he too was part of the *Goodnight Sweetheart* family.'

During the casting process for the *Goodnight Sweetheart* special, Emma was given an unexpected revelation. 'Susie Parriss rang me and said Yvonne now had a sixteen-year-old daughter,' the actress explained. 'She had seen my daughter Esme Coy in a play and asked if I minded if she suggested her for the role. I kept very much out of all the casting. Esme had three recalls for the part of Ellie. I was, of course, so pleased when they offered her the role.' Nicholas was equally pleased with the casting. 'I was delighted that Esme played our daughter,' he enthused.

Esme can still recall a moment during the audition process that she believes helped her to win the role. 'I remember the final audition with the producer, director and casting director,' she said. 'They were so lovely and friendly. I had to do the scene where Ellie is with Gary, her dad, at the bus stop. Apparently, they liked the way I said my final line. It felt like it left the scene on a cliffhanger and would make the viewers wonder if the characters will see each other again.'

The special was Esme's first multi-camera sitcom. 'I felt massively daunted about joining such an established and popular programme,' said the actress. 'It felt reassuring to join at the same time as Tim Preston, who played Michael. Being similar in age, Tim and I had a laugh during rehearsals, and it was one of his first television jobs too. So being a newbie with him took the pressure off!'

Esme's second of two scenes was filmed on location. 'We rehearsed the bus stop scene before we went to Arlington Square,' she said. 'But this was my first time in front of camera, so I was super nervous. It was amazing to be able to work with Nick who totally put me at ease off and on camera. I remember it being really windy on location but it kind of worked with the whole "Winds of Change" vibe to the scene!'

Despite the stress of the week leading up to the main recording day, there was still time for some good-hearted banter between Esme and her mother, Emma. 'One of my abiding memories of the rehearsal period was getting annoyed at my mum for giving me a note,' she remembered. 'So, as daughters and mothers do, we bickered a bit (jokingly of course!), but the costume and make-up team overheard. They didn't know we were related, so they just thought I was being a bratty young actress! When my mum and I were in the make-up chair before the show, they said how much we looked alike. "Wait," I said. "Did you guys not realise that we're related!?" They hadn't realised because we have different acting surnames. Thankfully, this stopped them thinking of me as a prima donna after they found out!'

Working on this episode of *Goodnight Sweetheart* was a unique learning curve for Esme. 'Fortunately, I had Nick, Vic and my mum to talk me through how to play to a studio audience, while also trying to stay natural for the small screen,' she said. 'It was a little odd acting with my mum – especially when I had to be so rude to her in my first scene! We all had so much fun doing it, though. It was extremely hard to try and contain the giggles!'

Victor was more than happy to mentor the actress where he could while making the special. 'For me, the biggest highlight of making the special was Emma's daughter, Esme, appearing in the cast,' he said. 'It really helped make the cast feel like a family.'

One piece of advice that Victor gave to Esme on the recording day has stayed with her. 'Before I went on for the last take of the studio scene, Vic said to me backstage, "Just really go for it!",' she said. 'That extra push made me give the performance that you see in the episode.'

Esme continues to build her profile and credits as an actress. Her theatre roles include playing Laura in the Andrew Braidford play *Relative* at the Lyric Hammersmith, London, Celia in the William Shakespeare comedy *As You Like it* at the Anatomy Museum, King's College, London, and Ella in Angel Adeoye's short play *Ella and Louis* at the Bomb Factory Art Foundation, London. Her other television credits include Megan Gold in the medical drama *Doctors*, Rowella in the period drama *Poldark*, and Miss Goring in the Emmy-nominated drama *Bridgerton*. Esme's film appearances include playing a goth in the short comedy *Test Case*.

The new thirty-minute special of *Goodnight Sweetheart* was broadcast by BBC One on Friday 2 September 2016 at 9.00pm. The reaction on social media was incredible, with the overriding verdict being that viewers had not only enjoyed the special but were keen to see a full series commissioned. The gamble had paid off for all concerned. But despite there being an appetite for more episodes, the BBC appeared to have other ideas. 'The reason had little to do with the popularity of the one-off,' said Laurence. 'Charlotte Moore, BBC One's controller of programmes, had been given a "beating" when she took to the stage at the Edinburgh International Television Festival. She was asked why she felt the need to return "classic" comedy to the screen rather than making new shows. It unnerved her and she felt she couldn't possibly make another series of *Goodnight Sweetheart*, largely because she had already committed to remaking *Porridge*. It was widely acknowledged that Charlotte Moore had made the wrong choice, for the viewing figures screamed out to her, "More *Goodnight Sweetheart*!" We had the original cast. *Porridge* didn't. Therefore, it was deemed a failure. We have to say we were astonished when we heard the news that Charlotte didn't commission a new series.'

Nicholas was disappointed that a new series of *Goodnight Sweetheart* wasn't commissioned by the BBC. 'Making the special made me thoughtful,' he said.

'It was like another chance to say thank you and goodbye to the sitcom. It would have been nice to have made another series if we'd had the same cast. I wouldn't have wanted to work with different people. I know Lo and Mo could have written it. I was surprised that the BBC chose to commission *Porridge* as I read that a RadioTimes.com poll said that sixty-five per cent of nearly four thousand voters named it the classic sitcom pilot they'd most like to see as a full series. I think the main problem was that the BBC wouldn't be able to provide the kind of budget that we would need to make it to the same standard as we did with the other six series.

'There was nothing like *Goodnight Sweetheart* and there still isn't. It was the most labour-intensive job I've ever worked on, but it was a joy to go to work every day. I miss working with the cast. Vic and I remain in touch to this day. I love him, he's brilliant. I would really like to work with him again. Same with Chris. He has perfect timing, as do Liz and Emma. I'm fortunate to call them all friends.

'We didn't think the series would be so popular with children, but to this day I still receive lots of fan mail from children.'

Elizabeth was surprised that the BBC didn't choose to proceed with a new series. 'The feedback after the episode was shown was phenomenal and we trended on Twitter for a couple of days,' said the actress. 'Sadly, the decision was made by the powers that be not to commission a full series. I must admit this surprised me and the rest of the cast.

'Everyone from the entire cast and crew was incredibly kind. It was a dream job. We have all stayed in touch. In fact, all of the gang came to my fiftieth birthday in Brighton.'

Also despondent at the outcome was Emma. 'We were all very disappointed we didn't go for another series,' she said. 'But we all still remain firm friends, supporting each other with whatever life throws at us.'

Despite the BBC's ruling on another series, Victor still remembers *Goodnight Sweetheart* as being one of his happiest jobs to date. 'There was a nice buzz all the time,' he confirmed. 'I count all the cast as dear friends.'

Christopher had been keen to play Reg again. 'Although the character was none too bright, he was a lovely, sweet man who had a heart as big as a house,' the actor said. 'I think it's a great, great shame that the BBC missed the boat to do another series back in 2017. Being in such a popular series meant I got taken more seriously and that led to roles I would not normally get offered.'

For the new cast members, Tim and Esme, the absence of a new series was particularly a shame. 'I would have liked to have made more episodes,' said Tim. 'At the time, there was definitely a feeling, even an assumption, that we should be making a series.'

Although the viewers have been left wondering if Ellie would ever find out the true identity of her father, there is another storyline that Esme was keen to explore. 'I would have wanted Ellie and Michael to turn out to be time travellers too!' she said.

Looking back, Julie Sykes realises how lucky she was to work on such an important series. 'I learned so much from the fantastic crew,' said Julie. 'I have since gone on to work with most of the crew on various other sitcoms over the last twenty years, and many have become good friends. Likewise, I have formed friendships with the cast members, and have had the very great pleasure of working with some of them on other projects over the years.

'There was a magic with *Goodnight Sweetheart*. The scripts were brilliant, the cast were always hardworking, and much fun to work with, and the crew were highly skilled. There was always a lovely atmosphere in the studio. This was down to the calmness of the producers and the directors, the funny scripts, and the total respect that the crew had for the cast, and more importantly the respect that the cast had for the crew. We laughed all the time. We formed our own family, and I, for one, was devastated that the series finished. I could happily have continued to spend three months every year in the company of these wonderful people.'

The idea of the sitcom being remade outside of the UK was considered. 'Both the US and Germany expressed serious interest in making their own version of *Goodnight Sweetheart*,' said Laurence. 'We visited Berlin to have serious discussions with a network, who wanted to set it in Berlin during the Second World War. Of course, the stakes were so much higher for Gary – he would have had the Gestapo on his tail – and that may well have increased the drama. But, as my notes remind me, the Germans became sensitive (and rightly so) about setting a comedy in Nazi Germany. As for the US, because they never saw warfare in the country during the Second World War, it was felt we should set it in another era. They kept leaning towards Prohibition, but for us that never quite worked. So goodbye USA.'

The idea of creating stage versions of sitcoms is nothing new. *Dad's Army*, *It Ain't Half Hot Mum* and *Bread* are just three series that were adapted for the theatre. Indeed, Marks and Gran's *Birds of a Feather* successfully made the transition. So why not *Goodnight Sweetheart*? 'The musical idea came to us while we were making the television series,' revealed Laurence. 'We thought no more of it until 2007, when we got together with an internationally renowned composer to write an "original" stage musical. However, people in the theatre couldn't understand why we would want original songs when the songs of the Second World War were just so moving and evocative. We said farewell to the composer and rewrote the book and included some wartime gems as well as hit songs of the 1980s, which was to be our "Now".'

A semi-professional try-out production of the musical debuted at the Brookside Theatre in Romford, Essex, on Wednesday 12 September 2018 and ran until Saturday 22 September 2018. This short run gave Laurence and Maurice a chance to see which parts of the musical worked and those that needed changing. 'The musical went through many further rewrites, moving the "Now" from the 1980s to present day, until we realised the music wasn't nearly as evocative,' said Laurence. 'Everyone who read the book of the musical became very excited by it but nothing else happened. It was to go into production in 2020, but then we were visited by Covid-19 and once more the show was thwarted.

'But at the back end of 2022 a top theatre producer by chance read the book and instantly said, "I really want to bring this to the stage!" We met, we discussed it with him, and with a following wind it might be that a large-scale production of *Goodnight Sweetheart – The Musical* could open in 2025.'

Thanks to the repeats on television, including the channel That's TV, and streaming services, including Britbox and ITVX, and DVD releases, *Goodnight Sweetheart* continues to be enjoyed and discovered by new generations.

'We really do receive at least five emails a week from all over the world, asking when the series is coming back,' confirmed Laurence. 'It certainly has touched the hearts of so many people. In terms of an idea, I would say it's the most inventive series we have ever created. We somehow managed to execute what seemed to us nigh on impossible. It was certainly up there with the best shows we created and wrote, and I still don't understand what it was about it that touched so many people of all ages. The series didn't die the day the war ended. It has a strange heartbeat that won't stop. We would do it again in a heartbeat.'

List of Episodes

Series 1

1. Rites of Passage

First broadcast: BBC One,
Thursday 18 November 1993, 8.30pm
UK viewers: 10.49 million

Cast

Gary Sparrow	Nicholas Lyndhurst
Phoebe Bamford	Dervla Kirwan
Yvonne Sparrow	Michelle Holmes
Eric Elward	David Ryall
Ron Wheatcroft	Victor McGuire
PC Reg Deadman/Reg's Grandson	Christopher Ettridge
Old Codger	John Rapley
OU Lecturer	Pete Drummond

Production Team

Written by	Laurence Marks, Maurice Gran
Music by	Anthony and Gaynor Sadler
Theme song performed by	Nick Curtis
Casting	Susie Parriss, Paddy Stern
Script Associate	Micheál Jacob
Costume Designer	Diana Moseley
Make-Up Designer	Gabrielle Hamilton
Graphic Designer	Paul Peppiate
Technical Manager	Derek Oliver
Vision Control	Andy Newton
Vision Mixer	Barbara Hicks
Location Manager	Julia Morpeth
Production Secretary	Roz Davidson
First Assistant Directors	Peter Errington, Simon Haveland
Art Director	Lou Beaumont
Videotape Editor	Chris Wadsworth
Dubbing Editors	John Howell, Dave Thompson
Production Manager	Nick Mortimer
Properties Master	Andy Beales
Production Buyer	Laurie Law
Stage Manager	Robert Crossley
Script Supervisor	Emma Thomas
Camera Supervisor	Phil Palmer
Sound Supervisor	Ted Scott
Lighting Director	Christopher Clayton
Production Designer	Roger Andrews
Executive Producer	Allan McKeown
Producer	John Bartlett
Director	Robin Nash

2. Fools Rush In

First broadcast: BBC One,
Thursday 25 November 1993, 8.30pm
UK viewers: 9.76 million

Cast

Gary Sparrow	Nicholas Lyndhurst
Phoebe Bamford	Dervla Kirwan
Yvonne Sparrow	Michelle Holmes
Eric Elward	David Ryall
Ron Wheatcroft	Victor McGuire
Edna	Pamela Cundell
Donald Bamford	Ben Lobb
Old Codger	John Rapley
Barman	Freddie Stuart
Marty Harty	Roger Kitter
Listener	Karen Frawley
Band	Les Brown and His Music

Production Team

Written by	Laurence Marks, Maurice Gran
Music by	Anthony and Gaynor Sadler
Theme song performed by	Nick Curtis
Casting	Susie Parriss, Paddy Stern
Costume Designer	Diana Moseley
Make-Up Designer	Gabrielle Hamilton
Graphic Designer	Paul Peppiate
Technical Manager	Derek Oliver
Vision Control	Andy Newton
Vision Mixer	Barbara Hicks
Location Manager	Julia Morpeth
First Assistant Directors	Peter Errington, Simon Haveland
Videotape Editor	Chris Wadsworth
Dubbing Editors	John Howell, Dave Thompson
Production Manager	Nick Mortimer
Properties Master	Andy Beales
Production Buyer	Laurie Law
Stage Manager	Robert Crossley
Script Supervisor	Emma Thomas
Camera Supervisor	Phil Palmer
Sound Supervisor	Ted Scott
Lighting Director	Christopher Clayton
Production Designer	Roger Andrews
Executive Producer	Allan McKeown
Producer	John Bartlett
Director	Robin Nash

Goodnight Sweetheart: A Guide to the Classic Sitcom

3. Is Your Journey Really Necessary?

First broadcast: BBC One,
Thursday 2 December 1993, 8.30pm
UK viewers: 9.33 million

Cast

Gary Sparrow	Nicholas Lyndhurst
Phoebe Bamford	Dervla Kirwan
Yvonne Sparrow	Michelle Holmes
Eric Elward	David Ryall
Ron Wheatcroft	Victor McGuire
PC Reg Deadman/Reg's Grandson	Christopher Ettridge
The Spiv	Peter Cellier
DI Howard	Anthony Pedley
Emanuel 'Manny' Solomons	Harry Landis
DS Martin	Michael Garner
Pregnant Girl	Maria Gough
Station Mistress	Maggie Guess
Nurse	Jean Challis
Newscaster	Tanveer Ghani

Production Team

Written by	Laurence Marks, Maurice Gran
Music by	Anthony and Gaynor Sadler
Theme song performed by	Nick Curtis
Casting	Susie Parriss, Paddy Stern
Costume Designer	Diana Moseley
Make-Up Designer	Gabrielle Hamilton
Graphic Designer	Paul Peppiate
Technical Manager	Derek Oliver
Vision Control	Terry Watson
Vision Mixer	Barbara Hicks
Location Manager	Julia Morpeth
First Assistant Directors	Peter Errington, Simon Haveland
Videotape Editor	Chris Wadsworth
Dubbing Editors	John Howell, Dave Thompson
Production Manager	Julian Meers
Properties Master	Andy Beales
Production Buyer	Laurie Law
Stage Manager	Robert Crossley
Script Supervisor	Emma Thomas
Camera Supervisor	Phil Palmer
Sound Supervisor	Ted Scott
Lighting Director	Christopher Clayton
Production Designer	Roger Andrews
Executive Producer	Allan McKeown
Producer	John Bartlett
Director	Robin Nash

4. The More I See You

First broadcast: BBC One,
Thursday 9 December 1993, 8.30pm
UK viewers: 9.06 million

Cast

Gary Sparrow	Nicholas Lyndhurst
Phoebe Bamford	Dervla Kirwan
Yvonne Sparrow	Michelle Holmes
Eric Elward	David Ryall
Ron Wheatcroft	Victor McGuire
Security Guard	Martyn Whitby
Kid	Bobby Coombes
Car Mechanic	Nirjay Mahindru

Production Team

Written by	Laurence Marks, Maurice Gran
Music by	Anthony and Gaynor Sadler
Theme song performed by	Nick Curtis
Casting	Susie Parriss, Paddy Stern
Costume Designer	Diana Moseley
Make-Up Designer	Gabrielle Hamilton
Graphic Designer	Paul Peppiate
Technical Manager	Derek Oliver
Vision Control	Richard Waiting
Vision Mixer	Barbara Hicks
Location Manager	Julia Morpeth
First Assistant Directors	Peter Errington, Simon Haveland
Videotape Editor	Chris Wadsworth
Dubbing Editors	John Howell, Dave Thompson
Production Manager	Julian Meers
Properties Master	Andy Beales
Production Buyer	Laurie Law
Stage Manager	Robert Crossley
Script Supervisor	Emma Thomas
Camera Supervisor	Phil Palmer
Sound Supervisor	Ted Scott
Lighting Director	Christopher Clayton
Production Designer	Roger Andrews
Executive Producer	Allan McKeown
Producer	John Bartlett
Director	Robin Nash

List of Episodes

5. I Get Along Without You Very Well

First broadcast: BBC One,
Thursday 16 December 1993, 8.30pm
UK viewers: 8.96 million

Cast

Gary Sparrow	Nicholas Lyndhurst
Phoebe Bamford	Dervla Kirwan
Yvonne Sparrow	Michelle Holmes
Eric Elward	David Ryall
Ron Wheatcroft	Victor McGuire
PC Reg Deadman	Christopher Ettridge
Old Lady	Hilda Fenemore
Phoebe Sparrow	Peggy Phango
Hazel	Rachael Weaver
Newsreader	Claire Williamson

Production Team

Written by	Laurence Marks, Maurice Gran
Music by	Anthony and Gaynor Sadler
Theme song performed by	Nick Curtis
Casting	Susie Parriss, Paddy Stern
Costume Designer	Diana Moseley
Make-Up Designer	Gabrielle Hamilton
Graphic Designer	Paul Peppiate
Technical Manager	Derek Oliver
Vision Control	Andy Newton
Vision Mixer	Barbara Hicks
Location Manager	Julia Morpeth
First Assistant Directors	Peter Errington, Simon Haveland
Videotape Editor	Chris Wadsworth
Dubbing Editor	John Howell
Production Manager	Julian Meers
Properties Master	Andy Beales
Production Buyer	Laurie Law
Stage Manager	Robert Crossley
Script Supervisor	Emma Thomas
Camera Supervisor	Phil Palmer
Sound Supervisor	Ted Scott
Lighting Director	Christopher Clayton
Production Designer	Roger Andrews
Executive Producer	Allan McKeown
Producer	John Bartlett
Director	Robin Nash

6. In the Mood

First broadcast: BBC One,
Thursday 23 December 1993, 8.30pm
UK viewers: 8.58 million

Cast

Gary Sparrow	Nicholas Lyndhurst
Phoebe Bamford	Dervla Kirwan
Yvonne Sparrow	Michelle Holmes
Eric Elward	David Ryall
Ron Wheatcroft	Victor McGuire
PC Reg Deadman	Christopher Ettridge
Emanuel 'Manny' Solomons	Harry Landis
Head Waiter	Roger Brierley
Doctor	Jerome Willis
Old Codger	John Rapley
Commentator	Aaron Aardvark

Production Team

Written by	Laurence Marks, Maurice Gran
Music by	Anthony and Gaynor Sadler
Theme song performed by	Nick Curtis
Casting	Susie Parriss, Paddy Stern
Costume Designer	Diana Moseley
Make-Up Designer	Gabrielle Hamilton
Graphic Designer	Paul Peppiate
Technical Manager	Derek Oliver
Vision Control	Andy Newton
Vision Mixer	Barbara Hicks
Production Secretary	Roz Davidson
First Assistant Director	Peter Errington
Art Director	Lou Beaumont
Videotape Editor	Chris Wadsworth
Dubbing Editors	John Howell, Dave Thompson
Production Manager	Julian Meers
Properties Master	Andy Beales
Production Buyer	Laurie Law
Stage Manager	Robert Crossley
Script Supervisor	Emma Thomas
Camera Supervisor	Phil Palmer
Sound Supervisor	Ted Scott
Lighting Director	Christopher Clayton
Production Designer	Roger Andrews
Executive Producer	Allan McKeown
Producer	John Bartlett
Director	Robin Nash

Goodnight Sweetheart: A Guide to the Classic Sitcom

Series 2

1. Don't Get Around Much Anymore

First broadcast: BBC One,
Monday 20 February 1995, 8.30pm
UK viewers: 12.73 million

Cast

Gary Sparrow	Nicholas Lyndhurst
Phoebe Bamford	Dervla Kirwan
Yvonne Sparrow	Michelle Holmes
Ron Wheatcroft	Victor McGuire
Reg Deadman/Reg's Grandson	Christopher Ettridge
Mainwaring	Alec Linstead
Wilson	Terrence Hardiman
Thursfield	Eamonn Walker
Major	Max Digby
Old Codger	John Rapley

Production Team

Written by	Laurence Marks, Maurice Gran
Theme song performed by	Nick Curtis
Script Editor	Micheál Jacob
Casting	Susie Parriss, Paddy Stern
Costume Designer	Diana Moseley
Make-Up Designer	Gabrielle Hamilton
Graphic Designer	Paul Peppiate
Technical Manager	Derek Oliver
Vision Control	Andy Newton
Vision Mixer	Angela Beveridge
Location Manager	Chris D'Oyly-John
Production Co-ordinator	Mia Jupp
First Assistant Director	Nick Kirkpatrick
Art Director	Lou Beaumont
Videotape Editor	Chris Wadsworth
Dubbing Editor	Richard Churchill
Production Manager	Christopher Miles
Properties	Andy Beales
Property Buyer	Laurie Law
Stage Manager	Robert Crossley
Script Supervisor	Emma Thomas
Camera Supervisor	Phil Palmer
OB Camera Operator	Tony Keene
Sound Supervisor	Ted Scott
Lighting Director	Christopher Clayton
Production Designer	Roger Andrews
Supervising Producers	Laurence Marks, Maurice Gran
Executive Producer	Allan McKeown
Producer	John Bartlett
Director	Robin Nash

2. I Got It Bad and That Ain't Good

First broadcast: BBC One,
Monday 27 February 1995
UK viewers: 13.45 million

Cast

Gary Sparrow	Nicholas Lyndhurst
Phoebe Bamford	Dervla Kirwan
Yvonne Sparrow	Michelle Holmes
Ron Wheatcroft	Victor McGuire
Reg Deadman/Reg's Grandson	Christopher Ettridge
Ludo	Jonathan Cake
Frederick	Paul Shearer
Joe	Patrick Pearson
Old Codger	John Rapley
Girl in Boat	Alison Beattie
Stall Holder	Duncan Faber
Shopper	Louise Tomkins

Production Team

Written by	Laurence Marks, Maurice Gran
Theme song performed by	Nick Curtis
Script Editor	Micheál Jacob
Casting	Susie Parriss, Paddy Stern
Costume Designer	Diana Moseley
Make-Up Designer	Gabrielle Hamilton
Graphic Designer	Paul Peppiate
Technical Manager	Derek Oliver
Vision Control	Andy Newton
Vision Mixer	Angela Beveridge
Location Manager	Chris D'Oyly-John
Production Co-ordinator	Mia Jupp
First Assistant Director	Nick Kirkpatrick
Art Director	Lou Beaumont
Videotape Editor	Chris Wadsworth
Dubbing Editor	Richard Churchill
Production Manager	Christopher Miles
Properties	Andy Beales
Property Buyer	Laurie Law
Stage Manager	Robert Crossley
Script Supervisor	Emma Thomas
Camera Supervisor	Phil Palmer
OB Camera Operator	Tony Keene
Sound Supervisor	Ted Scott
Lighting Director	Christopher Clayton
Production Designer	Roger Andrews
Supervising Producers	Laurence Marks, Maurice Gran
Executive Producer	Allan McKeown
Producer	John Bartlett
Director	Robin Nash

3. Just One More Chance

First broadcast: BBC One,
Monday 6 March 1995, 8.30pm
UK viewers: 12.79 million

Cast

Gary Sparrow	Nicholas Lyndhurst
Phoebe Bamford	Dervla Kirwan
Yvonne Sparrow	Michelle Holmes
Ron Wheatcroft	Victor McGuire
Reg Deadman	Christopher Ettridge
Jenny	Clare Cathcart

Production Team

Created by	Laurence Marks, Maurice Gran
Written by	Paul Makin
Theme song performed by	Nick Curtis
Script Editor	Micheál Jacob
Casting	Susie Parriss, Paddy Stern
Costume Designer	Diana Moseley
Make-Up Designer	Gabrielle Hamilton
Graphic Designer	Paul Peppiate
Technical Manager	Derek Oliver
Vision Control	Andy Newton
Vision Mixer	Angela Beveridge
Location Manager	Chris D'Oyly-John
Production Co-ordinator	Mia Jupp
First Assistant Director	Nick Kirkpatrick
Art Director	Lou Beaumont
Videotape Editor	Chris Wadsworth
Dubbing Editor	Richard Churchill
Production Manager	Christopher Miles
Properties	Andy Beales
Property Buyer	Laurie Law
Stage Manager	Robert Crossley
Script Supervisor	Emma Thomas
Camera Supervisor	Phil Palmer
OB Camera Operator	Tony Keene
Sound Supervisor	Ted Scott
Lighting Director	Christopher Clayton
Production Designer	Roger Andrews
Supervising Producers	Laurence Marks, Maurice Gran
Executive Producer	Allan McKeown
Producer	John Bartlett
Director	Robin Nash

4. Who's Taking You Home Tonight?

First broadcast: BBC One,
Monday 13 March 1995, 8.30pm
UK viewers: 12.72 million

Cast

Gary Sparrow	Nicholas Lyndhurst
Phoebe Bamford	Dervla Kirwan
Yvonne Sparrow	Michelle Holmes
Ron Wheatcroft	Victor McGuire
Sanjay	Raj Patel
Sella	Nimmy March

Production Team

Created by	Laurence Marks, Maurice Gran
Written by	Gary Lawson, John Phelps
Theme song performed by	Nick Curtis
Script Editor	Micheál Jacob
Casting	Susie Parriss, Paddy Stern
Costume Designer	Diana Moseley
Make-Up Designer	Gabrielle Hamilton
Graphic Designer	Paul Peppiate
Technical Manager	Derek Oliver
Vision Control	Richard Waiting
Vision Mixer	Barbara Hicks
Location Manager	Chris D'Oyly-John
Production Co-ordinator	Mia Jupp
First Assistant Director	Nick Kirkpatrick
Art Director	Lou Beaumont
Videotape Editor	Chris Wadsworth
Dubbing Editor	Richard Churchill
Production Manager	Christopher Miles
Properties	Andy Beales
Property Buyer	Laurie Law
Stage Manager	Robert Crossley
Script Supervisor	Emma Thomas
Camera Supervisor	Phil Palmer
OB Camera Operator	Tony Keene
Sound Supervisor	Ted Scott
Lighting Director	Christopher Clayton
Production Designer	Roger Andrews
Supervising Producers	Laurence Marks, Maurice Gran
Executive Producer	Allan McKeown
Producer	John Bartlett
Director	Robin Nash

5. Wish Me Luck...

First broadcast: BBC One,
Monday 20 March 1995, 8.30pm
UK viewers: 12.87 million

Cast

Gary Sparrow	Nicholas Lyndhurst
Phoebe Bamford	Dervla Kirwan
Yvonne Sparrow	Michelle Holmes
Ron Wheatcroft	Victor McGuire
Reg Deadman	Christopher Ettridge
Injured Man	Colin Spaull
Mrs Bloss	Yvonne D'Alpra

Production Team

Created by	Laurence Marks, Maurice Gran
Written by	Gary Lawson, John Phelps
Theme song performed by	Nick Curtis
Script Editor	Micheál Jacob
Casting	Susie Parriss, Paddy Stern
Costume Designer	Diana Moseley
Make-Up Designer	Gabrielle Hamilton
Graphic Designer	Paul Peppiate
Technical Manager	Derek Oliver
Vision Control	Andy Newton
Vision Mixer	Barbara Hicks
Location Manager	Chris D'Oyly-John
Production Co-ordinator	Mia Jupp
First Assistant Director	Nick Kirkpatrick
Art Director	Lou Beaumont
Videotape Editor	Chris Wadsworth
Dubbing Editor	Richard Churchill
Production Manager	Christopher Miles
Properties	Andy Beales
Property Buyer	Laurie Law
Stage Manager	Robert Crossley
Script Supervisor	Emma Thomas
Camera Supervisor	Phil Palmer
OB Camera Operator	Tony Keene
Sound Supervisor	Ted Scott
Lighting Director	Christopher Clayton
Production Designer	Roger Andrews
Supervising Producers	Laurence Marks, Maurice Gran
Executive Producer	Allan McKeown
Producer	John Bartlett
Director	Robin Nash

6. ...As You Wave Me Goodbye

First broadcast: BBC One,
Monday 27 March 1995, 8.30pm
UK viewers: 12.64 million

Cast

Gary Sparrow	Nicholas Lyndhurst
Phoebe Bamford	Dervla Kirwan
Yvonne Sparrow	Michelle Holmes
Ron Wheatcroft	Victor McGuire
Reg Deadman	Christopher Ettridge
Mrs Bloss	Yvonne D'Alpra
Stan	John Rapley
Wendy	Amanda Richardson
Café Waitress	Maria Pastel

Production Team

Created by	Laurence Marks, Maurice Gran
Written by	Gary Lawson, John Phelps
Theme song performed by	Nick Curtis
Script Editor	Micheál Jacob
Casting	Susie Parriss, Paddy Stern
Costume Designer	Diana Moseley
Make-Up Designer	Gabrielle Hamilton
Graphic Designer	Paul Peppiate
Technical Manager	Derek Oliver
Vision Control	Andy Newton
Vision Mixer	Barbara Hicks
Location Manager	Chris D'Oyly-John
Production Co-ordinator	Mia Jupp
First Assistant Director	Nick Kirkpatrick
Art Director	Lou Beaumont
Videotape Editor	Chris Wadsworth
Dubbing Editor	Richard Churchill
Production Manager	Christopher Miles
Properties	Andy Beales
Property Buyer	Laurie Law
Stage Manager	Robert Crossley
Script Supervisor	Emma Thomas
Camera Supervisor	Phil Palmer
Sound Supervisor	Ted Scott
Lighting Director	Christopher Clayton
Production Designer	Roger Andrews
Supervising Producers	Laurence Marks, Maurice Gran
Executive Producer	Allan McKeown
Producer	John Bartlett
Director	Robin Nash

List of Episodes

7. Would You Like to Swing on a Star

First broadcast: BBC One,
Monday 3 April 1995, 8.30pm
UK viewers: 13.04 million

Cast

Gary Sparrow	Nicholas Lyndhurst
Phoebe Bamford	Dervla Kirwan
Yvonne Sparrow	Michelle Holmes
Ron Wheatcroft	Victor McGuire
Reg Deadman	Christopher Ettridge
Sidney Wix	Ronnie Stevens
Gregory	Peter Blythe
Lance	Robin Lermitte
Stall Holder	Nicola Redmond
Record Assistant	Natasha Gardiner
Dick	Len Howe
Autograph Seeker	Michelle Cattini

Production Team

Written by	Laurence Marks, Maurice Gran
Theme song performed by	Nick Curtis
Script Editor	Micheál Jacob
Casting	Susie Parriss, Paddy Stern
Costume Designer	Diana Moseley
Make-Up Designer	Gabrielle Hamilton
Graphic Designer	Paul Peppiate
Technical Manager	Derek Oliver
Vision Control	Andy Newton
Vision Mixers	Barbara Hicks, Angela Beveridge
Location Manager	Julia Morpeth
Production Co-ordinator	Mia Jupp
First Assistant Director	Nick Kirkpatrick
Art Director	Lou Beaumont
Videotape Editor	Chris Wadsworth
Dubbing Editor	Richard Churchill
Production Manager	Christopher Miles
Properties	Andy Beales
Property Buyer	Laurie Law
Stage Manager	Robert Crossley
Script Supervisor	Emma Thomas
Camera Supervisor	Phil Palmer
Sound Supervisor	Ted Scott
Lighting Director	Christopher Clayton
Production Designer	Roger Andrews
Supervising Producers	Laurence Marks, Maurice Gran
Executive Producer	Allan McKeown
Producer	John Bartlett
Director	Robin Nash

8. Nice Work If You Can Get it

First broadcast: BBC One,
Monday 10 April 1995, 8.30pm
UK viewers: 12.42 million

Cast

Gary Sparrow	Nicholas Lyndhurst
Phoebe Bamford	Dervla Kirwan
Yvonne Sparrow	Michelle Holmes
Ron Wheatcroft	Victor McGuire
Reg Deadman	Christopher Ettridge
Gregory	Peter Blythe
Sidney Wix	Ronnie Stevens
Dr Jakowitz	David de Keyser
Phil McCavity	Steven Speirs

Production Team

Written by	Laurence Marks, Maurice Gran
Theme song performed by	Nick Curtis
Script Editor	Micheál Jacob
Casting	Susie Parriss, Paddy Stern
Costume Designer	Diana Moseley
Make-Up Designer	Gabrielle Hamilton
Graphic Designer	Paul Peppiate
Technical Manager	Derek Oliver
Vision Control	Richard Waiting
Vision Mixers	Angela Beveridge, Barbara Hicks
Location Manager	Julia Morpeth
Production Co-ordinator	Mia Jupp
First Assistant Director	Nick Kirkpatrick
Art Director	Lou Beaumont
Videotape Editor	Chris Wadsworth
Dubbing Editor	Richard Churchill
Production Manager	Christopher Miles
Properties	Andy Beales
Property Buyer	Laurie Law
Stage Manager	Robert Crossley
Script Supervisor	Emma Thomas
Camera Supervisor	Phil Palmer
Sound Supervisor	Ted Scott
Lighting Director	Christopher Clayton
Production Designer	Roger Andrews
Supervising Producers	Laurence Marks, Maurice Gran
Executive Producer	Allan McKeown
Producer	John Bartlett
Director	Robin Nash

Goodnight Sweetheart: A Guide to the Classic Sitcom

9. Let Yourself Go

First broadcast: BBC One,
Monday 24 April 1995, 8.30pm
UK viewers: 12.76 million

Cast

Gary Sparrow	Nicholas Lyndhurst
Phoebe Bamford	Dervla Kirwan
Yvonne Sparrow	Michelle Holmes
Ron Wheatcroft	Victor McGuire
Reg Deadman	Christopher Ettridge
Harry	Adam Henderson
Sally	Katie Donnison
Television Presenter	Steve Rider
Television Commentator	John Motson
Mrs French	Jeannie Crowther
Peter	Chase Marks

Production Team

Created by	Laurence Marks, Maurice Gran
Written by	Paul Makin
Theme song performed by	Nick Curtis
Script Editor	Micheál Jacob
Casting	Susie Parriss, Paddy Stern
Costume Designer	Diana Moseley
Make-Up Designer	Gabrielle Hamilton
Graphic Designer	Paul Peppiate
Technical Manager	Derek Oliver
Vision Control	Andy Newton
Vision Mixer	Barbara Hicks
Location Manager	Julia Morpeth
Production Co-ordinator	Mia Jupp
First Assistant Director	Nick Kirkpatrick
Art Director	Lou Beaumont
Videotape Editor	Chris Wadsworth
Dubbing Editor	Richard Churchill
Production Manager	Christopher Miles
Properties	Andy Beales
Property Buyer	Laurie Law
Stage Manager	Robert Crossley
Script Supervisor	Emma Thomas
Camera Supervisor	Phil Palmer
Sound Supervisor	Ted Scott
Lighting Director	Christopher Clayton
Production Designer	Roger Andrews
Supervising Producers	Laurence Marks, Maurice Gran
Executive Producer	Allan McKeown
Producer	John Bartlett
Director	Robin Nash

10. Don't Fence Me in

First broadcast: BBC One,
Monday 1 May 1995, 8.30pm
UK viewers: 12.50 million

Cast

Gary Sparrow	Nicholas Lyndhurst
Phoebe Bamford	Dervla Kirwan
Yvonne Sparrow	Michelle Holmes
Ron Wheatcroft	Victor McGuire
Reg Deadman	Christopher Ettridge
George Harrison	Michael Troughton
Foreman	Jonathan Stratt
Worker	Glen Davies
Pete	Wayne Goddard
Mike	Scott Mitchell
Old Woman	Fanny Carby
Television Presenter	Suzy Aitchison
Television Presenter	Don Gallagher

Production Team

Written by	Laurence Marks, Maurice Gran
Theme song performed by	Nick Curtis
Script Editor	Micheál Jacob
Casting	Susie Parriss, Paddy Stern
Costume Designer	Diana Moseley
Make-Up Designer	Gabrielle Hamilton
Graphic Designer	Paul Peppiate
Technical Manager	Derek Oliver
Vision Control	Andy Newton
Vision Mixer	Barbara Hicks
Location Manager	Julia Morpeth
Production Co-ordinator	Mia Jupp
First Assistant Director	Nick Kirkpatrick
Art Director	Lou Beaumont
Videotape Editor	Chris Wadsworth
Dubbing Editor	Richard Churchill
Production Manager	Christopher Miles
Properties	Andy Beales
Property Buyer	Laurie Law
Stage Manager	Robert Crossley
Script Supervisor	Emma Thomas
Camera Supervisor	Phil Palmer
Sound Supervisor	Ted Scott
Lighting Director	Christopher Clayton
Production Designer	Roger Andrews
Supervising Producers	Laurence Marks, Maurice Gran
Executive Producer	Allan McKeown
Producer	John Bartlett
Director	Robin Nash

List of Episodes

Series 3

1. Between the Devil and the Deep Blue Sea

First broadcast: BBC One,
Tuesday 26 December 1995, 8.00pm
UK viewers: 10.66 million

Cast

Gary Sparrow	Nicholas Lyndhurst
Phoebe Bamford	Dervla Kirwan
Yvonne Sparrow	Michelle Holmes
Ron Wheatcroft	Victor McGuire
Reg Deadman	Christopher Ettridge
Jayne Mansfield	Diana Kent
Ed Murrow	Michael J. Shannon
Guy Burgess	Tim Dutton
Nippie	Josie Kidd
Wilfred Pickles	Jon Glover
Winston Churchill	John Evans

Production Team

Written by	Laurence Marks, Maurice Gran
Theme song performed by	Nick Curtis
Script Editor	Micheál Jacob
Casting	Susie Parriss, Paddy Stern
Costume Designer	Diana Moseley
Make-Up Designer	Gabrielle Hamilton
Graphic Designer	Paul Peppiate
Production Accountant	Sue Landsberger
Technical Manager	Derek Oliver
Vision Control	Andy Newton
Vision Mixer	Barbara Hicks
Console Operator	Terry Watson
Gaffer	Colin McCarthy
Location Manager	Julia Morpeth
Production Co-ordinator	Pip Haddow
First Assistant Director	Nick Rae
Art Director	Judith Lang
Videotape Editor	Chris Wadsworth
Properties	Andy Beales
Property Buyer	Laurie Law
Dubbing Editor	Richard Churchill
Production Manager	Christopher Miles
Stage Manager	Robert Crossley
Script Supervisor	Jenny Bowman
Camera Supervisor	Phil Palmer
Sound Supervisor	Paul Gartrell
Lighting Director	Christopher Clayton
Production Designer	Roger Andrews
Associate Producer	Julian Meers
Supervising Producers	Laurence Marks, Maurice Gran
Executive Producers	Allan McKeown, Claire Hinson
Producer	John Bartlett
Director	Robin Nash

2. It Ain't Necessarily So

First broadcast: BBC One,
Monday 1 January 1996, 8.30pm
UK viewers: 10.76 million

Cast

Gary Sparrow	Nicholas Lyndhurst
Phoebe Bamford	Dervla Kirwan
Yvonne Sparrow	Michelle Holmes
Ron Wheatcroft	Victor McGuire
Reg Deadman	Christopher Ettridge
Stella Wheatcroft	Nimmy March
Mrs Bloss	Yvonne D'Alpra
Curator	Charles Simon
Minicab Driver	Malcolm McFee

Production Team

Written by	Laurence Marks, Maurice Gran
Theme song performed by	Nick Curtis
Script Editor	Micheál Jacob
Casting	Paddy Stern, Susie Parriss
Costume Designer	Diana Moseley
Make-Up Designer	Gabrielle Hamilton
Graphic Designer	Paul Peppiate
Technical Manager	Derek Oliver
Vision Control	Andy Newton
Vision Mixer	Barbara Hicks
Location Manager	Julia Morpeth
Production Co-ordinator	Pip Haddow
First Assistant Director	Nick Rae
Art Director	Lou Beaumont
Videotape Editor	Phil Moss
Properties	Andy Beales
Property Buyer	Laurie Law
Dubbing Editor	Richard Churchill
Production Manager	Christopher Miles
Stage Manager	Robert Crossley
Script Supervisor	Jenny Bowman
Camera Supervisor	Phil Palmer
OB Camera Operator	Tony Keene
Sound Supervisor	Paul Gartrell
OB Sound Supervisor	Bob Newton
Lighting Director	Christopher Clayton
Production Designer	Roger Andrews
Associate Producer	Julian Meers
Supervising Producers	Laurence Marks, Maurice Gran
Executive Producers	Allan McKeown, Claire Hinson
Producer	John Bartlett
Director	Terry Kinane

Goodnight Sweetheart: A Guide to the Classic Sitcom

3. One O'Clock Jump

First broadcast: BBC One,
Monday 8 January 1996, 8.30pm
UK viewers: 11.08 million

Cast

Gary Sparrow	Nicholas Lyndhurst
Phoebe Bamford	Dervla Kirwan
Yvonne Sparrow	Michelle Holmes
Ron Wheatcroft	Victor McGuire
Reg Deadman	Christopher Ettridge
Margie Hook	Eve Bland
Mr Shik	Eddie Yeoh
Bus Inspector	Nick Bayly
Mr Hook	David Aldous
Mrs Shik	Nana Takahashi
Frank	Alfie Ettridge Rogers

Production Team

Written by	Laurence Marks, Maurice Gran
Theme song performed by	Nick Curtis
Script Editor	Micheál Jacob
Casting	Paddy Stern, Susie Parriss
Costume Designer	Diana Moseley
Make-Up Designer	Gabrielle Hamilton
Graphic Designer	Paul Peppiate
Technical Manager	Derek Oliver
Vision Control	Andy Newton
Vision Mixer	Naomi Neufeld
Location Manager	Julia Morpeth
Production Co-ordinator	Pip Haddow
First Assistant Director	Nick Rae
Art Director	Lou Beaumont
Videotape Editor	Phil Moss
Properties	Andy Beales
Property Buyer	Laurie Law
Dubbing Editor	Richard Churchill
Production Manager	Christopher Miles
Stage Manager	Robert Crossley
Script Supervisor	Jenny Bowman
Camera Supervisor	Phil Palmer
OB Camera Operator	Tony Keene
Sound Supervisor	Paul Gartrell
OB Sound Supervisor	Bob Newton
Lighting Director	Christopher Clayton
Production Designer	Roger Andrews
Associate Producer	Julian Meers
Supervising Producers	Laurence Marks, Maurice Gran
Executive Producers	Allan McKeown, Claire Hinson
Producer	John Bartlett
Director	Terry Kinane

4. It's a Sin to Tell a Lie

First broadcast: BBC One,
Monday 15 January 1996, 8.30pm
UK viewers: 11.28 million

Cast

Gary Sparrow	Nicholas Lyndhurst
Phoebe Bamford	Dervla Kirwan
Yvonne Sparrow	Michelle Holmes
Ron Wheatcroft	Victor McGuire
Reg Deadman	Christopher Ettridge
Owen Jones	Ken Jones
Guard	John Bardon
Mrs Bloss	Yvonne D'Alpra
Woman	Charmaine Parsons

Production Team

Created by	Laurence Marks, Maurice Gran
Written by	Gary Lawson, John Phelps
Theme song performed by	Nick Curtis
Script Editor	Micheál Jacob
Casting	Paddy Stern, Susie Parriss
Costume Designer	Diana Moseley
Make-Up Designer	Gabrielle Hamilton
Graphic Designer	Paul Peppiate
Technical Manager	Derek Oliver
Vision Control	Andy Newton
Vision Mixer	Barbara Hicks
Location Manager	Julia Morpeth
Production Co-ordinator	Pip Haddow
First Assistant Director	Nick Rae
Art Director	Lou Beaumont
Videotape Editor	Phil Moss
Properties	Andy Beales
Property Buyer	Laurie Law
Dubbing Editor	Richard Churchill
Production Manager	Christopher Miles
Stage Manager	Robert Crossley
Script Supervisor	Jenny Bowman
Camera Supervisor	Phil Palmer
Sound Supervisor	Paul Gartrell
Lighting Director	Christopher Clayton
Production Designer	Roger Andrews
Associate Producer	Julian Meers
Supervising Producers	Laurence Marks, Maurice Gran
Executive Producers	Allan McKeown, Claire Hinson
Producer	John Bartlett
Director	Terry Kinane

List of Episodes

5. Change Partners

First broadcast: BBC One,
Monday 22 January 1996, 8.30pm
UK viewers: 11.22 million

Cast

Gary Sparrow	Nicholas Lyndhurst
Phoebe Bamford	Dervla Kirwan
Yvonne Sparrow	Michelle Holmes
Ron Wheatcroft	Victor McGuire
Reg Deadman	Christopher Ettridge
Stella Wheatcroft	Nimmy March
Violet Bigby	Regina Freedman
Tom	Bryan Lawrence
Harry	Darren Bancroft
Gillian	Harriet Thorpe
Ken	Angus Kennedy
Customer	Paul Beech

Production Team

Created by	Laurence Marks, Maurice Gran
Written by	Gary Lawson, John Phelps
Theme song performed by	Nick Curtis
Script Editor	Micheál Jacob
Casting	Paddy Stern, Susie Parriss
Costume Designer	Diana Moseley
Make-Up Designer	Gabrielle Hamilton
Musical Director	Barry Francis
Choreographer	Mandy Demitriou
Graphic Designer	Paul Peppiate
Technical Manager	Derek Oliver
Vision Control	Andy Newton
Vision Mixer	Barbara Hicks
Production Co-ordinator	Pip Haddow
First Assistant Director	Nick Rae
Art Director	Judith Lang
Videotape Editor	Chis Wadsworth
Properties	Andy Beales
Property Buyer	Laurie Law
Dubbing Editor	Richard Churchill
Production Manager	Christopher Miles
Stage Manager	Robert Crossley
Script Supervisor	Jenny Bowman
Camera Supervisor	Phil Palmer
Sound Supervisor	Paul Gartrell
Lighting Director	Christopher Clayton
Production Designer	Roger Andrews
Associate Producer	Julian Meers
Supervising Producers	Laurence Marks, Maurice Gran
Executive Producers	Allan McKeown, Claire Hinson
Producer	John Bartlett
Director	Robin Nash

6. Goodnight Children Everywhere

First broadcast: BBC One,
Monday 29 January 1996, 8.30pm
UK viewers: 12.20 million

Cast

Gary Sparrow	Nicholas Lyndhurst
Phoebe Bamford	Dervla Kirwan
Yvonne Sparrow	Michelle Holmes
Ron Wheatcroft	Victor McGuire
Reg Deadman	Christopher Ettridge
Mrs Cooper	Kim Clifford
Mrs French	Jeannie Crowther
Sally	Katie Donnison
Peter	Chase Marks

Production Team

Created by	Laurence Marks, Maurice Gran
Written by	Geoff Rowley
Theme song performed by	Nick Curtis
Script Editor	Micheál Jacob
Casting	Paddy Stern, Susie Parriss
Costume Designer	Diana Moseley
Make-Up Designer	Gabrielle Hamilton
Graphic Designer	Paul Peppiate
Technical Manager	Derek Oliver
Vision Control	Andy Newton
Vision Mixer	Barbara Hicks
Production Co-ordinator	Pip Haddow
First Assistant Director	Nick Rae
Art Director	Lou Beaumont
Videotape Editor	Phil Moss
Properties	Andy Beales
Property Buyer	Laurie Law
Dubbing Editor	Richard Churchill
Production Manager	Christopher Miles
Stage Manager	Robert Crossley
Script Supervisor	Jenny Bowman
Camera Supervisor	Phil Palmer
OB Camera Supervisor	Tony Keene
Sound Supervisor	Paul Gartrell
OB Sound Supervisor	Bob Newton
Lighting Director	Christopher Clayton
Production Designer	Roger Andrews
Associate Producer	Julian Meers
Supervising Producers	Laurence Marks, Maurice Gran
Executive Producers	Allan McKeown, Claire Hinson
Producer	John Bartlett
Director	Terry Kinane

Goodnight Sweetheart: A Guide to the Classic Sitcom

7. Turned Out Nice Again

First broadcast: BBC One,
Monday 5 February 1996, 8.30pm
UK viewers: 12.12 million

Cast

Gary Sparrow	Nicholas Lyndhurst
Phoebe Bamford	Dervla Kirwan
Yvonne Sparrow	Michelle Holmes
Ron Wheatcroft	Victor McGuire
Reg Deadman	Christopher Ettridge
Sidney Wix	Ronnie Stevens
Beryl Formby	Polly Hemingway
George Formby	Phil Nice
Stella Wheatcroft	Nimmy March

Production Team

Created by	Laurence Marks, Maurice Gran
Written by	Geoff Rowley
Theme song performed by	Nick Curtis
Script Editor	Micheál Jacob
Casting	Paddy Stern, Susie Parriss
Costume Designer	Diana Moseley
Make-Up Designer	Gabrielle Hamilton
Graphic Designer	Paul Peppiate
Technical Manager	Derek Oliver
Vision Control	Andy Newton
Vision Mixer	Barbara Hicks
Location Manager	Julia Morpeth
Production Co-ordinator	Pip Haddow
First Assistant Director	Nick Rae
Art Director	Judith Lang
Videotape Editor	Phil Moss
Properties	Andy Beales
Property Buyer	Laurie Law
Dubbing Editor	Richard Churchill
Production Manager	Christopher Miles
Stage Manager	Robert Crossley
Script Supervisor	Jenny Bowman
Camera Supervisor	Phil Palmer
OB Camera Supervisor	Tony Keene
Sound Supervisor	Paul Gartrell
OB Sound Supervisor	Bob Newton
Lighting Director	Christopher Clayton
Production Designer	Roger Andrews
Associate Producer	Julian Meers
Supervising Producers	Laurence Marks, Maurice Gran
Executive Producers	Allan McKeown, Claire Hinson
Producer	John Bartlett
Director	Terry Kinane

8. There's Something About a Soldier

First broadcast: BBC One,
Monday 12 February 1996, 8.30pm
UK viewers: 12.19 million

Cast

Gary Sparrow	Nicholas Lyndhurst
Phoebe Bamford	Dervla Kirwan
Yvonne Sparrow	Michelle Holmes
Ron Wheatcroft	Victor McGuire
Reg Deadman	Christopher Ettridge
Donald Bamford	Ralph Ineson
Newsagent	Arthur White

Production Team

Created by	Laurence Marks, Maurice Gran
Written by	Paul Makin
Theme song performed by	Nick Curtis
Script Editor	Micheál Jacob
Casting	Paddy Stern, Susie Parriss
Costume Designer	Diana Moseley
Make-Up Designer	Gabrielle Hamilton
Graphic Designer	Paul Peppiate
Technical Manager	Derek Oliver
Vision Control	Andy Newton
Vision Mixer	Barbara Hicks
Location Manager	Julia Morpeth
Production Co-ordinator	Pip Haddow
First Assistant Director	Nick Rae
Art Director	Judith Lang
Videotape Editor	Chris Wadsworth
Properties	Andy Beales
Property Buyer	Laurie Law
Dubbing Editor	Richard Churchill
Production Manager	Christopher Miles
Stage Manager	Robert Crossley
Script Supervisor	Jenny Bowman
Camera Supervisor	Phil Palmer
Sound Supervisor	Paul Gartrell
Lighting Director	Christopher Clayton
Production Designer	Roger Andrews
Associate Producer	Julian Meers
Supervising Producers	Laurence Marks, Maurice Gran
Executive Producers	Allan McKeown, Claire Hinson
Producer	John Bartlett
Director	Robin Nash

List of Episodes

9. Someone to Watch Over Me

First broadcast: BBC One,
Monday 19 February 1996, 8.30pm
UK viewers: 13.06 million

Cast

Gary Sparrow	Nicholas Lyndhurst
Phoebe Bamford	Dervla Kirwan
Yvonne Sparrow	Michelle Holmes
Ron Wheatcroft	Victor McGuire
Reg Deadman	Christopher Ettridge
Doctor Stone	Jon Glover
Nurse Williams	Helena Calvert

Production Team

Created by	Laurence Marks, Maurice Gran
Written by	Paul Makin
Theme song performed by	Nick Curtis
Script Editor	Micheál Jacob
Casting	Paddy Stern, Susie Parriss
Costume Designer	Diana Moseley
Make-Up Designer	Gabrielle Hamilton
Graphic Designer	Paul Peppiate
Technical Manager	Derek Oliver
Vision Control	Andy Newton
Vision Mixer	Barbara Hicks
Location Manager	Julia Morpeth
Production Co-ordinator	Pip Haddow
First Assistant Director	Nick Rae
Art Director	Judith Lang
Videotape Editor	Chris Wadsworth
Properties	Andy Beales
Property Buyer	Laurie Law
Dubbing Editor	Richard Churchill
Production Manager	Christopher Miles
Stage Manager	Robert Crossley
Script Supervisor	Jenny Bowman
Camera Supervisor	Phil Palmer
Sound Supervisor	Paul Gartrell
Lighting Director	Christopher Clayton
Production Designer	Roger Andrews
Associate Producer	Julian Meers
Supervising Producers	Laurence Marks, Maurice Gran
Executive Producers	Allan McKeown, Claire Hinson
Producer	John Bartlett
Director	Robin Nash

10. The Yanks Are Coming

First broadcast: BBC One,
Monday 26 February 1996, 8.30pm
UK viewers: 10.98 million

Cast

Gary Sparrow	Nicholas Lyndhurst
Phoebe Bamford	Dervla Kirwan
Yvonne Sparrow	Michelle Holmes
Ron Wheatcroft	Victor McGuire
Reg Deadman	Christopher Ettridge
Billy Joe McCarthy	Sam Douglas
Zeffirelli	Matt Rippy
James T	Rhashan Stone
Niles	Tee Jaye
Vanessa Masterson	Belinda Stewart-Wilson

Production Team

Created by	Laurence Marks, Maurice Gran
Written by	Gary Lawson, John Phelps
Theme song performed by	Nick Curtis
Script Editor	Micheál Jacob
Casting	Paddy Stern, Susie Parriss
Costume Designer	Diana Moseley
Make-Up Designer	Gabrielle Hamilton
Graphic Designer	Paul Peppiate
Technical Manager	Derek Oliver
Vision Control	Andy Newton
Vision Mixer	Barbara Hicks
Location Manager	Julia Morpeth
Production Co-ordinator	Pip Haddow
First Assistant Director	Nick Rae
Art Director	Judith Lang
Videotape Editor	Chris Wadsworth
Properties	Andy Beales
Property Buyer	Laurie Law
Dubbing Editor	Richard Churchill
Production Manager	Christopher Miles
Stage Manager	Robert Crossley
Script Supervisor	Jenny Bowman
Camera Supervisor	Phil Palmer
Sound Supervisor	Paul Gartrell
Lighting Director	Christopher Clayton
Production Designer	Roger Andrews
Associate Producer	Julian Meers
Supervising Producers	Laurence Marks, Maurice Gran
Executive Producers	Allan McKeown, Claire Hinson
Producer	John Bartlett
Director	Robin Nash

Goodnight Sweetheart: A Guide to the Classic Sitcom

11. Let's Get Away from it All

First broadcast: BBC One,
Monday 4 March 1996
UK viewers: 10.88 million

Cast

Gary Sparrow	Nicholas Lyndhurst
Phoebe Bamford	Dervla Kirwan
Yvonne Sparrow	Michelle Holmes
Ron Wheatcroft	Victor McGuire
Reg Deadman	Christopher Ettridge
Woman	Maggie Jones

Production Team

Created by	Laurence Marks, Maurice Gran
Written by	Paul Makin
Theme song performed by	Nick Curtis
Script Editor	Micheál Jacob
Casting	Paddy Stern, Susie Parriss
Costume Designer	Diana Moseley
Make-Up Designer	Gabrielle Hamilton
Graphic Designer	Paul Peppiate
Technical Manager	Derek Oliver
Vision Control	Andy Newton
Vision Mixer	Barbara Hicks
Location Manager	Julia Morpeth
Production Co-ordinator	Pip Haddow
First Assistant Director	Nick Rae
Art Director	Judith Lang
Videotape Editor	Chris Wadsworth
Properties	Andy Beales
Property Buyer	Laurie Law
Dubbing Editor	Richard Churchill
Production Manager	Christopher Miles
Stage Manager	Robert Crossley
Script Supervisor	Jenny Bowman
Camera Supervisor	Phil Palmer
Sound Supervisor	Paul Gartrell
Lighting Director	Christopher Clayton
Production Designer	Roger Andrews
Associate Producer	Julian Meers
Supervising Producers	Laurence Marks, Maurice Gran
Executive Producers	Allan McKeown, Claire Hinson
Producer	John Bartlett
Director	Robin Nash

Series 4

1. You're Driving Me Crazy

First broadcast: BBC One,
Monday 3 March 1997, 8.30pm
UK viewers: 9.47 million

Cast

Gary Sparrow	Nicholas Lyndhurst
Yvonne Sparrow	Emma Amos
Phoebe Bamford	Elizabeth Carling
Ron Wheatcroft	Victor McGuire
Reg Deadman	Christopher Ettridge
Dr Jakowitz	David de Keyser
Clifford	Tim Stern
Tommy Kingdom	Nick Stringer
Soldier	Danny Swanson

Production Team

Written by	Laurence Marks, Maurice Gran
Theme song performed by	Nick Curtis
Script Editor	Micheál Jacob
Casting	Paddy Stern, Susie Parriss
Costume Designer	Diana Moseley
Make-Up Designer	Gabrielle Hamilton
Graphic Designer	Paul Peppiate
Production Accountant	Sue Landsberger
Technical Manager	Derek Oliver
Vision Control	Andy Newton
Vision Mixer	Barbara Hicks
Console Operator	Terry Watson
Gaffer	Colin McCarthy
Location Manager	Julia Morpeth
Production Co-ordinator	Claire Newton
First Assistant Director	Julie Sykes
Art Director	Judith Lang
Videotape Editors	Chris Wadsworth, Howard Denyer
Properties	Andy Beales
Property Buyer	Laurie Law
Production Manager	Mia Jupp
Stage Manager	Robert Crossley
Script Supervisor	Diane Taylor
Camera Supervisor	Tony Keene
Sound Supervisor	Paul Gartrell
Lighting Director	Christopher Clayton
Production Designer	Roger Andrews
Associate Producer	Julian Meers
Supervising Producers	Laurence Marks, Maurice Gran
Executive Producer	Claire Hinson
Producer	John Bartlett
Director	Robin Nash

2. In the Mood

First broadcast: BBC One,
Monday 10 March 1997, 8.30pm
UK viewers: 8.94 million

Cast

Gary Sparrow	Nicholas Lyndhurst
Phoebe Bamford	Elizabeth Carling
Yvonne Sparrow	Emma Amos
Ron Wheatcroft	Victor McGuire
Reg Deadman/Reg's Grandson	Christopher Ettridge
Cabbie	Richard Albrecht
George	Zak Maguire
Arthur	Elliot Henderson-Boyle
Big Kid	James Craise

Production Team

Created by	Laurence Marks, Maurice Gran
Written by	Sam Lawrence
Theme song performed by	Nick Curtis
Script Editor	Micheál Jacob
Casting	Paddy Stern, Susie Parriss
Costume Designer	Diana Moseley
Make-Up Designer	Gabrielle Hamilton
Graphic Designer	Paul Peppiate
Production Accountant	Sue Landsberger
Technical Manager	Derek Oliver
Vision Control	Andy Newton
Vision Mixer	Barbara Hicks
Console Operator	Terry Watson
Gaffer	Colin McCarthy
Location Manager	Julia Morpeth
Production Co-ordinator	Claire Newton
First Assistant Director	Julie Sykes
Art Director	Judith Lang
Videotape Editors	Chris Wadsworth, Howard Denyer
Properties	Andy Beales
Property Buyer	Laurie Law
Production Manager	Mia Jupp
Stage Manager	Robert Crossley
Script Supervisor	Diane Taylor
Camera Supervisor	Tony Keene
Sound Supervisor	Paul Gartrell
Lighting Director	Christopher Clayton
Production Designer	Roger Andrews
Associate Producer	Julian Meers
Supervising Producers	Laurence Marks, Maurice Gran
Executive Producer	Claire Hinson
Producer	John Bartlett
Director	Robin Nash

Goodnight Sweetheart: A Guide to the Classic Sitcom

3. Out of Town

First broadcast: BBC One,
Monday 17 March 1997, 8.30pm
UK viewers: 9.46 million

Cast

Gary Sparrow	Nicholas Lyndhurst
Yvonne Sparrow	Emma Amos
Phoebe Bamford	Elizabeth Carling
Ron Wheatcroft	Victor McGuire
Reg Deadman	Christopher Ettridge
George Sparrow	Roger Sloman

Production Team

Created by	Laurence Marks, Maurice Gran
Written by	Sam Lawrence
Theme song performed by	Nick Curtis
Script Editor	Micheál Jacob
Casting	Paddy Stern, Susie Parriss
Costume Designer	Diana Moseley
Make-Up Designer	Gabrielle Hamilton
Graphic Designer	Paul Peppiate
Production Accountant	Sue Landsberger
Technical Manager	Derek Oliver
Vision Control	Andy Newton
Vision Mixer	Barbara Hicks
Console Operator	Terry Watson
Gaffer	Colin McCarthy
Location Manager	Julia Morpeth
Production Co-ordinator	Claire Newton
First Assistant Directors	Tristram Shapeero, Robert Crossley
Art Director	Judith Lang
Videotape Editors	Chris Wadsworth, Howard Denyer
Properties	Andy Beales
Property Buyer	Laurie Law
Production Manager	Mia Jupp
Stage Manager	Robert Crossley
Script Supervisor	Diane Taylor
Camera Supervisor	Tony Keene
Sound Supervisor	Paul Gartrell
Lighting Director	Christopher Clayton
Production Designer	Roger Andrews
Associate Producer	Julian Meers
Supervising Producers	Laurence Marks, Maurice Gran
Executive Producer	Claire Hinson
Producer	John Bartlett
Director	Robin Nash

4. And Mother Came Too

First broadcast: BBC One,
Monday 24 March 1997, 8.30pm
UK viewers: 8.26 million

Cast

Gary Sparrow	Nicholas Lyndhurst
Phoebe Bamford	Elizabeth Carling
Ron Wheatcroft	Victor McGuire
Reg Deadman	Christopher Ettridge
Dolly Bamford	Rowena Cooper
Vicar	Peter Halliday
Magistrate	Jane Briers
Ron's Solicitor	Sebastian Abineri
Policeman	Martin Beaumont
Prosecution	Ellen O'Grady
Transvestite	Kerry Angus

Production Team

Created by	Laurence Marks, Maurice Gran
Written by	Gary Lawson, John Phelps
Theme song performed by	Nick Curtis
Script Editor	Micheál Jacob
Casting	Paddy Stern, Susie Parriss
Costume Designer	Diana Moseley
Make-Up Designer	Gabrielle Hamilton
Graphic Designer	Paul Peppiate
Production Accountant	Sue Landsberger
Technical Manager	Derek Oliver
Vision Control	Andy Newton
Vision Mixer	Barbara Hicks
Console Operator	Terry Watson
Gaffer	Colin McCarthy
Location Manager	Julia Morpeth
Production Co-ordinator	Claire Newton
First Assistant Directors	Tristram Shapeero, Robert Crossley
Art Director	Judith Lang
Videotape Editors	Chris Wadsworth, Howard Denyer
Properties	Andy Beales
Property Buyer	Laurie Law
Production Manager	Mia Jupp
Stage Manager	Robert Crossley
Script Supervisor	Diane Taylor
Camera Supervisor	Tony Keene
Sound Supervisor	Paul Gartrell
Lighting Director	Christopher Clayton
Production Designer	Roger Andrews
Associate Producer	Julian Meers
Supervising Producers	Laurence Marks, Maurice Gran
Executive Producer	Claire Hinson
Producer	John Bartlett
Director	Robin Nash

5. The Leaving of Liverpool

First broadcast: BBC One,
Tuesday 8 April 1997, 8.30pm
UK viewers: 7.43 million

Cast

Gary Sparrow	Nicholas Lyndhurst
Yvonne Sparrow	Emma Amos
Phoebe Bamford	Elizabeth Carling
Ron Wheatcroft	Victor McGuire
Reg Deadman	Christopher Ettridge
Gran	Carmel McSharry
Landlord	Kenneth Cope
Albert Wheatcroft	Vic Noir

Production Team

Created by	Laurence Marks, Maurice Gran
Written by	Geoff Rowley
Theme song performed by	Nick Curtis
Script Editor	Micheál Jacob
Casting	Paddy Stern, Susie Parriss
Costume Designer	Diana Moseley
Make-Up Designer	Gabrielle Hamilton
Graphic Designer	Paul Peppiate
Production Accountant	Sue Landsberger
Technical Manager	Derek Oliver
Vision Control	Andy Newton
Vision Mixer	Barbara Hicks
Console Operator	Terry Watson
Gaffer	Colin McCarthy
Location Manager	Julia Morpeth
Production Co-ordinator	Claire Newton
First Assistant Directors	Tristram Shapeero, Robert Crossley
Art Director	Judith Lang
Videotape Editors	Chris Wadsworth, Howard Denyer
Properties	Andy Beales
Property Buyer	Laurie Law
Production Manager	Mia Jupp
Stage Manager	Robert Crossley
Script Supervisor	Diane Taylor
Camera Supervisor	Tony Keene
Sound Supervisor	Paul Gartrell
Lighting Director	Christopher Clayton
Production Designer	Roger Andrews
Associate Producer	Julian Meers
Supervising Producers	Laurence Marks, Maurice Gran
Executive Producer	Claire Hinson
Producer	John Bartlett
Director	Robin Nash

6. How Long Has this Been Going On

First broadcast: BBC One,
Tuesday 15 April 1997, 8.30pm
UK viewers: 6.84 million

Cast

Gary Sparrow	Nicholas Lyndhurst
Phoebe Bamford	Elizabeth Carling
Yvonne Sparrow	Emma Amos
Ron Wheatcroft	Victor McGuire
Reg Deadman	Christopher Ettridge
Helen Shackleton	Susan Tracy
Margie Hook	Eve Bland
Jackie Hook	Gordon Winter
Stanley	Doug Fisher
Dr Obote	Cyril Nri

Production Team

Written by	Laurence Marks, Maurice Gran
Theme song performed by	Nick Curtis
Script Editor	Micheál Jacob
Casting	Paddy Stern, Susie Parriss
Costume Designer	Diana Moseley
Make-Up Designer	Gabrielle Hamilton
Graphic Designer	Paul Peppiate
Production Accountant	Sue Landsberger
Technical Manager	Derek Oliver
Vision Control	Richard Waiting
Vision Mixer	Barbara Hicks
Console Operator	Terry Watson
Gaffer	Colin McCarthy
Production Co-ordinator	Claire Newton
First Assistant Director	Julie Sykes
Art Director	Judith Lang
Videotape Editors	Chris Wadsworth, Howard Denyer
Properties	Andy Beales
Property Buyer	Laurie Law
Production Manager	Mia Jupp
Stage Manager	Robert Crossley
Script Supervisor	Diane Taylor
Camera Supervisor	Tony Keene
Sound Supervisor	Paul Gartrell
Lighting Director	Christopher Clayton
Production Designer	Roger Andrews
Associate Producer	Julian Meers
Supervising Producers	Laurence Marks, Maurice Gran
Executive Producer	Claire Hinson
Producer	John Bartlett
Director	Robin Nash

Goodnight Sweetheart: A Guide to the Classic Sitcom

7. Easy Living

First broadcast: BBC One,
Tuesday 22 April 1997, 8.30pm
UK viewers: 6.68 million

Cast

Gary Sparrow	Nicholas Lyndhurst
Yvonne Sparrow	Emma Amos
Phoebe Bamford	Elizabeth Carling
Ron Wheatcroft	Victor McGuire
Reg Deadman	Christopher Ettridge
Vicar	Peter Halliday
Police Sergeant	Jonathan Hackett

Production Team

Created by	Laurence Marks, Maurice Gran
Written by	Geoff Rowley
Theme song performed by	Nick Curtis
Script Editor	Micheál Jacob
Casting	Paddy Stern, Susie Parriss
Costume Designer	Jo Allman
Make-Up Designer	Gabrielle Hamilton
Graphic Designer	Paul Peppiate
Production Accountant	Sue Landsberger
Technical Manager	Derek Oliver
Vision Control	Richard Waiting
Vision Mixer	Barbara Hicks
Console Operator	Terry Watson
Gaffer	Colin McCarthy
Production Co-Ordinator	Claire Newton
First Assistant Director	Julie Sykes
Art Director	Judith Lang
Videotape Editor	Phil Moss
Properties	Andy Beales
Property Buyer	Laurie Law
Production Manager	Mia Jupp
Stage Manager	Robert Crossley
Script Supervisor	Diane Taylor
Camera Supervisor	Tony Keene
Sound Supervisor	Paul Gartrell
Lighting Director	Christopher Clayton
Production Designer	Roger Andrews
Associate Producer	Julian Meers
Supervising Producers	Laurence Marks, Maurice Gran
Executive Producer	Claire Hinson
Producer	John Bartlett
Director	Terry Kinane

8. Come Fly with Me

First broadcast: BBC One,
Tuesday 29 April 1997, 8.30pm
UK viewers: 6.00 million

Cast

Gary Sparrow	Nicholas Lyndhurst
Phoebe Bamford	Elizabeth Carling
Yvonne Sparrow	Emma Amos
Ron Wheatcroft	Victor McGuire
Reg Deadman	Christopher Ettridge
Steve	Chris Humphreys
Mike	John Fitzgerald-Jay
Joe	Jay Simon
Stripper	Danielle Tarento

Production Team

Created by	Laurence Marks, Maurice Gran
Written by	Sam Lawrence
Theme song performed by	Nick Curtis
Script Editor	Micheál Jacob
Casting	Paddy Stern, Susie Parriss
Costume Designer	Jo Allman
Make-Up Designer	Gabrielle Hamilton
Graphic Designer	Paul Peppiate
Production Accountant	Sue Landsberger
Technical Manager	Derek Oliver
Vision Control	Richard Waiting
Vision Mixer	Barbara Hicks
Console Operator	Terry Watson
Gaffer	Colin McCarthy
Production Co-ordinator	Claire Newton
First Assistant Director	Julie Sykes
Art Director	Judith Lang
Dubbing Mixer	Richard Churchill
Videotape Editors	Phil Moss, Howard Denyer
Properties	Andy Beales
Property Buyer	Laurie Law
Production Manager	Mia Jupp
Stage Manager	Robert Crossley
Script Supervisor	Diane Taylor
Camera Supervisor	Tony Keene
Sound Supervisor	Paul Gartrell
Lighting Director	Christopher Clayton
Production Designer	Roger Andrews
Associate Producer	Julian Meers
Supervising Producers	Laurence Marks, Maurice Gran
Executive Producer	Claire Hinson
Producer	John Bartlett
Director	Terry Kinane

9. Heartaches

First broadcast: BBC One,
Tuesday 6 May 1997, 8.30pm
UK viewers: 7.90 million

Cast

Gary Sparrow	Nicholas Lyndhurst
Yvonne Sparrow	Emma Amos
Phoebe Bamford/Sparrow	Elizabeth Carling
Ron Wheatcroft	Victor McGuire
Reg Deadman	Christopher Ettridge
Vicar	Peter Halliday
Margie Deadman	Eve Bland
Steve	Chris Humphreys
Stanley	Doug Fisher
Mrs Bloss	Yvonne D'Alpra
Peter	Chase Marks
Sally	Katie Donnison
Mrs French	Jeannie Crowther
Violet Bigby	Regina Freedman

Production Team

Created by	Laurence Marks, Maurice Gran
Written by	Paul Makin
Theme song performed by	Nick Curtis
Script Editor	Micheál Jacob
Casting	Paddy Stern, Susie Parriss
Costume Designer	Jo Allman
Make-Up Designer	Gabrielle Hamilton
Graphic Designer	Paul Peppiate
Production Accountant	Sue Landsberger
Technical Manager	Derek Oliver
Vision Control	Richard Waiting
Vision Mixer	Barbara Hicks
Console Operator	Terry Watson
Gaffer	Colin McCarthy
Production Co-ordinator	Claire Newton
First Assistant Director	Julie Sykes
Art Director	Judith Lang
Dubbing Mixer	Richard Churchill
Videotape Editors	Phil Moss, Howard Denyer
Properties	Andy Beales
Property Buyer	Laurie Law
Production Manager	Mia Jupp
Stage Manager	Robert Crossley
Script Supervisor	Diane Taylor
Camera Supervisor	Tony Keene
Sound Supervisor	Paul Gartrell
Lighting Director	Christopher Clayton
Production Designer	Roger Andrews
Associate Producer	Julian Meers
Supervising Producers	Laurence Marks, Maurice Gran
Executive Producer	Claire Hinson
Producer	John Bartlett
Director	Terry Kinane

10. Careless Talk…

First broadcast: BBC One,
Tuesday 13 May 1997, 8.30pm
UK viewers: 7.12 million

Cast

Gary Sparrow	Nicholas Lyndhurst
Phoebe Sparrow	Elizabeth Carling
Yvonne Sparrow	Emma Amos
Ron Wheatcroft	Victor McGuire
Reg Deadman	Christopher Ettridge
Kate	Allie Byrne
Shop Assistant	Peter Hughes

Production Team

Created by	Laurence Marks, Maurice Gran
Written by	Gary Lawson, John Phelps
Theme song performed by	Nick Curtis
Script Editor	Micheál Jacob
Casting	Paddy Stern, Susie Parriss
Costume Designer	Jo Allman
Make-Up Designer	Gabrielle Hamilton
Graphic Designer	Paul Peppiate
Production Accountant	Sue Landsberger
Technical Manager	Derek Oliver
Vision Control	Richard Waiting
Vision Mixer	Sandra Vardy
Console Operator	Terry Watson
Gaffer	Colin McCarthy
Production Co-ordinator	Claire Newton
First Assistant Director	Julie Sykes
Art Director	Judith Lang
Dubbing Mixer	Richard Churchill
Videotape Editors	Phil Moss, Howard Denyer
Properties	Andy Beales
Property Buyer	Laurie Law
Production Manager	Mia Jupp
Stage Manager	Robert Crossley
Script Supervisor	Diane Taylor
Camera Supervisor	Tony Keene
Sound Supervisor	Paul Gartrell
Lighting Director	Christopher Clayton
Production Designer	Roger Andrews
Associate Producer	Julian Meers
Supervising Producers	Laurence Marks, Maurice Gran
Executive Producer	Claire Hinson
Producer	John Bartlett
Director	Terry Kinane

Goodnight Sweetheart: A Guide to the Classic Sitcom

11. The Bells Are Ringing

First broadcast: BBC One,
Tuesday 20 May 1997, 8.30pm
UK viewers: 7.09 million

Cast

Gary Sparrow	Nicholas Lyndhurst
Yvonne Sparrow	Emma Amos
Phoebe Sparrow	Elizabeth Carling
Reg Deadman	Christopher Ettridge
Ron Wheatcroft	Victor McGuire
Margie Deadman	Eve Bland
Miss Weatherell	Brenda Cowling

Production Team

Created by	Laurence Marks, Maurice Gran
Written by	Paul Makin
Theme song performed by	Nick Curtis
Script Editor	Micheál Jacob
Casting	Paddy Stern, Susie Parriss
Costume Designers	Jo Allman, Phil Rainforth
Make-Up Designers	Gabrielle Hamilton, Shelley Greenham
Graphic Designer	Paul Peppiate
Production Accountant	Sue Landsberger
Technical Manager	Derek Oliver
Vision Control	Richard Waiting
Vision Mixer	Sandra Vardy
Console Operator	Terry Watson
Gaffer	Colin McCarthy
Production Co-ordinator	Claire Newton
First Assistant Director	Julie Sykes
Art Director	Judith Lang
Dubbing Mixer	Richard Churchill
Videotape Editors	Phil Moss, Howard Denyer
Properties	Andy Beales
Property Buyer	Laurie Law
Production Manager	Mia Jupp
Stage Manager	Robert Crossley
Script Supervisor	Diane Taylor
Camera Supervisor	Tony Keene
Sound Supervisor	Paul Gartrell
Lighting Directors	Christopher Clayton, Jared Clayton
Production Designer	Roger Andrews
Associate Producer	Julian Meers
Supervising Producers	Laurence Marks, Maurice Gran
Executive Producer	Claire Hinson
Producer	John Bartlett
Director	Terry Kinane

List of Episodes

Series 5

1. A Room with a View

First broadcast: BBC One,
Monday 23 February 1998, 8.30pm
UK viewers: 8.85 million

Cast

Gary Sparrow	Nicholas Lyndhurst
Yvonne Sparrow	Emma Amos
Phoebe Sparrow	Elizabeth Carling
Reg Deadman	Christopher Ettridge
Ron Wheatcroft	Victor McGuire
Mr Rutley	James Grout
Noël Coward	David Benson
George	Richard Syms
Rescue Worker	Alan Turner

Production Team

Written by	Laurence Marks, Maurice Gran
Theme song performed by	Nick Curtis
Script Editor	Micheál Jacob
Casting	Susie Parriss
Costume Designer	Jo Rainforth
Make-Up Designer	Gabrielle Hamilton
Graphic Designer	Paul Peppiate
Production Accountant	Sue Landsberger
Technical Manager	Derek Oliver
Vision Control	Andrew Newton
Vision Mixer	Barbara Hicks
Gaffer	Colin McCarthy
Location Manager	Garance Rawinsky
Production Co-ordinator	Emily Freshwater
First Assistant Director	Julie Sykes
Art Director	Judith Lang
Videotape Editor	Graham Carr
Property Master	Andy Beales
Properties	Bert Mackay
Stage Manager	Robert Crossley
Script Supervisor	Diane Taylor
Visual Effects	David Payne
Camera Supervisor	Tony Keene
Sound Supervisor	Paul Gartrell
Lighting Director	Christopher Clayton
Production Designer	Roger Andrews
Line Producer	Julian Meers
Supervising Producers	Laurence Marks, Maurice Gran
Executive Producer	Claire Hinson
Producer	John Bartlett
Director	Terry Kinane

2. London Pride

First broadcast: BBC One,
Monday 2 March 1998, 8.30pm
UK viewers: 7.86 million

Cast

Gary Sparrow	Nicholas Lyndhurst
Phoebe Sparrow	Elizabeth Carling
Yvonne Sparrow	Emma Amos
Ron Wheatcroft	Victor McGuire
Reg Deadman	Christopher Ettridge
Noël Coward	David Benson
Butcher	Lloyd McGuire
Mr Hornby	Nick Lucas
Interviewer	Esther McVey
Policewoman	Penelope Solomon
Mrs Greig	Toni Palmer

Production Team

Written by	Laurence Marks, Maurice Gran
Theme song performed by	Nick Curtis
Script Editor	Micheál Jacob
Casting	Susie Parriss
Costume Designer	Jo Rainforth
Make-Up Designer	Gabrielle Hamilton
Graphic Designer	Paul Peppiate
Production Accountant	Sue Landsberger
Technical Manager	Derek Oliver
Vision Control	Andrew Newton
Vision Mixer	Barbara Hicks
Gaffer	Tony Greatorex
Location Manager	Garance Rawinsky
Production Co-ordinator	Emily Freshwater
First Assistant Director	Julie Sykes
Art Director	Judith Lang
Videotape Editor	Graham Carr
Property Master	Andy Beales
Properties	Bert Mackay
Stage Manager	Robert Crossley
Script Supervisor	Diane Taylor
Camera Supervisor	Tony Keene
Sound Supervisor	Paul Gartrell
Lighting Director	Christopher Clayton
Production Designer	Roger Andrews
Line Producer	Julian Meers
Supervising Producers	Laurence Marks, Maurice Gran
Executive Producer	Claire Hinson
Producer	John Bartlett
Director	Terry Kinane

Goodnight Sweetheart: A Guide to the Classic Sitcom

3. When Two Worlds Collide

First broadcast: BBC One,
Monday 9 March 1998, 8.30pm
UK viewers: 8.89 million

Cast

Gary Sparrow	Nicholas Lyndhurst
Yvonne Sparrow	Emma Amos
Phoebe Bamford	Elizabeth Carling
Reg Deadman	Christopher Ettridge
Ron Wheatcroft	Victor McGuire

Production Team

Created by	Laurence Marks, Maurice Gran
Written by	Gary Lawson, John Phelps
Theme song performed by	Nick Curtis
Script Editor	Micheál Jacob
Casting	Susie Parriss
Costume Designer	Jo Rainforth
Make-Up Designer	Gabrielle Hamilton
Graphic Designer	Paul Peppiate
Production Accountant	Sue Landsberger
Technical Manager	Derek Oliver
Vision Control	Andrew Newton
Vision Mixer	Barbara Hicks
Gaffer	Colin McCarthy
Location Manager	Garance Rawinsky
Production Co-ordinator	Emily Freshwater
First Assistant Director	Julie Sykes
Art Director	Judith Lang
Videotape Editor	Graham Carr
Property Master	Andy Beales
Properties	Bert Mackay
Stage Manager	Robert Crossley
Script Supervisor	Diane Taylor
Visual Effects	David Payne
Stuntman	Lee Sheward
Camera Supervisor	Tony Keene
Sound Supervisor	Paul Gartrell
Lighting Director	Christopher Clayton
Production Designer	Roger Andrews
Line Producer	Julian Meers
Supervising Producers	Laurence Marks, Maurice Gran
Executive Producer	Claire Hinson
Producer	John Bartlett
Director	Terry Kinane

4. Mairzy Doats

First broadcast: BBC One,
Monday 16 March 1998, 8.30pm
UK viewers: 8.82 million

Cast

Gary Sparrow	Nicholas Lyndhurst
Phoebe Sparrow	Elizabeth Carling
Yvonne Sparrow	Emma Amos
Ron Wheatcroft	Victor McGuire
Reg Deadman	Christopher Ettridge
Margie Deadman	Eve Bland
George	Richard Syms
Violet Bigby	Regina Freedman
Nightclub Owner	David Simeon

Production Team

Created by	Laurence Marks, Maurice Gran
Written by	Geoff Rowley
Theme song performed by	Nick Curtis
Choreography	Brian Rogers
Script Editor	Micheál Jacob
Casting	Susie Parriss
Costume Designer	Jo Rainforth
Make-Up Designer	Gabrielle Hamilton
Graphic Designer	Paul Peppiate
Production Accountant	Sue Landsberger
Technical Manager	Derek Oliver
Vision Control	Andrew Newton
Vision Mixer	Barbara Hicks
Gaffer	Colin McCarthy
Production Co-ordinator	Emily Freshwater
First Assistant Director	Julie Sykes
Art Director	Judith Lang
Videotape Editor	Graham Carr
Property Master	Andy Beales
Properties	Bert Mackay
Stage Manager	Robert Crossley
Script Supervisor	Diane Taylor
Visual Effects	David Payne
Stunts	Lee Sheward
Camera Supervisor	Tony Keene
Sound Supervisor	Paul Gartrell
Lighting Director	Christopher Clayton
Production Designer	Roger Andrews
Line Producer	Julian Meers
Supervising Producers	Laurence Marks, Maurice Gran
Executive Producer	Claire Hinson
Producer	John Bartlett
Director	Terry Kinane

5. Pennies from Heaven

First broadcast: BBC One,
Monday 23 March 1998, 8.30pm
UK viewers: 8.66 million

Cast

Gary Sparrow	Nicholas Lyndhurst
Yvonne Sparrow	Emma Amos
Phoebe Sparrow	Elizabeth Carling
Reg Deadman	Christopher Ettridge
Ron Wheatcroft	Victor McGuire
Mrs Flanagan	Pippa Haywood
Bookie	David Ross
DS Bruce	Robert Perkins
Punter	Nick Carpenter

Production Team

Created by	Laurence Marks, Maurice Gran
Written by	Geoff Rowley
Theme song performed by	Nick Curtis
Script Editor	Micheál Jacob
Casting	Susie Parriss
Costume Designer	Jo Rainforth
Make-Up Designer	Gabrielle Hamilton
Graphic Designer	Paul Peppiate
Production Accountant	Sue Landsberger
Technical Manager	Derek Oliver
Vision Control	Andrew Newton
Vision Mixer	Barbara Hicks
Gaffer	Colin McCarthy
Location Manager	Garance Rawinsky
Production Co-ordinator	Emily Freshwater
First Assistant Director	Julie Sykes
Art Director	Judith Lang
Videotape Editor	Graham Carr
Property Master	Andy Beales
Properties	Bert Mackay
Stage Manager	Robert Crossley
Script Supervisor	Diane Taylor
Camera Supervisor	Tony Keene
Sound Supervisor	Paul Gartrell
Lighting Director	Christopher Clayton
Production Designer	Roger Andrews
Line Producer	Julian Meers
Supervising Producers	Laurence Marks, Maurice Gran
Executive Producer	Claire Hinson
Producer	John Bartlett
Director	Terry Kinane

6. We Don't Want to Lose You...

First broadcast: BBC One,
Monday 30 March 1998, 8.30pm
UK viewers: 8.28 million

Cast

Gary Sparrow	Nicholas Lyndhurst
Phoebe Sparrow	Elizabeth Carling
Yvonne Sparrow	Emma Amos
Ron Wheatcroft	Victor McGuire
Reg Deadman	Christopher Ettridge
Tufty McDuff	Timothy West

Production Team

Created by	Laurence Marks, Maurice Gran
Written by	Sam Lawrence
Theme song performed by	Nick Curtis
Script Editor	Micheál Jacob
Casting	Susie Parriss
Costume Designer	Jo Rainforth
Make-Up Designers	Gabrielle Hamilton
Graphic Designer	Paul Peppiate
Production Accountant	Sue Landsberger
Technical Manager	Derek Oliver
Vision Control	Andrew Newton
Vision Mixer	Barbara Hicks
Gaffer	Colin McCarthy
Location Manager	Garance Rawinsky
Production Co-ordinator	Emily Freshwater
First Assistant Director	Julie Sykes
Art Director	Judith Lang
Videotape Editor	Graham Carr
Property Master	Andy Beales
Properties	Bert Mackay
Stage Manager	Robert Crossley
Script Supervisor	Diane Taylor
Camera Supervisor	Tony Keene
Sound Supervisor	Paul Gartrell
Lighting Directors	Christopher Clayton
Production Designer	Roger Andrews
Line Producer	Julian Meers
Supervising Producers	Laurence Marks, Maurice Gran
Executive Producer	Claire Hinson
Producer	John Bartlett
Director	Robin Nash

Goodnight Sweetheart: A Guide to the Classic Sitcom

7. ...But We Think You Have to Go

First broadcast: BBC One,
Monday 6 April 1998, 8.30pm
UK viewers: 8.18 million

Cast

Gary Sparrow/Colonel Henri Dupont	Nicholas Lyndhurst
Yvonne Sparrow	Emma Amos
Phoebe Sparrow	Elizabeth Carling
Reg Deadman	Christopher Ettridge
Ron Wheatcroft	Victor McGuire
Tufty McDuff	Timothy West
Celeste	Sally Dexter
Weiss	Peter Czajkowski
Simone Sutherland	Rae Baker
Holz	Jason Hall

Production Team

Created by	Laurence Marks, Maurice Gran
Written by	Sam Lawrence
Theme song performed by	Nick Curtis
Script Editor	Micheál Jacob
Casting	Susie Parriss
Costume Designer	Jo Rainforth
Make-Up Designer	Gabrielle Hamilton
Graphic Designer	Paul Peppiate
Production Accountant	Sue Landsberger
Engineering Manager	Derek Oliver
Vision Control	Andrew Newton
Vision Mixer	Barbara Hicks
Gaffer	Colin McCarthy
Location Manager	Garance Rawinsky
Production Co-Ordinator	Emily Freshwater
First Assistant Director	Julie Sykes
Art Director	Judith Lang
Videotape Editor	Graham Carr
Property Master	Andy Beales
Properties	Bert Mackay
Stage Manager	Robert Crossley
Script Supervisor	Diane Taylor
Stunts	Jamie Edgell
Camera Supervisor	Tony Keene
Sound Supervisor	Paul Gartrell
Lighting Director	Christopher Clayton
Production Designer	Roger Andrews
Line Producer	Julian Meers
Supervising Producers	Laurence Marks, Maurice Gran
Executive Producer	Claire Hinson
Producer	John Bartlett
Director	Robin Nash

8. Have You Ever Seen a Dream Walking

First broadcast: BBC One,
Monday 13 April 1998, 8.30pm
UK viewers: 7.39 million

Cast

Gary Sparrow	Nicholas Lyndhurst
Phoebe Sparrow	Elizabeth Carling
Yvonne Sparrow	Emma Amos
Ron Wheatcroft	Victor McGuire
Reg Deadman	Christopher Ettridge
Therapist	Penelope Solomon
Mrs Hardcore	Anna Karen
Guest Appearance	Rolf Harris

Production Team

Created by	Laurence Marks, Maurice Gran
Written by	Gary Lawson, John Phelps
Theme song performed by	Nick Curtis
Script Editor	Micheál Jacob
Casting	Susie Parriss
Costume Designer	Jo Rainforth
Make-Up Designer	Gabrielle Hamilton
Graphic Designer	Paul Peppiate
Production Accountant	Sue Landsberger
Engineering Manager	Derek Oliver
Vision Control	Andrew Newton
Vision Mixer	Barbara Hicks
Gaffer	Colin McCarthy
Production Co-ordinator	Emily Freshwater
First Assistant Director	Julie Sykes
Art Director	Judith Lang
Videotape Editor	Graham Carr
Property Master	Andy Beales
Properties	Bert Mackay
Stage Manager	Robert Crossley
Script Supervisor	Diane Taylor
Camera Supervisor	Tony Keene
Sound Supervisor	Paul Gartrell
Lighting Director	Christopher Clayton
Production Designer	Roger Andrews
Line Producer	Julian Meers
Supervising Producers	Laurence Marks, Maurice Gran
Executive Producer	Claire Hinson
Producer	John Bartlett
Director	Robin Nash

9. Love the One You're With

First broadcast: BBC One,
Monday 20 April 1998, 8.30pm
UK viewers: 8.17 million

Cast

Gary Sparrow	Nicholas Lyndhurst
Yvonne Sparrow	Emma Amos
Phoebe Sparrow	Elizabeth Carling
Reg Deadman	Christopher Ettridge
Ron Wheatcroft	Victor McGuire
Mr Rutley	James Grout
Margie Deadman	Eve Bland
Noël Coward	David Benson
Porter	Brian Rawlinson
Nurse	Liz Whiting

Production Team

Written by	Laurence Marks, Maurice Gran
Theme song performed by	Nick Curtis
Script Editor	Micheál Jacob
Casting	Susie Parriss
Costume Designer	Jo Rainforth
Make-Up Designer	Gabrielle Hamilton
Graphic Designer	Paul Peppiate
Production Accountant	Sue Landsberger
Engineering Manager	Derek Oliver
Vision Control	Andrew Newton
Vision Mixer	Barbara Hicks
Gaffer	Colin McCarthy
Production Co-ordinator	Emily Freshwater
First Assistant Director	Julie Sykes
Art Director	Judith Lang
Videotape Editor	Graham Carr
Property Master	Andy Beales
Properties	Bert Mackay
Stage Manager	Robert Crossley
Script Supervisor	Diane Taylor
Camera Supervisor	Tony Keene
Sound Supervisor	Paul Gartrell
Lighting Director	Christopher Clayton
Production Designer	Roger Andrews
Line Producer	Julian Meers
Supervising Producers	Laurence Marks, Maurice Gran
Executive Producer	Claire Hinson
Producer	John Bartlett
Director	Robin Nash

10. My Heart Belongs to Daddy

First broadcast: BBC One,
Monday 27 April 1998, 8.30pm
UK viewers: 7.29 million

Cast

Gary Sparrow	Nicholas Lyndhurst
Phoebe Sparrow	Elizabeth Carling
Yvonne Sparrow	Emma Amos
Ron Wheatcroft	Victor McGuire
Reg Deadman	Christopher Ettridge
Michael Sparrow	Ian Lavender
Noël Coward	David Benson
Knacker John	David Bauckham

Production Team

Created by	Laurence Marks, Maurice Gran
Written by	Sam Lawrence
Theme song performed by	Nick Curtis
'Phoebe's Song' by David Harsent, Mark Bastable	
Script Editor	Micheál Jacob
Casting	Susie Parriss
Costume Designer	Jo Rainforth
Make-Up Designers	Gabrielle Hamilton, Shelley Greenham
Graphic Designers	Paul Peppiate, Graham Walker
Production Accountant	Sue Landsberger
Engineering Manager	Derek Oliver
Vision Control	Andrew Newton
Vision Mixer	Barbara Hicks
Gaffer	Colin McCarthy
Production Co-ordinator	Emily Freshwater
First Assistant Director	Julie Sykes
Art Director	Judith Lang
Videotape Editors	Graham Carr, Graham Portbury, Howard Denyer
Property Master	Andy Beales
Properties	Bert Mackay
Stage Manager	Robert Crossley
Script Supervisor	Diane Taylor
Camera Supervisor	Tony Keene
Sound Supervisor	Paul Gartrell
Lighting Directors	Christopher Clayton, Jared Clayton
Production Designer	Roger Andrews
Line Producer	Julian Meers
Supervising Producers	Laurence Marks, Maurice Gran
Executive Producer	Claire Hinson
Producer	John Bartlett
Director	Robin Nash

Goodnight Sweetheart: A Guide to the Classic Sitcom

Series 6

1. Mine's a Double

First broadcast: BBC One,
Sunday 18 April 1999, 8.30pm
UK viewers: 7.83 million

Cast

Gary Sparrow/Bad Gary/Good Gary	Nicholas Lyndhurst
Phoebe Sparrow	Elizabeth Carling
Yvonne Sparrow	Emma Amos
Ron Wheatcroft	Victor McGuire
Reg Deadman	Christopher Ettridge

Production Team

Created by	Laurence Marks, Maurice Gran
Written by	Gary Lawson, John Phelps
Theme song performed by	Nick Curtis
Script Editor	Victoria Grew
Casting	Susie Parriss
Costume Designer	Jo Rainforth
Make-Up Designer	Sue Ayling
Graphic Designer	Paul Peppiate
Production Accountant	Sue Landsberger
Engineering Manager	Derek Oliver
Vision Control	Andrew Newton
Vision Mixer	Peter Phillips
Gaffer	Peter Dale
Location Manager	Garance Rawinsky
Production Co-ordinator	Debbie Stafford
First Assistant Director	Julie Sykes
Art Director	Heather Gibson
Dubbing Mixer	Adrian Smith
Videotape Editor	Phil Moss
Property Master	Andy Beales
Properties	Bert Mackay
Stage Manager	Clare Brown
Script Supervisor	Diane Taylor
Camera Supervisor	Tony Keene
Sound Supervisor	Paul Gartrell
Lighting Director	Christopher Clayton
Production Designer	David Ferris
Production Manager	Chris Iliffe
Line Producer	Julian Meers
Supervising Producers	Laurence Marks, Maurice Gran
Executive Producer	Claire Hinson
Produced and Directed by	Nic Phillips

2. All About Yvonne

First broadcast: BBC One,
Sunday 25 April 1999, 8.30pm
UK viewers: 6.96 million

Cast

Gary Sparrow	Nicholas Lyndhurst
Yvonne Sparrow	Emma Amos
Phoebe Sparrow	Elizabeth Carling
Reg Deadman	Christopher Ettridge
Ron Wheatcroft	Victor McGuire
Flic	Sonya Walger
Roberto	Gavin Abbott

Production Team

Created by	Laurence Marks, Maurice Gran
Written by	Gary Lawson, John Phelps
Theme song performed by	Nick Curtis
Script Editor	Victoria Grew
Casting	Susie Parriss
Costume Designer	Jo Rainforth
Make-Up Designer	Sue Ayling
Graphic Designer	Paul Peppiate
Production Accountant	Sue Landsberger
Engineering Manager	Derek Oliver
Vision Control	Andrew Newton
Vision Mixer	Barbara Hicks
Gaffer	Colin McCarthy
Production Co-ordinator	Debbie Stafford
First Assistant Director	Julie Sykes
Art Director	Heather Gibson
Dubbing Mixer	Adrian Smith
Videotape Editor	Phil Moss
Property Master	Andy Beales
Properties	Bert Mackay
Stage Manager	Clare Brown
Script Supervisor	Diane Taylor
Camera Supervisor	Tony Keene
Sound Supervisor	Paul Gartrell
Lighting Director	Christopher Clayton
Production Designer	David Ferris
Production Manager	Chris Iliffe
Line Producer	Julian Meers
Supervising Producers	Laurence Marks, Maurice Gran
Executive Producer	Claire Hinson
Produced and Directed by	Nic Phillips

3. California Dreamin'

First broadcast: BBC One,
Sunday 2 May 1999, 8.30pm
UK viewers: 5.70 million

Cast

Gary Sparrow	Nicholas Lyndhurst
Yvonne Sparrow	Emma Amos
Phoebe Sparrow	Elizabeth Carling
Reg Deadman	Christopher Ettridge
Ron Wheatcroft	Victor McGuire
Flic	Sonya Walger
Fred	Gary Lammin
Daisy	Tabitha Wady
Angus	Donald Douglas

Production Team

Created by	Laurence Marks, Maurice Gran
Written by	Sam Lawrence
Theme song performed by	Nick Curtis
Script Editor	Victoria Grew
Music Arranged by	Logorhythm Music
Casting	Susie Parriss
Costume Designer	Jo Rainforth
Make-Up Designer	Sue Ayling
Graphic Designer	Paul Peppiate
Production Accountant	Sue Landsberger
Engineering Manager	Derek Oliver
Vision Control	Andrew Newton
Vision Mixer	Barbara Hicks
Gaffer	Dick Crane
Location Manager	Garance Rawinsky
Production Co-ordinator	Debbie Stafford
First Assistant Director	Julie Sykes
Art Director	Heather Gibson
Dubbing Mixer	Adrian Smith
Videotape Editor	Phil Moss
Property Master	Andy Beales
Properties	Bert Mackay
Stage Manager	Clare Brown
Script Supervisor	Diane Taylor
Camera Supervisor	Tony Keene
Sound Supervisor	Paul Gartrell
Lighting Director	Christopher Clayton
Production Designer	David Ferris
Production Manager	Chris Iliffe
Line Producer	Julian Meers
Supervising Producers	Laurence Marks, Maurice Gran
Executive Producer	Claire Hinson
Produced and Directed by	Nic Phillips

4. Grief Encounter

First broadcast: BBC One,
Sunday 16 May 1999, 8.30pm
UK viewers: 5.66 million

Cast

Gary Sparrow	Nicholas Lyndhurst
Phoebe Sparrow	Elizabeth Carling
Yvonne Sparrow	Emma Amos
Ron Wheatcroft	Victor McGuire
Reg Deadman	Christopher Ettridge
Noël Coward	David Benson
Anthony Blair	Paul Goodwin
Murray	Rolf Saxon
Celia Johnson	Dolly Wells
Trevor Howard	Andrew Havill
David Lean	Richard Braine

Production Team

Written by	Laurence Marks, Maurice Gran
Brief Encounter	Courtesy of Carlton International Media Limited
'Tony's Song' composed by	David Harsent, Logorhythm Music
Theme song performed by	Nick Curtis
Script Editor	Victoria Grew
Music Arranged by	Logorhythm Music
Casting	Susie Parriss
Costume Designer	Jo Rainforth
Make-Up Designer	Sue Ayling
Graphic Designer	Paul Peppiate
Production Accountant	Sue Landsberger
Engineering Manager	Derek Oliver
Vision Control	Andrew Newton
Vision Mixer	Barbara Hicks
Gaffer	Dick Crane
Location Manager	Garance Rawinsky
Production Co-ordinator	Debbie Stafford
First Assistant Director	Julie Sykes
Art Director	Heather Gibson
Dubbing Mixer	Adrian Smith
Videotape Editor	Phil Moss
Property Master	Andy Beales
Properties	Bert Mackay
Stage Manager	Clare Brown
Script Supervisor	Diane Taylor
Camera Supervisor	Tony Keene
Sound Supervisor	Paul Gartrell
Lighting Director	Christopher Clayton
Production Designer	David Ferris
Production Manager	Chris Iliffe
Line Producer	Julian Meers
Supervising Producers	Laurence Marks, Maurice Gran
Executive Producer	Claire Hinson
Produced and Directed by	Nic Phillips

Goodnight Sweetheart: A Guide to the Classic Sitcom

5. The 'Ouses in Between

First broadcast: BBC One,
Sunday 23 May 1999, 8.30pm
UK viewers: 6.20 million

Cast

Gary Sparrow	Nicholas Lyndhurst
Yvonne Sparrow/Marie Lloyd	Emma Amos
Phoebe Sparrow	Elizabeth Carling
Reg Deadman/Isambard Deadman	
	Christopher Ettridge
Ron Wheatcroft	Victor McGuire
Jack the Ripper	Nicholas Day
Detective	John Harding
MC	Mike Savage
Woman	Sophie-Louise Dann
Taxi Driver	Alex Leppard
Heckler	Terry Bird

Production Team

Created by	Laurence Marks, Maurice Gran
Written by	Geoff Rowley
Theme song performed by	Nick Curtis
Script Editor	Victoria Grew
Music Arranged by	Logorhythm Music
Casting	Susie Parriss
Costume Designer	Jo Rainforth
Make-Up Designer	Sue Ayling
Graphic Designer	Paul Peppiate
Production Accountant	Sue Landsberger
Engineering Manager	Derek Oliver
Vision Control	Andrew Newton
Vision Mixer	Barbara Hicks
Gaffer	Colin McCarthy
Location Manager	Garance Rawinsky
Production Co-ordinator	Debbie Stafford
First Assistant Director	Julie Sykes
Art Director	Heather Gibson
Dubbing Mixer	Adrian Smith
Videotape Editor	Phil Moss
Property Master	Andy Beales
Properties	Bert Mackay
Stage Manager	Clare Brown
Script Supervisor	Diane Taylor
Camera Supervisor	Tony Keene
Sound Supervisor	Paul Gartrell
Lighting Director	Christopher Clayton
Production Designer	David Ferris
Production Manager	Chris Iliffe
Line Producer	Julian Meers
Supervising Producers	Laurence Marks, Maurice Gran
Executive Producer	Claire Hinson
Produced and Directed by	Nic Phillips

6. Just in Time

First broadcast: BBC One,
Sunday 30 May 1999, 8.30pm
UK viewers: 6.10 million

Cast

Gary Sparrow	Nicholas Lyndhurst
Phoebe Sparrow	Elizabeth Carling
Yvonne Sparrow	Emma Amos
Ron Wheatcroft	Victor McGuire
Reg Deadman	Christopher Ettridge
Margie Deadman	Eve Bland
Sparks	Toby Whitehouse
Brick	Tom Goodman-Hill

Production Team

Created by	Laurence Marks, Maurice Gran
Written by	Geoff Rowley
Theme song performed by	Nick Curtis
Script Editor	Victoria Grew
Music Arranged by	Logorhythm Music
Casting	Susie Parriss
Costume Designer	Jo Rainforth
Make-Up Designer	Sue Ayling
Graphic Designer	Paul Peppiate
Production Accountant	Sue Landsberger
Engineering Manager	Derek Oliver
Vision Control	Andrew Newton
Vision Mixer	Barbara Hicks
Gaffer	Colin McCarthy
Location Manager	Garance Rawinsky
Production Co-ordinator	Debbie Stafford
First Assistant Director	Julie Sykes
Art Director	Heather Gibson
Dubbing Mixer	Adrian Smith
Videotape Editor	Mark Sangster
Property Master	Andy Beales
Properties	Bert Mackay
Stage Manager	Clare Brown
Script Supervisor	Diane Taylor
Camera Supervisor	Tony Keene
Sound Supervisor	Paul Gartrell
Lighting Director	Christopher Clayton
Production Designer	David Ferris
Production Manager	Chris Iliffe
Line Producer	Julian Meers
Supervising Producers	Laurence Marks, Maurice Gran
Executive Producer	Claire Hinson
Producer	Nic Phillips
Director	Robin Nash

List of Episodes

7. How I Won the War

First broadcast: BBC One,
Sunday 6 June 1999, 8.35pm
UK viewers: 6.44 million

Cast

Gary Sparrow	Nicholas Lyndhurst
Yvonne Sparrow	Emma Amos
Phoebe Sparrow	Elizabeth Carling
Reg Deadman	Christopher Ettridge
Ron Wheatcroft	Victor McGuire
Nancy Potter	Bonnie Langford
Flic	Sonya Walger
Nipper Smith	Simon Sherlock
Rock Justice	Gary Cady
Sid Potter	Paul Grunert
Brian Merry	Jim McManus

Production Team

Created by	Laurence Marks, Maurice Gran
Written by	Sam Lawrence
Theme song performed by	Nick Curtis
Script Editor	Victoria Grew
Casting	Susie Parriss
Costume Designer	Jo Rainforth
Make-Up Designer	Sue Ayling
Graphic Designer	Paul Peppiate
Production Accountant	Sue Landsberger
Engineering Manager	Derek Oliver
Vision Control	Andrew Newton
Vision Mixer	Barbara Hicks
Gaffer	Colin McCarthy
Location Manager	Garance Rawinsky
Production Co-ordinator	Debbie Stafford
First Assistant Director	Julie Sykes
Art Director	Heather Gibson
Dubbing Mixer	Phil Reed
Videotape Editor	Mark Sangster
Property Master	Alan Mesure
Properties	Bert Mackay
Stage Manager	Clare Brown
Script Supervisor	Diane Taylor
Visual Effects	Andy McVean
Camera Supervisor	Tony Keene
Sound Supervisor	Paul Gartrell
Lighting Director	Christopher Clayton
Production Designer	David Ferris
Production Manager	Chris Iliffe
Line Producer	Julian Meers
Supervising Producers	Laurence Marks, Maurice Gran
Executive Producer	Claire Hinson
Producer	Nic Phillips
Director	Robin Nash

8. Something Fishie

First broadcast: BBC One,
Sunday 13 June 1999, 9.25pm
UK viewers: 5.26 million

Cast

Gary Sparrow	Nicholas Lyndhurst
Phoebe Sparrow	Elizabeth Carling
Yvonne Sparrow	Emma Amos
Ron Wheatcroft	Victor McGuire
Reg Deadman	Christopher Ettridge
Mrs Green	Lynda Baron
Mr Smith	Leo Dolan
Mr Jones	Kenneth MacDonald
Priestley	Norman Eshley
Newsreader	Emily Bruni

Production Team

Created by	Laurence Marks, Maurice Gran
Written by	Sam Lawrence
Theme song performed by	Nick Curtis
Script Editor	Victoria Grew
Music Arranged by	Logorhythm Music
Casting	Susie Parriss
Costume Designer	Jo Rainforth
Make-Up Designer	Sue Ayling
Graphic Designer	Paul Peppiate
Production Accountant	Sue Landsberger
Engineering Manager	Derek Oliver
Vision Control	Andrew Newton
Vision Mixer	Barbara Hicks
Gaffer	Colin McCarthy
Location Manager	Garance Rawinsky
Production Co-ordinator	Debbie Stafford
First Assistant Director	Julie Sykes
Art Director	Heather Gibson
Dubbing Mixer	Phil Reed
Videotape Editor	Phil Moss
Property Master	Andy Beales
Properties	Bert Mackay
Stage Manager	Clare Brown
Script Supervisor	Diane Taylor
Camera Supervisor	Tony Keene
Sound Supervisor	Paul Gartrell
Lighting Director	Christopher Clayton
Production Designer	David Ferris
Production Manager	Chris Iliffe
Line Producer	Julian Meers
Supervising Producers	Laurence Marks, Maurice Gran
Executive Producer	Claire Hinson
Producer	Nic Phillips
Director	Terry Kinane

Goodnight Sweetheart: A Guide to the Classic Sitcom

9. Flash, Bang, Wallop

First broadcast: BBC One,
Monday 21 June 1999, 8.30pm
UK viewers: 6.86 million

Cast

Gary Sparrow	Nicholas Lyndhurst
Yvonne Sparrow	Emma Amos
Phoebe Sparrow	Elizabeth Carling
Reg Deadman	Christopher Ettridge
Ron Wheatcroft	Victor McGuire
Noël Coward	David Benson
PC Cotterill	Robert Whitelock
Mr Bannister	Robin Meredith
Holiday Rep	Dorothea Phillips

Production Team

Created by	Laurence Marks, Maurice Gran
Written by	Paul Alexander, Simon Braithwaite
Theme song performed by	Nick Curtis
Script Editor	Victoria Grew
Music Arranged by	Logorhythm Music
Casting	Susie Parriss
Costume Designer	Jo Rainforth
Make-Up Designer	Sue Ayling
Graphic Designer	Paul Peppiate
Production Accountant	Sue Landsberger
Engineering Manager	Derek Oliver
Vision Control	Andrew Newton
Vision Mixer	Barbara Hicks
Gaffer	Peter Dale
Location Manager	Garance Rawinsky
Production Co-ordinator	Debbie Stafford
First Assistant Director	Julie Sykes
Art Director	Heather Gibson
Dubbing Mixer	Adrian Smith
Videotape Editor	Phil Moss
Property Master	Andy Beales
Properties	Bert Mackay
Stage Manager	Clare Brown
Script Supervisor	Diane Taylor
Camera Supervisor	Tony Keene
Sound Supervisor	Paul Gartrell
Lighting Director	Jared Clayton
Production Designer	David Ferris
Production Manager	Chris Iliffe
Line Producer	Julian Meers
Supervising Producers	Laurence Marks, Maurice Gran
Executive Producer	Claire Hinson
Producer	Nic Phillips
Director	Terry Kinane

10. Accentuate the Positive

First broadcast: BBC One, BBC One,
Monday 28 June 1999, 8.30pm
UK viewers: 8.33 million

Cast

Gary Sparrow	Nicholas Lyndhurst
Phoebe Sparrow	Elizabeth Carling
Yvonne Sparrow	Emma Amos
Ron Wheatcroft	Victor McGuire
Reg Deadman	Christopher Ettridge
Clement Attlee MP	Alan David
Kenneth	Tony Millan

Production Team

Written by	Laurence Marks, Maurice Gran
Theme song performed by	Nick Curtis
Script Editor	Victoria Grew
Music Arranged by	Logorhythm Music
Casting	Susie Parriss
Costume Designers	Jo Rainforth, Phil Rainforth
Make-Up Designer	Sue Ayling
Graphic Designer	Paul Peppiate
Production Accountant	Sue Landsberger
Engineering Manager	Derek Oliver
Vision Control	Andrew Newton
Vision Mixer	Barbara Hicks
Gaffer	Stuart Davies
Location Manager	Garance Rawinsky
Production Co-ordinator	Debbie Stafford
First Assistant Director	Julie Sykes
Art Director	Heather Gibson
Dubbing Mixer	Phil Reed
Videotape Editors	Phil Moss, Howard Denyer
Property Master	Alan Mesure
Properties	Bert Mackay
Stage Manager	Clare Brown
Script Supervisor	Diane Taylor
Camera Supervisor	Paul Freeman
OB Camera	Tony Keene
Grip	Andy Young
Sound Supervisor	Paul Gartrell
OB Sound	Bob Newton
Lighting Director	Christopher Clayton
Production Designer	David Ferris
Production Manager	Chris Iliffe
Line Producer	Julian Meers
Supervising Producers	Laurence Marks, Maurice Gran
Executive Producer	Claire Hinson
Producer	Nic Phillips
Director	Terry Kinane

Special

Many Happy Returns

First broadcast: BBC One,
Friday 2 September 2016, 9.00pm
UK viewers: 4.66 million

Cast

Gary Sparrow	Nicholas Lyndhurst
Phoebe Sparrow	Elizabeth Carling
Yvonne Sparrow	Emma Amos
Ron Wheatcroft	Victor McGuire
Reg Deadman	Christopher Ettridge
Michael Sparrow	Tim Preston
George Sparrow	Liam Jeavons
Midwife	Angela Murray
Phone Salesman	Khali Best
Bouncer	Ted Robbins
Ellie	Esme Coy

Production Team

Written by	Laurence Marks, Maurice Gran
Goodnight Sweetheart composed by	Ray Noble, Jimmy Campbell, Reg Connelly
Arranged by	Keith Strachan, Matthew Strachan
Performed by	Damien Edwards
Casting Director	Susie Parriss
First Assistant Director/Floor Manager	Julie Sykes
First Assistant Director/Stage Manager	Helene Beauchamp
Third Assistant Director	Mark Nunn
Assistant Floor Manager	Kerrie Chandler
Make-Up Artists	Nicola Ogden Davies, Helen Black
Costumer Supervisors	Kat Cappellazzi, Jo Thompson
Costume Standbys	Bocca Williams, Rosa Diamond
Petty Cash Buyer	Laura Rose Konstam
Standby Props	Kenny Augustin, David Jones
Dressing Props	Ian Newton, Dempsey Cook
Prop Master	Gary Watson
Production Buyer	Terry Jones
Art Director	Siobhan Pemberton
Grip	Lee Naylor-Vane
Location Manager	Ben Mangham
Vision Mixer	Peter Phillips
Production Runner	Sam Allen
Production Secretary	Nick Dyne
Junior Production Co-ordinator	Emma-Jayne Cullen
Junior Production Manager	Cat Hadrill
Production Accountant	Margarita Piatek
Script Supervisor	Suzanne Baron
Costume Designer	Caroline Pitcher
Make-Up Designer	Carlene Gearing
Location Gaffer	Paul Barlow
Studio Gaffer	Matt Taylor
Camera Supervisor	Tony Keene
Location Sound Recordist	Sam Diamond
Sound Supervisor	Kevin Paice
Title Design	Works
Visual Effects	Hugh Johnson, Jan Meyer, Marcus Millichope
Dubbing Mixer	Glenn Calder
Editor	Anthony Boys
Online Editor	David Chisholm
Colourist	Vince Narduzzo
Production Designer	Anthea Nelson
Director of Photography/Lighting Director	Martin Hawkins
Head of Production	Rebecca Parkinson
Line Producer	Samantha McCole
Producer	Humphrey Barclay
Executive Producer	Jon Rolph
Director	Martin Dennis

Sources

Publications

Daily Express
The Guardian
Variety

Websites

BARB: www.barb.co.uk
BBC Genome: genome.ch.bbc.co.uk
Blog About the Box: blogaboutthebox.wordpress.com
Find That Location: findthatlocation.com
IMDb: www.imdb.com
Marks and Gran official website: www.marksandgran.com
Richmond Shakespeare Society: www.richmondshakespeare.org.uk
Spotlight: www.spotlight.com
TV Studio History: www.tvstudiohistory.co.uk

DVD

Goodnight Sweetheart: The Complete Series